Buffy
the Vampire Slayer™

OMNIBUS

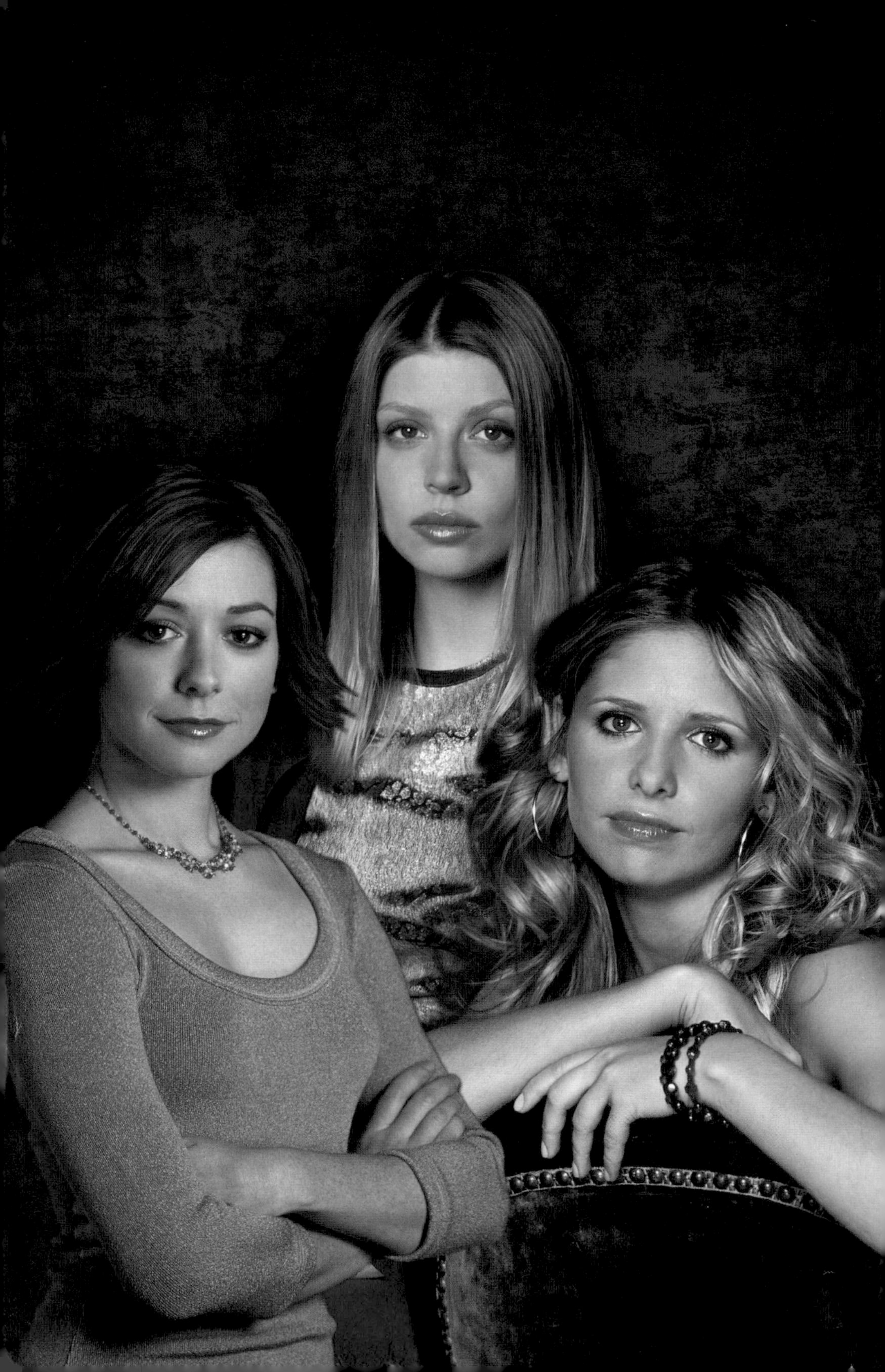

Buffy the Vampire Slayer™

OMNIBUS

VOLUME 6

AMBER BENSON
CHYNNA CLUGSTON
JANE ESPENSON
TOM FASSBENDER
CHRISTOPHER GOLDEN
TERRY MOORE
JIM PASCOE
ERIC POWELL
JAMIE S. RICH
CLIFF RICHARDS
TOM SNIEGOSKI
ANDI WATSON
CHRISTIAN ZANIER

Based on the television series created by Joss Whedon.

Angel *is based on the television series by Joss Whedon and David Greenwalt.*

These stories take place during Buffy the Vampire Slayer *Seasons Four and Five and* Angel *Season One.*

DARK HORSE BOOKS®

Publisher MIKE RICHARDSON
Series Editor SCOTT ALLIE
Collection Editor SIERRA HAHN
Assistant Editors on Original Series MATT DRYER, MIKE CARRIGLITTO & ADAM GALLARDO
Collection Designers LIA RIBACCHI & HEIDI WHITCOMB
Cover Illustration PAUL LEE & BRIAN HORTON

Special thanks to Debbie Olshan at Twentieth Century Fox, David Campiti at Glass House Graphics, Caroline Kallas, and George Snyder.

BUFFY THE VAMPIRE SLAYER™ OMNIBUS VOLUME SIX
Buffy the Vampire Slayer™ & © 2000, 2001, 2002, 2009 Twentieth Century Fox Film Corporation. All rights reserved. Buffy™ and all other prominently featured characters are trademarks of Twentieth Century Fox Film Corporation. Dark Horse Books® and the Dark Horse logo are registered trademarks of Dark Horse Comics, Inc. All rights reserved. No portion of this publication may be reproduced or transmitted, in any form or by any means, without the express written permission of Dark Horse Comics, Inc. Names, characters, places, and incidents featured in this publication either are the product of the author's imagination or are used fictitiously. Any resemblance to actual persons (living or dead), events, institutions, or locales, without satiric intent, is coincidental.

This volume reprints
Buffy the Vampire Slayer/Angel: Wizard ½, originally published in 2000;
Buffy the Vampire Slayer: Jonathan, originally published January 2001;
Buffy the Vampire Slayer: Giles, originally published October 2000;
Buffy the Vampire Slayer: Lover's Walk, originally published February 2001;
Buffy the Vampire Slayer #29–30, originally published January and February 2001;
Angel #15–16, originally published January and February 2001;
Buffy the Vampire Slayer #31–34, originally published March through June 2001;
Buffy the Vampire Slayer: Willow and Tara, "Wannablessedbe," originally published April 2001;
Dark Horse Extra: Buffy the Vampire Slayer, "Demonology," originally published May and June 2002;
and *Buffy the Vampire Slayer #35–38*, originally published July through November 2001;
all from Dark Horse Comics.

Published by Dark Horse Books
A division of Dark Horse Comics, Inc.
10956 SE Main Street
Milwaukie, OR 97222

darkhorse.com

To find a comics shop in your area, call the Comic Shop Locator Service toll-free at (888) 266-4226.

First edition: February 2009
ISBN 978-1-59582-242-0

10 9 8 7 6 5 4 3 2 1
Printed in Hong Kong

INTRODUCTION

The oldest story here, "City of Despair," was done for a promotional comic given out by *Wizard* magazine. This was Buffy's first introduction to the new Angel—who now had his own show. Tom Fassbender and Jim Pascoe were the writers I was most excited about at the time, and this was just one fun little adventure.

Some of the most fun we ever had, though, was the *Jonathan* one-shot. In the "Superstar" episode of the show, Jonathan Levinson—the littlest nerd among the Big Bads of Season Six—mysteriously became the coolest cat in Sunnydale. To demonstrate that coolness, Joss wanted Jonathan to have his own comic in the show, so Dark Horse contributed some props, with covers drawn by Jeff Matsuda. Jane Espenson, who'd written "Superstar," offered to continue what she'd started, and created an adventure set completely in that reality of Jonathan as superagent.

Around this time, I also realized my dream of doing a Giles comic. Chris Golden and Tom Sniegoski had brought Eric Powell into the fold for a couple issues of their *Angel* series, and I'd become a fan. The *Giles* one-shot was conceived around the idea of building Eric up with a heavily horror-themed issue. Eric's become one of Dark Horse's biggest stars, with his award-winning series *The Goon*.

Soon after, we did a romance-themed one-shot, "Lover's Walk." I wanted to establish Riley as a character, knowing that his relationship with Buffy was not popular with fans. Bringing P. Craig Russell in to ink Cliff Richards here made it popular with comics aficionados. I also wanted a Willow and Tara story, treating their relationship with the same simple dignity that Joss gave it on the show. Jamie Rich teamed with Chynna Clugston, who'd worked on *Buffy* before.

The opportunity to delve deeper into their relationship was presented when Chris Golden met Amber Benson, who had her own writing ambitions. Chris and Amber have worked together a lot since then, including a series of novels called *The Ghosts of Albion*, but "Wannablessedbe," the first Willow and Tara comic, was their first collaboration. We were lucky to get Terry Moore, the creator of the fantastic *Strangers in Paradise* series, to draw the book. To bring a little extra Willow and Tara to the table, Andi Watson, the original writer of the *Buffy* comic, wrote and drew a short tale for the short-lived *Dark Horse Extra*.

The real *Buffy* and *Angel* crossover was a serious undertaking, and drove everyone nuts. I had the bright idea of doing the four issues across the spread of two months of the regular *Buffy* and *Angel* monthlies, ignoring the fact that we could have sold the hell out of a miniseries called *Buffy/Angel*, kicking off with a #1. But since I didn't have a regular writer on the *Buffy* monthly at the time, and this would give both Christian Zanier, the artist on *Angel*, and Cliff, the artist on *Buffy*, a chance to handle both characters, it felt like a nice creative challenge.

Out of the Woodwork marked the beginning of Tom Fassbender and Jim Pascoe's run as the regular writers on the monthly series, which gave us some of my favorite pre–Season Eight stories. We brought Dawn into the comic, and Fassbender and Pascoe's second arc, *False Memories*, played with the idea that the characters would remember Dawn having been there in earlier adventures. I felt I was finally understanding what Joss was doing to elevate this genre stuff, so we took that supernatural notion of the false Dawn memories and explored the idea in more emotionally real ways for the characters. We re-created earlier scenes, giving Dawn significant roles in those scenes, thereby changing the spirit of what had happened. Readers have always been a little uncomfortable with the way the comic has inserted Dawn into the early years, but for me, not only does it make sense that characters would remember her being there, but it allowed us to do something the show never could—to go back.

Scott Allie

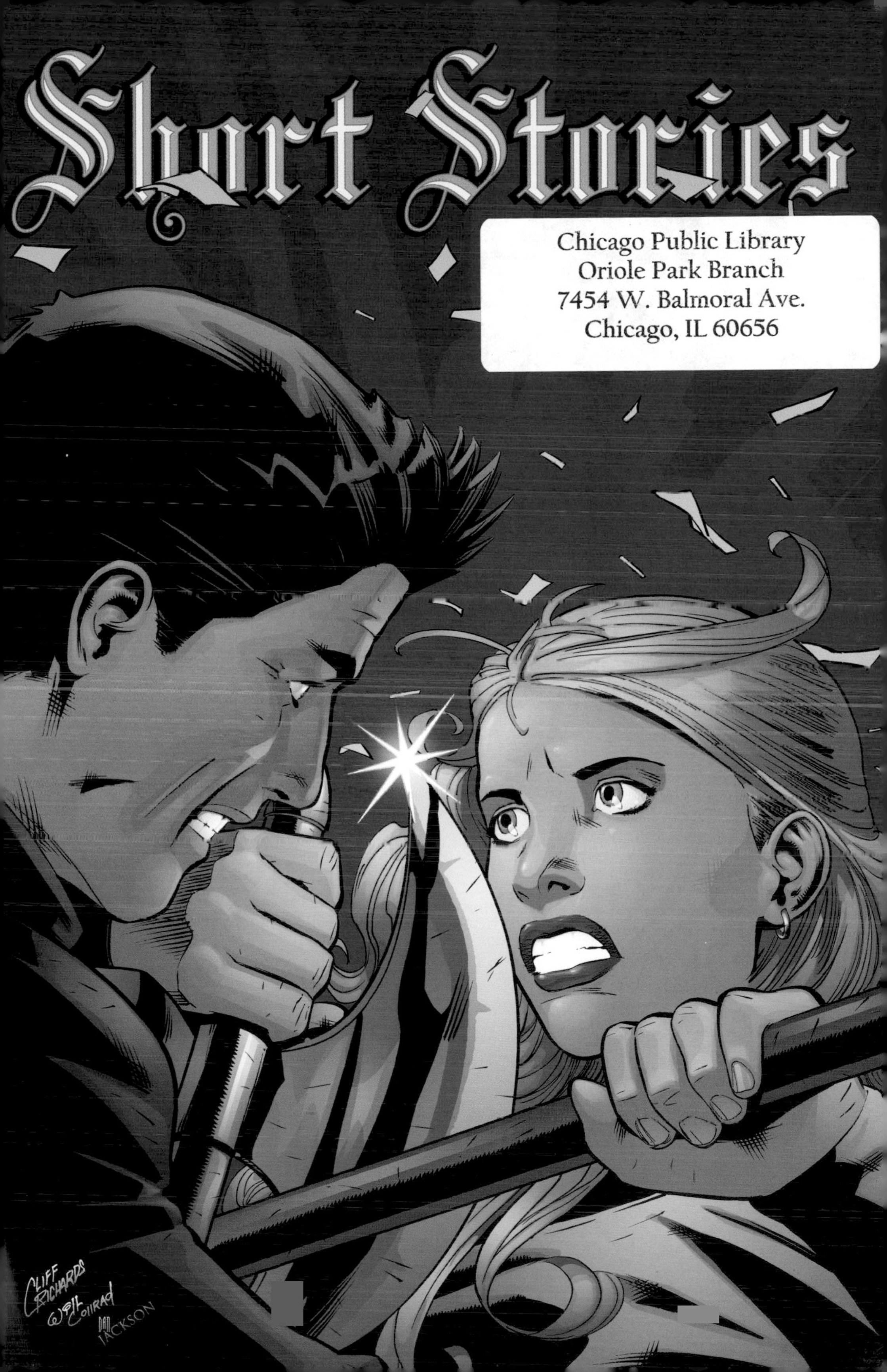
Short Stories
CLIFF RICHARDS
WILL CONRAD
DAN JACKSON

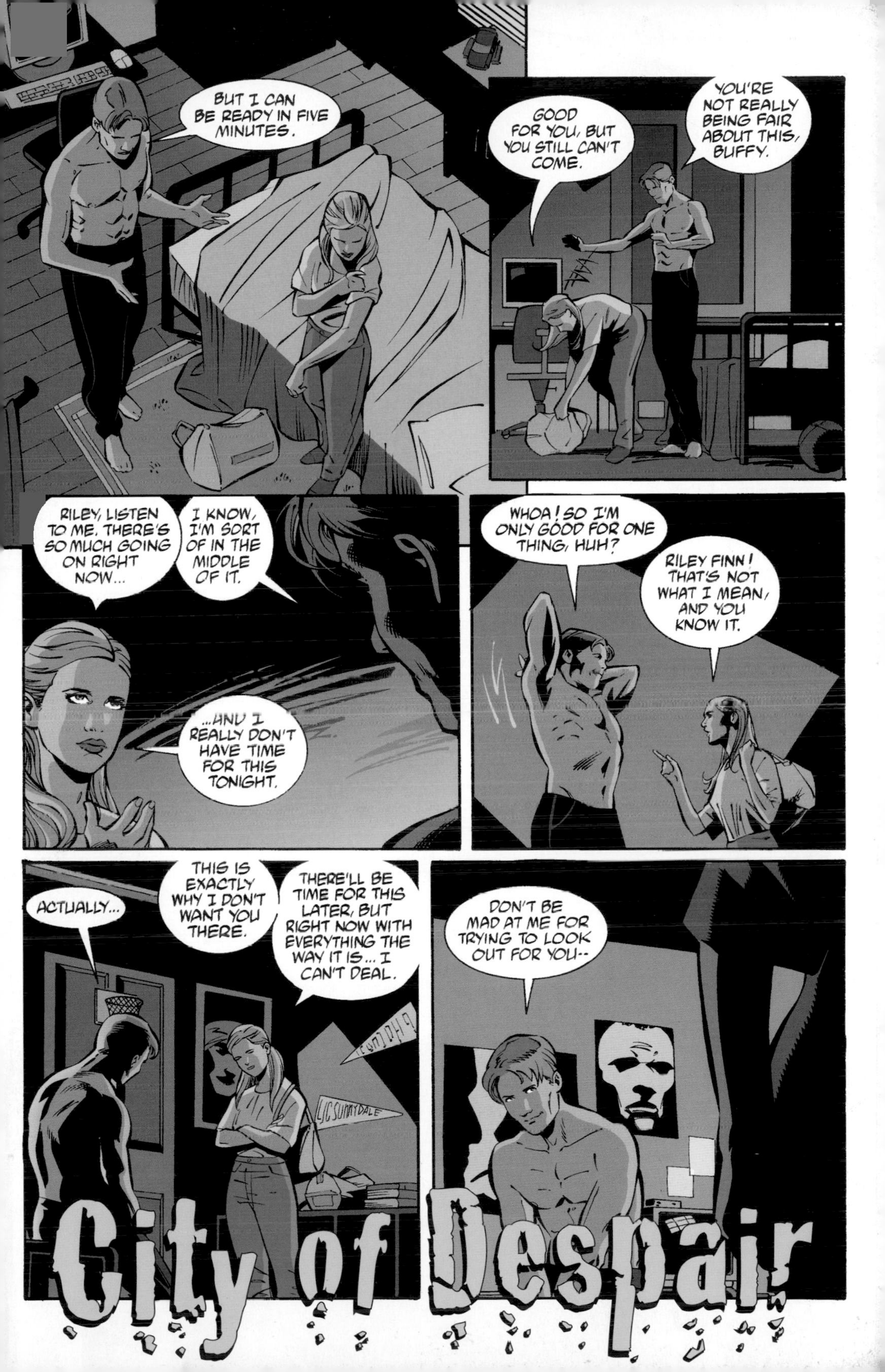
BUT I CAN BE READY IN FIVE MINUTES.
GOOD FOR YOU, BUT YOU STILL CAN'T COME.
YOU'RE NOT REALLY BEING FAIR ABOUT THIS, BUFFY.
RILEY, LISTEN TO ME. THERE'S SO MUCH GOING ON RIGHT NOW...
I KNOW, I'M SORT OF IN THE MIDDLE OF IT.
...AND I REALLY DON'T HAVE TIME FOR THIS TONIGHT.
WHOA! SO I'M ONLY GOOD FOR ONE THING, HUH?
RILEY FINN! THAT'S NOT WHAT I MEAN, AND YOU KNOW IT.
ACTUALLY...
THIS IS EXACTLY WHY I DON'T WANT YOU THERE.
THERE'LL BE TIME FOR THIS LATER, BUT RIGHT NOW WITH EVERYTHING THE WAY IT IS... I CAN'T DEAL.
U.C. SUNNYDALE
DON'T BE MAD AT ME FOR TRYING TO LOOK OUT FOR YOU--
City of Despair

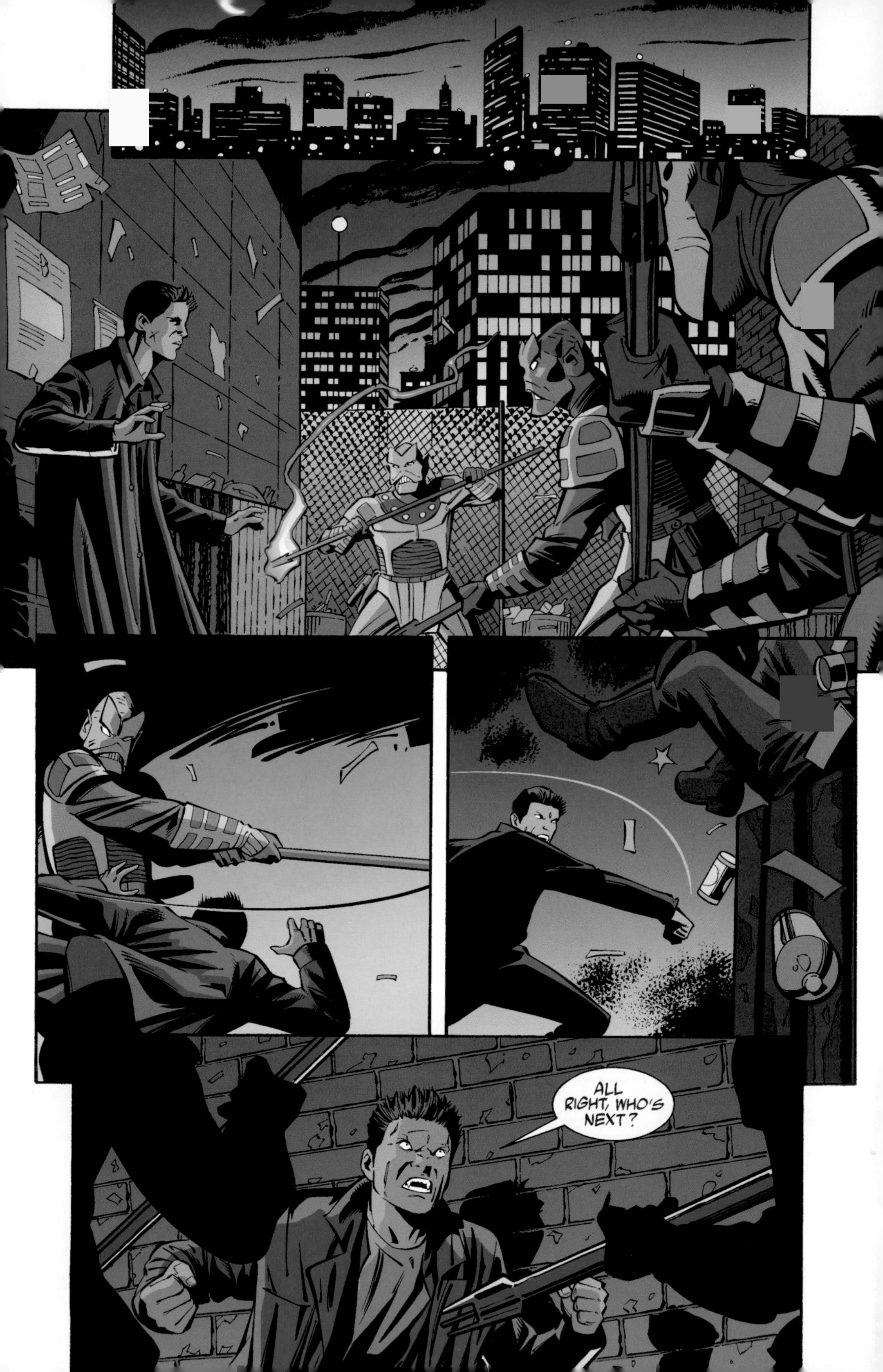
ALL RIGHT, WHO'S NEXT?

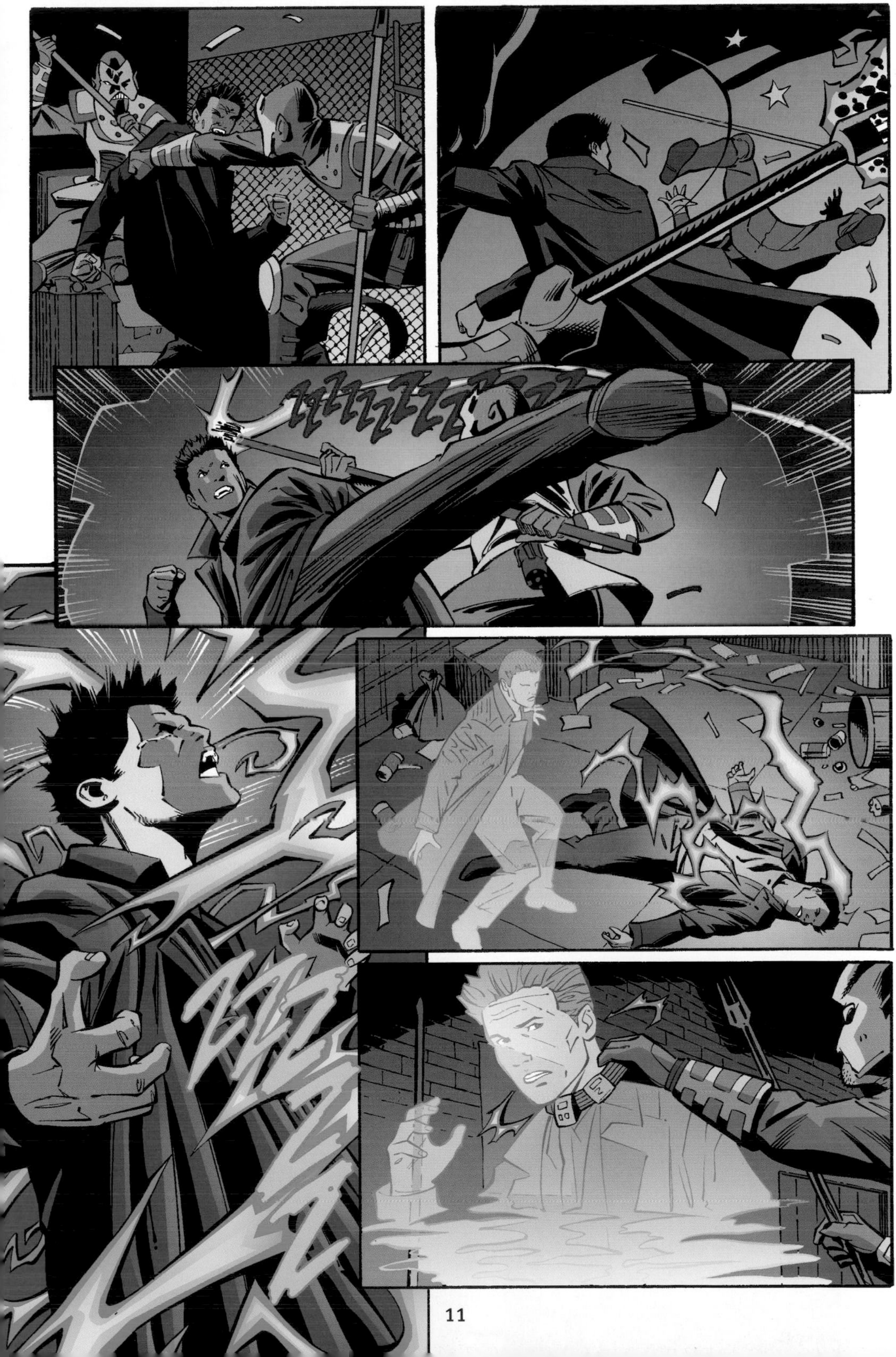

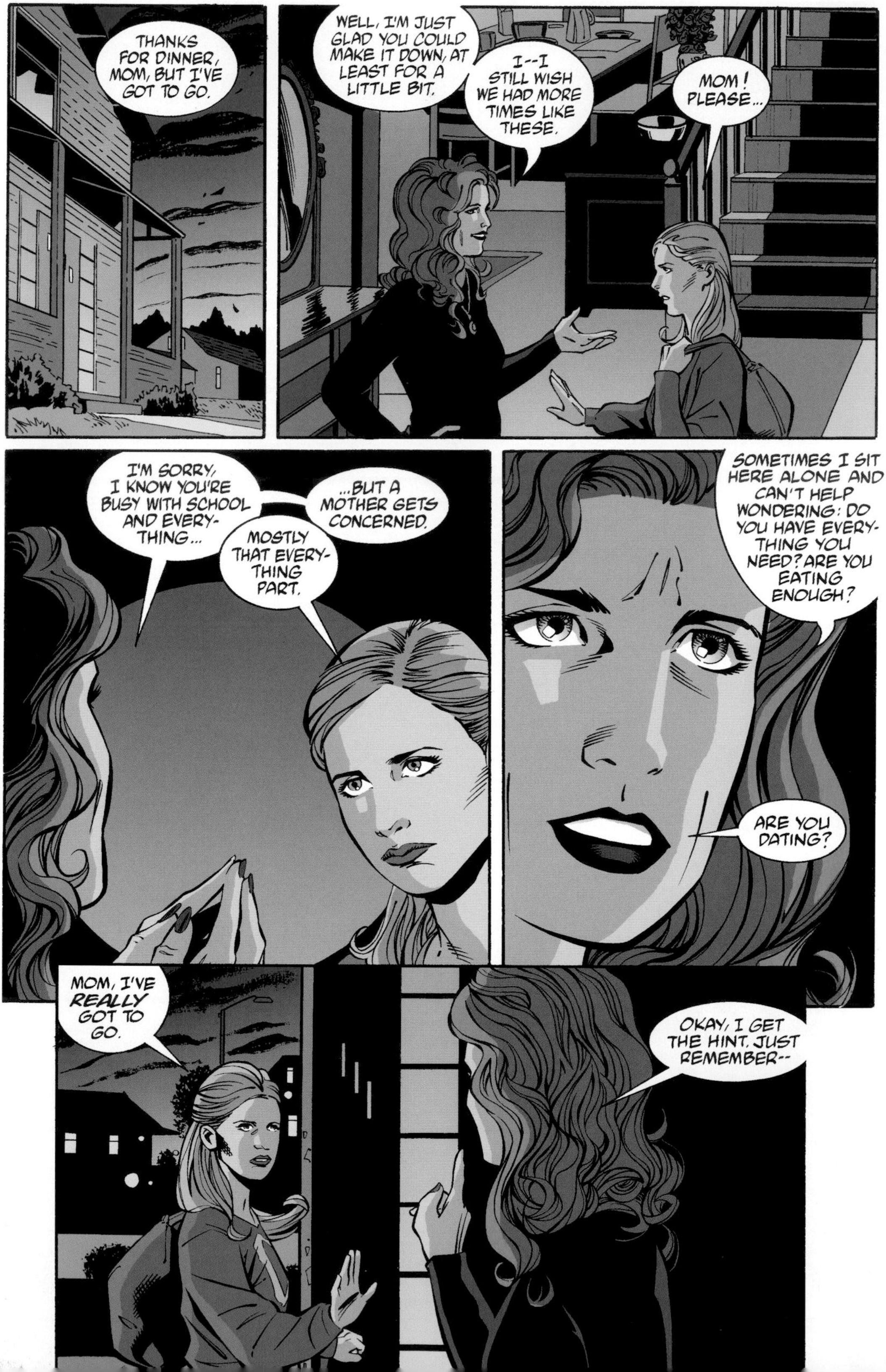
THANKS FOR DINNER, MOM, BUT I'VE GOT TO GO.
WELL, I'M JUST GLAD YOU COULD MAKE IT DOWN, AT LEAST FOR A LITTLE BIT.
I--I STILL WISH WE HAD MORE TIMES LIKE THESE.
MOM! PLEASE...
I'M SORRY, I KNOW YOU'RE BUSY WITH SCHOOL AND EVERY-THING...
...BUT A MOTHER GETS CONCERNED.
MOSTLY THAT EVERY-THING PART.
SOMETIMES I SIT HERE ALONE AND CAN'T HELP WONDERING: DO YOU HAVE EVERY-THING YOU NEED? ARE YOU EATING ENOUGH?
ARE YOU DATING?
MOM, I'VE REALLY GOT TO GO.
OKAY, I GET THE HINT. JUST REMEMBER--

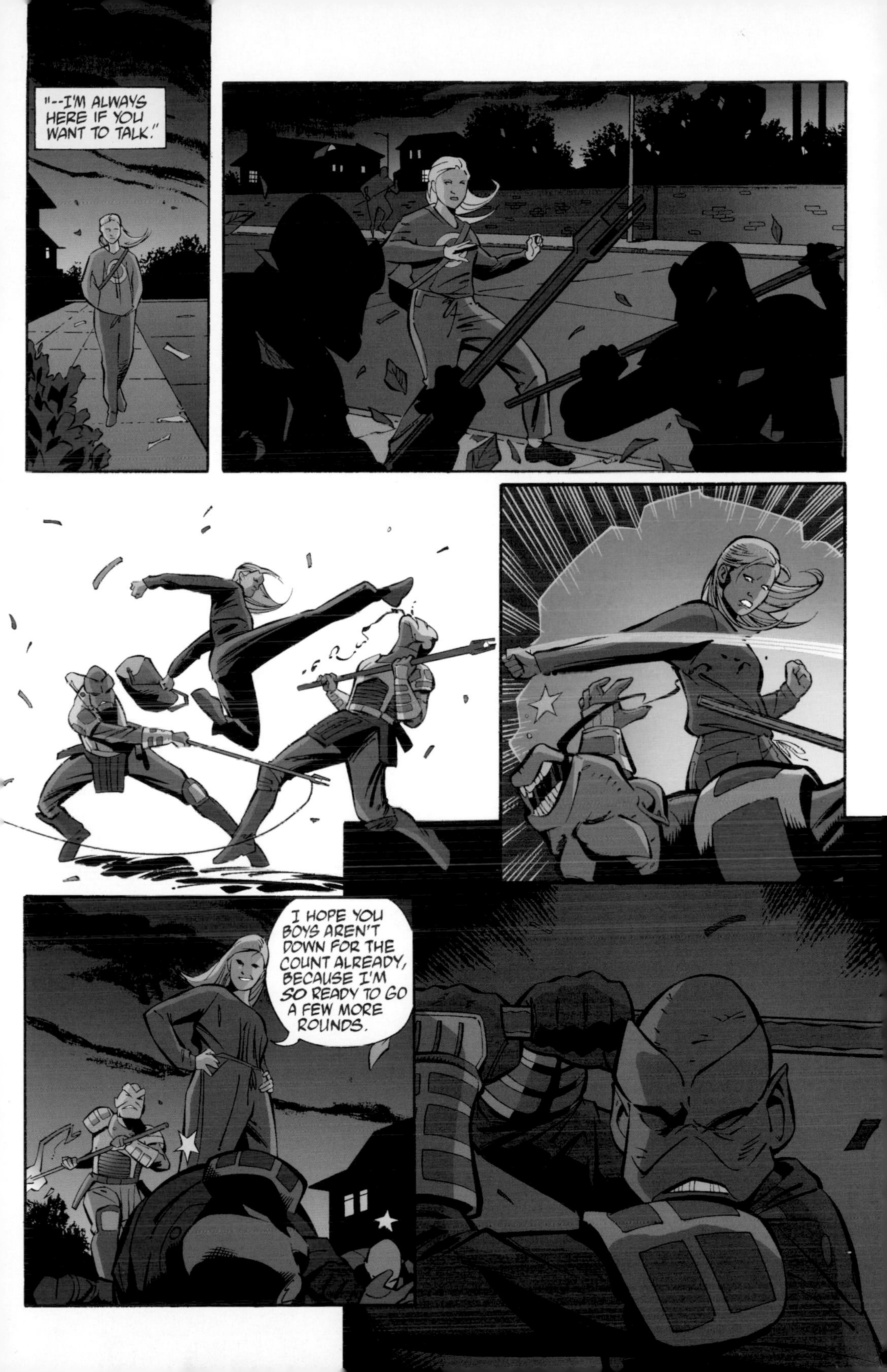
"--I'M ALWAYS HERE IF YOU WANT TO TALK."
I HOPE YOU BOYS AREN'T DOWN FOR THE COUNT ALREADY, BECAUSE I'M *SO* READY TO GO A FEW MORE ROUNDS.

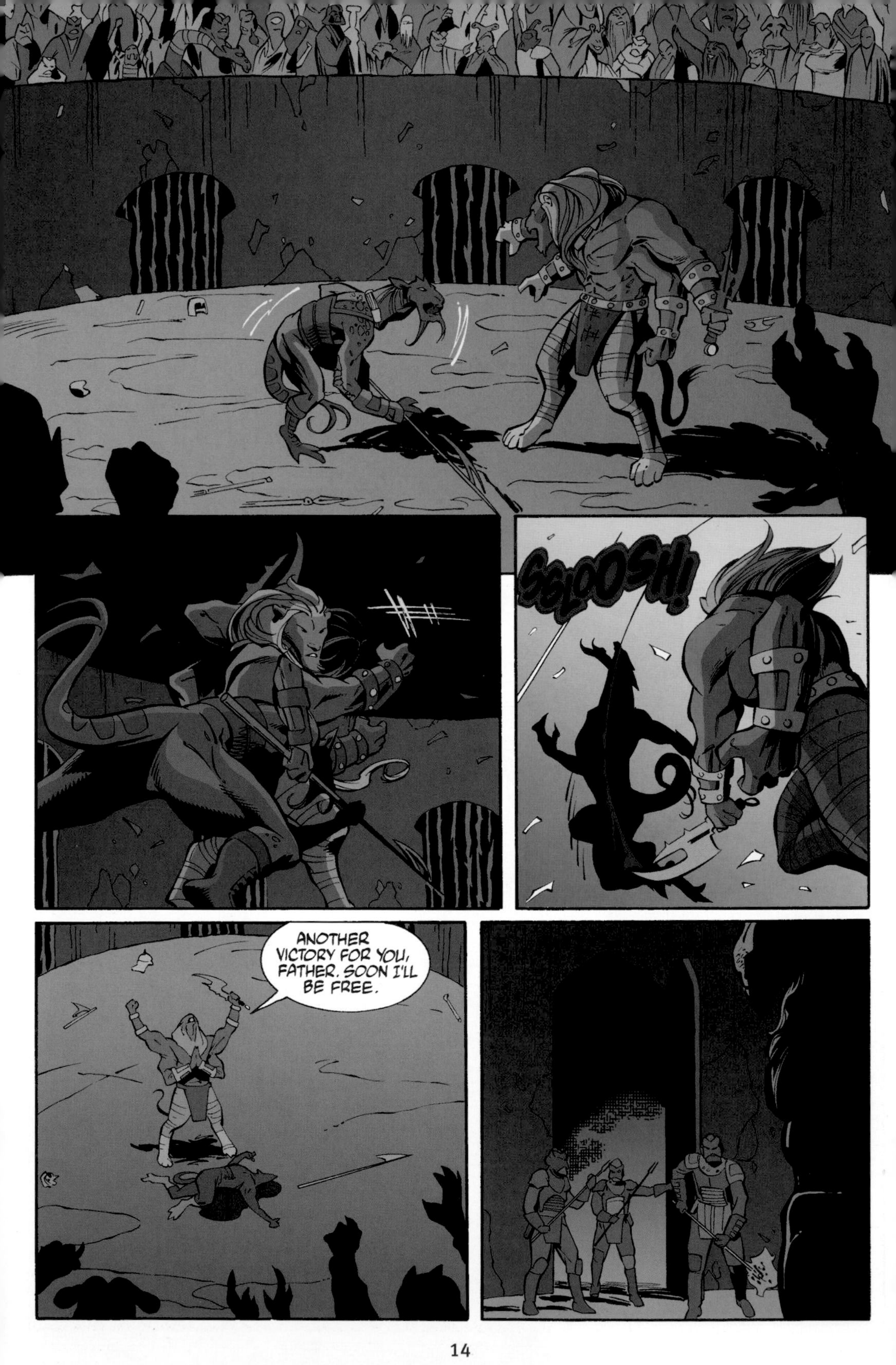
SGLOOSH!
ANOTHER VICTORY FOR YOU, FATHER. SOON I'LL BE FREE.

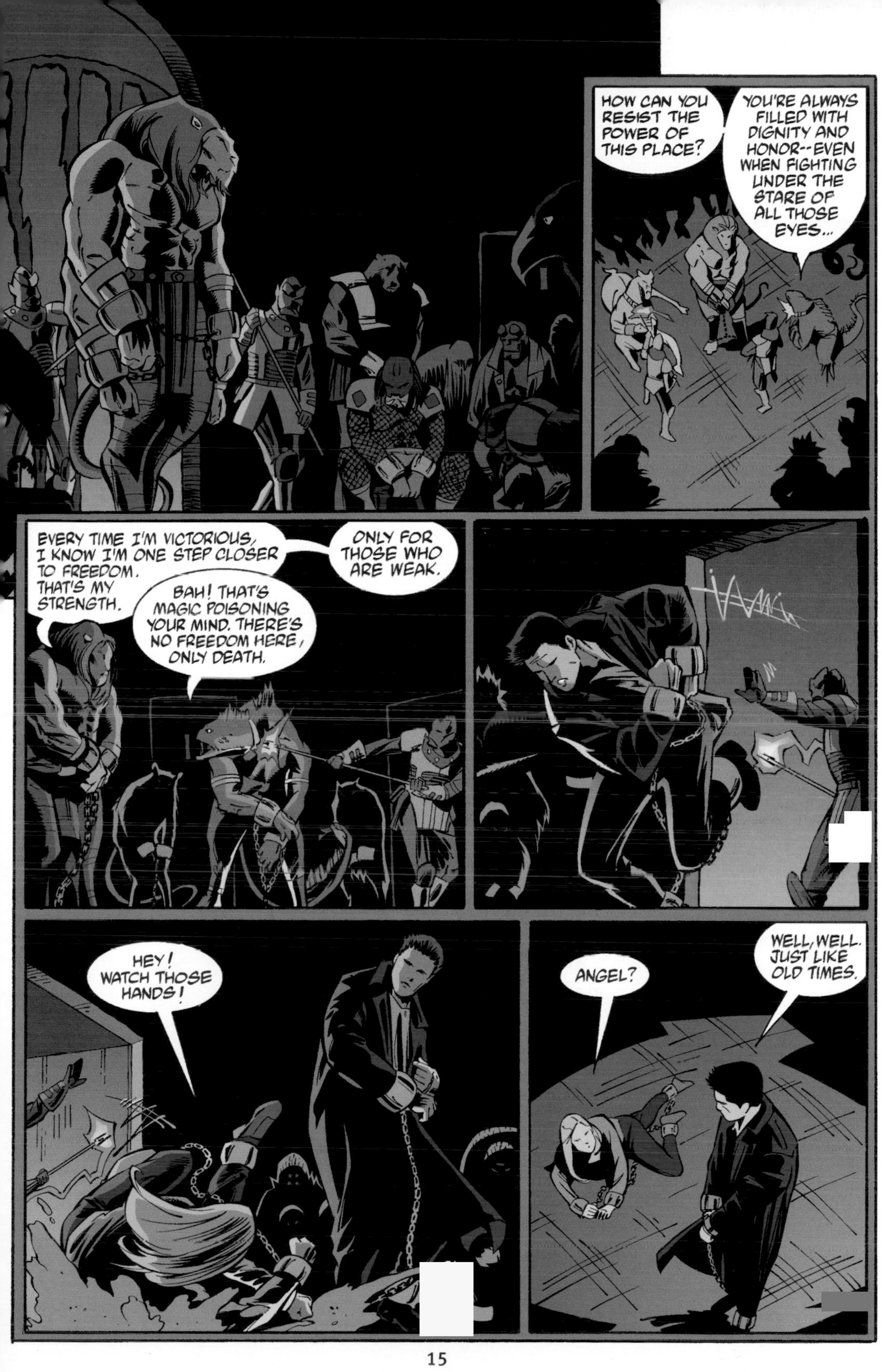
HOW CAN YOU RESIST THE POWER OF THIS PLACE?
YOU'RE ALWAYS FILLED WITH DIGNITY AND HONOR--EVEN WHEN FIGHTING UNDER THE STARE OF ALL THOSE EYES...
EVERY TIME I'M VICTORIOUS, I KNOW I'M ONE STEP CLOSER TO FREEDOM. THAT'S MY STRENGTH.
ONLY FOR THOSE WHO ARE WEAK.
BAH! THAT'S MAGIC POISONING YOUR MIND. THERE'S NO FREEDOM HERE, ONLY DEATH.
HEY! WATCH THOSE HANDS!
ANGEL?
WELL, WELL. JUST LIKE OLD TIMES.

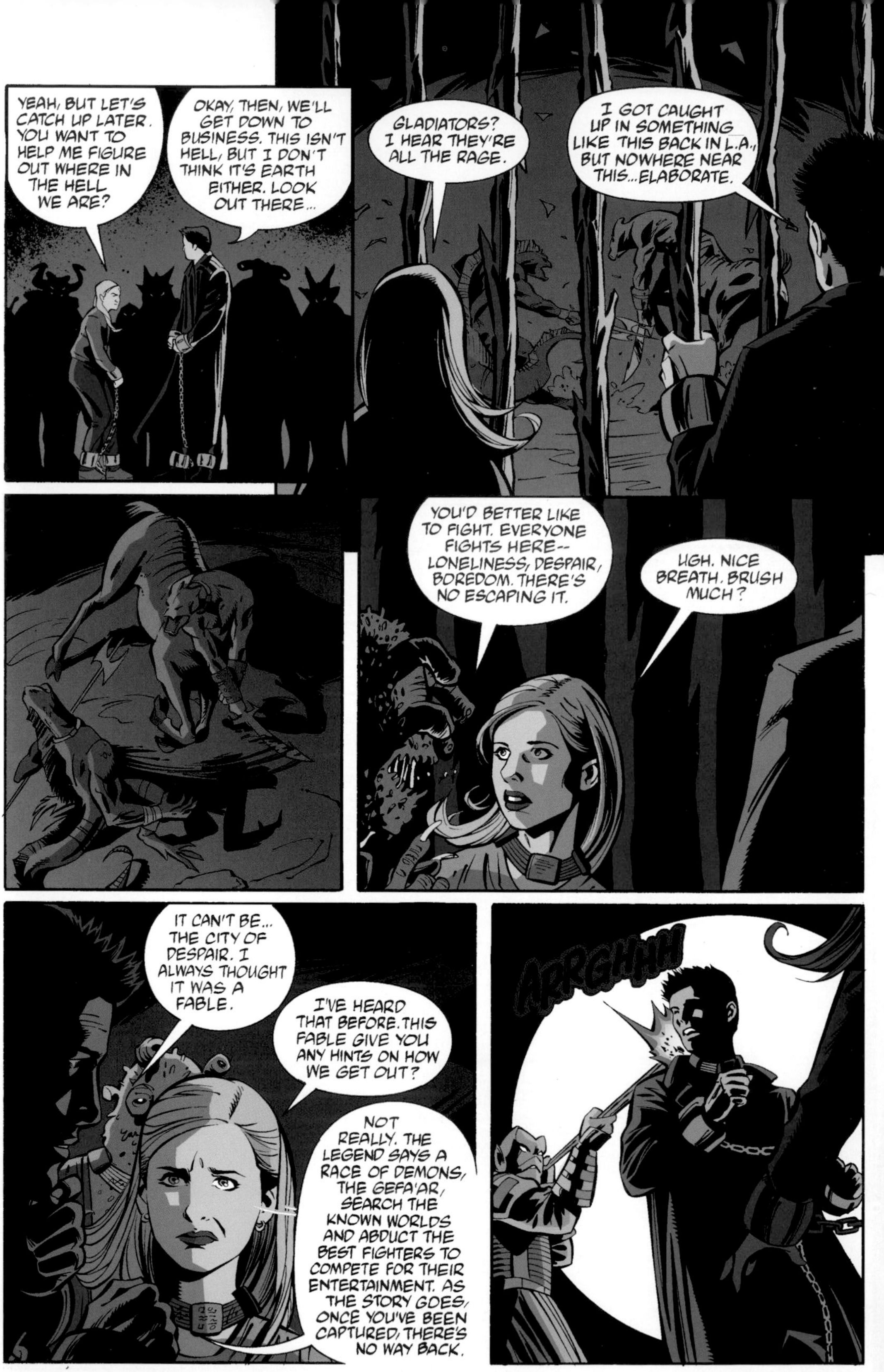
YEAH, BUT LET'S CATCH UP LATER. YOU WANT TO HELP ME FIGURE OUT WHERE IN THE HELL WE ARE?
OKAY, THEN, WE'LL GET DOWN TO BUSINESS. THIS ISN'T HELL, BUT I DON'T THINK IT'S EARTH EITHER. LOOK OUT THERE...
GLADIATORS? I HEAR THEY'RE ALL THE RAGE.
I GOT CAUGHT UP IN SOMETHING LIKE THIS BACK IN L.A., BUT NOWHERE NEAR THIS...ELABORATE.
YOU'D BETTER LIKE TO FIGHT. EVERYONE FIGHTS HERE-- LONELINESS, DESPAIR, BOREDOM. THERE'S NO ESCAPING IT.
UGH. NICE BREATH. BRUSH MUCH?
IT CAN'T BE... THE CITY OF DESPAIR. I ALWAYS THOUGHT IT WAS A FABLE.
I'VE HEARD THAT BEFORE. THIS FABLE GIVE YOU ANY HINTS ON HOW WE GET OUT?
NOT REALLY. THE LEGEND SAYS A RACE OF DEMONS, THE GEFA'AR, SEARCH THE KNOWN WORLDS AND ABDUCT THE BEST FIGHTERS TO COMPETE FOR THEIR ENTERTAINMENT. AS THE STORY GOES, ONCE YOU'VE BEEN CAPTURED, THERE'S NO WAY BACK.
ARRGHHH

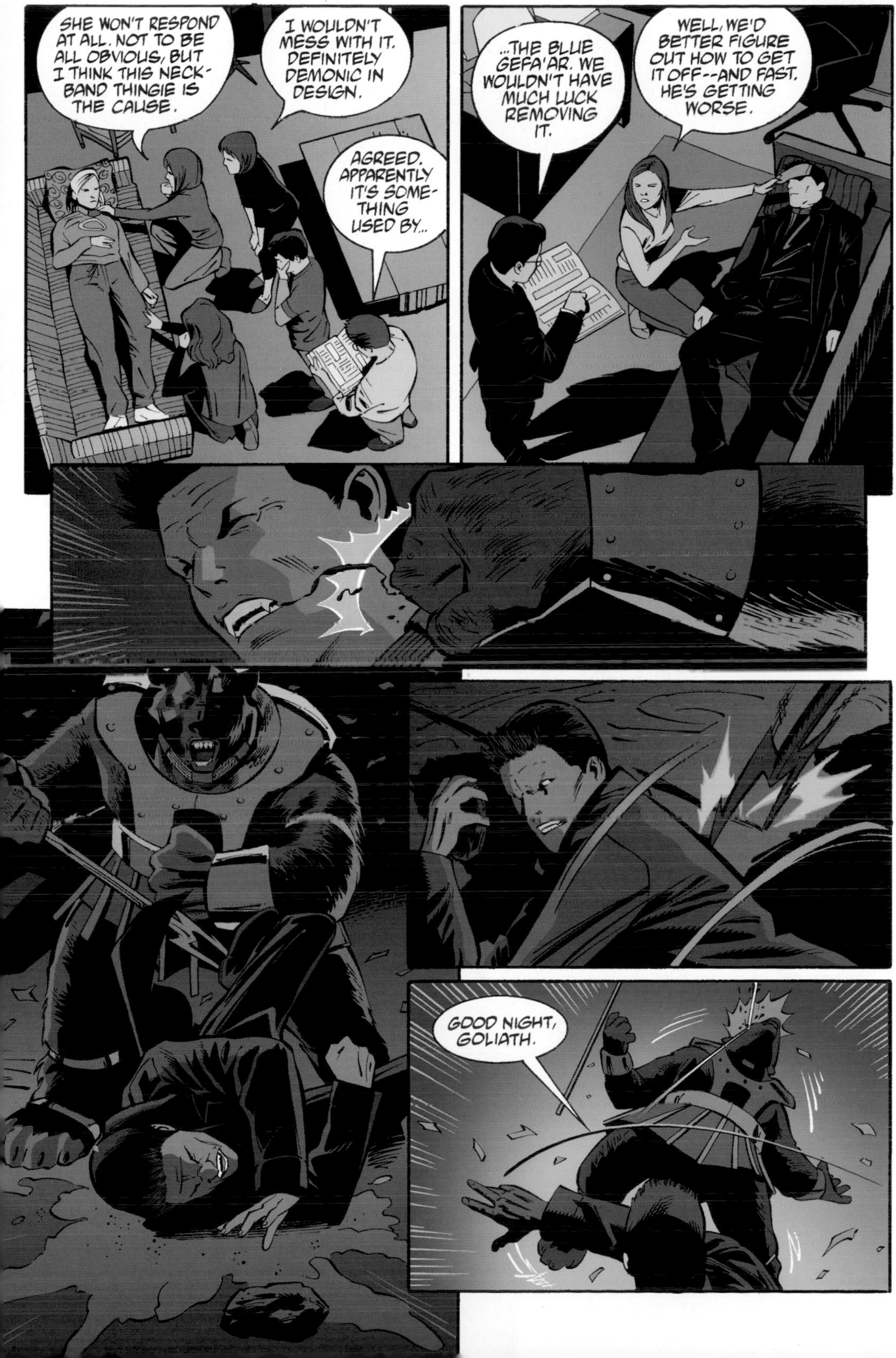
SHE WON'T RESPOND AT ALL. NOT TO BE ALL OBVIOUS, BUT I THINK THIS NECK-BAND THINGIE IS THE CAUSE.
I WOULDN'T MESS WITH IT. DEFINITELY DEMONIC IN DESIGN.
AGREED. APPARENTLY IT'S SOMETHING USED BY...
...THE BLUE GEFA'AR. WE WOULDN'T HAVE MUCH LUCK REMOVING IT.
WELL, WE'D BETTER FIGURE OUT HOW TO GET IT OFF--AND FAST. HE'S GETTING WORSE.
GOOD NIGHT, GOLIATH.

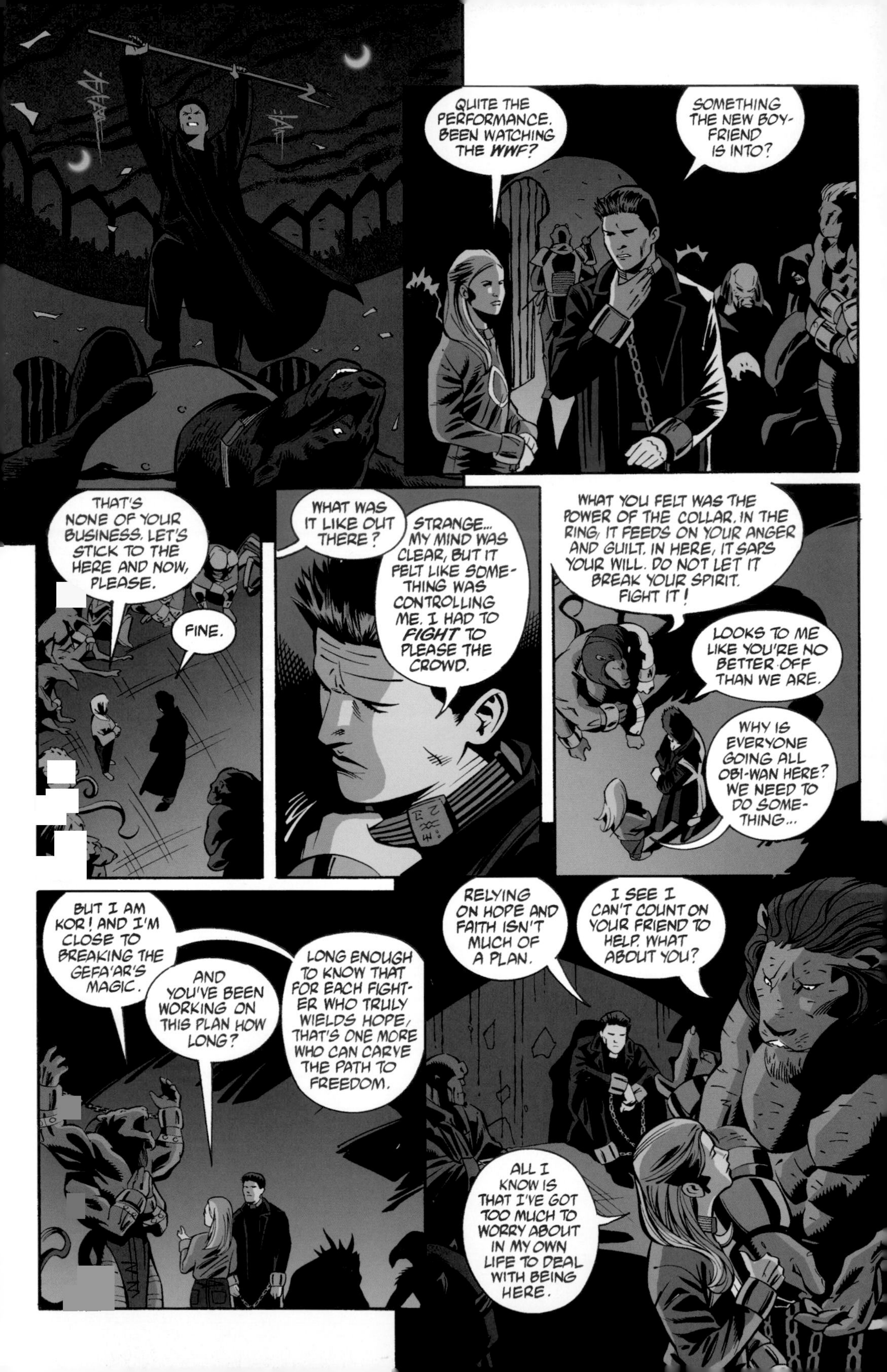

QUITE THE PERFORMANCE. BEEN WATCHING THE WWF?
SOMETHING THE NEW BOY-FRIEND IS INTO?
THAT'S NONE OF YOUR BUSINESS. LET'S STICK TO THE HERE AND NOW, PLEASE.
FINE.
WHAT WAS IT LIKE OUT THERE?
STRANGE... MY MIND WAS CLEAR, BUT IT FELT LIKE SOME-THING WAS CONTROLLING ME. I HAD TO FIGHT TO PLEASE THE CROWD.
WHAT YOU FELT WAS THE POWER OF THE COLLAR. IN THE RING, IT FEEDS ON YOUR ANGER AND GUILT. IN HERE, IT SAPS YOUR WILL. DO NOT LET IT BREAK YOUR SPIRIT. FIGHT IT!
LOOKS TO ME LIKE YOU'RE NO BETTER OFF THAN WE ARE.
WHY IS EVERYONE GOING ALL OBI-WAN HERE? WE NEED TO DO SOME-THING...
BUT I AM KOR! AND I'M CLOSE TO BREAKING THE GEFA'AR'S MAGIC.
AND YOU'VE BEEN WORKING ON THIS PLAN HOW LONG?
LONG ENOUGH TO KNOW THAT FOR EACH FIGHT-ER WHO TRULY WIELDS HOPE, THAT'S ONE MORE WHO CAN CARVE THE PATH TO FREEDOM.
RELYING ON HOPE AND FAITH ISN'T MUCH OF A PLAN.
I SEE I CAN'T COUNT ON YOUR FRIEND TO HELP. WHAT ABOUT YOU?
ALL I KNOW IS THAT I'VE GOT TOO MUCH TO WORRY ABOUT IN MY OWN LIFE TO DEAL WITH BEING HERE.

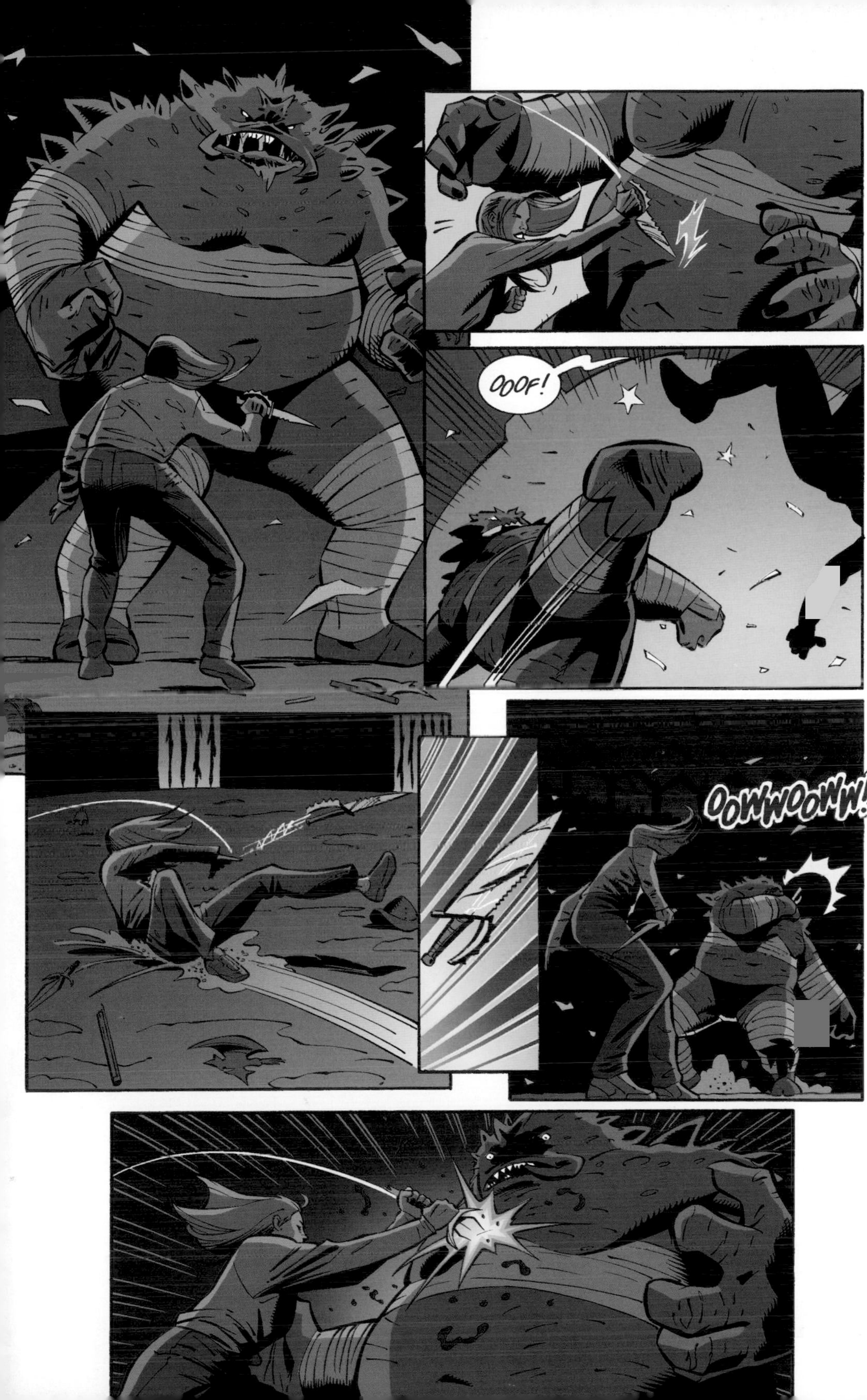
OOOF!
OOWWOOWW!

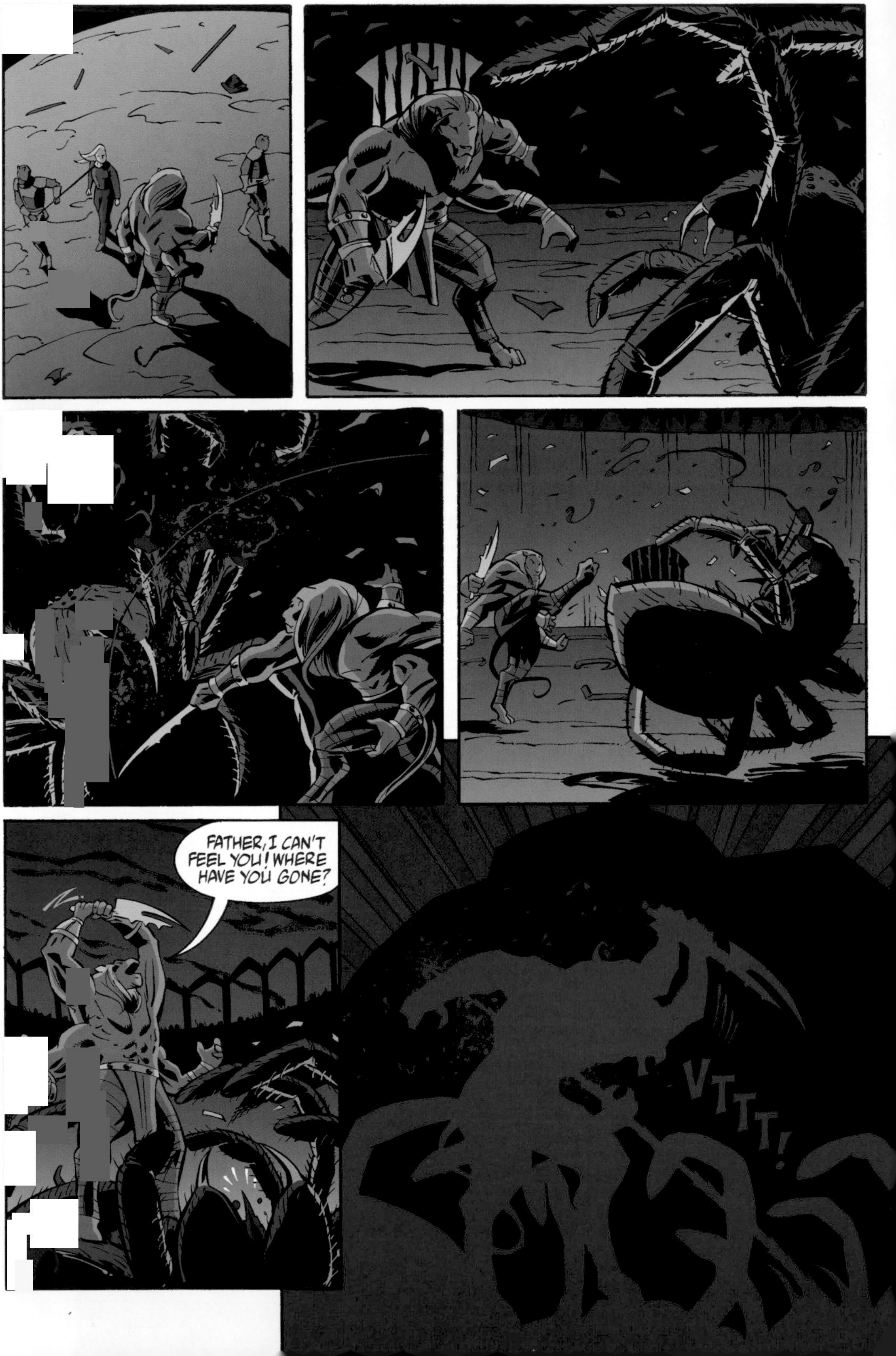
FATHER, I CAN'T FEEL YOU! WHERE HAVE YOU GONE?
VTTT!

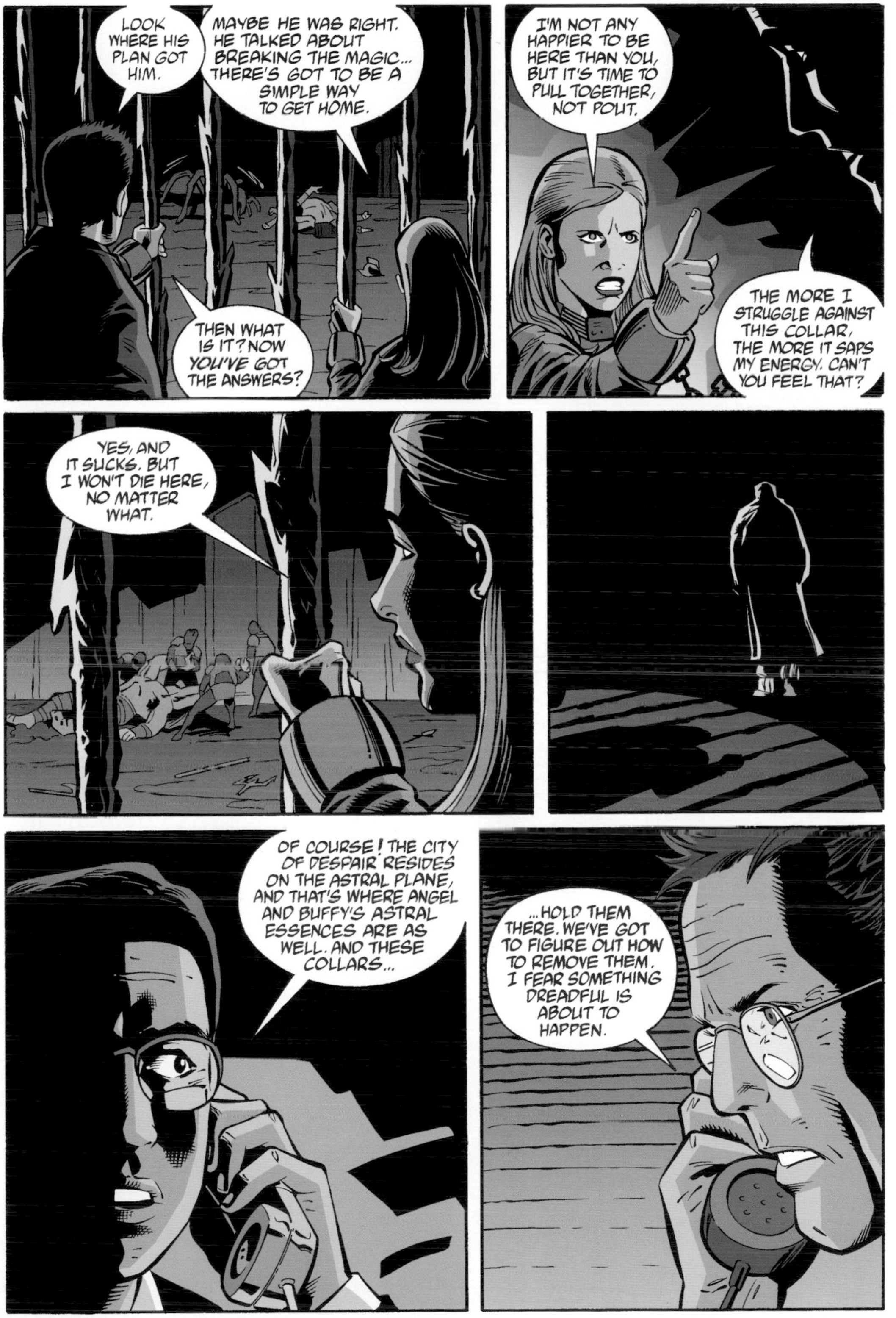
LOOK WHERE HIS PLAN GOT HIM.
MAYBE HE WAS RIGHT. HE TALKED ABOUT BREAKING THE MAGIC... THERE'S GOT TO BE A SIMPLE WAY TO GET HOME.
THEN WHAT IS IT? NOW YOU'VE GOT THE ANSWERS?
I'M NOT ANY HAPPIER TO BE HERE THAN YOU, BUT IT'S TIME TO PULL TOGETHER, NOT POUT.
THE MORE I STRUGGLE AGAINST THIS COLLAR, THE MORE IT SAPS MY ENERGY. CAN'T YOU FEEL THAT?
YES, AND IT SUCKS. BUT I WON'T DIE HERE, NO MATTER WHAT.
OF COURSE! THE CITY OF DESPAIR RESIDES ON THE ASTRAL PLANE, AND THAT'S WHERE ANGEL AND BUFFY'S ASTRAL ESSENCES ARE AS WELL. AND THESE COLLARS...
...HOLD THEM THERE. WE'VE GOT TO FIGURE OUT HOW TO REMOVE THEM. I FEAR SOMETHING DREADFUL IS ABOUT TO HAPPEN.

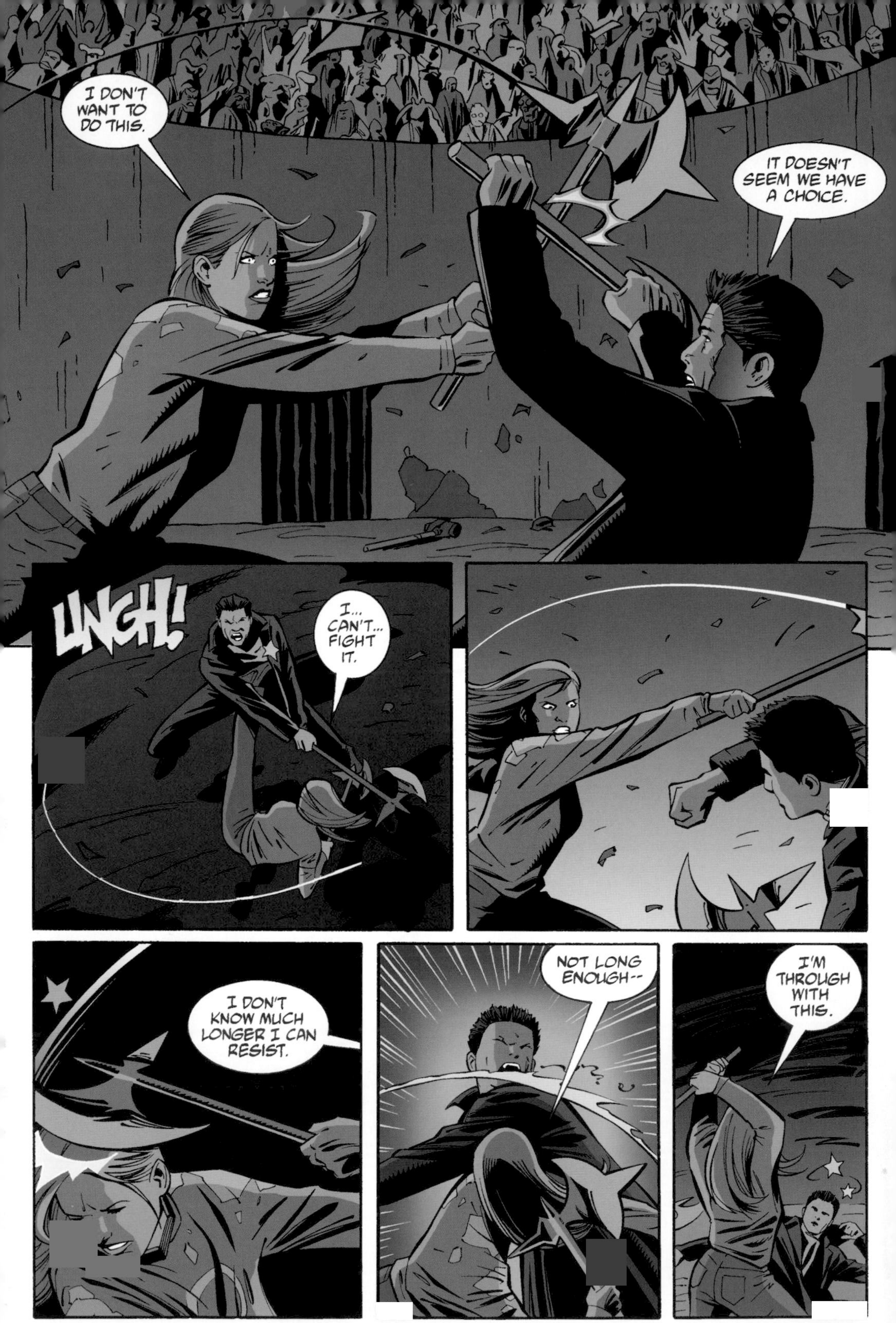

I DON'T WANT TO DO THIS.
IT DOESN'T SEEM WE HAVE A CHOICE.
UNGH!
I... CAN'T... FIGHT IT.
I DON'T KNOW MUCH LONGER I CAN RESIST.
NOT LONG ENOUGH--
I'M THROUGH WITH THIS.

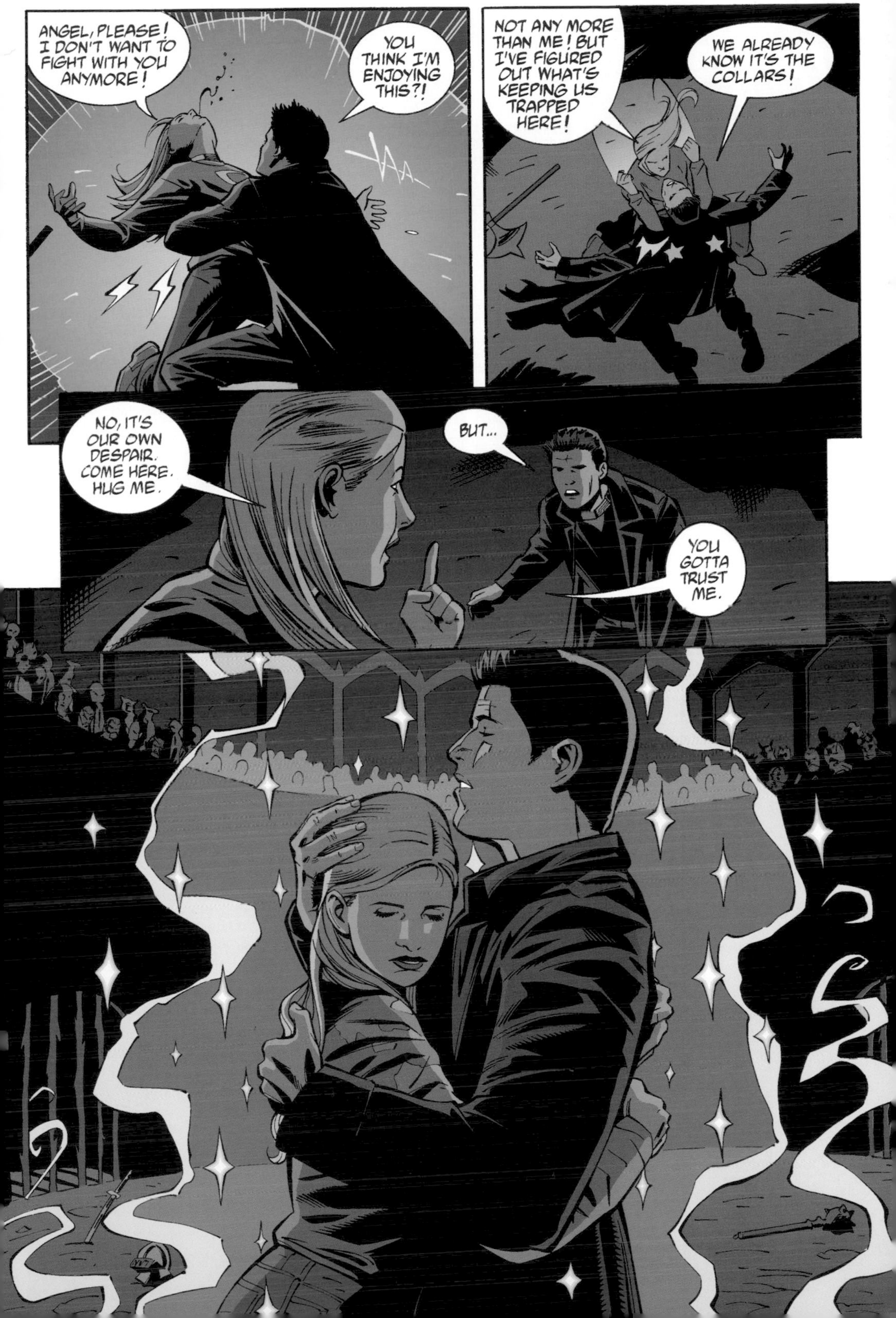
ANGEL, PLEASE! I DON'T WANT TO FIGHT WITH YOU ANYMORE!
YOU THINK I'M ENJOYING THIS?!
NOT ANY MORE THAN ME! BUT I'VE FIGURED OUT WHAT'S KEEPING US TRAPPED HERE!
WE ALREADY KNOW IT'S THE COLLARS!
NO, IT'S OUR OWN DESPAIR. COME HERE. HUG ME.
BUT...
YOU GOTTA TRUST ME.

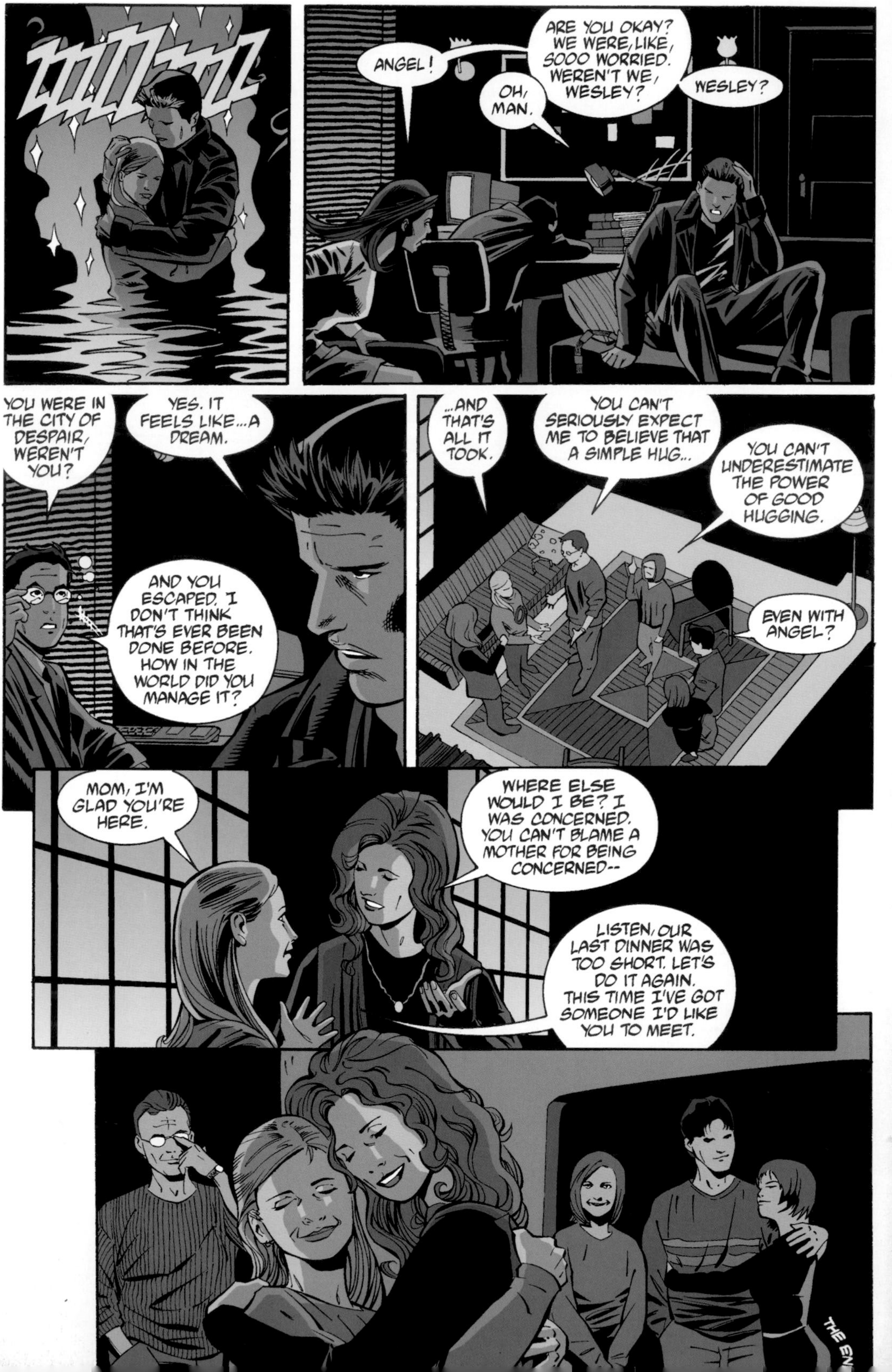
ANGEL!
ARE YOU OKAY? WE WERE, LIKE, SOOO WORRIED. WEREN'T WE, WESLEY?
OH, MAN.
WESLEY?
YOU WERE IN THE CITY OF DESPAIR, WEREN'T YOU?
YES. IT FEELS LIKE...A DREAM.
AND YOU ESCAPED. I DON'T THINK THAT'S EVER BEEN DONE BEFORE. HOW IN THE WORLD DID YOU MANAGE IT?
...AND THAT'S ALL IT TOOK.
YOU CAN'T SERIOUSLY EXPECT ME TO BELIEVE THAT A SIMPLE HUG...
YOU CAN'T UNDERESTIMATE THE POWER OF GOOD HUGGING.
EVEN WITH ANGEL?
MOM, I'M GLAD YOU'RE HERE.
WHERE ELSE WOULD I BE? I WAS CONCERNED. YOU CAN'T BLAME A MOTHER FOR BEING CONCERNED--
LISTEN, OUR LAST DINNER WAS TOO SHORT. LET'S DO IT AGAIN. THIS TIME I'VE GOT SOMEONE I'D LIKE YOU TO MEET.
THE EN

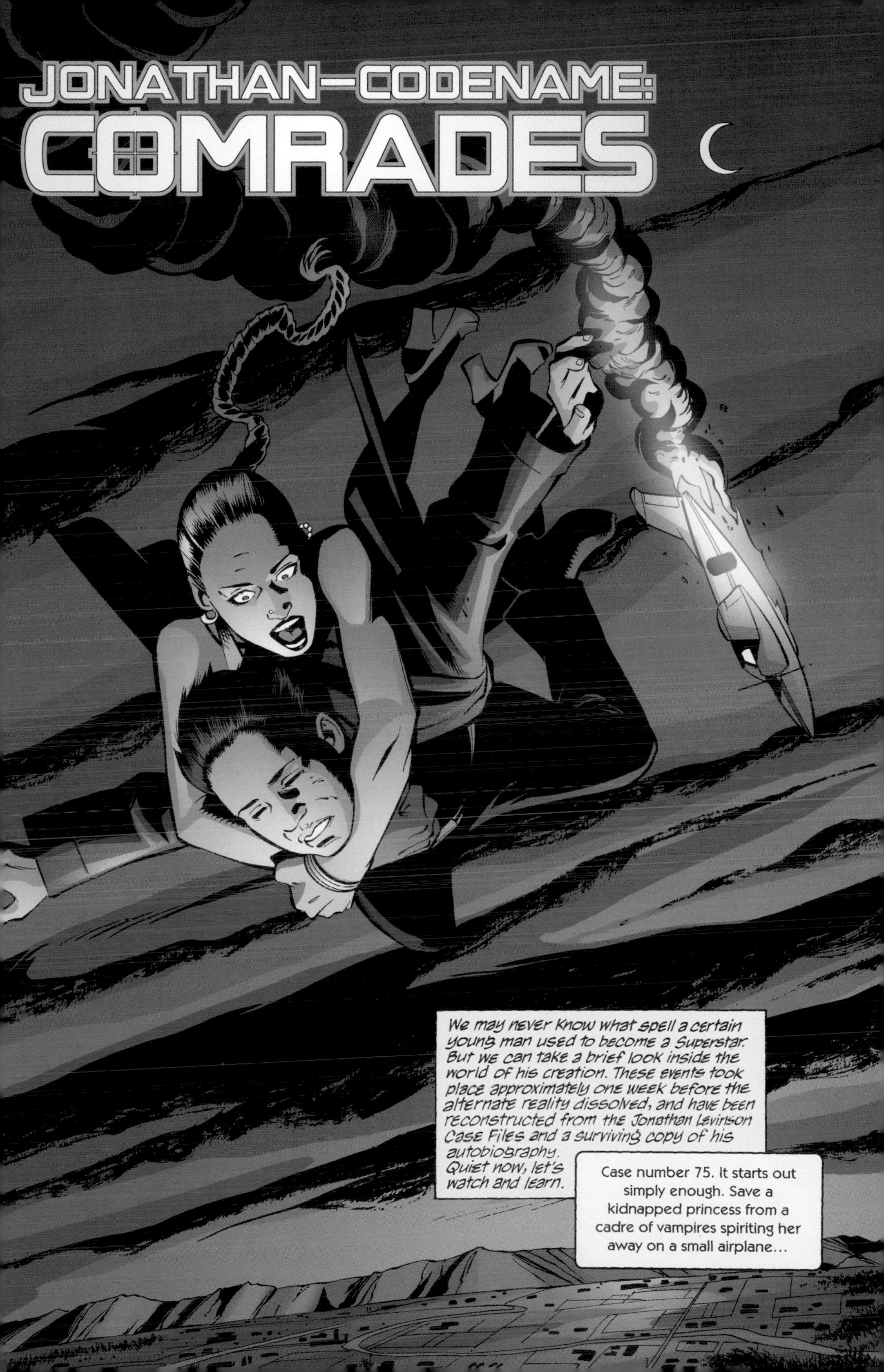
JONATHAN—CODENAME:
COMRADES
We may never know what spell a certain young man used to become a Superstar. But we can take a brief look inside the world of his creation. These events took place approximately one week before the alternate reality dissolved, and have been reconstructed from the Jonathan Levinson Case Files and a surviving copy of his autobiography.
Quiet now, let's watch and learn.
Case number 75. It starts out simply enough. Save a kidnapped princess from a cadre of vampires spiriting her away on a small airplane...

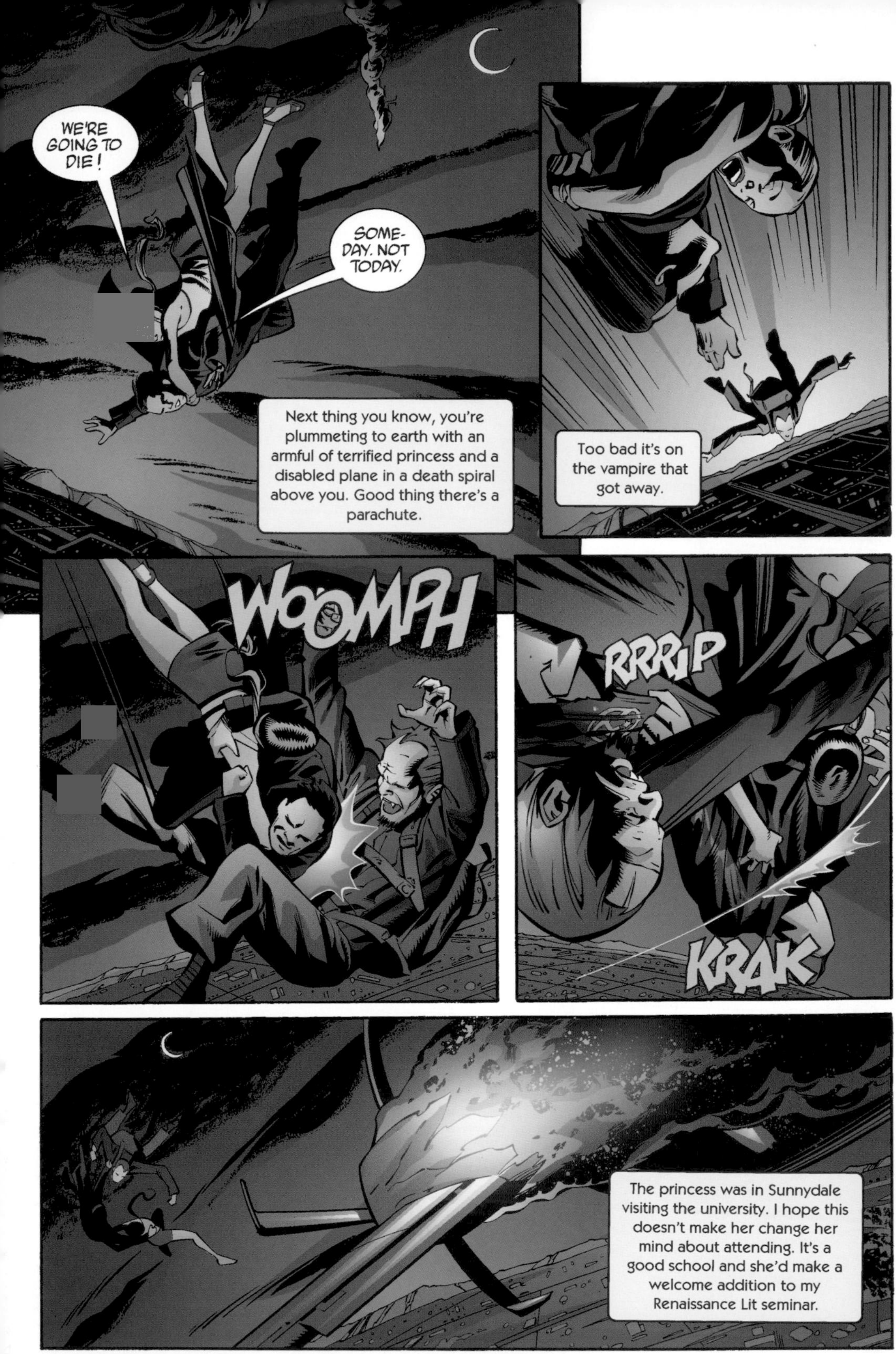
WE'RE GOING TO DIE!
SOME-DAY. NOT TODAY.
Next thing you know, you're plummeting to earth with an armful of terrified princess and a disabled plane in a death spiral above you. Good thing there's a parachute.
Too bad it's on the vampire that got away.
WOOMPH
RRRIP
KRAK
The princess was in Sunnydale visiting the university. I hope this doesn't make her change her mind about attending. It's a good school and she'd make a welcome addition to my Renaissance Lit seminar.

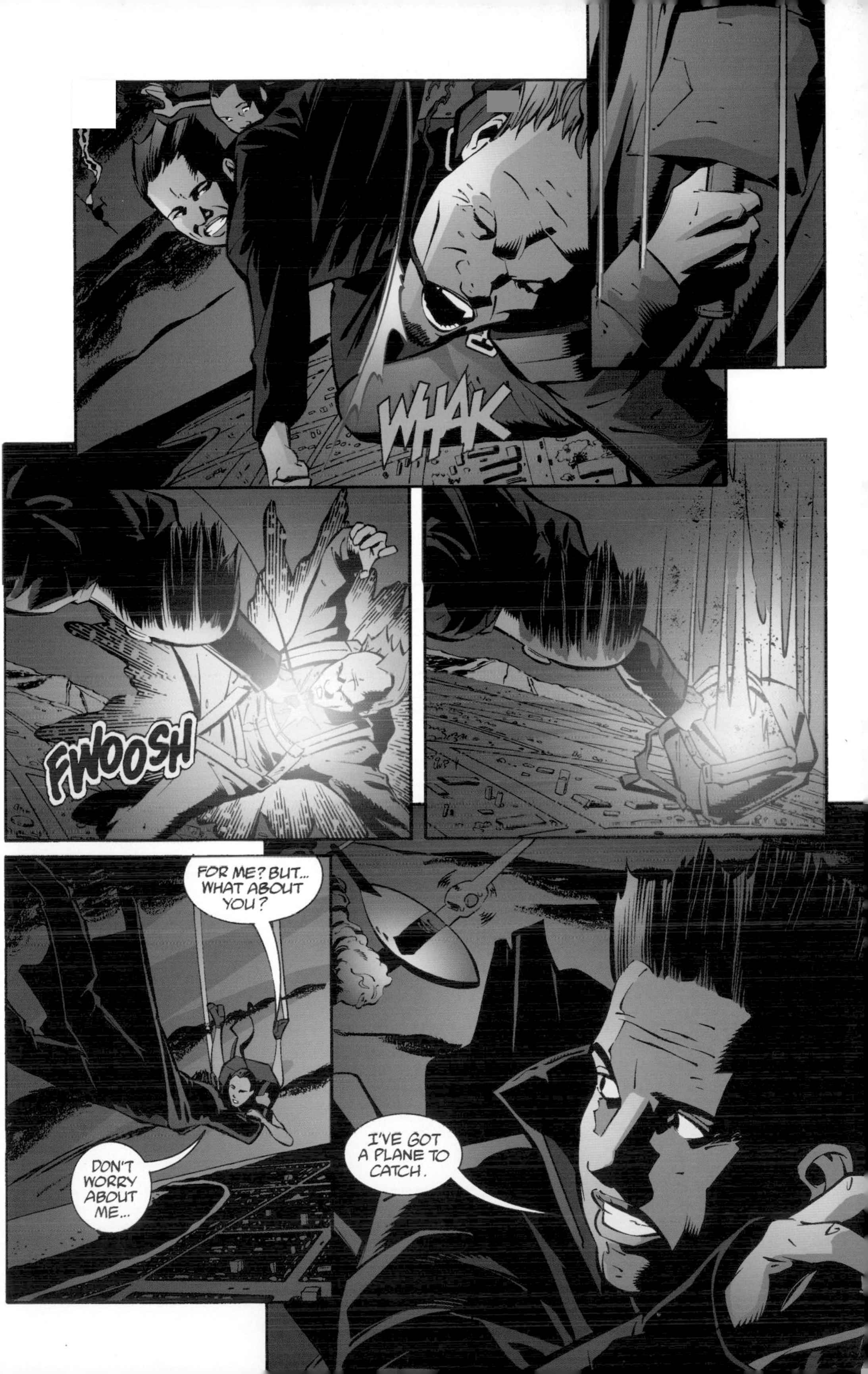
WHAK
FWOOSH
FOR ME? BUT... WHAT ABOUT YOU?
DON'T WORRY ABOUT ME...
I'VE GOT A PLANE TO CATCH.

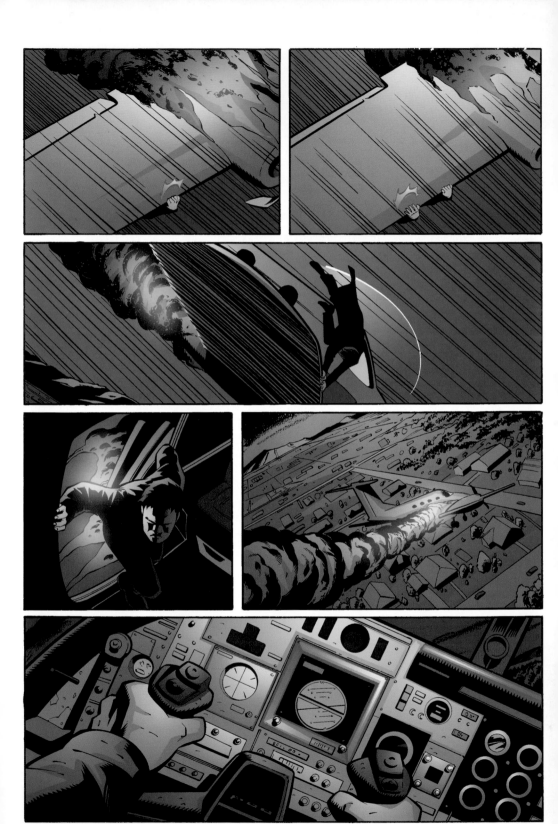

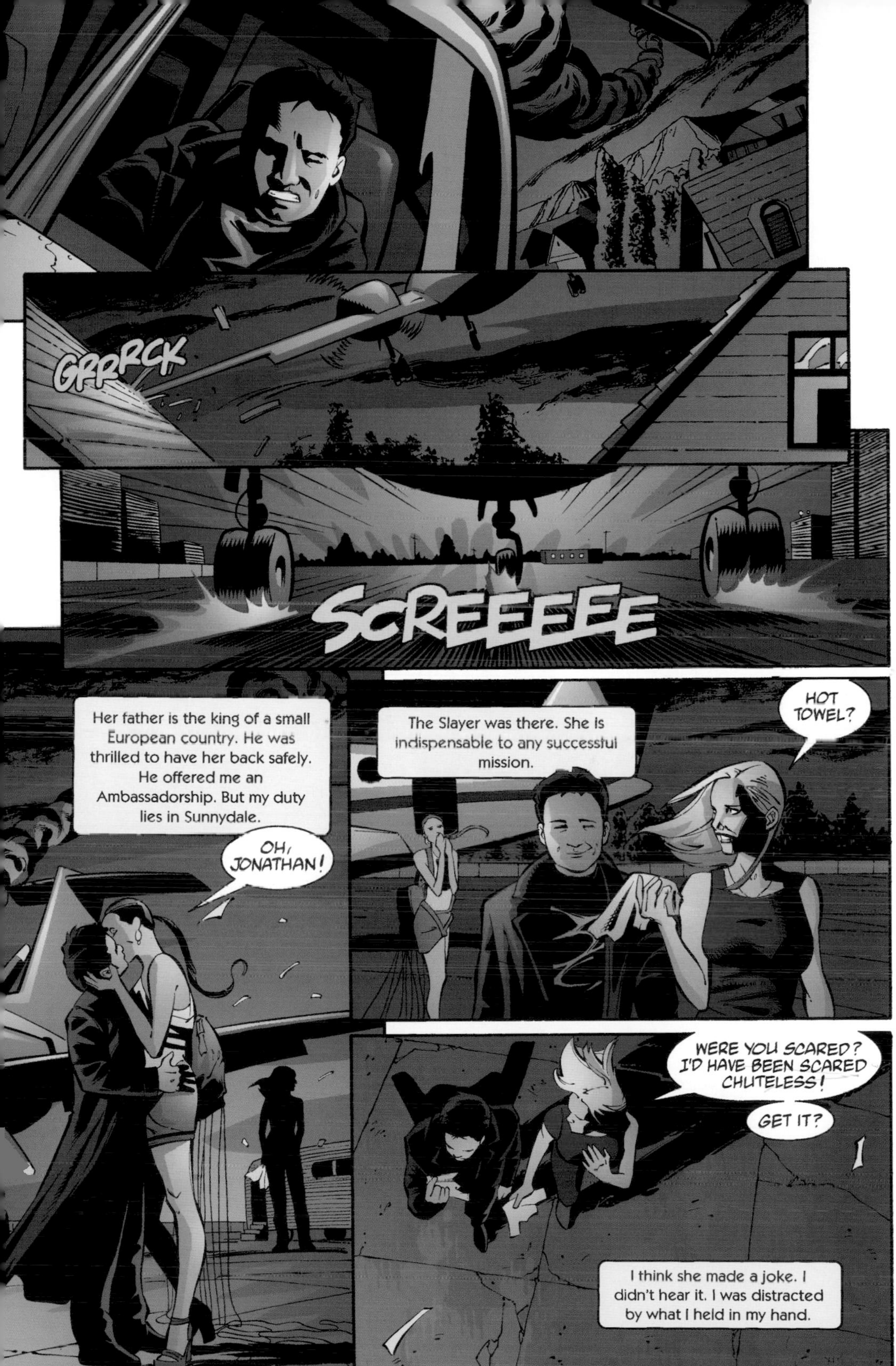
GRRRCK
SCREEEEEE
Her father is the king of a small European country. He was thrilled to have her back safely. He offered me an Ambassadorship. But my duty lies in Sunnydale.
OH, JONATHAN!
The Slayer was there. She is indispensable to any successful mission.
HOT TOWEL?
WERE YOU SCARED? I'D HAVE BEEN SCARED CHUTELESS!
GET IT?
I think she made a joke. I didn't hear it. I was distracted by what I held in my hand.

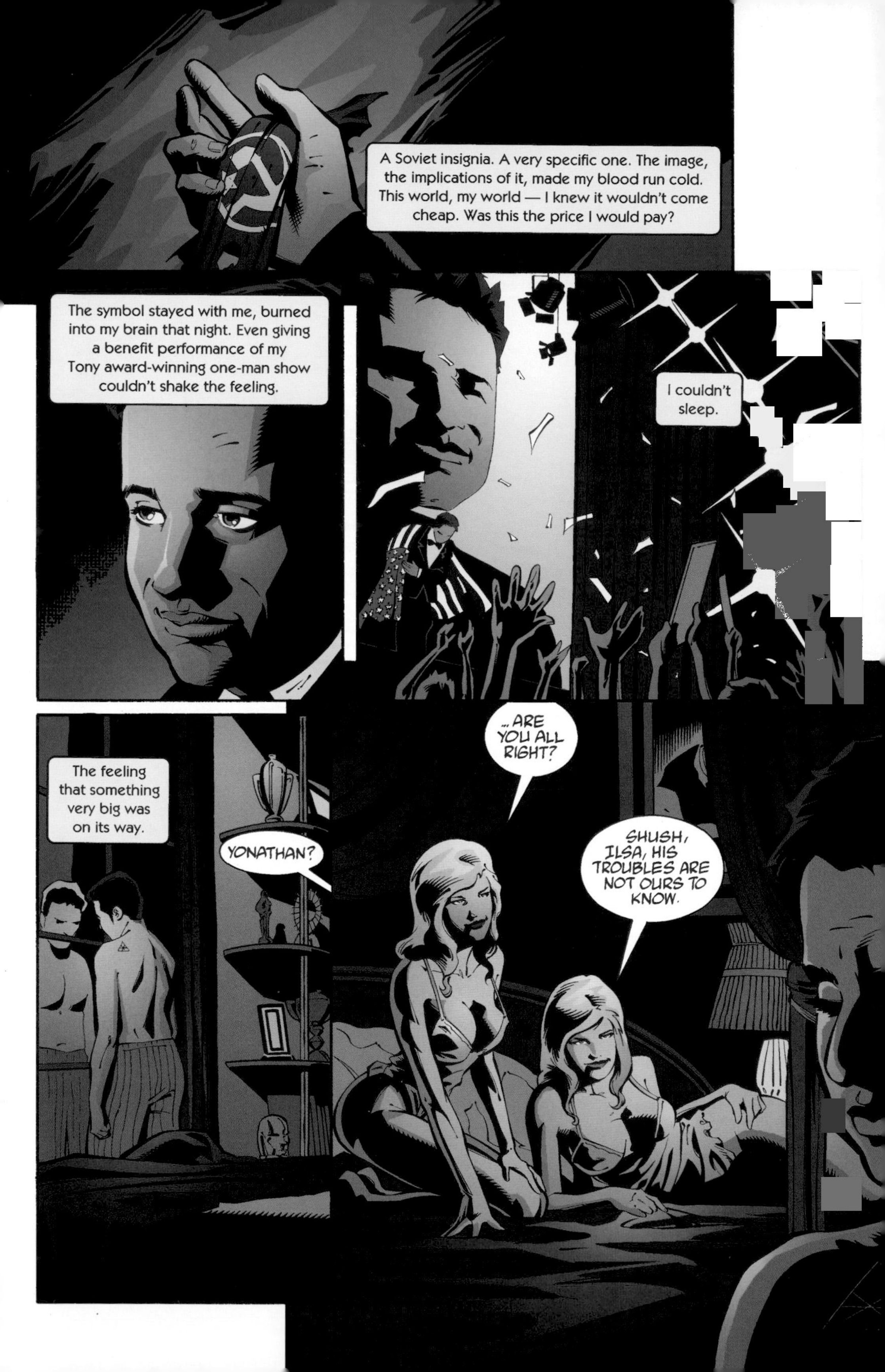

A Soviet insignia. A very specific one. The image, the implications of it, made my blood run cold. This world, my world — I knew it wouldn't come cheap. Was this the price I would pay?
The symbol stayed with me, burned into my brain that night. Even giving a benefit performance of my Tony award-winning one-man show couldn't shake the feeling.
I couldn't sleep.
The feeling that something very big was on its way.
YONATHAN?
...ARE YOU ALL RIGHT?
SHUSH, ILSA, HIS TROUBLES ARE NOT OURS TO KNOW.

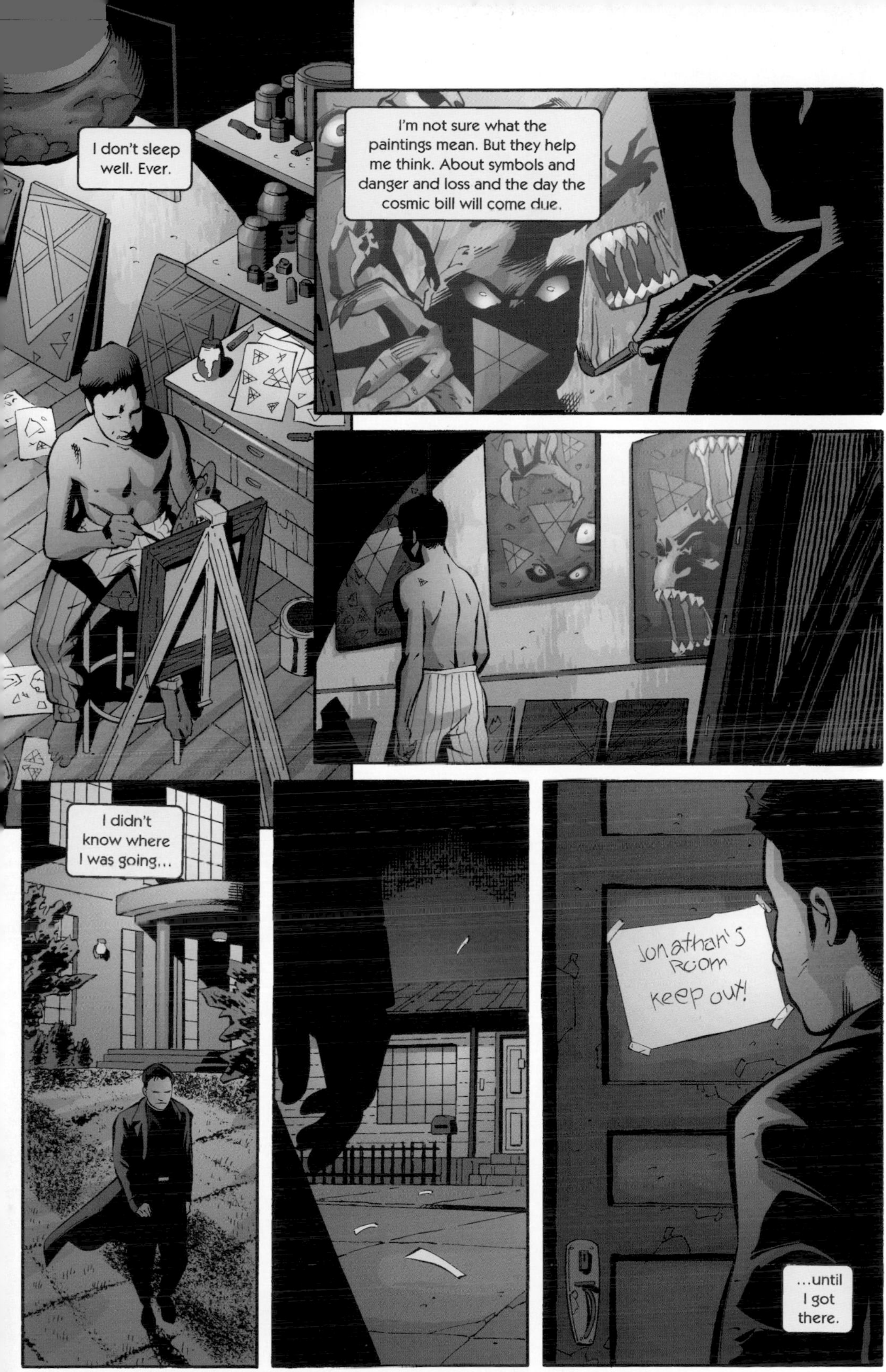
I don't sleep well. Ever.
I'm not sure what the paintings mean. But they help me think. About symbols and danger and loss and the day the cosmic bill will come due.
I didn't know where I was going...
Jonathan's Room
Keep out!
...until I got there.

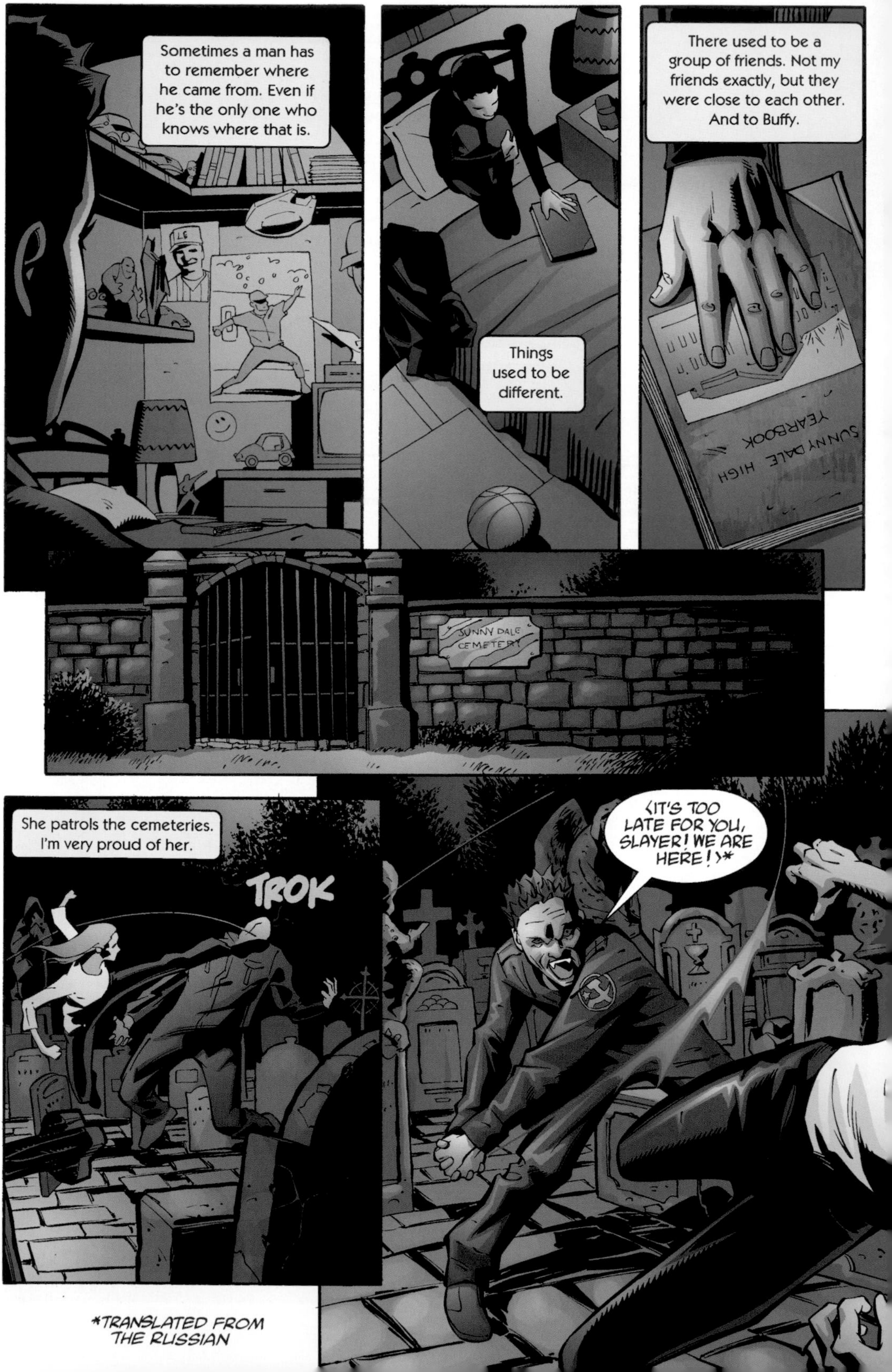
Sometimes a man has to remember where he came from. Even if he's the only one who knows where that is.
Things used to be different.
There used to be a group of friends. Not my friends exactly, but they were close to each other. And to Buffy.
SUNNYDALE HIGH YEARBOOK
SUNNYDALE CEMETERY
She patrols the cemeteries. I'm very proud of her.
TROK
‹IT'S TOO LATE FOR YOU, SLAYER! WE ARE HERE!›*
*TRANSLATED FROM THE RUSSIAN

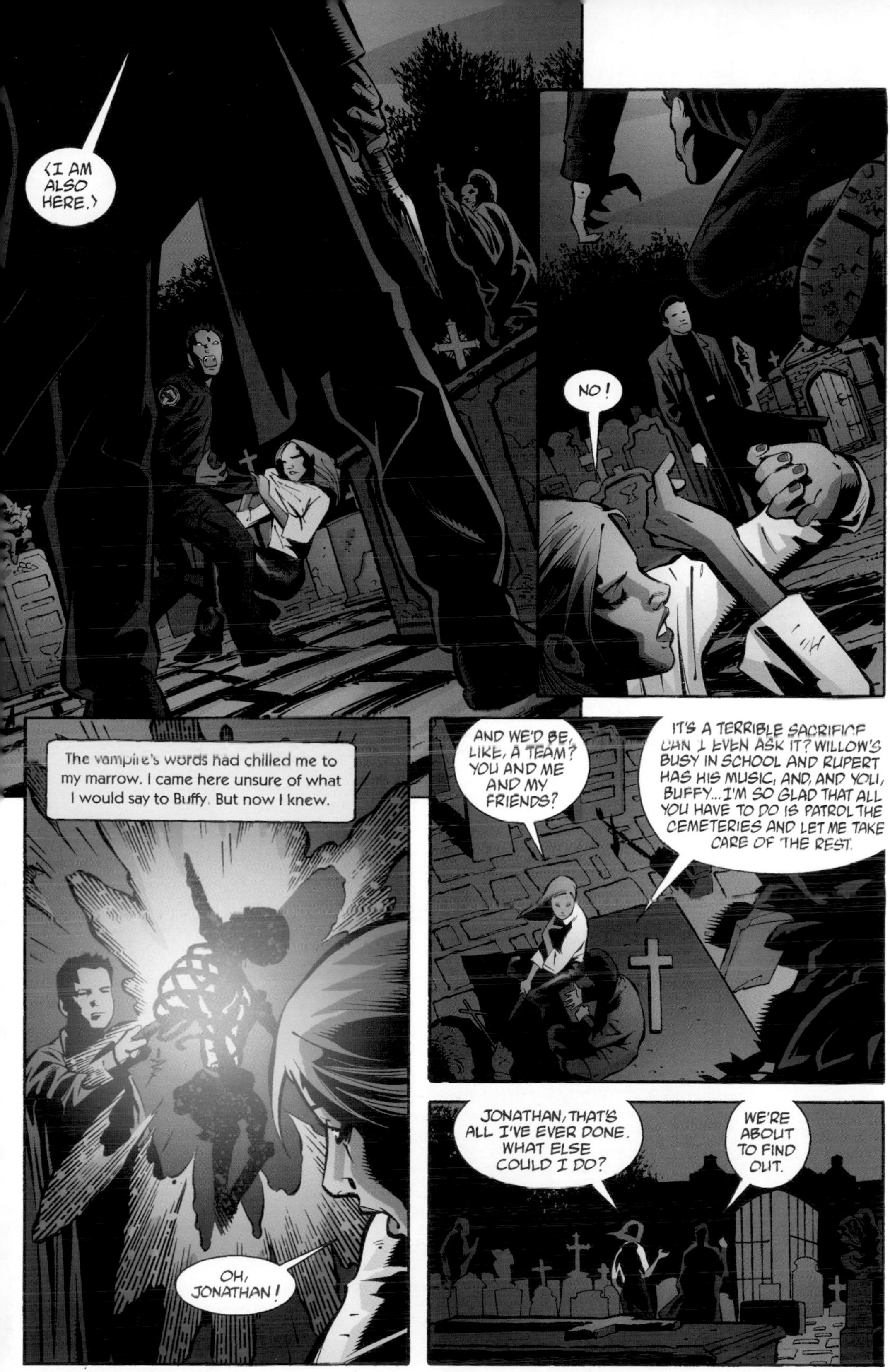

<I AM ALSO HERE.>
NO!
The vampire's words had chilled me to my marrow. I came here unsure of what I would say to Buffy. But now I knew.
OH, JONATHAN!
AND WE'D BE, LIKE, A TEAM? YOU AND ME AND MY FRIENDS?
IT'S A TERRIBLE SACRIFICE CAN I EVEN ASK IT? WILLOW'S BUSY IN SCHOOL AND RUPERT HAS HIS MUSIC, AND, AND YOU, BUFFY... I'M SO GLAD THAT ALL YOU HAVE TO DO IS PATROL THE CEMETERIES AND LET ME TAKE CARE OF THE REST.
JONATHAN, THAT'S ALL I'VE EVER DONE. WHAT ELSE COULD I DO?
WE'RE ABOUT TO FIND OUT.

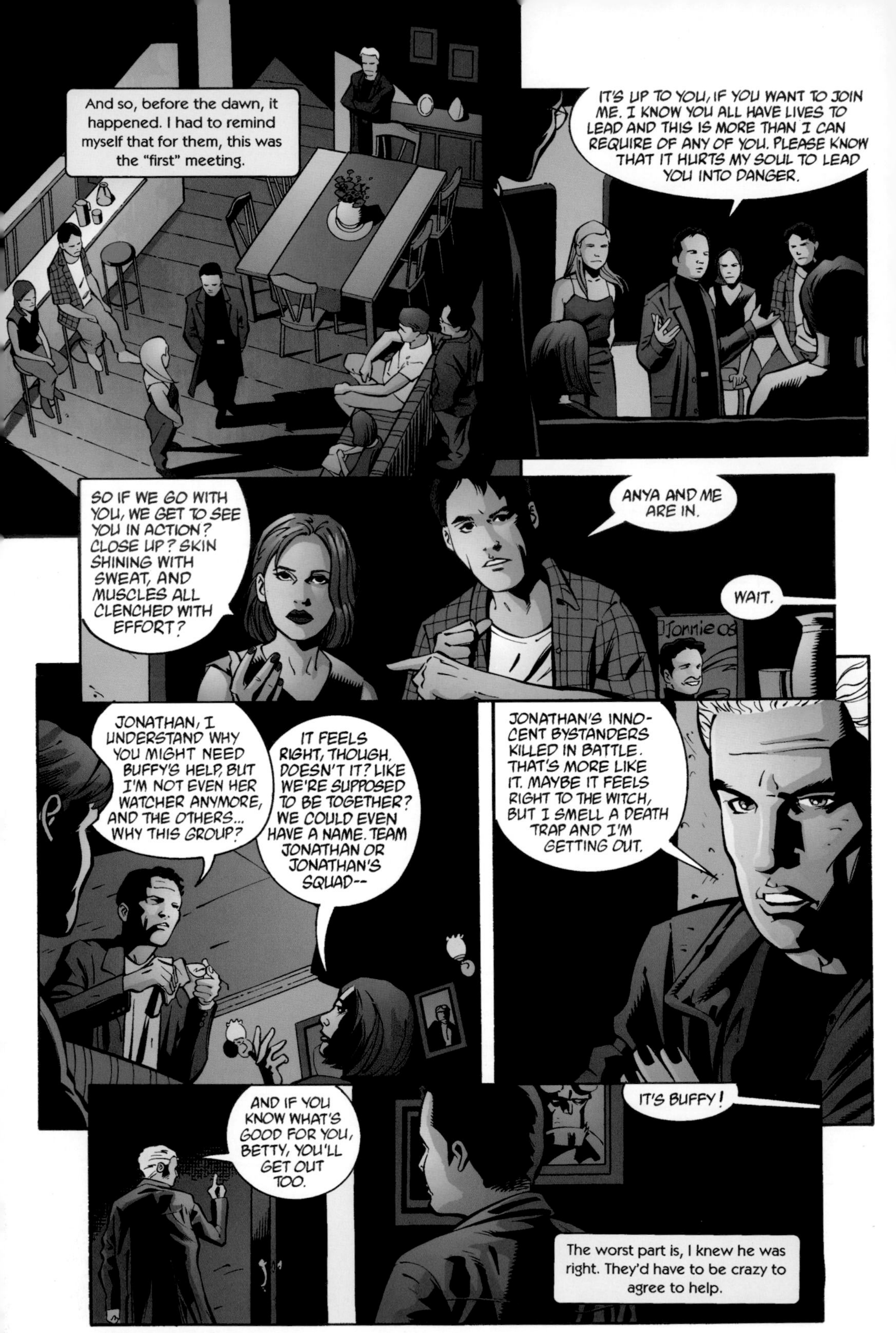
And so, before the dawn, it happened. I had to remind myself that for them, this was the "first" meeting.
IT'S UP TO YOU, IF YOU WANT TO JOIN ME. I KNOW YOU ALL HAVE LIVES TO LEAD AND THIS IS MORE THAN I CAN REQUIRE OF ANY OF YOU. PLEASE KNOW THAT IT HURTS MY SOUL TO LEAD YOU INTO DANGER.
SO IF WE GO WITH YOU, WE GET TO SEE YOU IN ACTION? CLOSE UP? SKIN SHINING WITH SWEAT, AND MUSCLES ALL CLENCHED WITH EFFORT?
ANYA AND ME ARE IN.
WAIT.
Jonnie 08
JONATHAN, I UNDERSTAND WHY YOU MIGHT NEED BUFFY'S HELP, BUT I'M NOT EVEN HER WATCHER ANYMORE, AND THE OTHERS... WHY THIS GROUP?
IT FEELS RIGHT, THOUGH, DOESN'T IT? LIKE WE'RE SUPPOSED TO BE TOGETHER? WE COULD EVEN HAVE A NAME. TEAM JONATHAN OR JONATHAN'S SQUAD--
JONATHAN'S INNOCENT BYSTANDERS KILLED IN BATTLE. THAT'S MORE LIKE IT. MAYBE IT FEELS RIGHT TO THE WITCH, BUT I SMELL A DEATH TRAP AND I'M GETTING OUT.
AND IF YOU KNOW WHAT'S GOOD FOR YOU, BETTY, YOU'LL GET OUT TOO.
IT'S BUFFY!
The worst part is, I knew he was right. They'd have to be crazy to agree to help.

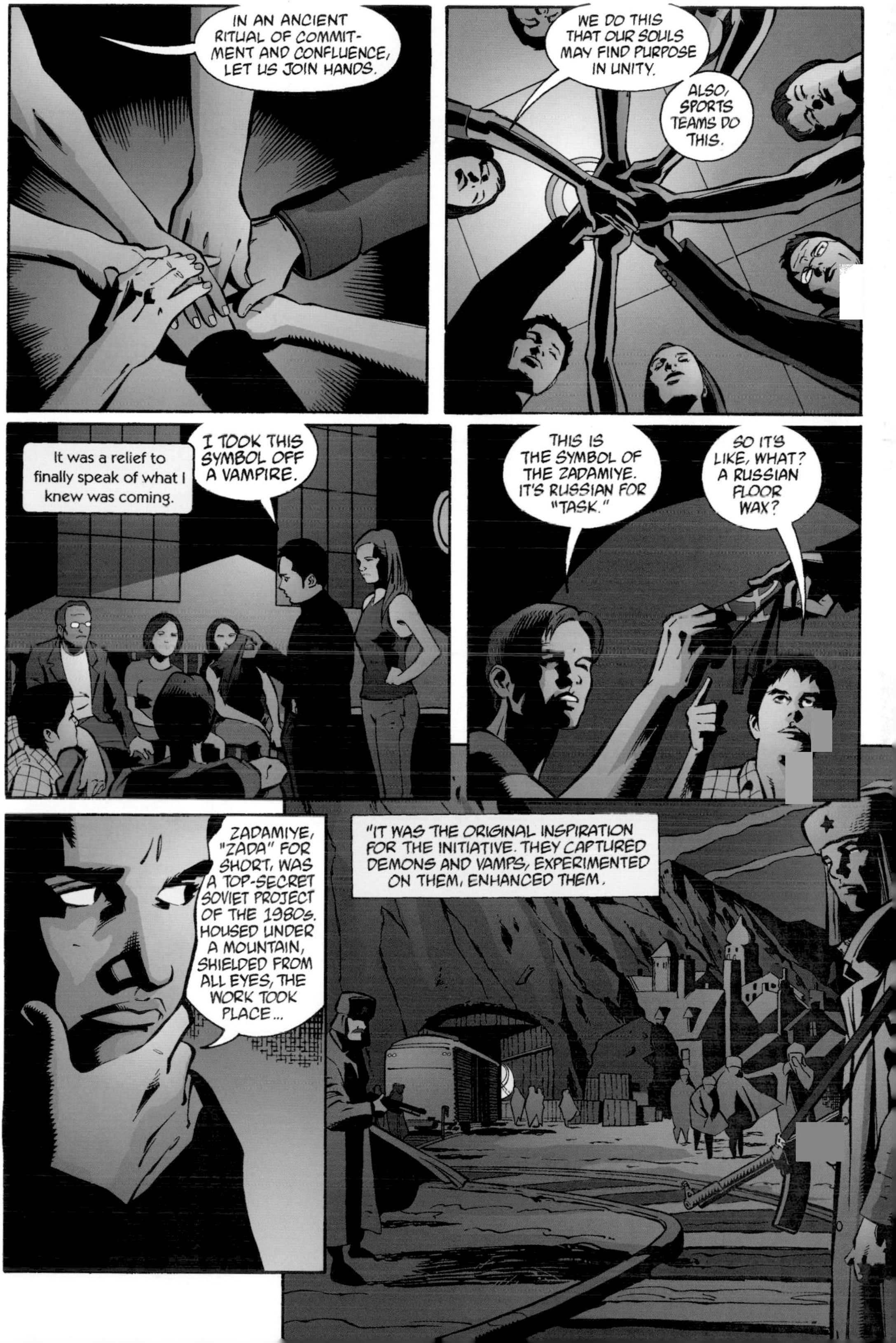
IN AN ANCIENT RITUAL OF COMMITMENT AND CONFLUENCE, LET US JOIN HANDS.
WE DO THIS THAT OUR SOULS MAY FIND PURPOSE IN UNITY.
ALSO, SPORTS TEAMS DO THIS.
It was a relief to finally speak of what I knew was coming.
I TOOK THIS SYMBOL OFF A VAMPIRE.
THIS IS THE SYMBOL OF THE ZADAMIYE. IT'S RUSSIAN FOR "TASK."
SO IT'S LIKE, WHAT? A RUSSIAN FLOOR WAX?
ZADAMIYE, "ZADA" FOR SHORT, WAS A TOP-SECRET SOVIET PROJECT OF THE 1980s. HOUSED UNDER A MOUNTAIN, SHIELDED FROM ALL EYES, THE WORK TOOK PLACE...
"IT WAS THE ORIGINAL INSPIRATION FOR THE INITIATIVE. THEY CAPTURED DEMONS AND VAMPS, EXPERIMENTED ON THEM, ENHANCED THEM.

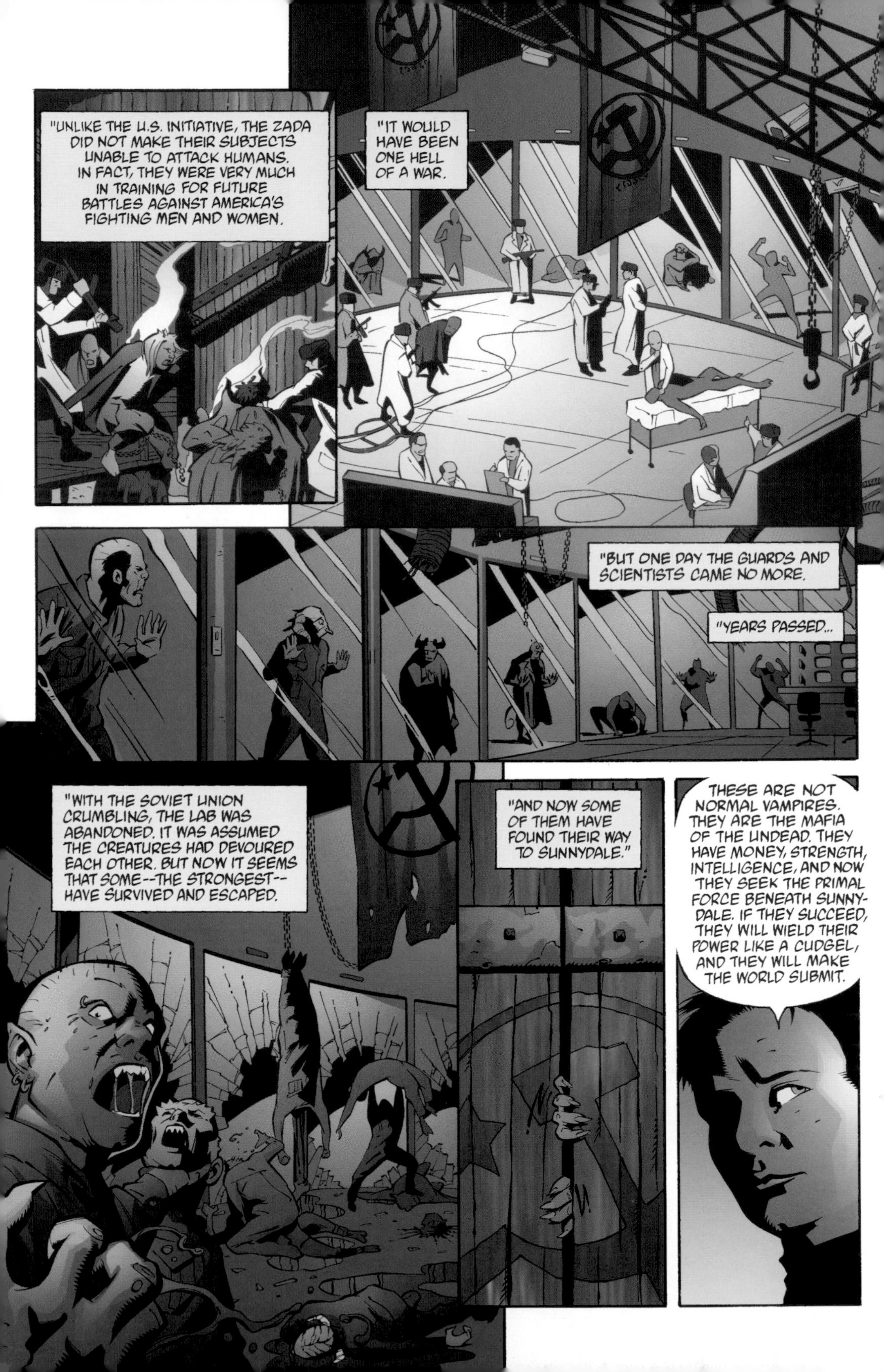
"UNLIKE THE U.S. INITIATIVE, THE ZADA DID NOT MAKE THEIR SUBJECTS UNABLE TO ATTACK HUMANS. IN FACT, THEY WERE VERY MUCH IN TRAINING FOR FUTURE BATTLES AGAINST AMERICA'S FIGHTING MEN AND WOMEN.
"IT WOULD HAVE BEEN ONE HELL OF A WAR.
"BUT ONE DAY THE GUARDS AND SCIENTISTS CAME NO MORE.
"YEARS PASSED...
"WITH THE SOVIET UNION CRUMBLING, THE LAB WAS ABANDONED. IT WAS ASSUMED THE CREATURES HAD DEVOURED EACH OTHER. BUT NOW IT SEEMS THAT SOME--THE STRONGEST--HAVE SURVIVED AND ESCAPED.
"AND NOW SOME OF THEM HAVE FOUND THEIR WAY TO SUNNYDALE."
THESE ARE NOT NORMAL VAMPIRES. THEY ARE THE MAFIA OF THE UNDEAD. THEY HAVE MONEY, STRENGTH, INTELLIGENCE, AND NOW THEY SEEK THE PRIMAL FORCE BENEATH SUNNYDALE. IF THEY SUCCEED, THEY WILL WIELD THEIR POWER LIKE A CUDGEL, AND THEY WILL MAKE THE WORLD SUBMIT.

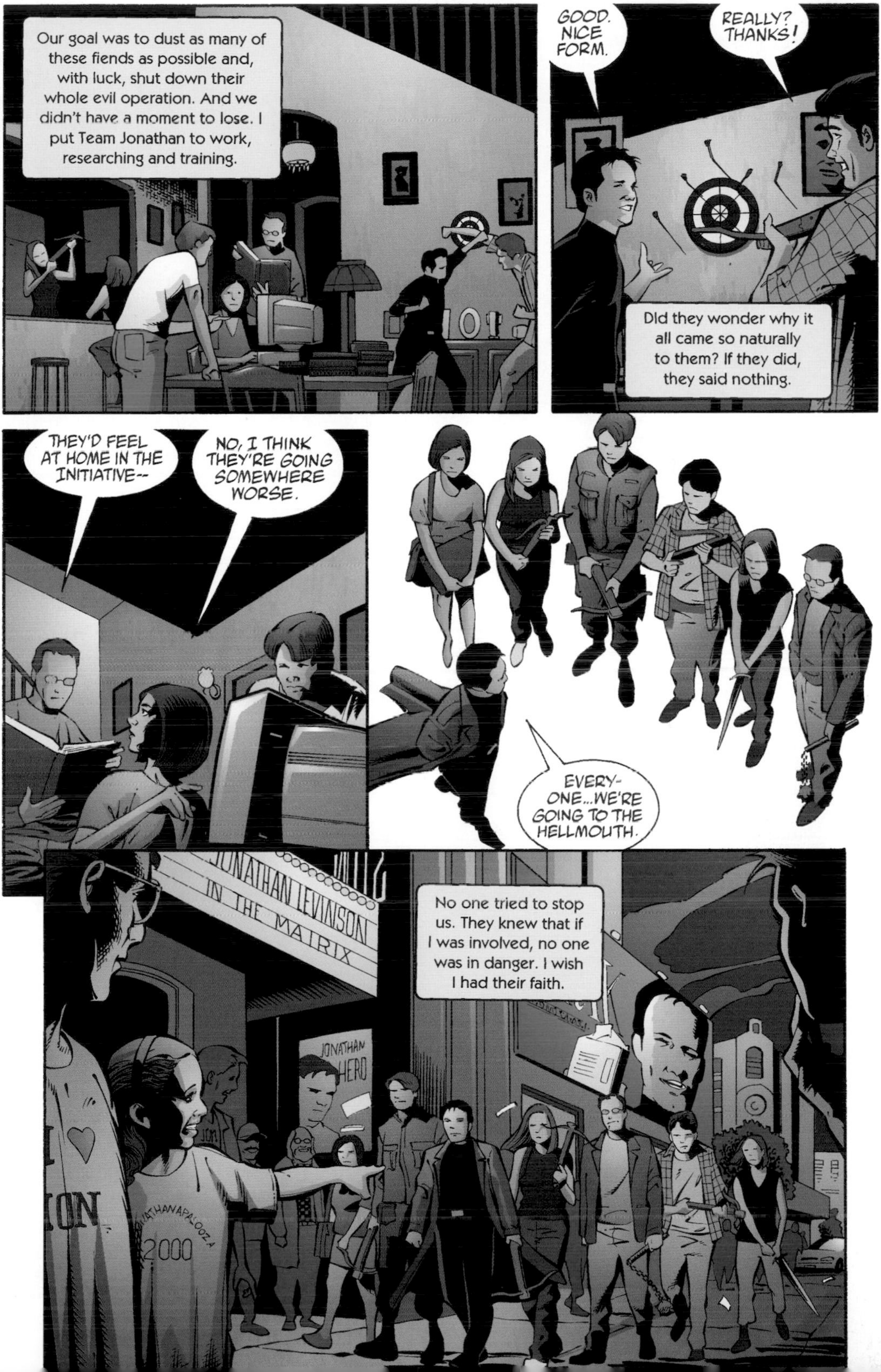

Our goal was to dust as many of these fiends as possible and, with luck, shut down their whole evil operation. And we didn't have a moment to lose. I put Team Jonathan to work, researching and training.
GOOD. NICE FORM.
REALLY? THANKS!
Did they wonder why it all came so naturally to them? If they did, they said nothing.
THEY'D FEEL AT HOME IN THE INITIATIVE--
NO, I THINK THEY'RE GOING SOMEWHERE WORSE.
EVERY-ONE...WE'RE GOING TO THE HELLMOUTH.
JONATHAN LEVINSON IN THE MATRIX
No one tried to stop us. They knew that if I was involved, no one was in danger. I wish I had their faith.
JONATHAN HERO
JONATHANAPALOOZA 2000

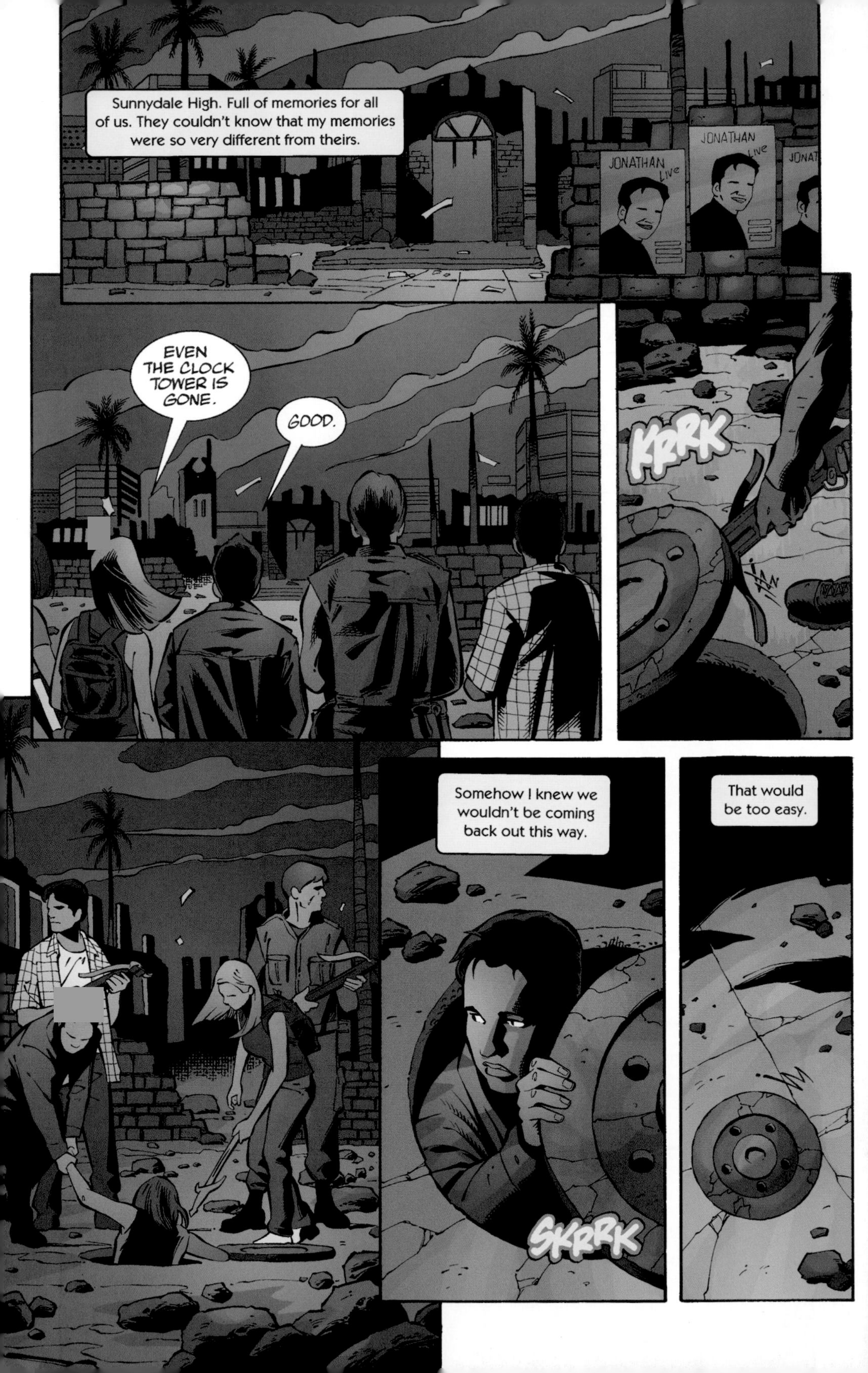
Sunnydale High. Full of memories for all of us. They couldn't know that my memories were so very different from theirs.
JONATHAN Live
JONATHAN Live
EVEN THE CLOCK TOWER IS GONE.
GOOD.
KRRK
Somehow I knew we wouldn't be coming back out this way.
SKRRK
That would be too easy.

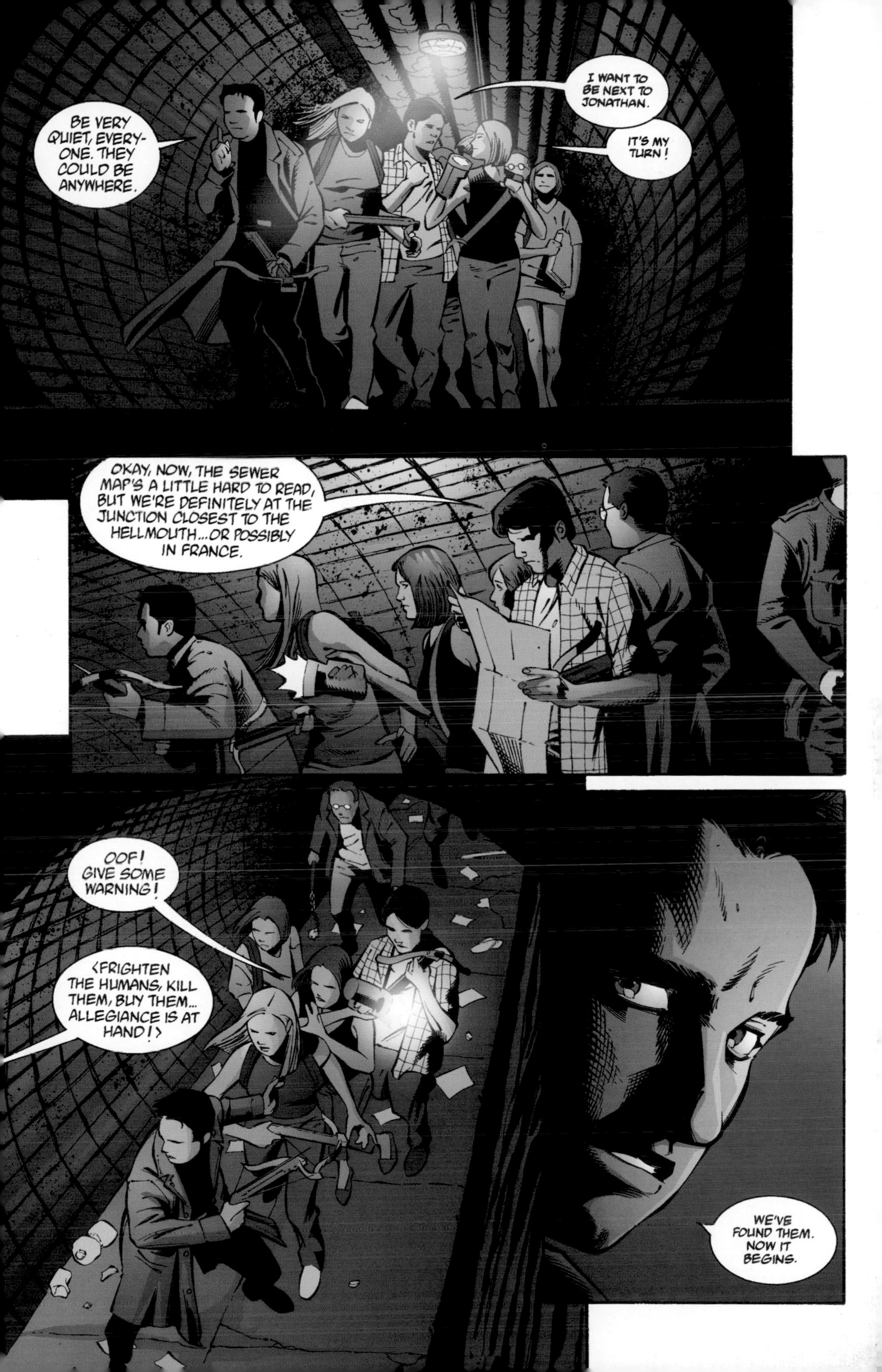
BE VERY QUIET, EVERY-ONE. THEY COULD BE ANYWHERE.
I WANT TO BE NEXT TO JONATHAN.
IT'S MY TURN!
OKAY, NOW, THE SEWER MAP'S A LITTLE HARD TO READ, BUT WE'RE DEFINITELY AT THE JUNCTION CLOSEST TO THE HELLMOUTH...OR POSSIBLY IN FRANCE.
OOF! GIVE SOME WARNING!
<FRIGHTEN THE HUMANS, KILL THEM, BUY THEM... ALLEGIANCE IS AT HAND!>
WE'VE FOUND THEM. NOW IT BEGINS.

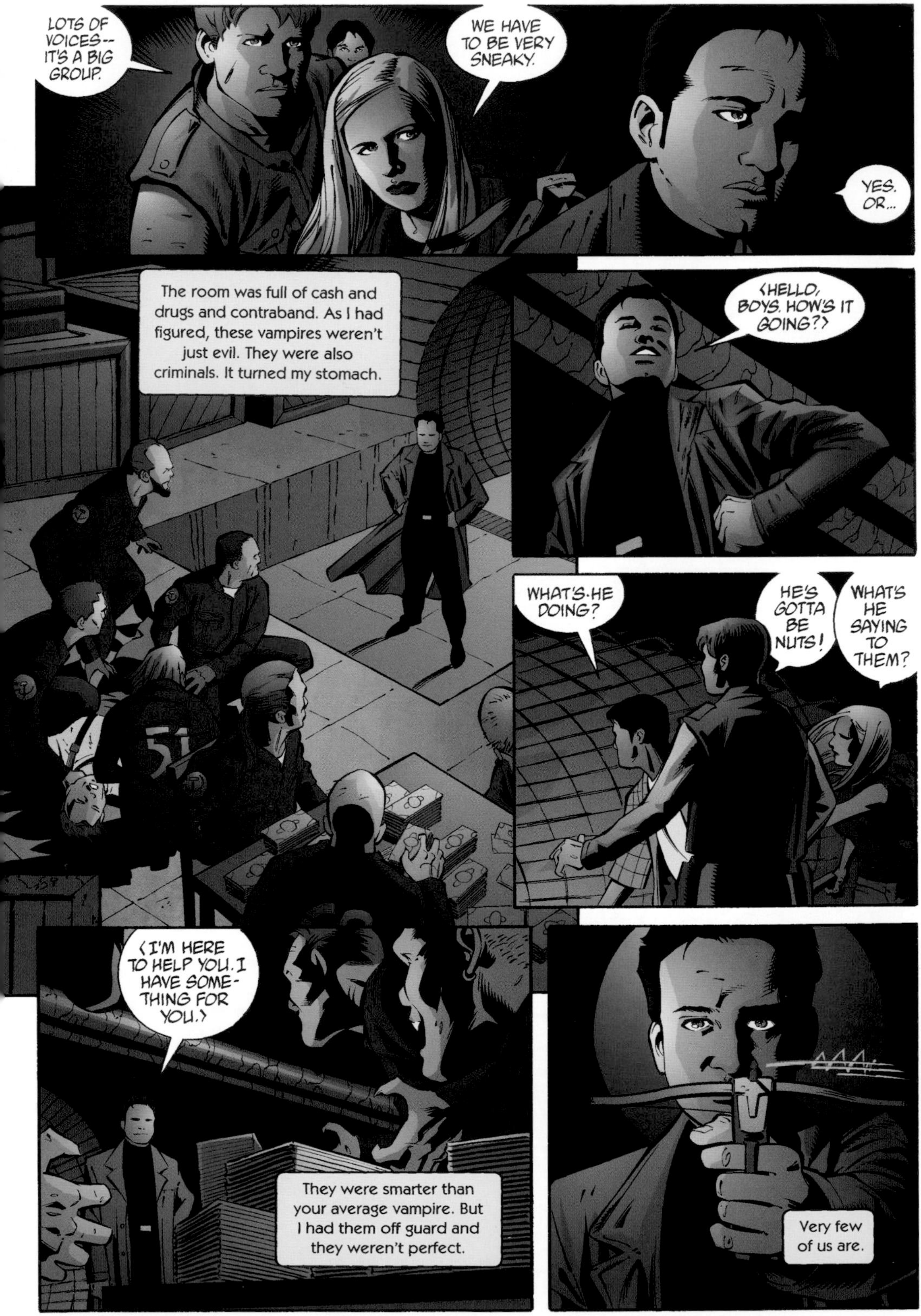
LOTS OF VOICES-- IT'S A BIG GROUP.
WE HAVE TO BE VERY SNEAKY.
YES. OR...
The room was full of cash and drugs and contraband. As I had figured, these vampires weren't just evil. They were also criminals. It turned my stomach.
‹HELLO, BOYS. HOW'S IT GOING?›
WHAT'S HE DOING?
HE'S GOTTA BE NUTS!
WHAT'S HE SAYING TO THEM?
‹I'M HERE TO HELP YOU. I HAVE SOMETHING FOR YOU.›
They were smarter than your average vampire. But I had them off guard and they weren't perfect.
Very few of us are.

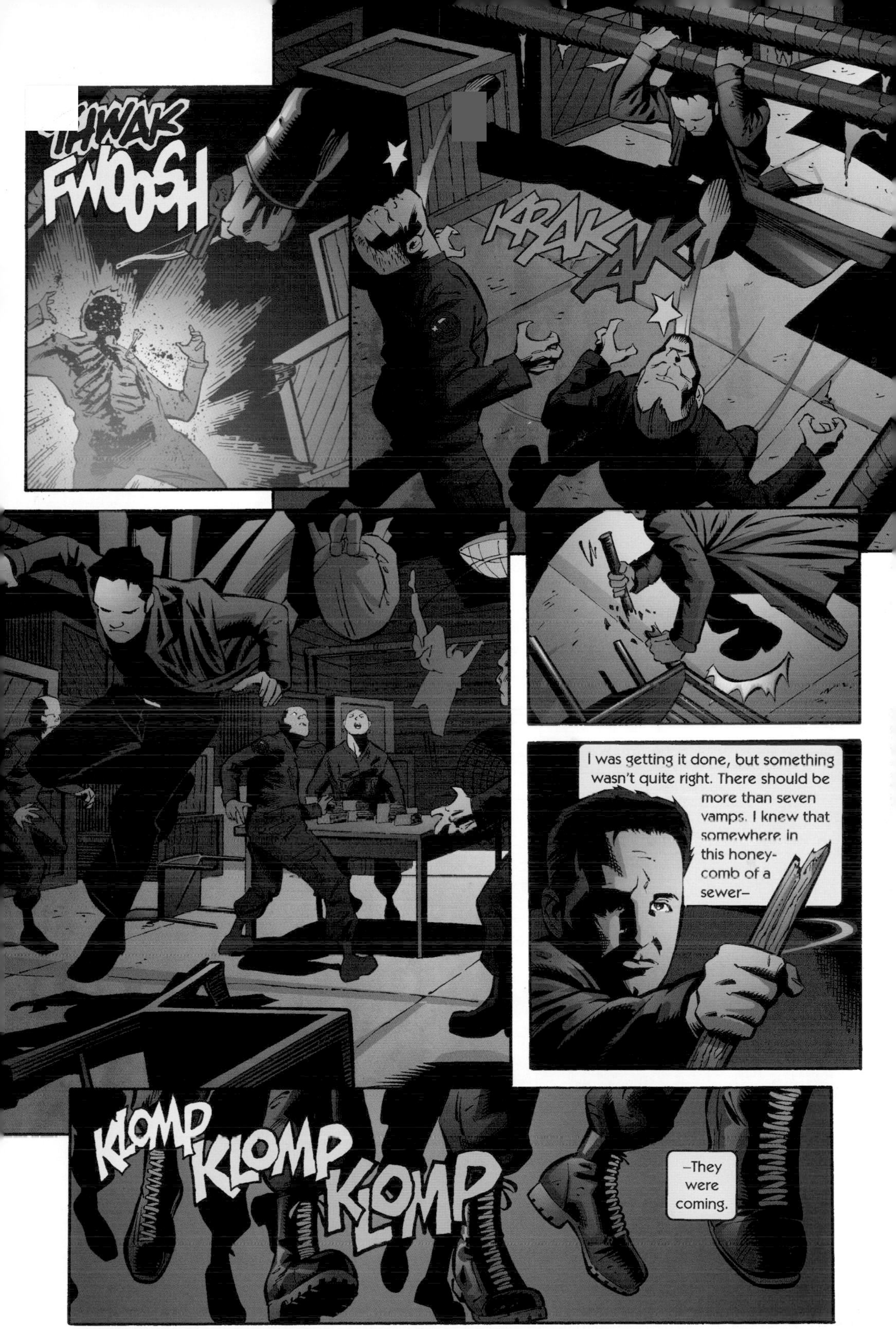
THWAK
FWOOSH
KRAKAKAK
I was getting it done, but something wasn't quite right. There should be more than seven vamps. I knew that somewhere in this honeycomb of a sewer–
KLOMP KLOMP KLOMP KLOMP
–They were coming.

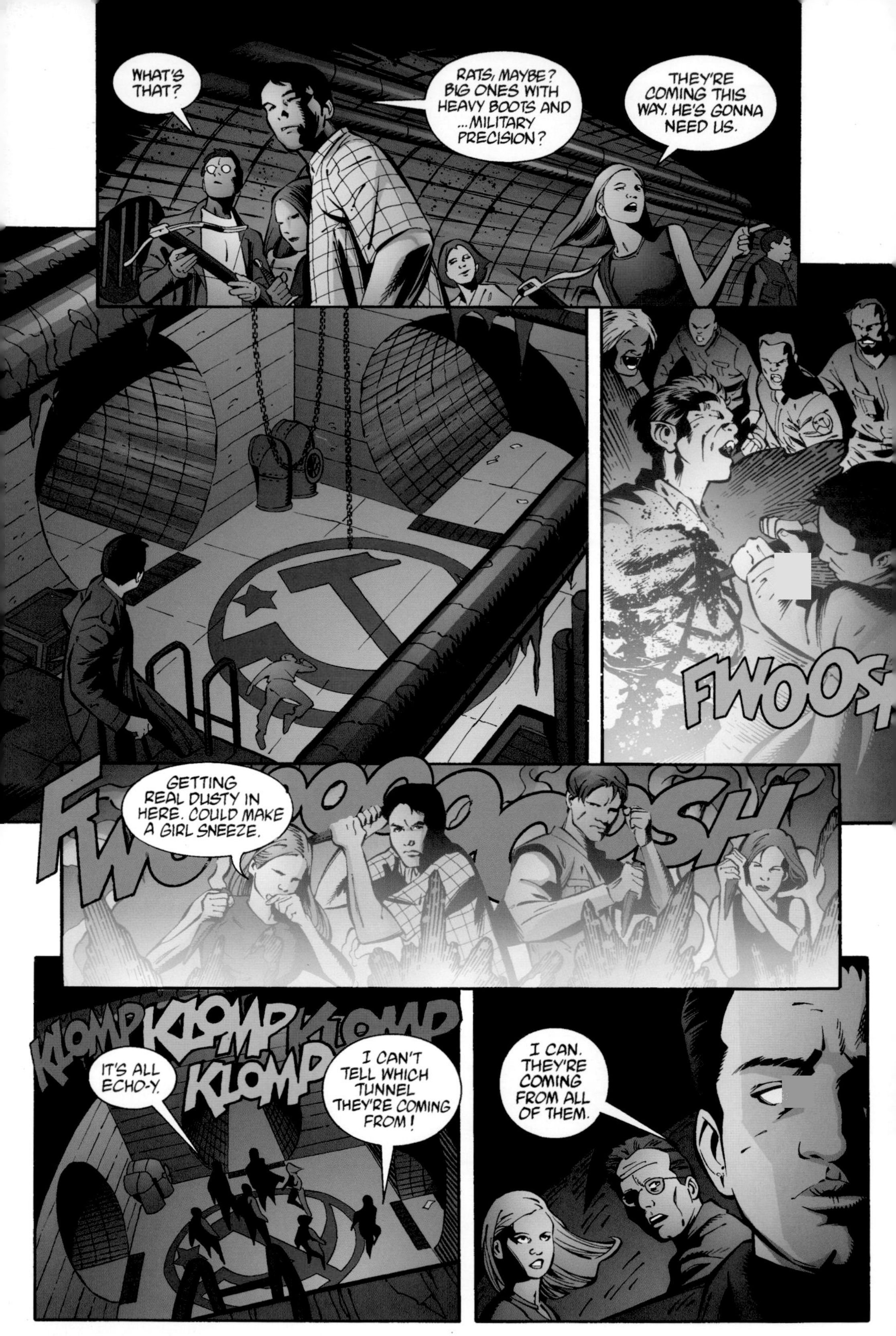
WHAT'S THAT?
RATS, MAYBE? BIG ONES WITH HEAVY BOOTS AND ...MILITARY PRECISION?
THEY'RE COMING THIS WAY. HE'S GONNA NEED US.
FWOOS
GETTING REAL DUSTY IN HERE. COULD MAKE A GIRL SNEEZE.
IT'S ALL ECHO-Y.
KLOMP
I CAN'T TELL WHICH TUNNEL THEY'RE COMING FROM!
I CAN. THEY'RE COMING FROM ALL OF THEM.

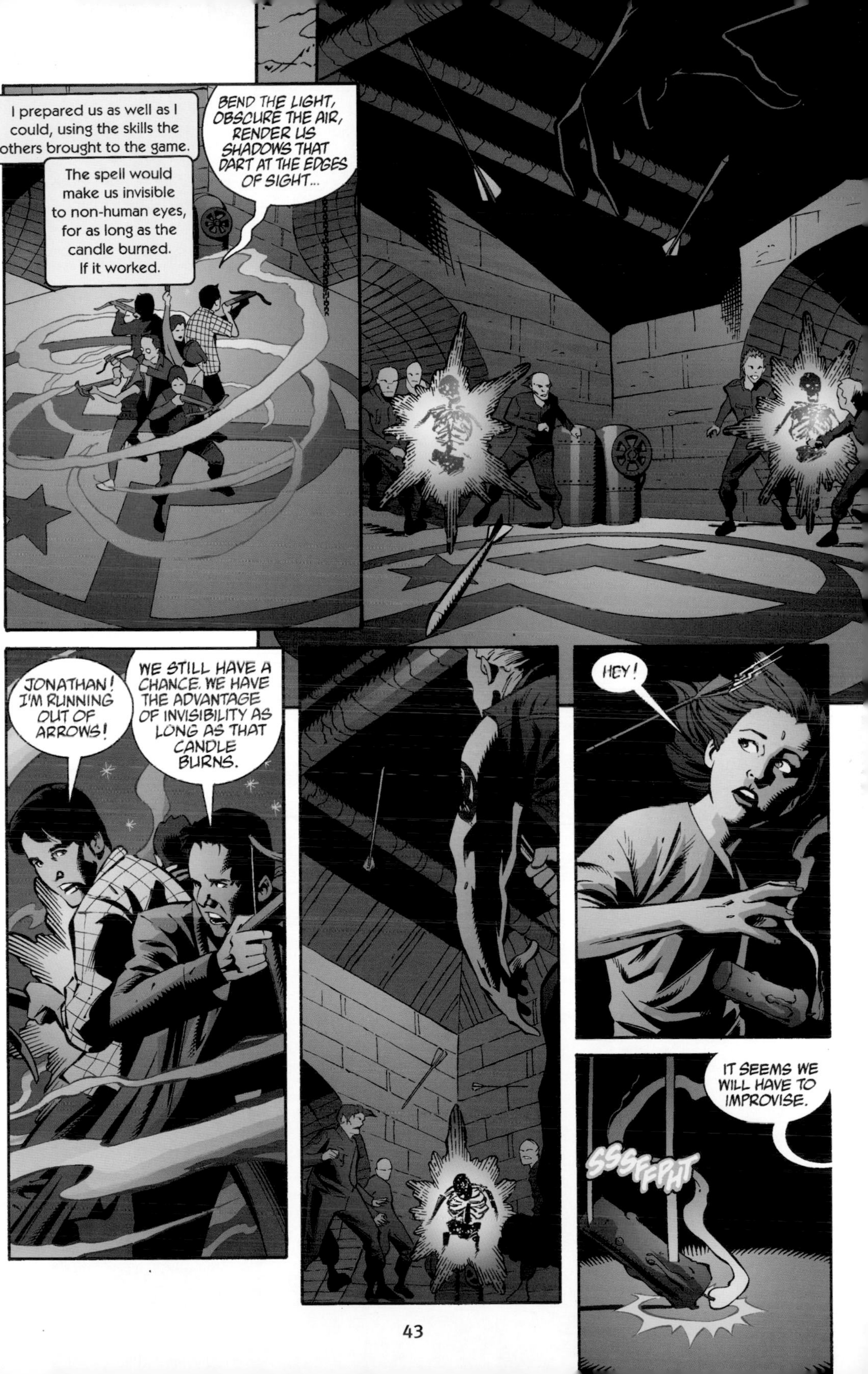
I prepared us as well as I could, using the skills the others brought to the game.
The spell would make us invisible to non-human eyes, for as long as the candle burned. If it worked.
BEND THE LIGHT, OBSCURE THE AIR, RENDER US SHADOWS THAT DART AT THE EDGES OF SIGHT...
JONATHAN! I'M RUNNING OUT OF ARROWS!
WE STILL HAVE A CHANCE. WE HAVE THE ADVANTAGE OF INVISIBILITY AS LONG AS THAT CANDLE BURNS.
HEY!
IT SEEMS WE WILL HAVE TO IMPROVISE.
SSSFFPHT

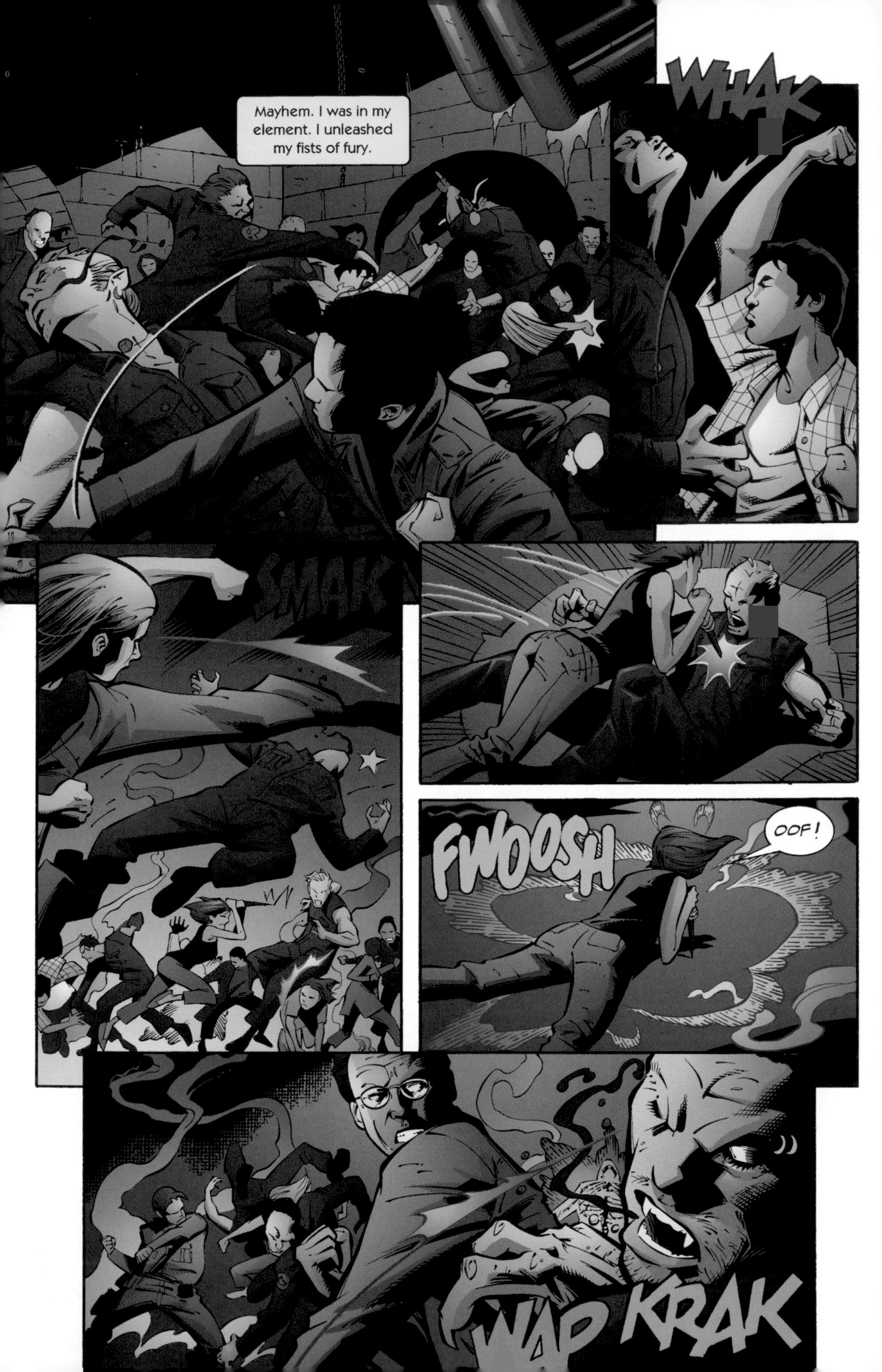
Mayhem. I was in my element. I unleashed my fists of fury.
WHAK
SMAK
FWOOSH
OOF!
WAP
KRAK

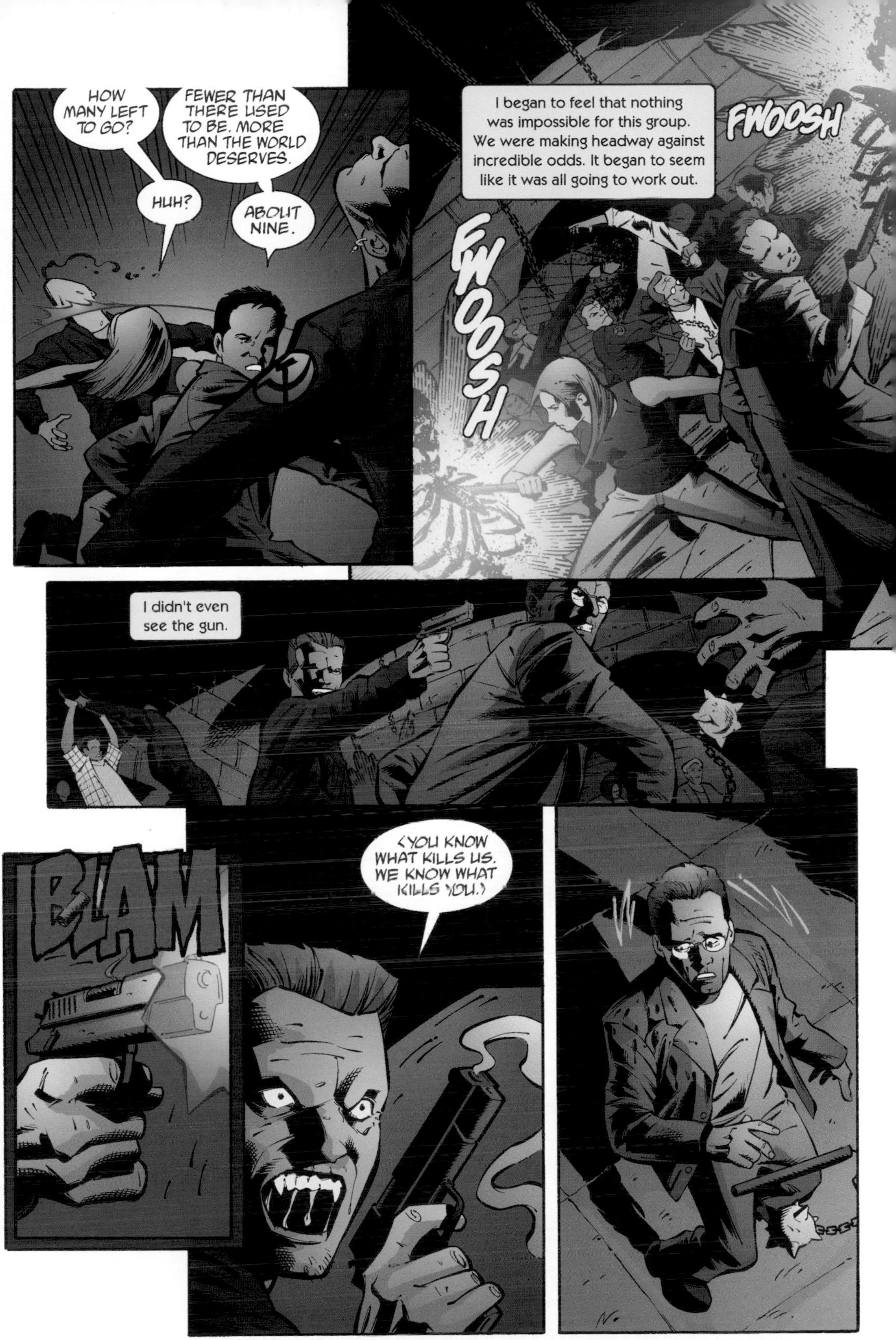
HOW MANY LEFT TO GO?
FEWER THAN THERE USED TO BE. MORE THAN THE WORLD DESERVES.
HUH?
ABOUT NINE.
I began to feel that nothing was impossible for this group. We were making headway against incredible odds. It began to seem like it was all going to work out.
FWOOSH
FWOOSH
I didn't even see the gun.
BLAM
<YOU KNOW WHAT KILLS US. WE KNOW WHAT KILLS YOU.>

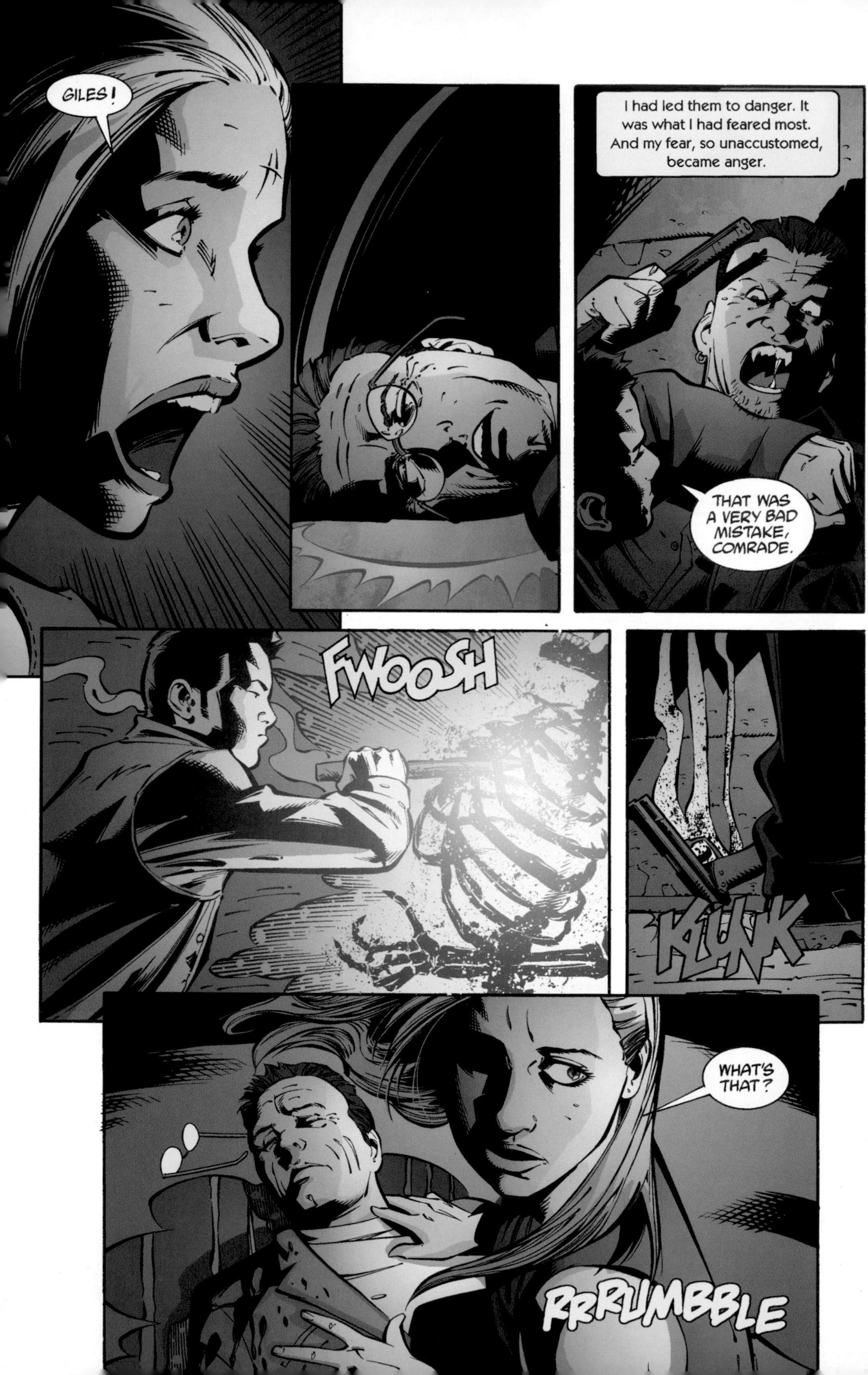
GILES!
I had led them to danger. It was what I had feared most. And my fear, so unaccustomed, became anger.
THAT WAS A VERY BAD MISTAKE, COMRADE.
FWOOSH
KLUNK
WHAT'S THAT?
RRRUMBBLE

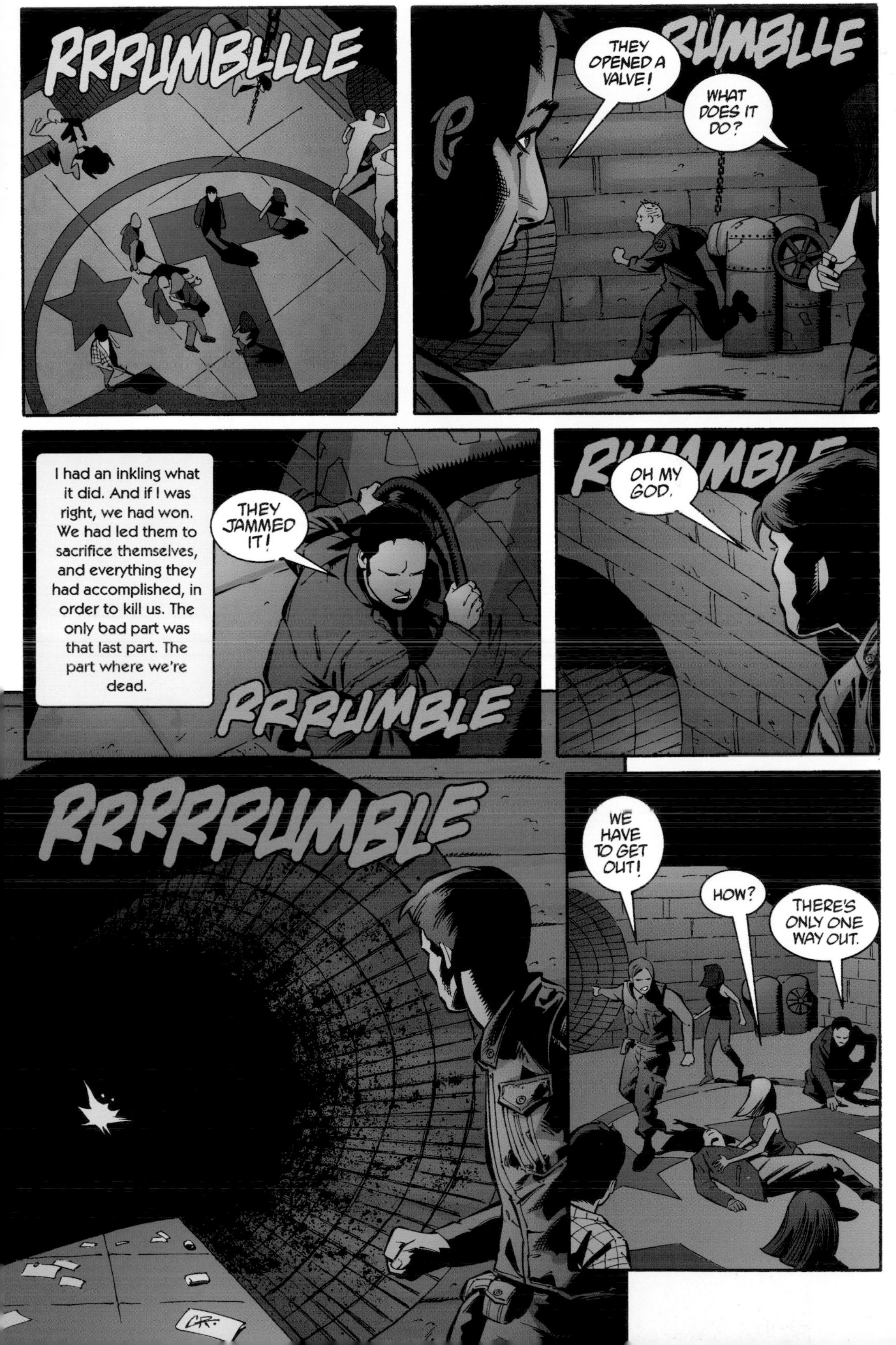
RRRUMBLLLE
RUMBLLE
THEY OPENED A VALVE!
WHAT DOES IT DO?
I had an inkling what it did. And if I was right, we had won. We had led them to sacrifice themselves, and everything they had accomplished, in order to kill us. The only bad part was that last part. The part where we're dead.
THEY JAMMED IT!
RRRUMBLE
OH MY GOD.
RRRRRRUMBLE
WE HAVE TO GET OUT!
HOW?
THERE'S ONLY ONE WAY OUT.
CR.

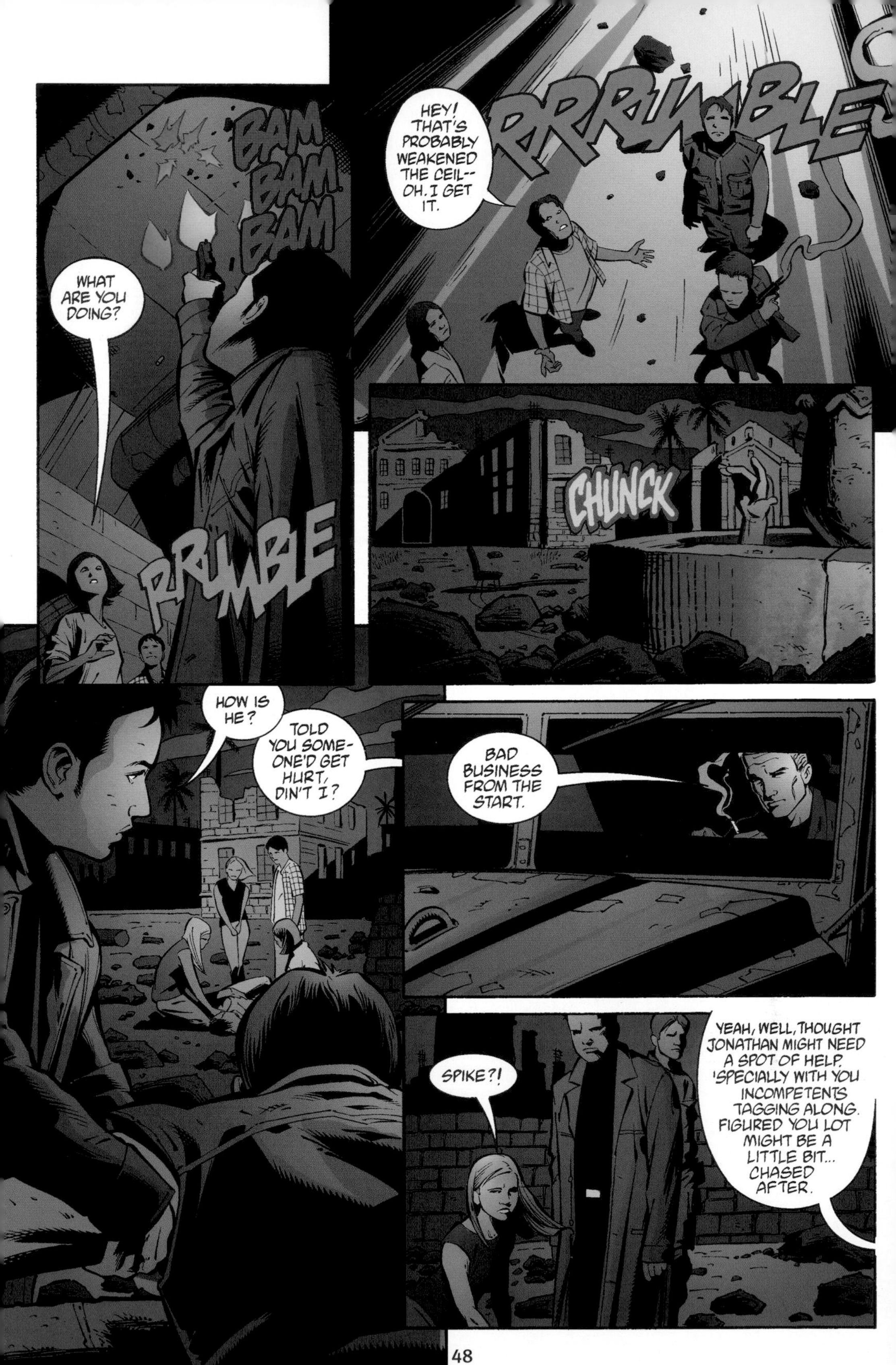
BAM BAM BAM
WHAT ARE YOU DOING?
RRUMBLE
HEY! THAT'S PROBABLY WEAKENED THE CEIL-- OH. I GET IT.
RRRUMBLE
CHUNCK
HOW IS HE?
TOLD YOU SOME-ONE'D GET HURT, DIN'T I?
BAD BUSINESS FROM THE START.
SPIKE?!
YEAH, WELL, THOUGHT JONATHAN MIGHT NEED A SPOT OF HELP. 'SPECIALLY WITH YOU INCOMPETENTS TAGGING ALONG. FIGURED YOU LOT MIGHT BE A LITTLE BIT... CHASED AFTER.

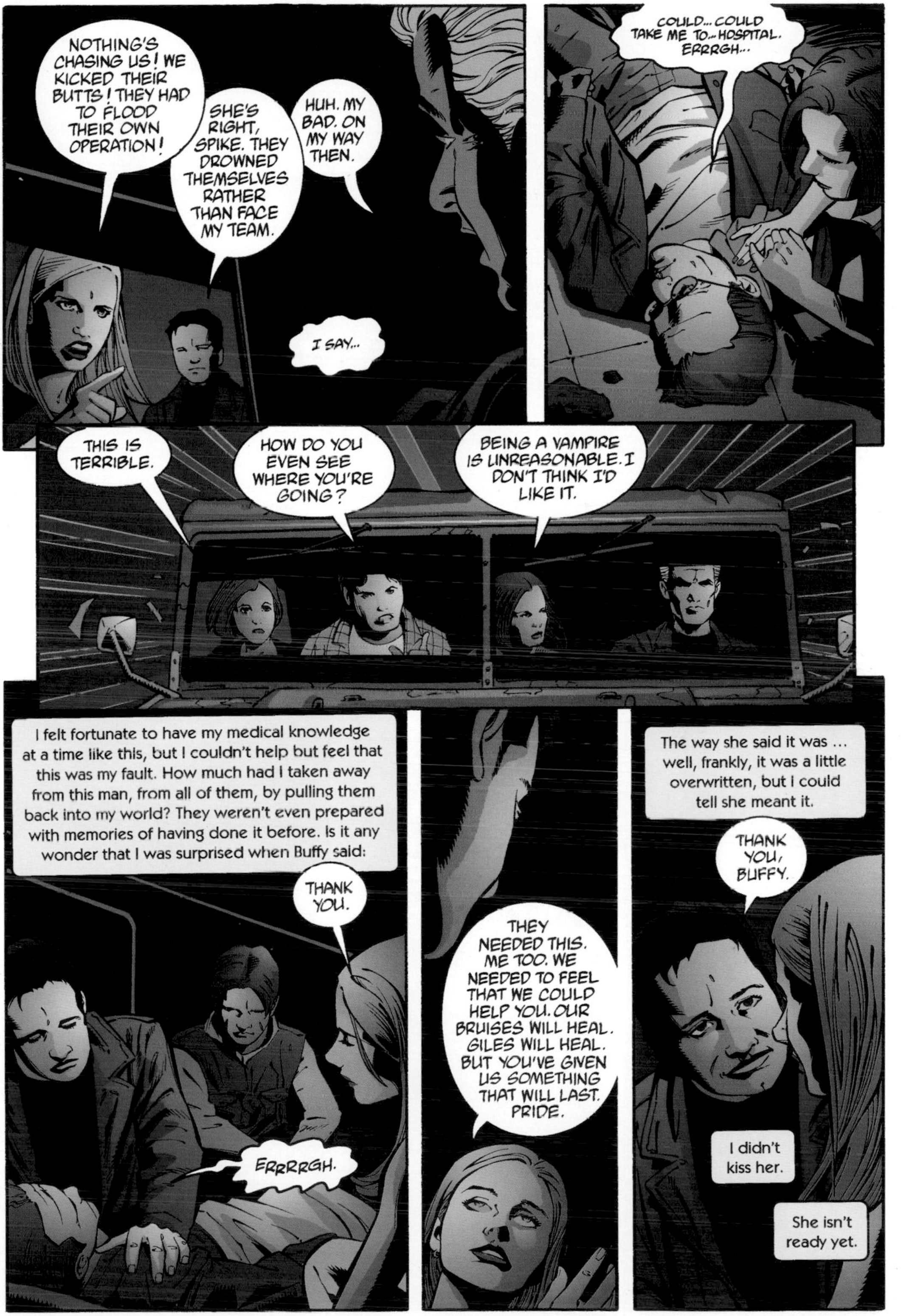
NOTHING'S CHASING US! WE KICKED THEIR BUTTS! THEY HAD TO FLOOD THEIR OWN OPERATION!
SHE'S RIGHT, SPIKE. THEY DROWNED THEMSELVES RATHER THAN FACE MY TEAM.
HUH. MY BAD. ON MY WAY THEN.
I SAY...
COULD... COULD TAKE ME TO... HOSPITAL. ERRRGH...
THIS IS TERRIBLE.
HOW DO YOU EVEN SEE WHERE YOU'RE GOING?
BEING A VAMPIRE IS UNREASONABLE. I DON'T THINK I'D LIKE IT.
I felt fortunate to have my medical knowledge at a time like this, but I couldn't help but feel that this was my fault. How much had I taken away from this man, from all of them, by pulling them back into my world? They weren't even prepared with memories of having done it before. Is it any wonder that I was surprised when Buffy said:
THANK YOU.
ERRRRGH.
THEY NEEDED THIS. ME TOO. WE NEEDED TO FEEL THAT WE COULD HELP YOU. OUR BRUISES WILL HEAL. GILES WILL HEAL. BUT YOU'VE GIVEN US SOMETHING THAT WILL LAST. PRIDE.
The way she said it was … well, frankly, it was a little overwritten, but I could tell she meant it.
THANK YOU, BUFFY.
I didn't kiss her.
She isn't ready yet.

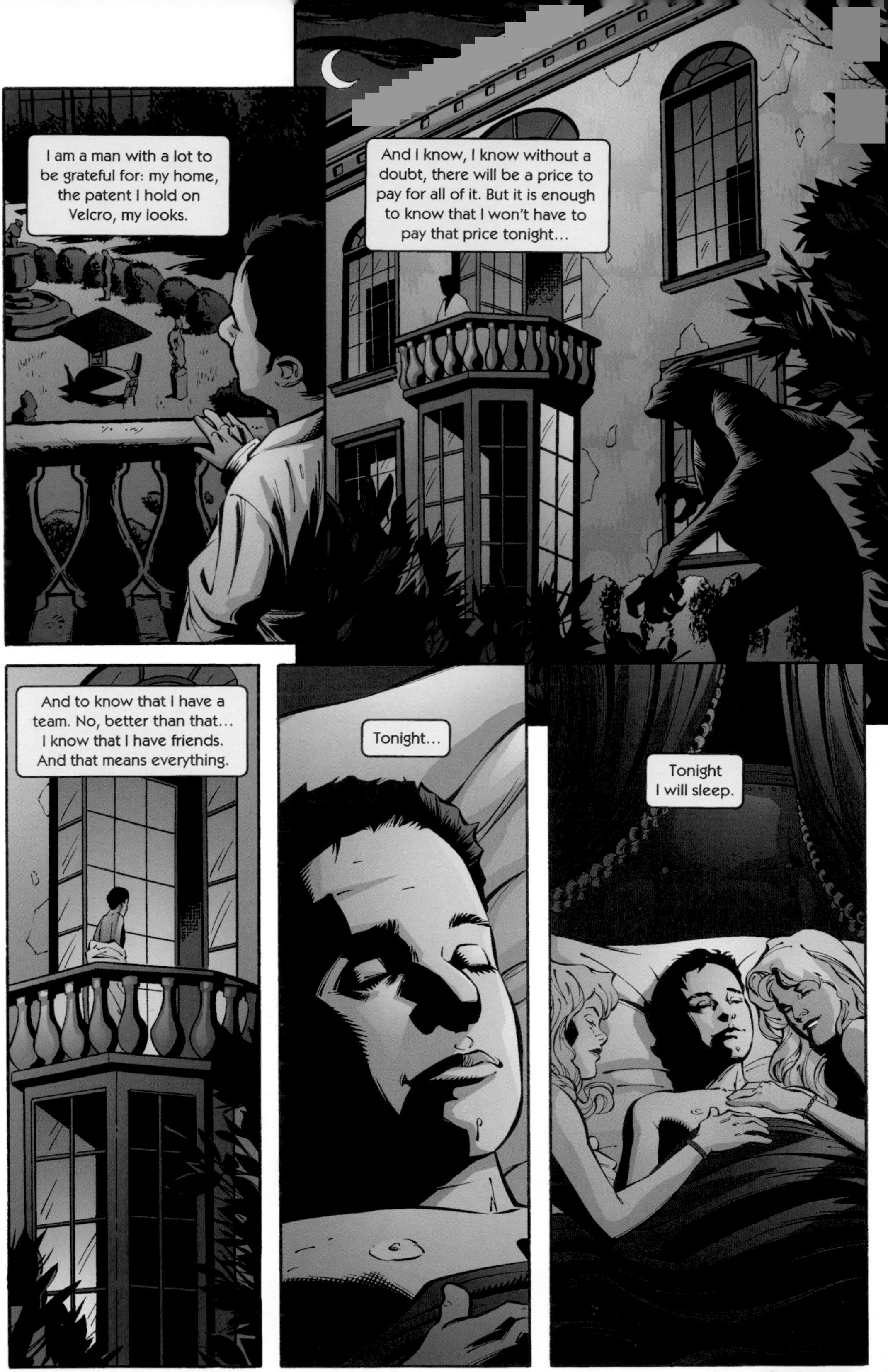
I am a man with a lot to be grateful for: my home, the patent I hold on Velcro, my looks.
And I know, I know without a doubt, there will be a price to pay for all of it. But it is enough to know that I won't have to pay that price tonight...
And to know that I have a team. No, better than that... I know that I have friends. And that means everything.
Tonight...
Tonight I will sleep.
THE END

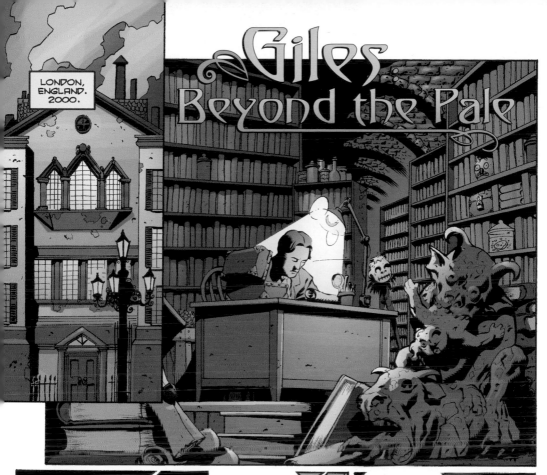

LONDON, ENGLAND. 2000.

Giles
Beyond the Pale

HMM. INTERESTING. NOTHING ABOUT THIS IN THE CATALOG.

BIG WOODEN BOX, SURE, BUT NOT A WORD ABOUT THE CONTENTS.

DID YOU SAY SOMETHING, THORTON?

I'VE JUST BEEN GOING THROUGH SOME OF THE MORE OBSCURE WATCHERS' JOURNALS.

51

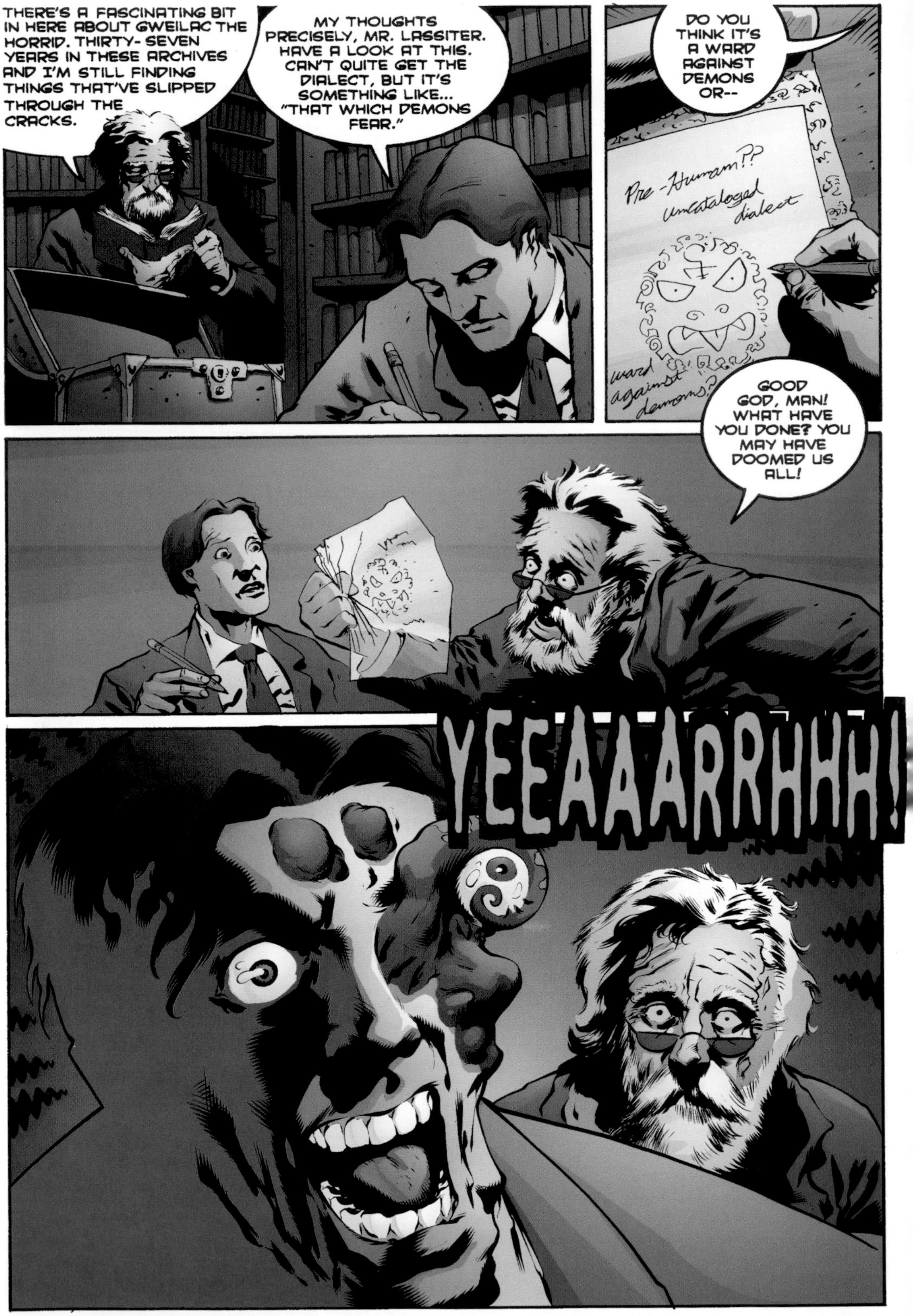
THERE'S A FASCINATING BIT IN HERE ABOUT GWEILAC THE HORRID. THIRTY- SEVEN YEARS IN THESE ARCHIVES AND I'M STILL FINDING THINGS THAT'VE SLIPPED THROUGH THE CRACKS.
MY THOUGHTS PRECISELY, MR. LASSITER. HAVE A LOOK AT THIS. CAN'T QUITE GET THE DIALECT, BUT IT'S SOMETHING LIKE... "THAT WHICH DEMONS FEAR."
DO YOU THINK IT'S A WARD AGAINST DEMONS OR--
Pre-Human??
uncataloged dialect
ward against demons?
GOOD GOD, MAN! WHAT HAVE YOU DONE? YOU MAY HAVE DOOMED US ALL!
YEEAAARRHHH!

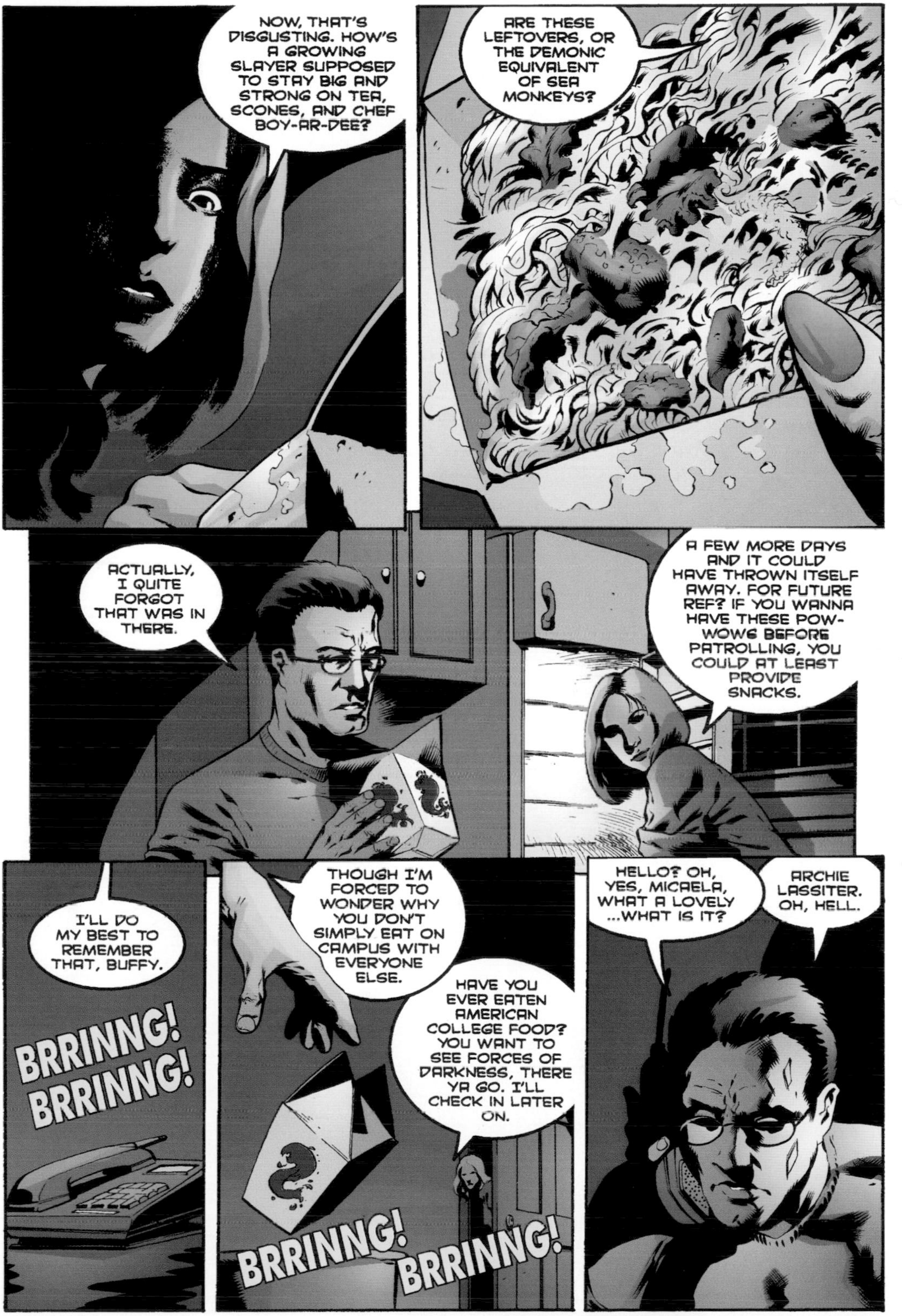
NOW, THAT'S DISGUSTING. HOW'S A GROWING SLAYER SUPPOSED TO STAY BIG AND STRONG ON TEA, SCONES, AND CHEF BOY-AR-DEE?
ARE THESE LEFTOVERS, OR THE DEMONIC EQUIVALENT OF SEA MONKEYS?
ACTUALLY, I QUITE FORGOT THAT WAS IN THERE.
A FEW MORE DAYS AND IT COULD HAVE THROWN ITSELF AWAY. FOR FUTURE REF? IF YOU WANNA HAVE THESE POW-WOWS BEFORE PATROLLING, YOU COULD AT LEAST PROVIDE SNACKS.
I'LL DO MY BEST TO REMEMBER THAT, BUFFY.
BRRINNG! BRRINNG!
THOUGH I'M FORCED TO WONDER WHY YOU DON'T SIMPLY EAT ON CAMPUS WITH EVERYONE ELSE.
HAVE YOU EVER EATEN AMERICAN COLLEGE FOOD? YOU WANT TO SEE FORCES OF DARKNESS, THERE YA GO. I'LL CHECK IN LATER ON.
BRRINNG! BRRINNG!
HELLO? OH, YES, MICAELA, WHAT A LOVELY ...WHAT IS IT?
ARCHIE LASSITER. OH, HELL.

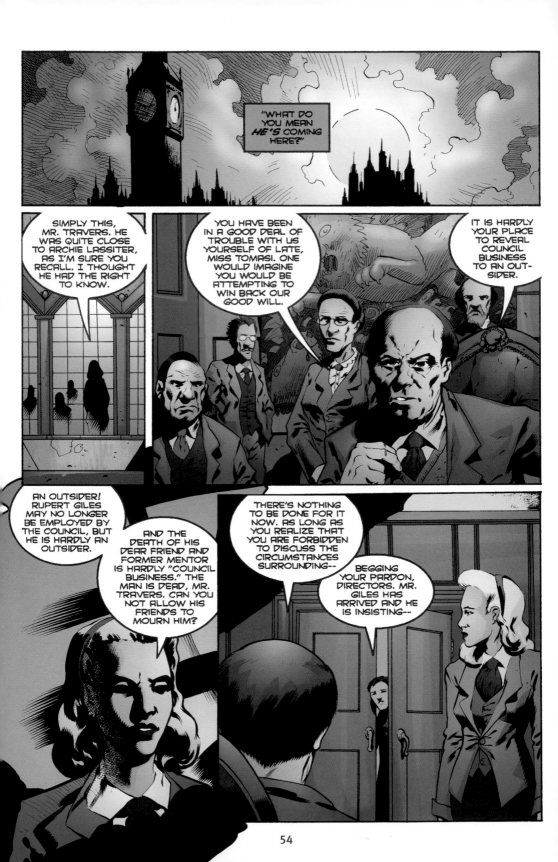

"WHAT DO YOU MEAN *HE'S* COMING HERE?"

SIMPLY THIS, MR. TRAVERS. HE WAS QUITE CLOSE TO ARCHIE LASSITER, AS I'M SURE YOU RECALL. I THOUGHT HE HAD THE RIGHT TO KNOW.

YOU HAVE BEEN IN A GOOD DEAL OF TROUBLE WITH US YOURSELF OF LATE, MISS TOMASI. ONE WOULD IMAGINE YOU WOULD BE ATTEMPTING TO WIN BACK OUR GOOD WILL.

IT IS HARDLY YOUR PLACE TO REVEAL COUNCIL BUSINESS TO AN OUT-SIDER.

AN OUTSIDER! RUPERT GILES MAY NO LONGER BE EMPLOYED BY THE COUNCIL, BUT HE IS HARDLY AN OUTSIDER.

AND THE DEATH OF HIS DEAR FRIEND AND FORMER MENTOR IS HARDLY "COUNCIL BUSINESS." THE MAN IS DEAD, MR. TRAVERS. CAN YOU NOT ALLOW HIS FRIENDS TO MOURN HIM?

THERE'S NOTHING TO BE DONE FOR IT NOW. AS LONG AS YOU REALIZE THAT YOU ARE FORBIDDEN TO DISCUSS THE CIRCUMSTANCES SURROUNDING--

BEGGING YOUR PARDON, DIRECTORS. MR. GILES HAS ARRIVED AND HE IS INSISTING--

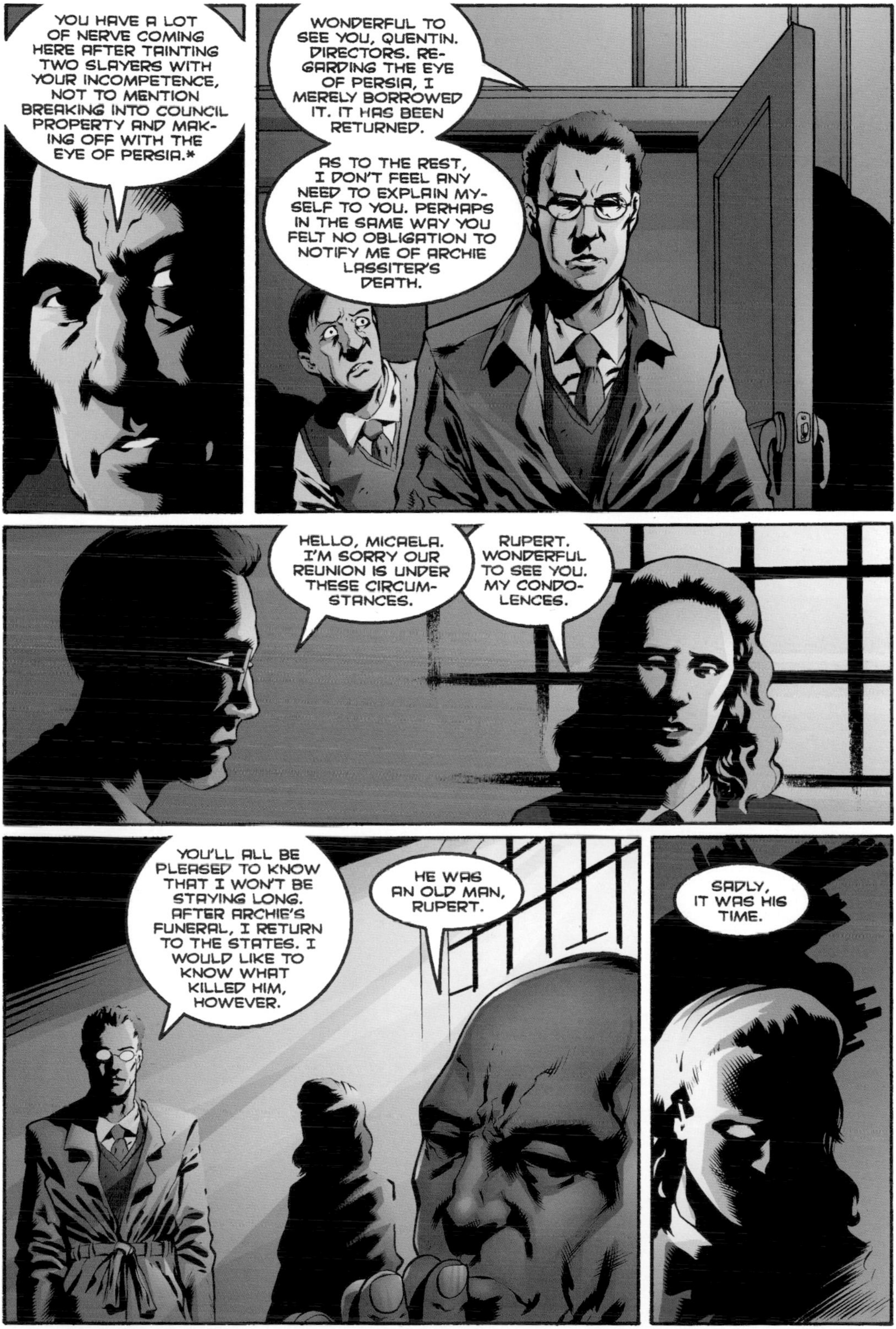
YOU HAVE A LOT OF NERVE COMING HERE AFTER TAINTING TWO SLAYERS WITH YOUR INCOMPETENCE, NOT TO MENTION BREAKING INTO COUNCIL PROPERTY AND MAKING OFF WITH THE EYE OF PERSIA.*
WONDERFUL TO SEE YOU, QUENTIN. DIRECTORS. REGARDING THE EYE OF PERSIA, I MERELY BORROWED IT. IT HAS BEEN RETURNED.
AS TO THE REST, I DON'T FEEL ANY NEED TO EXPLAIN MYSELF TO YOU. PERHAPS IN THE SAME WAY YOU FELT NO OBLIGATION TO NOTIFY ME OF ARCHIE LASSITER'S DEATH.
HELLO, MICAELA. I'M SORRY OUR REUNION IS UNDER THESE CIRCUMSTANCES.
RUPERT. WONDERFUL TO SEE YOU. MY CONDOLENCES.
YOU'LL ALL BE PLEASED TO KNOW THAT I WON'T BE STAYING LONG. AFTER ARCHIE'S FUNERAL, I RETURN TO THE STATES. I WOULD LIKE TO KNOW WHAT KILLED HIM, HOWEVER.
HE WAS AN OLD MAN, RUPERT.
SADLY, IT WAS HIS TIME.

*SEE BUFFY: THE BLOOD OF CARTHAGE, #21–#25

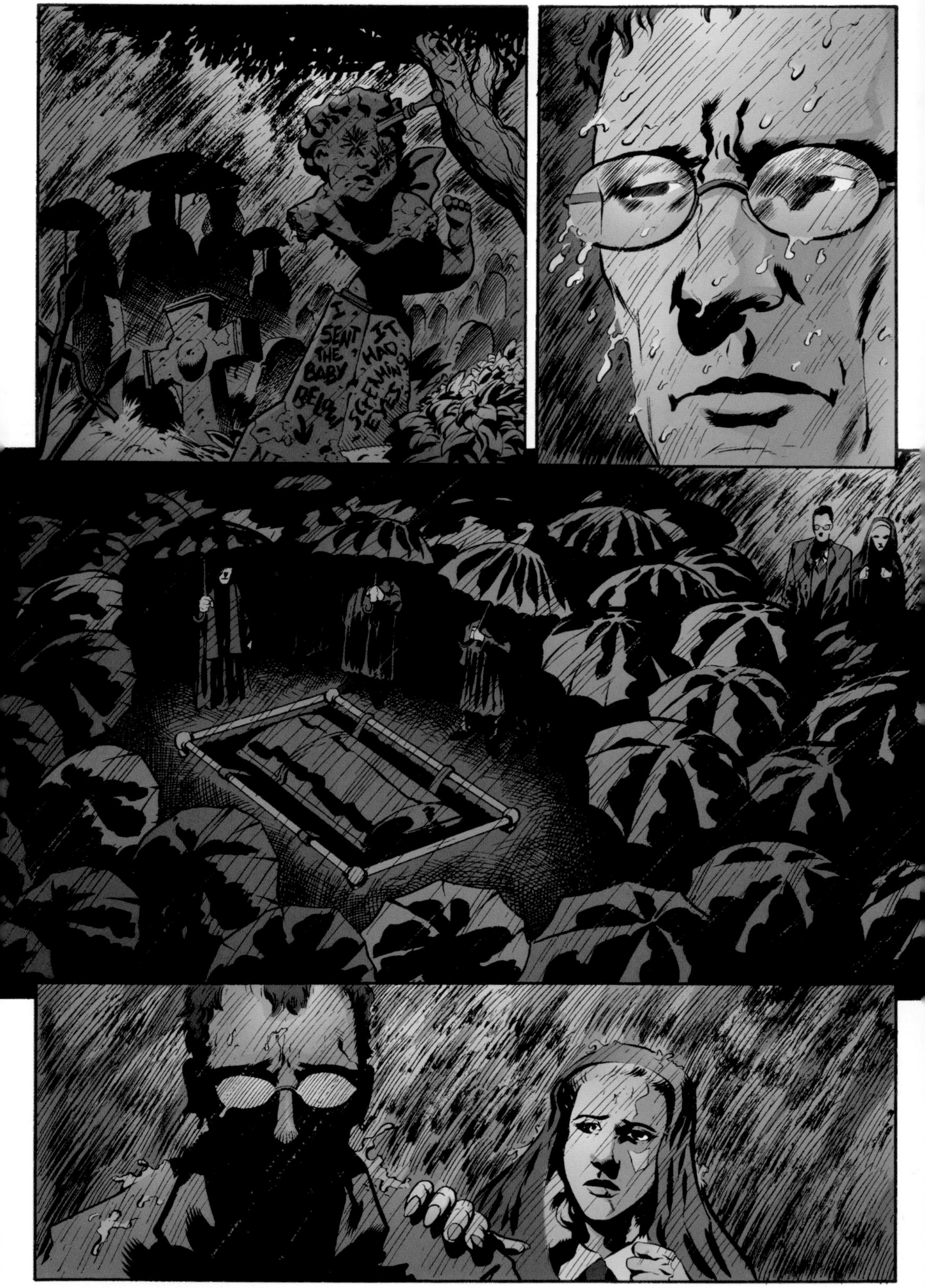
I SENT THE BABY BELOW
IT HAD SCREAMING EYES

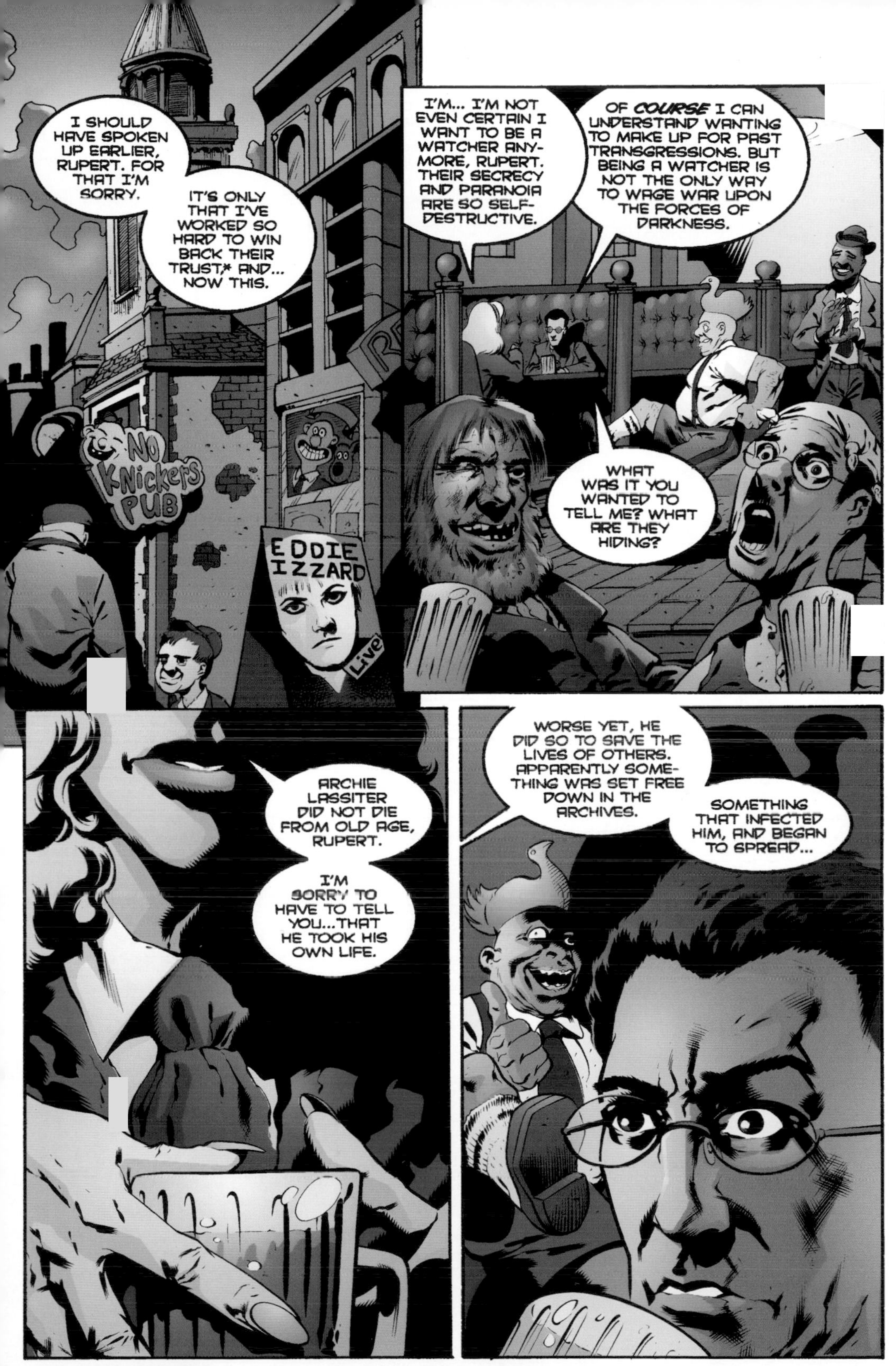
I SHOULD HAVE SPOKEN UP EARLIER, RUPERT. FOR THAT I'M SORRY.
IT'S ONLY THAT I'VE WORKED SO HARD TO WIN BACK THEIR TRUST,* AND... NOW THIS.
NO KNICKERS PUB
EDDIE IZZARD
LIVE
I'M... I'M NOT EVEN CERTAIN I WANT TO BE A WATCHER ANYMORE, RUPERT. THEIR SECRECY AND PARANOIA ARE SO SELF-DESTRUCTIVE.
OF COURSE I CAN UNDERSTAND WANTING TO MAKE UP FOR PAST TRANSGRESSIONS. BUT BEING A WATCHER IS NOT THE ONLY WAY TO WAGE WAR UPON THE FORCES OF DARKNESS.
WHAT WAS IT YOU WANTED TO TELL ME? WHAT ARE THEY HIDING?
ARCHIE LASSITER DID NOT DIE FROM OLD AGE, RUPERT.
I'M SORRY TO HAVE TO TELL YOU...THAT HE TOOK HIS OWN LIFE.
WORSE YET, HE DID SO TO SAVE THE LIVES OF OTHERS. APPARENTLY SOMETHING WAS SET FREE DOWN IN THE ARCHIVES.
SOMETHING THAT INFECTED HIM, AND BEGAN TO SPREAD...

*SEE THE GATEKEEPER TRILOGY FROM POCKET BOOKS

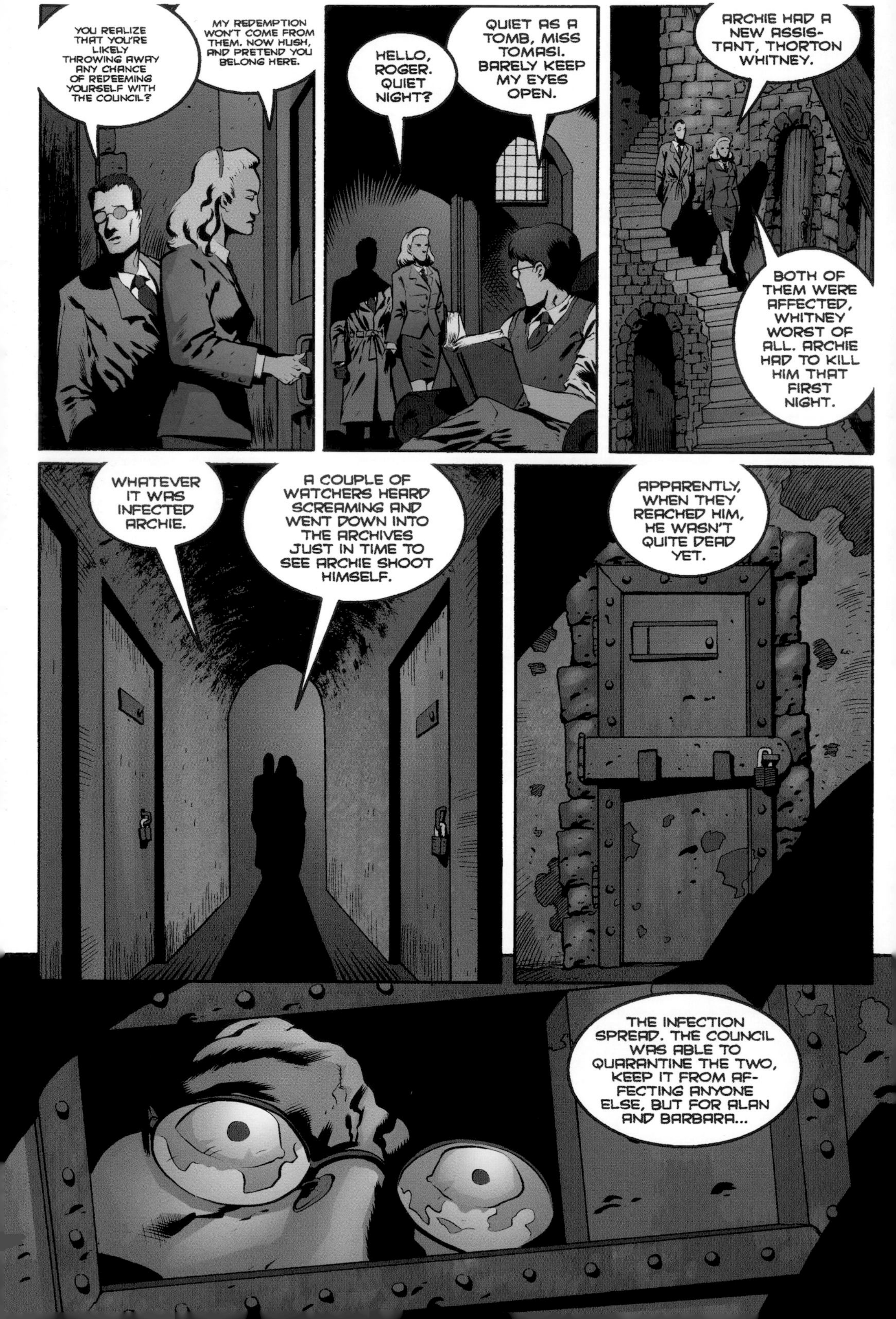
YOU REALIZE THAT YOU'RE LIKELY THROWING AWAY ANY CHANCE OF REDEEMING YOURSELF WITH THE COUNCIL?
MY REDEMPTION WON'T COME FROM THEM. NOW HUSH, AND PRETEND YOU BELONG HERE.
HELLO, ROGER. QUIET NIGHT?
QUIET AS A TOMB, MISS TOMASI. BARELY KEEP MY EYES OPEN.
ARCHIE HAD A NEW ASSISTANT, THORTON WHITNEY.
BOTH OF THEM WERE AFFECTED, WHITNEY WORST OF ALL. ARCHIE HAD TO KILL HIM THAT FIRST NIGHT.
WHATEVER IT WAS INFECTED ARCHIE.
A COUPLE OF WATCHERS HEARD SCREAMING AND WENT DOWN INTO THE ARCHIVES JUST IN TIME TO SEE ARCHIE SHOOT HIMSELF.
APPARENTLY, WHEN THEY REACHED HIM, HE WASN'T QUITE DEAD YET.
THE INFECTION SPREAD. THE COUNCIL WAS ABLE TO QUARANTINE THE TWO, KEEP IT FROM AFFECTING ANYONE ELSE, BUT FOR ALAN AND BARBARA...

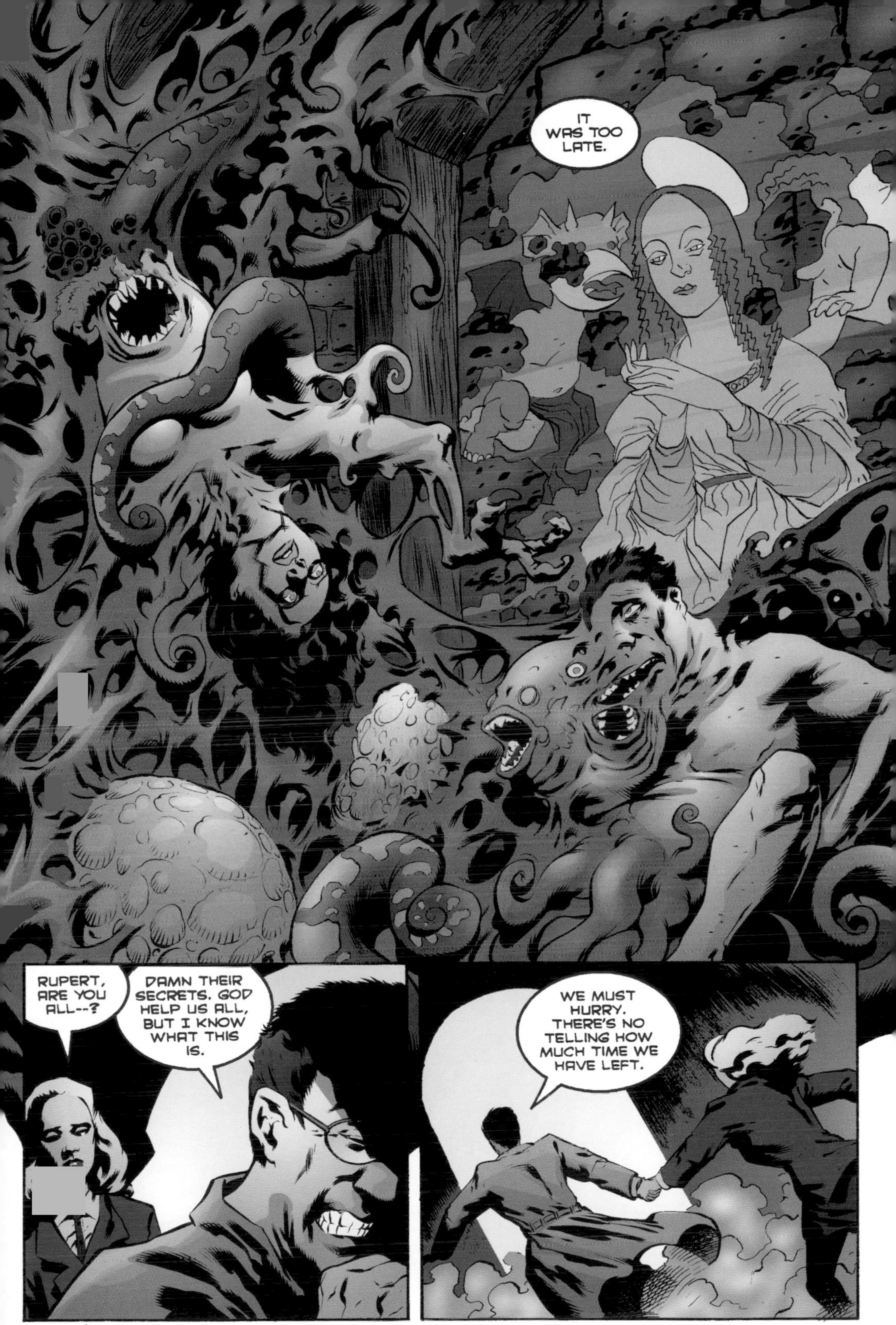
IT WAS TOO LATE.
RUPERT, ARE YOU ALL--?
DAMN THEIR SECRETS. GOD HELP US ALL, BUT I KNOW WHAT THIS IS.
WE MUST HURRY. THERE'S NO TELLING HOW MUCH TIME WE HAVE LEFT.

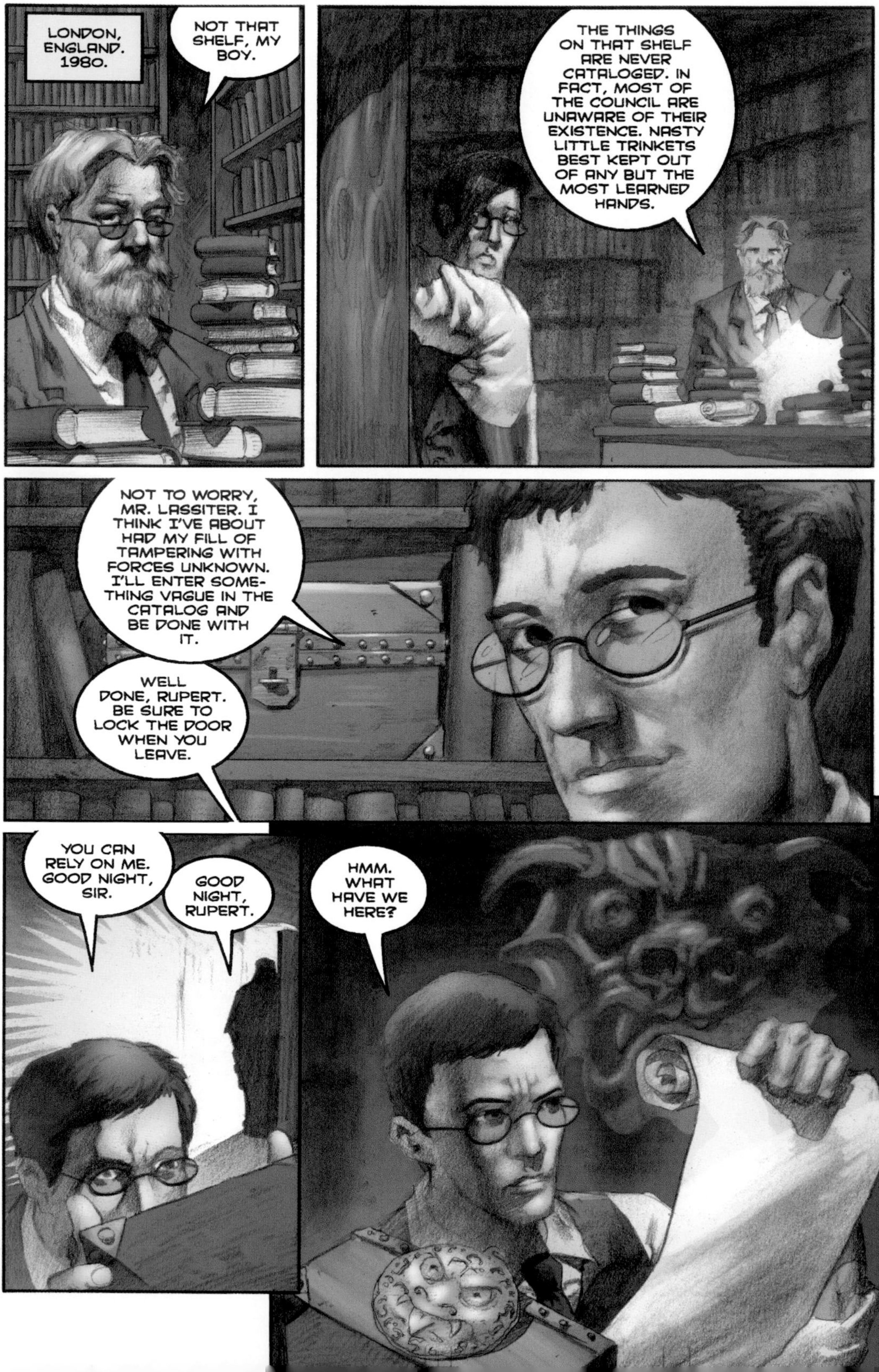
LONDON, ENGLAND. 1980.
NOT THAT SHELF, MY BOY.
THE THINGS ON THAT SHELF ARE NEVER CATALOGED. IN FACT, MOST OF THE COUNCIL ARE UNAWARE OF THEIR EXISTENCE. NASTY LITTLE TRINKETS BEST KEPT OUT OF ANY BUT THE MOST LEARNED HANDS.
NOT TO WORRY, MR. LASSITER. I THINK I'VE ABOUT HAD MY FILL OF TAMPERING WITH FORCES UNKNOWN. I'LL ENTER SOME-THING VAGUE IN THE CATALOG AND BE DONE WITH IT.
WELL DONE, RUPERT. BE SURE TO LOCK THE DOOR WHEN YOU LEAVE.
YOU CAN RELY ON ME. GOOD NIGHT, SIR.
GOOD NIGHT, RUPERT.
HMM. WHAT HAVE WE HERE?

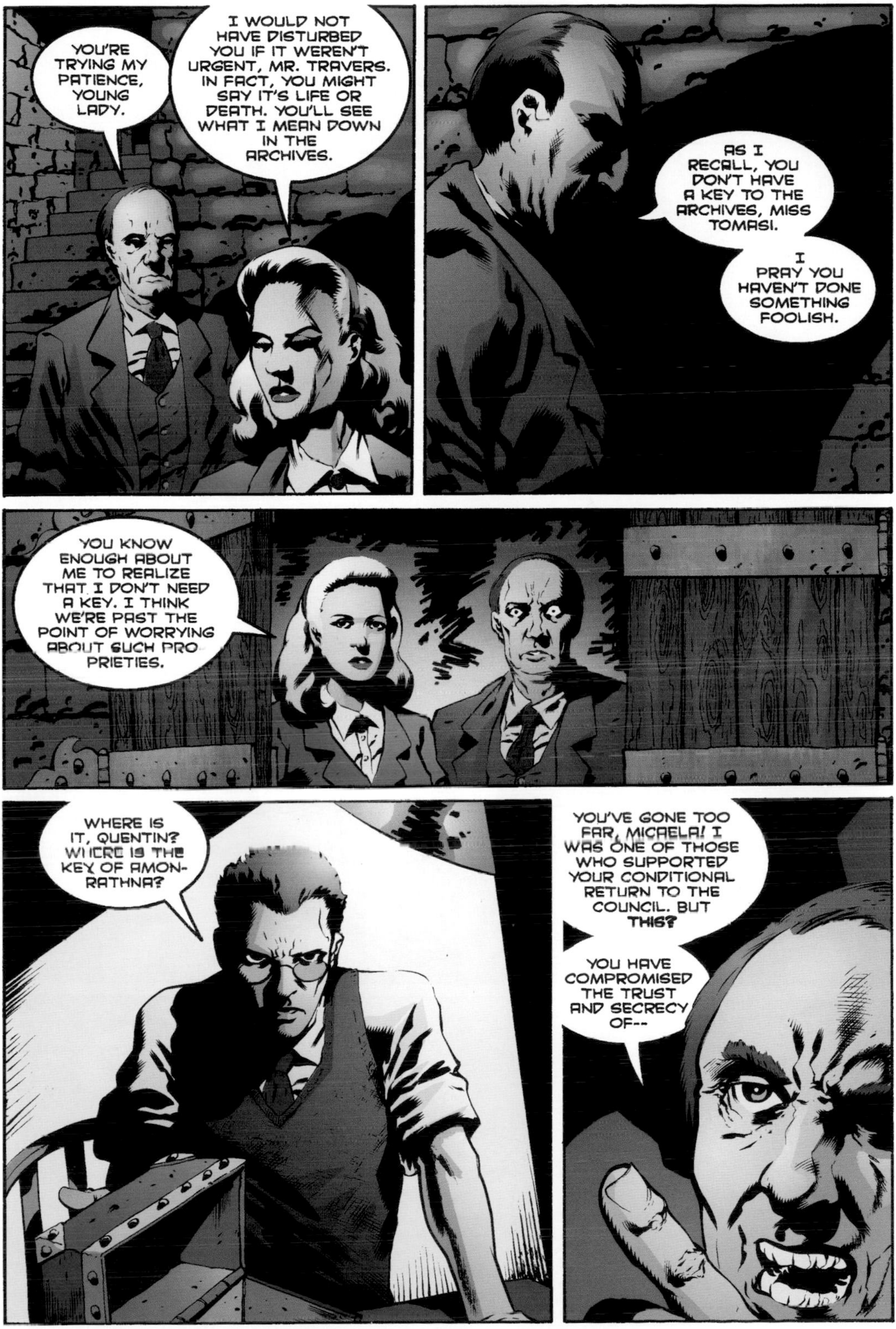
YOU'RE TRYING MY PATIENCE, YOUNG LADY.
I WOULD NOT HAVE DISTURBED YOU IF IT WEREN'T URGENT, MR. TRAVERS. IN FACT, YOU MIGHT SAY IT'S LIFE OR DEATH. YOU'LL SEE WHAT I MEAN DOWN IN THE ARCHIVES.
AS I RECALL, YOU DON'T HAVE A KEY TO THE ARCHIVES, MISS TOMASI.
I PRAY YOU HAVEN'T DONE SOMETHING FOOLISH.
YOU KNOW ENOUGH ABOUT ME TO REALIZE THAT I DON'T NEED A KEY. I THINK WE'RE PAST THE POINT OF WORRYING ABOUT SUCH PROPRIETIES.
WHERE IS IT, QUENTIN? WHERE IS THE KEY OF AMON-RATHNA?
YOU'VE GONE TOO FAR, MICAELA! I WAS ONE OF THOSE WHO SUPPORTED YOUR CONDITIONAL RETURN TO THE COUNCIL. BUT **THIS?**
YOU HAVE COMPROMISED THE TRUST AND SECRECY OF--

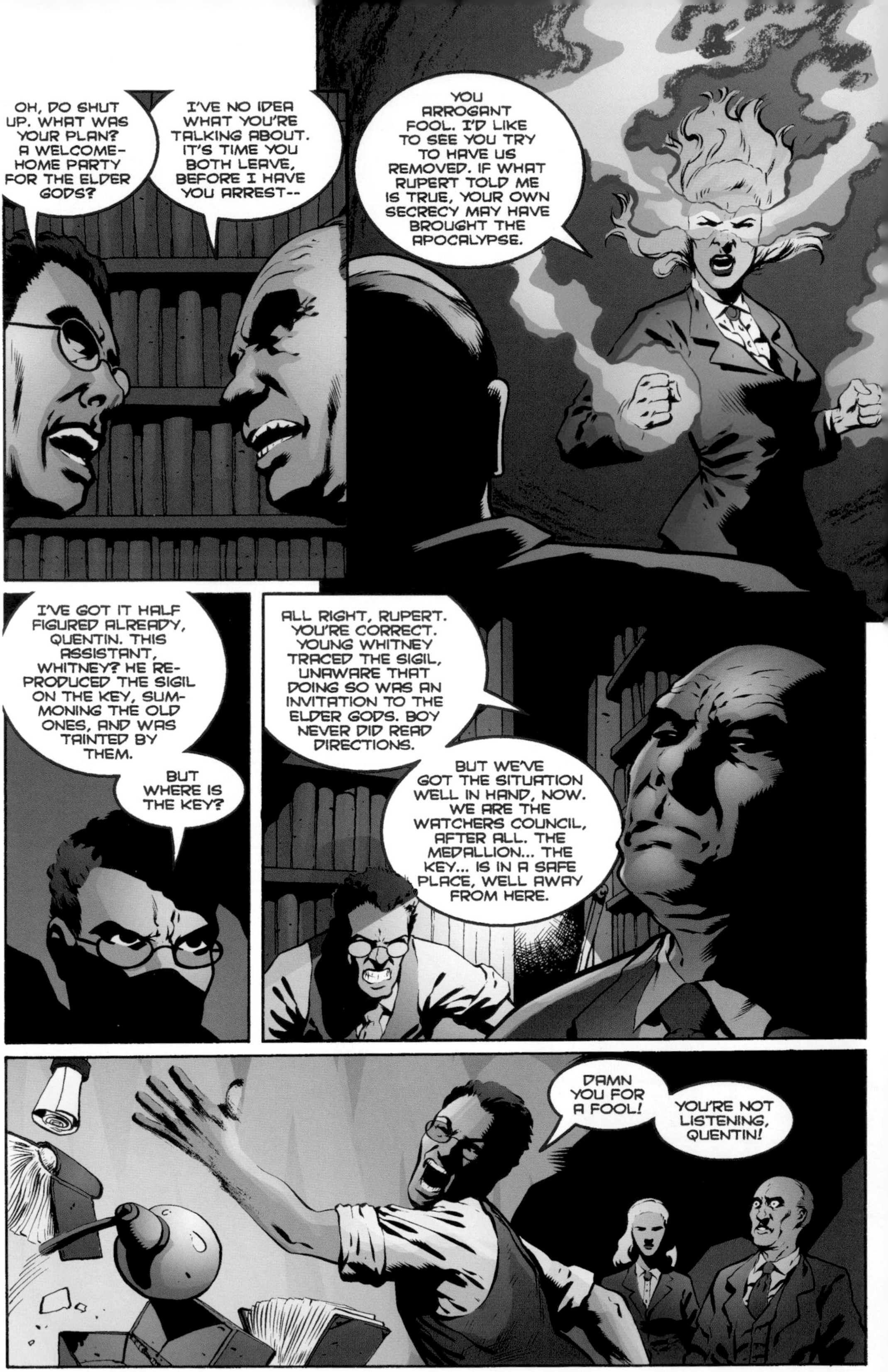
OH, DO SHUT UP. WHAT WAS YOUR PLAN? A WELCOME-HOME PARTY FOR THE ELDER GODS?
I'VE NO IDEA WHAT YOU'RE TALKING ABOUT. IT'S TIME YOU BOTH LEAVE, BEFORE I HAVE YOU ARREST--
YOU ARROGANT FOOL. I'D LIKE TO SEE YOU TRY TO HAVE US REMOVED. IF WHAT RUPERT TOLD ME IS TRUE, YOUR OWN SECRECY MAY HAVE BROUGHT THE APOCALYPSE.
I'VE GOT IT HALF FIGURED ALREADY, QUENTIN. THIS ASSISTANT, WHITNEY? HE REPRODUCED THE SIGIL ON THE KEY, SUMMONING THE OLD ONES, AND WAS TAINTED BY THEM.
BUT WHERE IS THE KEY?
ALL RIGHT, RUPERT. YOU'RE CORRECT. YOUNG WHITNEY TRACED THE SIGIL, UNAWARE THAT DOING SO WAS AN INVITATION TO THE ELDER GODS. BOY NEVER DID READ DIRECTIONS.
BUT WE'VE GOT THE SITUATION WELL IN HAND, NOW. WE ARE THE WATCHERS COUNCIL, AFTER ALL. THE MEDALLION... THE KEY... IS IN A SAFE PLACE, WELL AWAY FROM HERE.
DAMN YOU FOR A FOOL!
YOU'RE NOT LISTENING, QUENTIN!

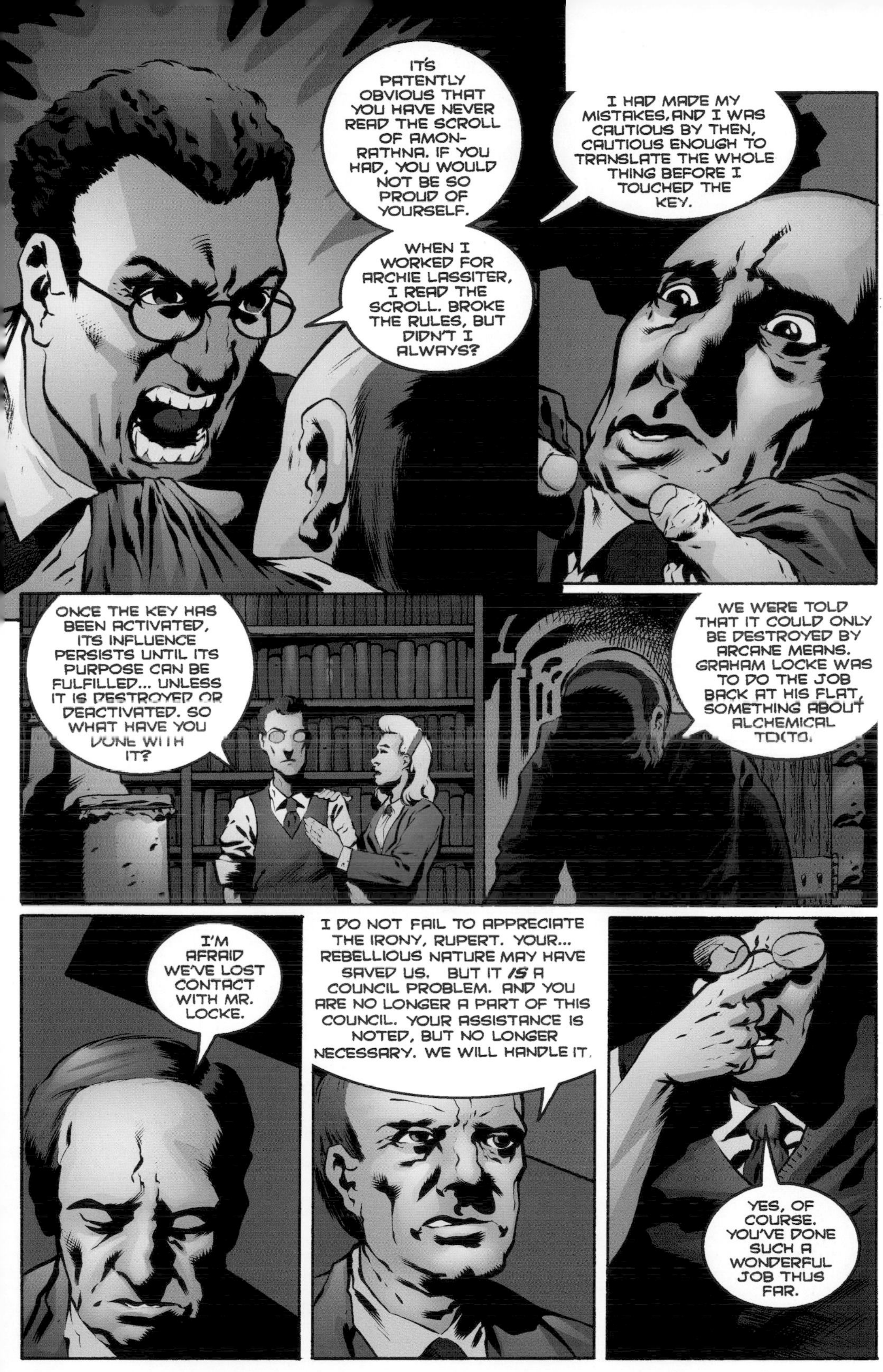
IT'S PATENTLY OBVIOUS THAT YOU HAVE NEVER READ THE SCROLL OF AMON-RATHNA. IF YOU HAD, YOU WOULD NOT BE SO PROUD OF YOURSELF.
WHEN I WORKED FOR ARCHIE LASSITER, I READ THE SCROLL. BROKE THE RULES, BUT DIDN'T I ALWAYS?
I HAD MADE MY MISTAKES, AND I WAS CAUTIOUS BY THEN, CAUTIOUS ENOUGH TO TRANSLATE THE WHOLE THING BEFORE I TOUCHED THE KEY.
ONCE THE KEY HAS BEEN ACTIVATED, ITS INFLUENCE PERSISTS UNTIL ITS PURPOSE CAN BE FULFILLED... UNLESS IT IS DESTROYED OR DEACTIVATED. SO WHAT HAVE YOU DONE WITH IT?
WE WERE TOLD THAT IT COULD ONLY BE DESTROYED BY ARCANE MEANS. GRAHAM LOCKE WAS TO DO THE JOB BACK AT HIS FLAT, SOMETHING ABOUT ALCHEMICAL TEXTS.
I'M AFRAID WE'VE LOST CONTACT WITH MR. LOCKE.
I DO NOT FAIL TO APPRECIATE THE IRONY, RUPERT. YOUR... REBELLIOUS NATURE MAY HAVE SAVED US. BUT IT IS A COUNCIL PROBLEM. AND YOU ARE NO LONGER A PART OF THIS COUNCIL. YOUR ASSISTANCE IS NOTED, BUT NO LONGER NECESSARY. WE WILL HANDLE IT.
YES, OF COURSE. YOU'VE DONE SUCH A WONDERFUL JOB THUS FAR.

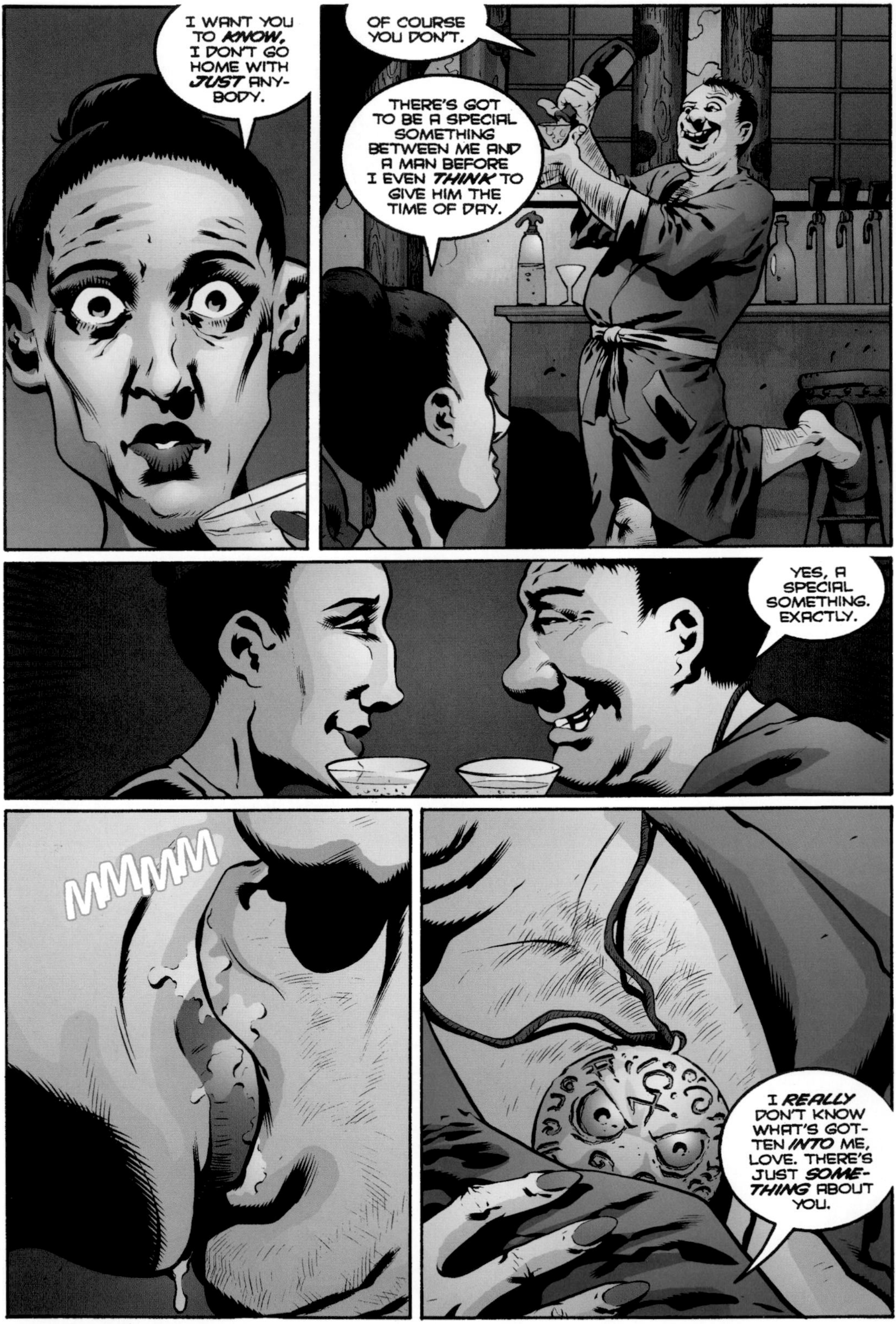
I WANT YOU TO KNOW, I DON'T GO HOME WITH JUST ANY-BODY.
OF COURSE YOU DON'T.
THERE'S GOT TO BE A SPECIAL SOMETHING BETWEEN ME AND A MAN BEFORE I EVEN THINK TO GIVE HIM THE TIME OF DAY.
YES, A SPECIAL SOMETHING. EXACTLY.
MMMMM
I REALLY DON'T KNOW WHAT'S GOT-TEN INTO ME, LOVE. THERE'S JUST SOME-THING ABOUT YOU.

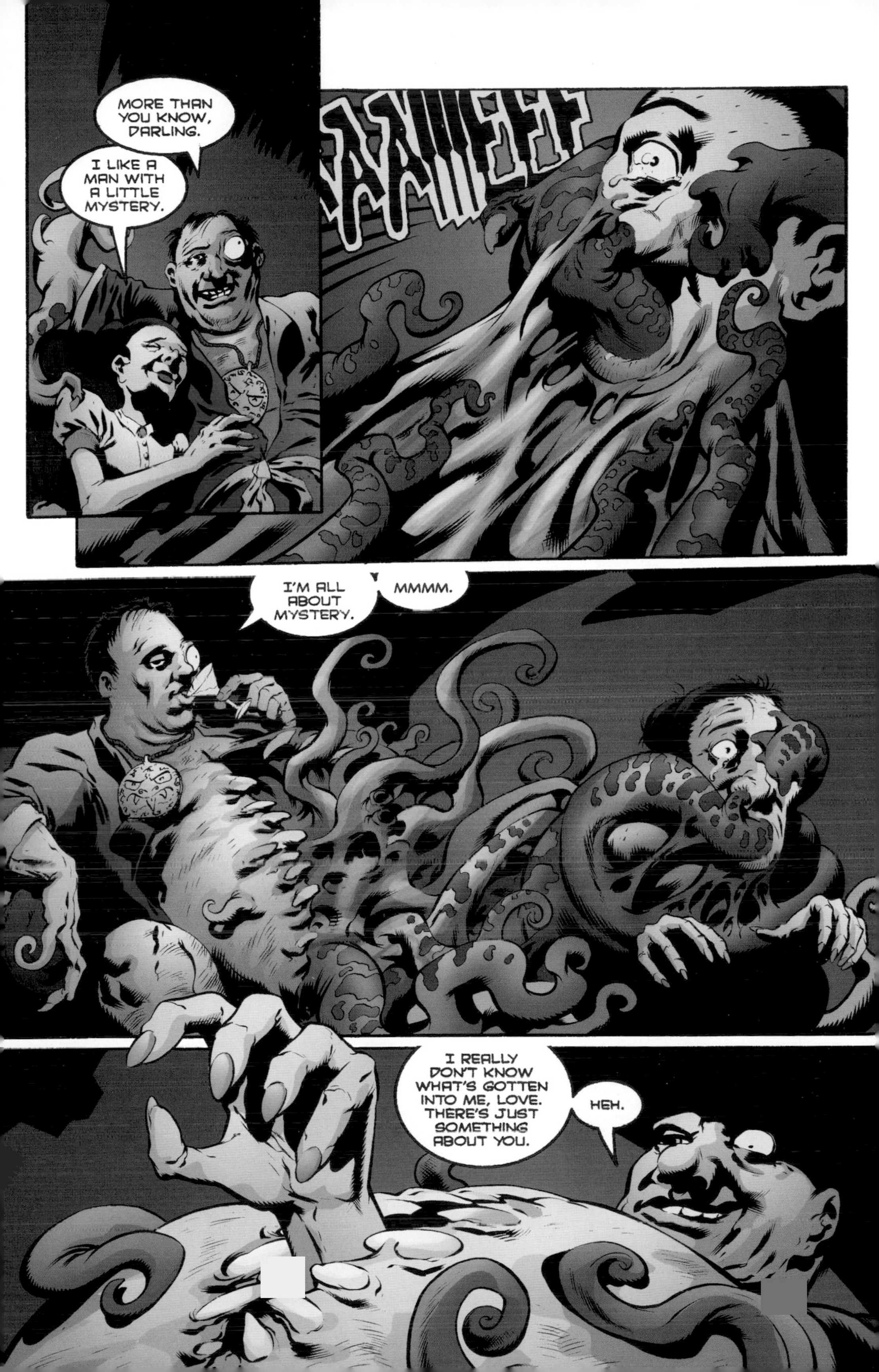

MORE THAN YOU KNOW, DARLING.
I LIKE A MAN WITH A LITTLE MYSTERY.
I'M ALL ABOUT MYSTERY.
MMMM.
I REALLY DON'T KNOW WHAT'S GOTTEN INTO ME, LOVE. THERE'S JUST SOMETHING ABOUT YOU.
HEH.

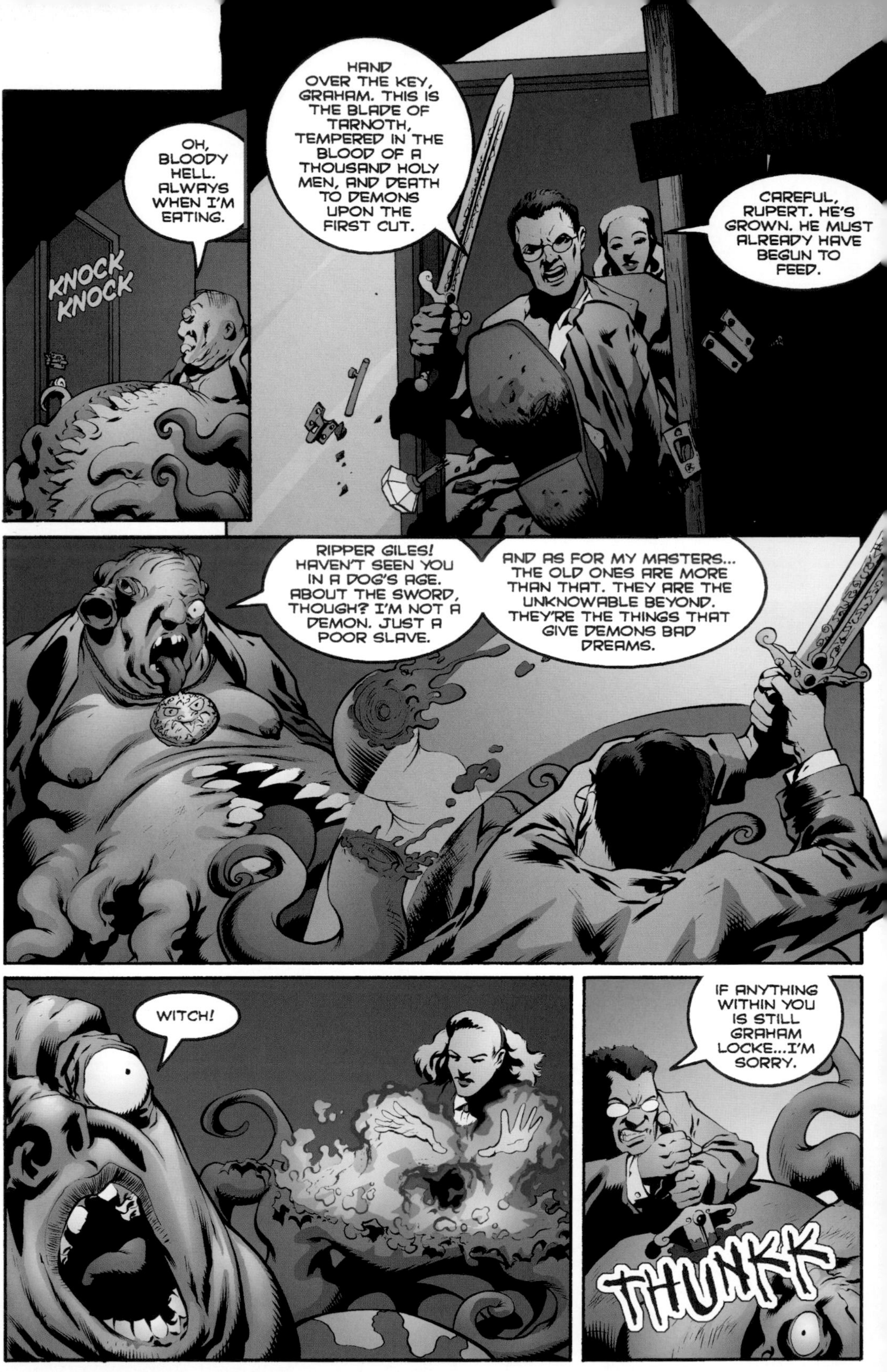
OH, BLOODY HELL. ALWAYS WHEN I'M EATING.
KNOCK KNOCK
HAND OVER THE KEY, GRAHAM. THIS IS THE BLADE OF TARNOTH, TEMPERED IN THE BLOOD OF A THOUSAND HOLY MEN, AND DEATH TO DEMONS UPON THE FIRST CUT.
CAREFUL, RUPERT. HE'S GROWN. HE MUST ALREADY HAVE BEGUN TO FEED.
RIPPER GILES! HAVEN'T SEEN YOU IN A DOG'S AGE. ABOUT THE SWORD, THOUGH? I'M NOT A DEMON. JUST A POOR SLAVE.
AND AS FOR MY MASTERS... THE OLD ONES ARE MORE THAN THAT. THEY ARE THE UNKNOWABLE BEYOND. THEY'RE THE THINGS THAT GIVE DEMONS BAD DREAMS.
WITCH!
IF ANYTHING WITHIN YOU IS STILL GRAHAM LOCKE...I'M SORRY.
THUNKK

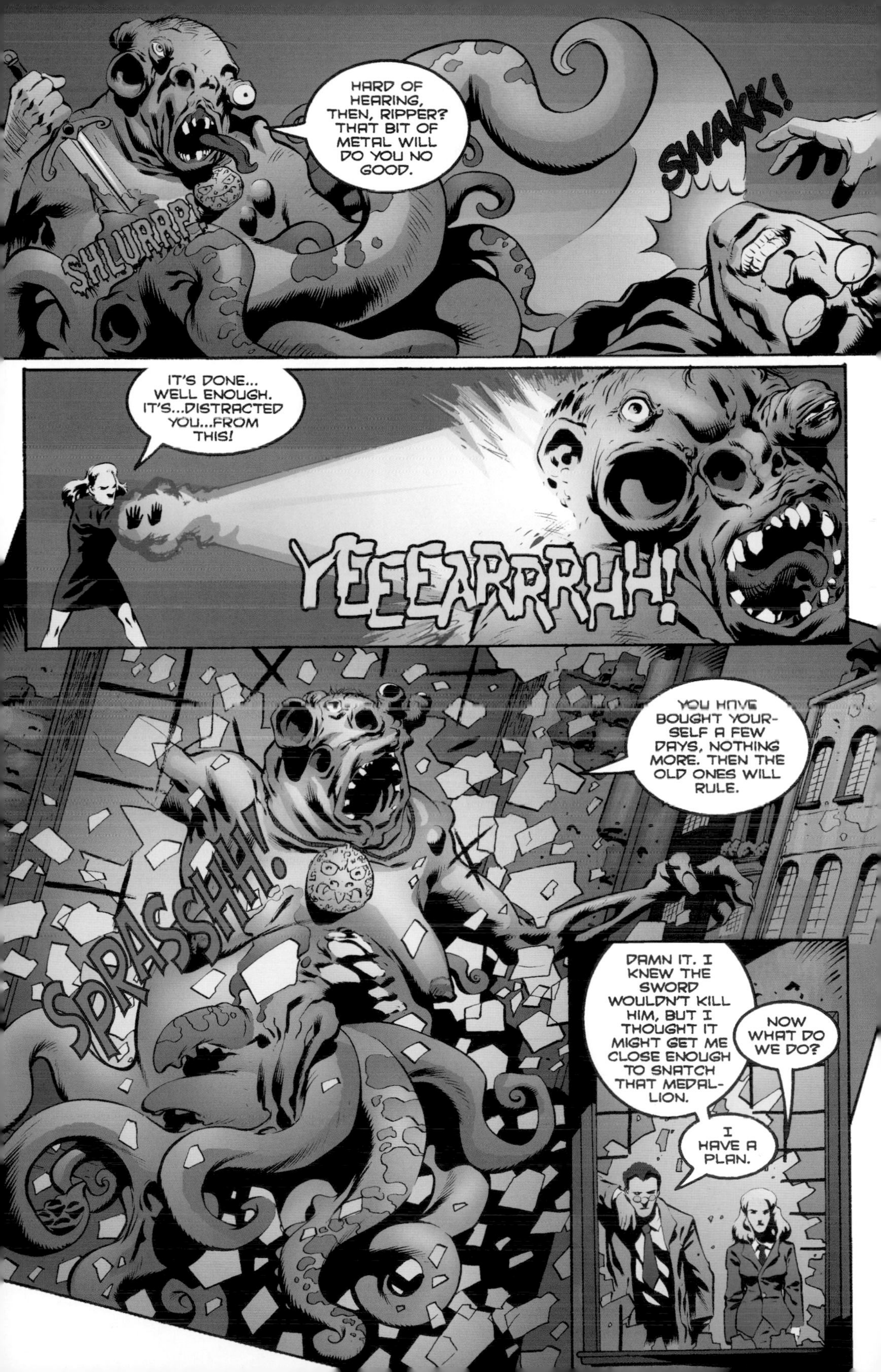
HARD OF HEARING, THEN, RIPPER? THAT BIT OF METAL WILL DO YOU NO GOOD.
SWAKK!
SHLURRP!
IT'S DONE... WELL ENOUGH. IT'S...DISTRACTED YOU...FROM THIS!
YEEEARRRUH!
YOU HAVE BOUGHT YOURSELF A FEW DAYS, NOTHING MORE. THEN THE OLD ONES WILL RULE.
SPRASSHH!
DAMN IT. I KNEW THE SWORD WOULDN'T KILL HIM, BUT I THOUGHT IT MIGHT GET ME CLOSE ENOUGH TO SNATCH THAT MEDALLION.
NOW WHAT DO WE DO?
I HAVE A PLAN.

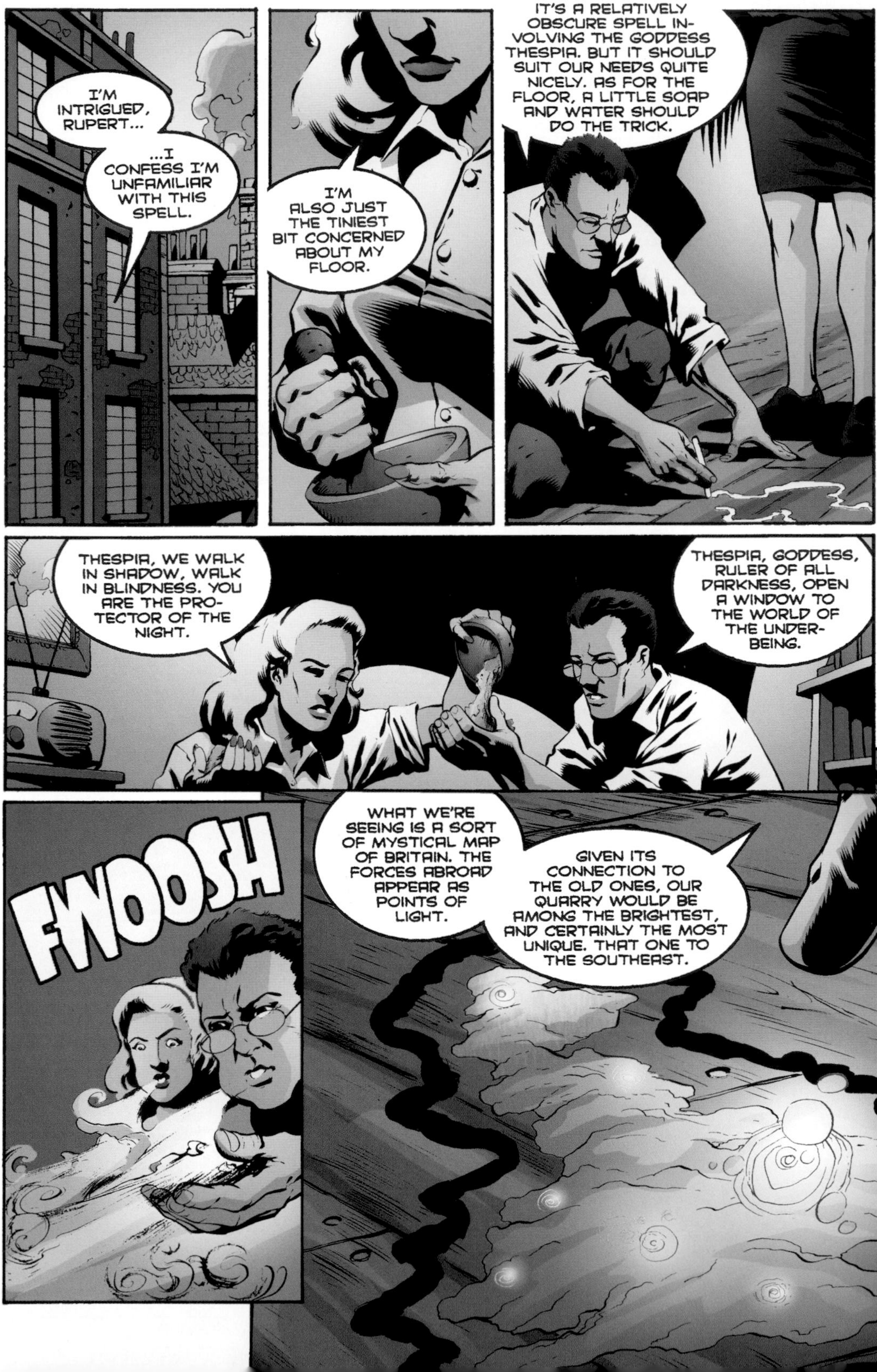
I'M INTRIGUED, RUPERT...
...I CONFESS I'M UNFAMILIAR WITH THIS SPELL.
I'M ALSO JUST THE TINIEST BIT CONCERNED ABOUT MY FLOOR.
IT'S A RELATIVELY OBSCURE SPELL INVOLVING THE GODDESS THESPIA. BUT IT SHOULD SUIT OUR NEEDS QUITE NICELY. AS FOR THE FLOOR, A LITTLE SOAP AND WATER SHOULD DO THE TRICK.
THESPIA, WE WALK IN SHADOW, WALK IN BLINDNESS. YOU ARE THE PROTECTOR OF THE NIGHT.
THESPIA, GODDESS, RULER OF ALL DARKNESS, OPEN A WINDOW TO THE WORLD OF THE UNDERBEING.
FWOOSH
WHAT WE'RE SEEING IS A SORT OF MYSTICAL MAP OF BRITAIN. THE FORCES ABROAD APPEAR AS POINTS OF LIGHT.
GIVEN ITS CONNECTION TO THE OLD ONES, OUR QUARRY WOULD BE AMONG THE BRIGHTEST, AND CERTAINLY THE MOST UNIQUE. THAT ONE TO THE SOUTHEAST.

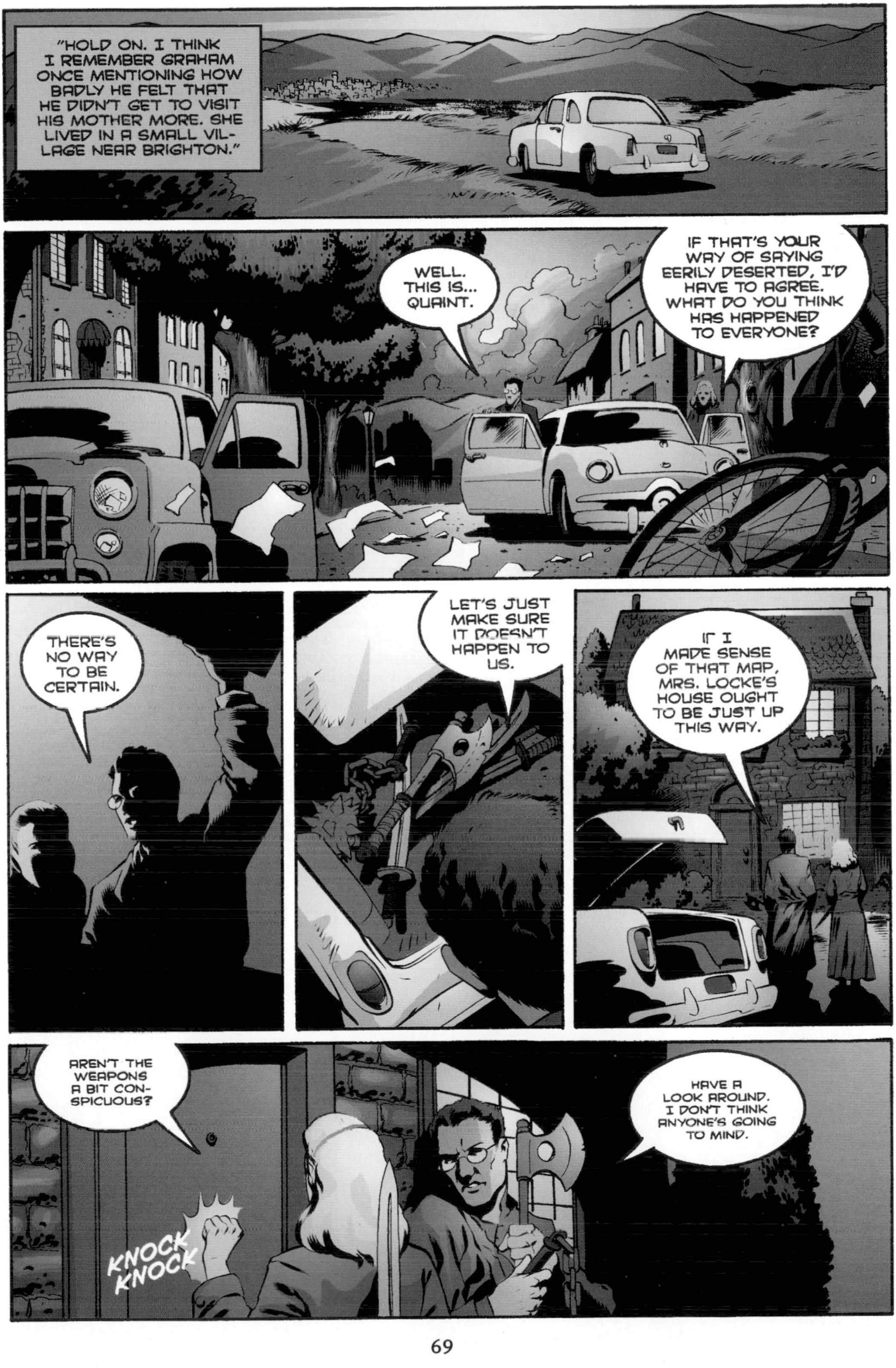
"HOLD ON. I THINK I REMEMBER GRAHAM ONCE MENTIONING HOW BADLY HE FELT THAT HE DIDN'T GET TO VISIT HIS MOTHER MORE. SHE LIVED IN A SMALL VILLAGE NEAR BRIGHTON."
WELL. THIS IS... QUAINT.
IF THAT'S YOUR WAY OF SAYING EERILY DESERTED, I'D HAVE TO AGREE. WHAT DO YOU THINK HAS HAPPENED TO EVERYONE?
THERE'S NO WAY TO BE CERTAIN.
LET'S JUST MAKE SURE IT DOESN'T HAPPEN TO US.
IF I MADE SENSE OF THAT MAP, MRS. LOCKE'S HOUSE OUGHT TO BE JUST UP THIS WAY.
AREN'T THE WEAPONS A BIT CONSPICUOUS?
HAVE A LOOK AROUND. I DON'T THINK ANYONE'S GOING TO MIND.
KNOCK KNOCK

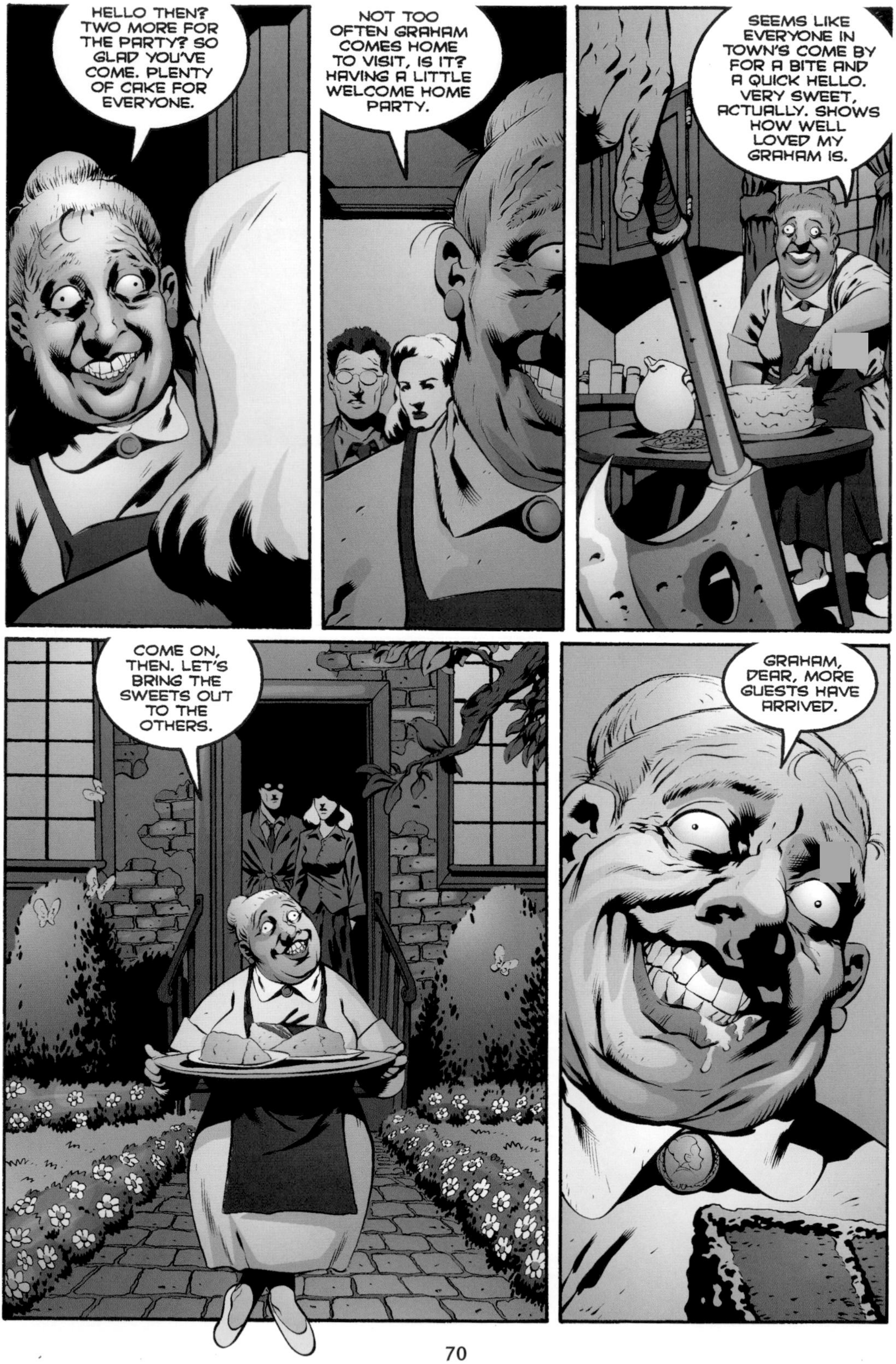
HELLO THEN? TWO MORE FOR THE PARTY? SO GLAD YOU'VE COME. PLENTY OF CAKE FOR EVERYONE.
NOT TOO OFTEN GRAHAM COMES HOME TO VISIT, IS IT? HAVING A LITTLE WELCOME HOME PARTY.
SEEMS LIKE EVERYONE IN TOWN'S COME BY FOR A BITE AND A QUICK HELLO. VERY SWEET, ACTUALLY. SHOWS HOW WELL LOVED MY GRAHAM IS.
COME ON, THEN. LET'S BRING THE SWEETS OUT TO THE OTHERS.
GRAHAM, DEAR, MORE GUESTS HAVE ARRIVED.

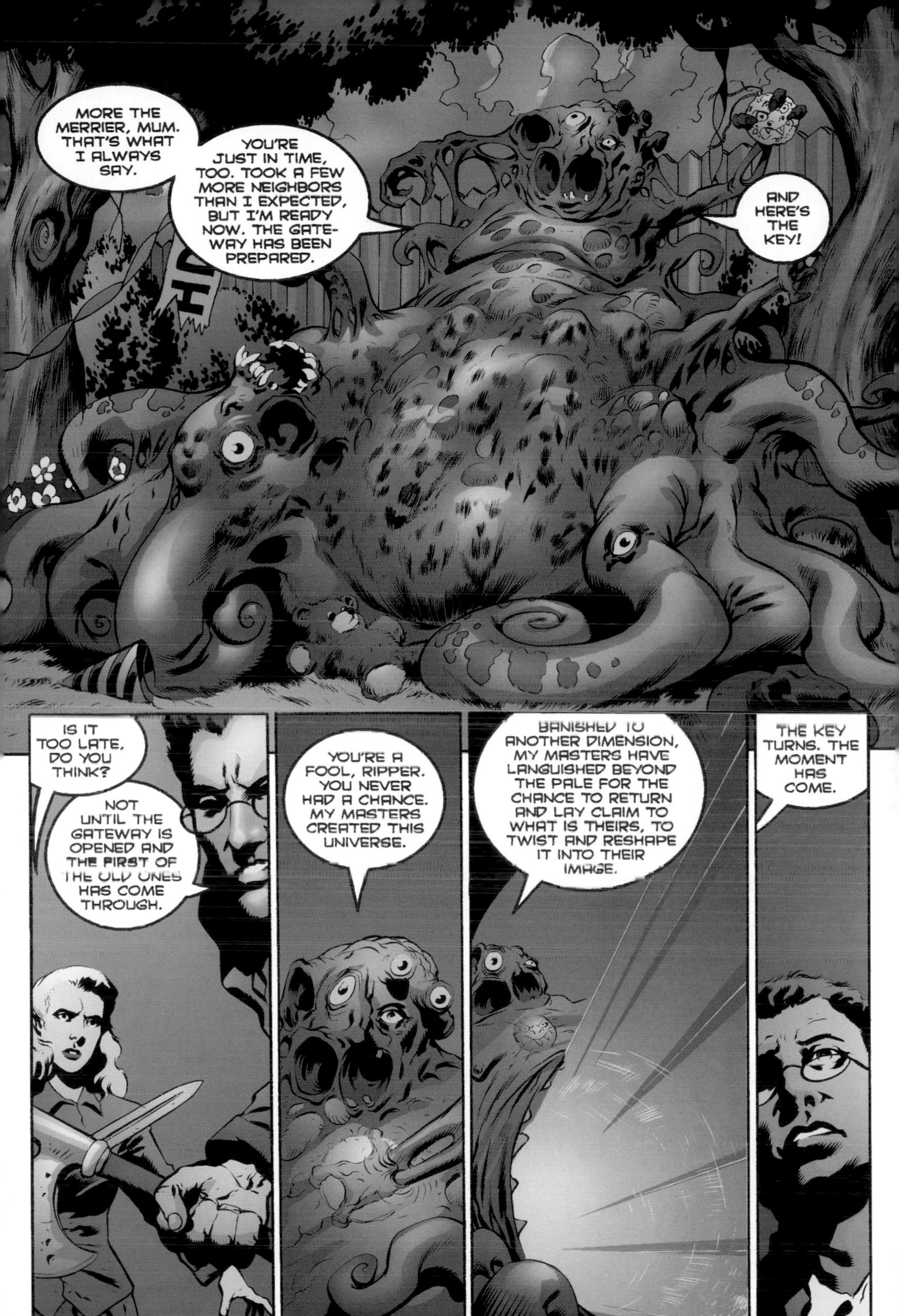

MORE THE MERRIER, MUM. THAT'S WHAT I ALWAYS SAY.
YOU'RE JUST IN TIME, TOO. TOOK A FEW MORE NEIGHBORS THAN I EXPECTED, BUT I'M READY NOW. THE GATEWAY HAS BEEN PREPARED.
AND HERE'S THE KEY!
IS IT TOO LATE, DO YOU THINK?
NOT UNTIL THE GATEWAY IS OPENED AND THE FIRST OF THE OLD ONES HAS COME THROUGH.
YOU'RE A FOOL, RIPPER. YOU NEVER HAD A CHANCE. MY MASTERS CREATED THIS UNIVERSE.
BANISHED TO ANOTHER DIMENSION, MY MASTERS HAVE LANGUISHED BEYOND THE PALE FOR THE CHANCE TO RETURN AND LAY CLAIM TO WHAT IS THEIRS, TO TWIST AND RESHAPE IT INTO THEIR IMAGE.
THE KEY TURNS. THE MOMENT HAS COME.

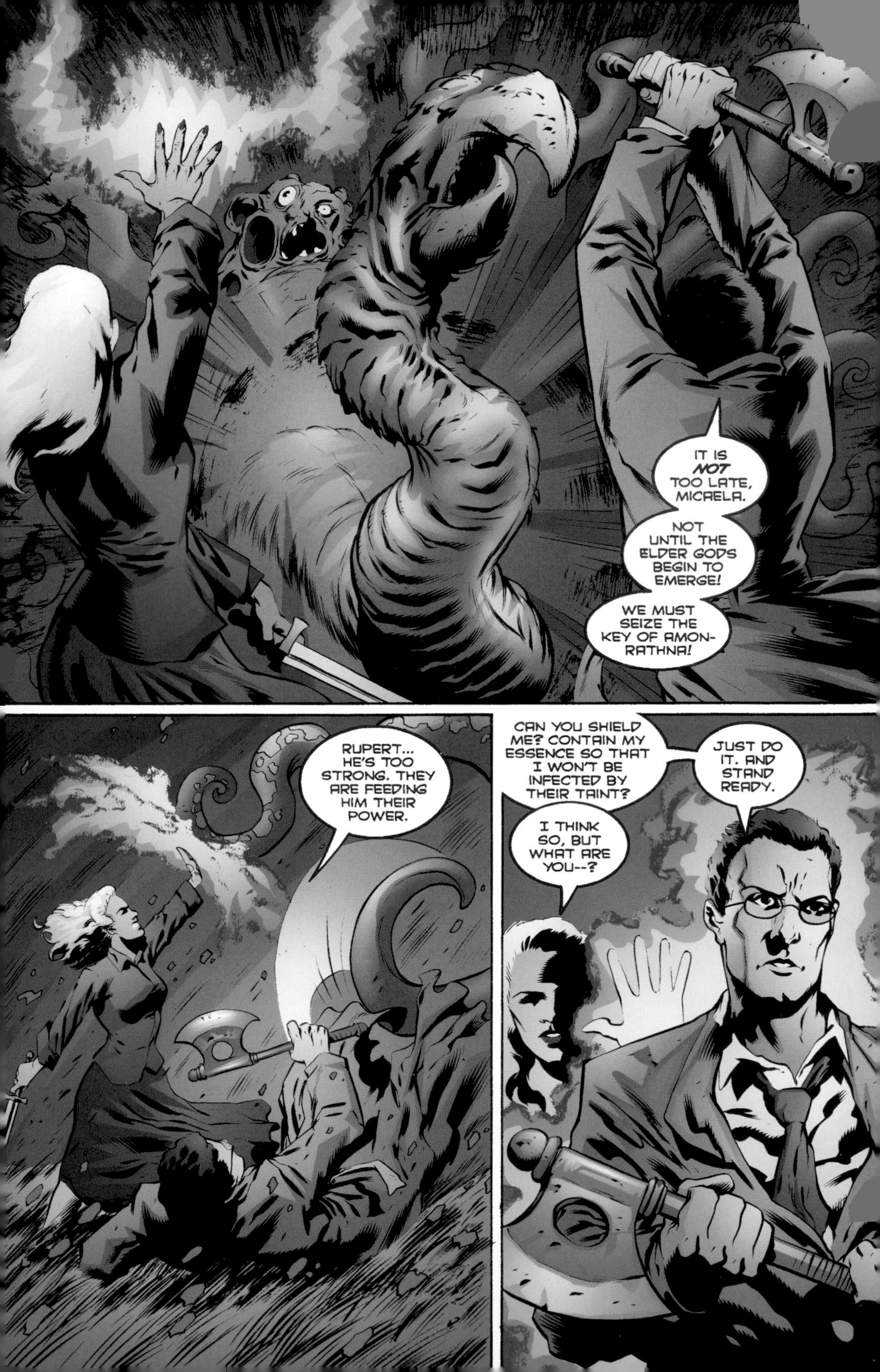
IT IS NOT TOO LATE, MICAELA.
NOT UNTIL THE ELDER GODS BEGIN TO EMERGE!
WE MUST SEIZE THE KEY OF AMON-RATHNA!
RUPERT... HE'S TOO STRONG. THEY ARE FEEDING HIM THEIR POWER.
CAN YOU SHIELD ME? CONTAIN MY ESSENCE SO THAT I WON'T BE INFECTED BY THEIR TAINT?
I THINK SO, BUT WHAT ARE YOU--?
JUST DO IT. AND STAND READY.

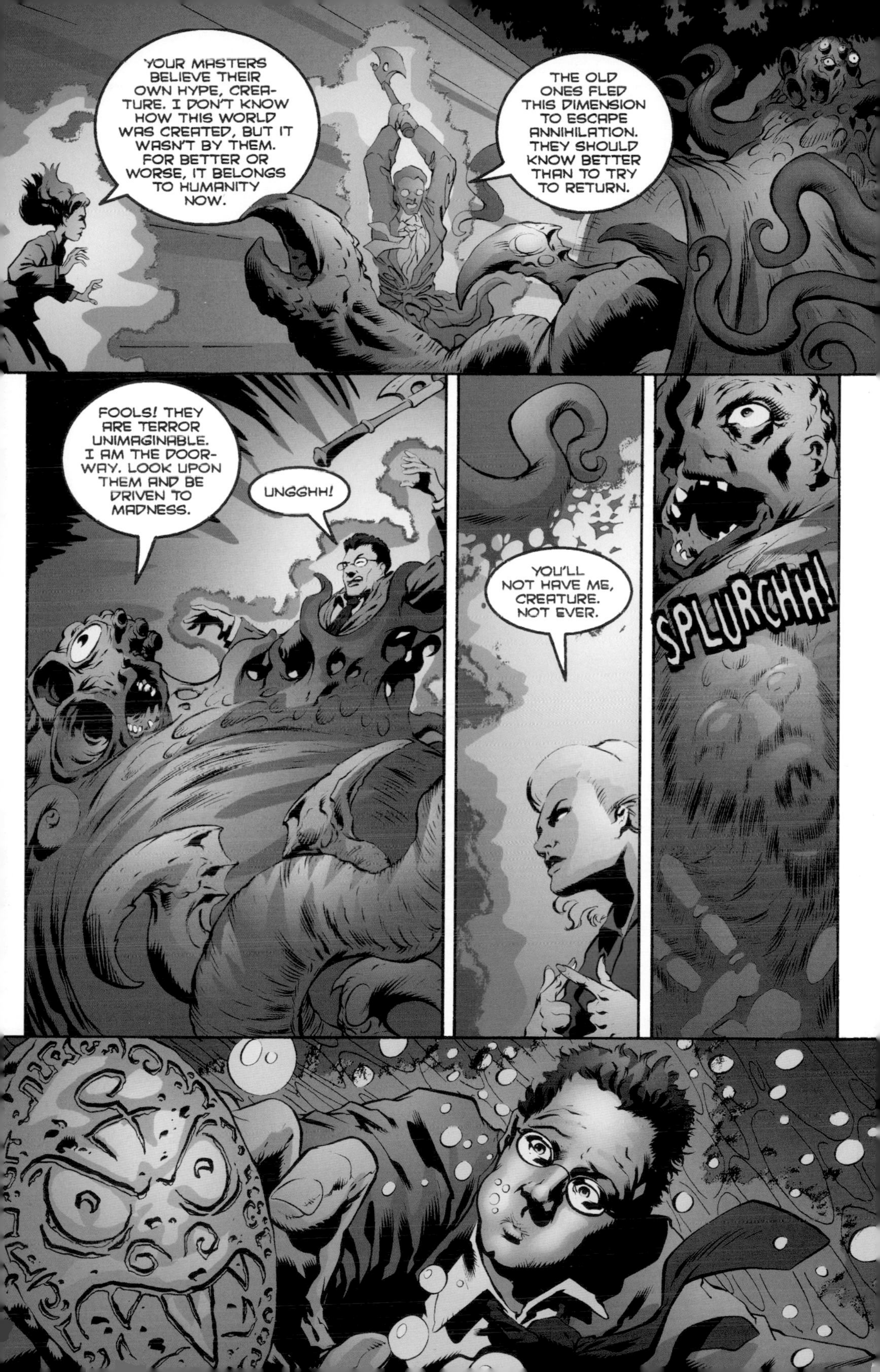
YOUR MASTERS BELIEVE THEIR OWN HYPE, CREA- TURE. I DON'T KNOW HOW THIS WORLD WAS CREATED, BUT IT WASN'T BY THEM. FOR BETTER OR WORSE, IT BELONGS TO HUMANITY NOW.
THE OLD ONES FLED THIS DIMENSION TO ESCAPE ANNIHILATION. THEY SHOULD KNOW BETTER THAN TO TRY TO RETURN.
FOOLS! THEY ARE TERROR UNIMAGINABLE. I AM THE DOOR- WAY. LOOK UPON THEM AND BE DRIVEN TO MADNESS.
UNGGHH!
YOU'LL NOT HAVE ME, CREATURE. NOT EVER.
SPLURCHH!

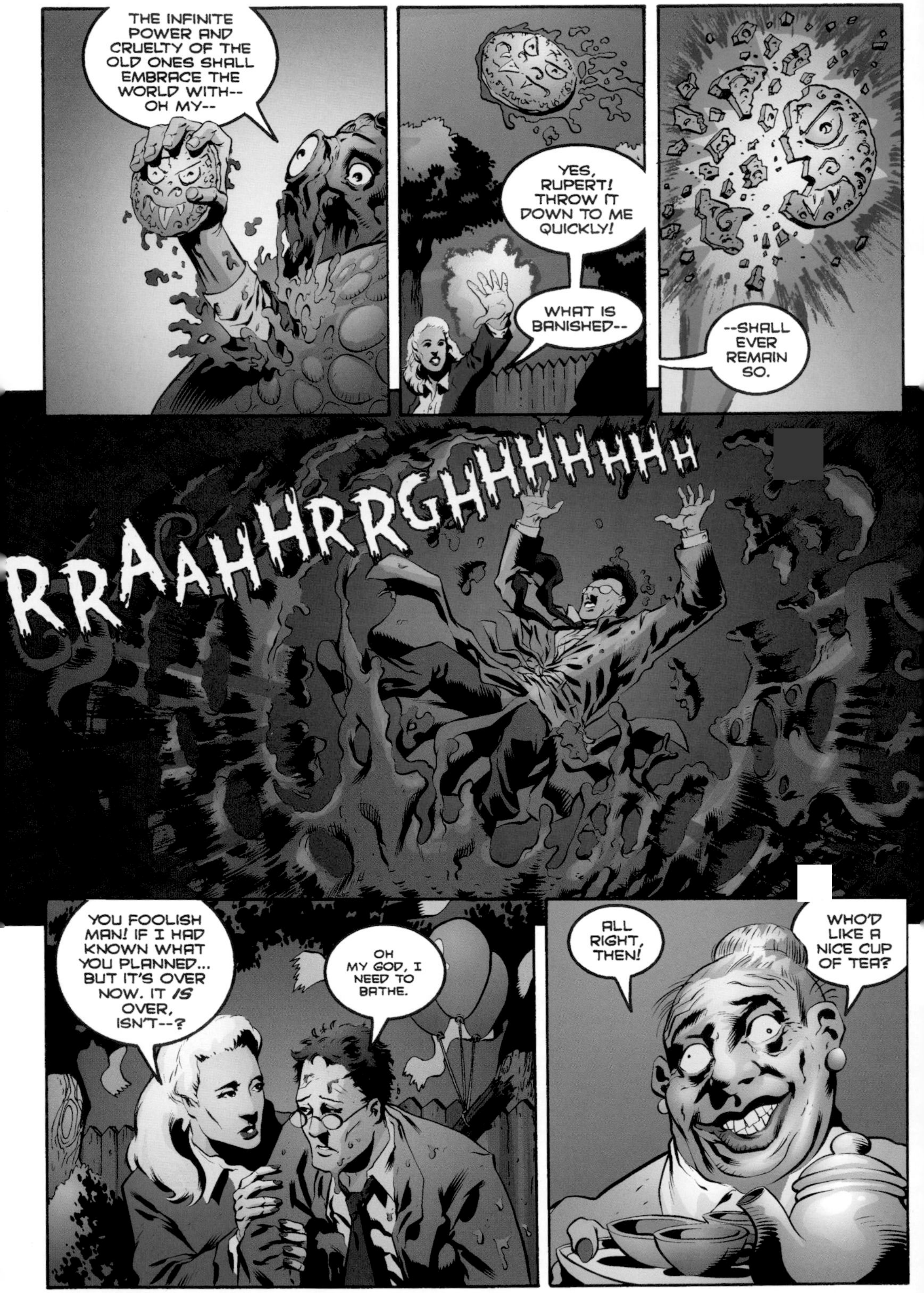
THE INFINITE POWER AND CRUELTY OF THE OLD ONES SHALL EMBRACE THE WORLD WITH-- OH MY--
YES, RUPERT! THROW IT DOWN TO ME QUICKLY!
WHAT IS BANISHED--
--SHALL EVER REMAIN SO.
RRAAHHRRGHHHHHHH
YOU FOOLISH MAN! IF I HAD KNOWN WHAT YOU PLANNED... BUT IT'S OVER NOW. IT *IS* OVER, ISN'T--?
OH MY GOD, I NEED TO BATHE.
ALL RIGHT, THEN!
WHO'D LIKE A NICE CUP OF TEA?

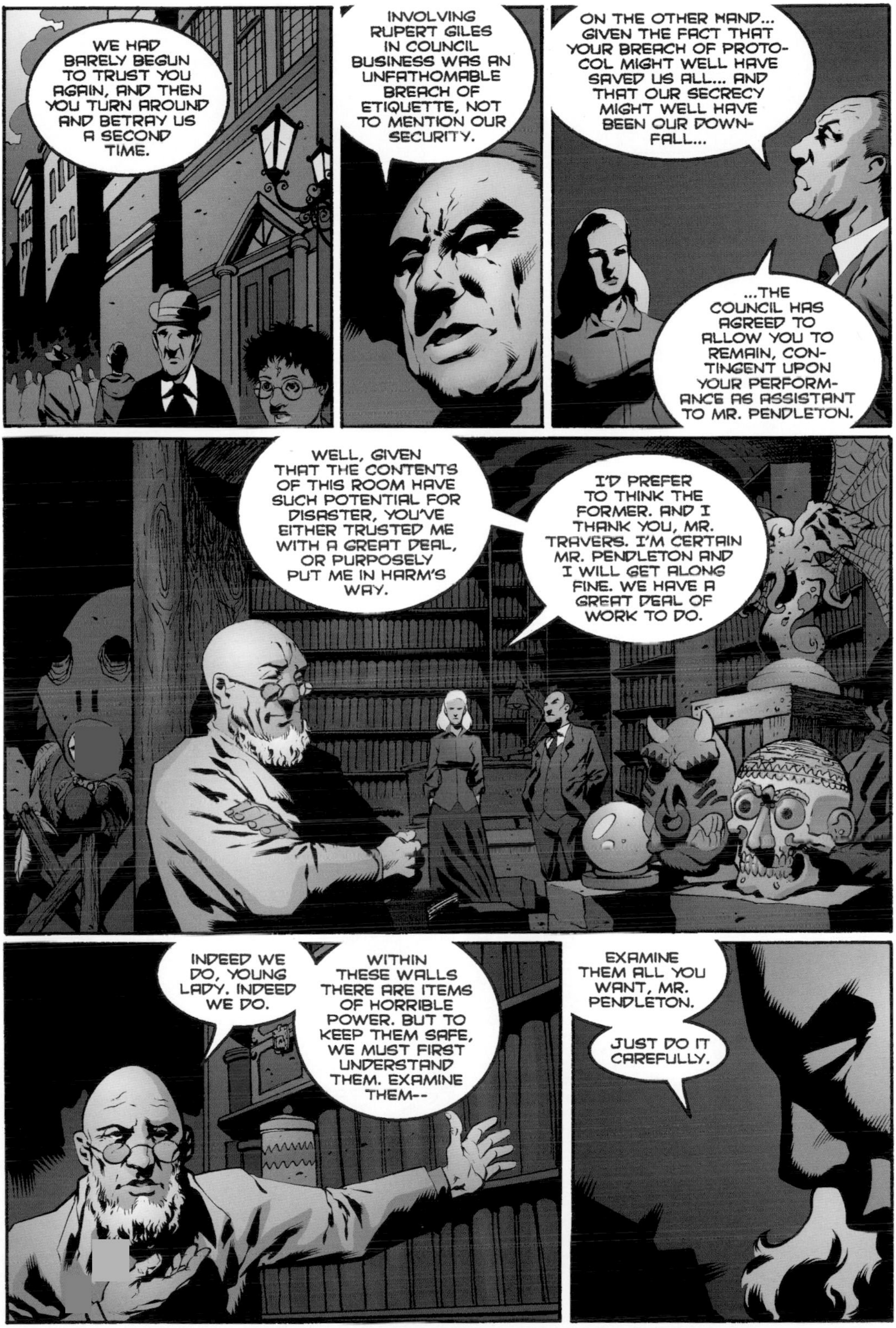
WE HAD BARELY BEGUN TO TRUST YOU AGAIN, AND THEN YOU TURN AROUND AND BETRAY US A SECOND TIME.
INVOLVING RUPERT GILES IN COUNCIL BUSINESS WAS AN UNFATHOMABLE BREACH OF ETIQUETTE, NOT TO MENTION OUR SECURITY.
ON THE OTHER HAND... GIVEN THE FACT THAT YOUR BREACH OF PROTOCOL MIGHT WELL HAVE SAVED US ALL... AND THAT OUR SECRECY MIGHT WELL HAVE BEEN OUR DOWNFALL...
...THE COUNCIL HAS AGREED TO ALLOW YOU TO REMAIN, CONTINGENT UPON YOUR PERFORMANCE AS ASSISTANT TO MR. PENDLETON.
WELL, GIVEN THAT THE CONTENTS OF THIS ROOM HAVE SUCH POTENTIAL FOR DISASTER, YOU'VE EITHER TRUSTED ME WITH A GREAT DEAL, OR PURPOSELY PUT ME IN HARM'S WAY.
I'D PREFER TO THINK THE FORMER. AND I THANK YOU, MR. TRAVERS. I'M CERTAIN MR. PENDLETON AND I WILL GET ALONG FINE. WE HAVE A GREAT DEAL OF WORK TO DO.
INDEED WE DO, YOUNG LADY. INDEED WE DO.
WITHIN THESE WALLS THERE ARE ITEMS OF HORRIBLE POWER. BUT TO KEEP THEM SAFE, WE MUST FIRST UNDERSTAND THEM. EXAMINE THEM--
EXAMINE THEM ALL YOU WANT, MR. PENDLETON.
JUST DO IT CAREFULLY.

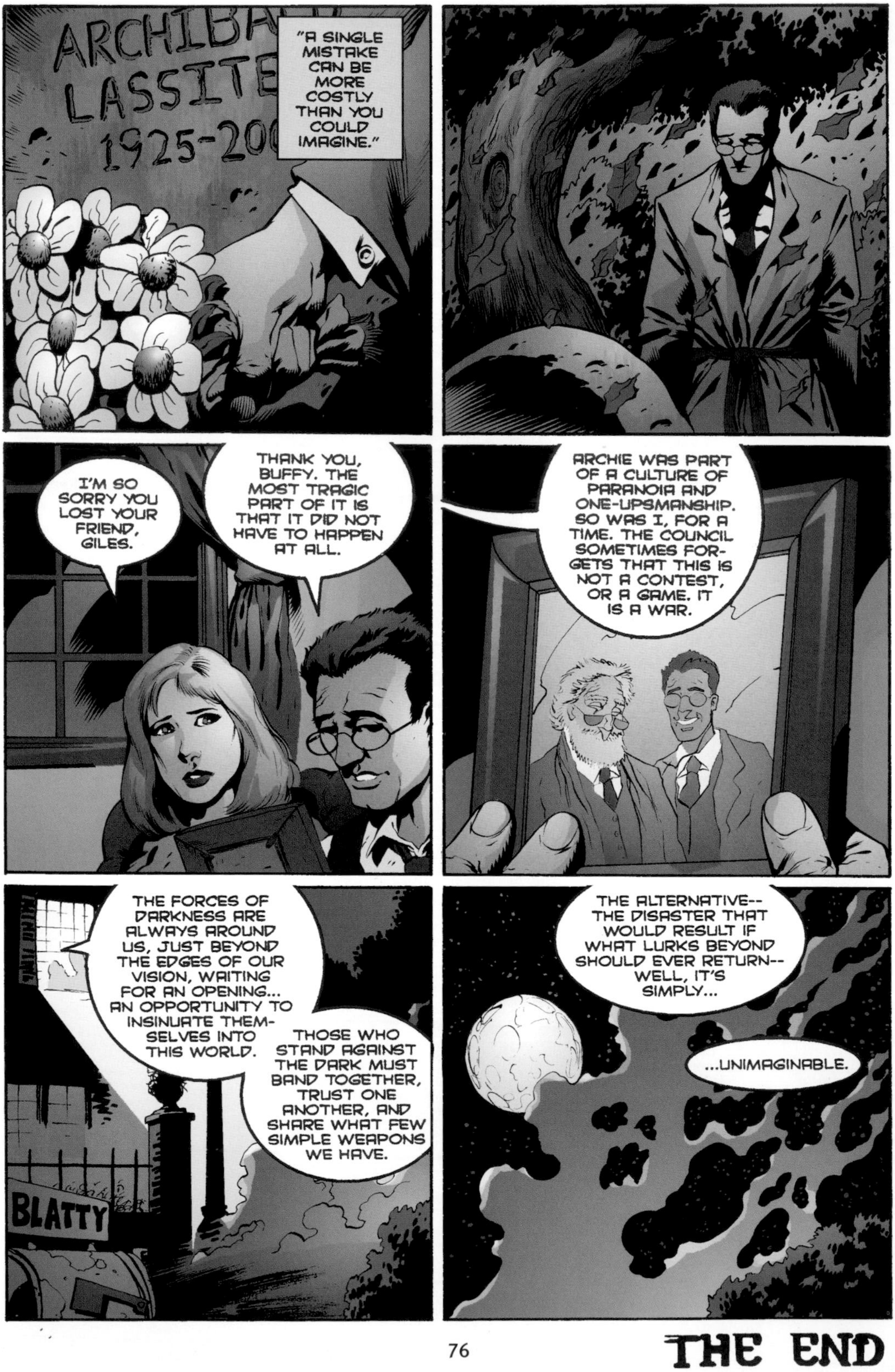
ARCHIBA
LASSITE
1925-200
"A SINGLE MISTAKE CAN BE MORE COSTLY THAN YOU COULD IMAGINE."
I'M SO SORRY YOU LOST YOUR FRIEND, GILES.
THANK YOU, BUFFY. THE MOST TRAGIC PART OF IT IS THAT IT DID NOT HAVE TO HAPPEN AT ALL.
ARCHIE WAS PART OF A CULTURE OF PARANOIA AND ONE-UPSMANSHIP. SO WAS I, FOR A TIME. THE COUNCIL SOMETIMES FOR-GETS THAT THIS IS NOT A CONTEST, OR A GAME. IT IS A WAR.
THE FORCES OF DARKNESS ARE ALWAYS AROUND US, JUST BEYOND THE EDGES OF OUR VISION, WAITING FOR AN OPENING... AN OPPORTUNITY TO INSINUATE THEM-SELVES INTO THIS WORLD.
THOSE WHO STAND AGAINST THE DARK MUST BAND TOGETHER, TRUST ONE ANOTHER, AND SHARE WHAT FEW SIMPLE WEAPONS WE HAVE.
BLATTY
THE ALTERNATIVE-- THE DISASTER THAT WOULD RESULT IF WHAT LURKS BEYOND SHOULD EVER RETURN-- WELL, IT'S SIMPLY...
...UNIMAGINABLE.
THE END

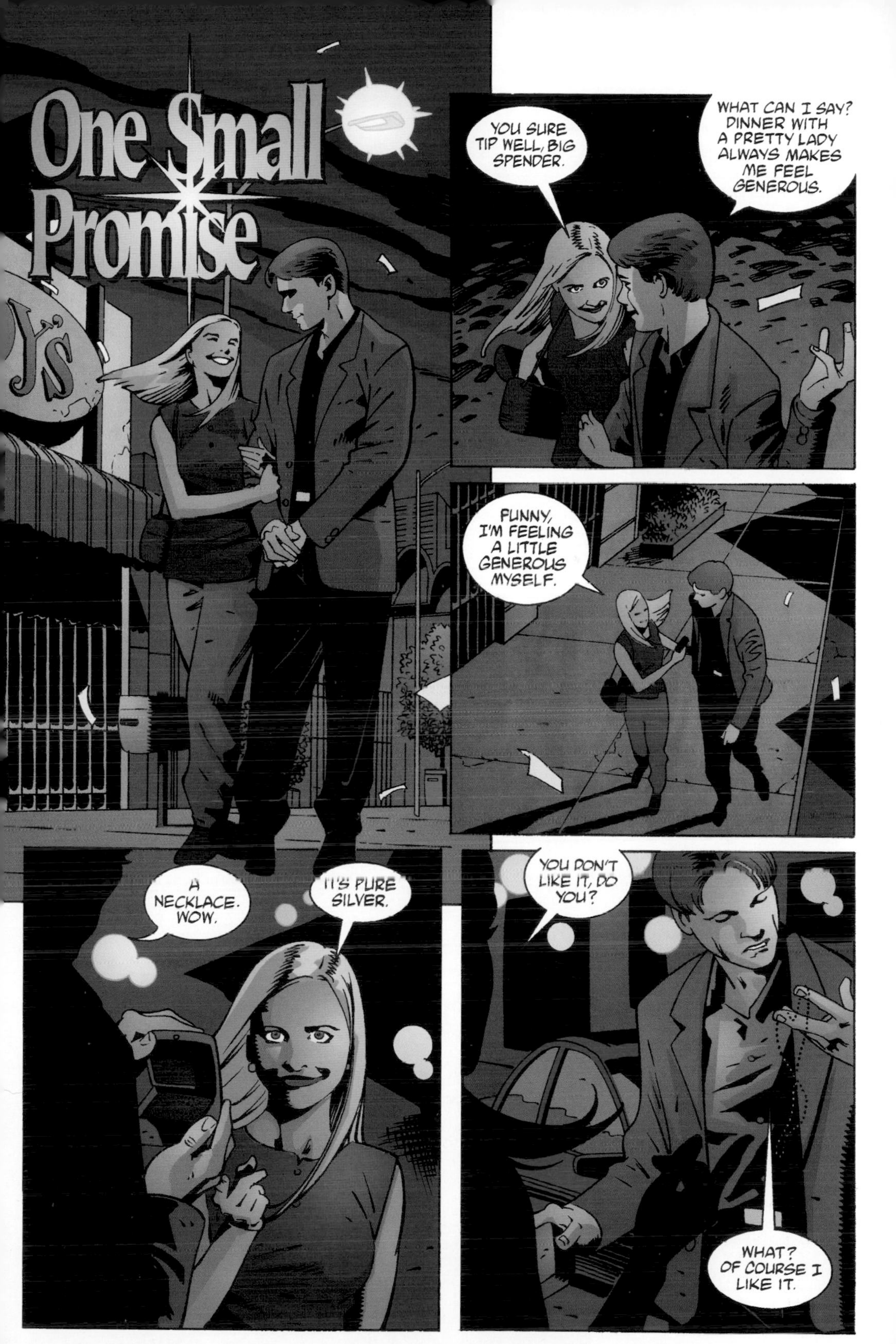
One Small Promise
YOU SURE TIP WELL, BIG SPENDER.
WHAT CAN I SAY? DINNER WITH A PRETTY LADY ALWAYS MAKES ME FEEL GENEROUS.
FUNNY, I'M FEELING A LITTLE GENEROUS MYSELF.
A NECKLACE. WOW.
IT'S PURE SILVER.
YOU DON'T LIKE IT, DO YOU?
WHAT? OF COURSE I LIKE IT.

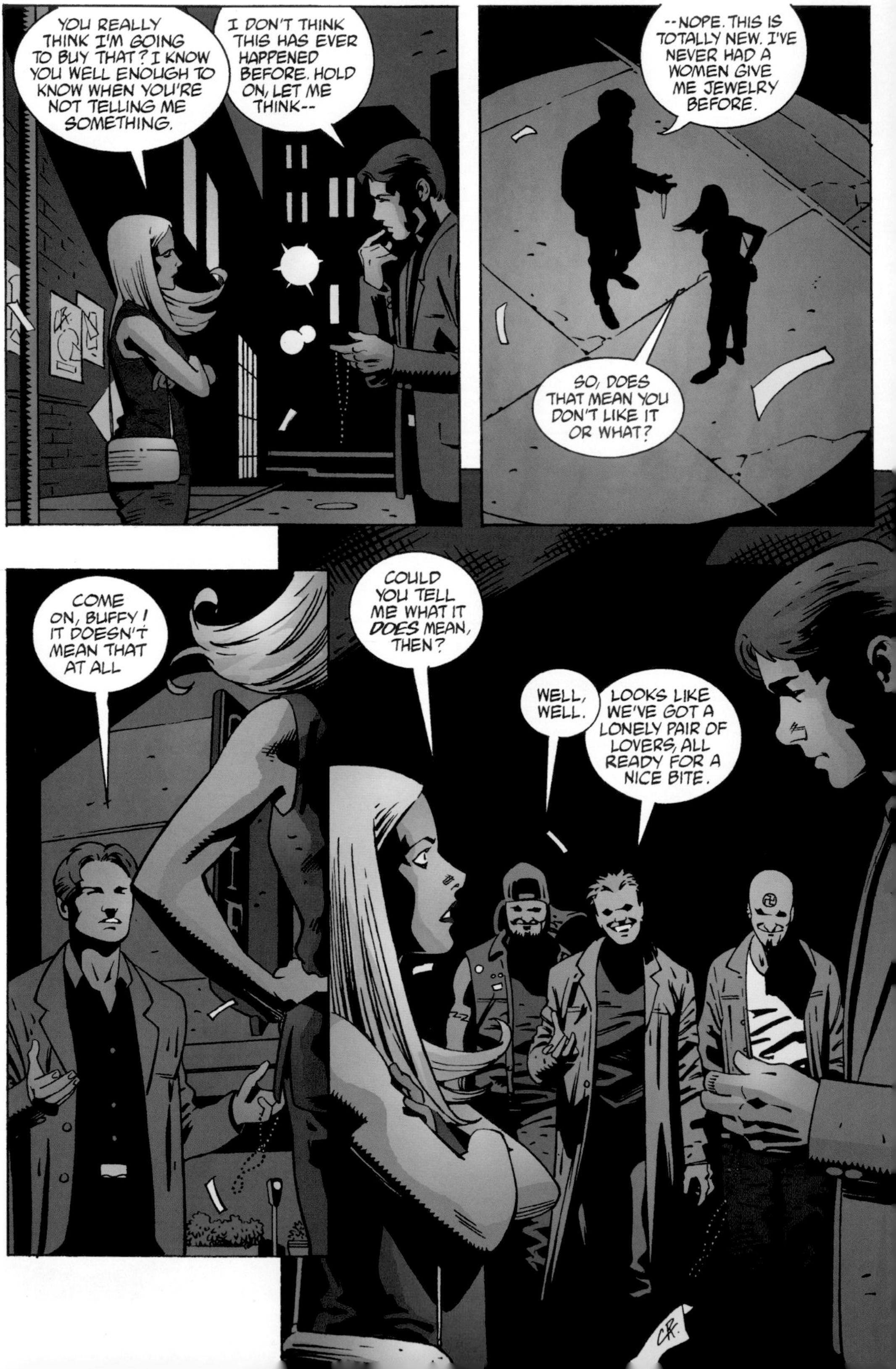
YOU REALLY THINK I'M GOING TO BUY THAT? I KNOW YOU WELL ENOUGH TO KNOW WHEN YOU'RE NOT TELLING ME SOMETHING.
I DON'T THINK THIS HAS EVER HAPPENED BEFORE. HOLD ON, LET ME THINK--
--NOPE. THIS IS TOTALLY NEW. I'VE NEVER HAD A WOMEN GIVE ME JEWELRY BEFORE.
SO, DOES THAT MEAN YOU DON'T LIKE IT OR WHAT?
COME ON, BUFFY! IT DOESN'T MEAN THAT AT ALL
COULD YOU TELL ME WHAT IT DOES MEAN, THEN?
WELL, WELL.
LOOKS LIKE WE'VE GOT A LONELY PAIR OF LOVERS, ALL READY FOR A NICE BITE.
CR.

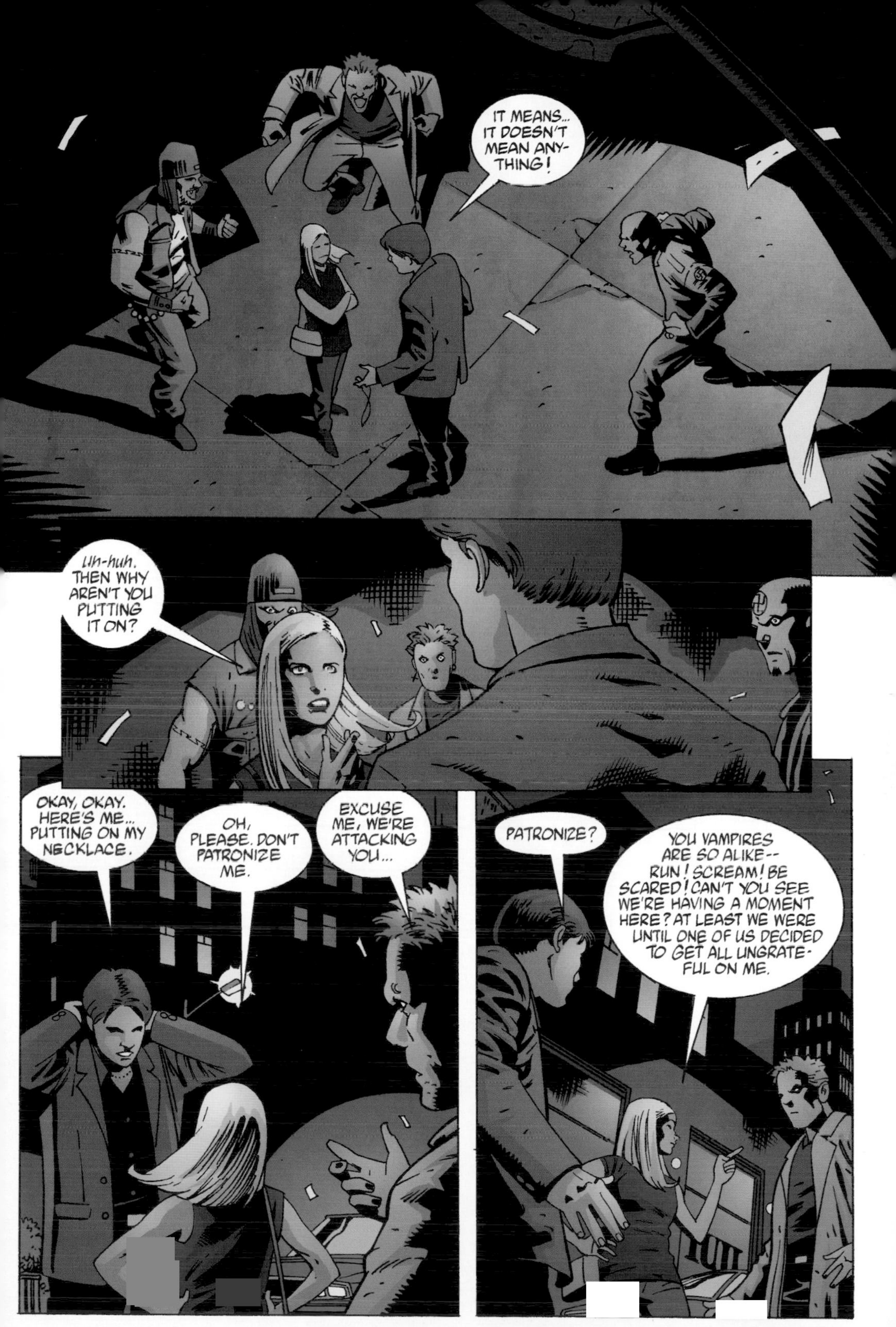
IT MEANS... IT DOESN'T MEAN ANYTHING!
Uh-huh. THEN WHY AREN'T YOU PUTTING IT ON?
OKAY, OKAY. HERE'S ME... PUTTING ON MY NECKLACE.
OH, PLEASE. DON'T PATRONIZE ME.
EXCUSE ME, WE'RE ATTACKING YOU...
PATRONIZE?
YOU VAMPIRES ARE SO ALIKE-- RUN! SCREAM! BE SCARED! CAN'T YOU SEE WE'RE HAVING A MOMENT HERE? AT LEAST WE WERE UNTIL ONE OF US DECIDED TO GET ALL UNGRATEFUL ON ME.

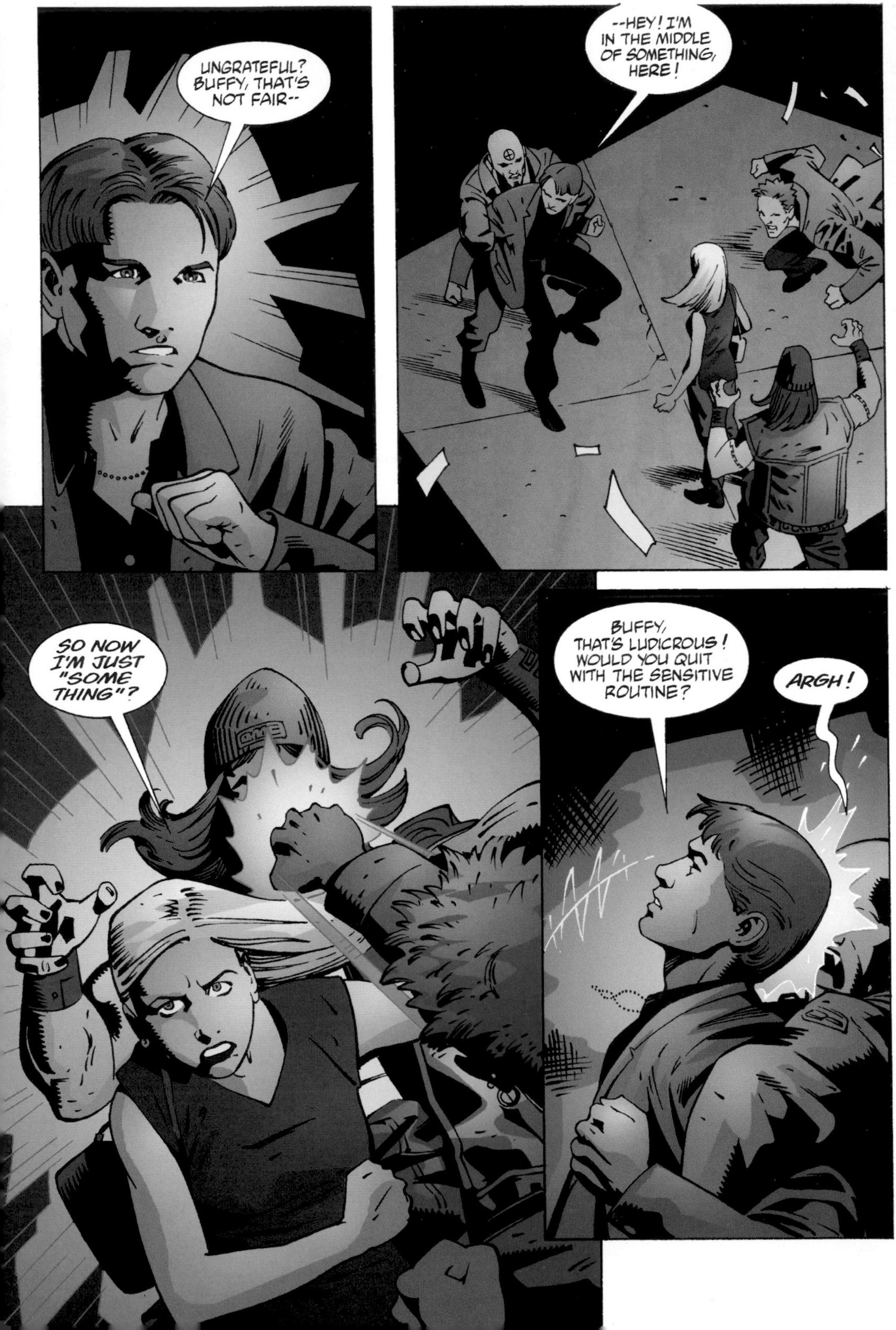
UNGRATEFUL? BUFFY, THAT'S NOT FAIR--
--HEY! I'M IN THE MIDDLE OF SOMETHING, HERE!
SO NOW I'M JUST "SOME THING"?
BUFFY, THAT'S LUDICROUS! WOULD YOU QUIT WITH THE SENSITIVE ROUTINE?
ARGH!

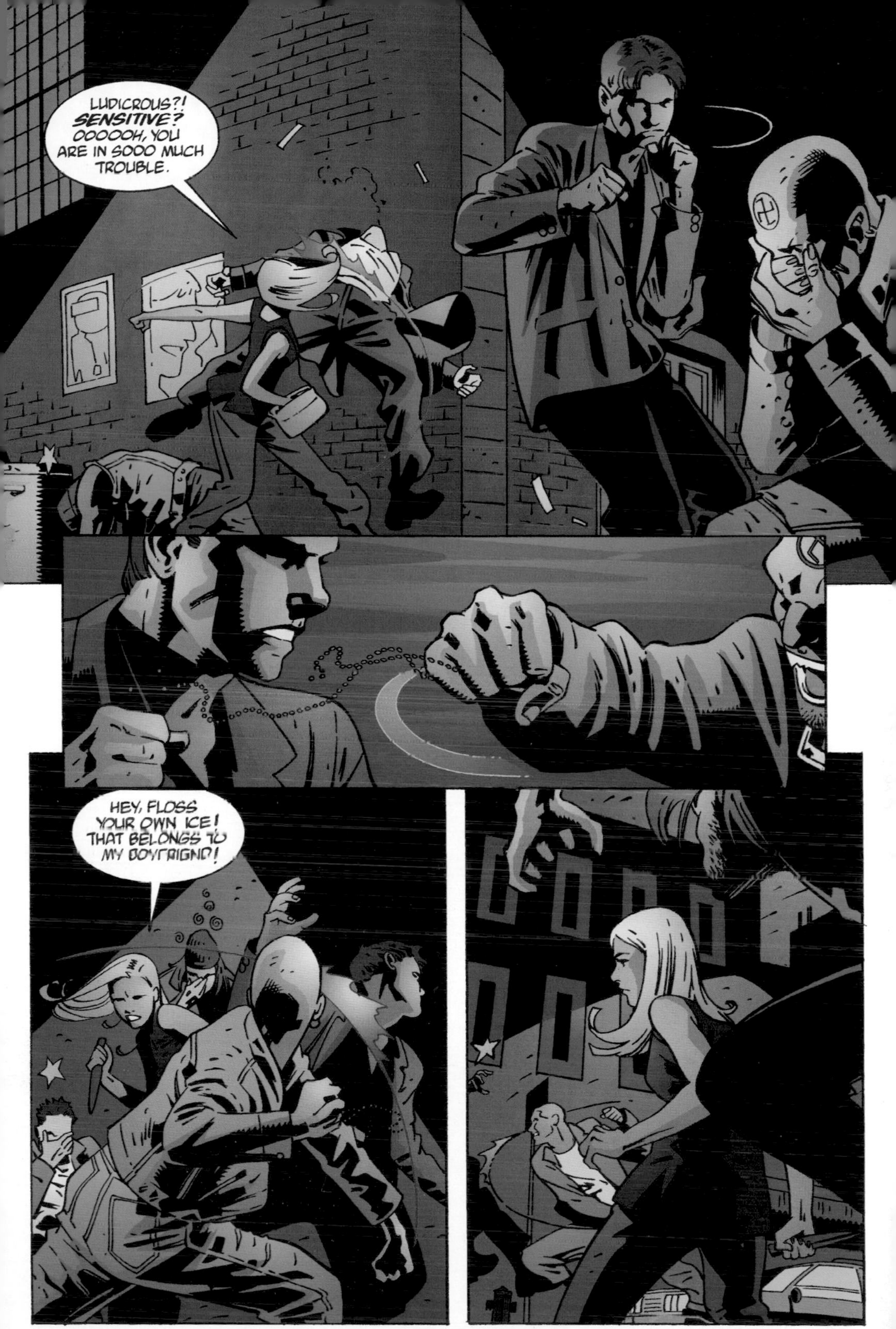
LUDICROUS?! SENSITIVE? OOOOOH, YOU ARE IN SOOO MUCH TROUBLE.
HEY, FLOSS YOUR OWN ICE! THAT BELONGS TO MY BOYFRIEND!

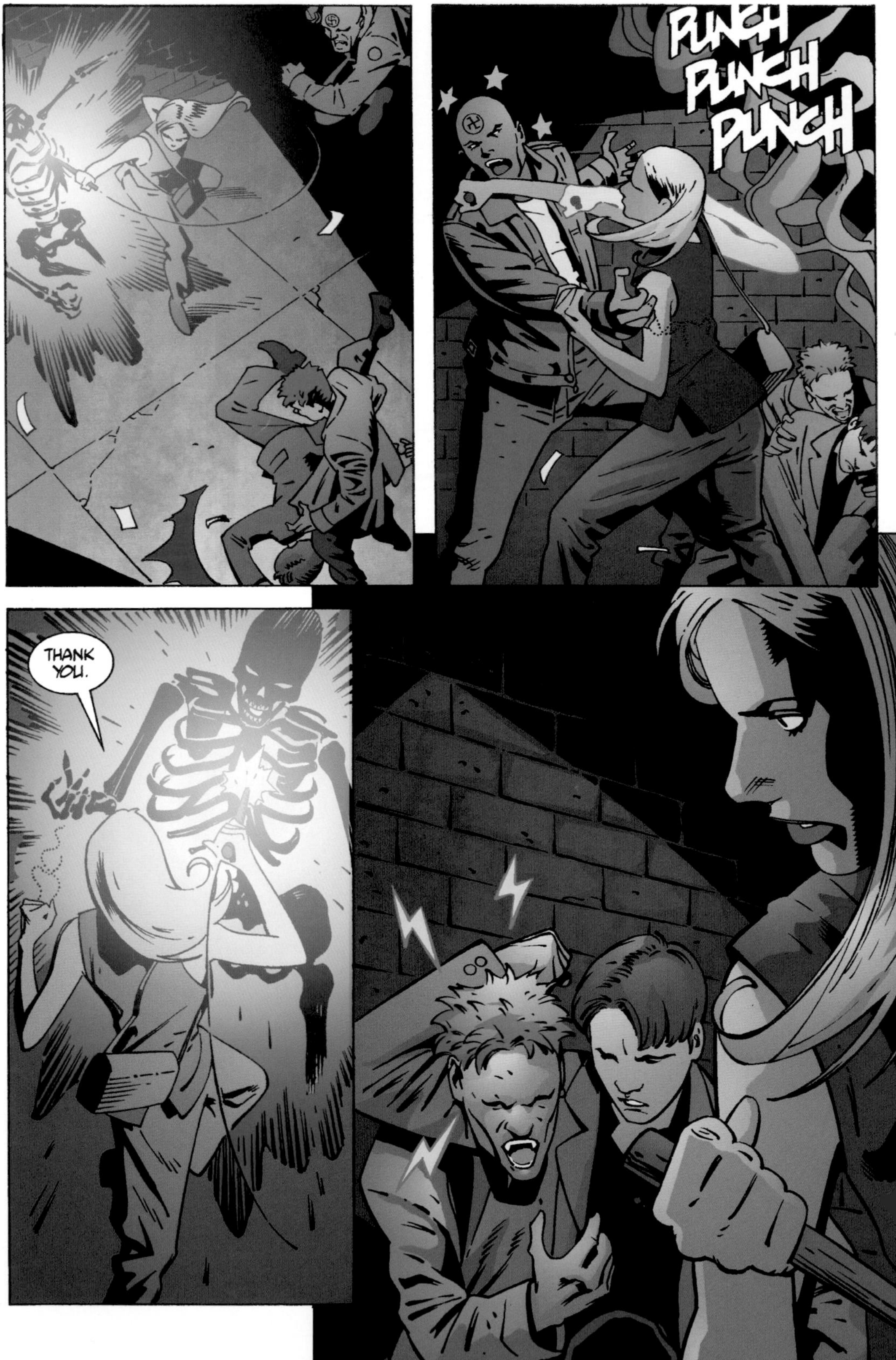
PUNCH
PUNCH
PUNCH
THANK YOU.

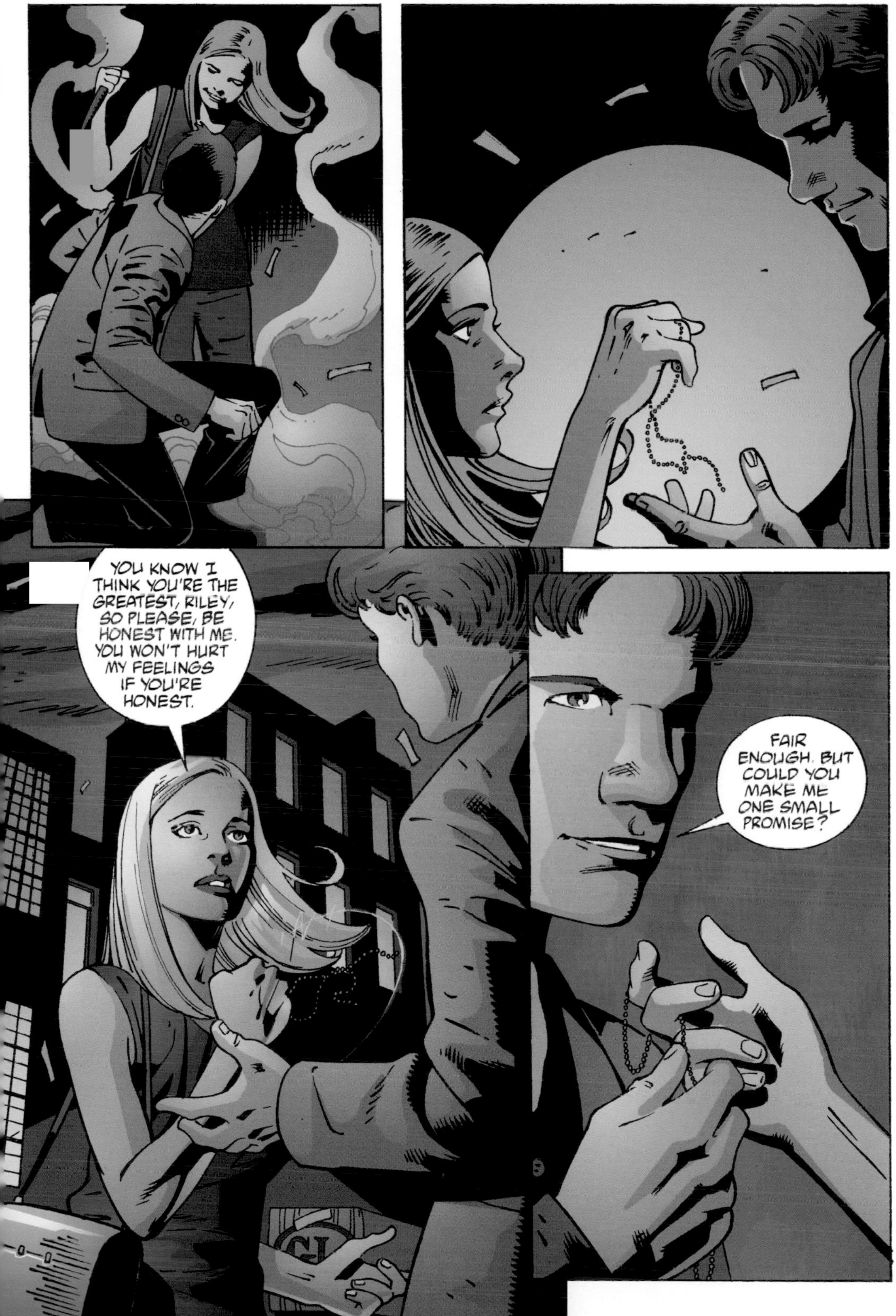
YOU KNOW I THINK YOU'RE THE GREATEST, RILEY, SO PLEASE, BE HONEST WITH ME. YOU WON'T HURT MY FEELINGS IF YOU'RE HONEST.
FAIR ENOUGH. BUT COULD YOU MAKE ME ONE SMALL PROMISE?

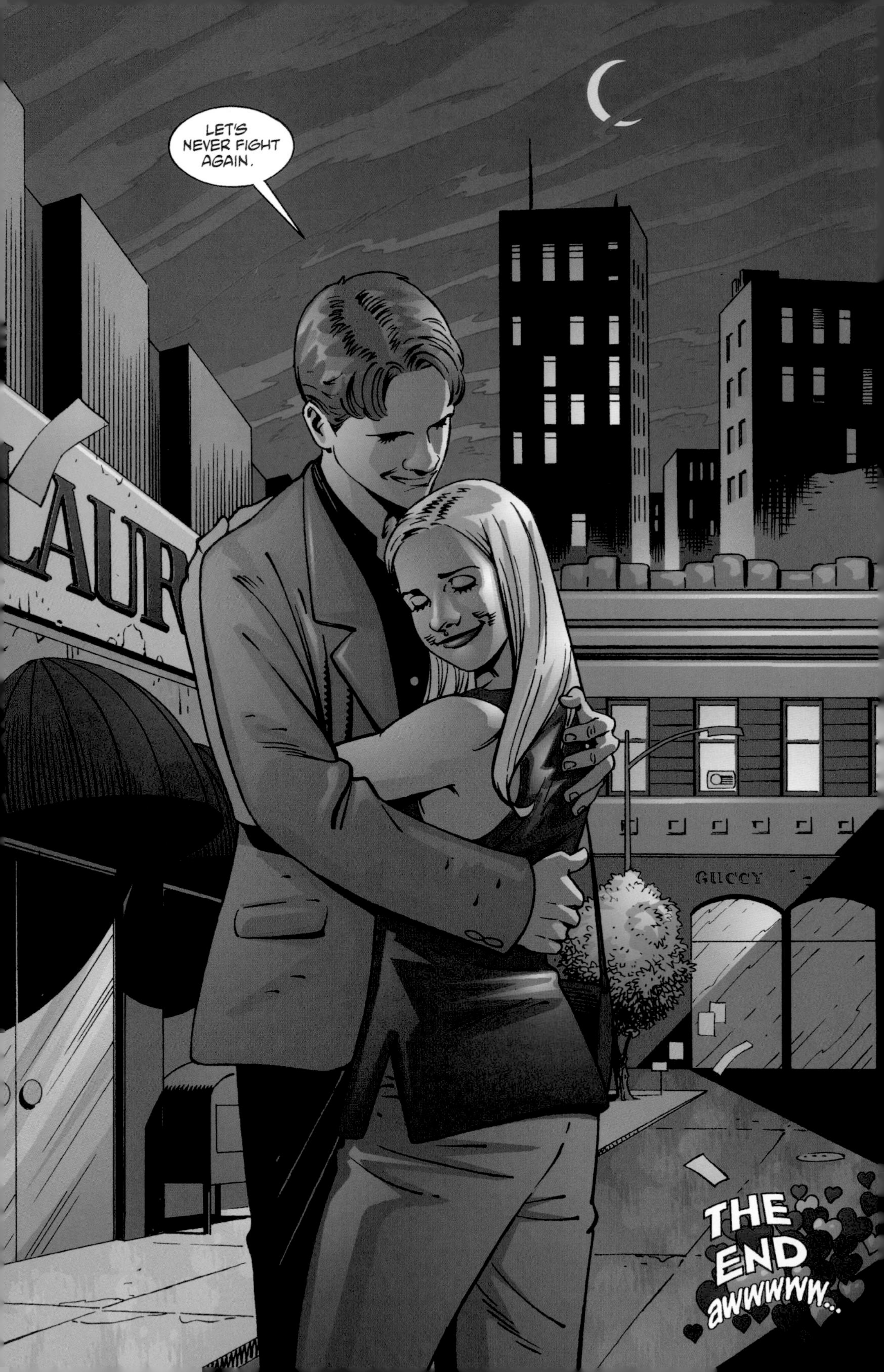
LET'S NEVER FIGHT AGAIN.
LAUR
GUCCY
THE END
awwwww...

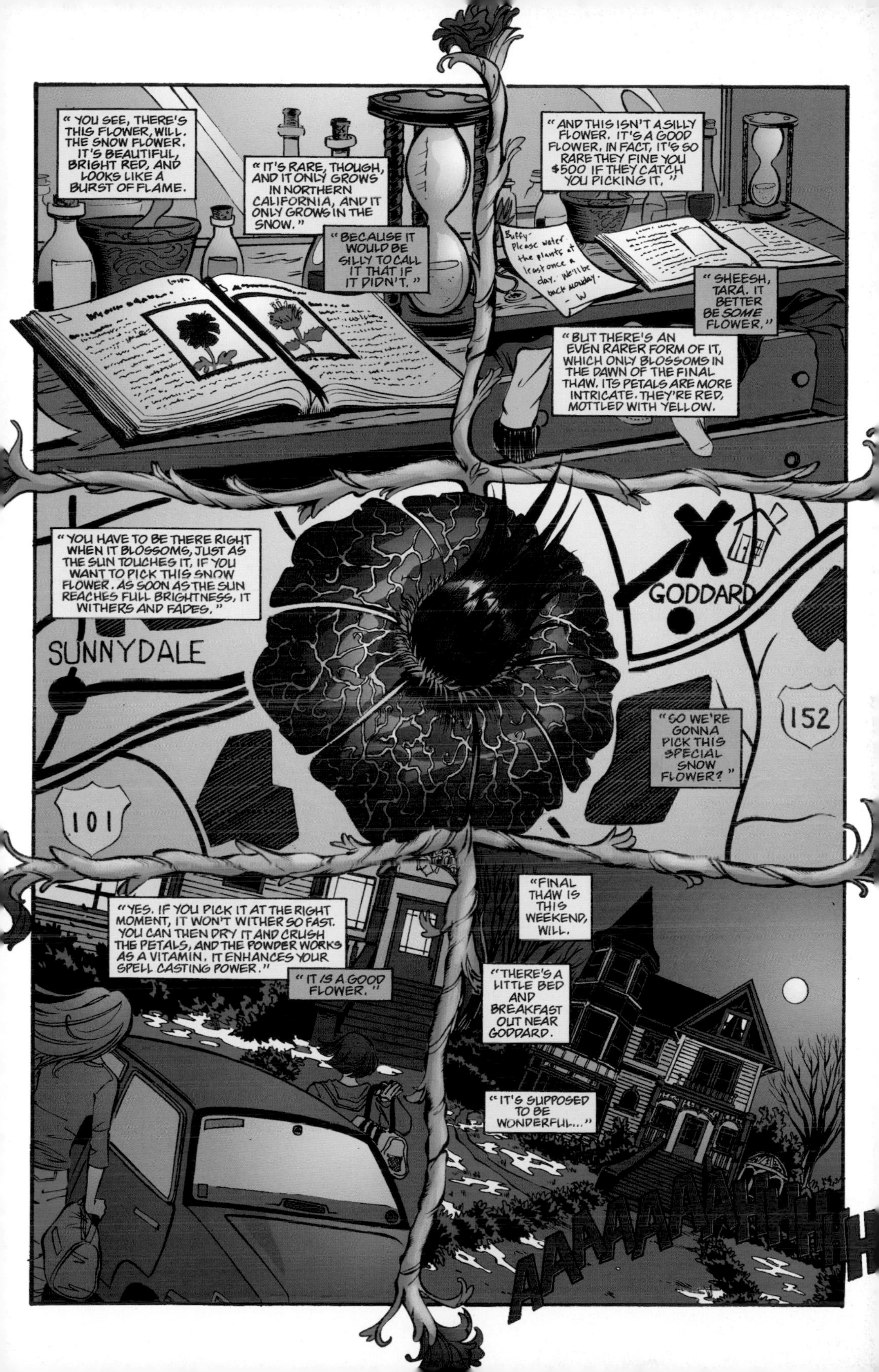

"YOU SEE, THERE'S THIS FLOWER, WILL. THE SNOW FLOWER. IT'S BEAUTIFUL, BRIGHT RED, AND LOOKS LIKE A BURST OF FLAME.
"IT'S RARE, THOUGH, AND IT ONLY GROWS IN NORTHERN CALIFORNIA, AND IT ONLY GROWS IN THE SNOW."
"BECAUSE IT WOULD BE SILLY TO CALL IT THAT IF IT DIDN'T."
"AND THIS ISN'T A SILLY FLOWER. IT'S A GOOD FLOWER. IN FACT, IT'S SO RARE THEY FINE YOU $500 IF THEY CATCH YOU PICKING IT."
Buffy- Please water the plants at least once a day. We'll be back Monday. - W
"SHEESH, TARA. IT BETTER BE SOME FLOWER."
"BUT THERE'S AN EVEN RARER FORM OF IT, WHICH ONLY BLOSSOMS IN THE DAWN OF THE FINAL THAW. ITS PETALS ARE MORE INTRICATE. THEY'RE RED, MOTTLED WITH YELLOW.
"YOU HAVE TO BE THERE RIGHT WHEN IT BLOSSOMS, JUST AS THE SUN TOUCHES IT, IF YOU WANT TO PICK THIS SNOW FLOWER. AS SOON AS THE SUN REACHES FULL BRIGHTNESS, IT WITHERS AND FADES."
GODDARD
SUNNYDALE
152
101
"SO WE'RE GONNA PICK THIS SPECIAL SNOW FLOWER?"
"YES. IF YOU PICK IT AT THE RIGHT MOMENT, IT WON'T WITHER SO FAST. YOU CAN THEN DRY IT AND CRUSH THE PETALS, AND THE POWDER WORKS AS A VITAMIN. IT ENHANCES YOUR SPELL CASTING POWER."
"IT IS A GOOD FLOWER."
"FINAL THAW IS THIS WEEKEND, WILL.
"THERE'S A LITTLE BED AND BREAKFAST OUT NEAR GODDARD.
"IT'S SUPPOSED TO BE WONDERFUL..."
AAAAAAAHHHHH

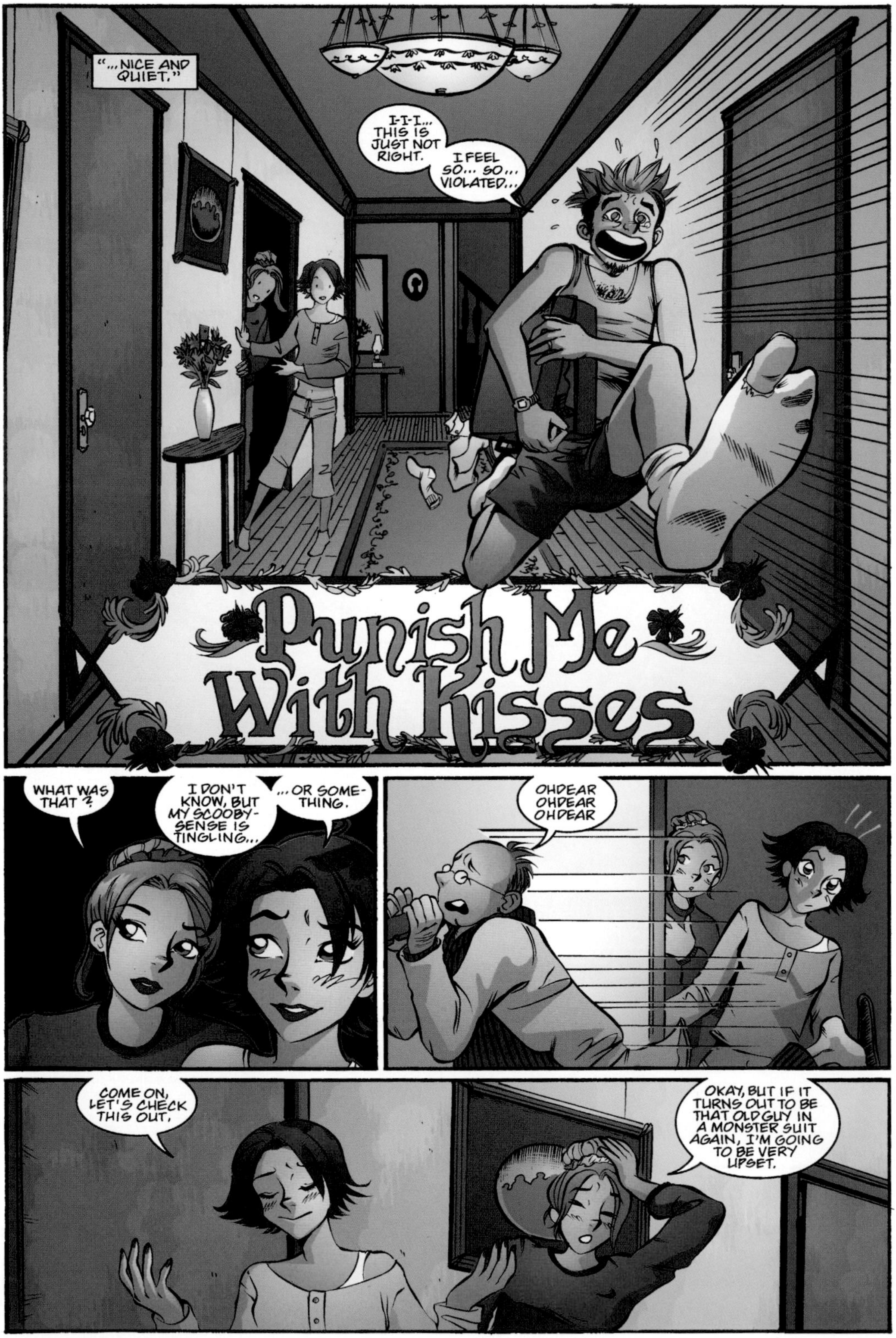
"...NICE AND QUIET."
I-I-I... THIS IS JUST NOT RIGHT.
I FEEL SO... SO... VIOLATED...
Punish Me With Kisses
WHAT WAS THAT?
I DON'T KNOW, BUT MY SCOOBY-SENSE IS TINGLING...
...OR SOME-THING.
OHDEAR OHDEAR OHDEAR
COME ON, LET'S CHECK THIS OUT.
OKAY, BUT IF IT TURNS OUT TO BE THAT OLD GUY IN A MONSTER SUIT AGAIN, I'M GOING TO BE VERY UPSET.

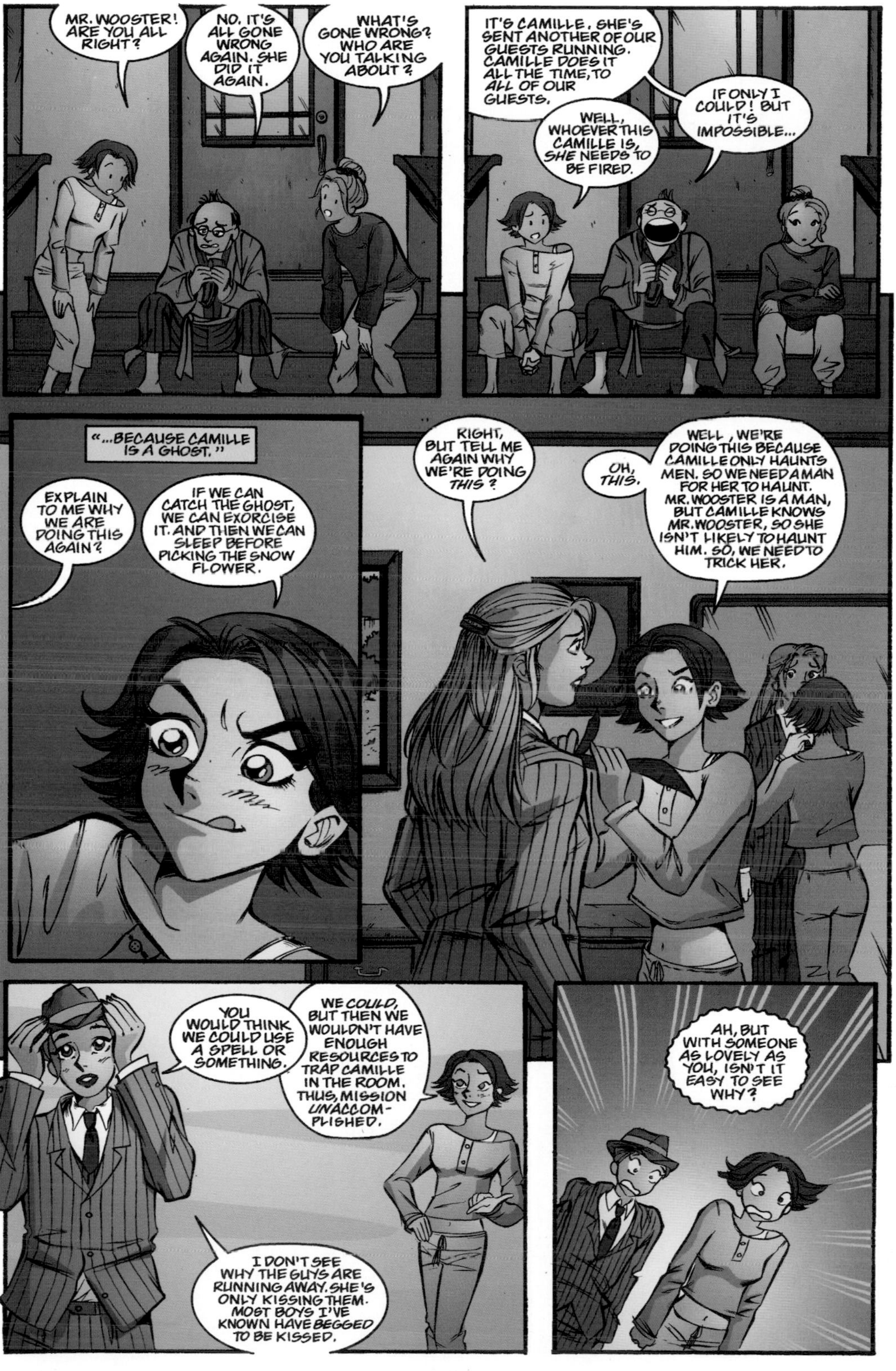
MR. WOOSTER! ARE YOU ALL RIGHT?
NO. IT'S ALL GONE WRONG AGAIN. SHE DID IT AGAIN.
WHAT'S GONE WRONG? WHO ARE YOU TALKING ABOUT?
IT'S CAMILLE. SHE'S SENT ANOTHER OF OUR GUESTS RUNNING. CAMILLE DOES IT ALL THE TIME, TO ALL OF OUR GUESTS.
WELL, WHOEVER THIS CAMILLE IS, SHE NEEDS TO BE FIRED.
IF ONLY I COULD! BUT IT'S IMPOSSIBLE...
"...BECAUSE CAMILLE IS A GHOST."
EXPLAIN TO ME WHY WE ARE DOING THIS AGAIN?
IF WE CAN CATCH THE GHOST, WE CAN EXORCISE IT. AND THEN WE CAN SLEEP BEFORE PICKING THE SNOW FLOWER.
RIGHT, BUT TELL ME AGAIN WHY WE'RE DOING THIS?
OH, THIS.
WELL, WE'RE DOING THIS BECAUSE CAMILLE ONLY HAUNTS MEN. SO WE NEED A MAN FOR HER TO HAUNT. MR. WOOSTER IS A MAN, BUT CAMILLE KNOWS MR. WOOSTER, SO SHE ISN'T LIKELY TO HAUNT HIM. SO, WE NEED TO TRICK HER.
YOU WOULD THINK WE COULD USE A SPELL OR SOMETHING.
WE COULD, BUT THEN WE WOULDN'T HAVE ENOUGH RESOURCES TO TRAP CAMILLE IN THE ROOM. THUS, MISSION UNACCOM-PLISHED.
I DON'T SEE WHY THE GUYS ARE RUNNING AWAY. SHE'S ONLY KISSING THEM. MOST BOYS I'VE KNOWN HAVE BEGGED TO BE KISSED.
AH, BUT WITH SOMEONE AS LOVELY AS YOU, ISN'T IT EASY TO SEE WHY?

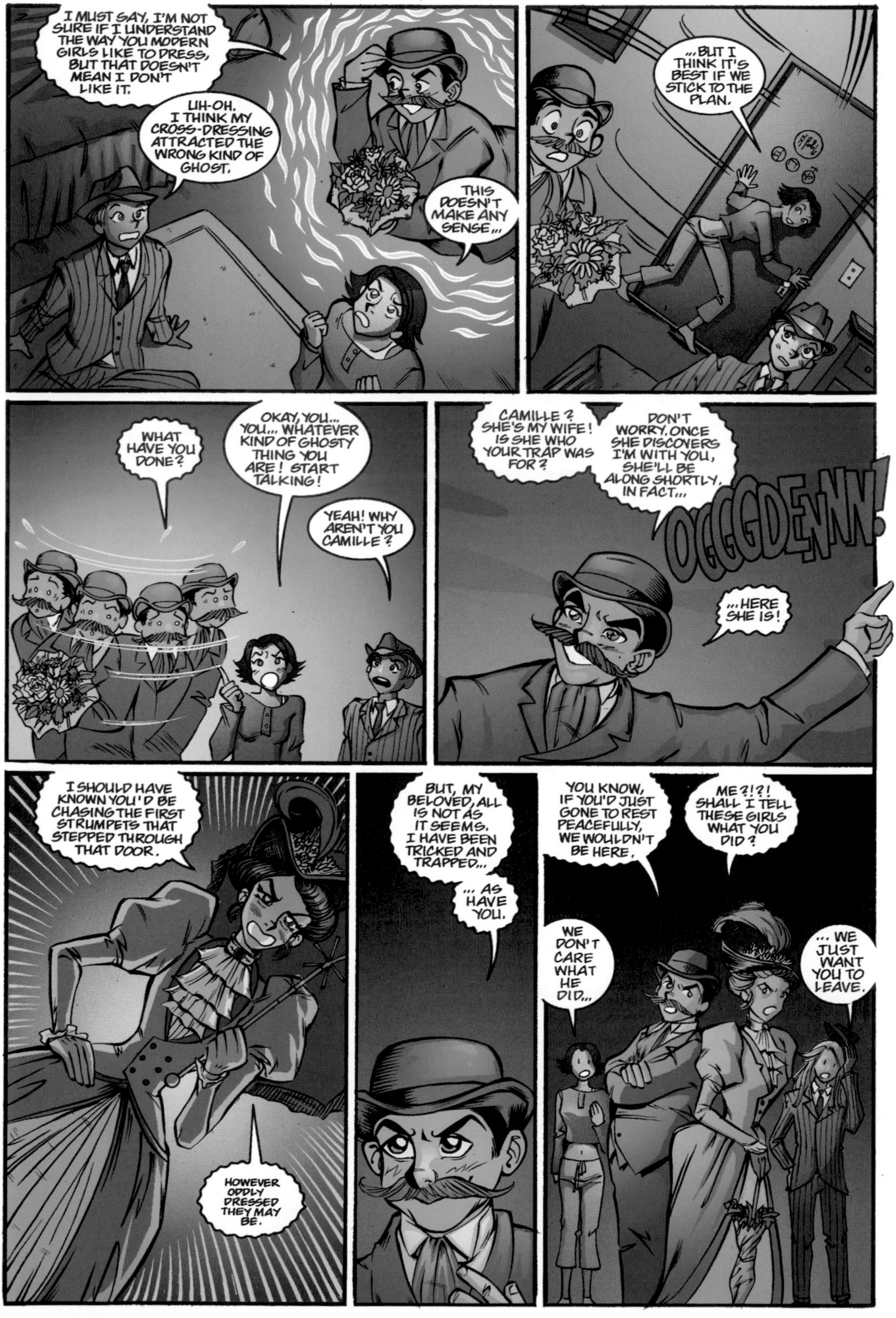
I MUST SAY, I'M NOT SURE IF I UNDERSTAND THE WAY YOU MODERN GIRLS LIKE TO DRESS, BUT THAT DOESN'T MEAN I DON'T LIKE IT.
UH-OH. I THINK MY CROSS-DRESSING ATTRACTED THE WRONG KIND OF GHOST.
THIS DOESN'T MAKE ANY SENSE...
...BUT I THINK IT'S BEST IF WE STICK TO THE PLAN.
WHAT HAVE YOU DONE?
OKAY, YOU... YOU... WHATEVER KIND OF GHOSTY THING YOU ARE! START TALKING!
YEAH! WHY AREN'T YOU CAMILLE?
CAMILLE? SHE'S MY WIFE! IS SHE WHO YOUR TRAP WAS FOR?
DON'T WORRY. ONCE SHE DISCOVERS I'M WITH YOU, SHE'LL BE ALONG SHORTLY. IN FACT...
OGGGDENNN!
...HERE SHE IS!
I SHOULD HAVE KNOWN YOU'D BE CHASING THE FIRST STRUMPETS THAT STEPPED THROUGH THAT DOOR.
HOWEVER ODDLY DRESSED THEY MAY BE.
BUT, MY BELOVED, ALL IS NOT AS IT SEEMS. I HAVE BEEN TRICKED AND TRAPPED...
... AS HAVE YOU.
YOU KNOW, IF YOU'D JUST GONE TO REST PEACEFULLY, WE WOULDN'T BE HERE.
ME?!?! SHALL I TELL THESE GIRLS WHAT YOU DID?
WE DON'T CARE WHAT HE DID...
... WE JUST WANT YOU TO LEAVE.

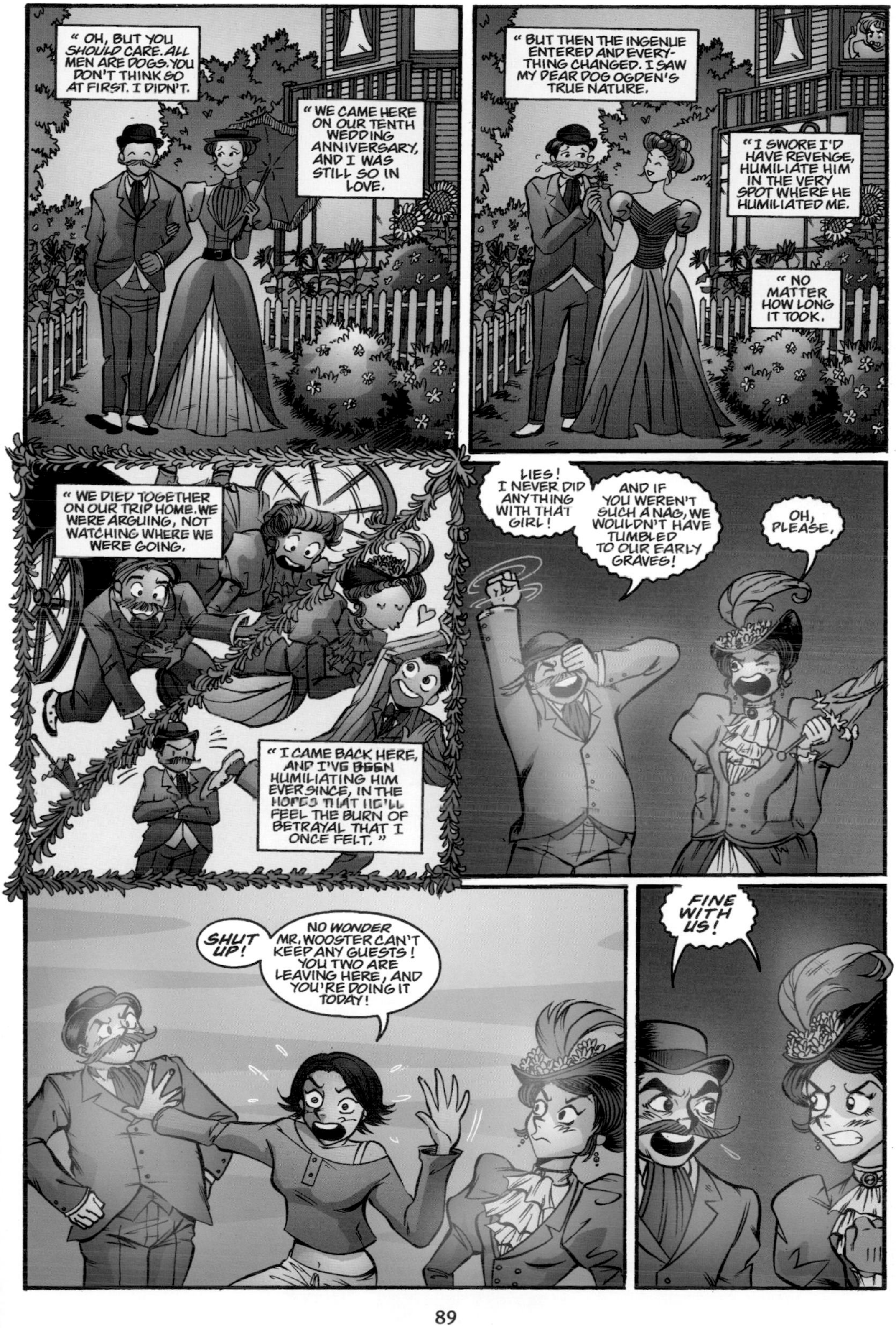

" OH, BUT YOU SHOULD CARE. ALL MEN ARE DOGS. YOU DON'T THINK SO AT FIRST. I DIDN'T.
" WE CAME HERE ON OUR TENTH WEDDING ANNIVERSARY, AND I WAS STILL SO IN LOVE.
" BUT THEN THE INGENUE ENTERED AND EVERYTHING CHANGED. I SAW MY DEAR DOG OGDEN'S TRUE NATURE.
" I SWORE I'D HAVE REVENGE, HUMILIATE HIM IN THE VERY SPOT WHERE HE HUMILIATED ME.
" NO MATTER HOW LONG IT TOOK.
" WE DIED TOGETHER ON OUR TRIP HOME. WE WERE ARGUING, NOT WATCHING WHERE WE WERE GOING.
" I CAME BACK HERE, AND I'VE BEEN HUMILIATING HIM EVER SINCE, IN THE HOPES THAT HE'LL FEEL THE BURN OF BETRAYAL THAT I ONCE FELT. "
LIES! I NEVER DID ANYTHING WITH THAT GIRL!
AND IF YOU WEREN'T SUCH A NAG, WE WOULDN'T HAVE TUMBLED TO OUR EARLY GRAVES!
OH, PLEASE.
SHUT UP!
NO WONDER MR. WOOSTER CAN'T KEEP ANY GUESTS! YOU TWO ARE LEAVING HERE, AND YOU'RE DOING IT TODAY!
FINE WITH US!

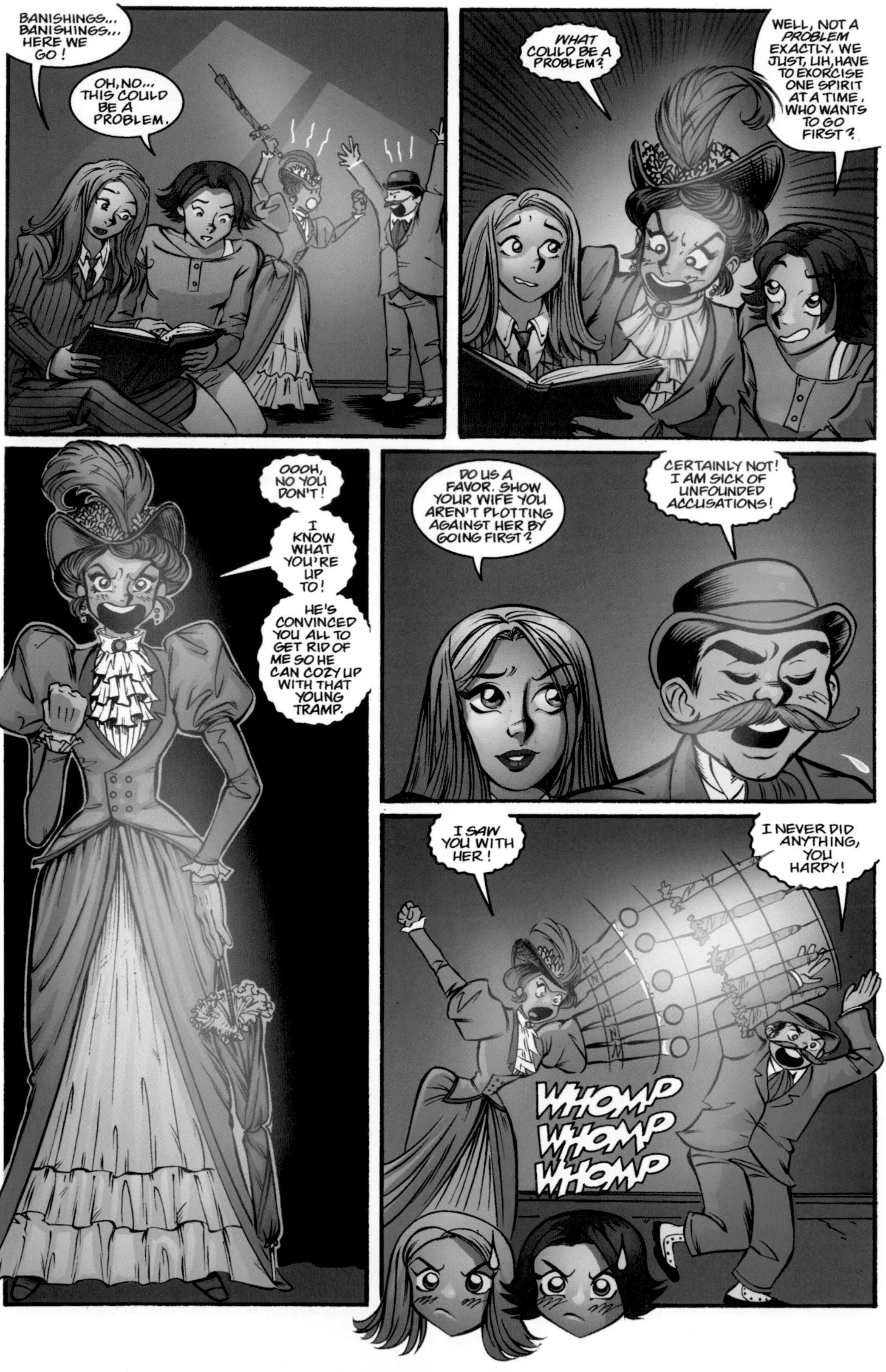
BANISHINGS... BANISHINGS... HERE WE GO!
OH, NO... THIS COULD BE A PROBLEM.
WHAT COULD BE A PROBLEM?
WELL, NOT A PROBLEM EXACTLY. WE JUST, UH, HAVE TO EXORCISE ONE SPIRIT AT A TIME. WHO WANTS TO GO FIRST?
OOOH, NO YOU DON'T!
I KNOW WHAT YOU'RE UP TO!
HE'S CONVINCED YOU ALL TO GET RID OF ME SO HE CAN COZY UP WITH THAT YOUNG TRAMP.
DO US A FAVOR. SHOW YOUR WIFE YOU AREN'T PLOTTING AGAINST HER BY GOING FIRST?
CERTAINLY NOT! I AM SICK OF UNFOUNDED ACCUSATIONS!
I SAW YOU WITH HER!
I NEVER DID ANYTHING, YOU HARPY!
WHOMP
WHOMP
WHOMP

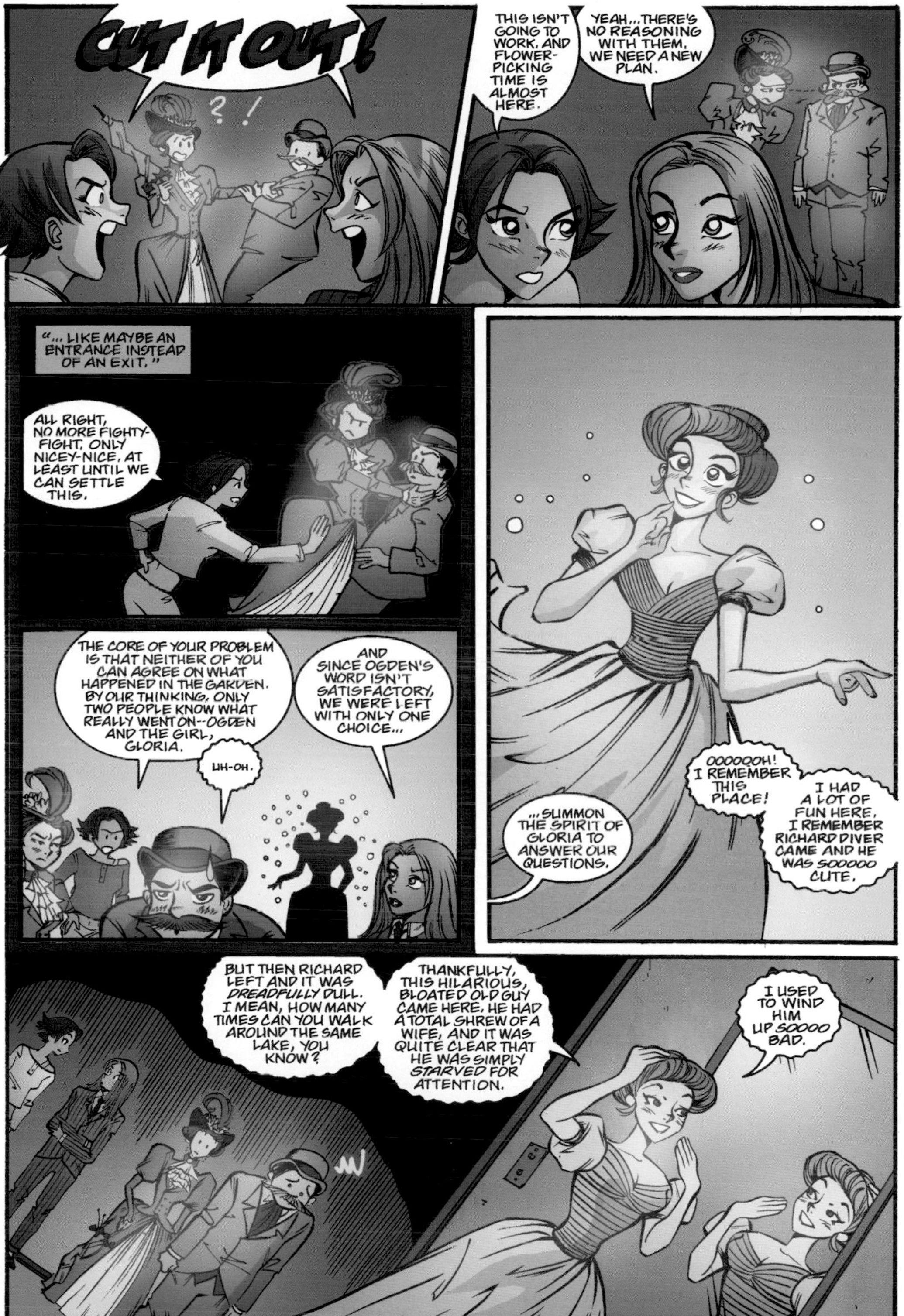
CUT IT OUT!
?!
THIS ISN'T GOING TO WORK, AND FLOWER-PICKING TIME IS ALMOST HERE.
YEAH... THERE'S NO REASONING WITH THEM. WE NEED A NEW PLAN.
"... LIKE MAYBE AN ENTRANCE INSTEAD OF AN EXIT."
ALL RIGHT, NO MORE FIGHTY-FIGHT, ONLY NICEY-NICE, AT LEAST UNTIL WE CAN SETTLE THIS.
THE CORE OF YOUR PROBLEM IS THAT NEITHER OF YOU CAN AGREE ON WHAT HAPPENED IN THE GARDEN. BY OUR THINKING, ONLY TWO PEOPLE KNOW WHAT REALLY WENT ON--OGDEN AND THE GIRL, GLORIA.
AND SINCE OGDEN'S WORD ISN'T SATISFACTORY, WE WERE LEFT WITH ONLY ONE CHOICE...
UH-OH.
...SUMMON THE SPIRIT OF GLORIA TO ANSWER OUR QUESTIONS.
OOOOOOH! I REMEMBER THIS PLACE!
I HAD A LOT OF FUN HERE. I REMEMBER RICHARD DIVER CAME AND HE WAS SOOOOO CUTE.
BUT THEN RICHARD LEFT AND IT WAS DREADFULLY DULL. I MEAN, HOW MANY TIMES CAN YOU WALK AROUND THE SAME LAKE, YOU KNOW?
THANKFULLY, THIS HILARIOUS, BLOATED OLD GUY CAME HERE. HE HAD A TOTAL SHREW OF A WIFE, AND IT WAS QUITE CLEAR THAT HE WAS SIMPLY STARVED FOR ATTENTION.
I USED TO WIND HIM UP SOOOO BAD.

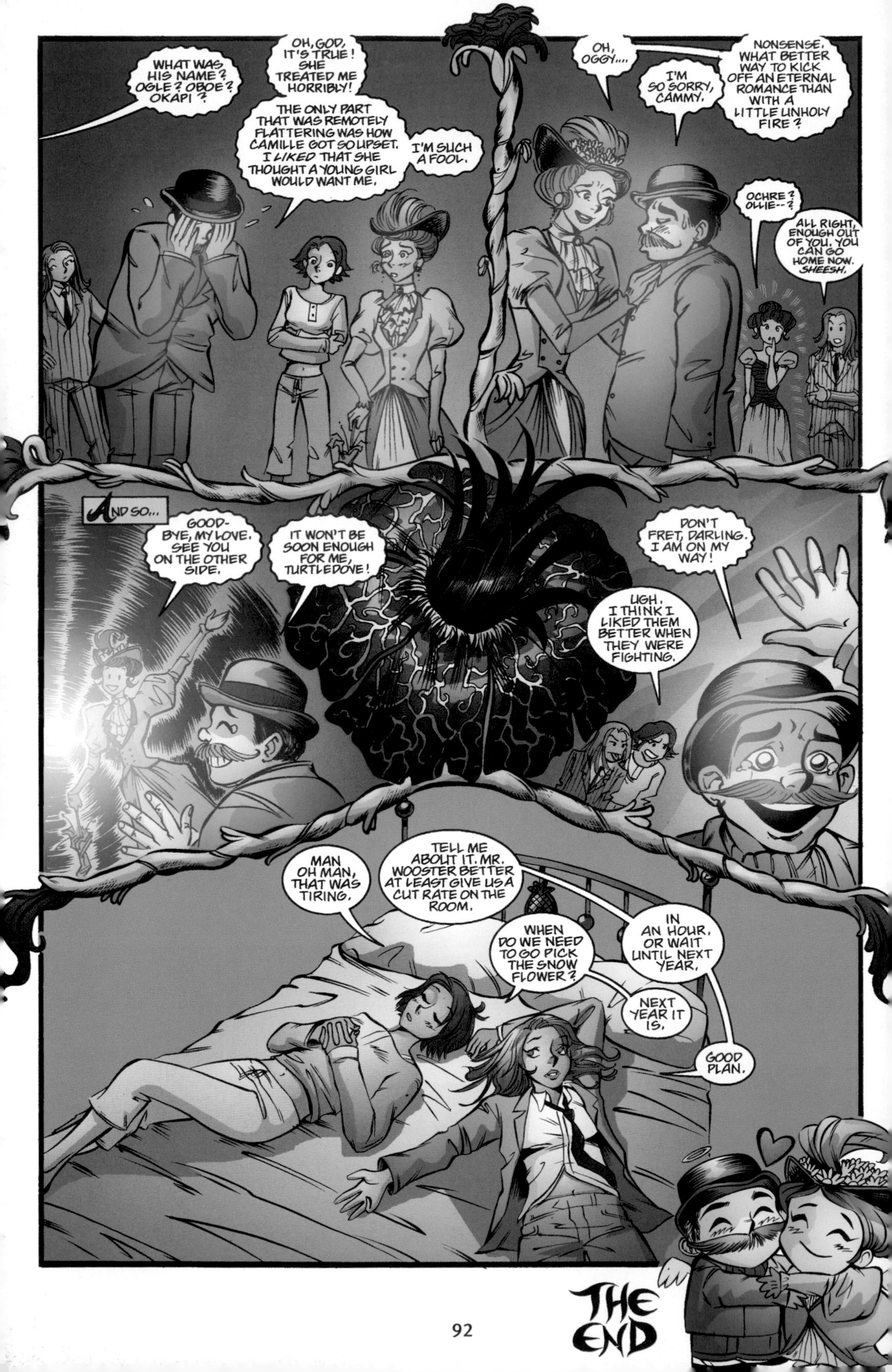
WHAT WAS HIS NAME? OGLE? OBOE? OKAPI?
OH, GOD, IT'S TRUE! SHE TREATED ME HORRIBLY!
THE ONLY PART THAT WAS REMOTELY FLATTERING WAS HOW CAMILLE GOT SO UPSET. I LIKED THAT SHE THOUGHT A YOUNG GIRL WOULD WANT ME.
I'M SUCH A FOOL.
OH, OGGY....
I'M SO SORRY, CAMMY.
NONSENSE, WHAT BETTER WAY TO KICK OFF AN ETERNAL ROMANCE THAN WITH A LITTLE UNHOLY FIRE?
OCHRE? OLLIE--?
ALL RIGHT, ENOUGH OUT OF YOU. YOU CAN GO HOME NOW. SHEESH.
AND SO...
GOOD-BYE, MY LOVE. SEE YOU ON THE OTHER SIDE.
IT WON'T BE SOON ENOUGH FOR ME, TURTLEDOVE!
DON'T FRET, DARLING. I AM ON MY WAY!
UGH. I THINK I LIKED THEM BETTER WHEN THEY WERE FIGHTING.
MAN OH MAN, THAT WAS TIRING.
TELL ME ABOUT IT. MR. WOOSTER BETTER AT LEAST GIVE US A CUT RATE ON THE ROOM.
WHEN DO WE NEED TO GO PICK THE SNOW FLOWER?
IN AN HOUR, OR WAIT UNTIL NEXT YEAR.
NEXT YEAR IT IS.
GOOD PLAN.
THE END

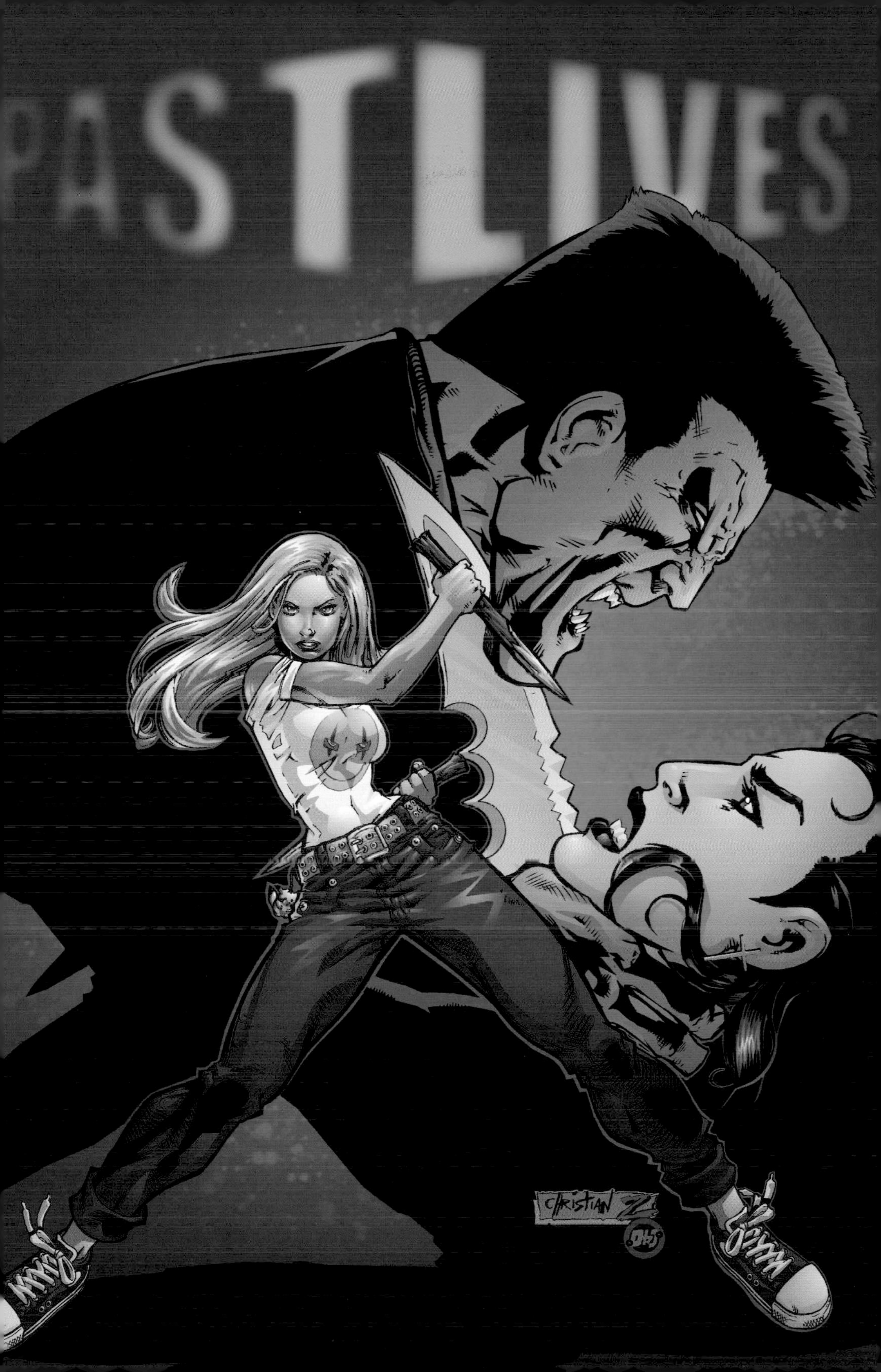
PAST LIVES
CHRISTIAN Z

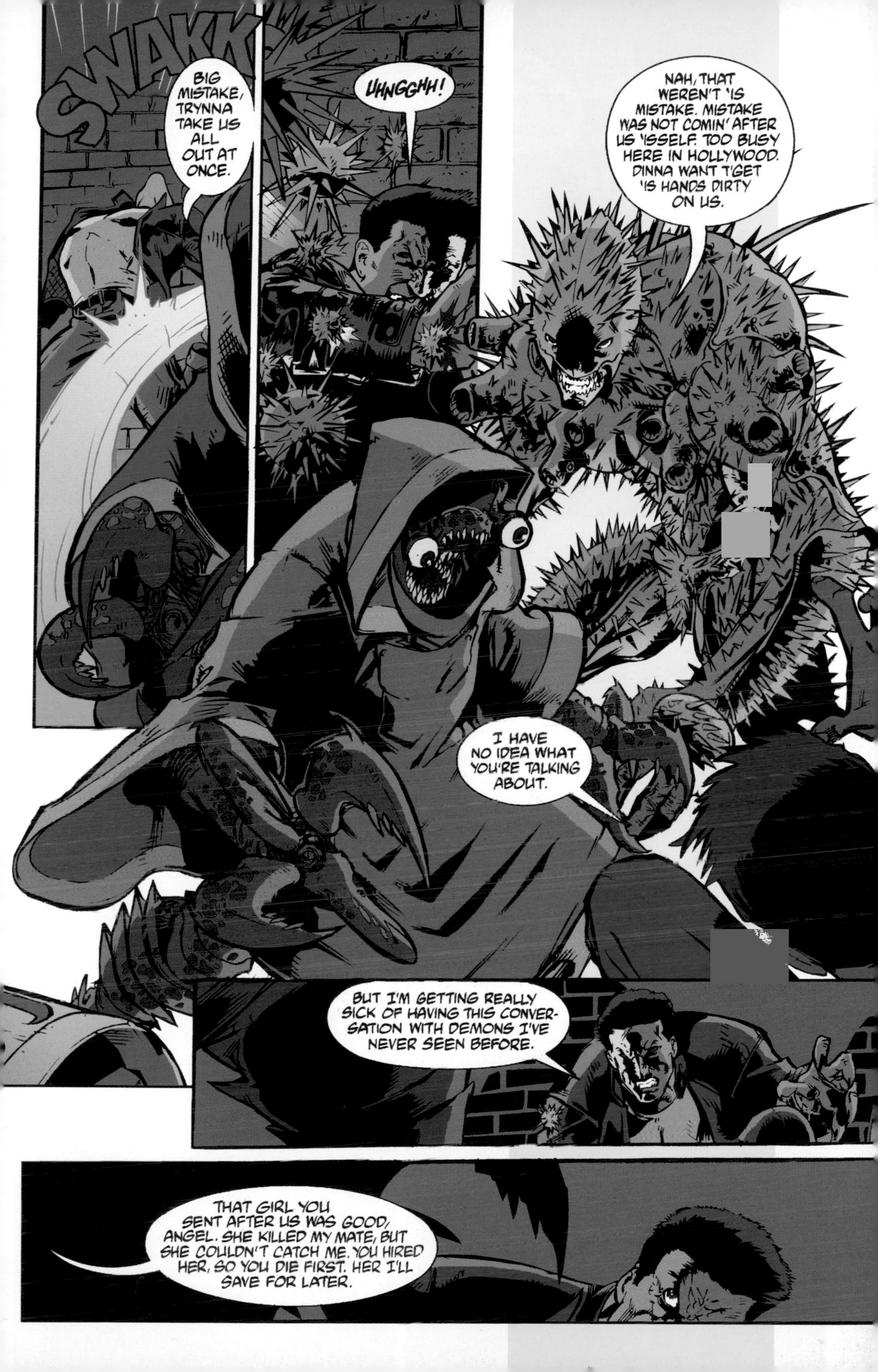
SWAKK
BIG MISTAKE, TRYNNA TAKE US ALL OUT AT ONCE.
UHNGGHH!
NAH, THAT WEREN'T 'IS MISTAKE. MISTAKE WAS NOT COMIN' AFTER US 'ISSELF. TOO BUSY HERE IN HOLLYWOOD. DINNA WANT T'GET 'IS HANDS DIRTY ON US.
I HAVE NO IDEA WHAT YOU'RE TALKING ABOUT.
BUT I'M GETTING REALLY SICK OF HAVING THIS CONVER-SATION WITH DEMONS I'VE NEVER SEEN BEFORE.
THAT GIRL YOU SENT AFTER US WAS GOOD, ANGEL. SHE KILLED MY MATE, BUT SHE COULDN'T CATCH ME. YOU HIRED HER, SO YOU DIE FIRST. HER I'LL SAVE FOR LATER.

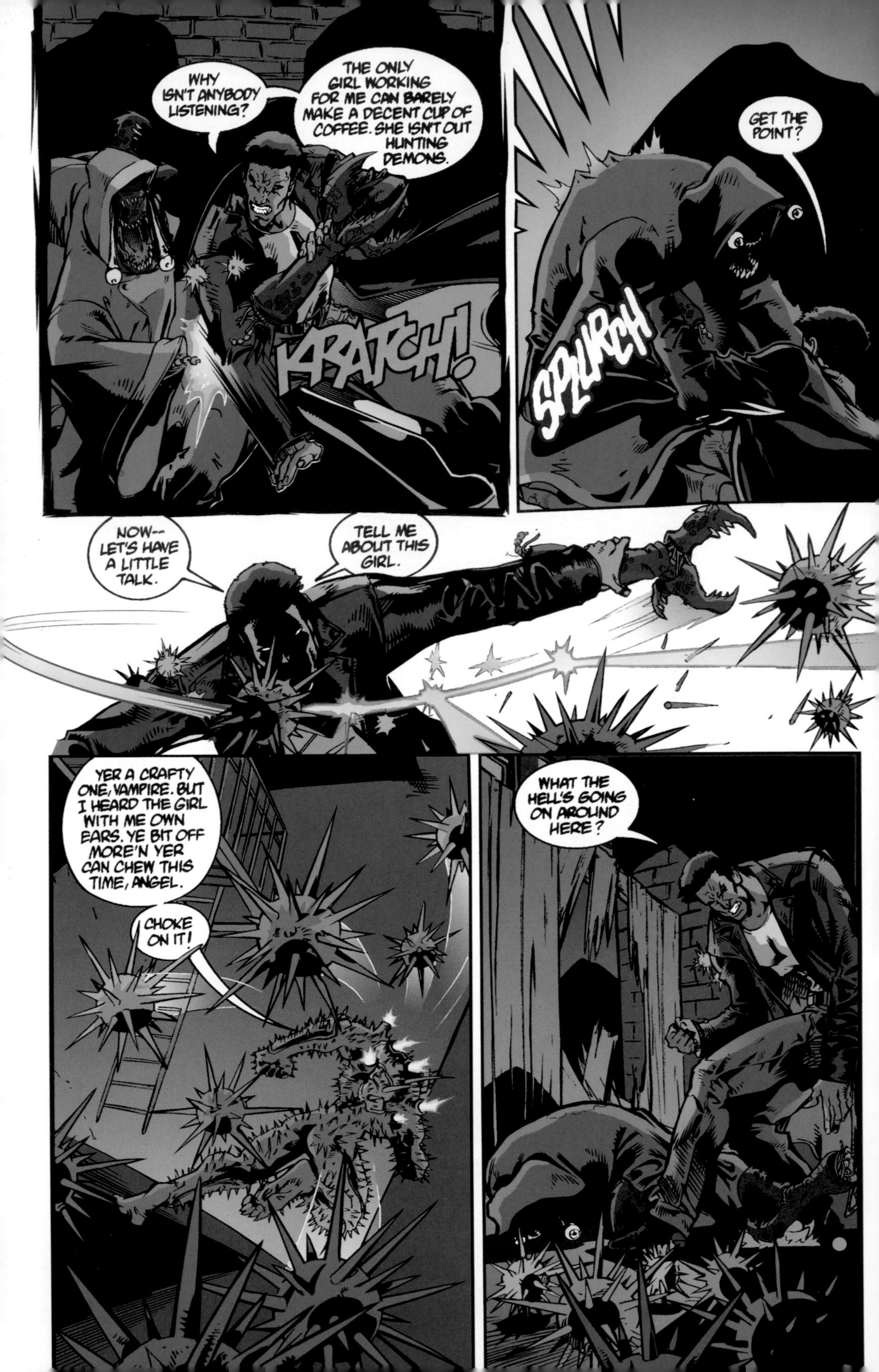
WHY ISN'T ANYBODY LISTENING?
THE ONLY GIRL WORKING FOR ME CAN BARELY MAKE A DECENT CUP OF COFFEE. SHE ISN'T OUT HUNTING DEMONS.
KRATCH!
GET THE POINT?
SPLURCH
NOW-- LET'S HAVE A LITTLE TALK.
TELL ME ABOUT THIS GIRL.
YER A CRAFTY ONE, VAMPIRE. BUT I HEARD THE GIRL WITH ME OWN EARS. YE BIT OFF MORE'N YER CAN CHEW THIS TIME, ANGEL.
CHOKE ON IT!
WHAT THE HELL'S GOING ON AROUND HERE?

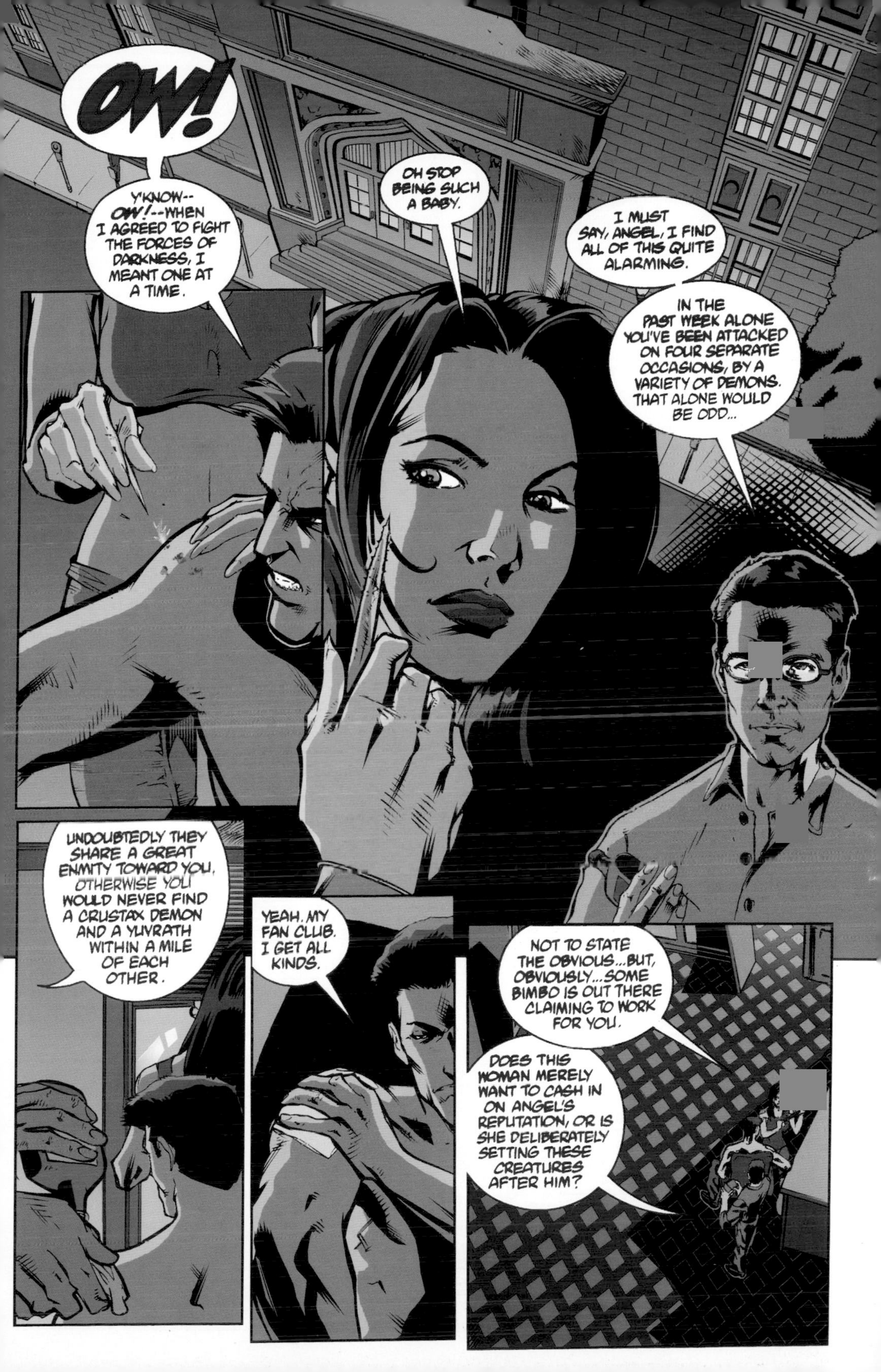
OW!
Y'KNOW-- OW!--WHEN I AGREED TO FIGHT THE FORCES OF DARKNESS, I MEANT ONE AT A TIME.
OH STOP BEING SUCH A BABY.
I MUST SAY, ANGEL, I FIND ALL OF THIS QUITE ALARMING.
IN THE PAST WEEK ALONE YOU'VE BEEN ATTACKED ON FOUR SEPARATE OCCASIONS, BY A VARIETY OF DEMONS. THAT ALONE WOULD BE ODD...
UNDOUBTEDLY THEY SHARE A GREAT ENMITY TOWARD YOU, OTHERWISE YOU WOULD NEVER FIND A CRUSTAX DEMON AND A YUVRATH WITHIN A MILE OF EACH OTHER.
YEAH. MY FAN CLUB. I GET ALL KINDS.
NOT TO STATE THE OBVIOUS...BUT, OBVIOUSLY...SOME BIMBO IS OUT THERE CLAIMING TO WORK FOR YOU.
DOES THIS WOMAN MERELY WANT TO CASH IN ON ANGEL'S REPUTATION, OR IS SHE DELIBERATELY SETTING THESE CREATURES AFTER HIM?

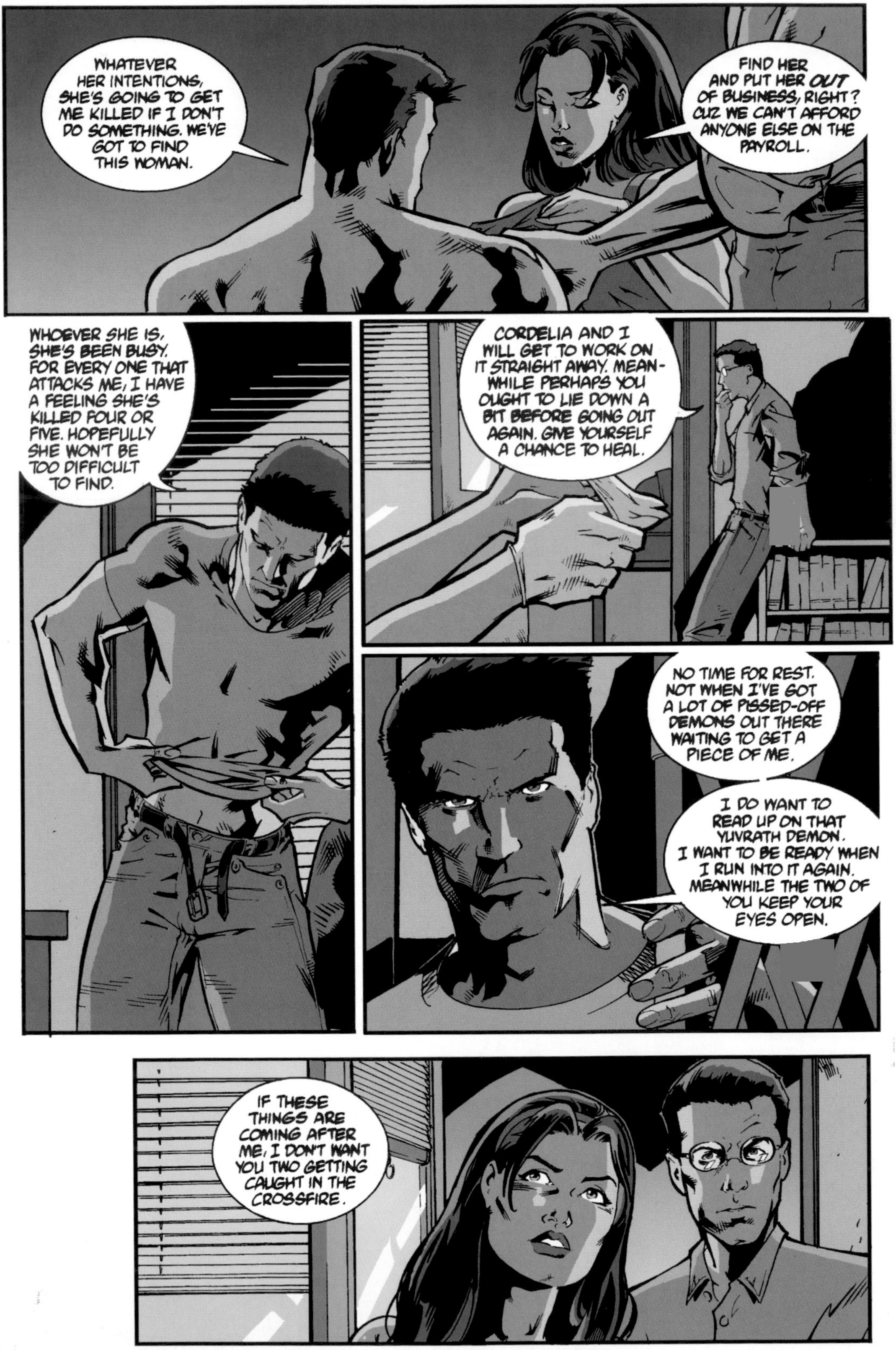
WHATEVER HER INTENTIONS, SHE'S GOING TO GET ME KILLED IF I DON'T DO SOMETHING. WE'VE GOT TO FIND THIS WOMAN.
FIND HER AND PUT HER OUT OF BUSINESS, RIGHT? CUZ WE CAN'T AFFORD ANYONE ELSE ON THE PAYROLL.
WHOEVER SHE IS, SHE'S BEEN BUSY. FOR EVERY ONE THAT ATTACKS ME, I HAVE A FEELING SHE'S KILLED FOUR OR FIVE. HOPEFULLY SHE WON'T BE TOO DIFFICULT TO FIND.
CORDELIA AND I WILL GET TO WORK ON IT STRAIGHT AWAY. MEAN-WHILE PERHAPS YOU OUGHT TO LIE DOWN A BIT BEFORE GOING OUT AGAIN. GIVE YOURSELF A CHANCE TO HEAL.
NO TIME FOR REST. NOT WHEN I'VE GOT A LOT OF PISSED-OFF DEMONS OUT THERE WAITING TO GET A PIECE OF ME.
I DO WANT TO READ UP ON THAT YUVRATH DEMON. I WANT TO BE READY WHEN I RUN INTO IT AGAIN. MEANWHILE THE TWO OF YOU KEEP YOUR EYES OPEN.
IF THESE THINGS ARE COMING AFTER ME, I DON'T WANT YOU TWO GETTING CAUGHT IN THE CROSSFIRE.

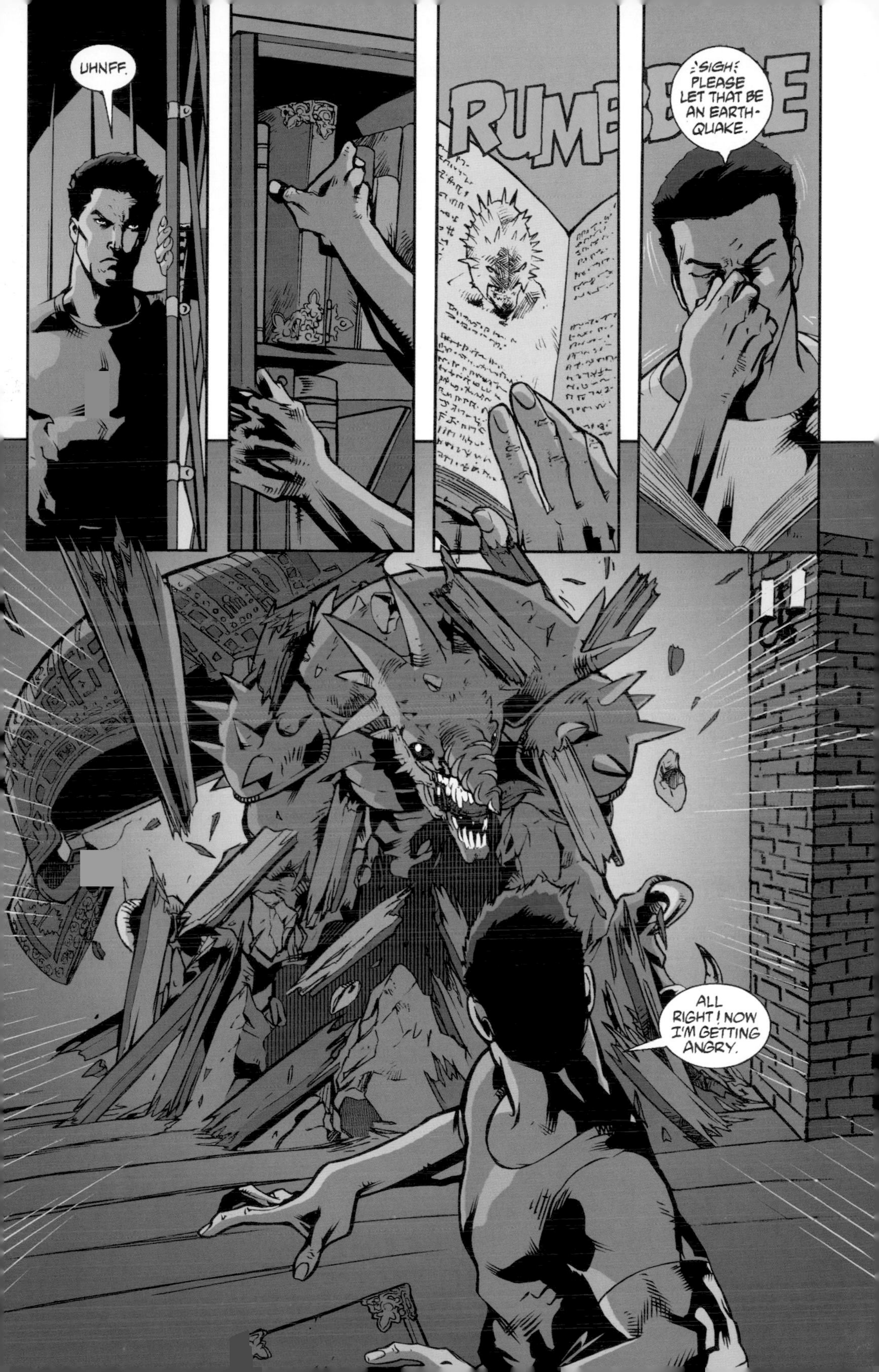
UHNFF.
RUMB
-SIGH- PLEASE LET THAT BE AN EARTH-QUAKE.
ALL RIGHT! NOW I'M GETTING ANGRY.

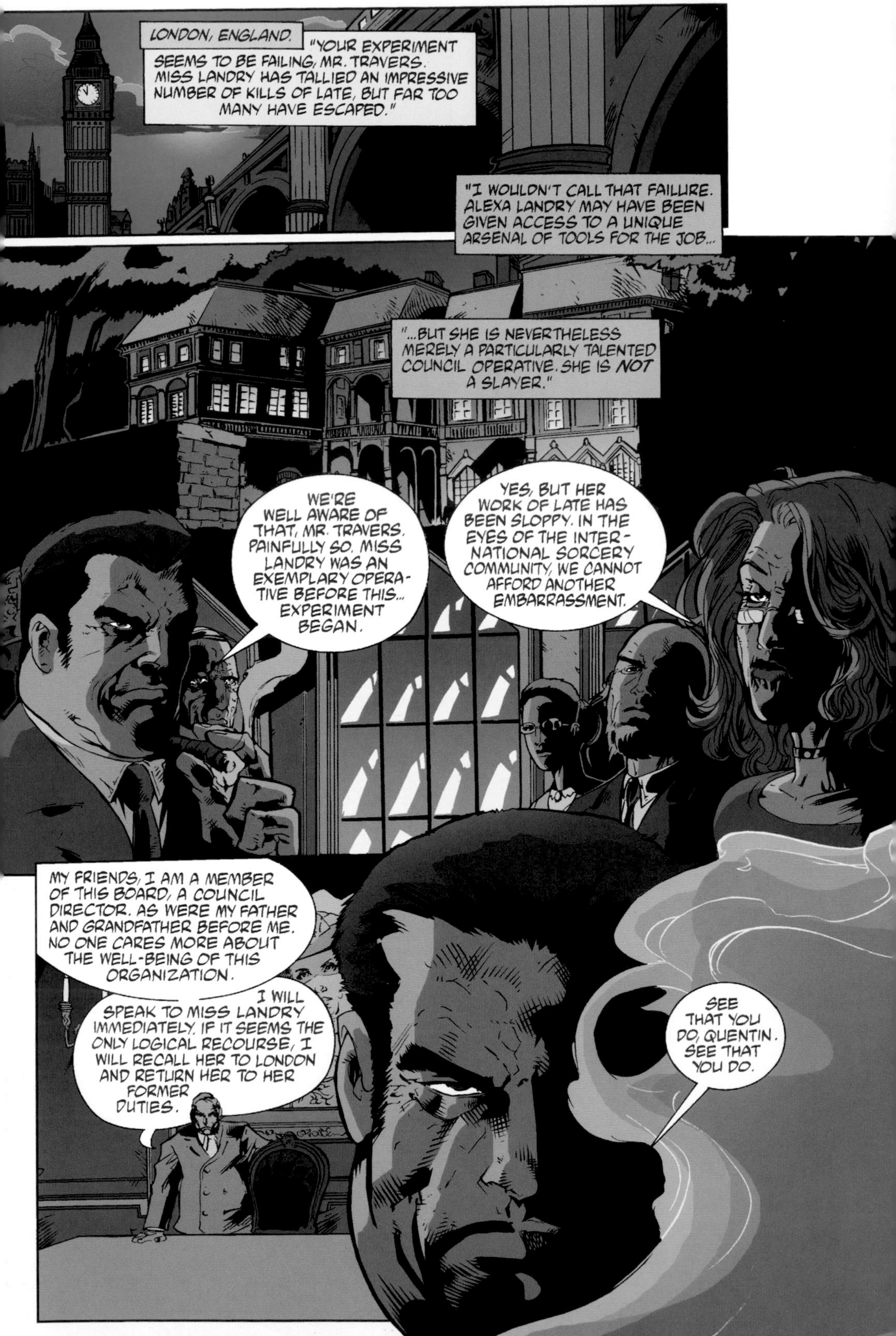
LONDON, ENGLAND.
"YOUR EXPERIMENT SEEMS TO BE FAILING, MR. TRAVERS. MISS LANDRY HAS TALLIED AN IMPRESSIVE NUMBER OF KILLS OF LATE, BUT FAR TOO MANY HAVE ESCAPED."
"I WOULDN'T CALL THAT FAILURE. ALEXA LANDRY MAY HAVE BEEN GIVEN ACCESS TO A UNIQUE ARSENAL OF TOOLS FOR THE JOB...
"...BUT SHE IS NEVERTHELESS MERELY A PARTICULARLY TALENTED COUNCIL OPERATIVE. SHE IS NOT A SLAYER."
WE'RE WELL AWARE OF THAT, MR. TRAVERS. PAINFULLY SO. MISS LANDRY WAS AN EXEMPLARY OPERATIVE BEFORE THIS... EXPERIMENT BEGAN.
YES, BUT HER WORK OF LATE HAS BEEN SLOPPY. IN THE EYES OF THE INTERNATIONAL SORCERY COMMUNITY, WE CANNOT AFFORD ANOTHER EMBARRASSMENT.
MY FRIENDS, I AM A MEMBER OF THIS BOARD, A COUNCIL DIRECTOR. AS WERE MY FATHER AND GRANDFATHER BEFORE ME. NO ONE CARES MORE ABOUT THE WELL-BEING OF THIS ORGANIZATION.
I WILL SPEAK TO MISS LANDRY IMMEDIATELY. IF IT SEEMS THE ONLY LOGICAL RECOURSE, I WILL RECALL HER TO LONDON AND RETURN HER TO HER FORMER DUTIES.
SEE THAT YOU DO, QUENTIN. SEE THAT YOU DO.

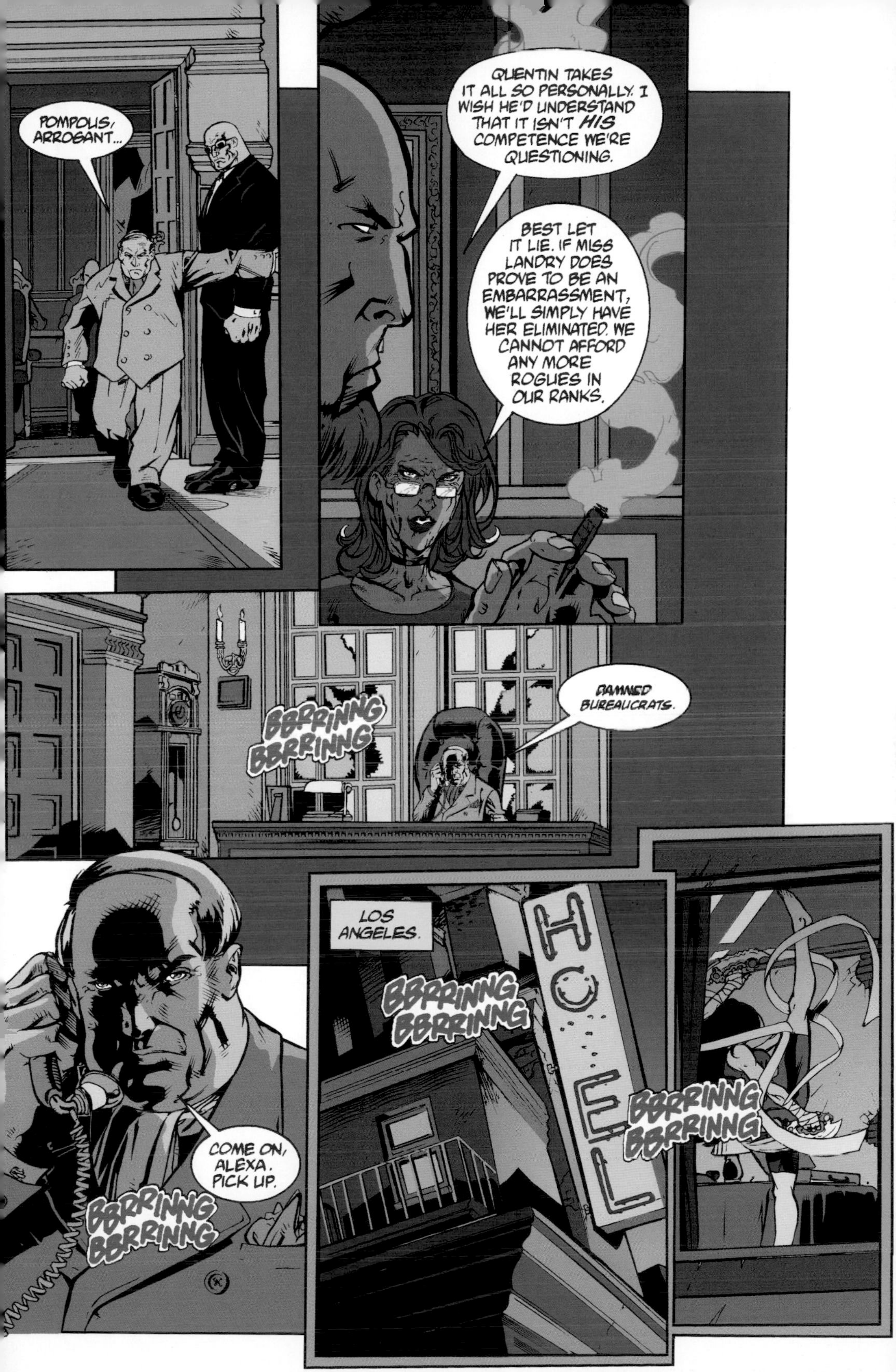
POMPOUS, ARROGANT...
QUENTIN TAKES IT ALL SO PERSONALLY. I WISH HE'D UNDERSTAND THAT IT ISN'T HIS COMPETENCE WE'RE QUESTIONING.
BEST LET IT LIE. IF MISS LANDRY DOES PROVE TO BE AN EMBARRASSMENT, WE'LL SIMPLY HAVE HER ELIMINATED. WE CANNOT AFFORD ANY MORE ROGUES IN OUR RANKS.
BBRRINNG BBRRINNG
DAMNED BUREAUCRATS.
COME ON, ALEXA. PICK UP.
BBRRINNG BBRRINNG
LOS ANGELES.
BBRRINNG BBRRINNG
BBRRINNG BBRRINNG

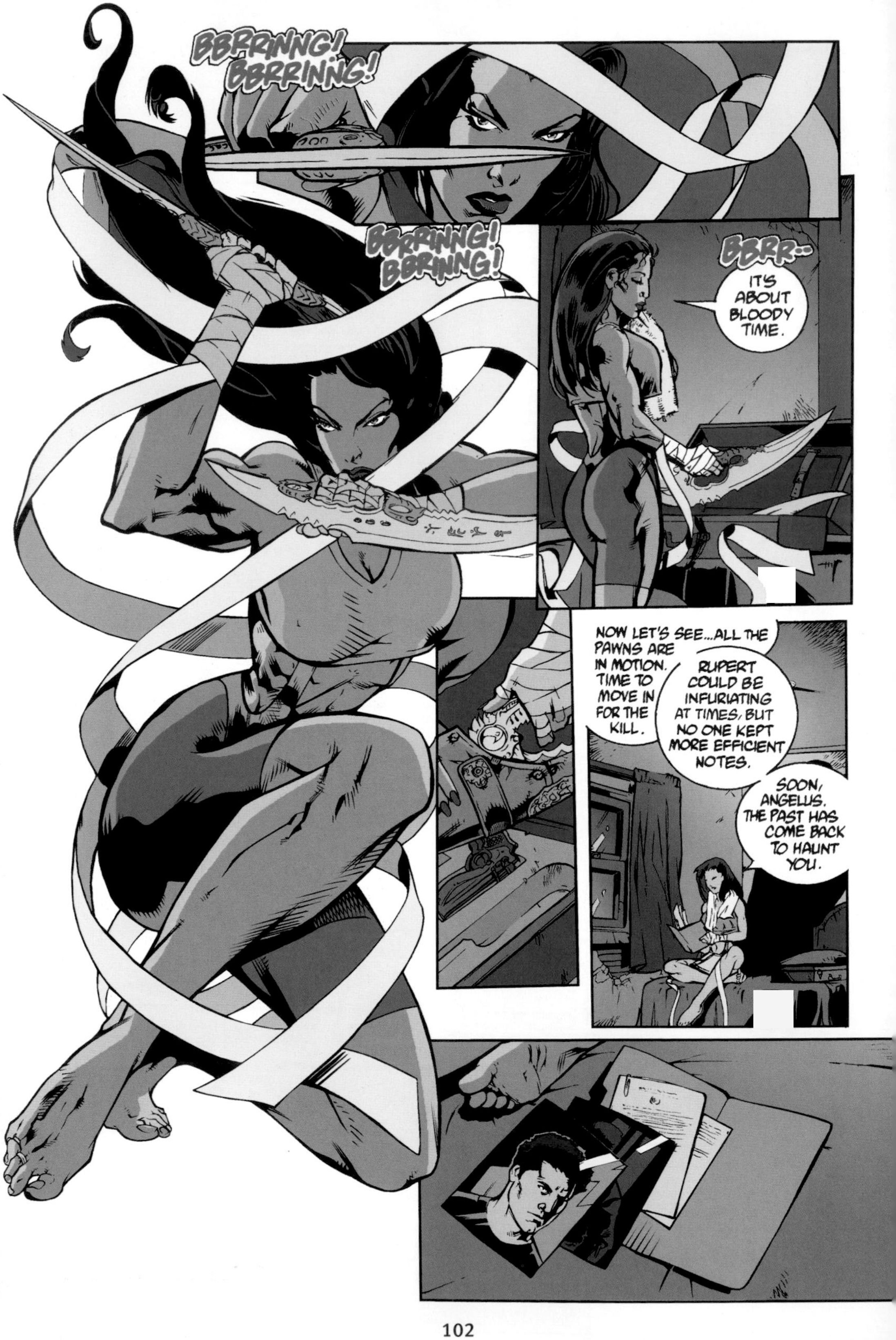
BBRRINNG! BBRRINNG!
BBRRINNG! BBRINNG!
BBRR--
IT'S ABOUT BLOODY TIME.
NOW LET'S SEE...ALL THE PAWNS ARE IN MOTION. TIME TO MOVE IN FOR THE KILL.
RUPERT COULD BE INFURIATING AT TIMES, BUT NO ONE KEPT MORE EFFICIENT NOTES.
SOON, ANGELUS. THE PAST HAS COME BACK TO HAUNT YOU.

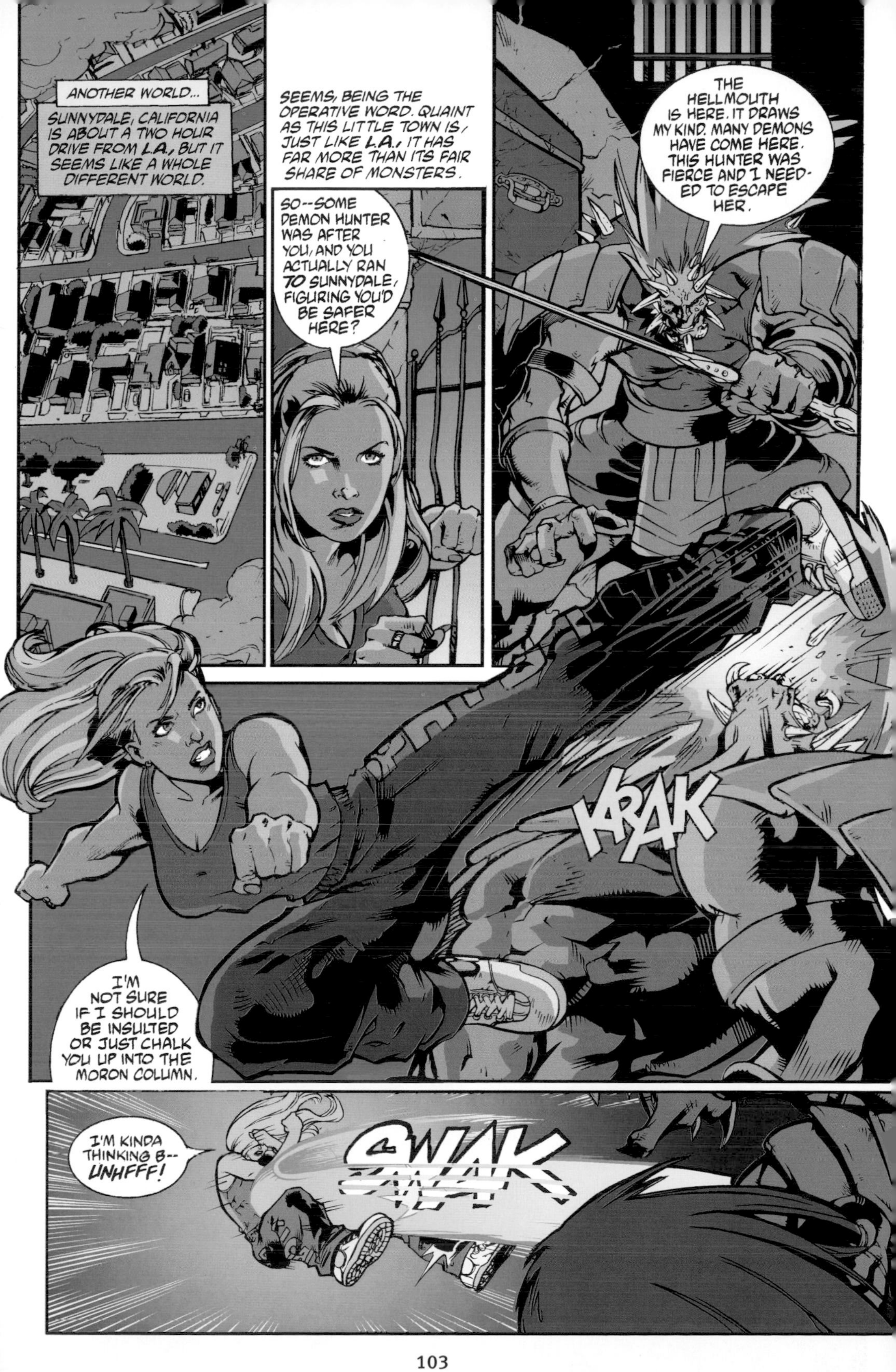
ANOTHER WORLD...
SUNNYDALE, CALIFORNIA IS ABOUT A TWO HOUR DRIVE FROM L.A., BUT IT SEEMS LIKE A WHOLE DIFFERENT WORLD.
SEEMS, BEING THE OPERATIVE WORD. QUAINT AS THIS LITTLE TOWN IS, JUST LIKE L.A., IT HAS FAR MORE THAN ITS FAIR SHARE OF MONSTERS.
SO--SOME DEMON HUNTER WAS AFTER YOU, AND YOU ACTUALLY RAN TO SUNNYDALE, FIGURING YOU'D BE SAFER HERE?
THE HELLMOUTH IS HERE. IT DRAWS MY KIND. MANY DEMONS HAVE COME HERE. THIS HUNTER WAS FIERCE AND I NEEDED TO ESCAPE HER.
KRAK
I'M NOT SURE IF I SHOULD BE INSULTED OR JUST CHALK YOU UP INTO THE MORON COLUMN.
I'M KINDA THINKING B-- UNHFFF!
SWAK

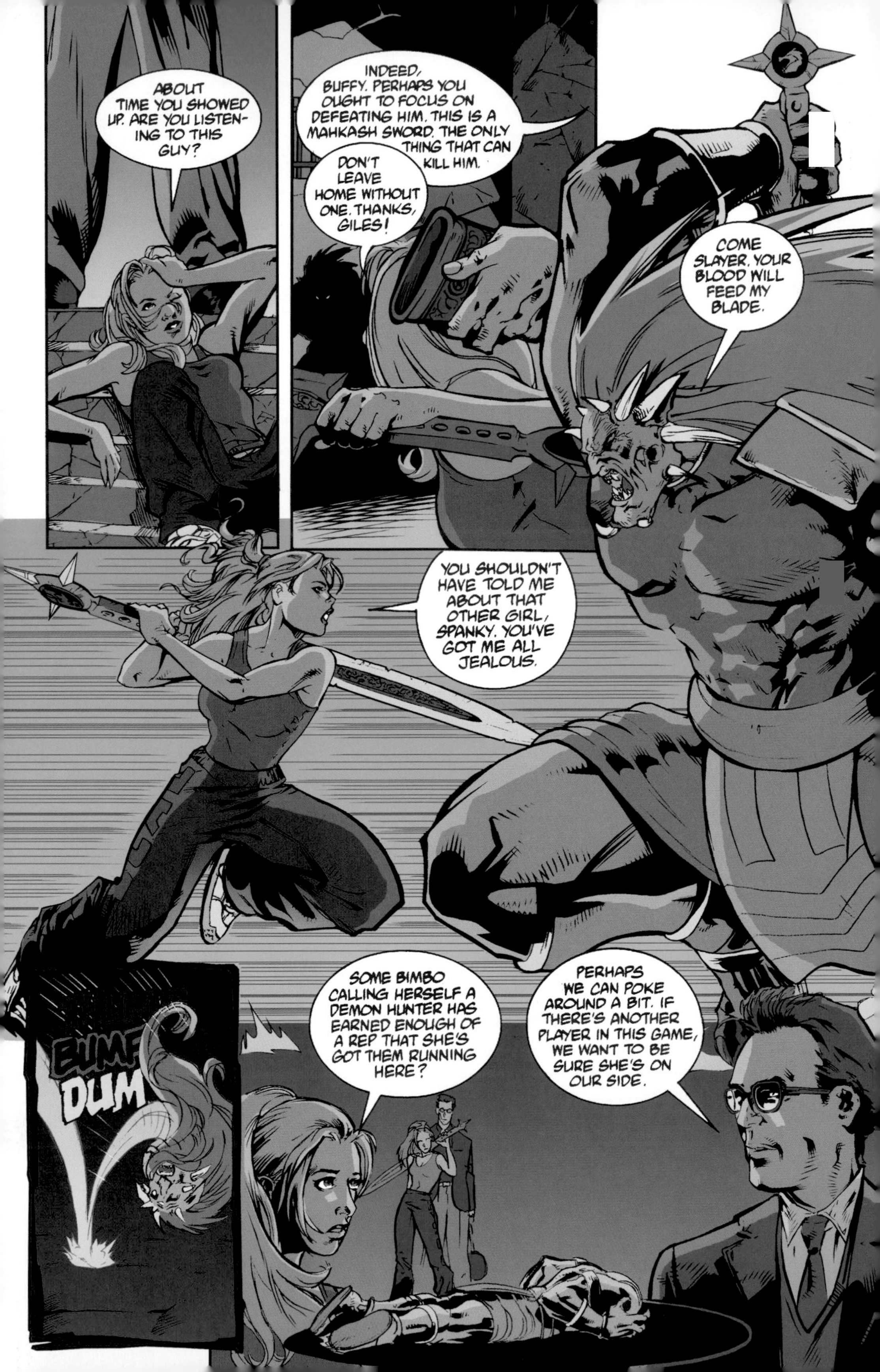
ABOUT TIME YOU SHOWED UP. ARE YOU LISTENING TO THIS GUY?
INDEED, BUFFY. PERHAPS YOU OUGHT TO FOCUS ON DEFEATING HIM. THIS IS A MAHKASH SWORD. THE ONLY THING THAT CAN KILL HIM.
DON'T LEAVE HOME WITHOUT ONE. THANKS, GILES!
COME SLAYER. YOUR BLOOD WILL FEED MY BLADE.
YOU SHOULDN'T HAVE TOLD ME ABOUT THAT OTHER GIRL, SPANKY. YOU'VE GOT ME ALL JEALOUS.
BUMP DUM
SOME BIMBO CALLING HERSELF A DEMON HUNTER HAS EARNED ENOUGH OF A REP THAT SHE'S GOT THEM RUNNING HERE?
PERHAPS WE CAN POKE AROUND A BIT. IF THERE'S ANOTHER PLAYER IN THIS GAME, WE WANT TO BE SURE SHE'S ON OUR SIDE.

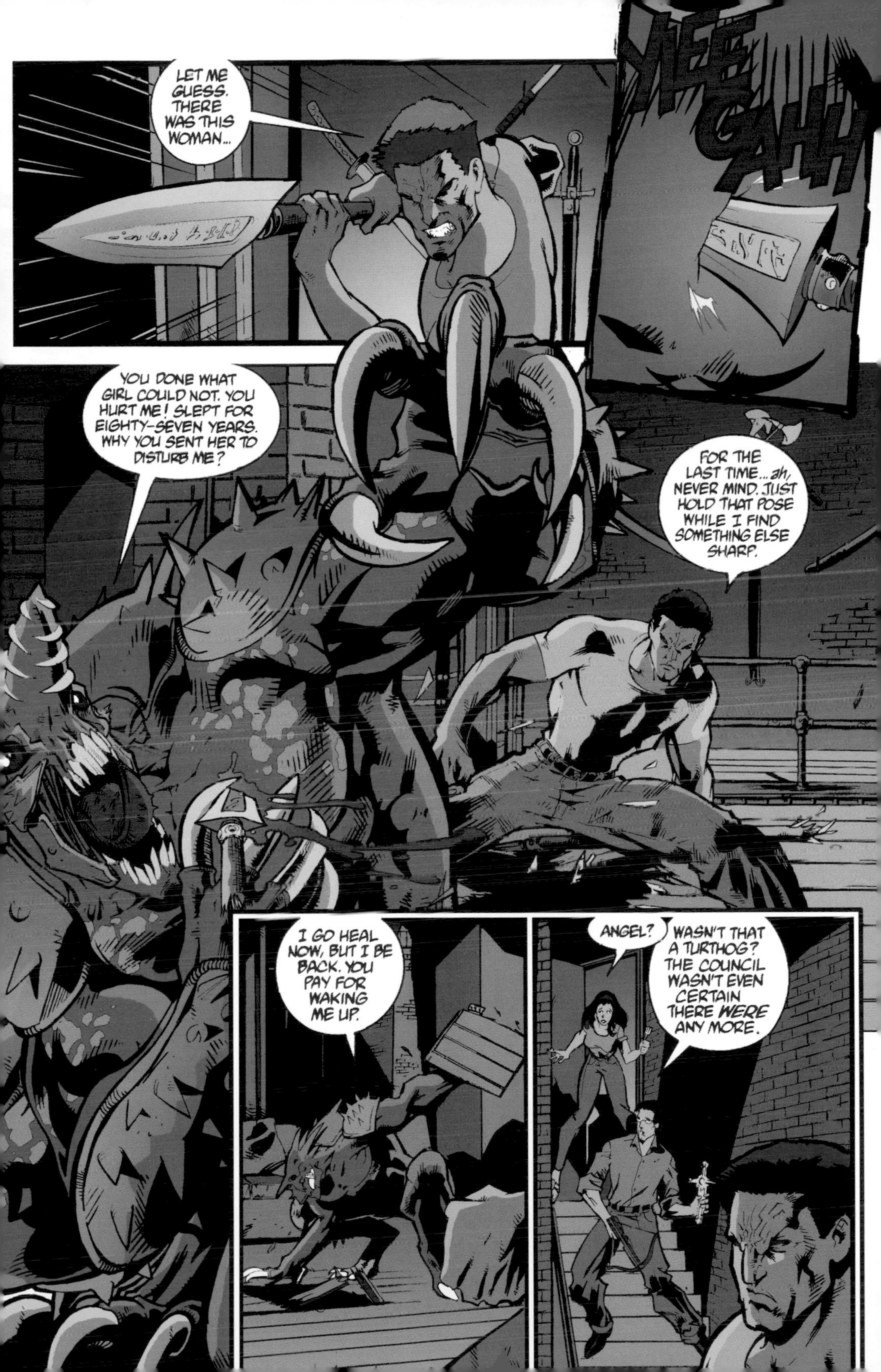
LET ME GUESS. THERE WAS THIS WOMAN...
YEEE GAHH
YOU DONE WHAT GIRL COULD NOT. YOU HURT ME! SLEPT FOR EIGHTY-SEVEN YEARS. WHY YOU SENT HER TO DISTURB ME?
FOR THE LAST TIME... ah, NEVER MIND. JUST HOLD THAT POSE WHILE I FIND SOMETHING ELSE SHARP.
I GO HEAL NOW, BUT I BE BACK. YOU PAY FOR WAKING ME UP.
ANGEL?
WASN'T THAT A TURTHOG? THE COUNCIL WASN'T EVEN CERTAIN THERE WERE ANY MORE.

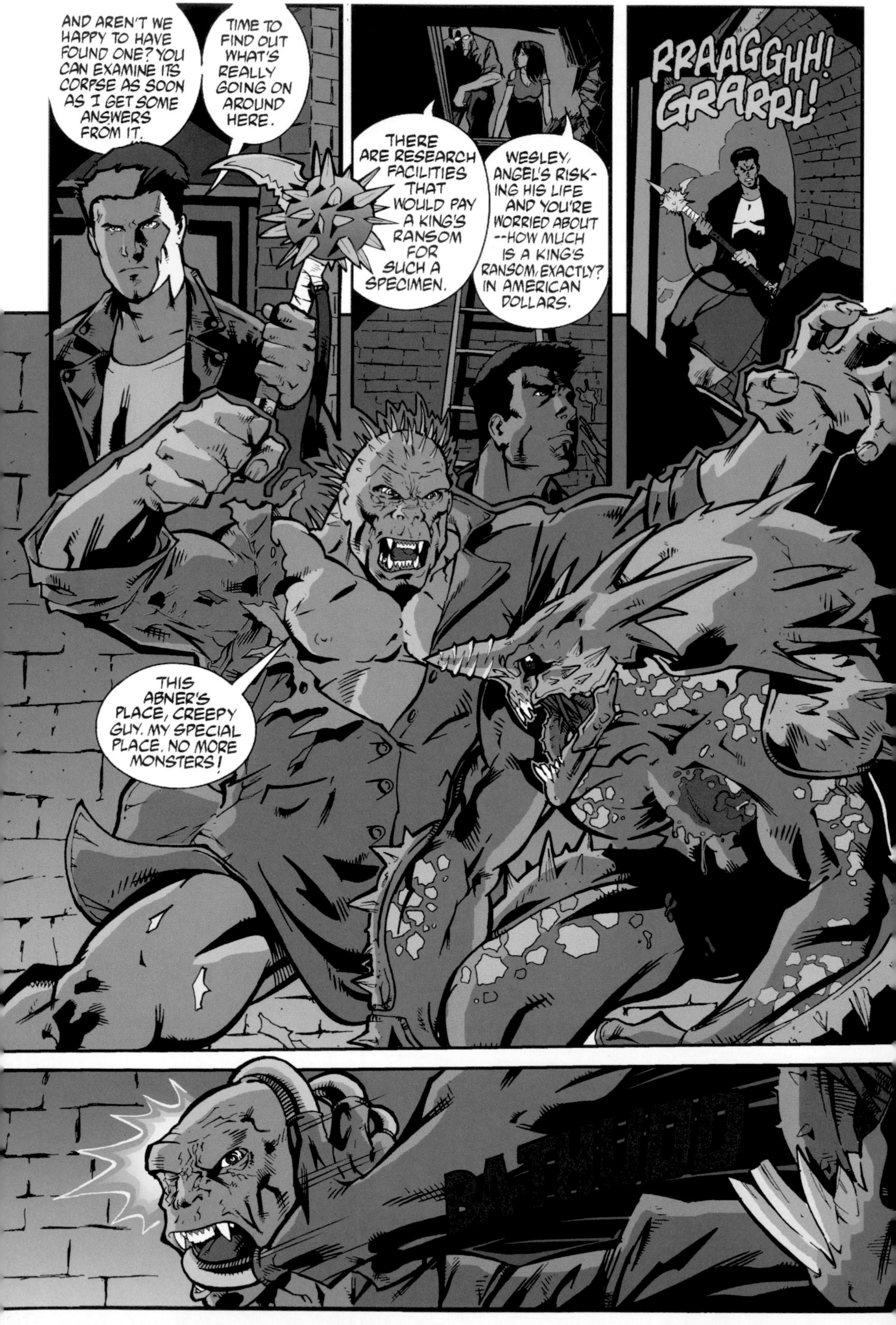
AND AREN'T WE HAPPY TO HAVE FOUND ONE? YOU CAN EXAMINE ITS CORPSE AS SOON AS I GET SOME ANSWERS FROM IT.
TIME TO FIND OUT WHAT'S REALLY GOING ON AROUND HERE.
THERE ARE RESEARCH FACILITIES THAT WOULD PAY A KING'S RANSOM FOR SUCH A SPECIMEN.
WESLEY, ANGEL'S RISKING HIS LIFE AND YOU'RE WORRIED ABOUT --HOW MUCH IS A KING'S RANSOM, EXACTLY? IN AMERICAN DOLLARS.
RRAAGGHH! GRARRL!
THIS ABNER'S PLACE, CREEPY GUY. MY SPECIAL PLACE. NO MORE MONSTERS!

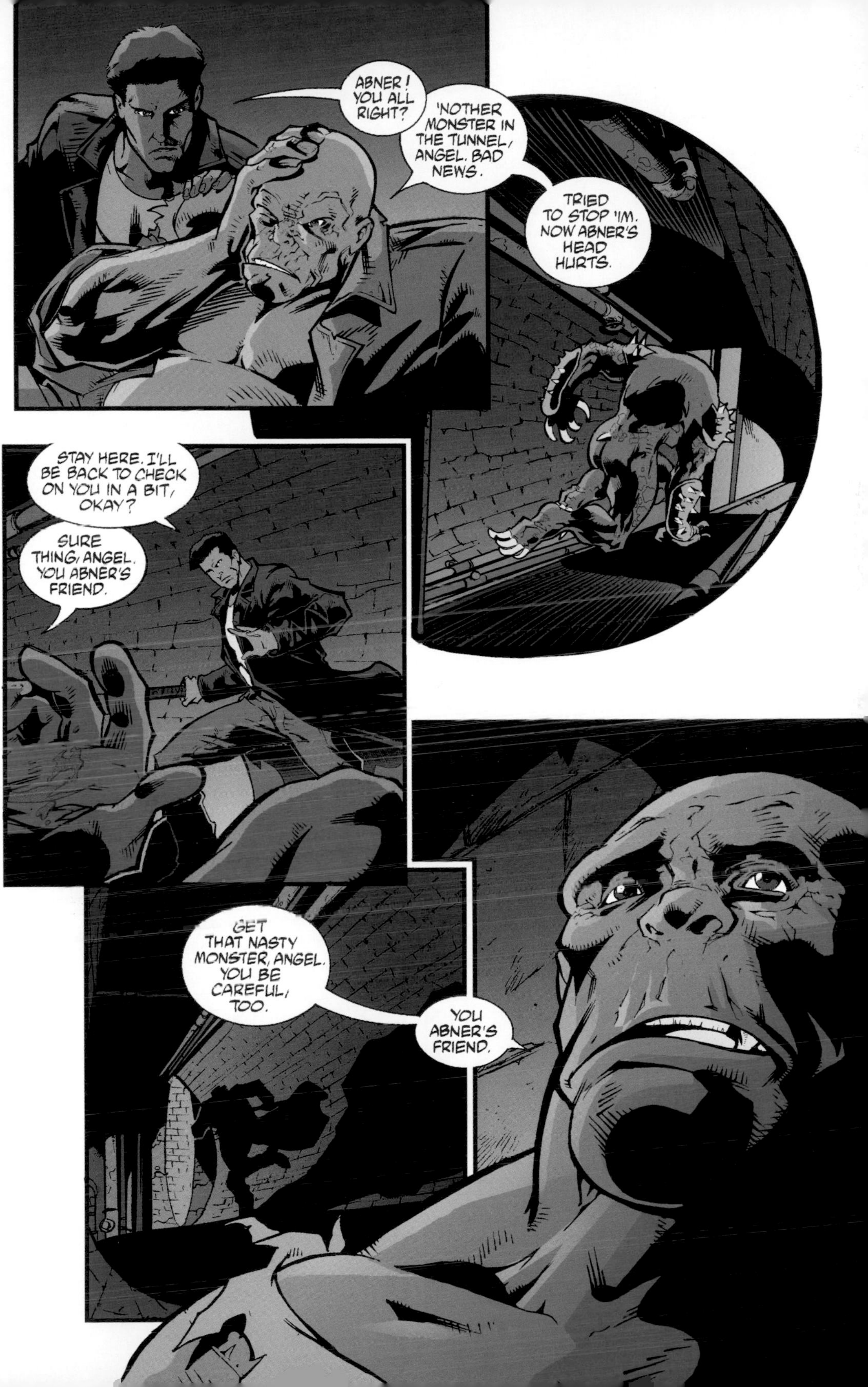
ABNER! YOU ALL RIGHT?
'NOTHER MONSTER IN THE TUNNEL, ANGEL. BAD NEWS.
TRIED TO STOP 'IM. NOW ABNER'S HEAD HURTS.
STAY HERE. I'LL BE BACK TO CHECK ON YOU IN A BIT, OKAY?
SURE THING, ANGEL. YOU ABNER'S FRIEND.
GET THAT NASTY MONSTER, ANGEL. YOU BE CAREFUL, TOO.
YOU ABNER'S FRIEND.

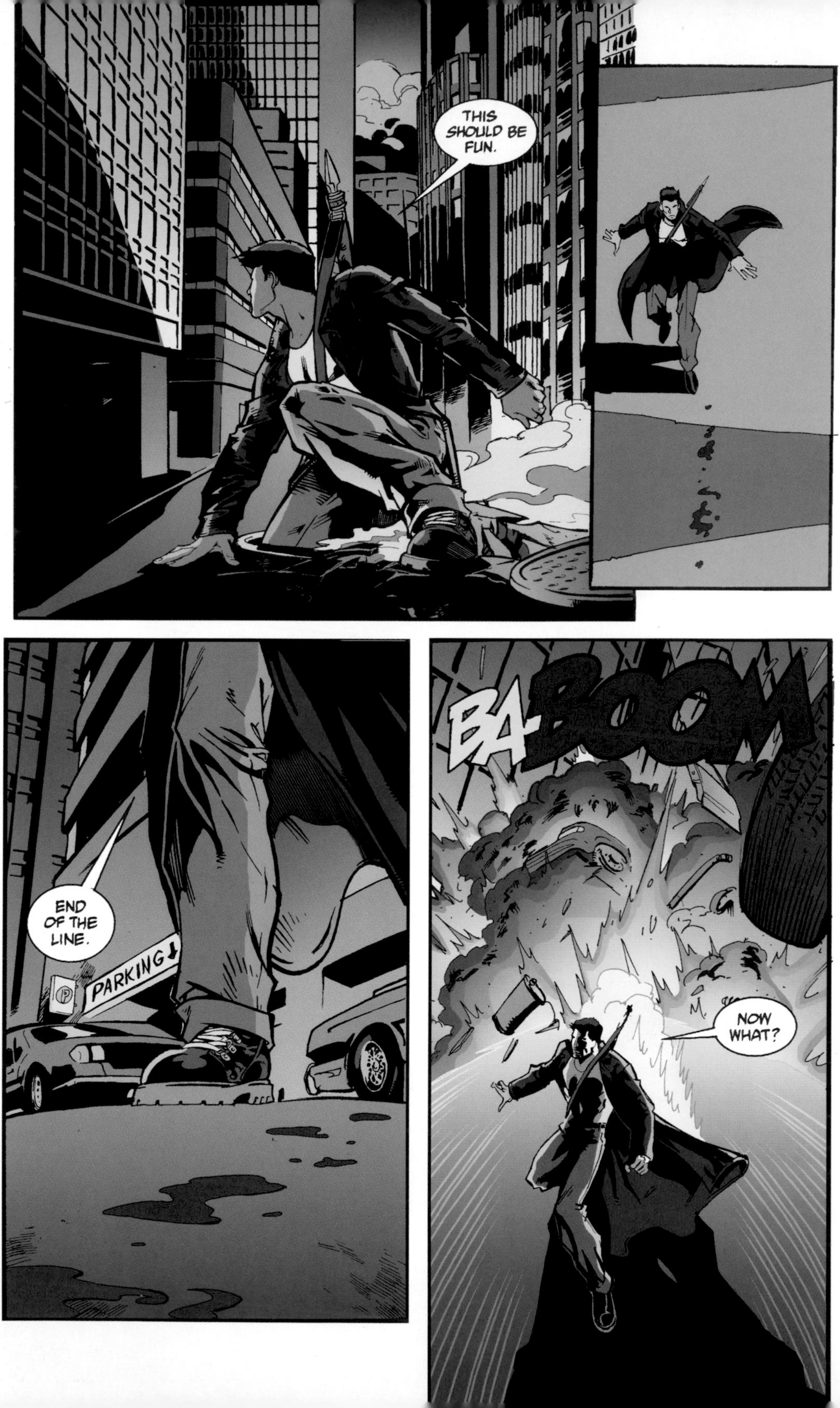
THIS SHOULD BE FUN.
END OF THE LINE.
PARKING
BA-BOOM
NOW WHAT?

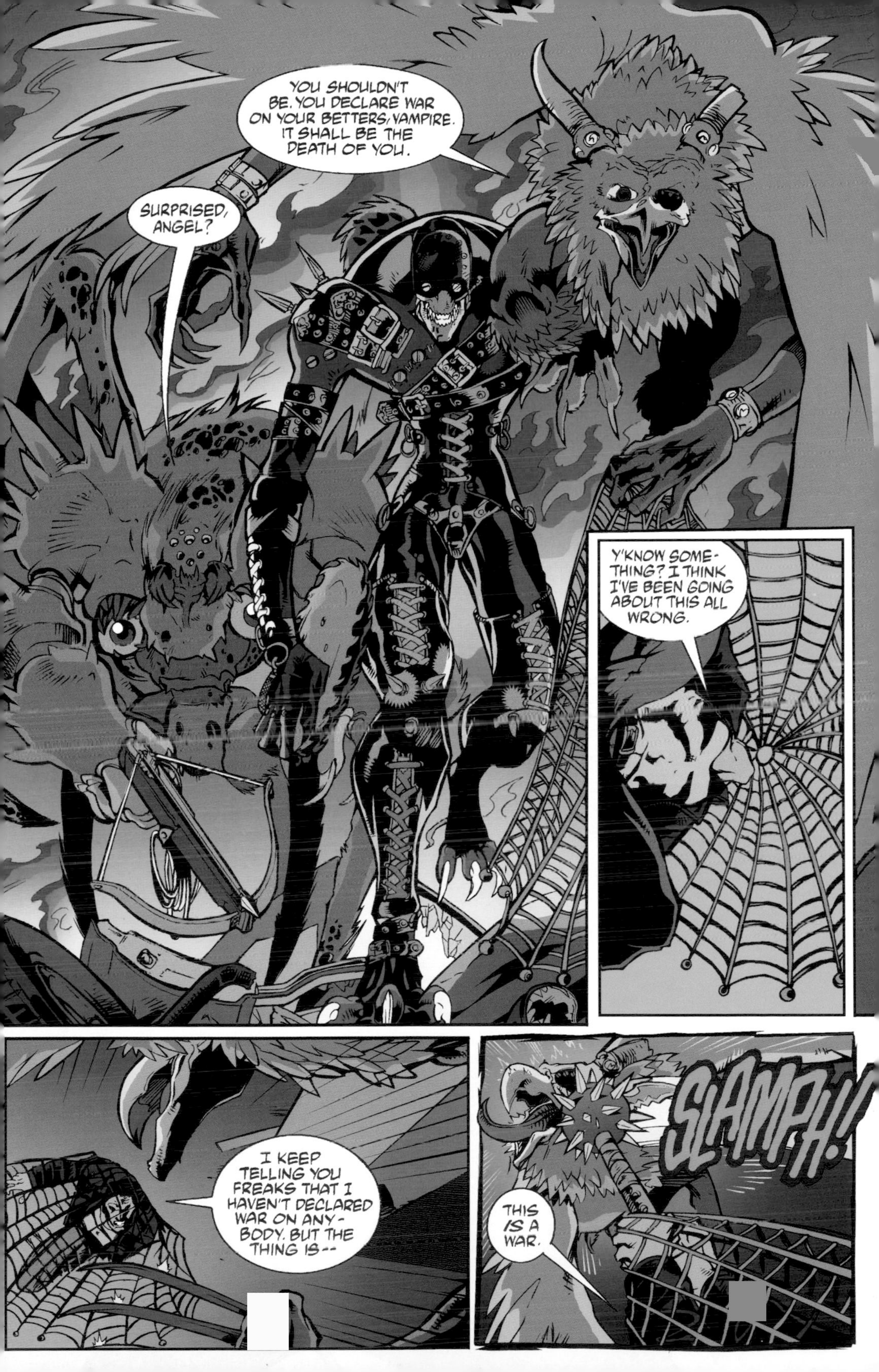
SURPRISED, ANGEL?
YOU SHOULDN'T BE. YOU DECLARE WAR ON YOUR BETTERS, VAMPIRE. IT SHALL BE THE DEATH OF YOU.
Y'KNOW SOMETHING? I THINK I'VE BEEN GOING ABOUT THIS ALL WRONG.
I KEEP TELLING YOU FREAKS THAT I HAVEN'T DECLARED WAR ON ANYBODY. BUT THE THING IS--
SLAMPH!!
THIS IS A WAR.

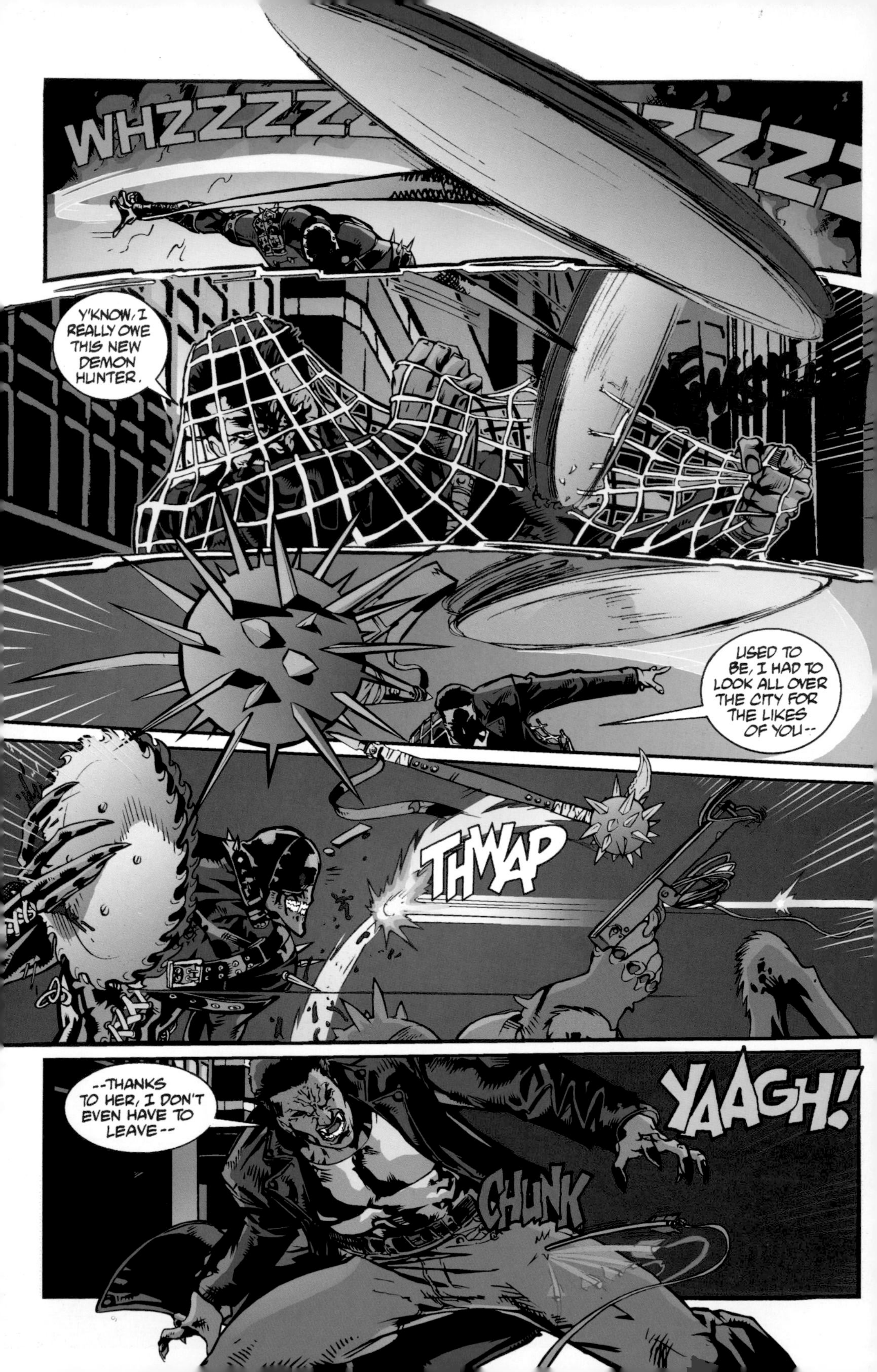
WHZZZZZ
Y'KNOW, I REALLY OWE THIS NEW DEMON HUNTER.
USED TO BE, I HAD TO LOOK ALL OVER THE CITY FOR THE LIKES OF YOU--
THWAP
--THANKS TO HER, I DON'T EVEN HAVE TO LEAVE--
YAAGH!
CHUNK

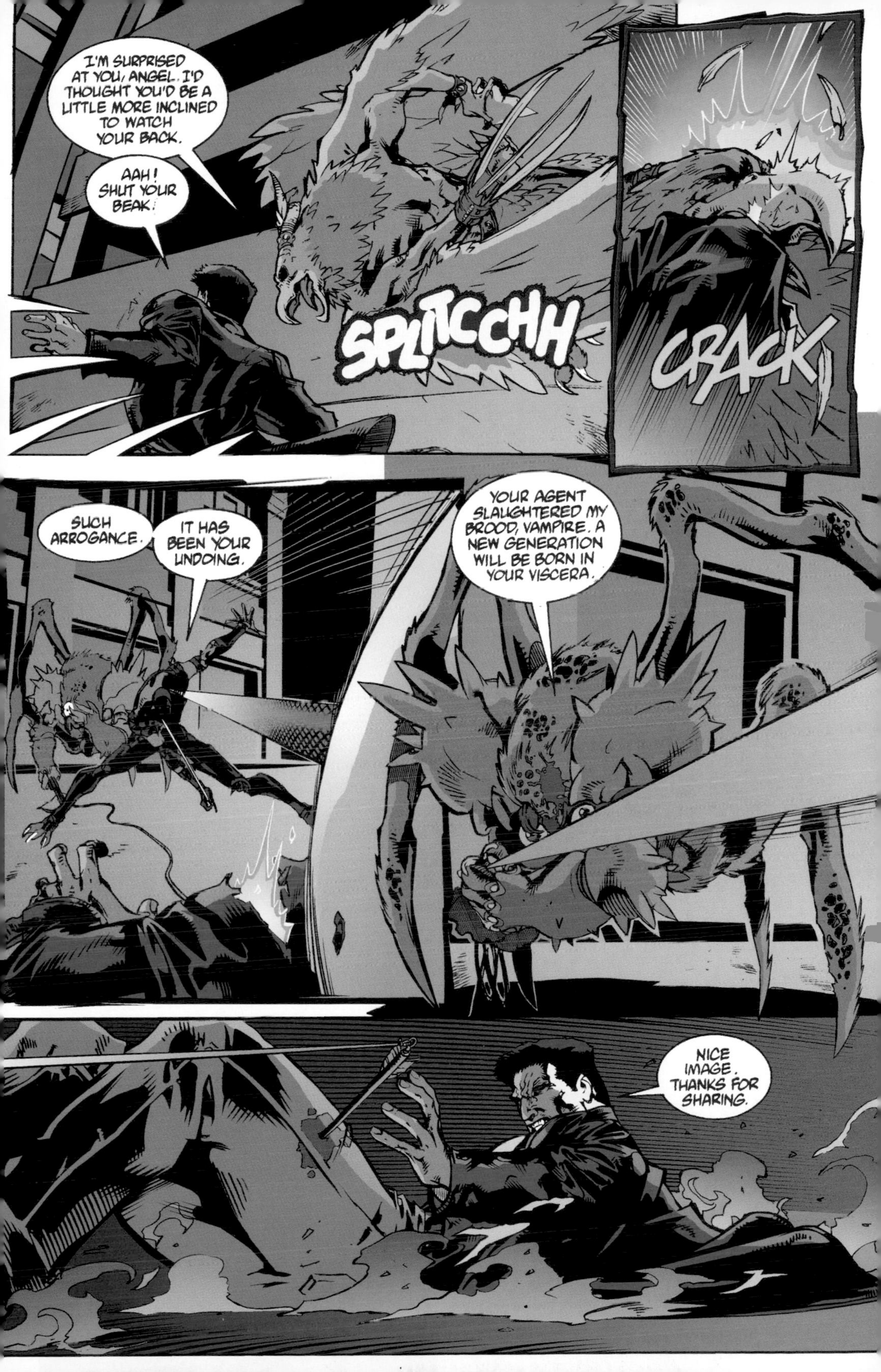
I'M SURPRISED AT YOU, ANGEL. I'D THOUGHT YOU'D BE A LITTLE MORE INCLINED TO WATCH YOUR BACK.
AAH! SHUT YOUR BEAK!
SPLITCCHH
CRACK
SUCH ARROGANCE.
IT HAS BEEN YOUR UNDOING.
YOUR AGENT SLAUGHTERED MY BROOD, VAMPIRE. A NEW GENERATION WILL BE BORN IN YOUR VISCERA.
NICE IMAGE. THANKS FOR SHARING.

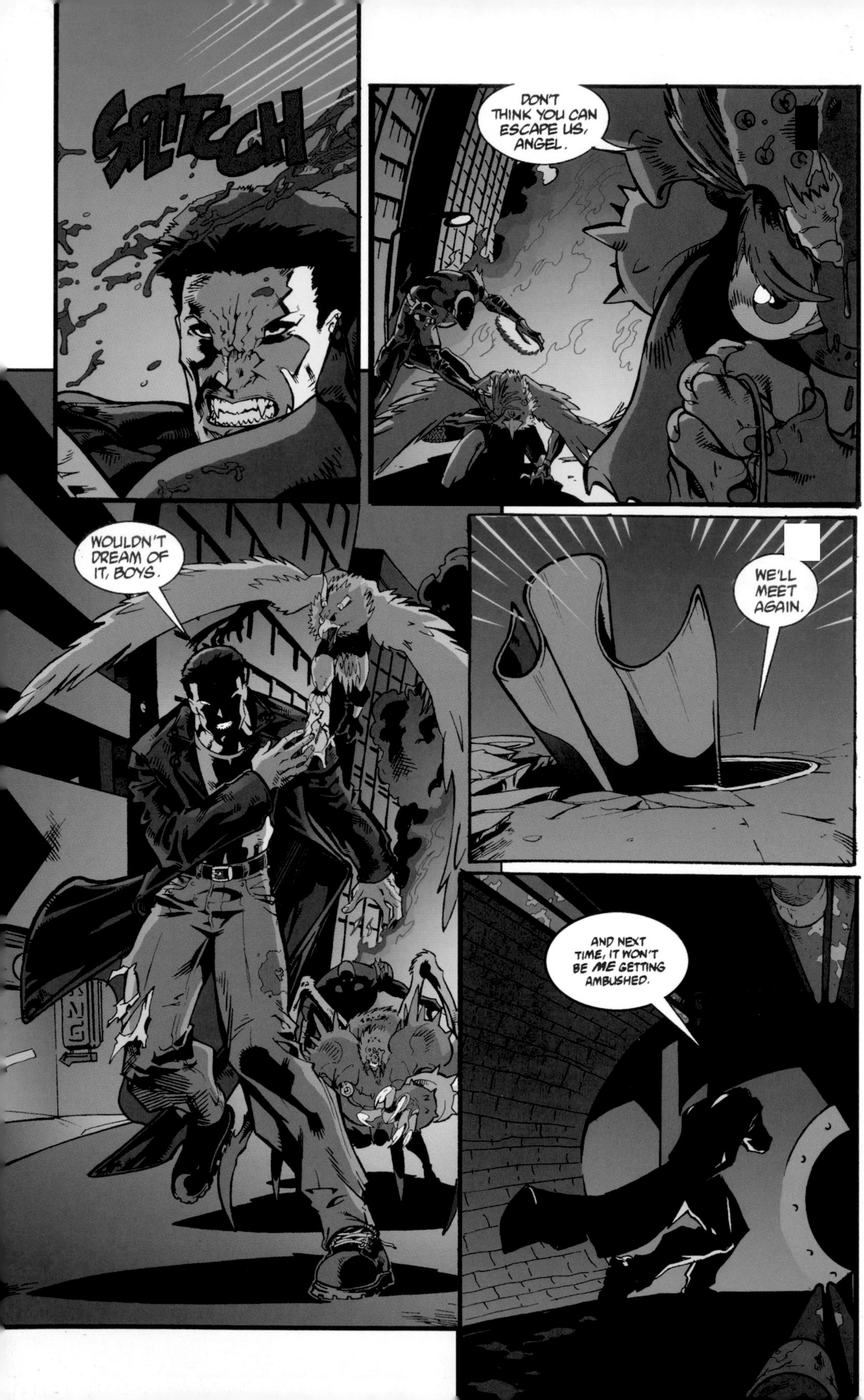
SPLITCCH
DON'T THINK YOU CAN ESCAPE US, ANGEL.
WOULDN'T DREAM OF IT, BOYS.
WE'LL MEET AGAIN.
AND NEXT TIME, IT WON'T BE ME GETTING AMBUSHED.

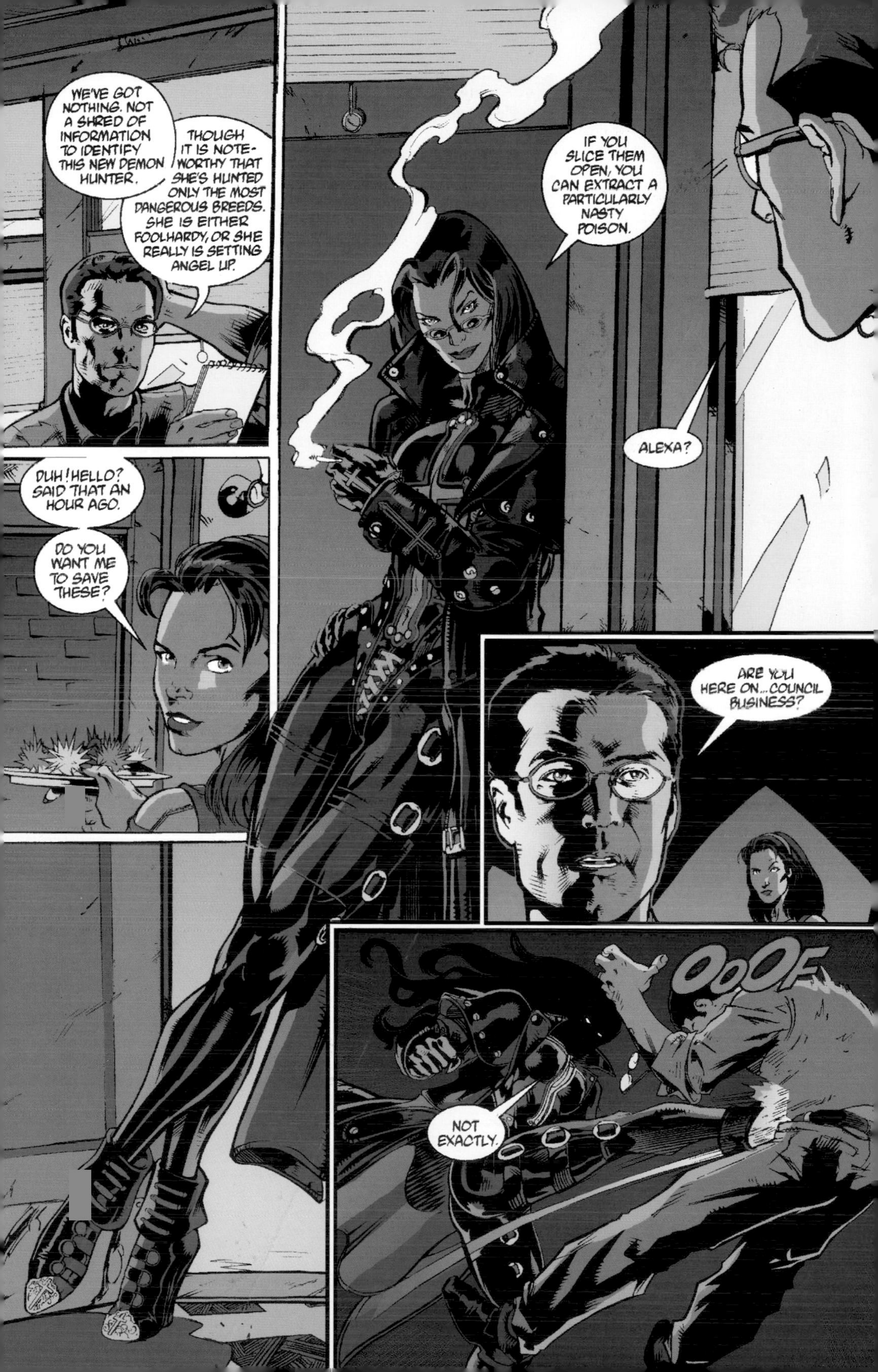
WE'VE GOT NOTHING. NOT A SHRED OF INFORMATION TO IDENTIFY THIS NEW DEMON HUNTER.
THOUGH IT IS NOTE-WORTHY THAT SHE'S HUNTED ONLY THE MOST DANGEROUS BREEDS. SHE IS EITHER FOOLHARDY, OR SHE REALLY IS SETTING ANGEL UP.
DUH! HELLO? SAID THAT AN HOUR AGO.
DO YOU WANT ME TO SAVE THESE?
IF YOU SLICE THEM OPEN, YOU CAN EXTRACT A PARTICULARLY NASTY POISON.
ALEXA?
ARE YOU HERE ON...COUNCIL BUSINESS?
OOOF
NOT EXACTLY.

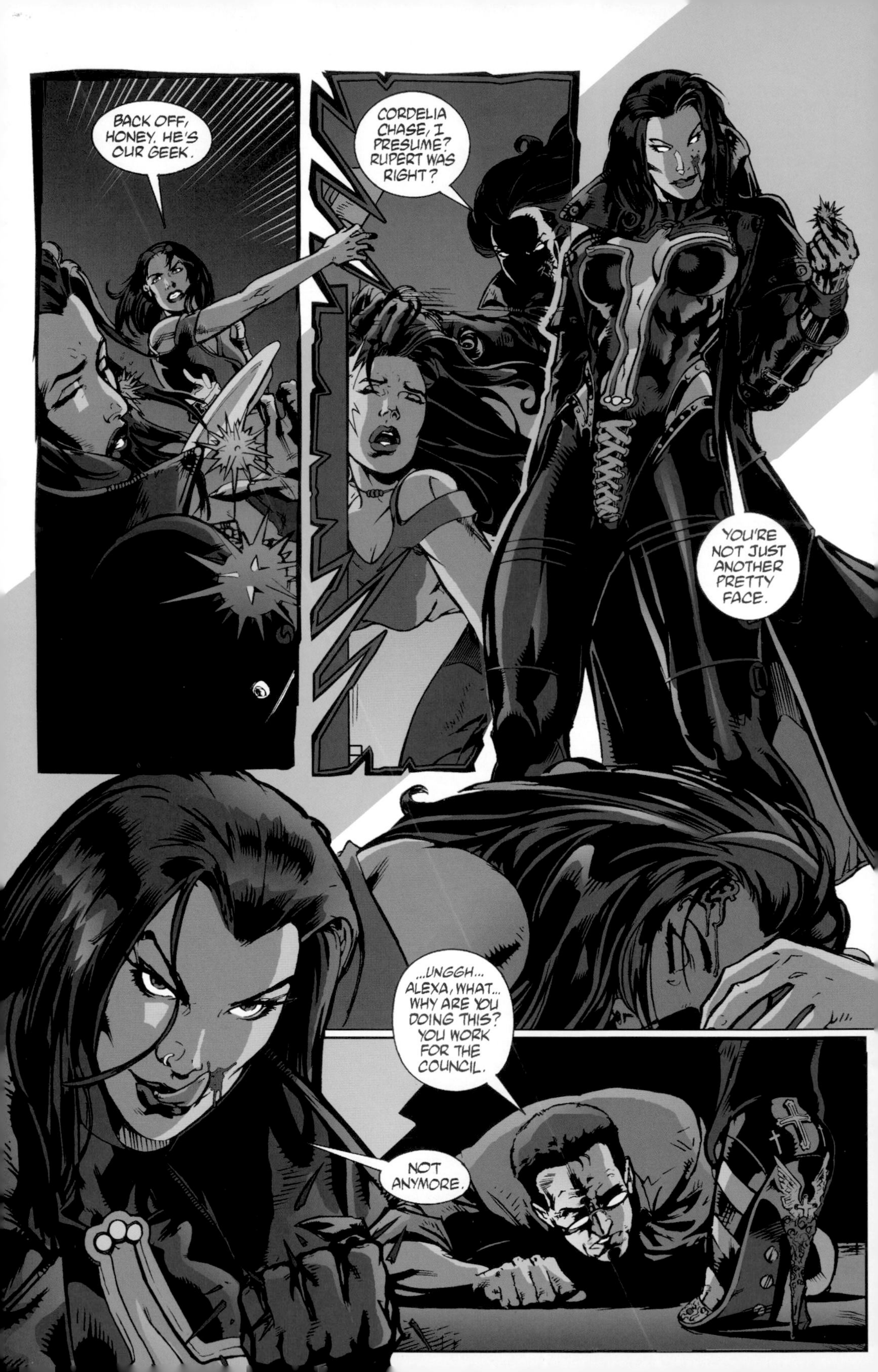
BACK OFF, HONEY. HE'S OUR GEEK.
CORDELIA CHASE, I PRESUME? RUPERT WAS RIGHT?
YOU'RE NOT JUST ANOTHER PRETTY FACE.
...UNGGH... ALEXA, WHAT... WHY ARE YOU DOING THIS? YOU WORK FOR THE COUNCIL.
NOT ANYMORE.

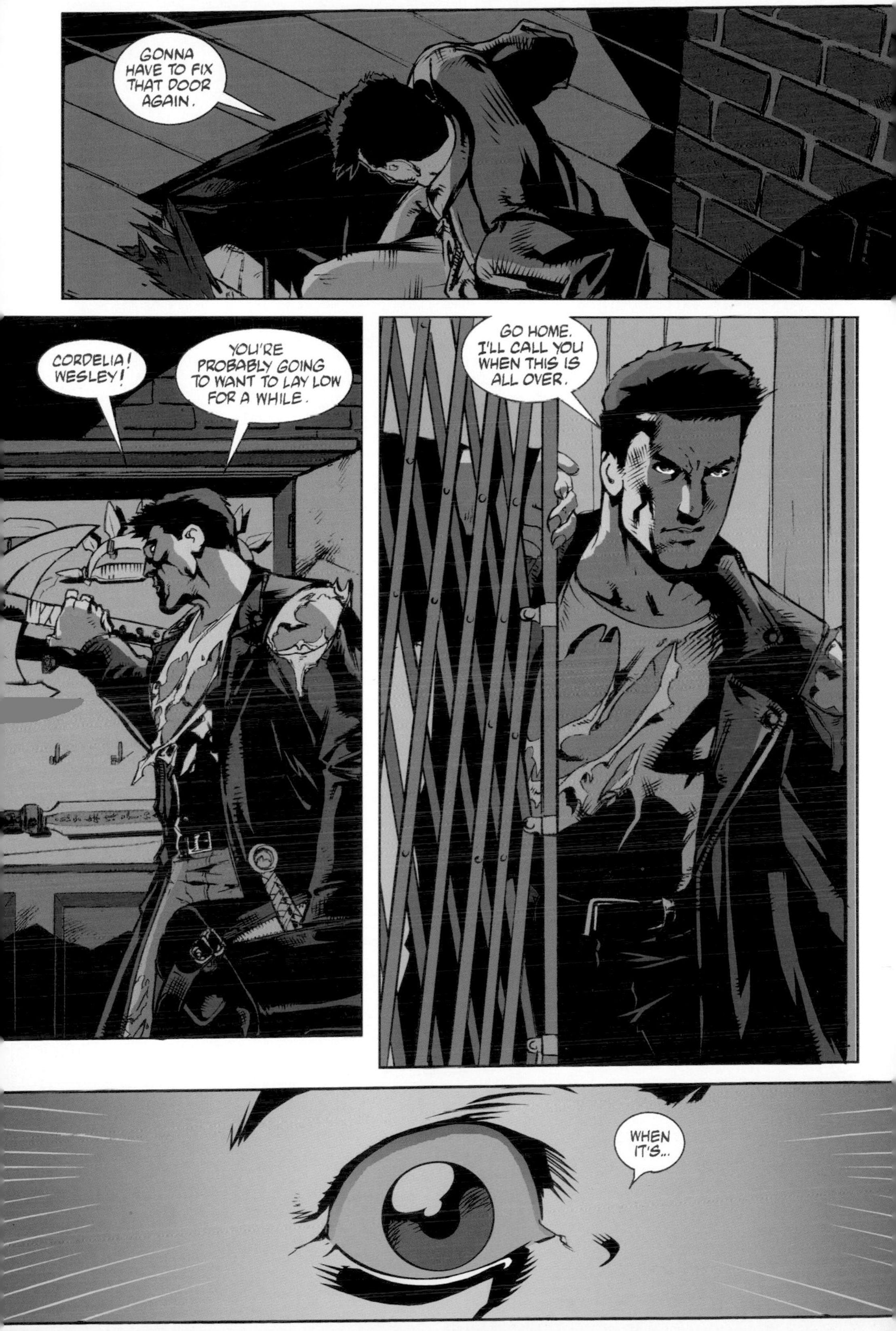
GONNA HAVE TO FIX THAT DOOR AGAIN.
CORDELIA! WESLEY!
YOU'RE PROBABLY GOING TO WANT TO LAY LOW FOR A WHILE.
GO HOME. I'LL CALL YOU WHEN THIS IS ALL OVER.
WHEN IT'S...

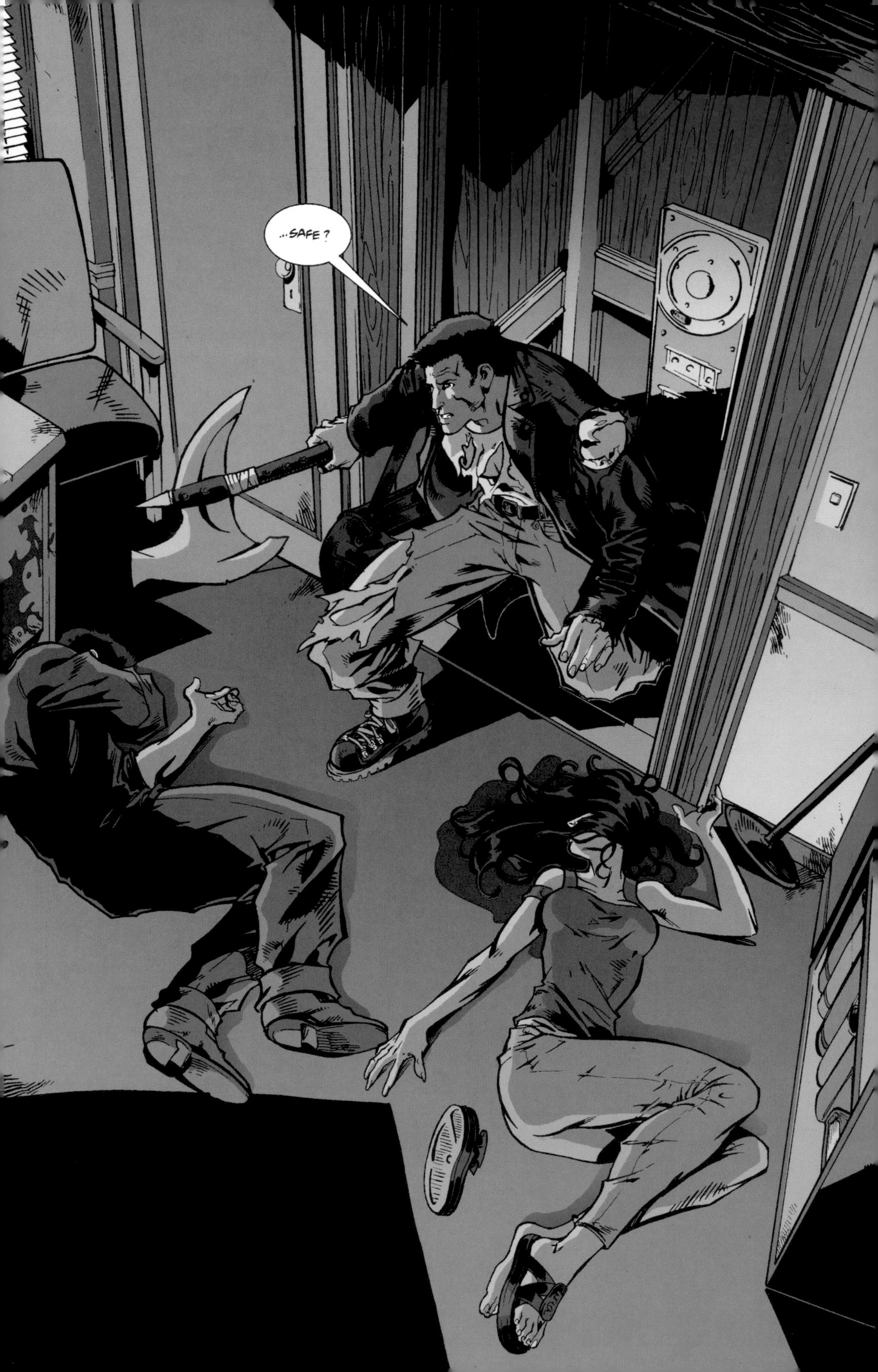
...SAFE ?

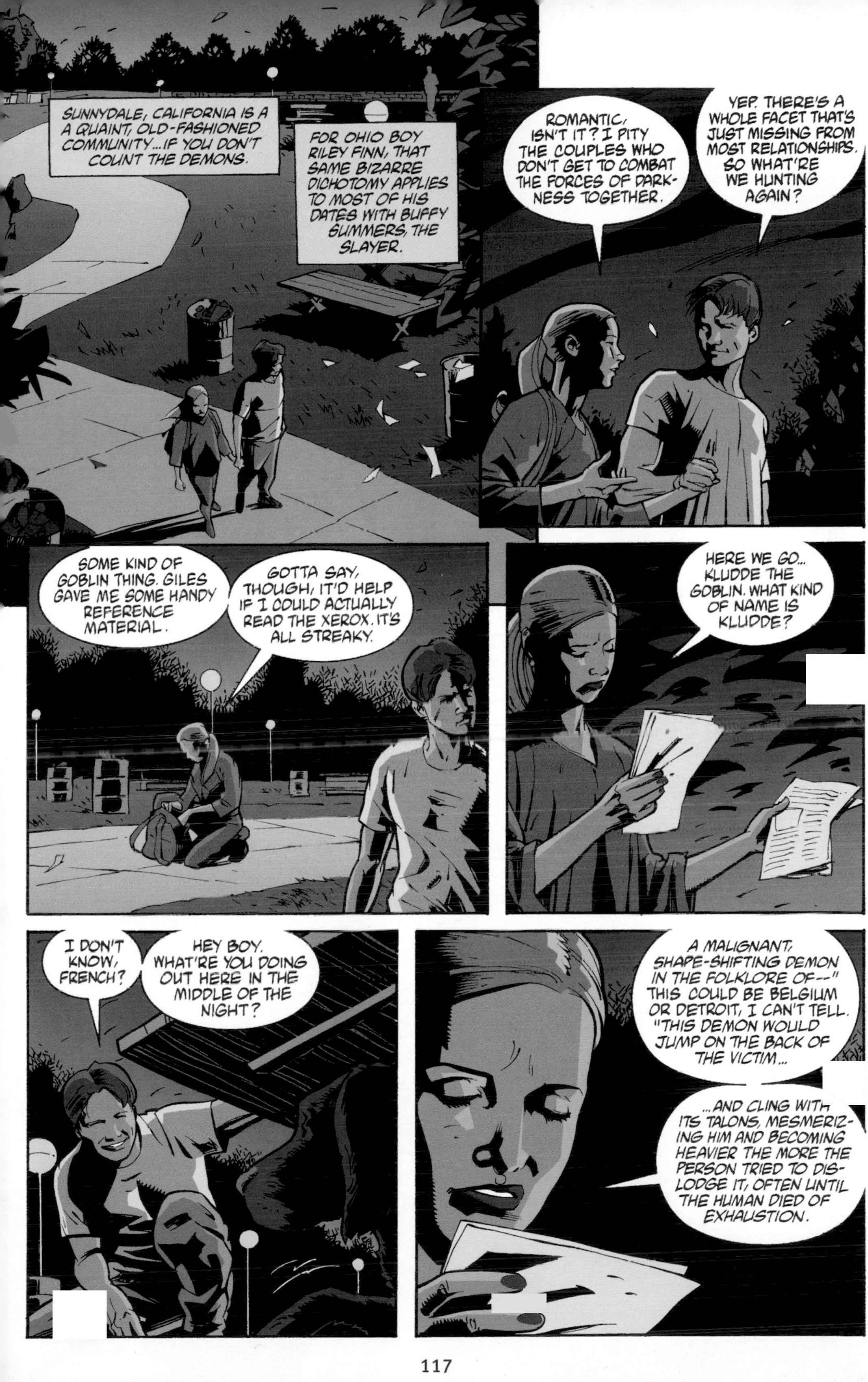
SUNNYDALE, CALIFORNIA IS A A QUAINT, OLD-FASHIONED COMMUNITY...IF YOU DON'T COUNT THE DEMONS.
FOR OHIO BOY RILEY FINN, THAT SAME BIZARRE DICHOTOMY APPLIES TO MOST OF HIS DATES WITH BUFFY SUMMERS, THE SLAYER.
ROMANTIC, ISN'T IT? I PITY THE COUPLES WHO DON'T GET TO COMBAT THE FORCES OF DARKNESS TOGETHER.
YEP. THERE'S A WHOLE FACET THAT'S JUST MISSING FROM MOST RELATIONSHIPS. SO WHAT'RE WE HUNTING AGAIN?
SOME KIND OF GOBLIN THING. GILES GAVE ME SOME HANDY REFERENCE MATERIAL.
GOTTA SAY, THOUGH, IT'D HELP IF I COULD ACTUALLY READ THE XEROX. IT'S ALL STREAKY.
HERE WE GO... KLUDDE THE GOBLIN. WHAT KIND OF NAME IS KLUDDE?
I DON'T KNOW, FRENCH?
HEY BOY. WHAT'RE YOU DOING OUT HERE IN THE MIDDLE OF THE NIGHT?
A MALIGNANT, SHAPE-SHIFTING DEMON IN THE FOLKLORE OF--" THIS COULD BE BELGIUM OR DETROIT, I CAN'T TELL. "THIS DEMON WOULD JUMP ON THE BACK OF THE VICTIM...
...AND CLING WITH ITS TALONS, MESMERIZING HIM AND BECOMING HEAVIER THE MORE THE PERSON TRIED TO DISLODGE IT, OFTEN UNTIL THE HUMAN DIED OF EXHAUSTION.

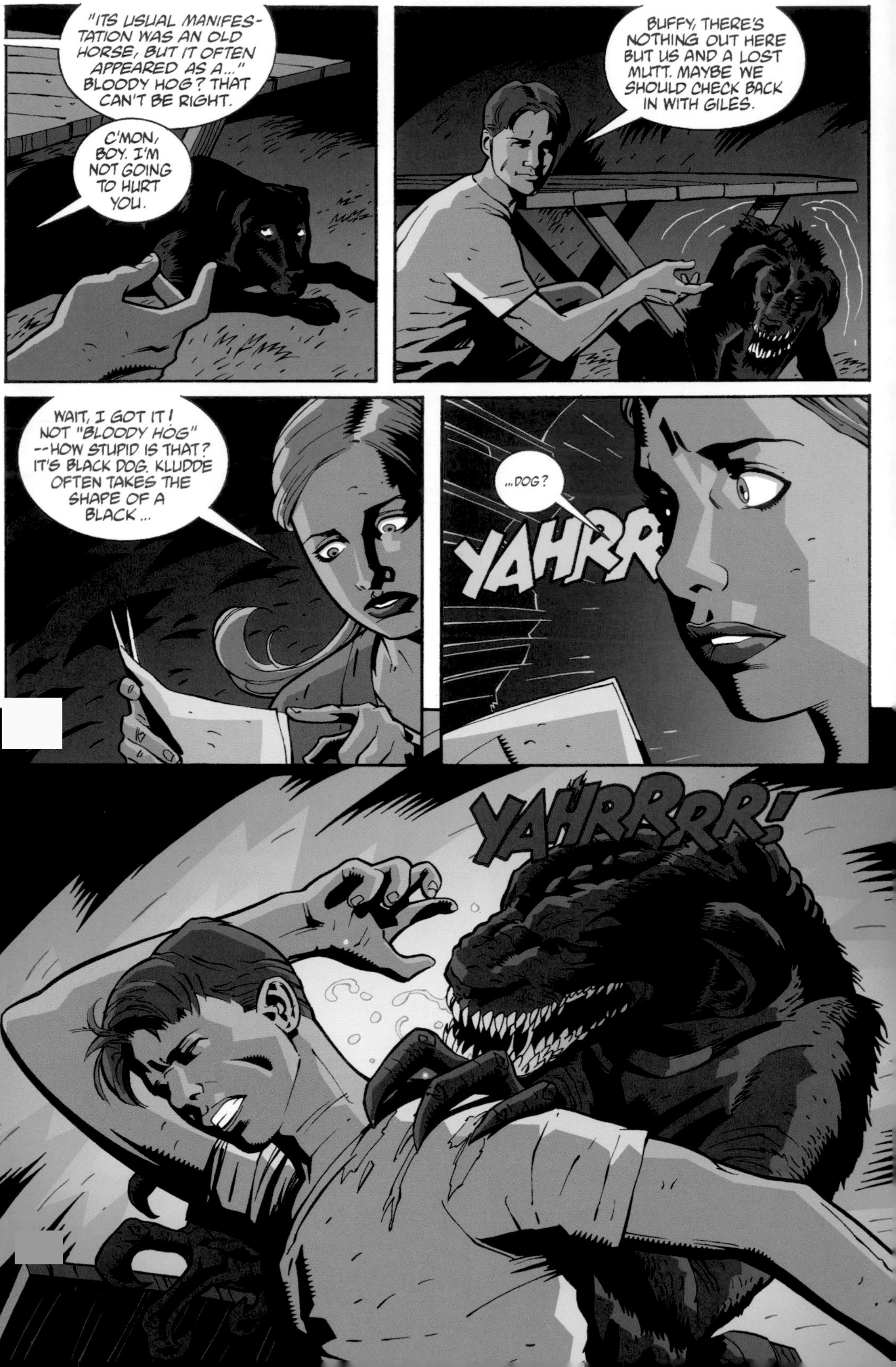
"ITS USUAL MANIFESTATION WAS AN OLD HORSE, BUT IT OFTEN APPEARED AS A..." BLOODY HOG? THAT CAN'T BE RIGHT.
C'MON, BOY. I'M NOT GOING TO HURT YOU.
BUFFY, THERE'S NOTHING OUT HERE BUT US AND A LOST MUTT. MAYBE WE SHOULD CHECK BACK IN WITH GILES.
WAIT, I GOT IT! NOT "BLOODY HOG" --HOW STUPID IS THAT? IT'S BLACK DOG. KLUDDE OFTEN TAKES THE SHAPE OF A BLACK...
...DOG?
YAHRR
YAHRRRR!

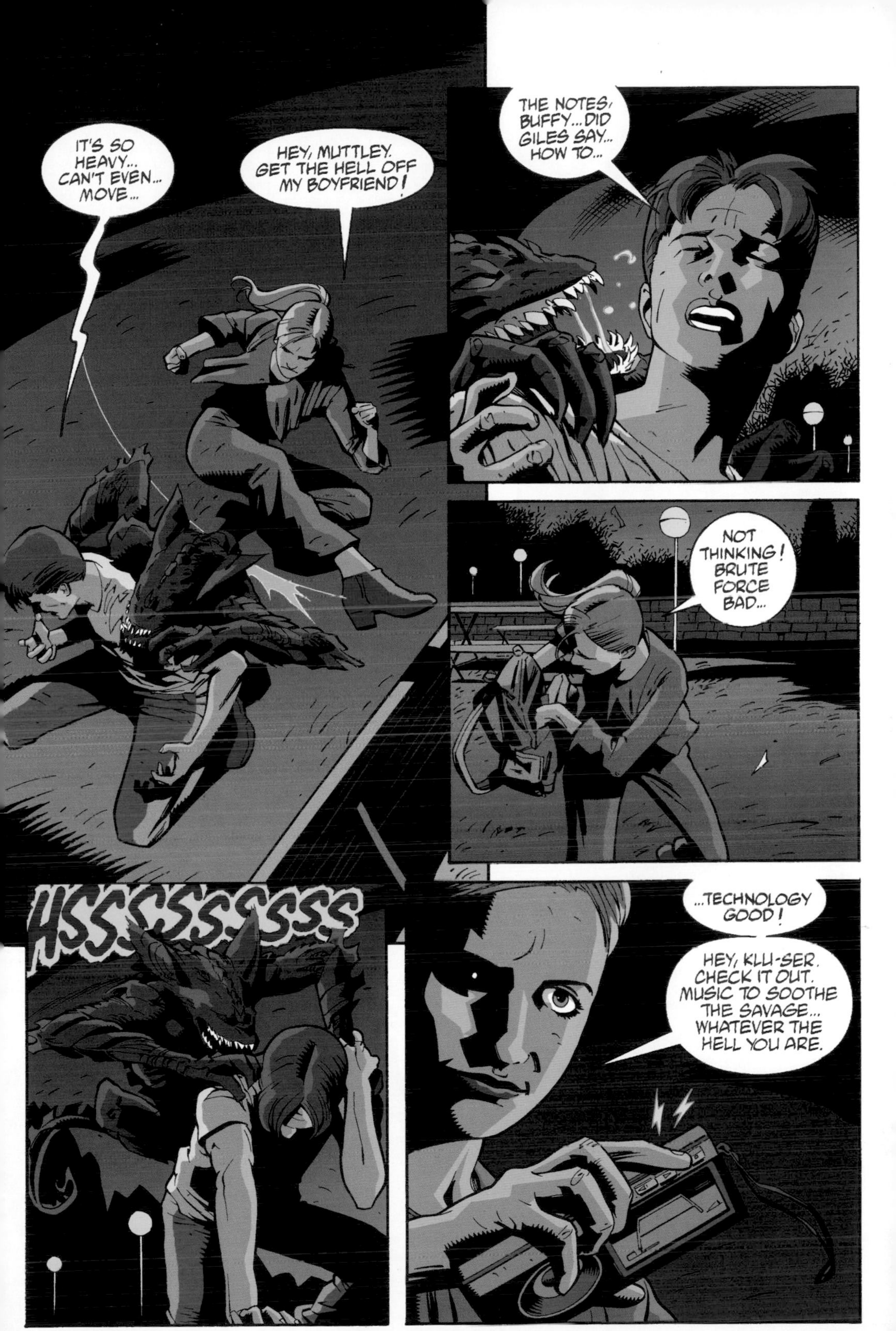
IT'S SO HEAVY... CAN'T EVEN... MOVE...
HEY, MUTTLEY. GET THE HELL OFF MY BOYFRIEND!
THE NOTES, BUFFY...DID GILES SAY... HOW TO...
NOT THINKING! BRUTE FORCE BAD...
HSSSSSSSSSS
...TECHNOLOGY GOOD!
HEY, KLU-SER. CHECK IT OUT. MUSIC TO SOOTHE THE SAVAGE... WHATEVER THE HELL YOU ARE.

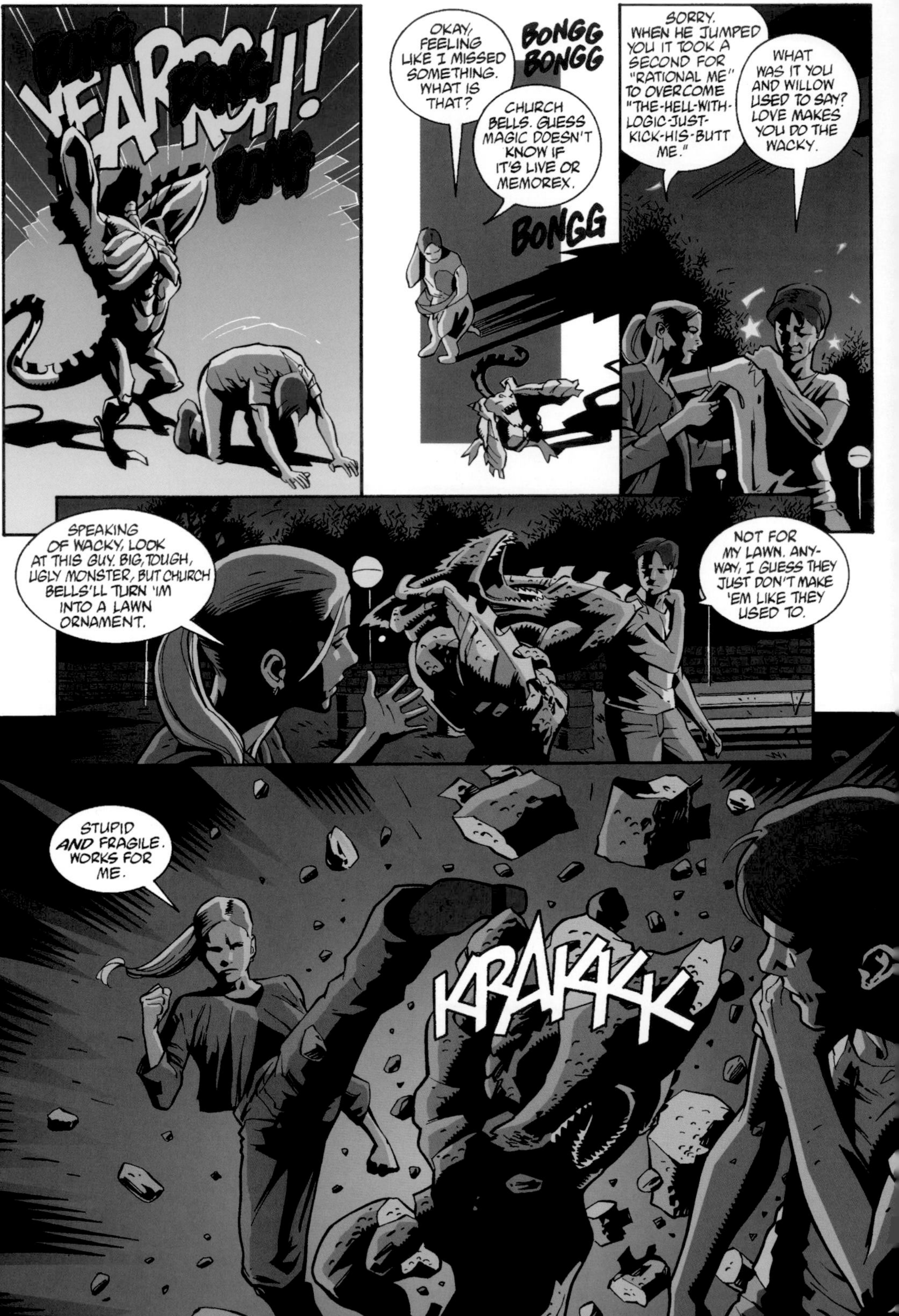
BONG
YEARRGH!
BONG
OKAY, FEELING LIKE I MISSED SOMETHING. WHAT IS THAT?
BONGG BONGG
CHURCH BELLS. GUESS MAGIC DOESN'T KNOW IF IT'S LIVE OR MEMOREX.
BONGG
SORRY. WHEN HE JUMPED YOU IT TOOK A SECOND FOR "RATIONAL ME" TO OVERCOME "THE-HELL-WITH-LOGIC-JUST-KICK-HIS-BUTT ME."
WHAT WAS IT YOU AND WILLOW USED TO SAY? LOVE MAKES YOU DO THE WACKY.
SPEAKING OF WACKY, LOOK AT THIS GUY. BIG, TOUGH, UGLY MONSTER, BUT CHURCH BELLS'LL TURN 'IM INTO A LAWN ORNAMENT.
NOT FOR MY LAWN. ANY-WAY, I GUESS THEY JUST DON'T MAKE 'EM LIKE THEY USED TO.
STUPID AND FRAGILE. WORKS FOR ME.
KRAKKK

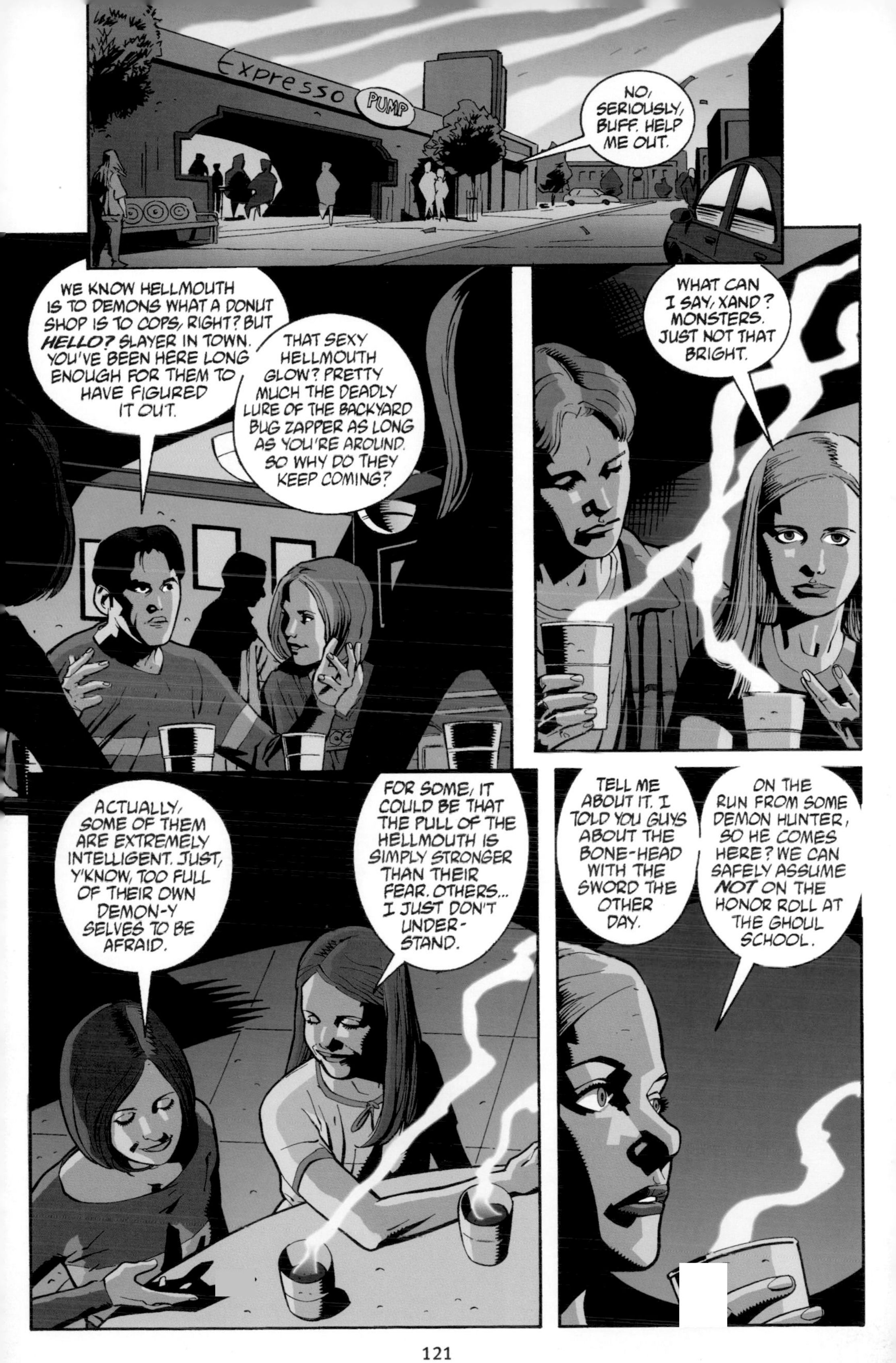
Expresso PUMP
NO, SERIOUSLY, BUFF. HELP ME OUT.
WE KNOW HELLMOUTH IS TO DEMONS WHAT A DONUT SHOP IS TO COPS, RIGHT? BUT *HELLO?* SLAYER IN TOWN. YOU'VE BEEN HERE LONG ENOUGH FOR THEM TO HAVE FIGURED IT OUT.
THAT SEXY HELLMOUTH GLOW? PRETTY MUCH THE DEADLY LURE OF THE BACKYARD BUG ZAPPER AS LONG AS YOU'RE AROUND. SO WHY DO THEY KEEP COMING?
WHAT CAN I SAY, XAND? MONSTERS. JUST NOT THAT BRIGHT.
ACTUALLY, SOME OF THEM ARE EXTREMELY INTELLIGENT. JUST, Y'KNOW, TOO FULL OF THEIR OWN DEMON-Y SELVES TO BE AFRAID.
FOR SOME, IT COULD BE THAT THE PULL OF THE HELLMOUTH IS SIMPLY STRONGER THAN THEIR FEAR. OTHERS... I JUST DON'T UNDER-STAND.
TELL ME ABOUT IT. I TOLD YOU GUYS ABOUT THE BONE-HEAD WITH THE SWORD THE OTHER DAY.
ON THE RUN FROM SOME DEMON HUNTER, SO HE COMES HERE? WE CAN SAFELY ASSUME *NOT* ON THE HONOR ROLL AT THE GHOUL SCHOOL.

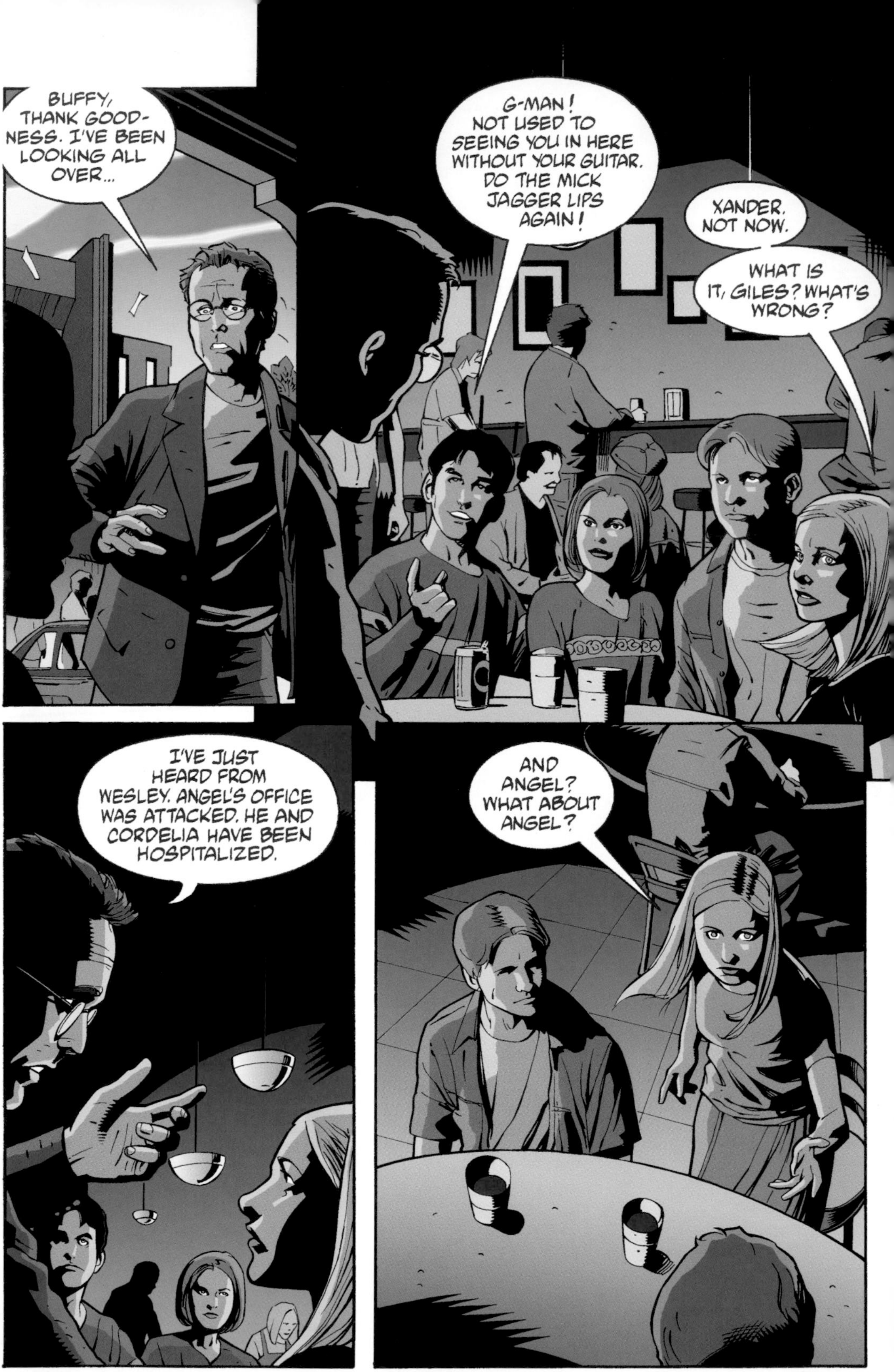
BUFFY, THANK GOODNESS. I'VE BEEN LOOKING ALL OVER...
G-MAN! NOT USED TO SEEING YOU IN HERE WITHOUT YOUR GUITAR. DO THE MICK JAGGER LIPS AGAIN!
XANDER. NOT NOW.
WHAT IS IT, GILES? WHAT'S WRONG?
I'VE JUST HEARD FROM WESLEY. ANGEL'S OFFICE WAS ATTACKED. HE AND CORDELIA HAVE BEEN HOSPITALIZED.
AND ANGEL? WHAT ABOUT ANGEL?

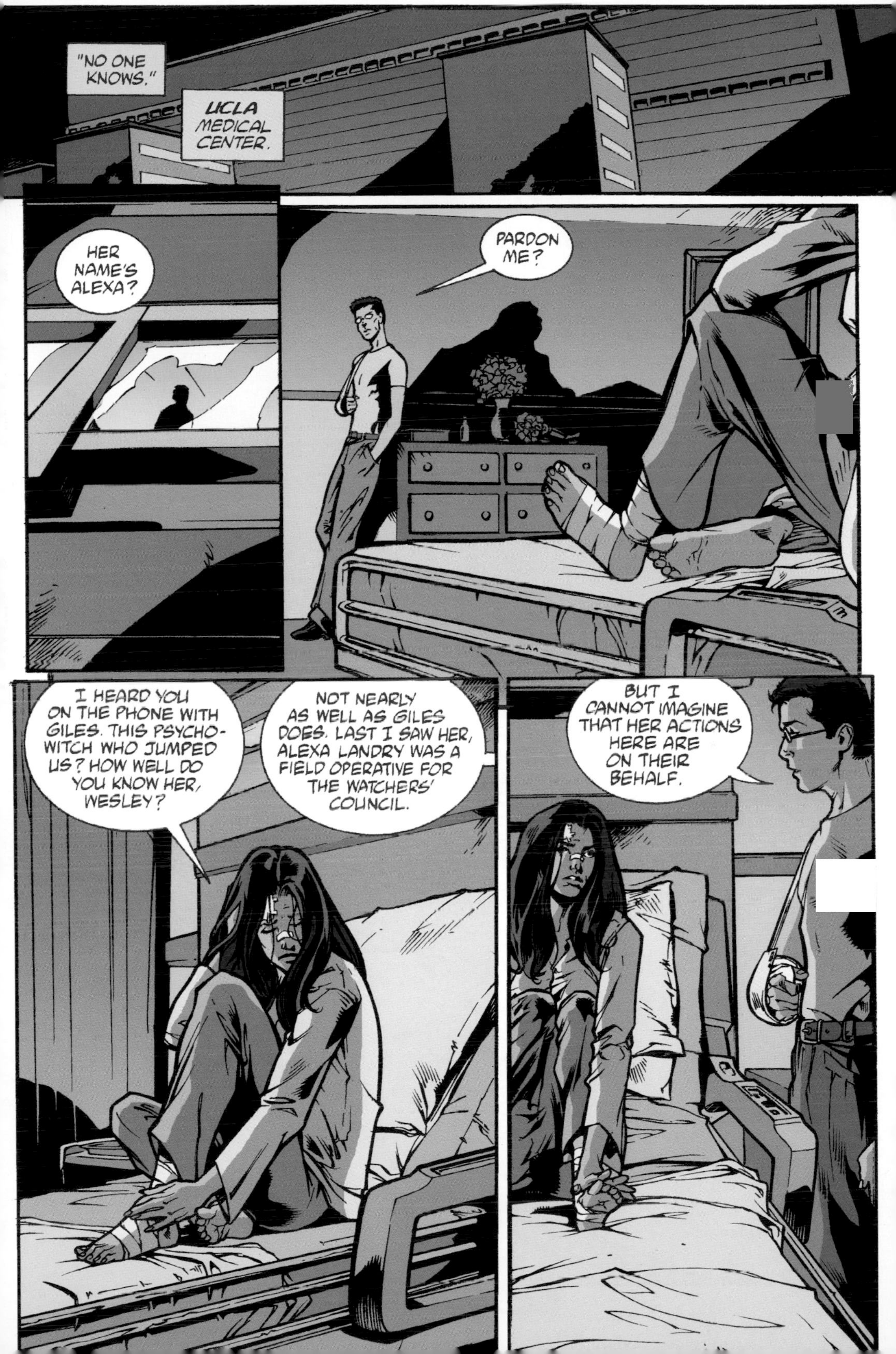

"NO ONE KNOWS."
UCLA MEDICAL CENTER.
HER NAME'S ALEXA?
PARDON ME?
I HEARD YOU ON THE PHONE WITH GILES. THIS PSYCHO-WITCH WHO JUMPED US? HOW WELL DO YOU KNOW HER, WESLEY?
NOT NEARLY AS WELL AS GILES DOES. LAST I SAW HER, ALEXA LANDRY WAS A FIELD OPERATIVE FOR THE WATCHERS' COUNCIL.
BUT I CANNOT IMAGINE THAT HER ACTIONS HERE ARE ON THEIR BEHALF.

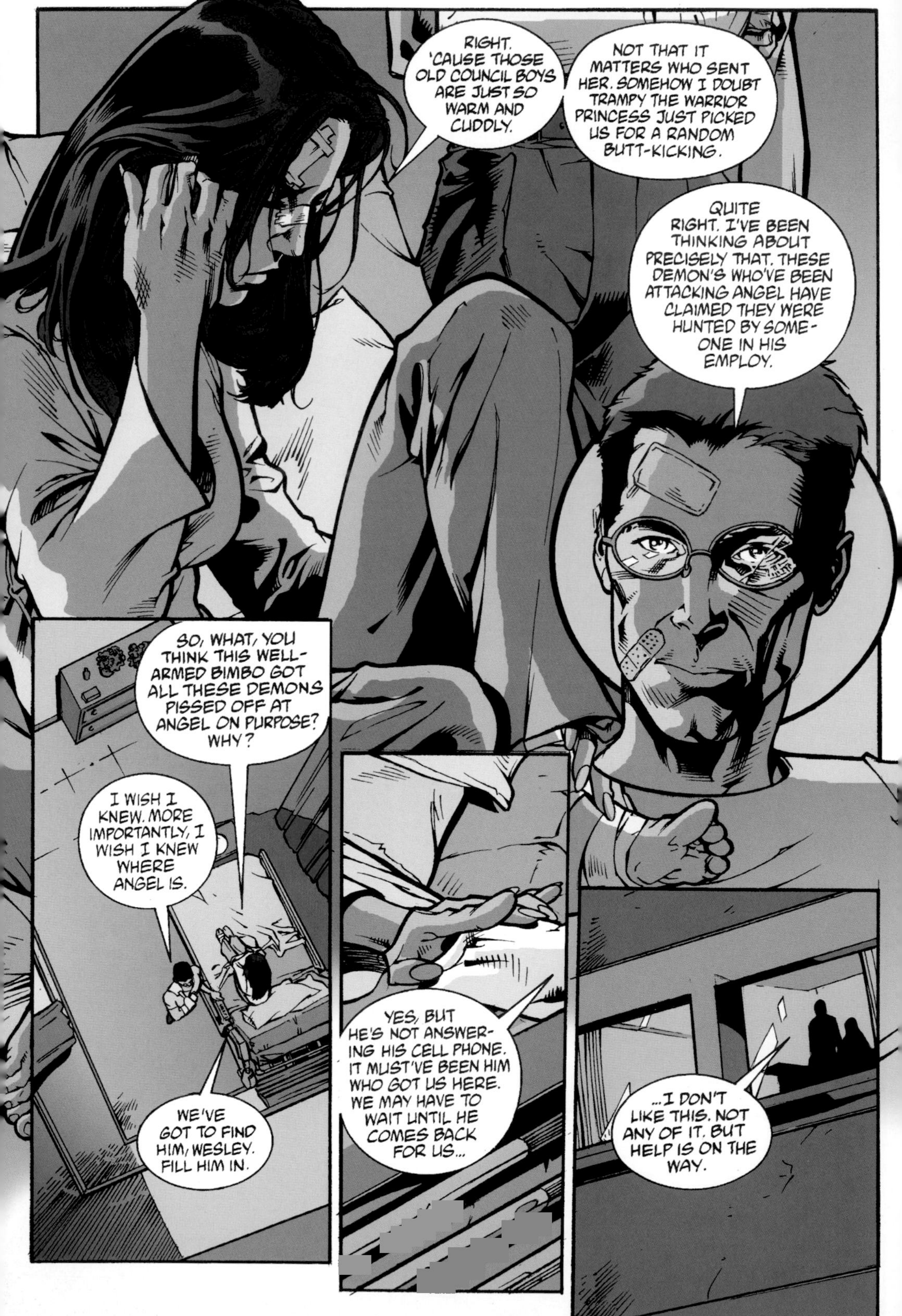
RIGHT. 'CAUSE THOSE OLD COUNCIL BOYS ARE JUST SO WARM AND CUDDLY.
NOT THAT IT MATTERS WHO SENT HER. SOMEHOW I DOUBT TRAMPY THE WARRIOR PRINCESS JUST PICKED US FOR A RANDOM BUTT-KICKING.
QUITE RIGHT. I'VE BEEN THINKING ABOUT PRECISELY THAT. THESE DEMON'S WHO'VE BEEN ATTACKING ANGEL HAVE CLAIMED THEY WERE HUNTED BY SOME-ONE IN HIS EMPLOY.
SO, WHAT, YOU THINK THIS WELL-ARMED BIMBO GOT ALL THESE DEMONS PISSED OFF AT ANGEL ON PURPOSE? WHY?
I WISH I KNEW. MORE IMPORTANTLY, I WISH I KNEW WHERE ANGEL IS.
WE'VE GOT TO FIND HIM, WESLEY. FILL HIM IN.
YES, BUT HE'S NOT ANSWER-ING HIS CELL PHONE. IT MUST'VE BEEN HIM WHO GOT US HERE. WE MAY HAVE TO WAIT UNTIL HE COMES BACK FOR US...
...I DON'T LIKE THIS. NOT ANY OF IT. BUT HELP IS ON THE WAY.

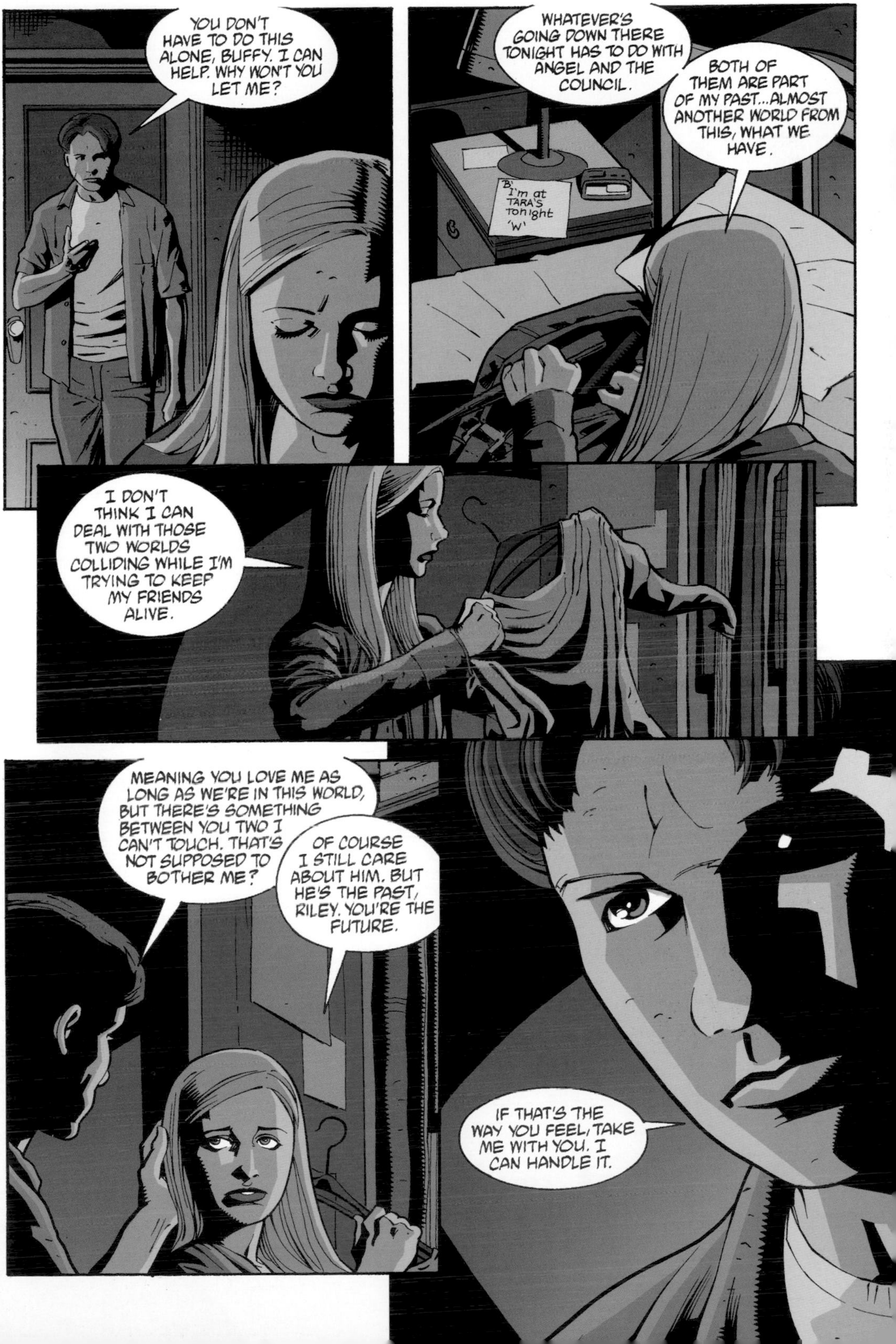
YOU DON'T HAVE TO DO THIS ALONE, BUFFY. I CAN HELP. WHY WON'T YOU LET ME?
WHATEVER'S GOING DOWN THERE TONIGHT HAS TO DO WITH ANGEL AND THE COUNCIL.
BOTH OF THEM ARE PART OF MY PAST...ALMOST ANOTHER WORLD FROM THIS, WHAT WE HAVE.
'B' I'm at TARA'S Tonight 'W'
I DON'T THINK I CAN DEAL WITH THOSE TWO WORLDS COLLIDING WHILE I'M TRYING TO KEEP MY FRIENDS ALIVE.
MEANING YOU LOVE ME AS LONG AS WE'RE IN THIS WORLD, BUT THERE'S SOMETHING BETWEEN YOU TWO I CAN'T TOUCH. THAT'S NOT SUPPOSED TO BOTHER ME?
OF COURSE I STILL CARE ABOUT HIM. BUT HE'S THE PAST, RILEY. YOU'RE THE FUTURE.
IF THAT'S THE WAY YOU FEEL, TAKE ME WITH YOU. I CAN HANDLE IT.

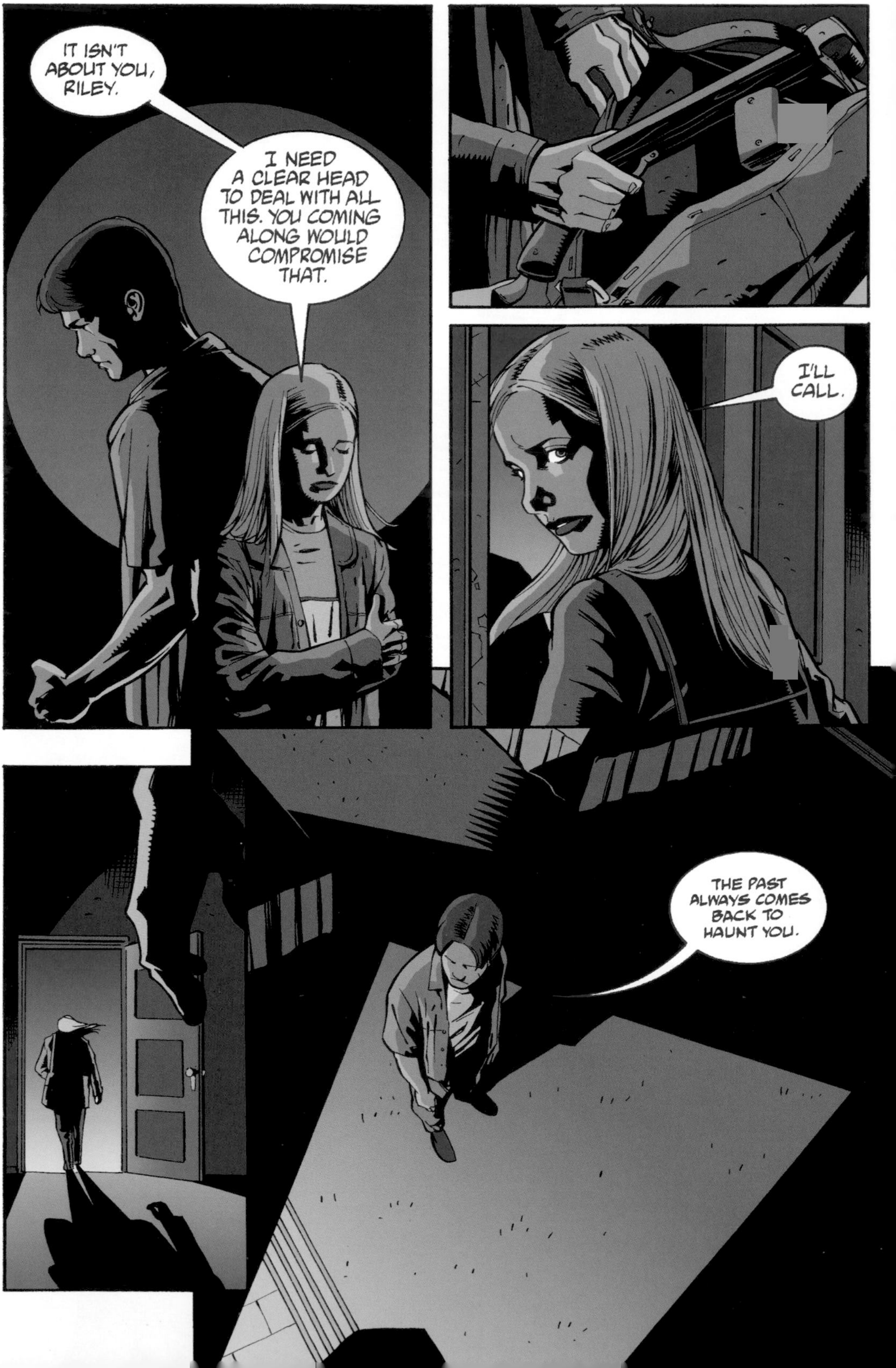
IT ISN'T ABOUT YOU, RILEY.
I NEED A CLEAR HEAD TO DEAL WITH ALL THIS. YOU COMING ALONG WOULD COMPROMISE THAT.
I'LL CALL.
THE PAST ALWAYS COMES BACK TO HAUNT YOU.

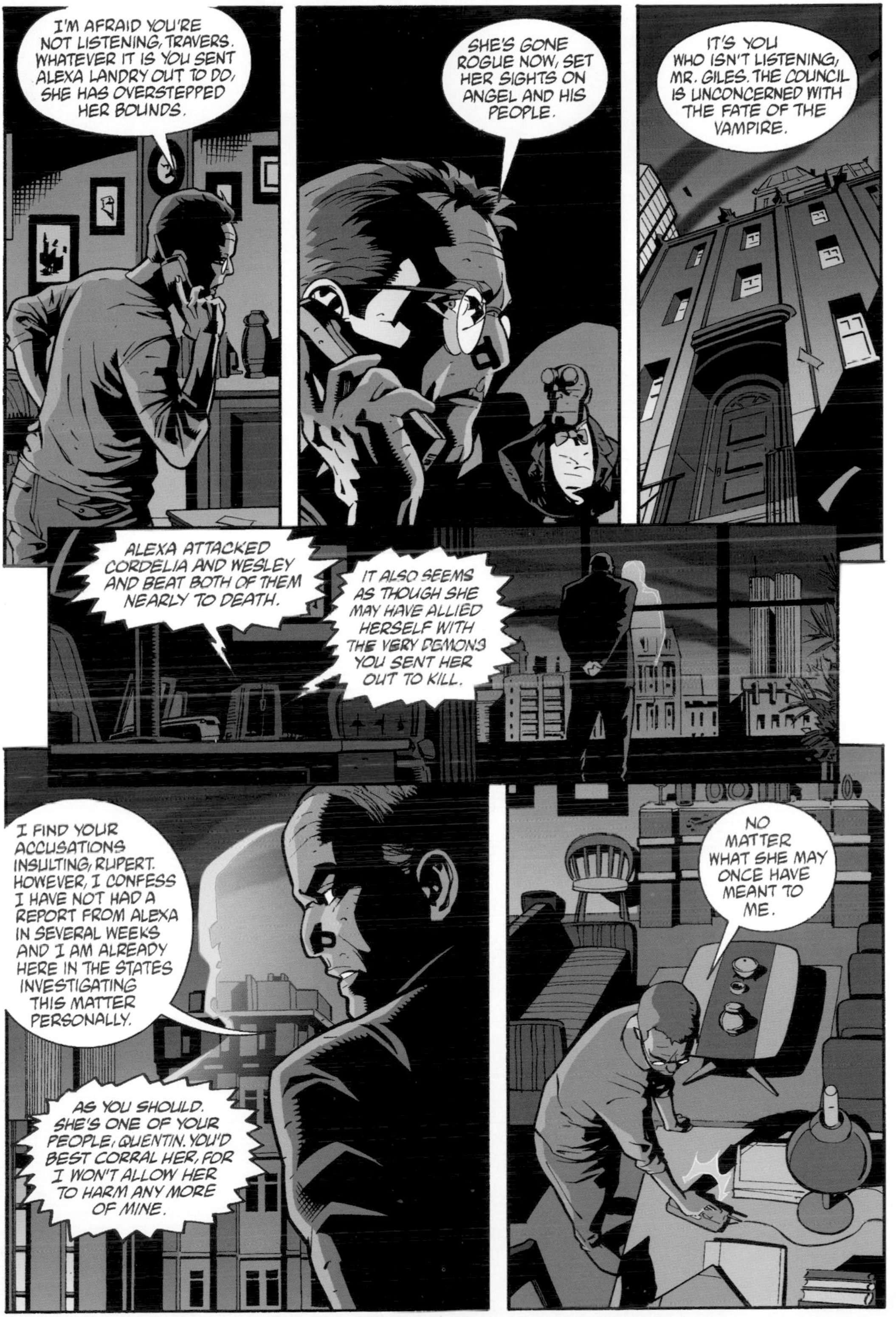

I'M AFRAID YOU'RE NOT LISTENING, TRAVERS. WHATEVER IT IS YOU SENT ALEXA LANDRY OUT TO DO, SHE HAS OVERSTEPPED HER BOUNDS.
SHE'S GONE ROGUE NOW, SET HER SIGHTS ON ANGEL AND HIS PEOPLE.
IT'S YOU WHO ISN'T LISTENING, MR. GILES. THE COUNCIL IS UNCONCERNED WITH THE FATE OF THE VAMPIRE.
ALEXA ATTACKED CORDELIA AND WESLEY AND BEAT BOTH OF THEM NEARLY TO DEATH.
IT ALSO SEEMS AS THOUGH SHE MAY HAVE ALLIED HERSELF WITH THE VERY DEMONS YOU SENT HER OUT TO KILL.
I FIND YOUR ACCUSATIONS INSULTING, RUPERT. HOWEVER, I CONFESS I HAVE NOT HAD A REPORT FROM ALEXA IN SEVERAL WEEKS AND I AM ALREADY HERE IN THE STATES INVESTIGATING THIS MATTER PERSONALLY.
AS YOU SHOULD. SHE'S ONE OF YOUR PEOPLE, QUENTIN. YOU'D BEST CORRAL HER, FOR I WON'T ALLOW HER TO HARM ANY MORE OF MINE.
NO MATTER WHAT SHE MAY ONCE HAVE MEANT TO ME.

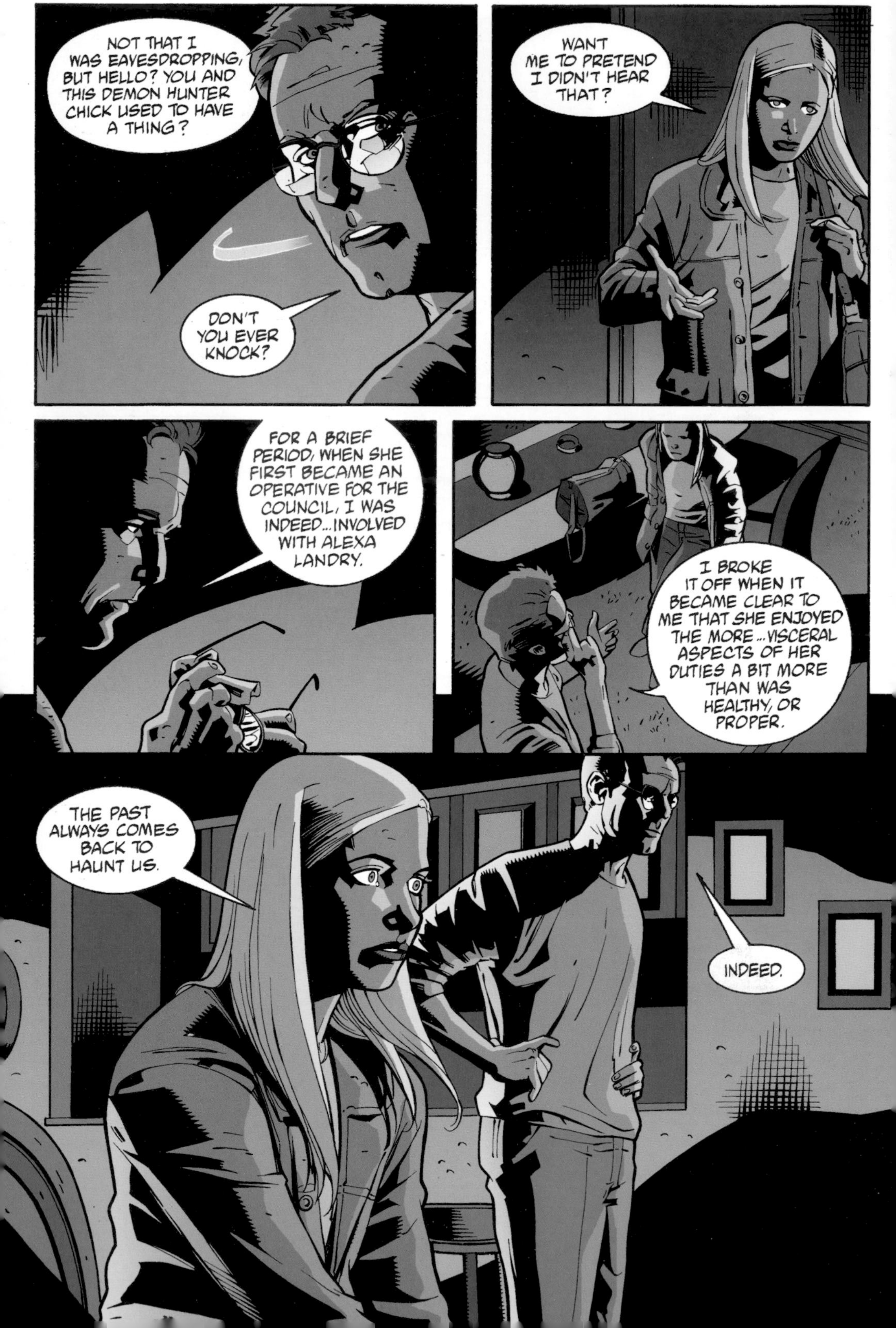
NOT THAT I WAS EAVESDROPPING, BUT HELLO? YOU AND THIS DEMON HUNTER CHICK USED TO HAVE A THING?
DON'T YOU EVER KNOCK?
WANT ME TO PRETEND I DIDN'T HEAR THAT?
FOR A BRIEF PERIOD, WHEN SHE FIRST BECAME AN OPERATIVE FOR THE COUNCIL, I WAS INDEED...INVOLVED WITH ALEXA LANDRY.
I BROKE IT OFF WHEN IT BECAME CLEAR TO ME THAT SHE ENJOYED THE MORE...VISCERAL ASPECTS OF HER DUTIES A BIT MORE THAN WAS HEALTHY, OR PROPER.
THE PAST ALWAYS COMES BACK TO HAUNT US.
INDEED.

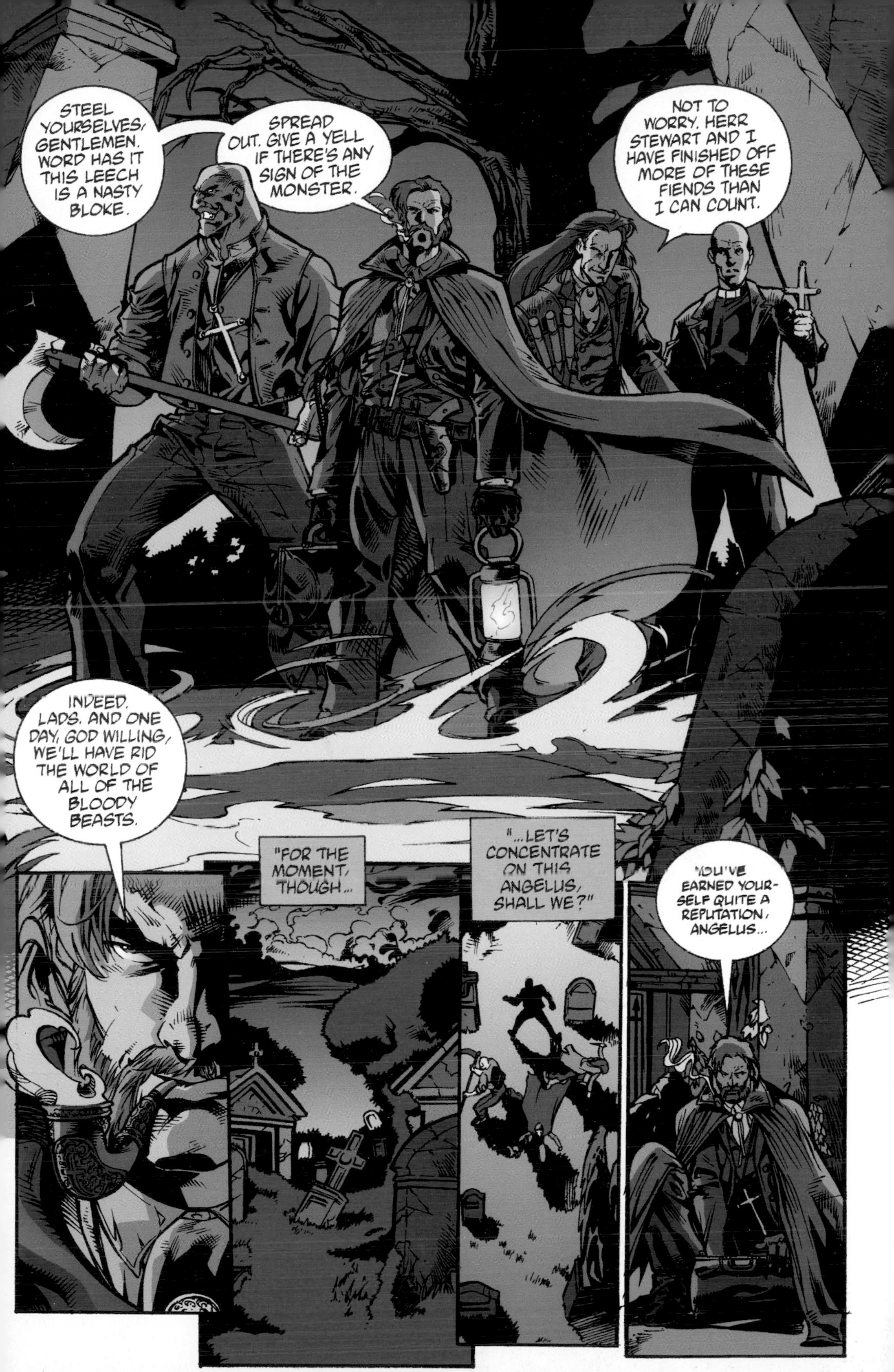
STEEL YOURSELVES, GENTLEMEN. WORD HAS IT THIS LEECH IS A NASTY BLOKE.
SPREAD OUT. GIVE A YELL IF THERE'S ANY SIGN OF THE MONSTER.
NOT TO WORRY. HERR STEWART AND I HAVE FINISHED OFF MORE OF THESE FIENDS THAN I CAN COUNT.
INDEED, LADS. AND ONE DAY, GOD WILLING, WE'LL HAVE RID THE WORLD OF ALL OF THE BLOODY BEASTS.
"FOR THE MOMENT, THOUGH...
"...LET'S CONCENTRATE ON THIS ANGELUS, SHALL WE?"
YOU'VE EARNED YOURSELF QUITE A REPUTATION, ANGELUS...

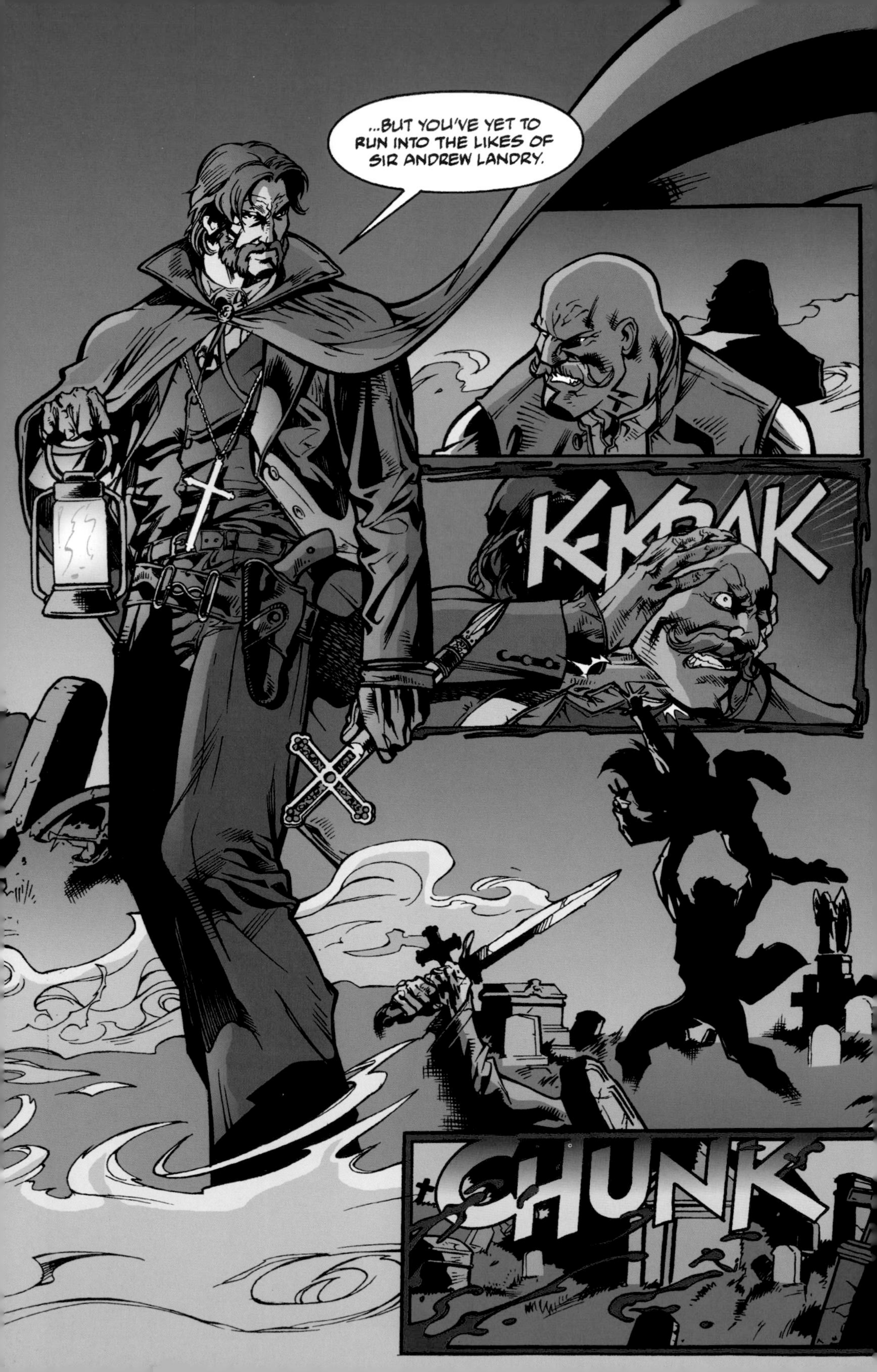
...BUT YOU'VE YET TO RUN INTO THE LIKES OF SIR ANDREW LANDRY.
K-KRAK
CHUNK

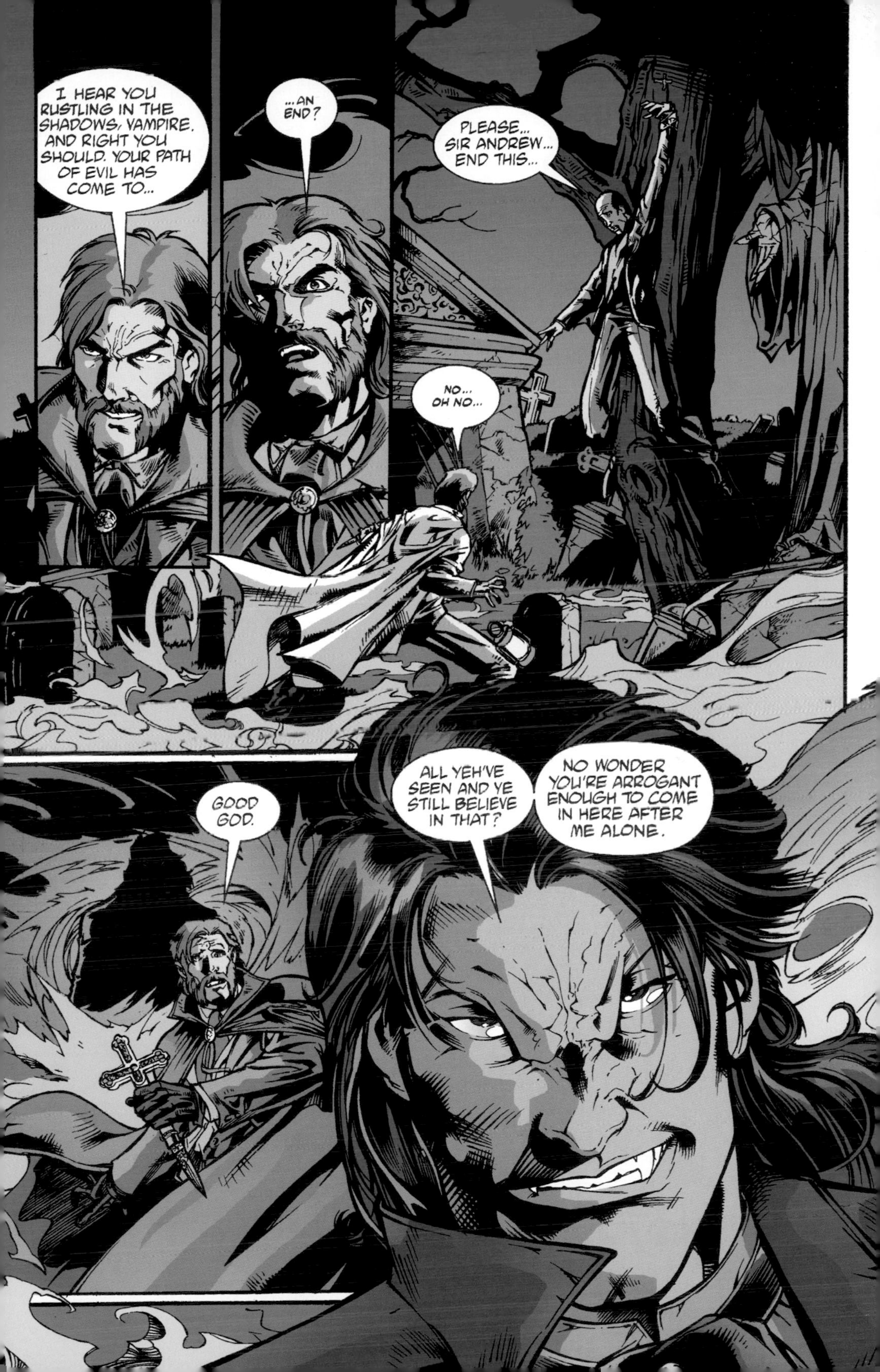
I HEAR YOU RUSTLING IN THE SHADOWS, VAMPIRE. AND RIGHT YOU SHOULD. YOUR PATH OF EVIL HAS COME TO...
...AN END?
PLEASE... SIR ANDREW... END THIS...
NO... OH NO...
GOOD GOD.
ALL YEH'VE SEEN AND YE STILL BELIEVE IN THAT?
NO WONDER YOU'RE ARROGANT ENOUGH TO COME IN HERE AFTER ME ALONE.

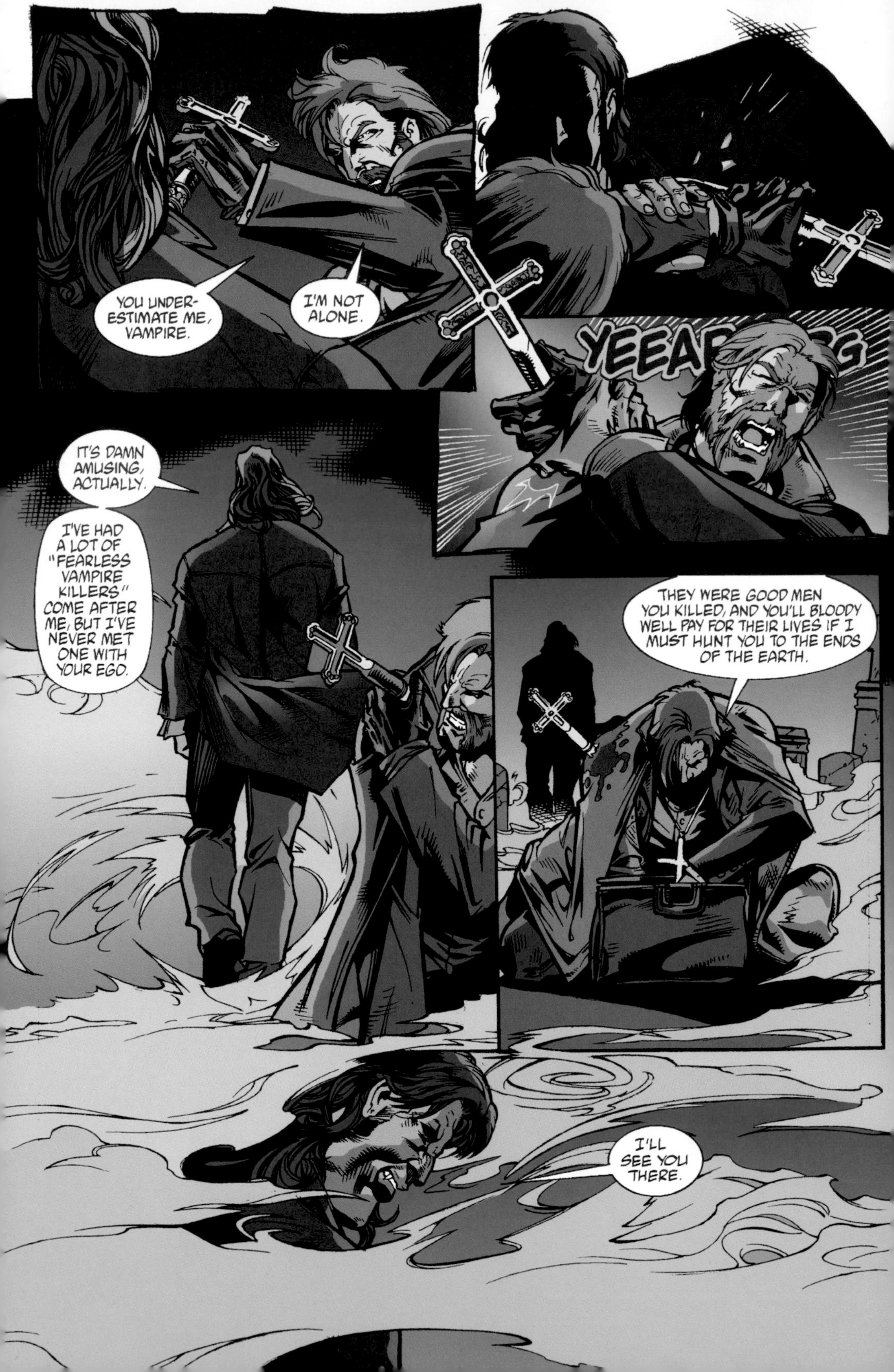
YOU UNDER-ESTIMATE ME, VAMPIRE.
I'M NOT ALONE.
YEEAARRGG
IT'S DAMN AMUSING, ACTUALLY.
I'VE HAD A LOT OF "FEARLESS VAMPIRE KILLERS" COME AFTER ME, BUT I'VE NEVER MET ONE WITH YOUR EGO.
THEY WERE GOOD MEN YOU KILLED, AND YOU'LL BLOODY WELL PAY FOR THEIR LIVES IF I MUST HUNT YOU TO THE ENDS OF THE EARTH.
I'LL SEE YOU THERE.

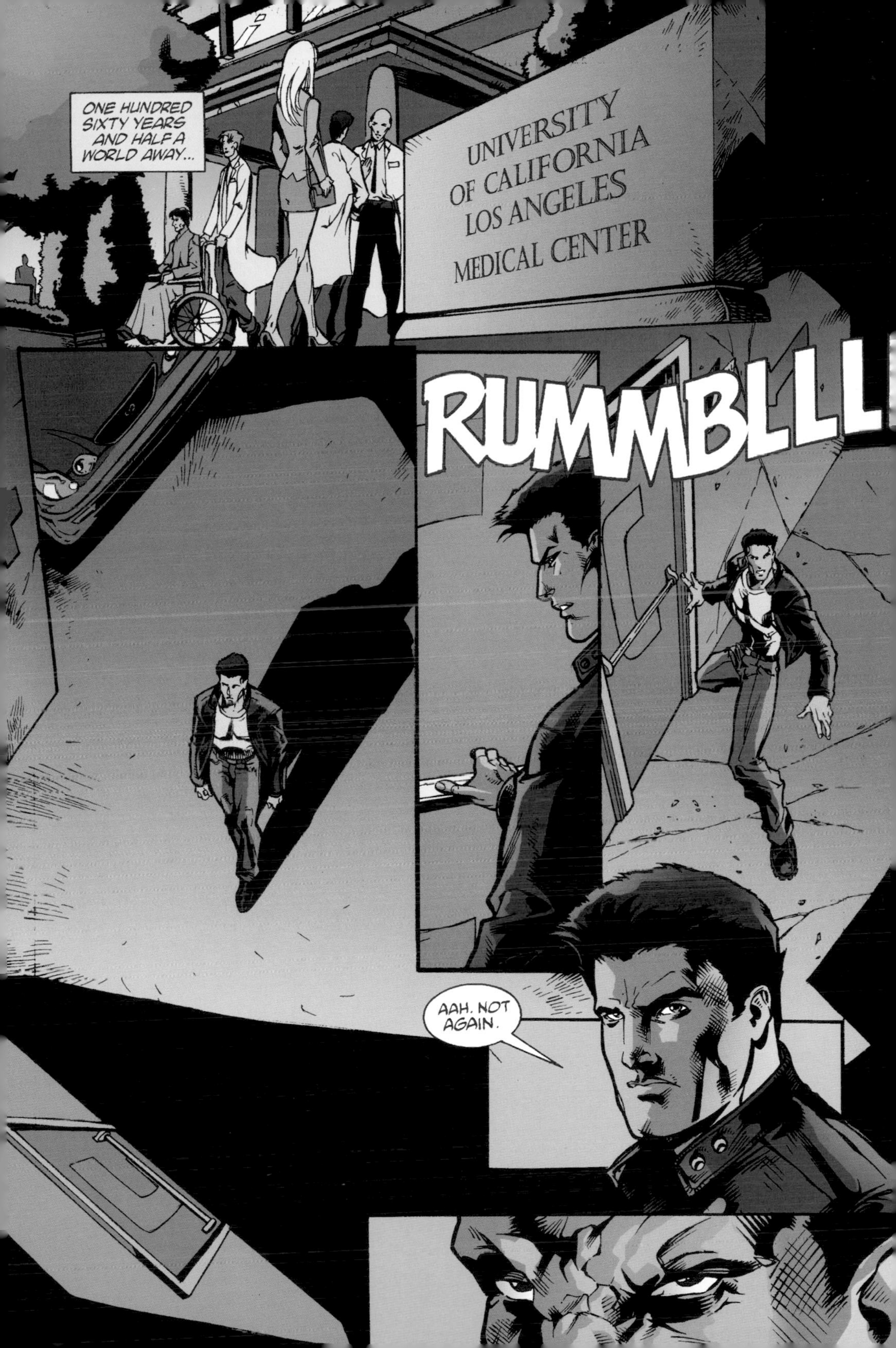
ONE HUNDRED SIXTY YEARS AND HALF A WORLD AWAY...
UNIVERSITY OF CALIFORNIA LOS ANGELES MEDICAL CENTER
RUMMBLLL
AAH. NOT AGAIN.

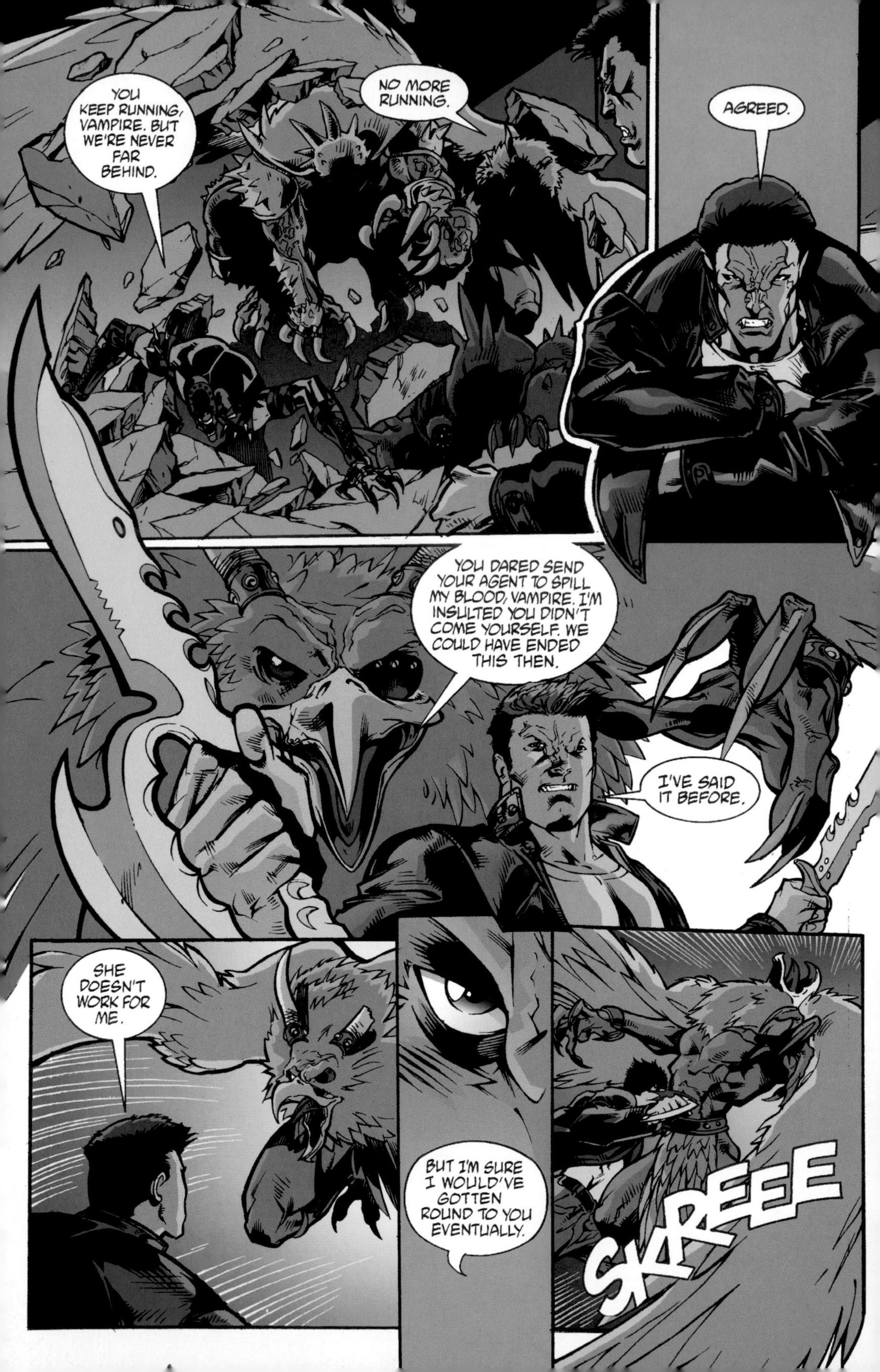
YOU KEEP RUNNING, VAMPIRE. BUT WE'RE NEVER FAR BEHIND.
NO MORE RUNNING.
AGREED.
YOU DARED SEND YOUR AGENT TO SPILL MY BLOOD, VAMPIRE. I'M INSULTED YOU DIDN'T COME YOURSELF. WE COULD HAVE ENDED THIS THEN.
I'VE SAID IT BEFORE.
SHE DOESN'T WORK FOR ME.
BUT I'M SURE I WOULD'VE GOTTEN ROUND TO YOU EVENTUALLY.
SKREEEE

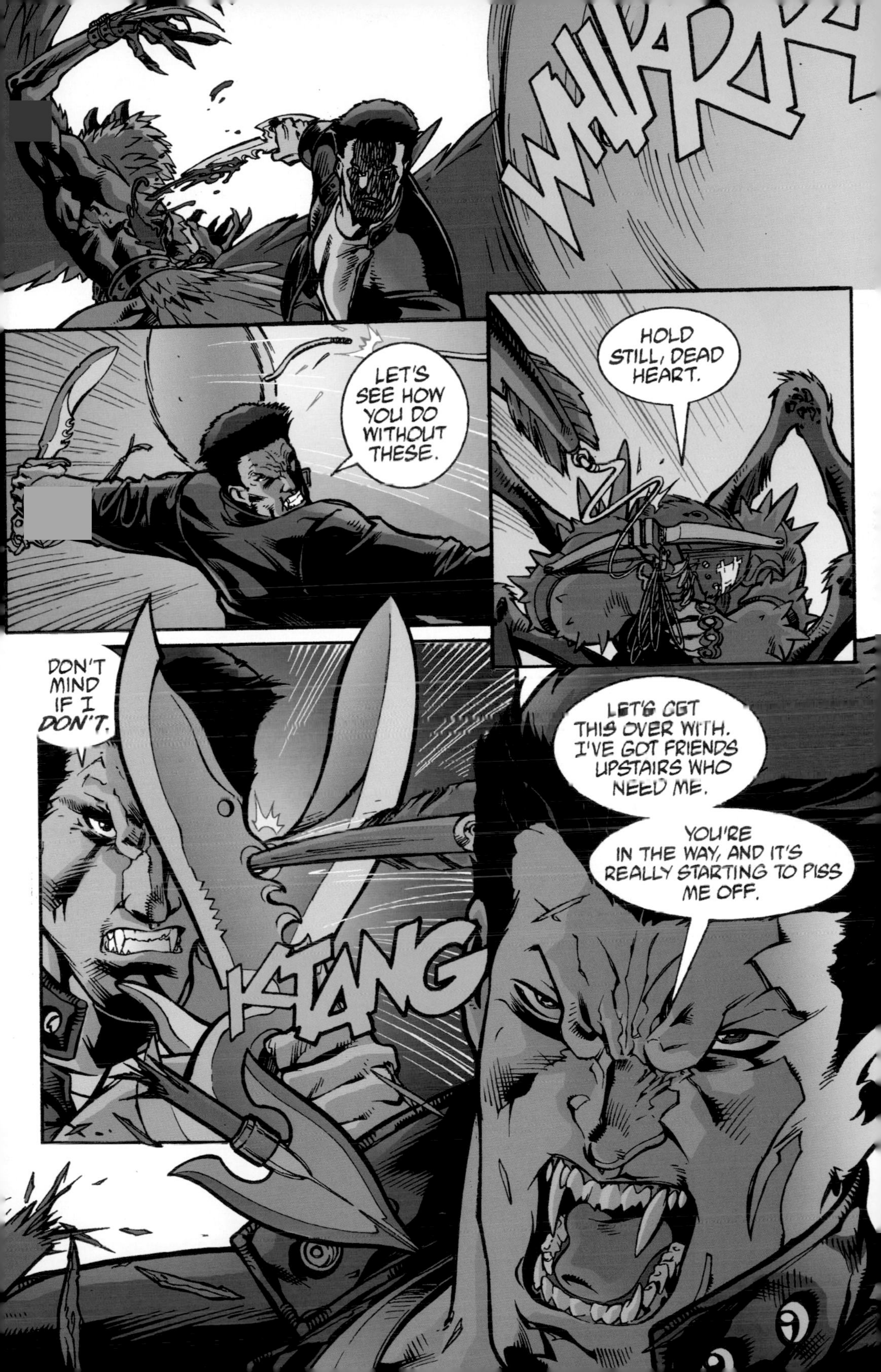
LET'S SEE HOW YOU DO WITHOUT THESE.
HOLD STILL, DEAD HEART.
DON'T MIND IF I *DON'T*.
KLANG
LET'S GET THIS OVER WITH. I'VE GOT FRIENDS UPSTAIRS WHO NEED ME.
YOU'RE IN THE WAY, AND IT'S REALLY STARTING TO PISS ME OFF.

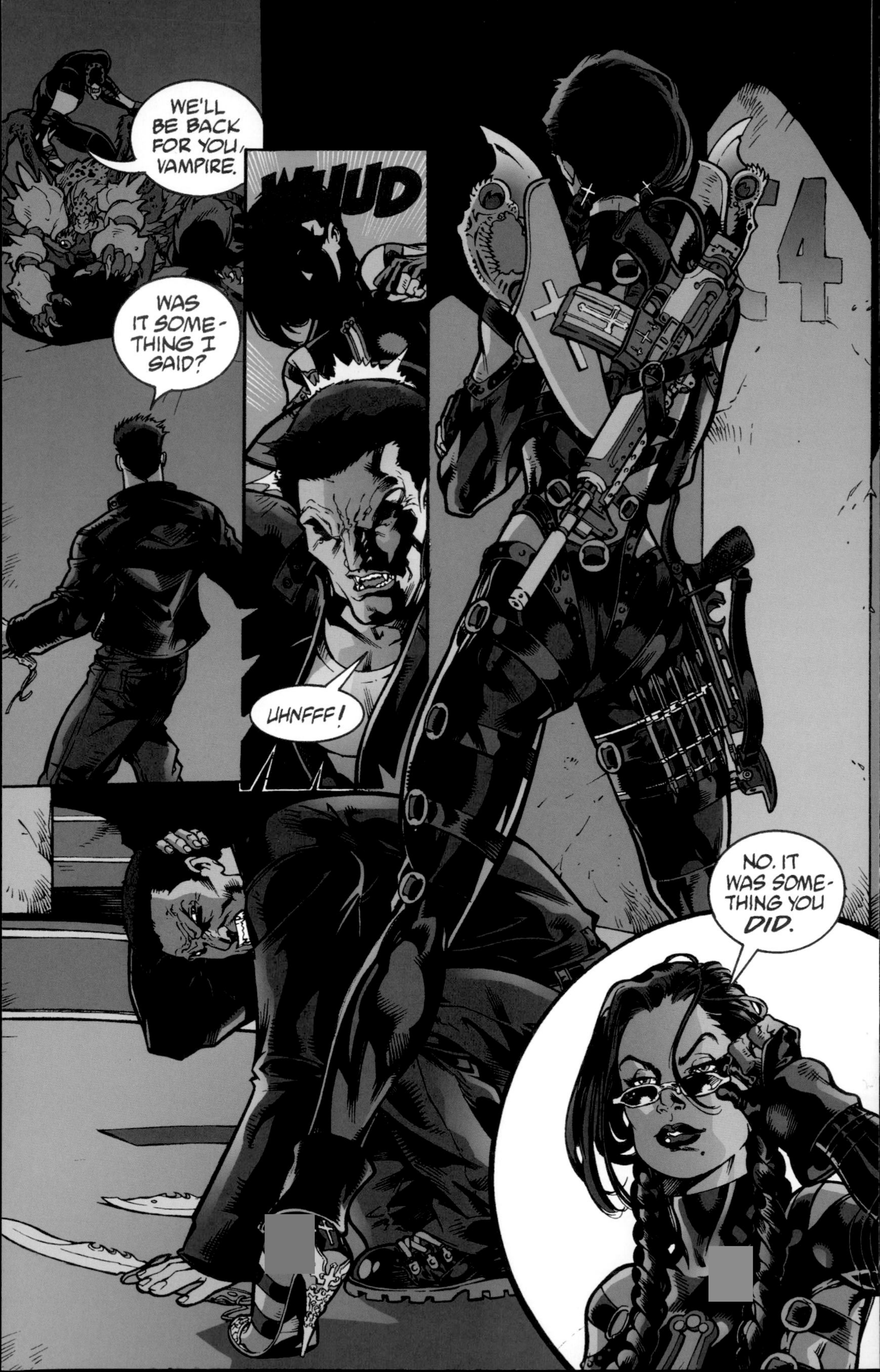
WE'LL BE BACK FOR YOU, VAMPIRE.
WHUD
WAS IT SOME-THING I SAID?
UHNFFF!
NO. IT WAS SOME-THING YOU DID.

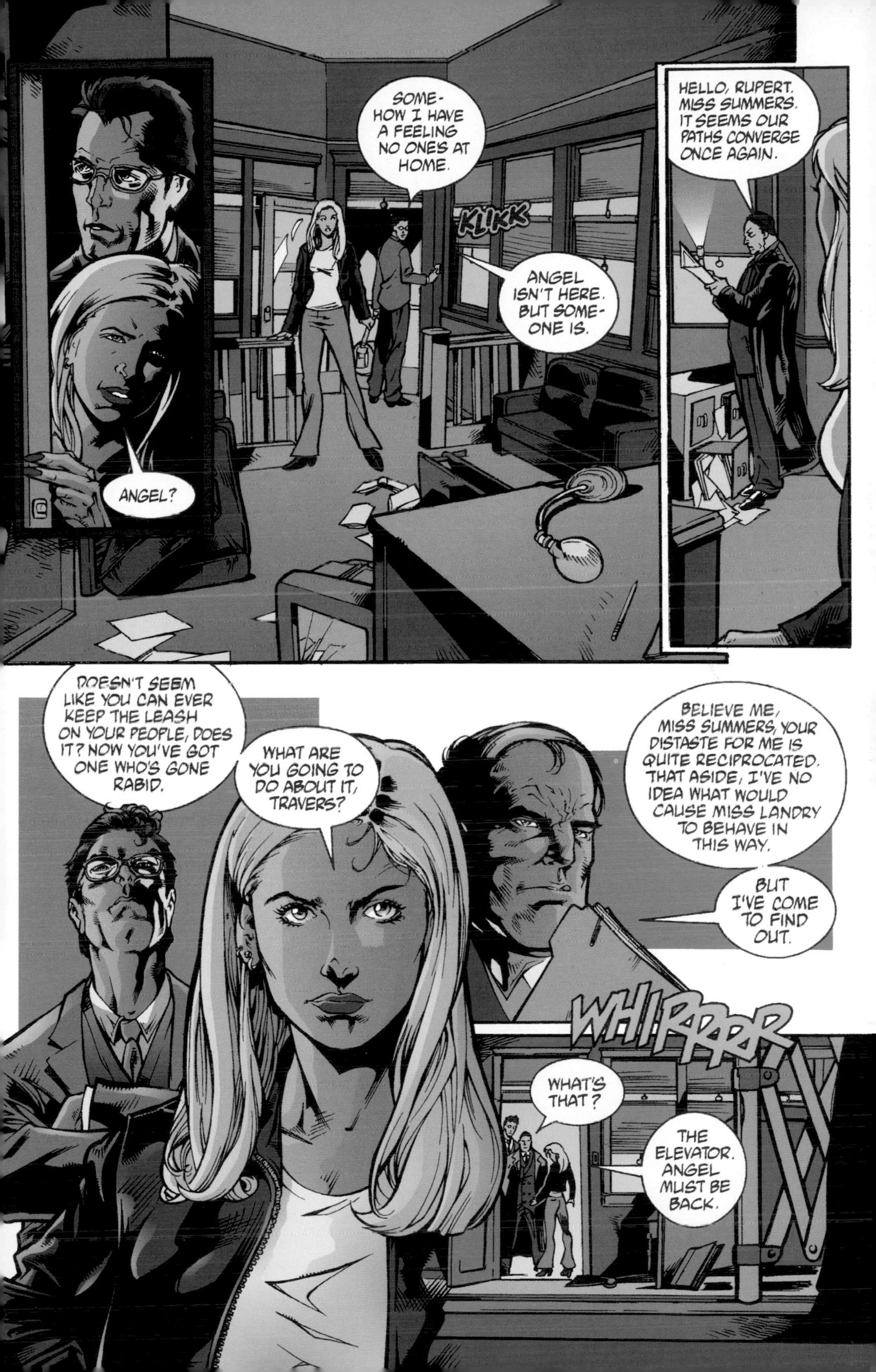
ANGEL?
SOME-HOW I HAVE A FEELING NO ONE'S AT HOME.
KLIKK
ANGEL ISN'T HERE. BUT SOME-ONE IS.
HELLO, RUPERT. MISS SUMMERS. IT SEEMS OUR PATHS CONVERGE ONCE AGAIN.
DOESN'T SEEM LIKE YOU CAN EVER KEEP THE LEASH ON YOUR PEOPLE, DOES IT? NOW YOU'VE GOT ONE WHO'S GONE RABID.
WHAT ARE YOU GOING TO DO ABOUT IT, TRAVERS?
BELIEVE ME, MISS SUMMERS, YOUR DISTASTE FOR ME IS QUITE RECIPROCATED. THAT ASIDE, I'VE NO IDEA WHAT WOULD CAUSE MISS LANDRY TO BEHAVE IN THIS WAY.
BUT I'VE COME TO FIND OUT.
WHIRRRR
WHAT'S THAT?
THE ELEVATOR. ANGEL MUST BE BACK.

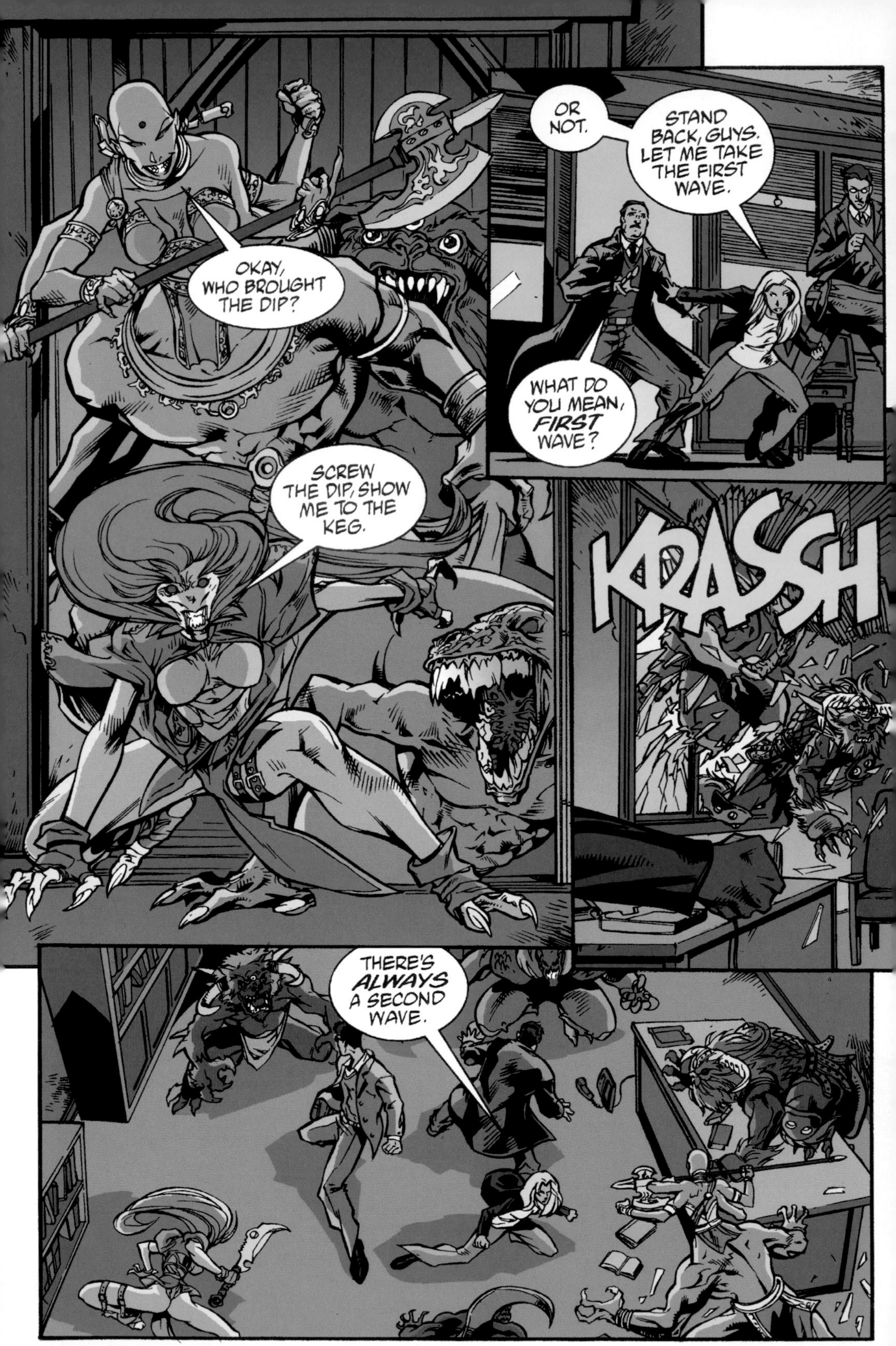
OKAY, WHO BROUGHT THE DIP?
SCREW THE DIP, SHOW ME TO THE KEG.
OR NOT.
STAND BACK, GUYS. LET ME TAKE THE FIRST WAVE.
WHAT DO YOU MEAN, **FIRST** WAVE?
KRASSH
THERE'S **ALWAYS** A SECOND WAVE.

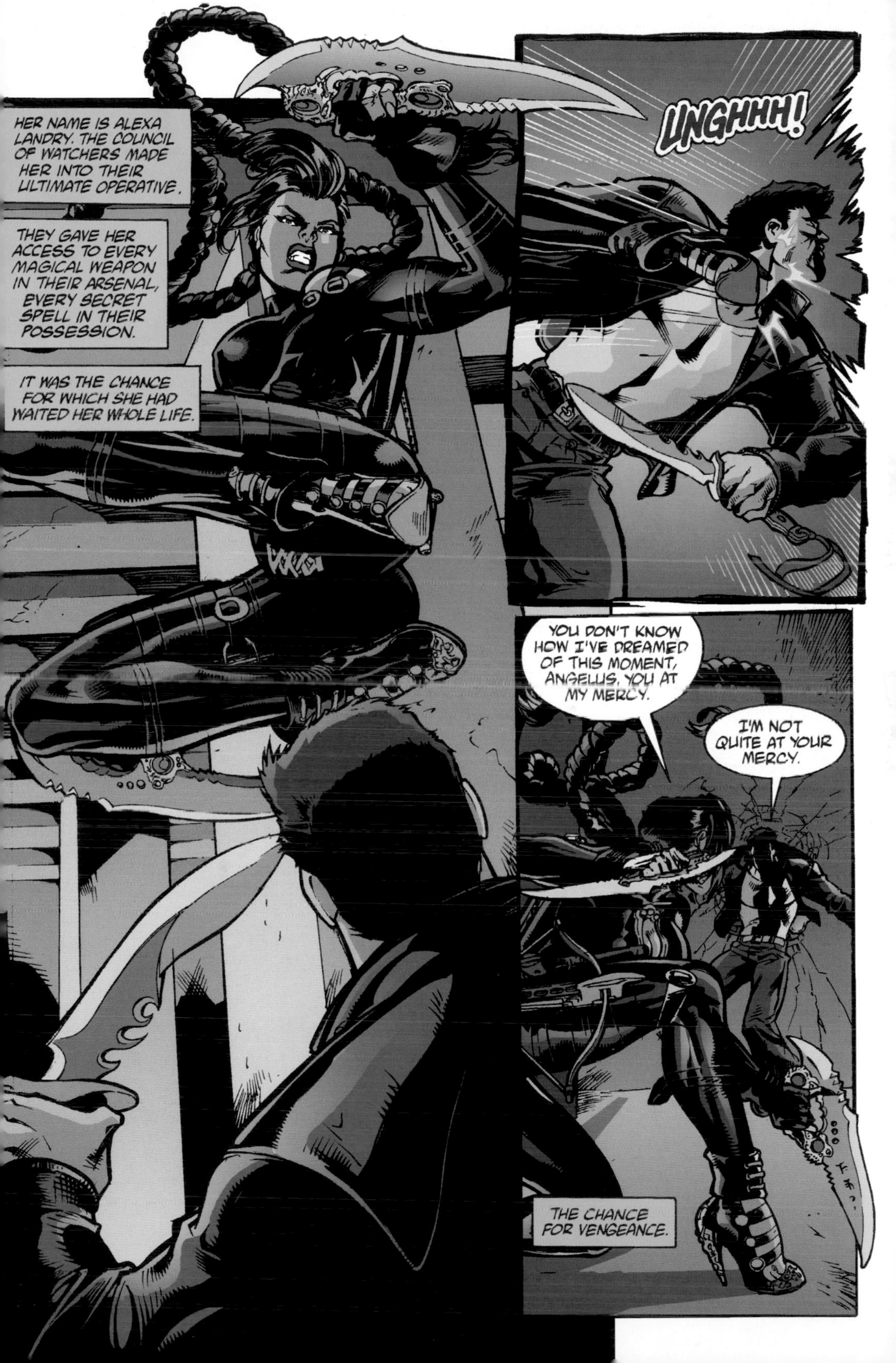
HER NAME IS ALEXA LANDRY. THE COUNCIL OF WATCHERS MADE HER INTO THEIR ULTIMATE OPERATIVE.
THEY GAVE HER ACCESS TO EVERY MAGICAL WEAPON IN THEIR ARSENAL, EVERY SECRET SPELL IN THEIR POSSESSION.
IT WAS THE CHANCE FOR WHICH SHE HAD WAITED HER WHOLE LIFE.
UNGHHH!
YOU DON'T KNOW HOW I'VE DREAMED OF THIS MOMENT, ANGELUS. YOU AT MY MERCY.
I'M NOT QUITE AT YOUR MERCY.
THE CHANCE FOR VENGEANCE.

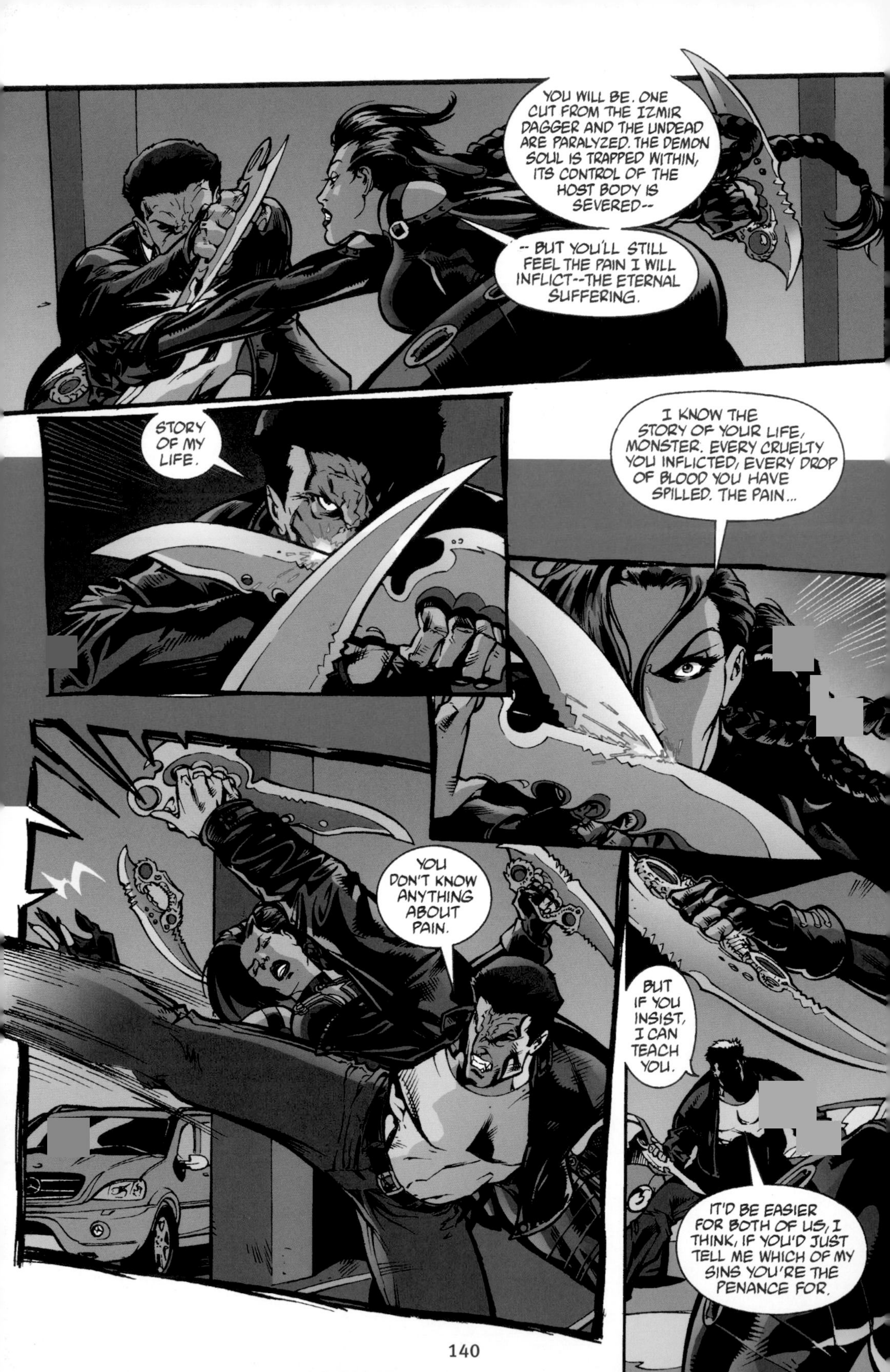
YOU WILL BE. ONE CUT FROM THE IZMIR DAGGER AND THE UNDEAD ARE PARALYZED. THE DEMON SOUL IS TRAPPED WITHIN, ITS CONTROL OF THE HOST BODY IS SEVERED--
-- BUT YOU'LL STILL FEEL THE PAIN I WILL INFLICT--THE ETERNAL SUFFERING.
STORY OF MY LIFE.
I KNOW THE STORY OF YOUR LIFE, MONSTER. EVERY CRUELTY YOU INFLICTED, EVERY DROP OF BLOOD YOU HAVE SPILLED. THE PAIN...
YOU DON'T KNOW ANYTHING ABOUT PAIN.
BUT IF YOU INSIST, I CAN TEACH YOU.
IT'D BE EASIER FOR BOTH OF US, I THINK, IF YOU'D JUST TELL ME WHICH OF MY SINS YOU'RE THE PENANCE FOR.

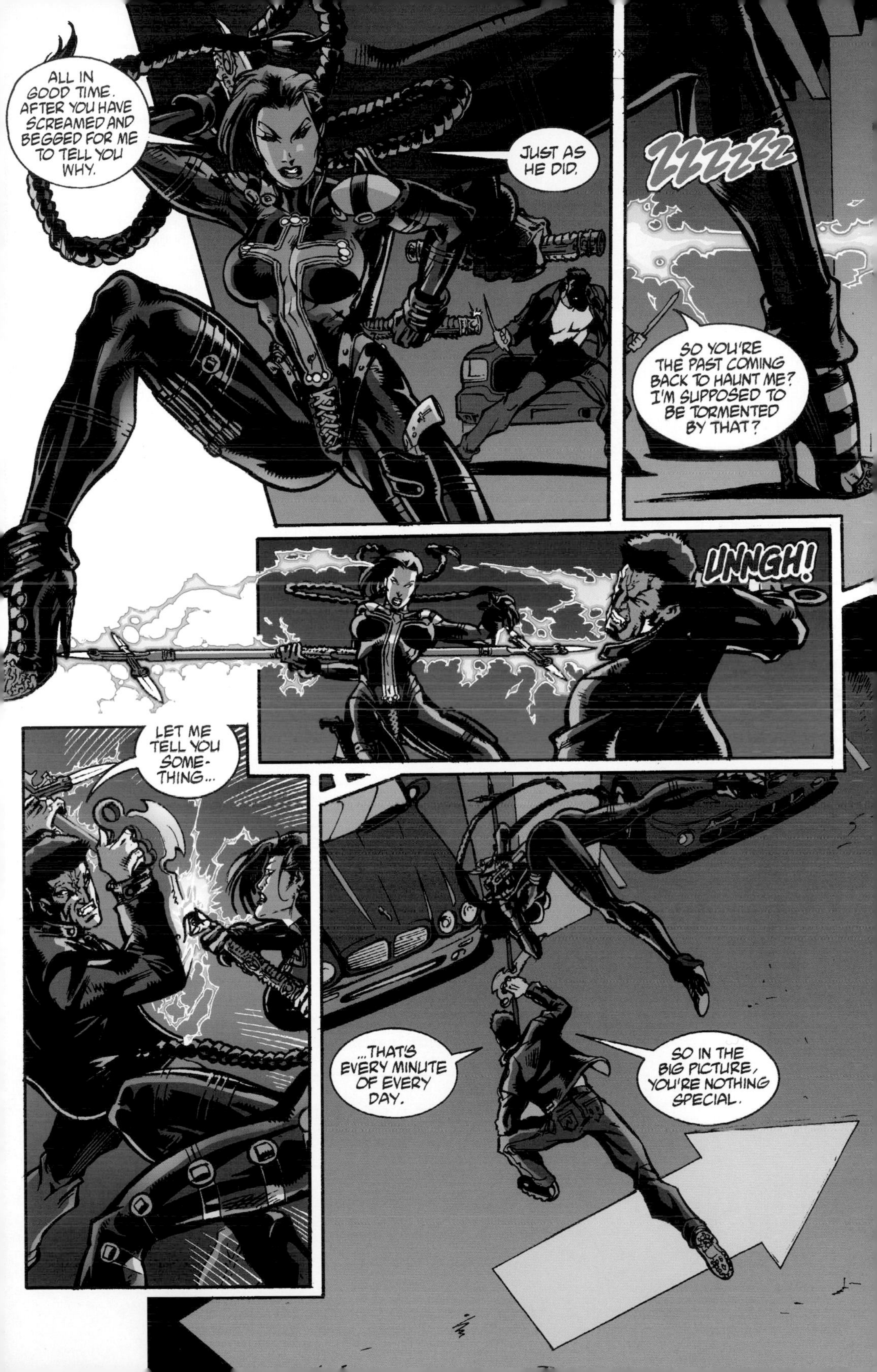
ALL IN GOOD TIME. AFTER YOU HAVE SCREAMED AND BEGGED FOR ME TO TELL YOU WHY.
JUST AS HE DID.
ZZZZZZ
SO YOU'RE THE PAST COMING BACK TO HAUNT ME? I'M SUPPOSED TO BE TORMENTED BY THAT?
UNNGH!
LET ME TELL YOU SOME-THING...
...THAT'S EVERY MINUTE OF EVERY DAY.
SO IN THE BIG PICTURE, YOU'RE NOTHING SPECIAL.

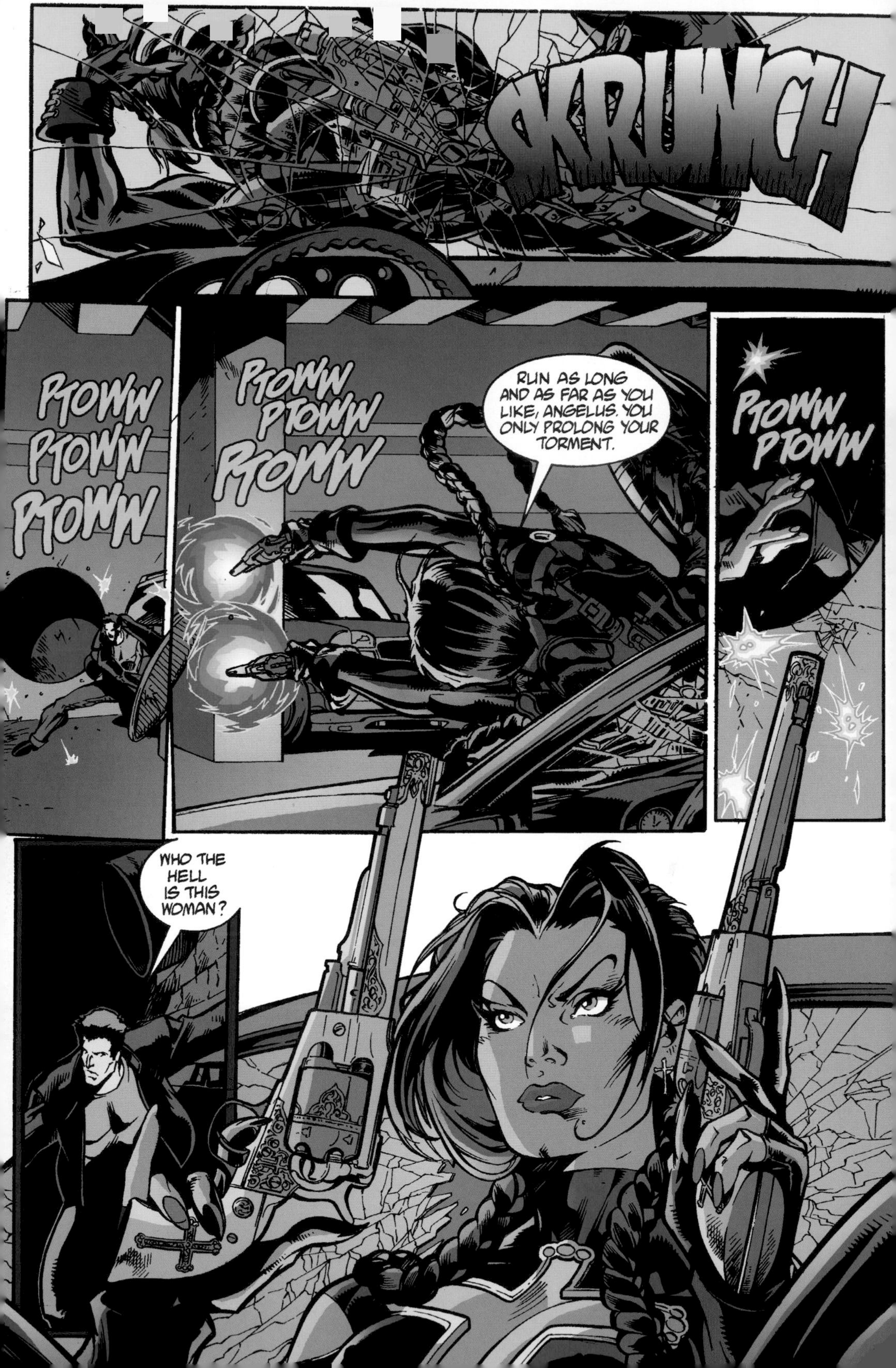
KRUNCH
PTOWW PTOWW PTOWW
PTOWW PTOWW PTOWW
RUN AS LONG AND AS FAR AS YOU LIKE, ANGELUS. YOU ONLY PROLONG YOUR TORMENT.
PTOWW PTOWW
WHO THE HELL IS THIS WOMAN?

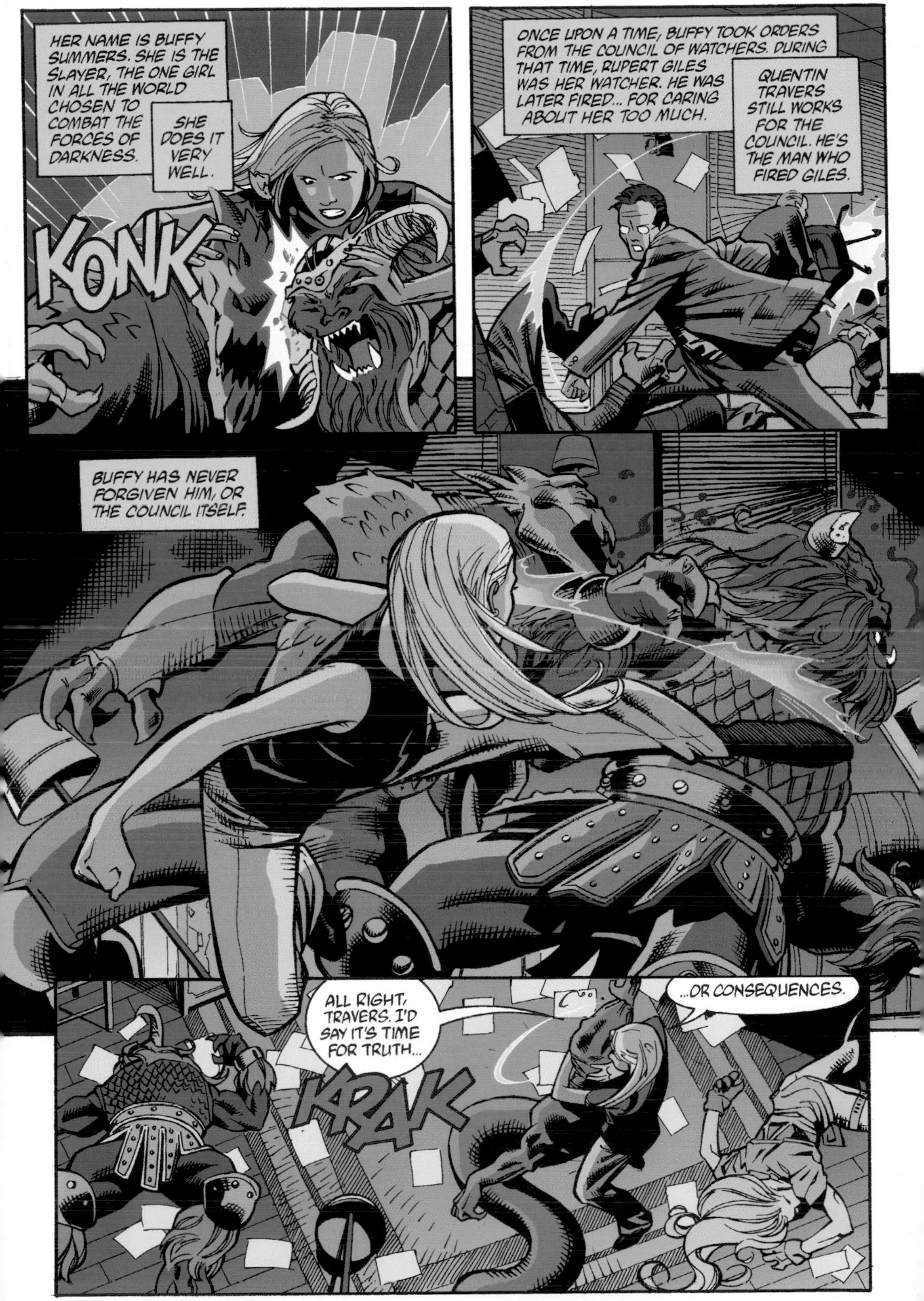
HER NAME IS BUFFY SUMMERS. SHE IS THE SLAYER, THE ONE GIRL IN ALL THE WORLD CHOSEN TO COMBAT THE FORCES OF DARKNESS.
SHE DOES IT VERY WELL.
KONK
ONCE UPON A TIME, BUFFY TOOK ORDERS FROM THE COUNCIL OF WATCHERS. DURING THAT TIME, RUPERT GILES WAS HER WATCHER. HE WAS LATER FIRED... FOR CARING ABOUT HER TOO MUCH.
QUENTIN TRAVERS STILL WORKS FOR THE COUNCIL. HE'S THE MAN WHO FIRED GILES.
BUFFY HAS NEVER FORGIVEN HIM, OR THE COUNCIL ITSELF.
ALL RIGHT, TRAVERS. I'D SAY IT'S TIME FOR TRUTH...
...OR CONSEQUENCES.
KRAK

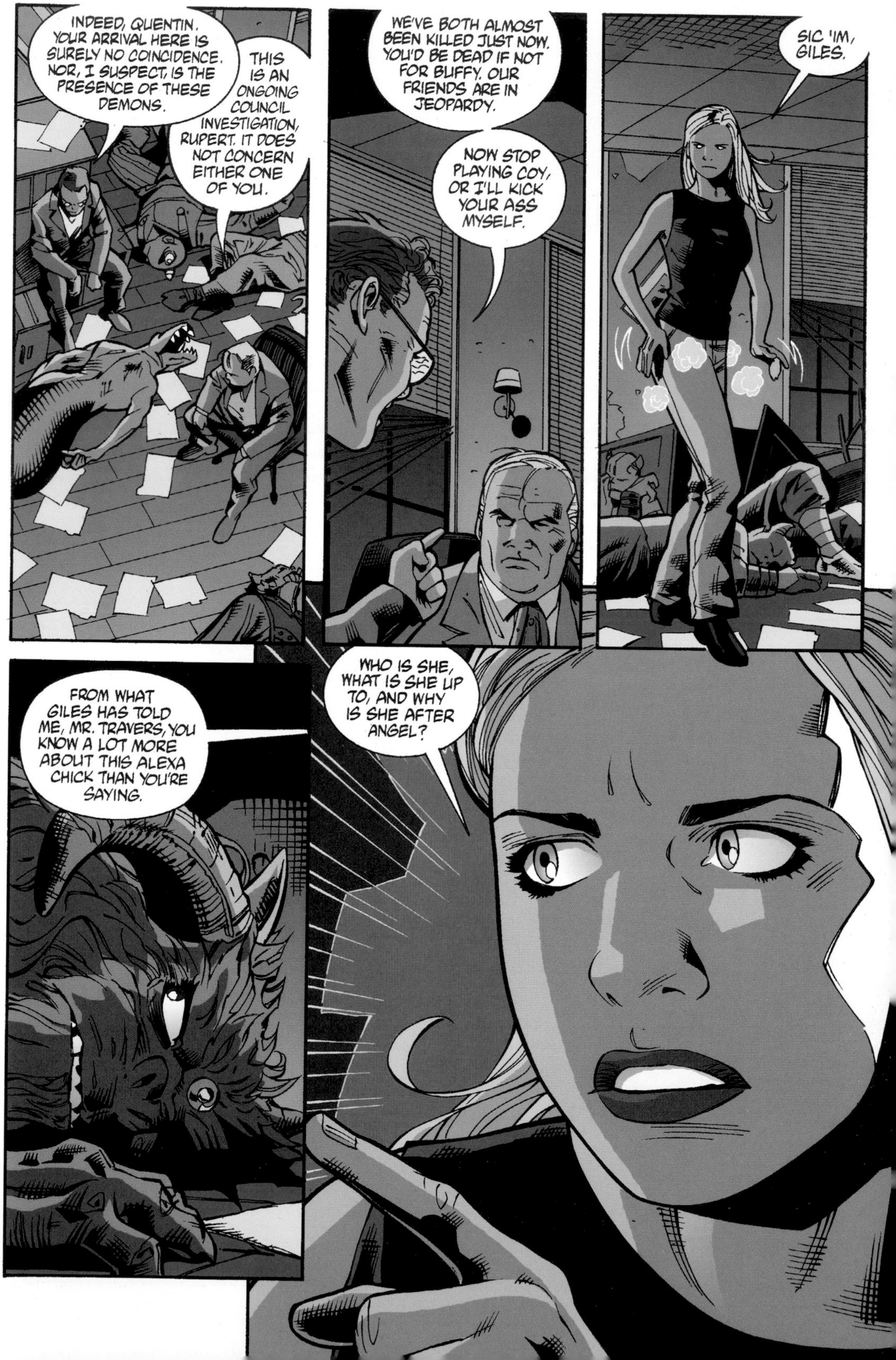
INDEED, QUENTIN. YOUR ARRIVAL HERE IS SURELY NO COINCIDENCE. NOR, I SUSPECT, IS THE PRESENCE OF THESE DEMONS.
THIS IS AN ONGOING COUNCIL INVESTIGATION, RUPERT. IT DOES NOT CONCERN EITHER ONE OF YOU.
WE'VE BOTH ALMOST BEEN KILLED JUST NOW. YOU'D BE DEAD IF NOT FOR BUFFY. OUR FRIENDS ARE IN JEOPARDY.
NOW STOP PLAYING COY, OR I'LL KICK YOUR ASS MYSELF.
SIC 'IM, GILES.
FROM WHAT GILES HAS TOLD ME, MR. TRAVERS, YOU KNOW A LOT MORE ABOUT THIS ALEXA CHICK THAN YOU'RE SAYING.
WHO IS SHE, WHAT IS SHE UP TO, AND WHY IS SHE AFTER ANGEL?

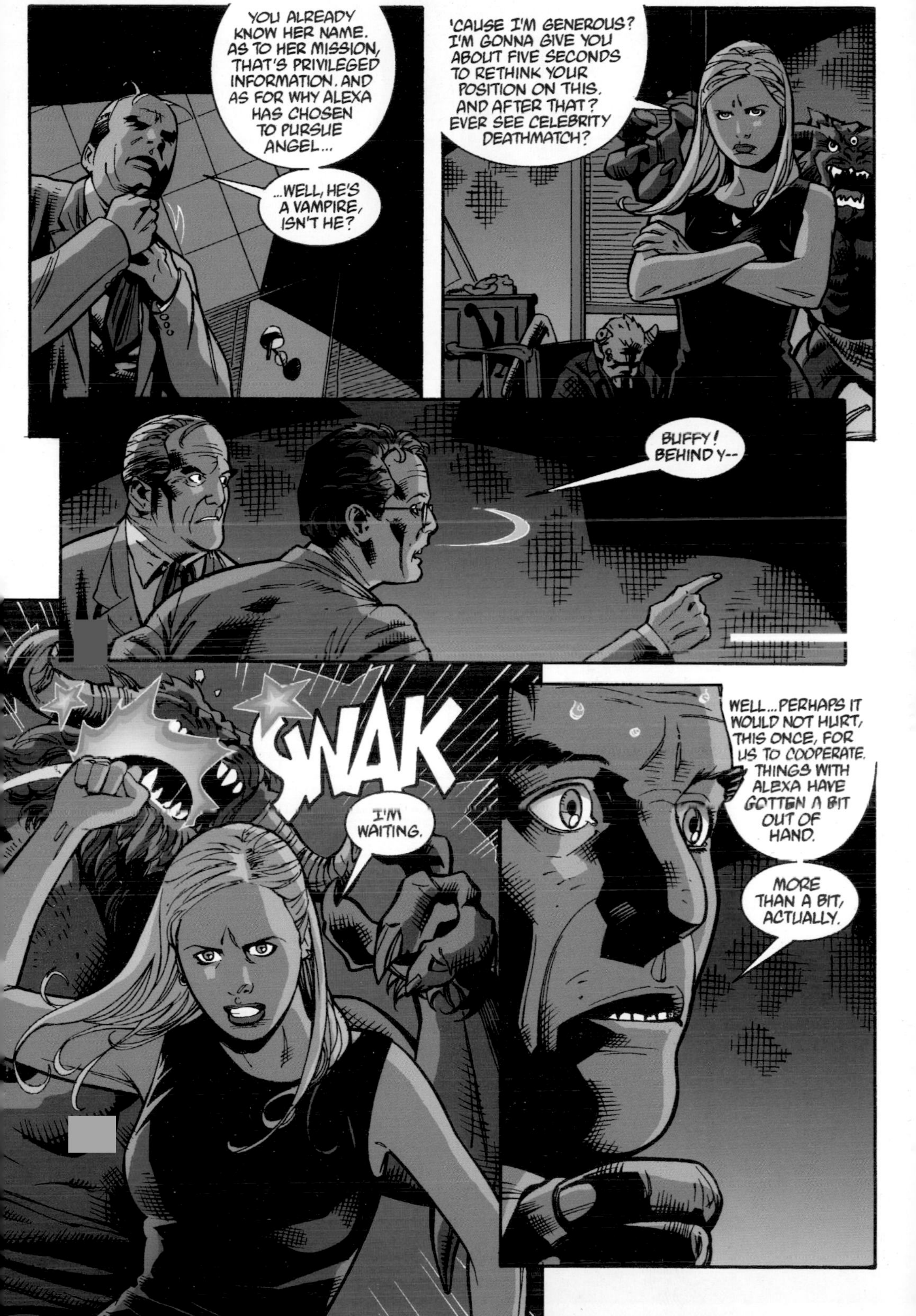

YOU ALREADY KNOW HER NAME. AS TO HER MISSION, THAT'S PRIVILEGED INFORMATION. AND AS FOR WHY ALEXA HAS CHOSEN TO PURSUE ANGEL...
...WELL, HE'S A VAMPIRE, ISN'T HE?
'CAUSE I'M GENEROUS? I'M GONNA GIVE YOU ABOUT FIVE SECONDS TO RETHINK YOUR POSITION ON THIS. AND AFTER THAT? EVER SEE CELEBRITY DEATHMATCH?
BUFFY! BEHIND Y--
SWAK
I'M WAITING.
WELL...PERHAPS IT WOULD NOT HURT, THIS ONCE, FOR US TO COOPERATE. THINGS WITH ALEXA HAVE GOTTEN A BIT OUT OF HAND.
MORE THAN A BIT, ACTUALLY.

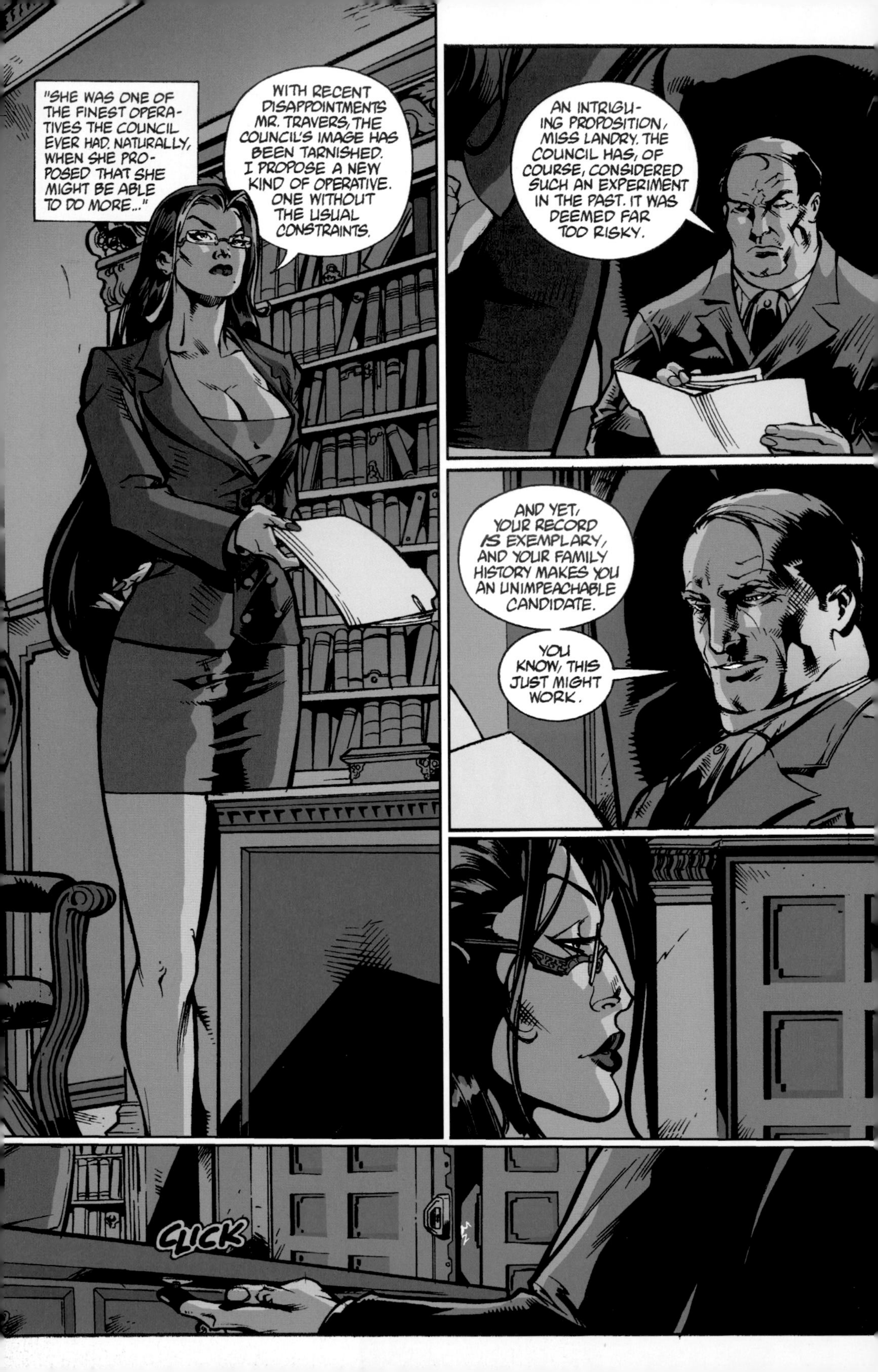
"SHE WAS ONE OF THE FINEST OPERATIVES THE COUNCIL EVER HAD. NATURALLY, WHEN SHE PROPOSED THAT SHE MIGHT BE ABLE TO DO MORE..."
WITH RECENT DISAPPOINTMENTS MR. TRAVERS, THE COUNCIL'S IMAGE HAS BEEN TARNISHED. I PROPOSE A NEW KIND OF OPERATIVE. ONE WITHOUT THE USUAL CONSTRAINTS.
AN INTRIGUING PROPOSITION, MISS LANDRY. THE COUNCIL HAS, OF COURSE, CONSIDERED SUCH AN EXPERIMENT IN THE PAST. IT WAS DEEMED FAR TOO RISKY.
AND YET, YOUR RECORD IS EXEMPLARY, AND YOUR FAMILY HISTORY MAKES YOU AN UNIMPEACHABLE CANDIDATE.
YOU KNOW, THIS JUST MIGHT WORK.
CLICK

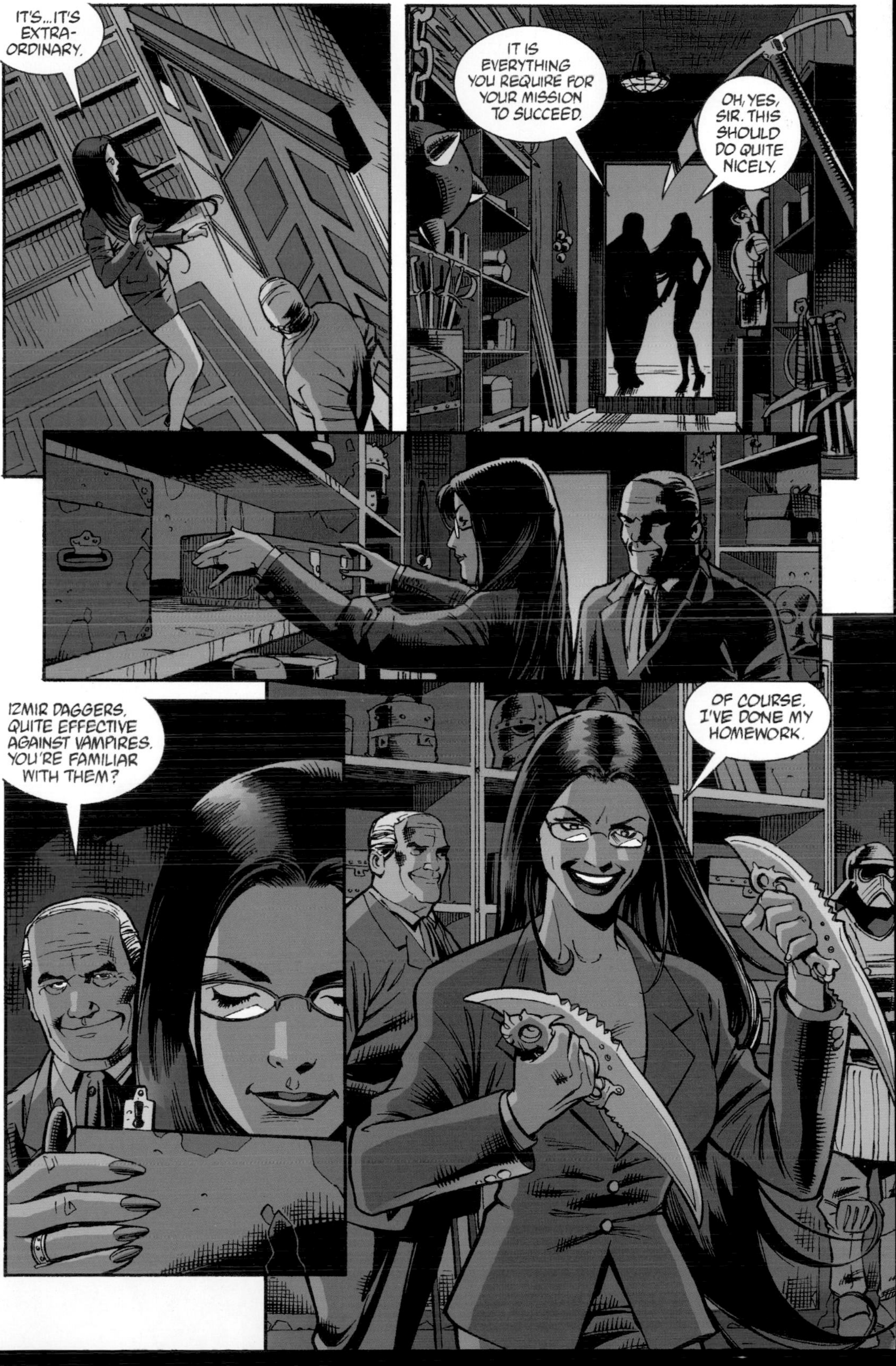
IT'S...IT'S EXTRA-ORDINARY.
IT IS EVERYTHING YOU REQUIRE FOR YOUR MISSION TO SUCCEED.
OH, YES, SIR. THIS SHOULD DO QUITE NICELY.
IZMIR DAGGERS. QUITE EFFECTIVE AGAINST VAMPIRES. YOU'RE FAMILIAR WITH THEM?
OF COURSE. I'VE DONE MY HOMEWORK.

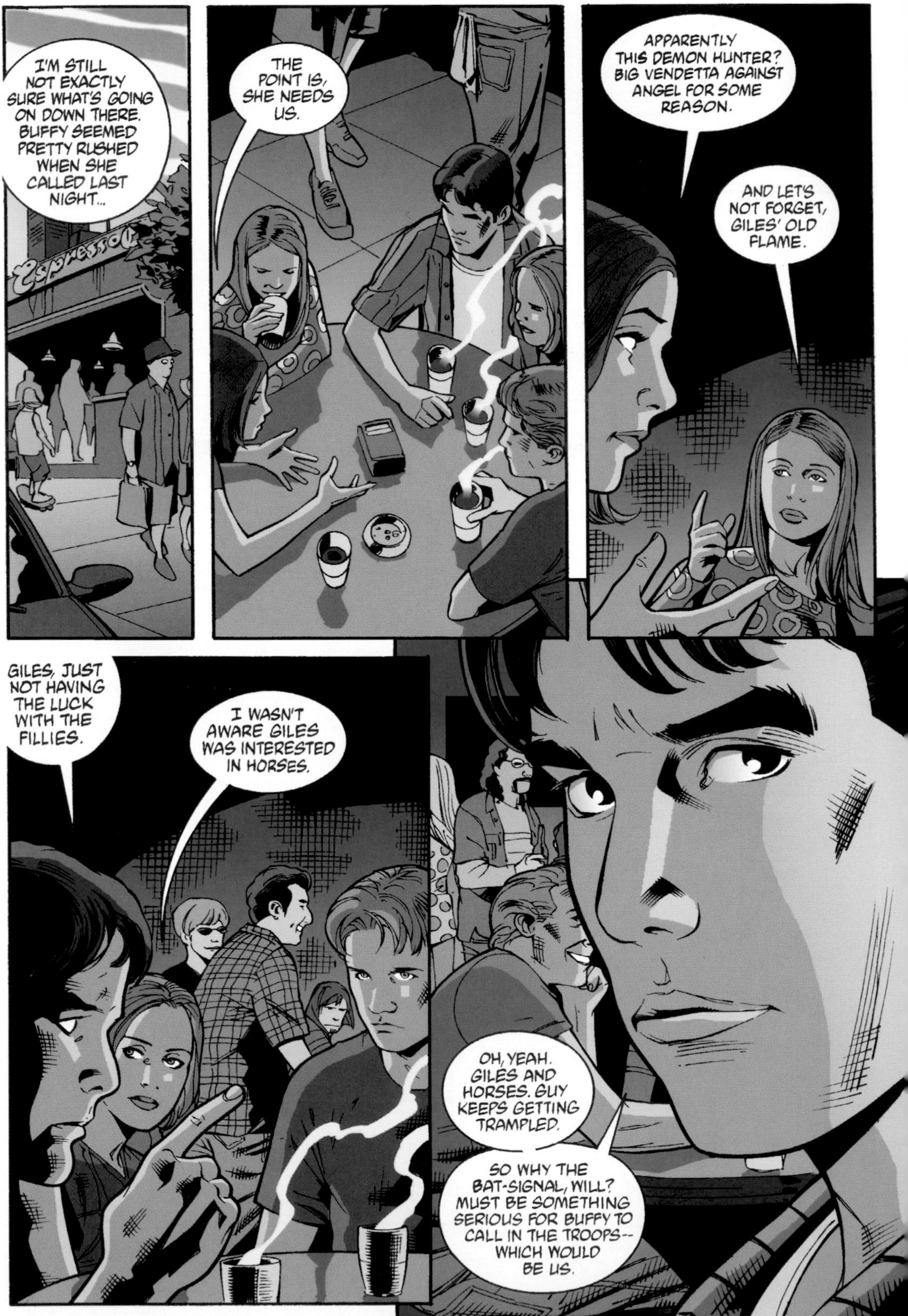
I'M STILL NOT EXACTLY SURE WHAT'S GOING ON DOWN THERE. BUFFY SEEMED PRETTY RUSHED WHEN SHE CALLED LAST NIGHT...
Espresso
THE POINT IS, SHE NEEDS US.
APPARENTLY THIS DEMON HUNTER? BIG VENDETTA AGAINST ANGEL FOR SOME REASON.
AND LET'S NOT FORGET, GILES' OLD FLAME.
GILES, JUST NOT HAVING THE LUCK WITH THE FILLIES.
I WASN'T AWARE GILES WAS INTERESTED IN HORSES.
OH, YEAH. GILES AND HORSES. GUY KEEPS GETTING TRAMPLED.
SO WHY THE BAT-SIGNAL, WILL? MUST BE SOMETHING SERIOUS FOR BUFFY TO CALL IN THE TROOPS-- WHICH WOULD BE US.

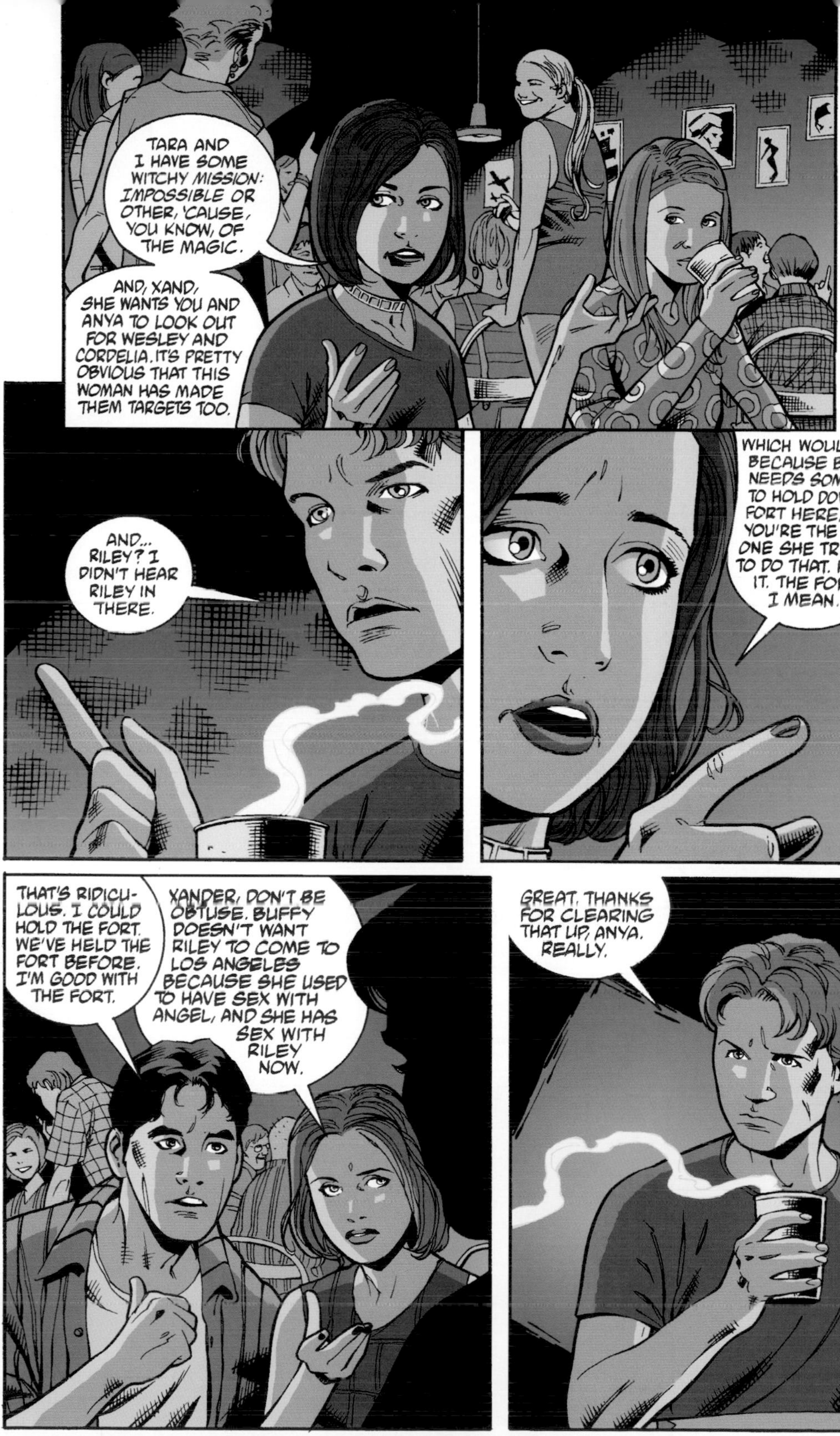
TARA AND I HAVE SOME WITCHY MISSION: IMPOSSIBLE OR OTHER, 'CAUSE, YOU KNOW, OF THE MAGIC.
AND, XAND, SHE WANTS YOU AND ANYA TO LOOK OUT FOR WESLEY AND CORDELIA. IT'S PRETTY OBVIOUS THAT THIS WOMAN HAS MADE THEM TARGETS TOO.
AND... RILEY? I DIDN'T HEAR RILEY IN THERE.
RIGHT. WHICH WOULD BE BECAUSE BUFFY NEEDS SOMEONE TO HOLD DOWN THE FORT HERE, AND YOU'RE THE ONLY ONE SHE TRUSTS TO DO THAT. HOLD IT. THE FORT, I MEAN.
THAT'S RIDICU-LOUS. I COULD HOLD THE FORT. WE'VE HELD THE FORT BEFORE. I'M GOOD WITH THE FORT.
XANDER, DON'T BE OBTUSE. BUFFY DOESN'T WANT RILEY TO COME TO LOS ANGELES BECAUSE SHE USED TO HAVE SEX WITH ANGEL, AND SHE HAS SEX WITH RILEY NOW.
GREAT. THANKS FOR CLEARING THAT UP, ANYA. REALLY.

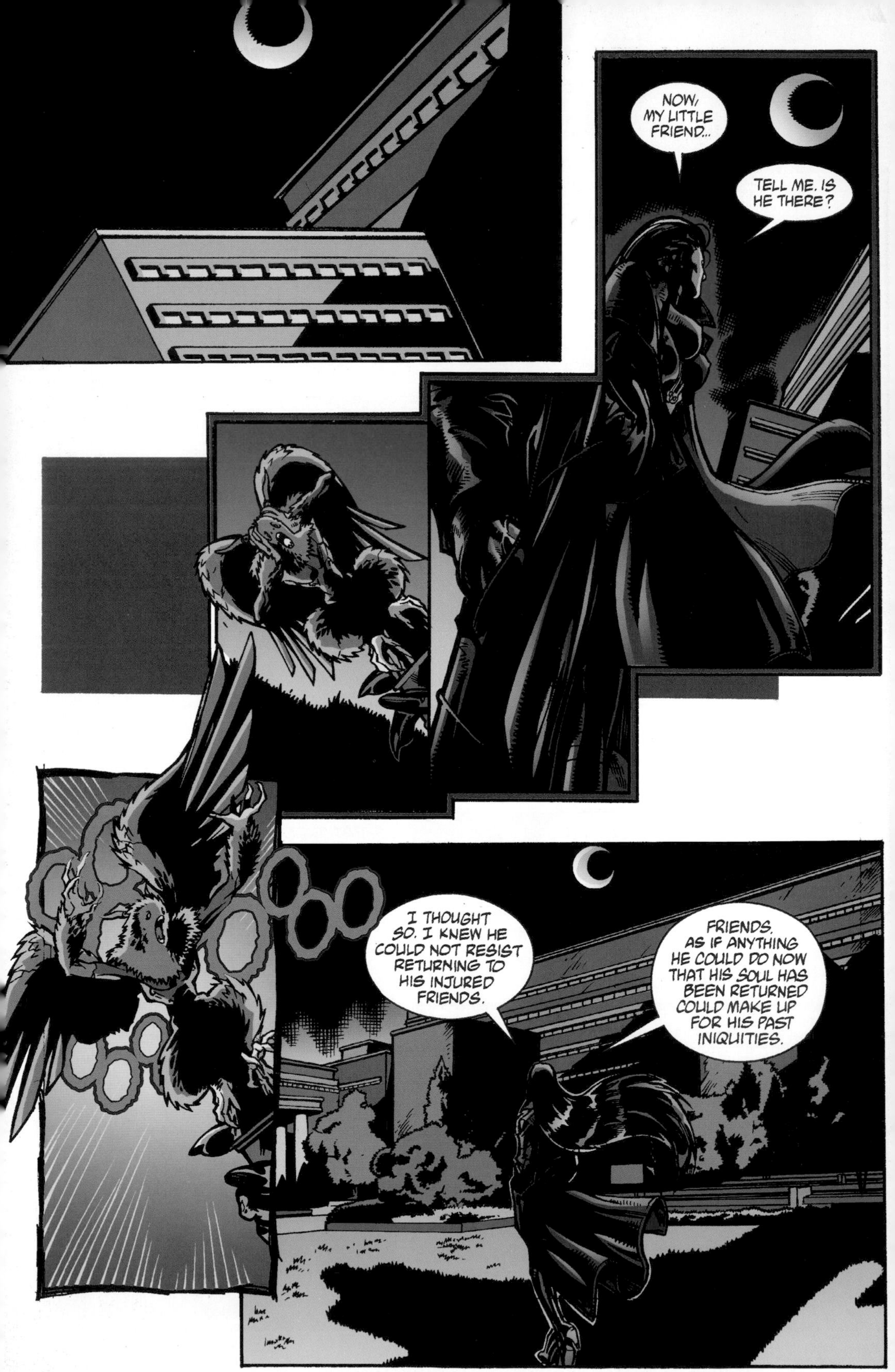
NOW, MY LITTLE FRIEND...
TELL ME. IS HE THERE?
I THOUGHT SO. I KNEW HE COULD NOT RESIST RETURNING TO HIS INJURED FRIENDS.
FRIENDS. AS IF ANYTHING HE COULD DO NOW THAT HIS SOUL HAS BEEN RETURNED COULD MAKE UP FOR HIS PAST INIQUITIES.

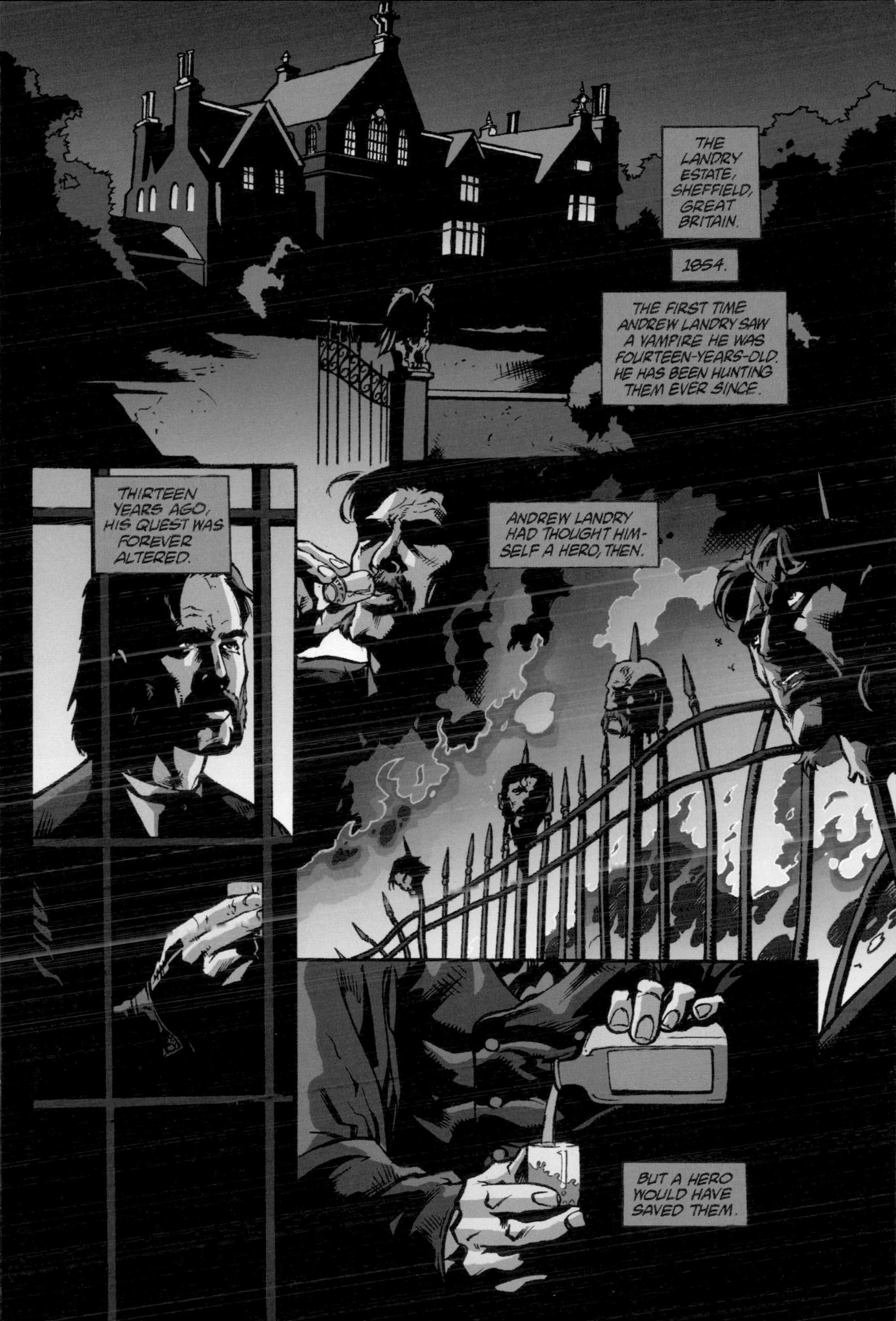
THE LANDRY ESTATE, SHEFFIELD, GREAT BRITAIN.
1854.
THE FIRST TIME ANDREW LANDRY SAW A VAMPIRE HE WAS FOURTEEN-YEARS-OLD. HE HAS BEEN HUNTING THEM EVER SINCE.
THIRTEEN YEARS AGO, HIS QUEST WAS FOREVER ALTERED.
ANDREW LANDRY HAD THOUGHT HIM-SELF A HERO, THEN.
BUT A HERO WOULD HAVE SAVED THEM.

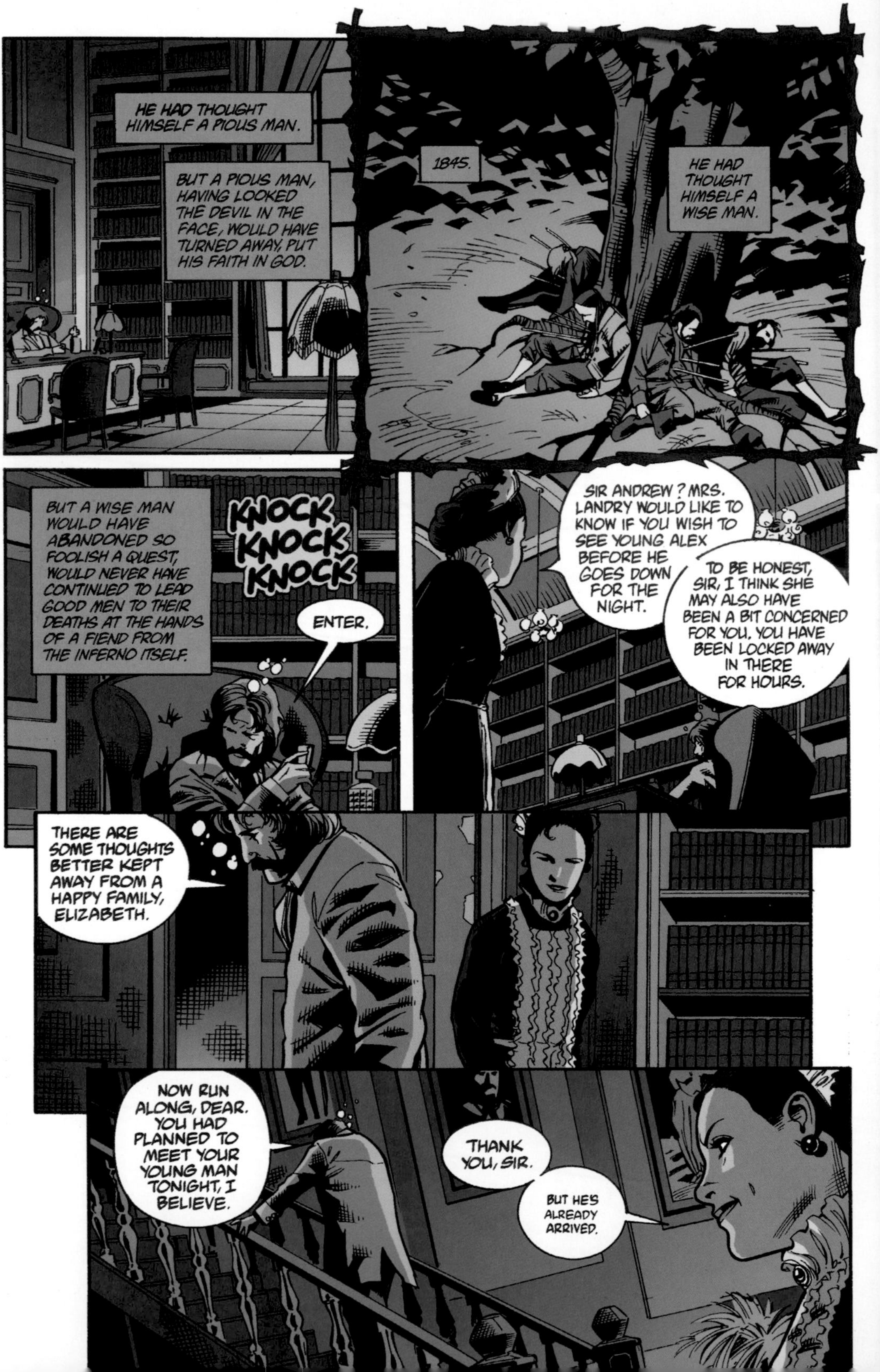

HE HAD THOUGHT HIMSELF A PIOUS MAN.
BUT A PIOUS MAN, HAVING LOOKED THE DEVIL IN THE FACE, WOULD HAVE TURNED AWAY, PUT HIS FAITH IN GOD.
1845.
HE HAD THOUGHT HIMSELF A WISE MAN.
BUT A WISE MAN WOULD HAVE ABANDONED SO FOOLISH A QUEST, WOULD NEVER HAVE CONTINUED TO LEAD GOOD MEN TO THEIR DEATHS AT THE HANDS OF A FIEND FROM THE INFERNO ITSELF.
KNOCK KNOCK KNOCK
ENTER.
SIR ANDREW? MRS. LANDRY WOULD LIKE TO KNOW IF YOU WISH TO SEE YOUNG ALEX BEFORE HE GOES DOWN FOR THE NIGHT.
TO BE HONEST, SIR, I THINK SHE MAY ALSO HAVE BEEN A BIT CONCERNED FOR YOU. YOU HAVE BEEN LOCKED AWAY IN THERE FOR HOURS.
THERE ARE SOME THOUGHTS BETTER KEPT AWAY FROM A HAPPY FAMILY, ELIZABETH.
NOW RUN ALONG, DEAR. YOU HAD PLANNED TO MEET YOUR YOUNG MAN TONIGHT, I BELIEVE.
THANK YOU, SIR.
BUT HE'S ALREADY ARRIVED.

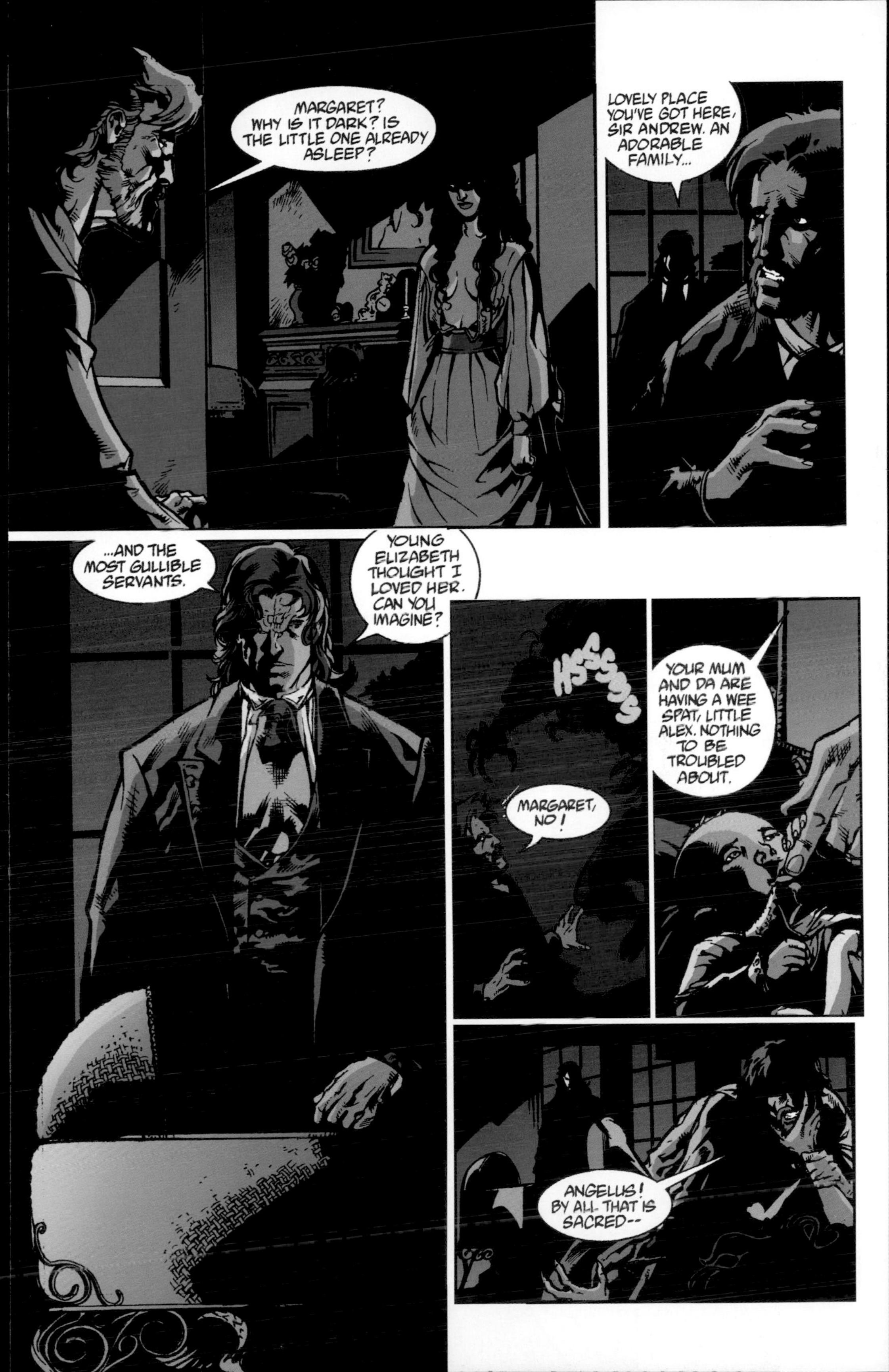
MARGARET? WHY IS IT DARK? IS THE LITTLE ONE ALREADY ASLEEP?
LOVELY PLACE YOU'VE GOT HERE, SIR ANDREW. AN ADORABLE FAMILY...
...AND THE MOST GULLIBLE SERVANTS.
YOUNG ELIZABETH THOUGHT I LOVED HER. CAN YOU IMAGINE?
HSSSSS
MARGARET, NO!
YOUR MUM AND DA ARE HAVING A WEE SPAT, LITTLE ALEX. NOTHING TO BE TROUBLED ABOUT.
ANGELUS! BY ALL THAT IS SACRED--

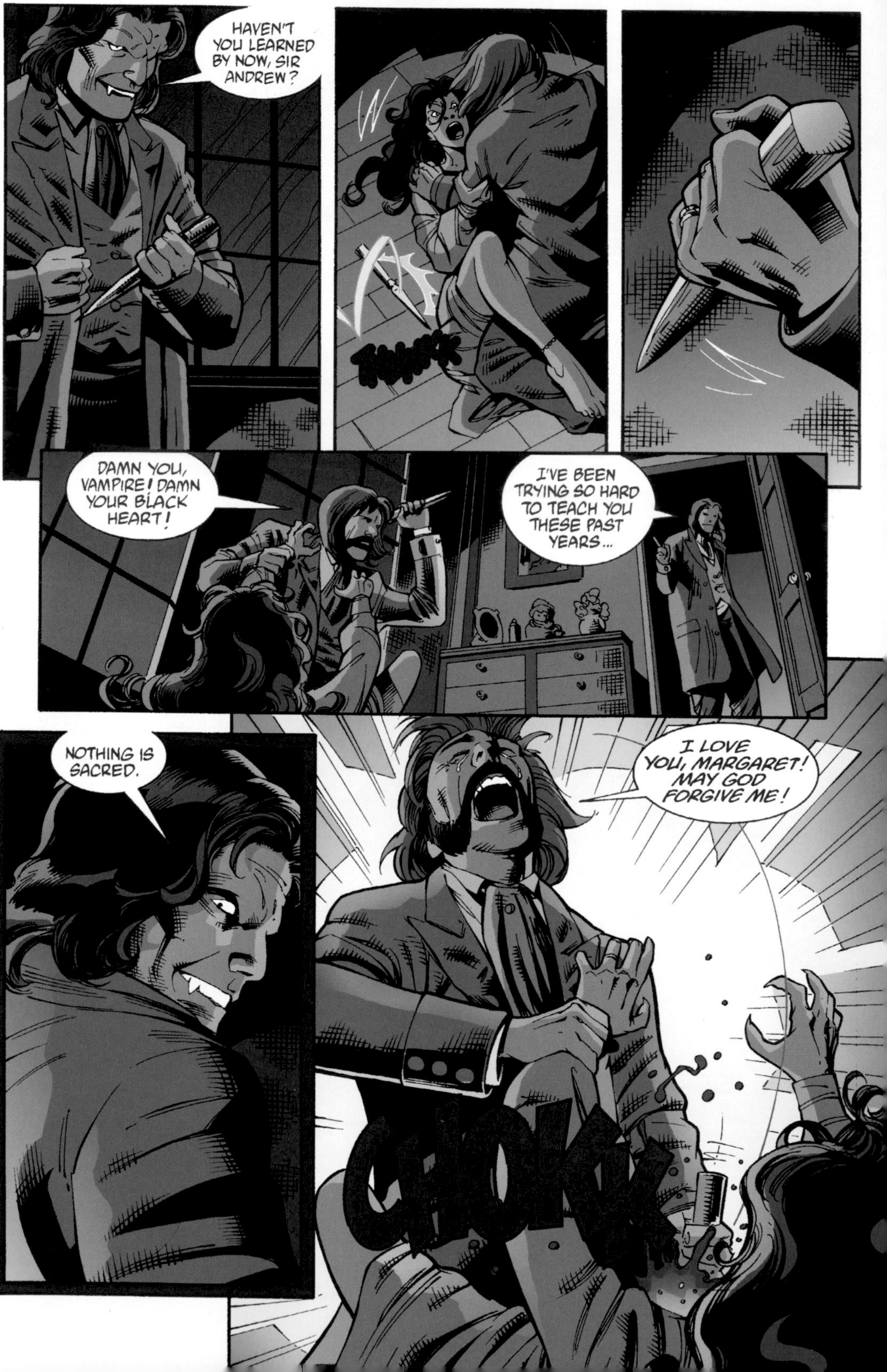
HAVEN'T YOU LEARNED BY NOW, SIR ANDREW?
THWAKK
DAMN YOU, VAMPIRE! DAMN YOUR BLACK HEART!
I'VE BEEN TRYING SO HARD TO TEACH YOU THESE PAST YEARS...
NOTHING IS SACRED.
I LOVE YOU, MARGARET! MAY GOD FORGIVE ME!

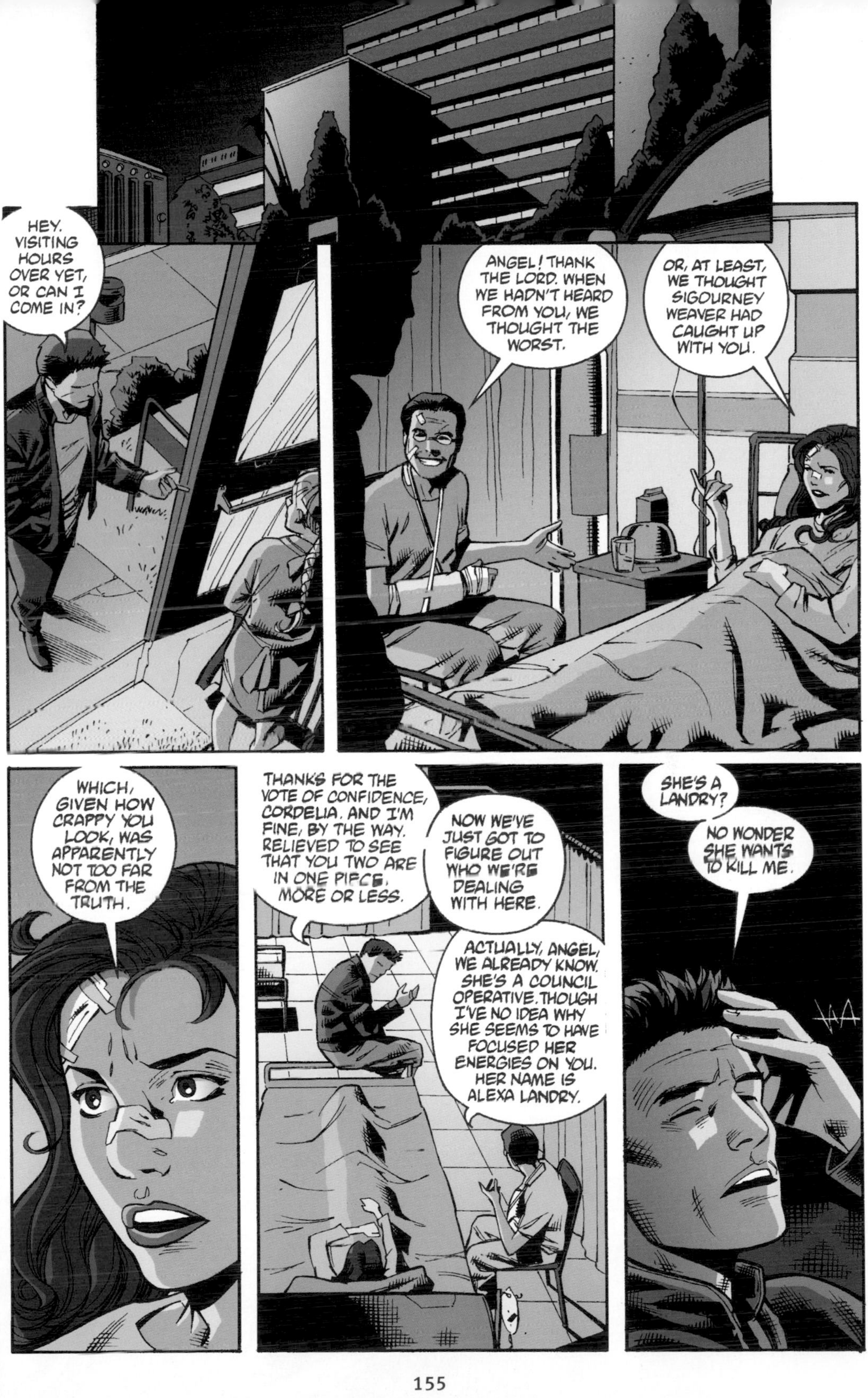
HEY. VISITING HOURS OVER YET, OR CAN I COME IN?
ANGEL! THANK THE LORD. WHEN WE HADN'T HEARD FROM YOU, WE THOUGHT THE WORST.
OR, AT LEAST, WE THOUGHT SIGOURNEY WEAVER HAD CAUGHT UP WITH YOU.
WHICH, GIVEN HOW CRAPPY YOU LOOK, WAS APPARENTLY NOT TOO FAR FROM THE TRUTH.
THANKS FOR THE VOTE OF CONFIDENCE, CORDELIA. AND I'M FINE, BY THE WAY. RELIEVED TO SEE THAT YOU TWO ARE IN ONE PIECE, MORE OR LESS.
NOW WE'VE JUST GOT TO FIGURE OUT WHO WE'RE DEALING WITH HERE.
ACTUALLY, ANGEL, WE ALREADY KNOW. SHE'S A COUNCIL OPERATIVE. THOUGH I'VE NO IDEA WHY SHE SEEMS TO HAVE FOCUSED HER ENERGIES ON YOU. HER NAME IS ALEXA LANDRY.
SHE'S A LANDRY?
NO WONDER SHE WANTS TO KILL ME.

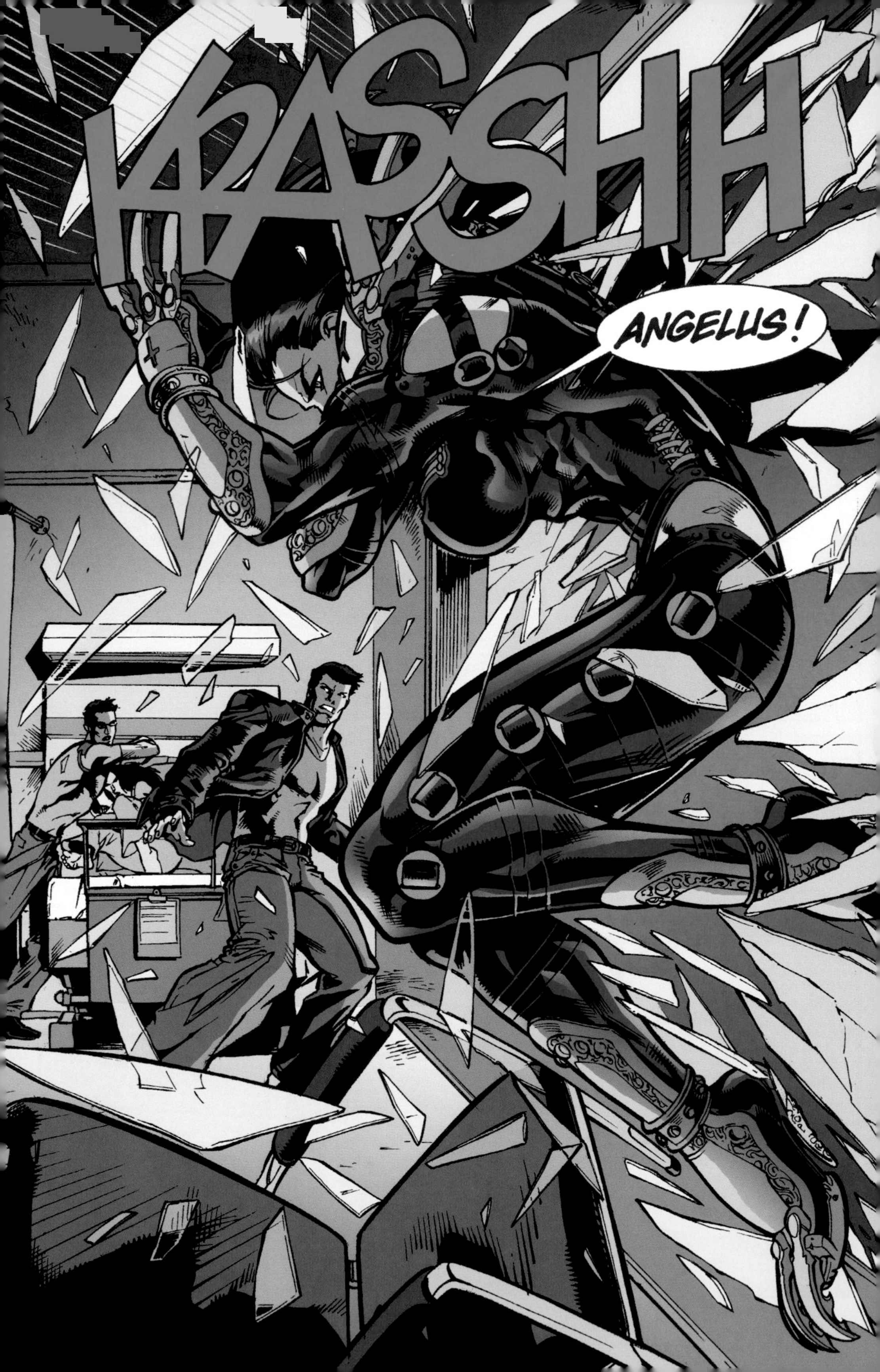
ANGELUS!

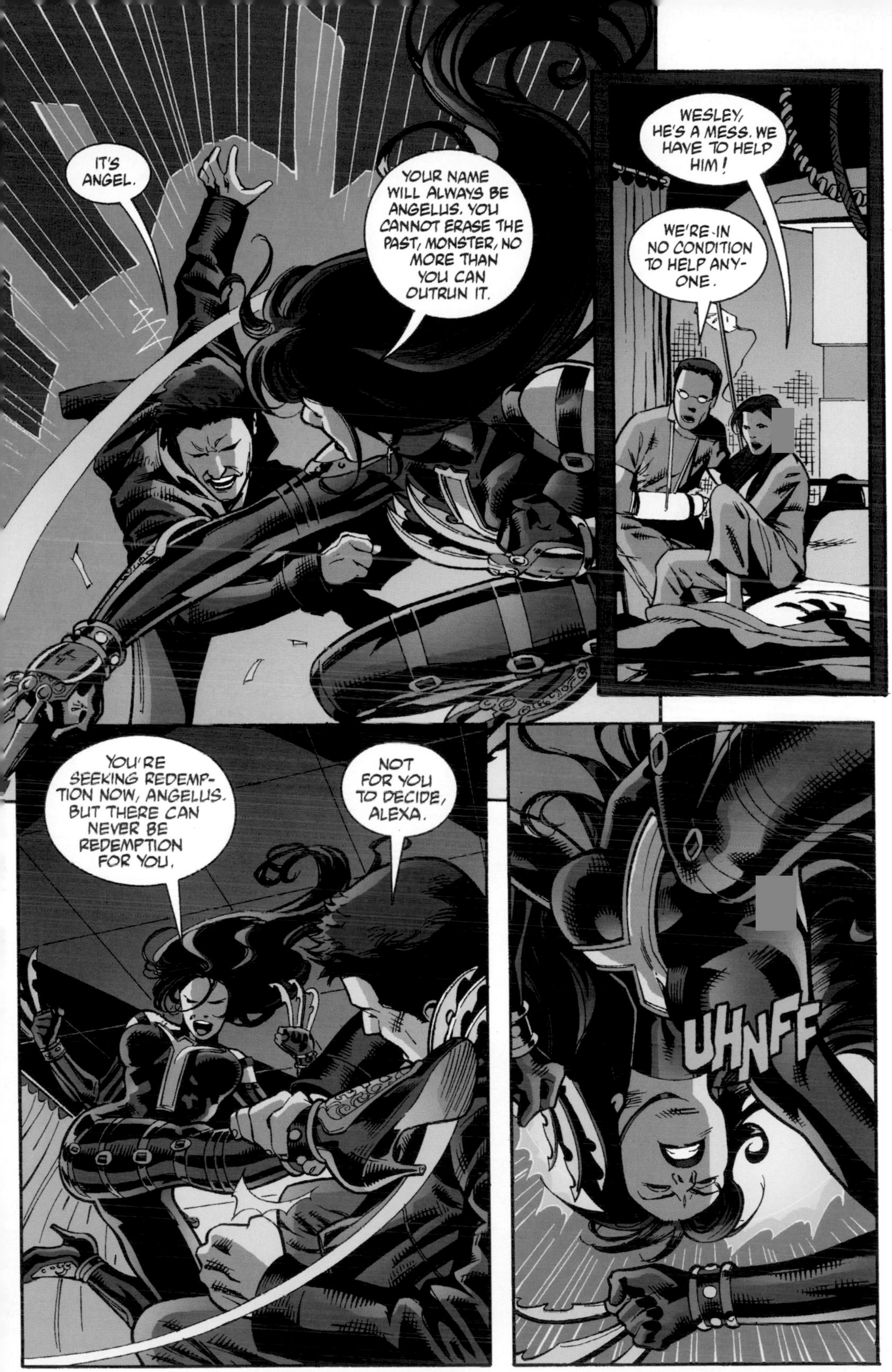
IT'S ANGEL.
YOUR NAME WILL ALWAYS BE ANGELUS. YOU CANNOT ERASE THE PAST, MONSTER, NO MORE THAN YOU CAN OUTRUN IT.
WESLEY, HE'S A MESS. WE HAVE TO HELP HIM!
WE'RE IN NO CONDITION TO HELP ANY-ONE.
YOU'RE SEEKING REDEMP-TION NOW, ANGELUS. BUT THERE CAN NEVER BE REDEMPTION FOR YOU.
NOT FOR YOU TO DECIDE, ALEXA.
UHNFF

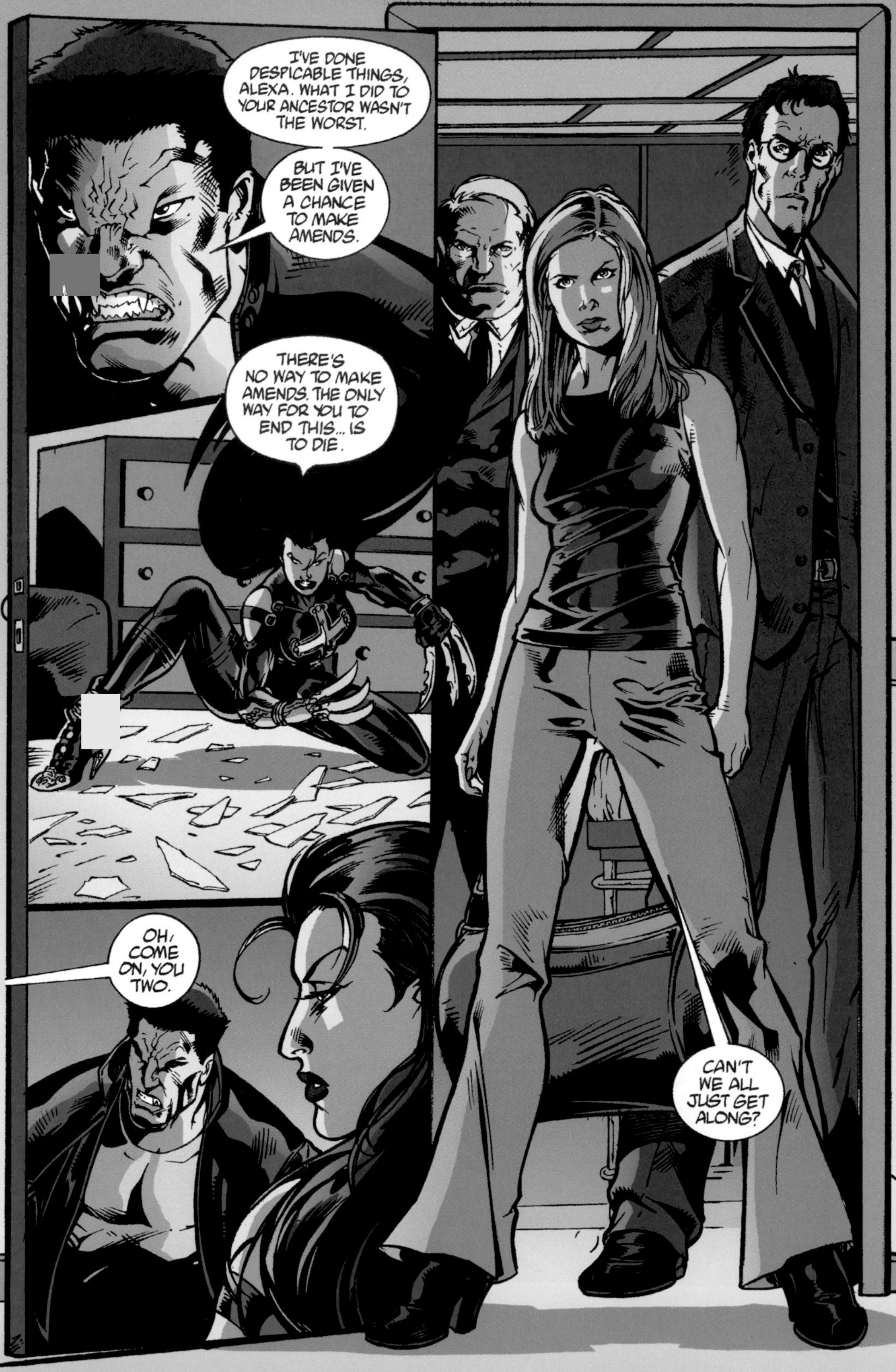
I'VE DONE DESPICABLE THINGS, ALEXA. WHAT I DID TO YOUR ANCESTOR WASN'T THE WORST.
BUT I'VE BEEN GIVEN A CHANCE TO MAKE AMENDS.
THERE'S NO WAY TO MAKE AMENDS. THE ONLY WAY FOR YOU TO END THIS... IS TO DIE.
OH, COME ON, YOU TWO.
CAN'T WE ALL JUST GET ALONG?

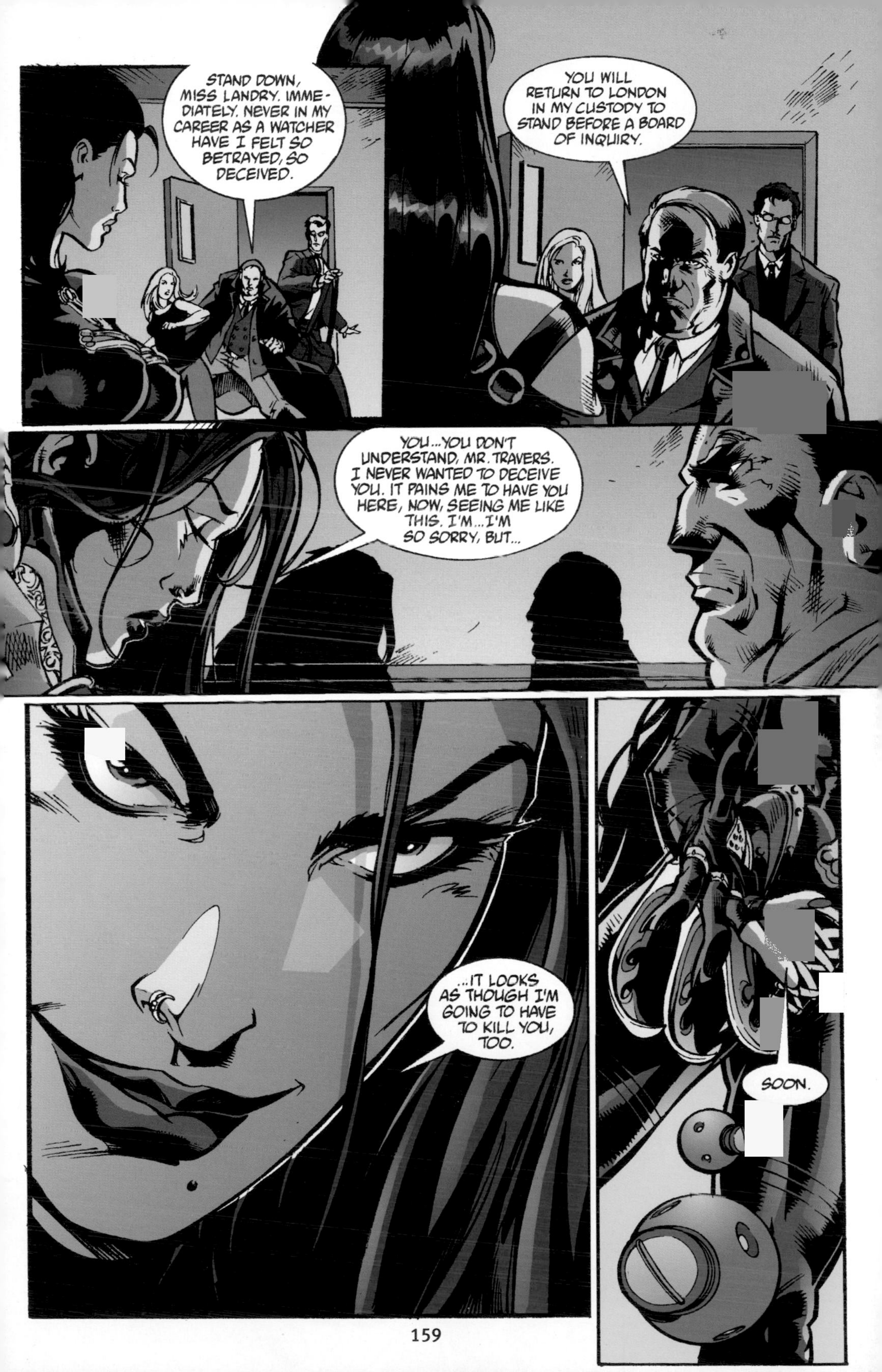
STAND DOWN, MISS LANDRY. IMME-DIATELY. NEVER IN MY CAREER AS A WATCHER HAVE I FELT SO BETRAYED, SO DECEIVED.
YOU WILL RETURN TO LONDON IN MY CUSTODY TO STAND BEFORE A BOARD OF INQUIRY.
YOU...YOU DON'T UNDERSTAND, MR. TRAVERS. I NEVER WANTED TO DECEIVE YOU. IT PAINS ME TO HAVE YOU HERE, NOW, SEEING ME LIKE THIS. I'M...I'M SO SORRY, BUT...
...IT LOOKS AS THOUGH I'M GOING TO HAVE TO KILL YOU, TOO.
SOON.

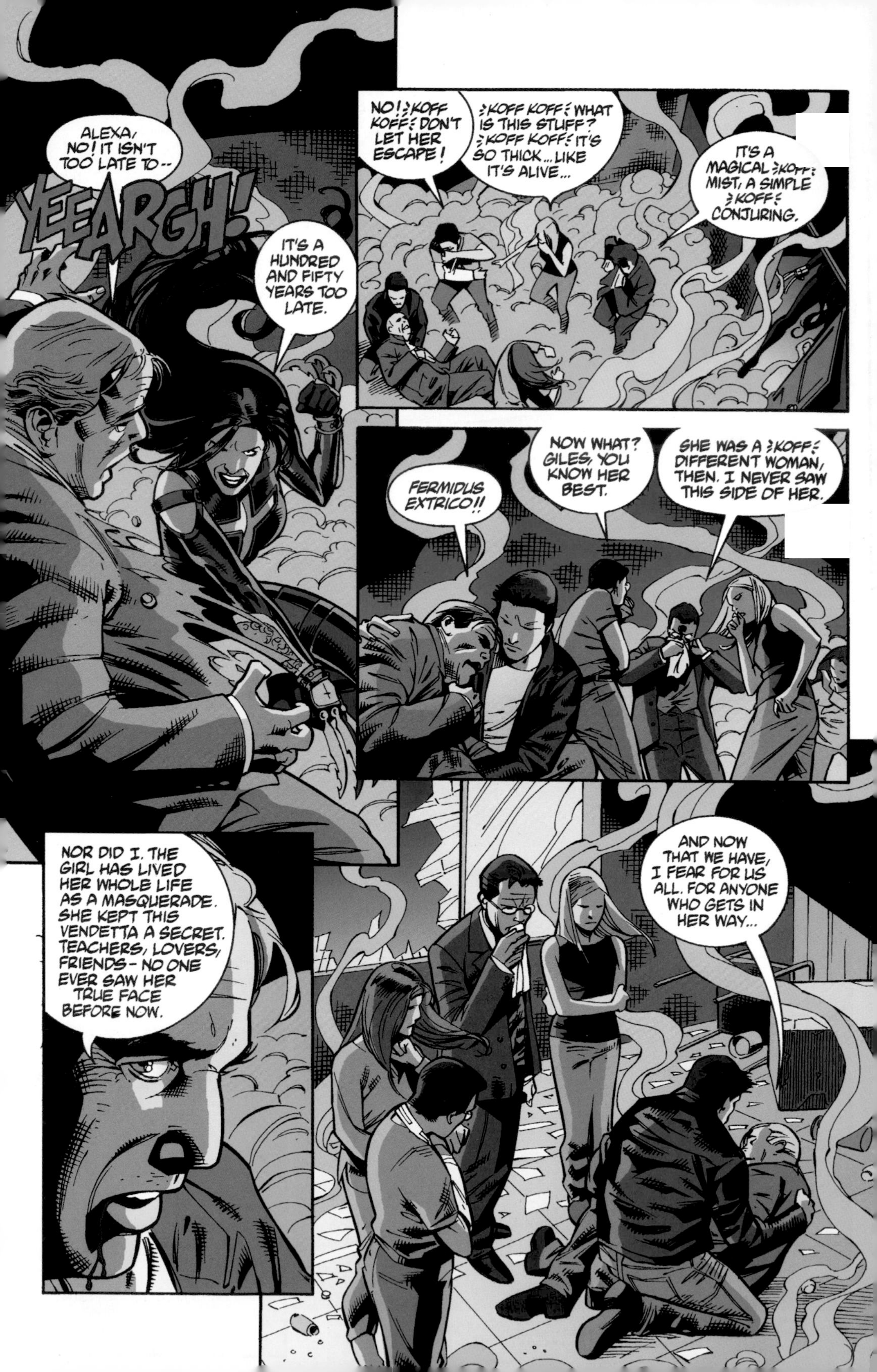
ALEXA, NO! IT ISN'T TOO LATE TO--
YEEARGH!
IT'S A HUNDRED AND FIFTY YEARS TOO LATE.
NO! *KOFF KOFF* DON'T LET HER ESCAPE!
KOFF KOFF WHAT IS THIS STUFF? *KOFF KOFF* IT'S SO THICK... LIKE IT'S ALIVE...
IT'S A MAGICAL *KOFF* MIST, A SIMPLE *KOFF* CONJURING.
FERMIDUS EXTRICO!!
NOW WHAT? GILES, YOU KNOW HER BEST.
SHE WAS A *KOFF* DIFFERENT WOMAN, THEN. I NEVER SAW THIS SIDE OF HER.
NOR DID I. THE GIRL HAS LIVED HER WHOLE LIFE AS A MASQUERADE. SHE KEPT THIS VENDETTA A SECRET. TEACHERS, LOVERS, FRIENDS-- NO ONE EVER SAW HER TRUE FACE BEFORE NOW.
AND NOW THAT WE HAVE, I FEAR FOR US ALL. FOR ANYONE WHO GETS IN HER WAY...

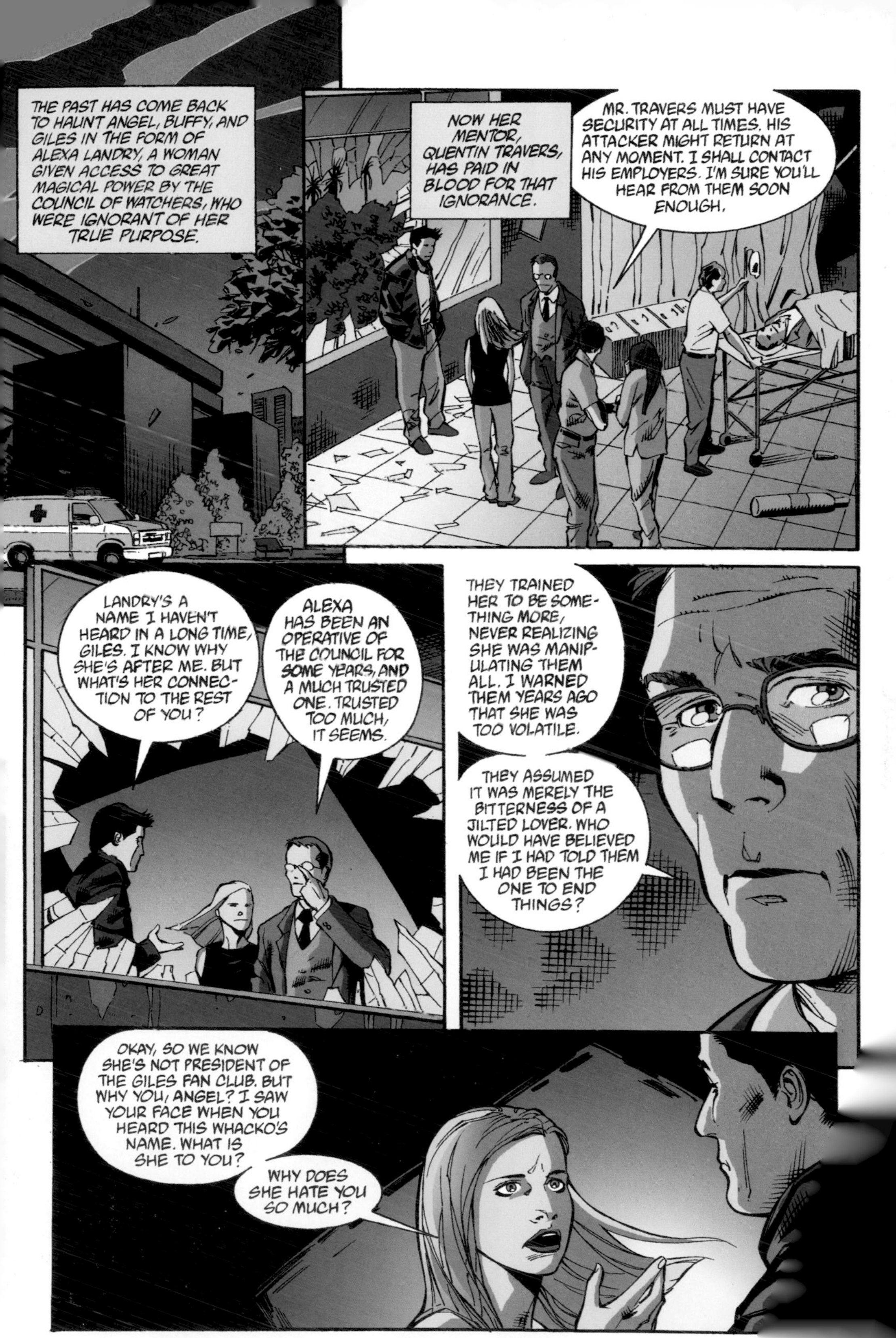
THE PAST HAS COME BACK TO HAUNT ANGEL, BUFFY, AND GILES IN THE FORM OF ALEXA LANDRY, A WOMAN GIVEN ACCESS TO GREAT MAGICAL POWER BY THE COUNCIL OF WATCHERS, WHO WERE IGNORANT OF HER TRUE PURPOSE.
NOW HER MENTOR, QUENTIN TRAVERS, HAS PAID IN BLOOD FOR THAT IGNORANCE.
MR. TRAVERS MUST HAVE SECURITY AT ALL TIMES. HIS ATTACKER MIGHT RETURN AT ANY MOMENT. I SHALL CONTACT HIS EMPLOYERS. I'M SURE YOU'LL HEAR FROM THEM SOON ENOUGH.
LANDRY'S A NAME I HAVEN'T HEARD IN A LONG TIME, GILES. I KNOW WHY SHE'S AFTER ME. BUT WHAT'S HER CONNECTION TO THE REST OF YOU?
ALEXA HAS BEEN AN OPERATIVE OF THE COUNCIL FOR SOME YEARS, AND A MUCH TRUSTED ONE. TRUSTED TOO MUCH, IT SEEMS.
THEY TRAINED HER TO BE SOMETHING MORE, NEVER REALIZING SHE WAS MANIPULATING THEM ALL. I WARNED THEM YEARS AGO THAT SHE WAS TOO VOLATILE.
THEY ASSUMED IT WAS MERELY THE BITTERNESS OF A JILTED LOVER. WHO WOULD HAVE BELIEVED ME IF I HAD TOLD THEM I HAD BEEN THE ONE TO END THINGS?
OKAY, SO WE KNOW SHE'S NOT PRESIDENT OF THE GILES FAN CLUB. BUT WHY YOU, ANGEL? I SAW YOUR FACE WHEN YOU HEARD THIS WHACKO'S NAME. WHAT IS SHE TO YOU?
WHY DOES SHE HATE YOU SO MUCH?

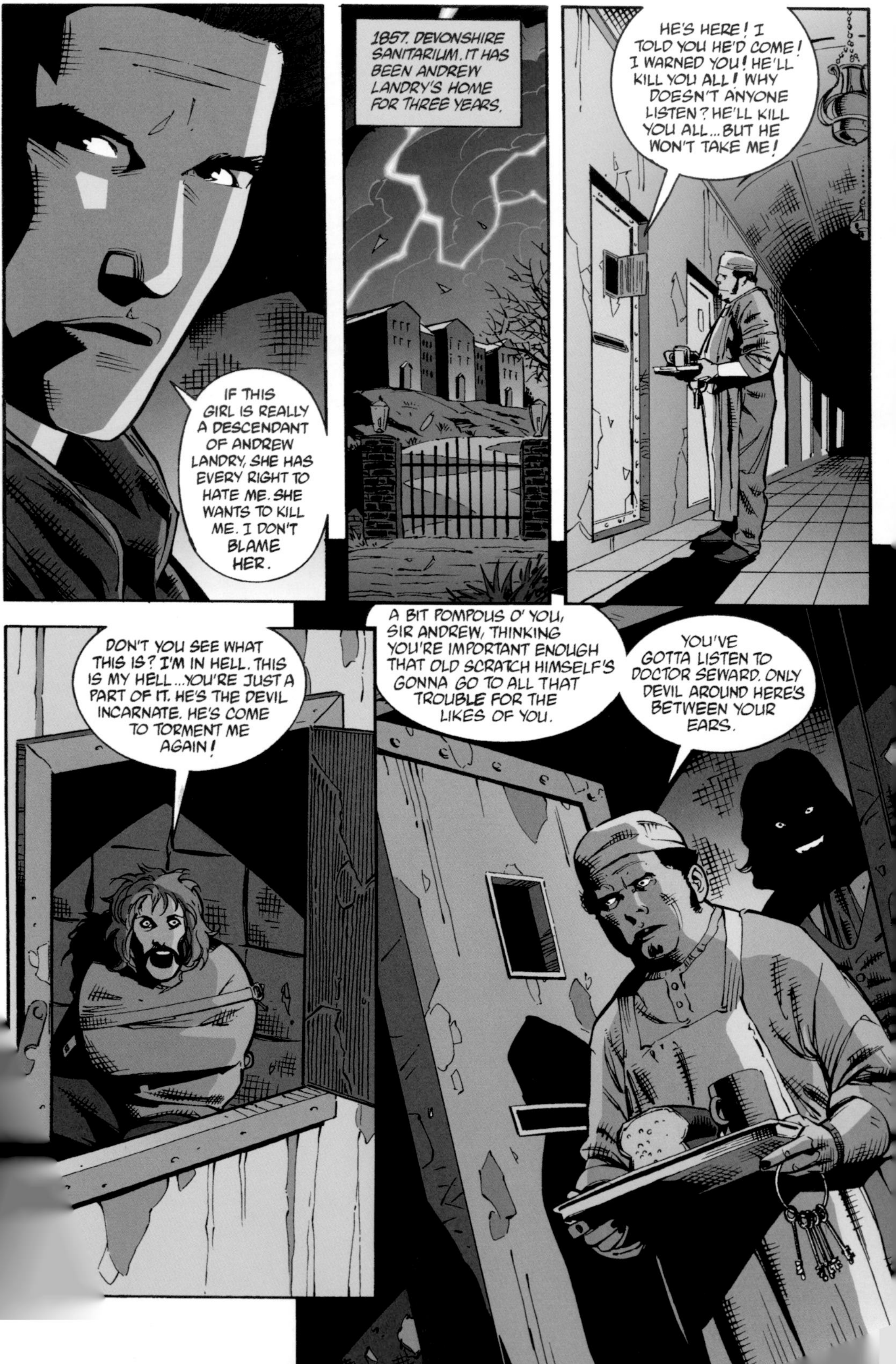
IF THIS GIRL IS REALLY A DESCENDANT OF ANDREW LANDRY, SHE HAS EVERY RIGHT TO HATE ME. SHE WANTS TO KILL ME. I DON'T BLAME HER.
1857. DEVONSHIRE SANITARIUM. IT HAS BEEN ANDREW LANDRY'S HOME FOR THREE YEARS.
HE'S HERE! I TOLD YOU HE'D COME! I WARNED YOU! HE'LL KILL YOU ALL! WHY DOESN'T ANYONE LISTEN? HE'LL KILL YOU ALL... BUT HE WON'T TAKE ME!
DON'T YOU SEE WHAT THIS IS? I'M IN HELL. THIS IS MY HELL... YOU'RE JUST A PART OF IT. HE'S THE DEVIL INCARNATE. HE'S COME TO TORMENT ME AGAIN!
A BIT POMPOUS O' YOU, SIR ANDREW, THINKING YOU'RE IMPORTANT ENOUGH THAT OLD SCRATCH HIMSELF'S GONNA GO TO ALL THAT TROUBLE FOR THE LIKES OF YOU.
YOU'VE GOTTA LISTEN TO DOCTOR SEWARD. ONLY DEVIL AROUND HERE'S BETWEEN YOUR EARS.

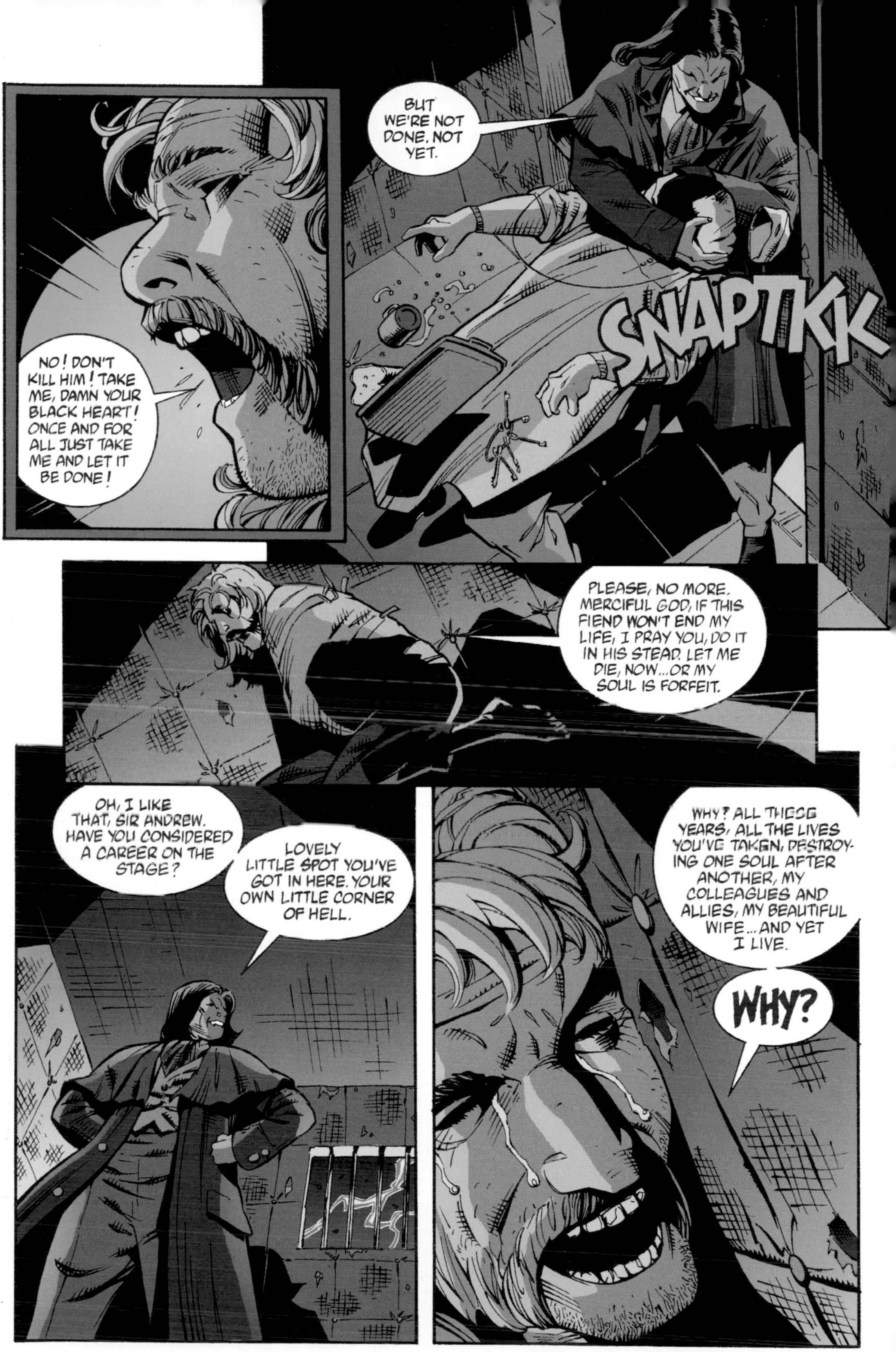
NO! DON'T KILL HIM! TAKE ME, DAMN YOUR BLACK HEART! ONCE AND FOR ALL JUST TAKE ME AND LET IT BE DONE!
BUT WE'RE NOT DONE. NOT YET.
SNAPTKK
PLEASE, NO MORE. MERCIFUL GOD, IF THIS FIEND WON'T END MY LIFE, I PRAY YOU, DO IT IN HIS STEAD. LET ME DIE, NOW...OR MY SOUL IS FORFEIT.
OH, I LIKE THAT, SIR ANDREW. HAVE YOU CONSIDERED A CAREER ON THE STAGE?
LOVELY LITTLE SPOT YOU'VE GOT IN HERE. YOUR OWN LITTLE CORNER OF HELL.
WHY? ALL THESE YEARS, ALL THE LIVES YOU'VE TAKEN, DESTROYING ONE SOUL AFTER ANOTHER, MY COLLEAGUES AND ALLIES, MY BEAUTIFUL WIFE...AND YET I LIVE.
WHY?

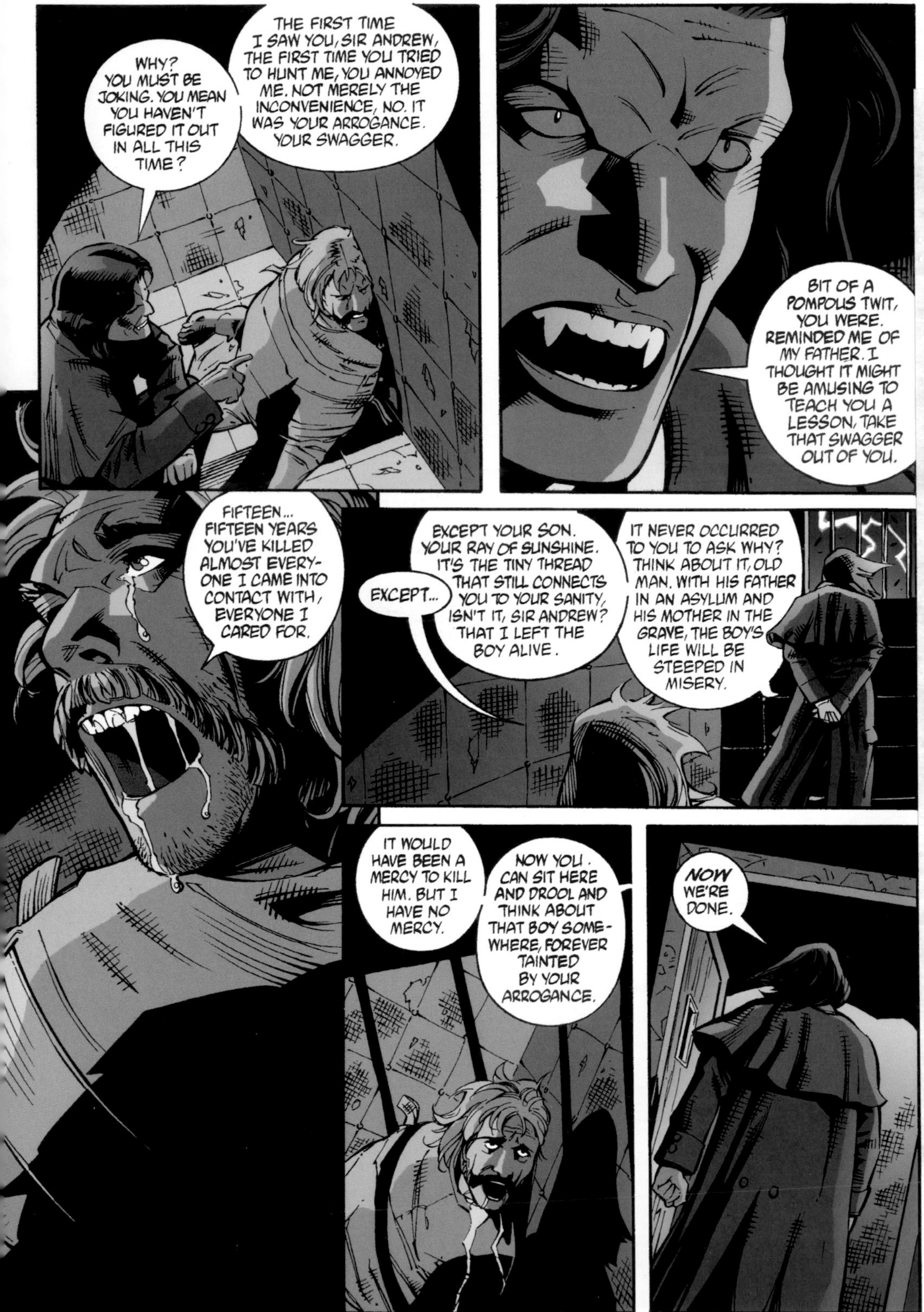
WHY? YOU MUST BE JOKING. YOU MEAN YOU HAVEN'T FIGURED IT OUT IN ALL THIS TIME?
THE FIRST TIME I SAW YOU, SIR ANDREW, THE FIRST TIME YOU TRIED TO HUNT ME, YOU ANNOYED ME. NOT MERELY THE INCONVENIENCE, NO. IT WAS YOUR ARROGANCE. YOUR SWAGGER.
BIT OF A POMPOUS TWIT, YOU WERE. REMINDED ME OF MY FATHER. I THOUGHT IT MIGHT BE AMUSING TO TEACH YOU A LESSON, TAKE THAT SWAGGER OUT OF YOU.
FIFTEEN... FIFTEEN YEARS YOU'VE KILLED ALMOST EVERY-ONE I CAME INTO CONTACT WITH, EVERYONE I CARED FOR.
EXCEPT...
EXCEPT YOUR SON. YOUR RAY OF SUNSHINE. IT'S THE TINY THREAD THAT STILL CONNECTS YOU TO YOUR SANITY, ISN'T IT, SIR ANDREW? THAT I LEFT THE BOY ALIVE.
IT NEVER OCCURRED TO YOU TO ASK WHY? THINK ABOUT IT, OLD MAN. WITH HIS FATHER IN AN ASYLUM AND HIS MOTHER IN THE GRAVE, THE BOY'S LIFE WILL BE STEEPED IN MISERY.
IT WOULD HAVE BEEN A MERCY TO KILL HIM. BUT I HAVE NO MERCY.
NOW YOU CAN SIT HERE AND DROOL AND THINK ABOUT THAT BOY SOME-WHERE, FOREVER TAINTED BY YOUR ARROGANCE.
NOW WE'RE DONE.

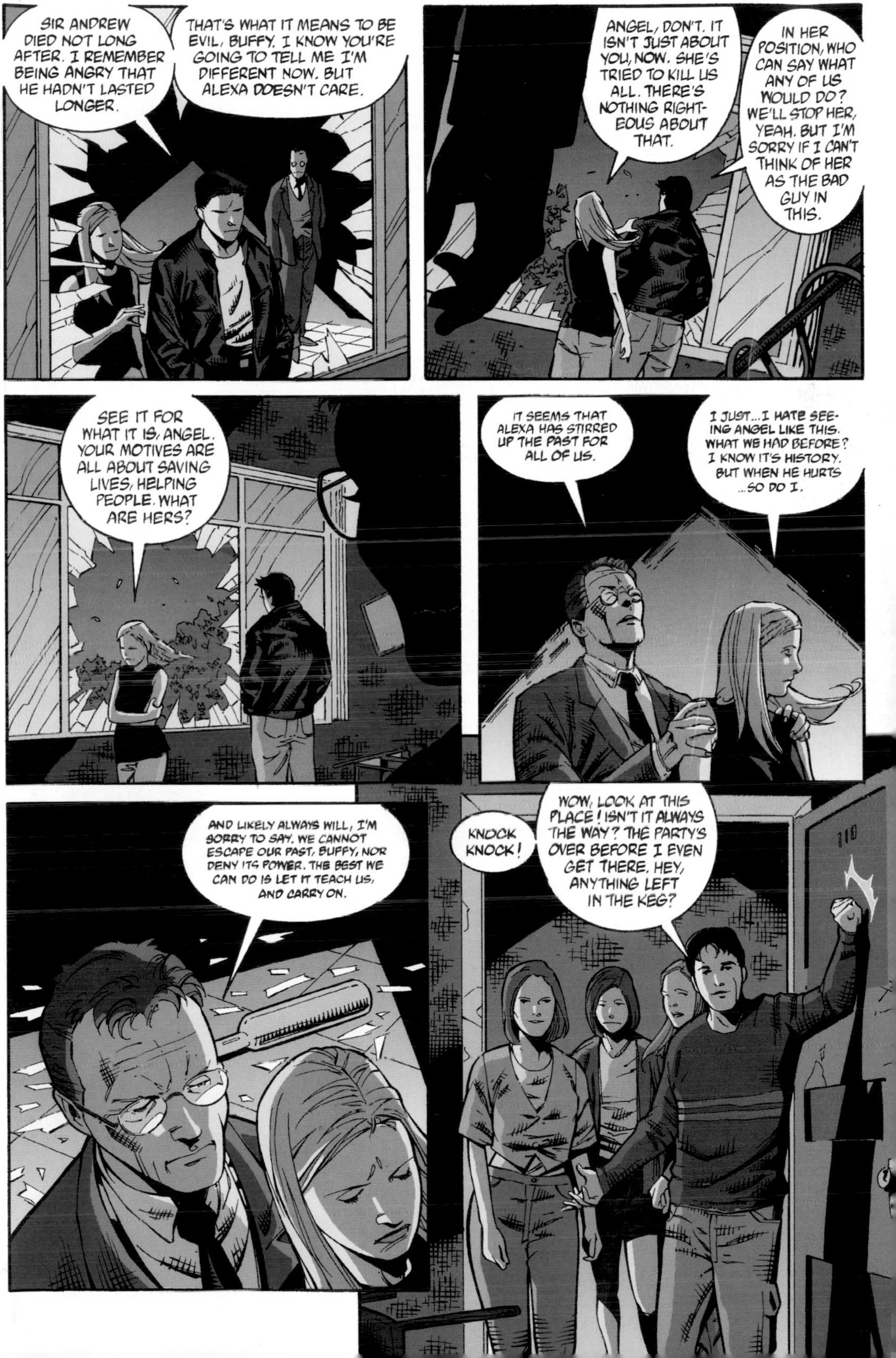
SIR ANDREW DIED NOT LONG AFTER. I REMEMBER BEING ANGRY THAT HE HADN'T LASTED LONGER.
THAT'S WHAT IT MEANS TO BE EVIL, BUFFY. I KNOW YOU'RE GOING TO TELL ME I'M DIFFERENT NOW. BUT ALEXA DOESN'T CARE.
ANGEL, DON'T. IT ISN'T JUST ABOUT YOU, NOW. SHE'S TRIED TO KILL US ALL. THERE'S NOTHING RIGHT-EOUS ABOUT THAT.
IN HER POSITION, WHO CAN SAY WHAT ANY OF US WOULD DO? WE'LL STOP HER, YEAH. BUT I'M SORRY IF I CAN'T THINK OF HER AS THE BAD GUY IN THIS.
SEE IT FOR WHAT IT IS, ANGEL. YOUR MOTIVES ARE ALL ABOUT SAVING LIVES, HELPING PEOPLE. WHAT ARE HERS?
IT SEEMS THAT ALEXA HAS STIRRED UP THE PAST FOR ALL OF US.
I JUST... I HATE SEE-ING ANGEL LIKE THIS. WHAT WE HAD BEFORE? I KNOW IT'S HISTORY. BUT WHEN HE HURTS ...SO DO I.
AND LIKELY ALWAYS WILL, I'M SORRY TO SAY. WE CANNOT ESCAPE OUR PAST, BUFFY, NOR DENY ITS POWER. THE BEST WE CAN DO IS LET IT TEACH US, AND CARRY ON.
KNOCK KNOCK!
WOW, LOOK AT THIS PLACE! ISN'T IT ALWAYS THE WAY? THE PARTY'S OVER BEFORE I EVEN GET THERE. HEY, ANYTHING LEFT IN THE KEG?

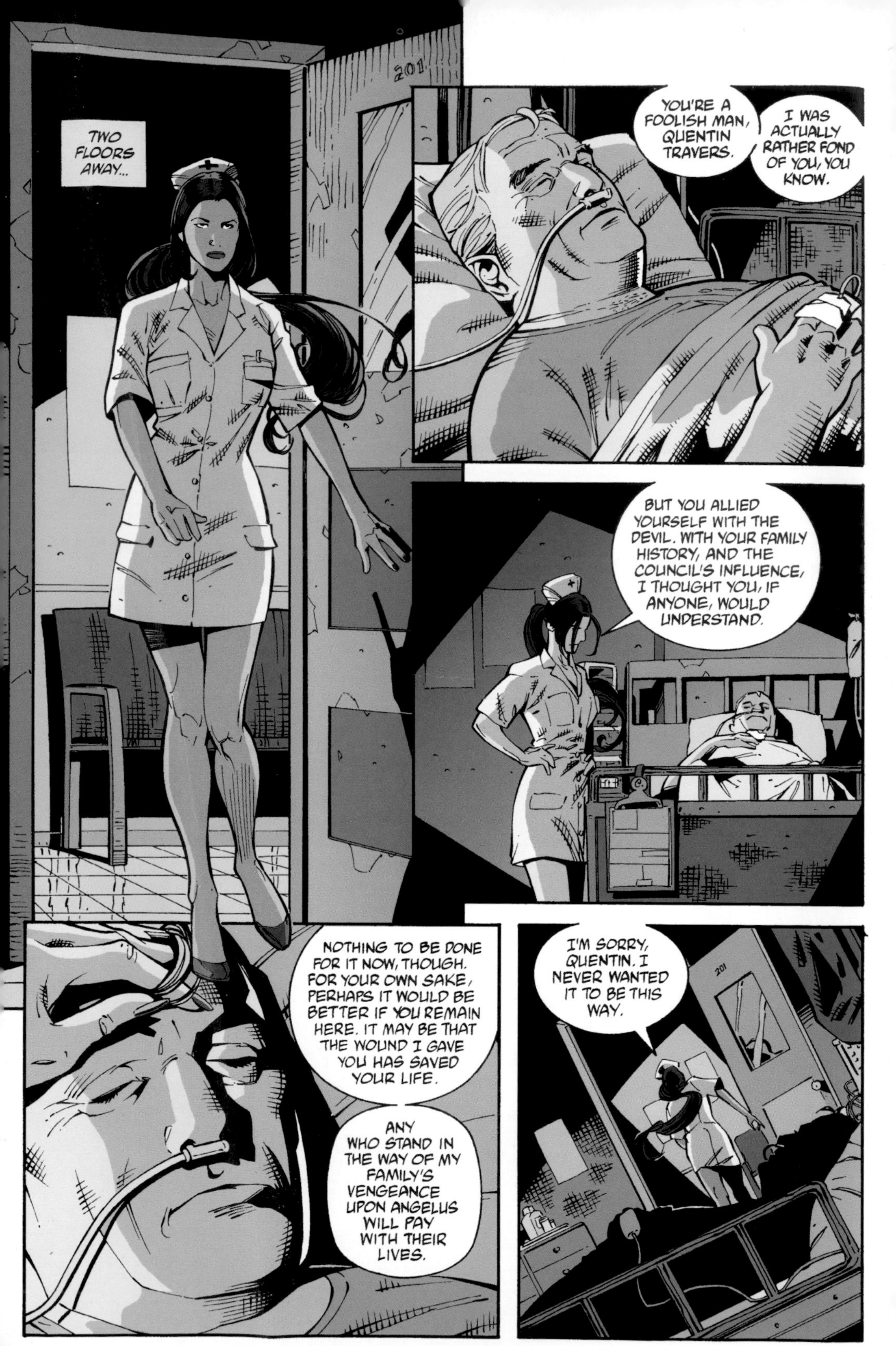
TWO FLOORS AWAY...
YOU'RE A FOOLISH MAN, QUENTIN TRAVERS.
I WAS ACTUALLY RATHER FOND OF YOU, YOU KNOW.
BUT YOU ALLIED YOURSELF WITH THE DEVIL. WITH YOUR FAMILY HISTORY, AND THE COUNCIL'S INFLUENCE, I THOUGHT YOU, IF ANYONE, WOULD UNDERSTAND.
NOTHING TO BE DONE FOR IT NOW, THOUGH. FOR YOUR OWN SAKE, PERHAPS IT WOULD BE BETTER IF YOU REMAIN HERE. IT MAY BE THAT THE WOUND I GAVE YOU HAS SAVED YOUR LIFE.
ANY WHO STAND IN THE WAY OF MY FAMILY'S VENGEANCE UPON ANGELUS WILL PAY WITH THEIR LIVES.
I'M SORRY, QUENTIN. I NEVER WANTED IT TO BE THIS WAY.

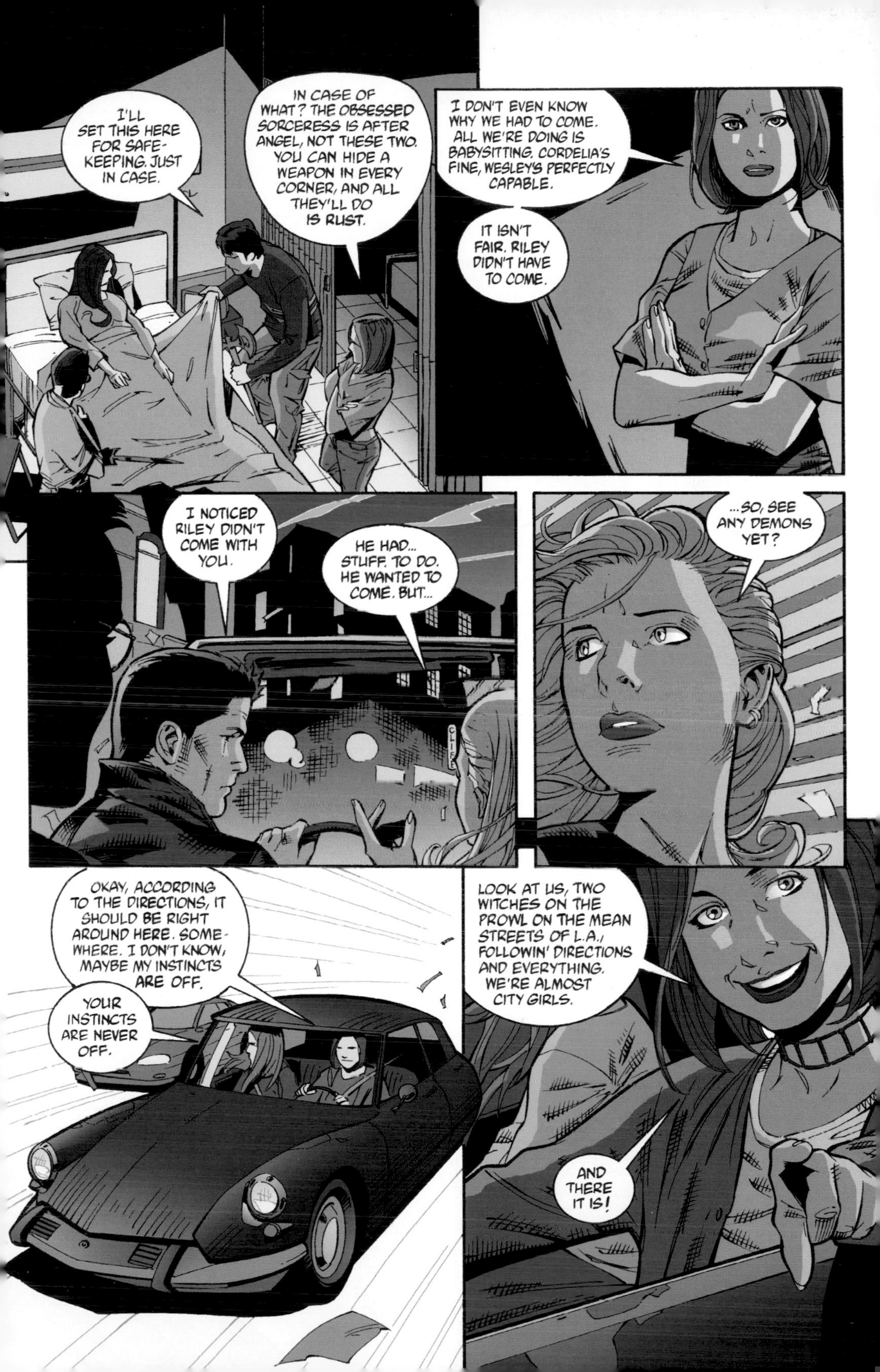
I'LL SET THIS HERE FOR SAFE-KEEPING. JUST IN CASE.
IN CASE OF WHAT? THE OBSESSED SORCERESS IS AFTER ANGEL, NOT THESE TWO. YOU CAN HIDE A WEAPON IN EVERY CORNER, AND ALL THEY'LL DO IS RUST.
I DON'T EVEN KNOW WHY WE HAD TO COME. ALL WE'RE DOING IS BABYSITTING. CORDELIA'S FINE, WESLEY'S PERFECTLY CAPABLE.
IT ISN'T FAIR. RILEY DIDN'T HAVE TO COME.
I NOTICED RILEY DIDN'T COME WITH YOU.
HE HAD... STUFF. TO DO. HE WANTED TO COME. BUT...
...SO, SEE ANY DEMONS YET?
OKAY, ACCORDING TO THE DIRECTIONS, IT SHOULD BE RIGHT AROUND HERE. SOME-WHERE. I DON'T KNOW, MAYBE MY INSTINCTS ARE OFF.
YOUR INSTINCTS ARE NEVER OFF.
LOOK AT US, TWO WITCHES ON THE PROWL ON THE MEAN STREETS OF L.A., FOLLOWIN' DIRECTIONS AND EVERYTHING. WE'RE ALMOST CITY GIRLS.
AND THERE IT IS!

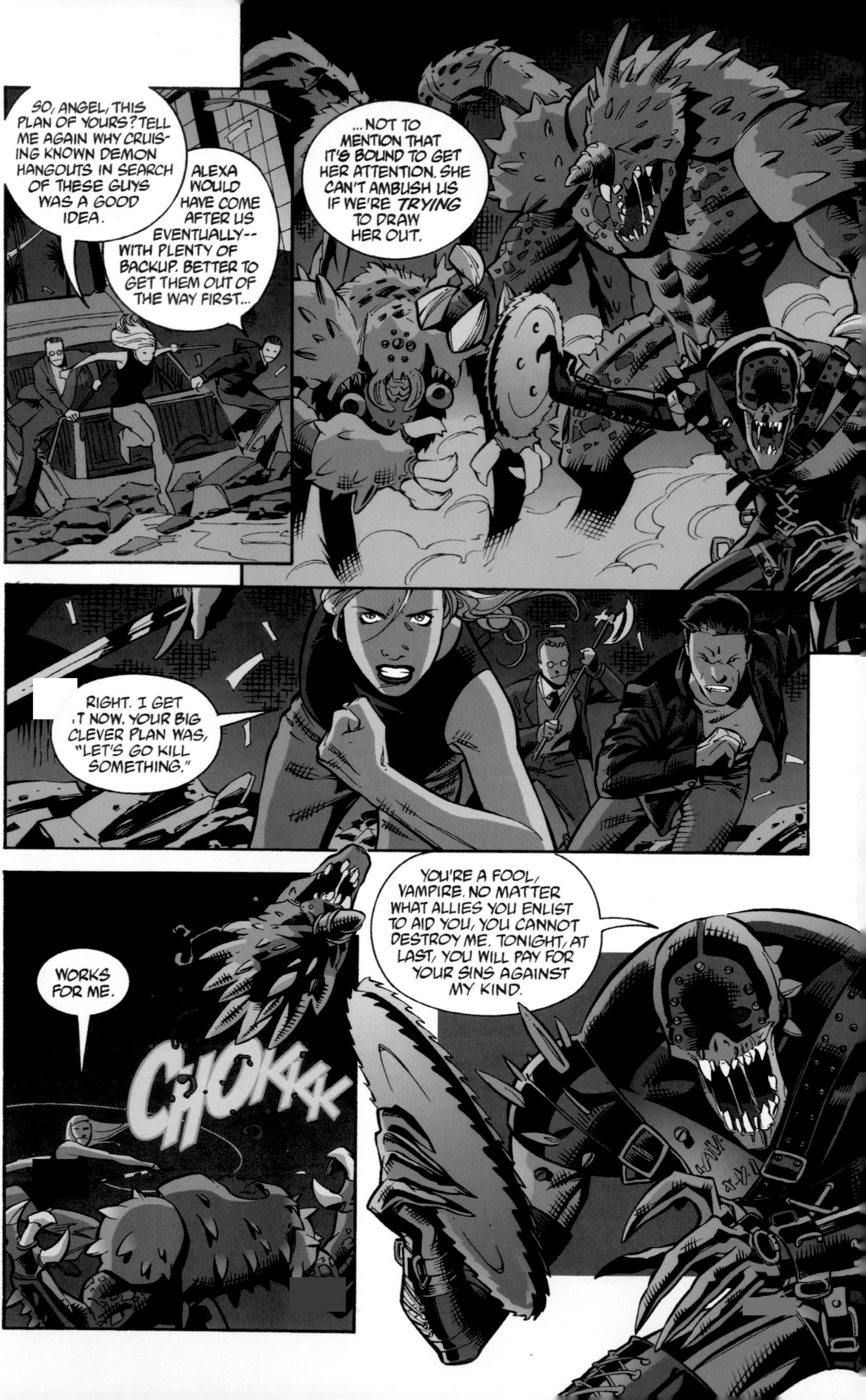
SO, ANGEL, THIS PLAN OF YOURS? TELL ME AGAIN WHY CRUISING KNOWN DEMON HANGOUTS IN SEARCH OF THESE GUYS WAS A GOOD IDEA.
ALEXA WOULD HAVE COME AFTER US EVENTUALLY-- WITH PLENTY OF BACKUP. BETTER TO GET THEM OUT OF THE WAY FIRST...
...NOT TO MENTION THAT IT'S BOUND TO GET HER ATTENTION. SHE CAN'T AMBUSH US IF WE'RE *TRYING* TO DRAW HER OUT.
RIGHT. I GET IT NOW. YOUR BIG CLEVER PLAN WAS, "LET'S GO KILL SOMETHING."
WORKS FOR ME.
CHOKKK
YOU'RE A FOOL, VAMPIRE. NO MATTER WHAT ALLIES YOU ENLIST TO AID YOU, YOU CANNOT DESTROY ME. TONIGHT, AT LAST, YOU WILL PAY FOR YOUR SINS AGAINST MY KIND.

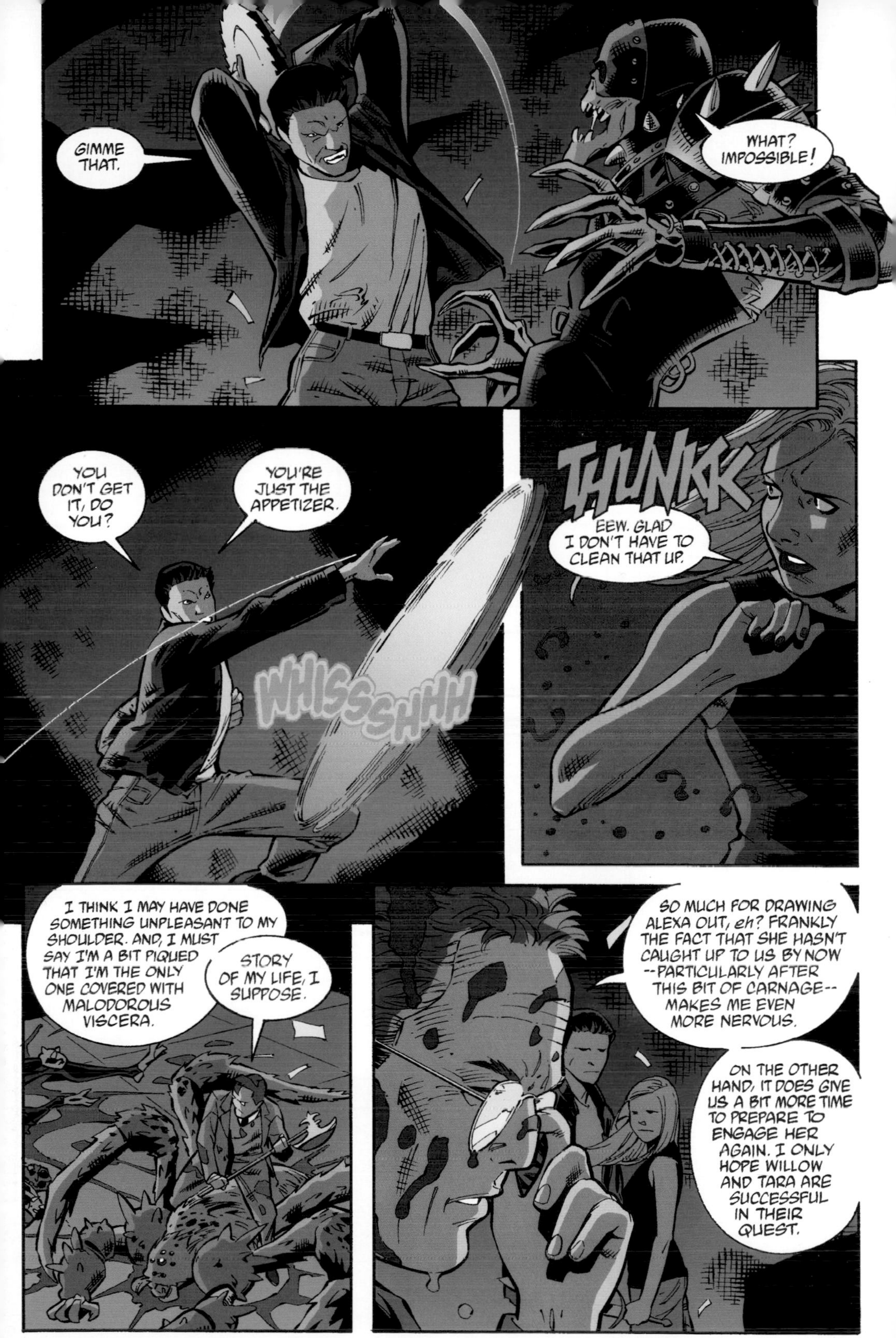
GIMME THAT.
WHAT? IMPOSSIBLE!
YOU DON'T GET IT, DO YOU?
YOU'RE JUST THE APPETIZER.
WHISSSHHH
THUNKK!
EEW. GLAD I DON'T HAVE TO CLEAN THAT UP.
I THINK I MAY HAVE DONE SOMETHING UNPLEASANT TO MY SHOULDER. AND, I MUST SAY I'M A BIT PIQUED THAT I'M THE ONLY ONE COVERED WITH MALODOROUS VISCERA.
STORY OF MY LIFE, I SUPPOSE.
SO MUCH FOR DRAWING ALEXA OUT, eh? FRANKLY THE FACT THAT SHE HASN'T CAUGHT UP TO US BY NOW --PARTICULARLY AFTER THIS BIT OF CARNAGE-- MAKES ME EVEN MORE NERVOUS.
ON THE OTHER HAND, IT DOES GIVE US A BIT MORE TIME TO PREPARE TO ENGAGE HER AGAIN. I ONLY HOPE WILLOW AND TARA ARE SUCCESSFUL IN THEIR QUEST.

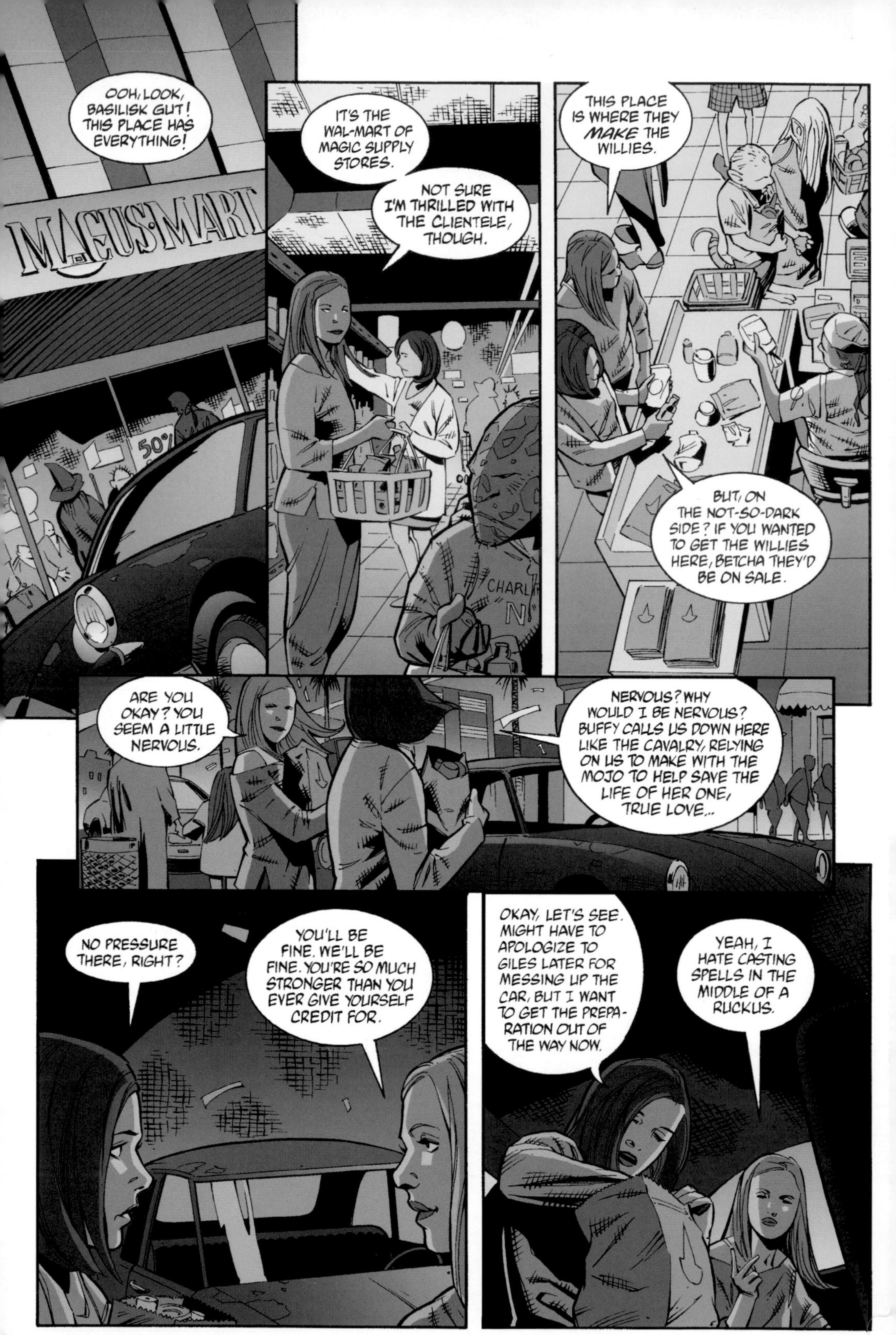
OOH, LOOK, BASILISK GUT! THIS PLACE HAS EVERYTHING!
MAGUS MART
50%
IT'S THE WAL-MART OF MAGIC SUPPLY STORES.
NOT SURE I'M THRILLED WITH THE CLIENTELE, THOUGH.
THIS PLACE IS WHERE THEY *MAKE* THE WILLIES.
BUT, ON THE NOT-SO-DARK SIDE? IF YOU WANTED TO GET THE WILLIES HERE, BETCHA THEY'D BE ON SALE.
ARE YOU OKAY? YOU SEEM A LITTLE NERVOUS.
NERVOUS? WHY WOULD I BE NERVOUS? BUFFY CALLS US DOWN HERE LIKE THE CAVALRY, RELYING ON US TO MAKE WITH THE MOJO TO HELP SAVE THE LIFE OF HER ONE, TRUE LOVE...
NO PRESSURE THERE, RIGHT?
YOU'LL BE FINE. WE'LL BE FINE. YOU'RE SO MUCH STRONGER THAN YOU EVER GIVE YOURSELF CREDIT FOR.
OKAY, LET'S SEE. MIGHT HAVE TO APOLOGIZE TO GILES LATER FOR MESSING UP THE CAR, BUT I WANT TO GET THE PREPARATION OUT OF THE WAY NOW.
YEAH, I HATE CASTING SPELLS IN THE MIDDLE OF A RUCKUS.

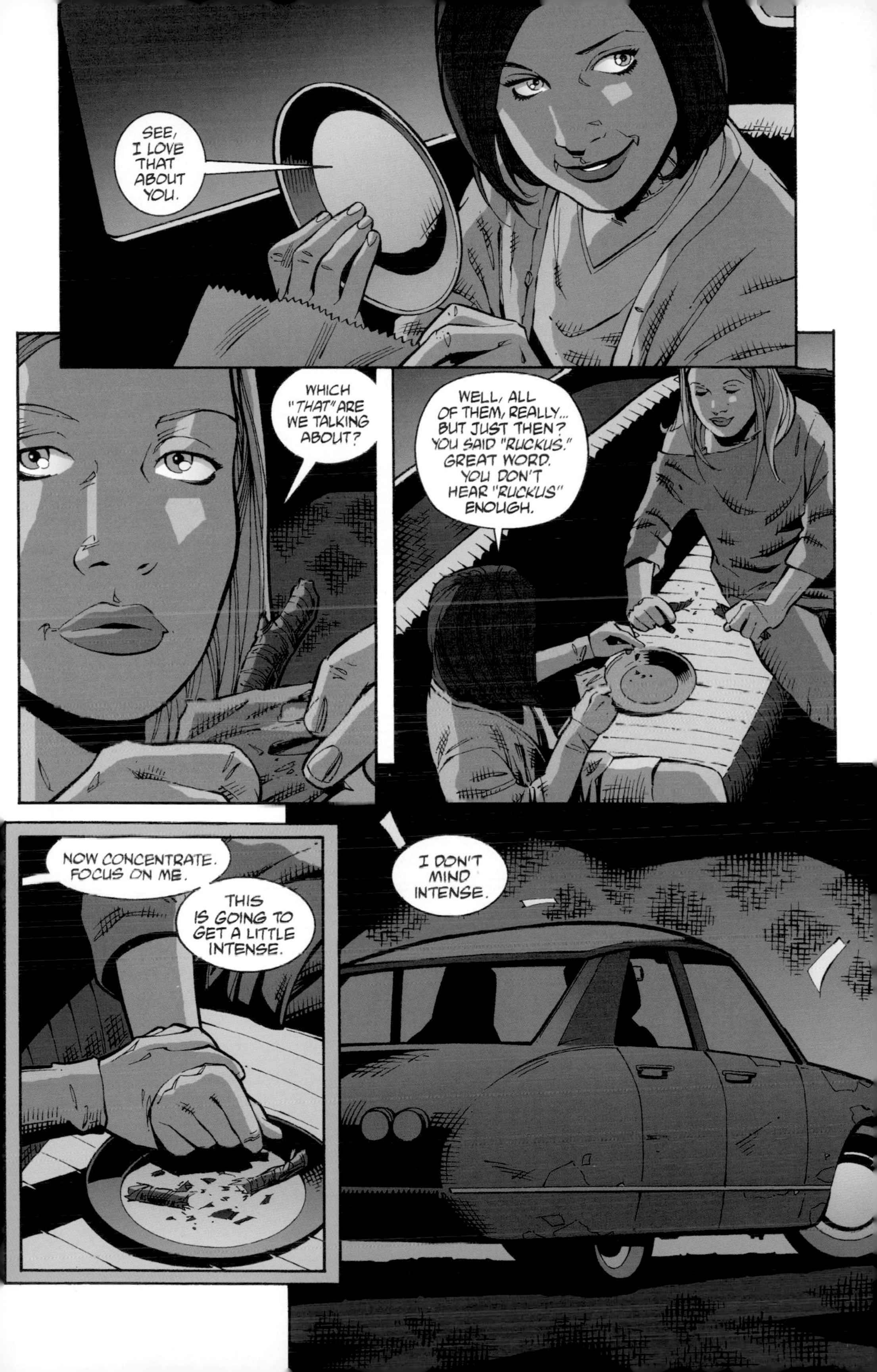
SEE, I LOVE THAT ABOUT YOU.
WHICH "THAT" ARE WE TALKING ABOUT?
WELL, ALL OF THEM, REALLY... BUT JUST THEN? YOU SAID "RUCKUS." GREAT WORD. YOU DON'T HEAR "RUCKUS" ENOUGH.
NOW CONCENTRATE. FOCUS ON ME.
THIS IS GOING TO GET A LITTLE INTENSE.
I DON'T MIND INTENSE.

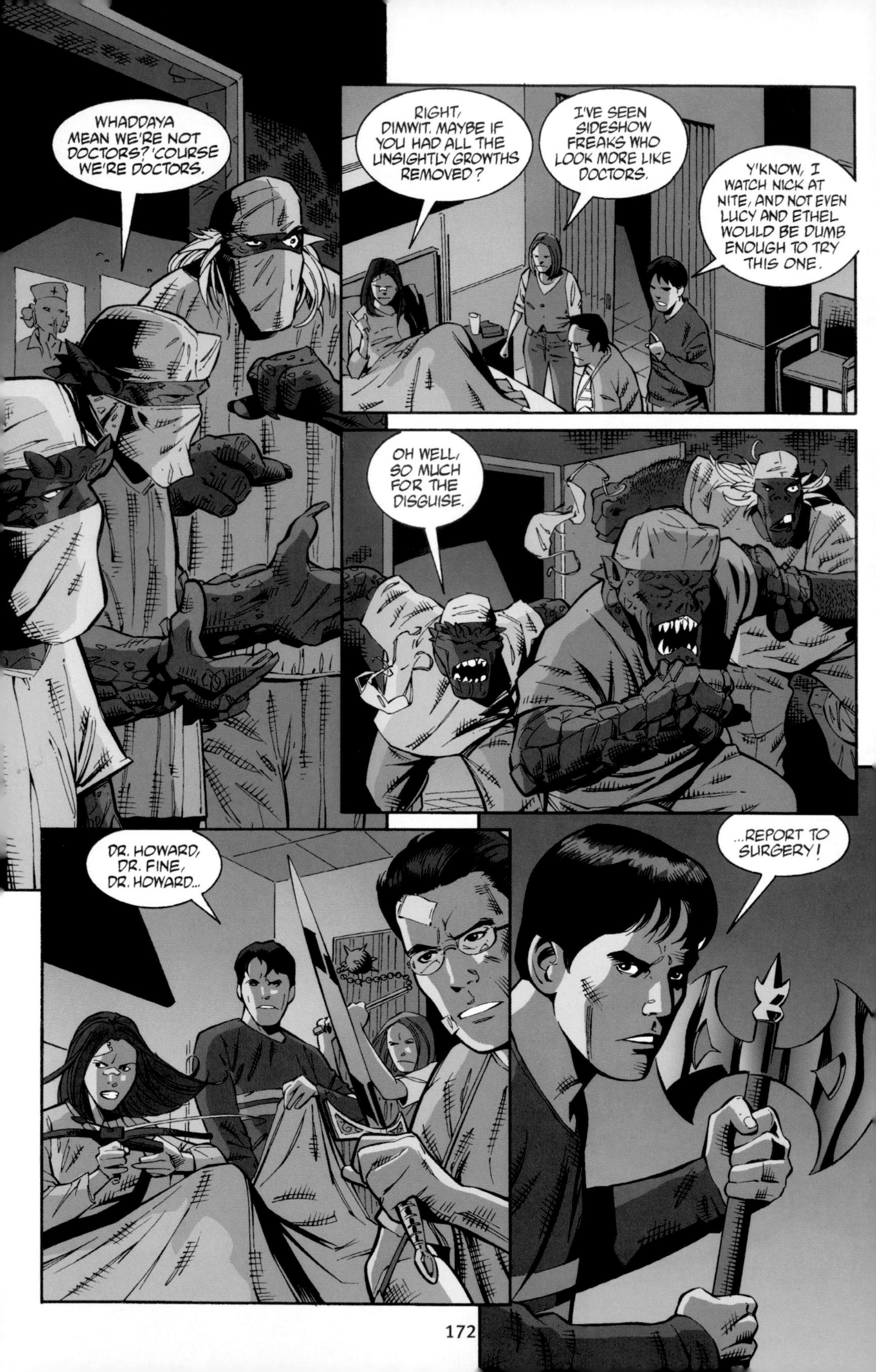
WHADDAYA MEAN WE'RE NOT DOCTORS? 'COURSE WE'RE DOCTORS.
RIGHT, DIMWIT. MAYBE IF YOU HAD ALL THE UNSIGHTLY GROWTHS REMOVED?
I'VE SEEN SIDESHOW FREAKS WHO LOOK MORE LIKE DOCTORS.
Y'KNOW, I WATCH NICK AT NITE, AND NOT EVEN LUCY AND ETHEL WOULD BE DUMB ENOUGH TO TRY THIS ONE.
OH WELL, SO MUCH FOR THE DISGUISE.
DR. HOWARD, DR. FINE, DR. HOWARD...
...REPORT TO SURGERY!

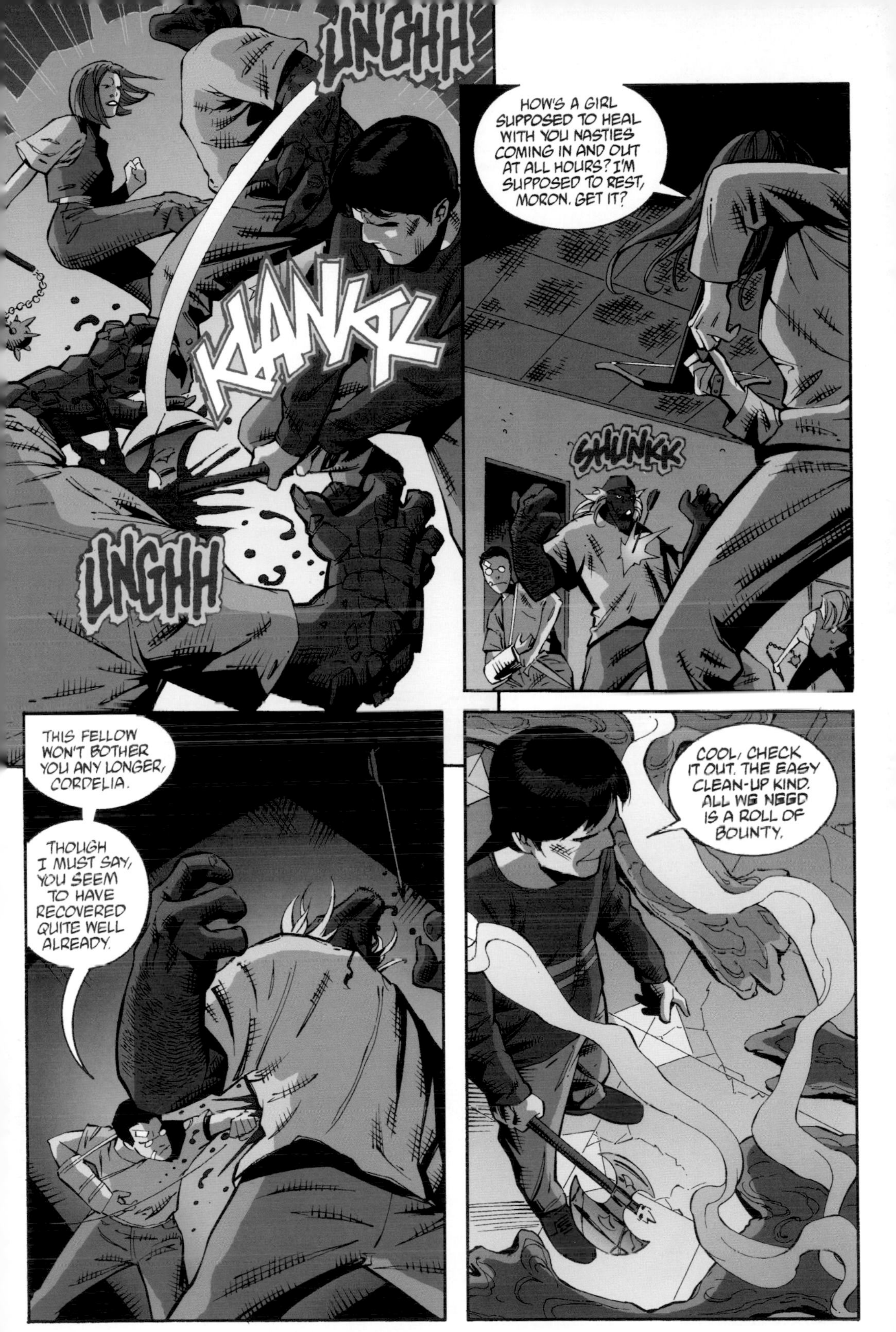
UNGHH
KLANKK
HOW'S A GIRL SUPPOSED TO HEAL WITH YOU NASTIES COMING IN AND OUT AT ALL HOURS? I'M SUPPOSED TO REST, MORON. GET IT?
UNGHH
SHUNKK
THIS FELLOW WON'T BOTHER YOU ANY LONGER, CORDELIA.
THOUGH I MUST SAY, YOU SEEM TO HAVE RECOVERED QUITE WELL ALREADY.
COOL, CHECK IT OUT. THE EASY CLEAN-UP KIND. ALL WE NEED IS A ROLL OF BOUNTY.

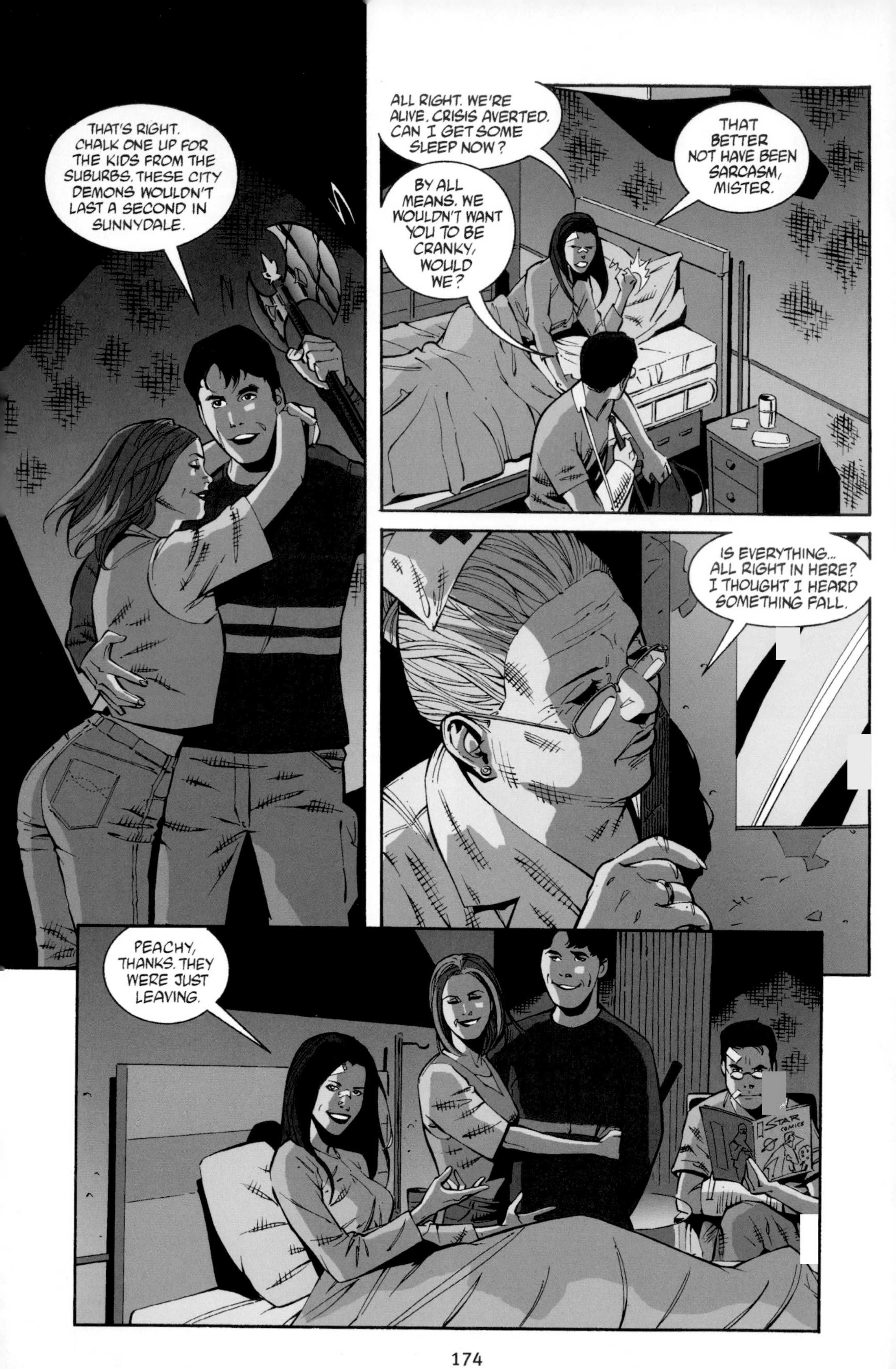
THAT'S RIGHT. CHALK ONE UP FOR THE KIDS FROM THE SUBURBS. THESE CITY DEMONS WOULDN'T LAST A SECOND IN SUNNYDALE.
ALL RIGHT. WE'RE ALIVE. CRISIS AVERTED. CAN I GET SOME SLEEP NOW?
BY ALL MEANS. WE WOULDN'T WANT YOU TO BE CRANKY, WOULD WE?
THAT BETTER NOT HAVE BEEN SARCASM, MISTER.
IS EVERYTHING... ALL RIGHT IN HERE? I THOUGHT I HEARD SOMETHING FALL.
PEACHY, THANKS. THEY WERE JUST LEAVING.
STAR COMICS

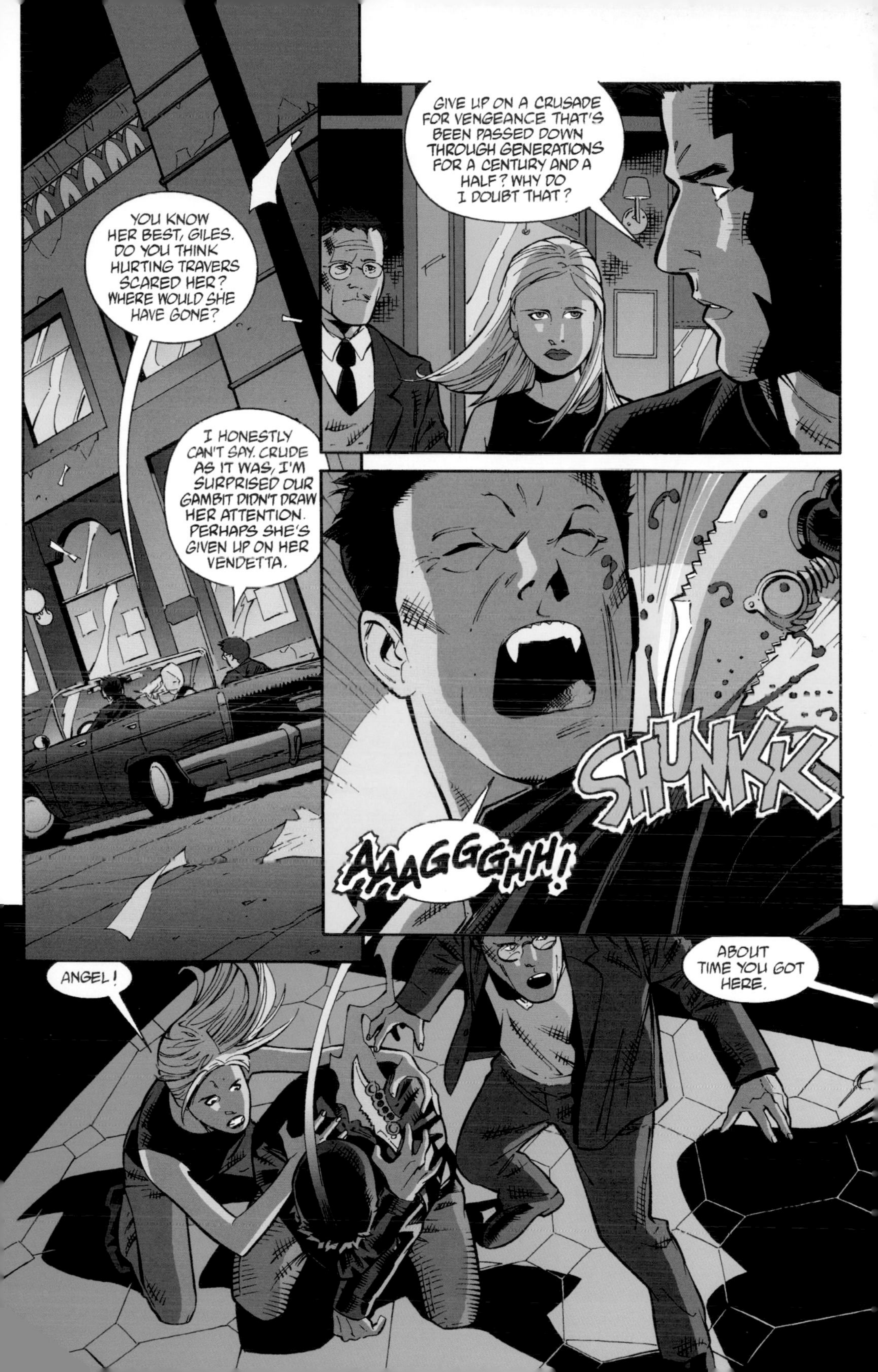
YOU KNOW HER BEST, GILES. DO YOU THINK HURTING TRAVERS SCARED HER? WHERE WOULD SHE HAVE GONE?
I HONESTLY CAN'T SAY. CRUDE AS IT WAS, I'M SURPRISED OUR GAMBIT DIDN'T DRAW HER ATTENTION. PERHAPS SHE'S GIVEN UP ON HER VENDETTA.
GIVE UP ON A CRUSADE FOR VENGEANCE THAT'S BEEN PASSED DOWN THROUGH GENERATIONS FOR A CENTURY AND A HALF? WHY DO I DOUBT THAT?
SHUNKK
AAAGGGHH!
ANGEL!
ABOUT TIME YOU GOT HERE.

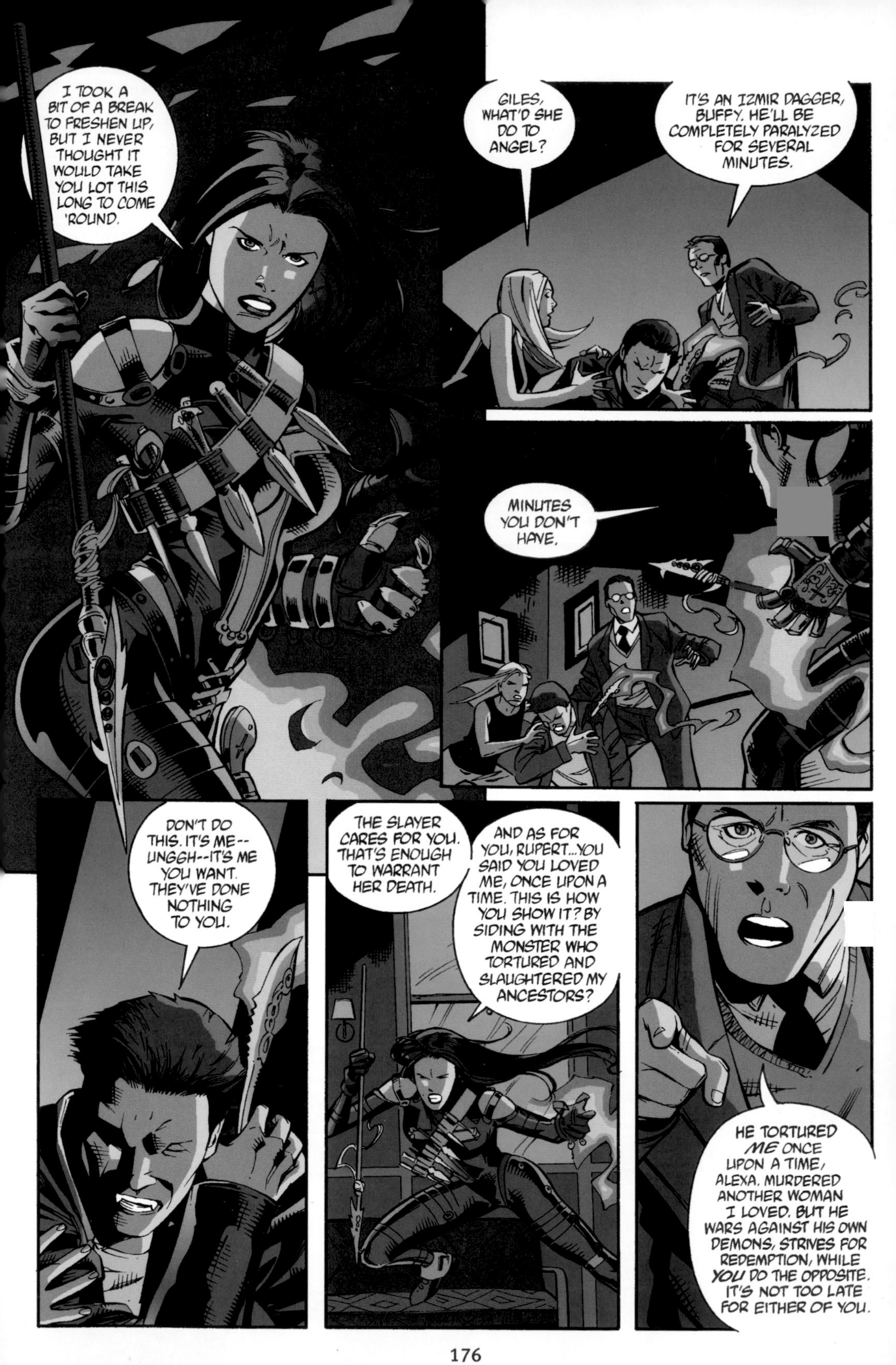
I TOOK A BIT OF A BREAK TO FRESHEN UP, BUT I NEVER THOUGHT IT WOULD TAKE YOU LOT THIS LONG TO COME 'ROUND.
GILES, WHAT'D SHE DO TO ANGEL?
IT'S AN IZMIR DAGGER, BUFFY. HE'LL BE COMPLETELY PARALYZED FOR SEVERAL MINUTES.
MINUTES YOU DON'T HAVE.
DON'T DO THIS. IT'S ME-- UNGGH--IT'S ME YOU WANT. THEY'VE DONE NOTHING TO YOU.
THE SLAYER CARES FOR YOU. THAT'S ENOUGH TO WARRANT HER DEATH.
AND AS FOR YOU, RUPERT...YOU SAID YOU LOVED ME, ONCE UPON A TIME. THIS IS HOW YOU SHOW IT? BY SIDING WITH THE MONSTER WHO TORTURED AND SLAUGHTERED MY ANCESTORS?
HE TORTURED *ME* ONCE UPON A TIME, ALEXA. MURDERED ANOTHER WOMAN I LOVED. BUT HE WARS AGAINST HIS OWN DEMONS, STRIVES FOR REDEMPTION, WHILE *YOU* DO THE OPPOSITE. IT'S NOT TOO LATE FOR EITHER OF YOU.

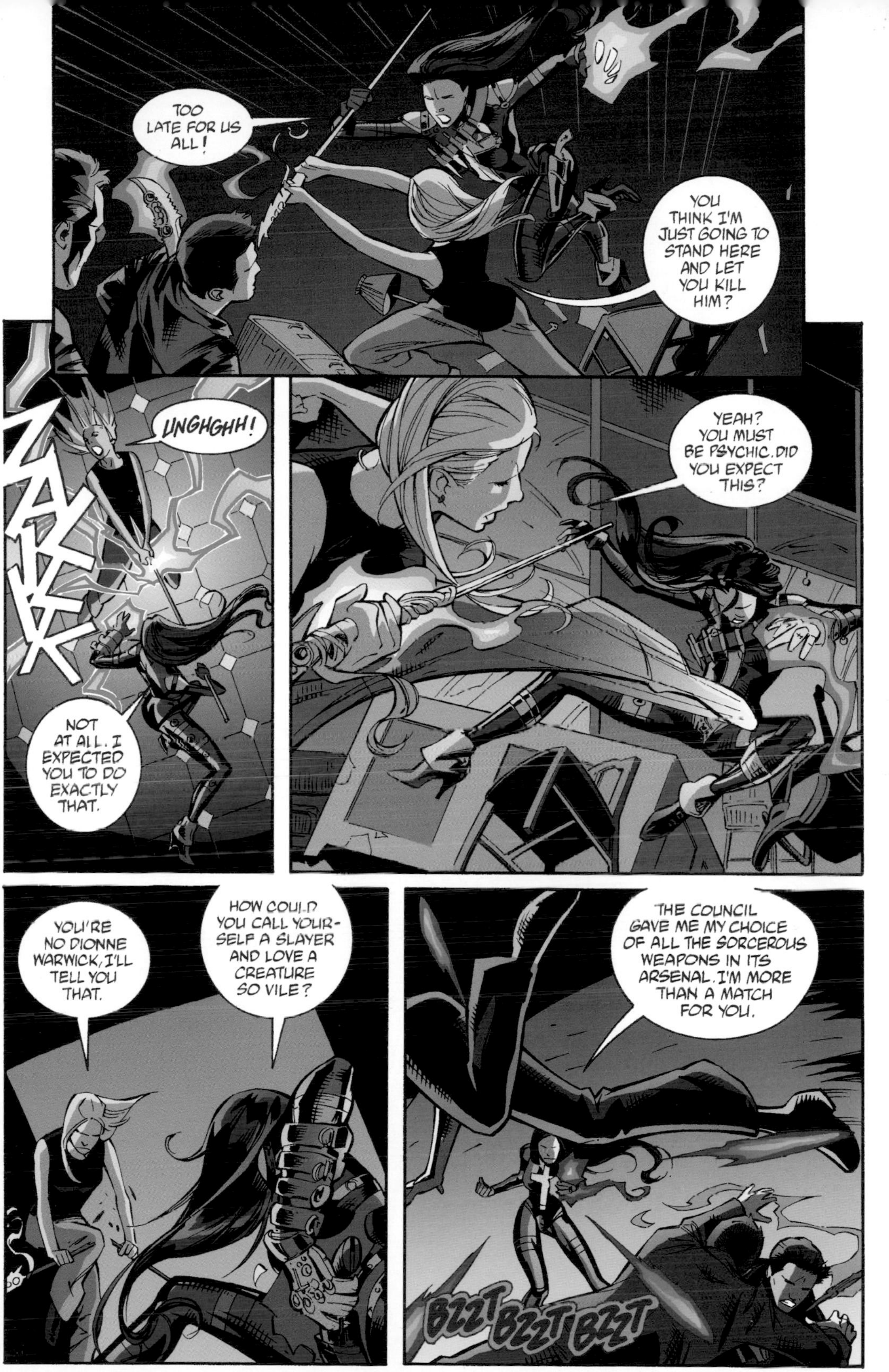

TOO LATE FOR US ALL!
YOU THINK I'M JUST GOING TO STAND HERE AND LET YOU KILL HIM?
YEAH? YOU MUST BE PSYCHIC. DID YOU EXPECT THIS?
UNGHGHH!
NOT AT ALL. I EXPECTED YOU TO DO EXACTLY THAT.
YOU'RE NO DIONNE WARWICK, I'LL TELL YOU THAT.
HOW COULD YOU CALL YOURSELF A SLAYER AND LOVE A CREATURE SO VILE?
THE COUNCIL GAVE ME MY CHOICE OF ALL THE SORCEROUS WEAPONS IN ITS ARSENAL. I'M MORE THAN A MATCH FOR YOU.
BZZT BZZT BZZT

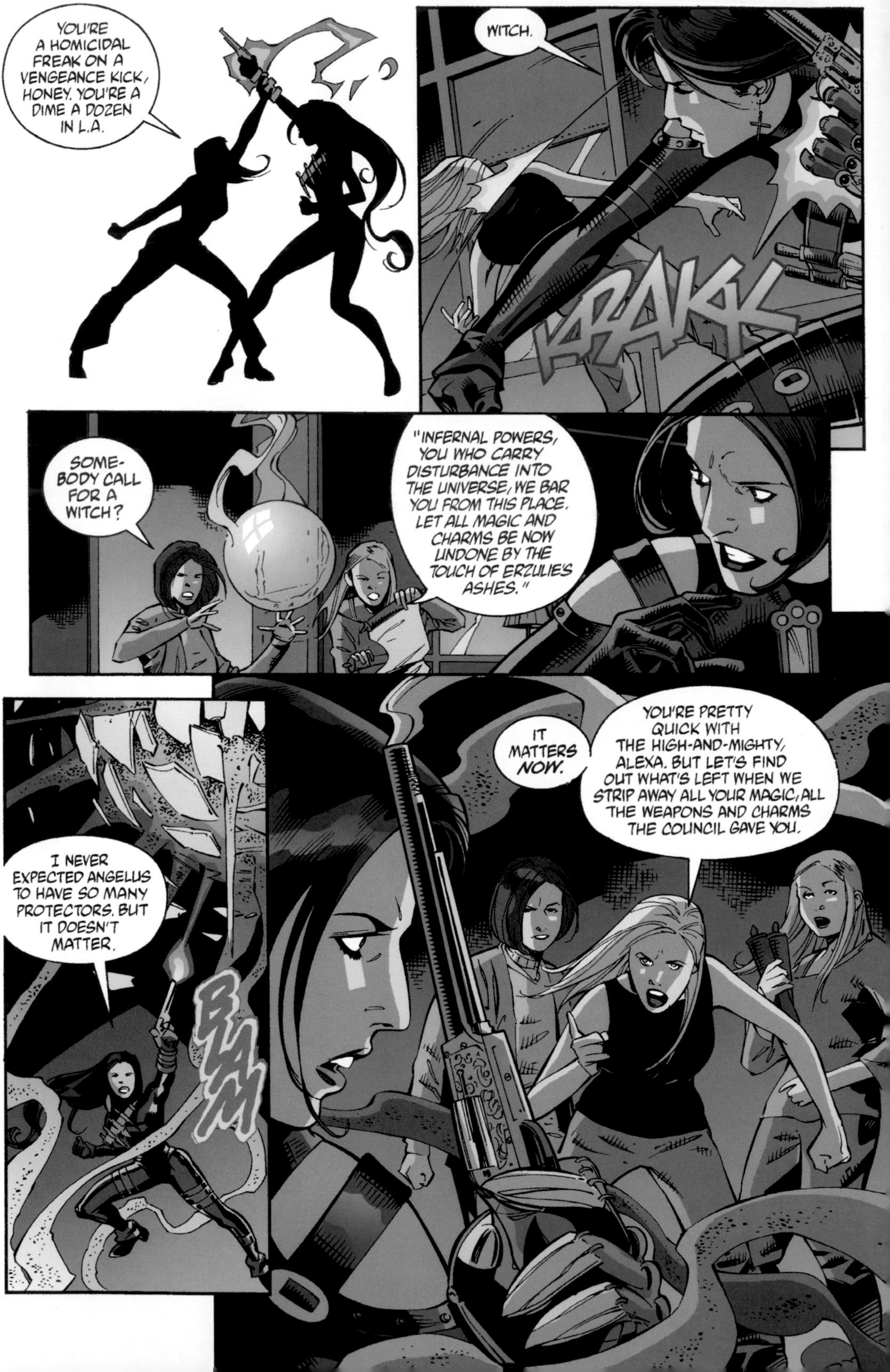
YOU'RE A HOMICIDAL FREAK ON A VENGEANCE KICK, HONEY. YOU'RE A DIME A DOZEN IN L.A.
WITCH.
KRAKAK
SOME-BODY CALL FOR A WITCH?
"INFERNAL POWERS, YOU WHO CARRY DISTURBANCE INTO THE UNIVERSE, WE BAR YOU FROM THIS PLACE. LET ALL MAGIC AND CHARMS BE NOW UNDONE BY THE TOUCH OF ERZULIE'S ASHES."
I NEVER EXPECTED ANGELUS TO HAVE SO MANY PROTECTORS. BUT IT DOESN'T MATTER.
BLAM
IT MATTERS NOW.
YOU'RE PRETTY QUICK WITH THE HIGH-AND-MIGHTY, ALEXA. BUT LET'S FIND OUT WHAT'S LEFT WHEN WE STRIP AWAY ALL YOUR MAGIC, ALL THE WEAPONS AND CHARMS THE COUNCIL GAVE YOU.

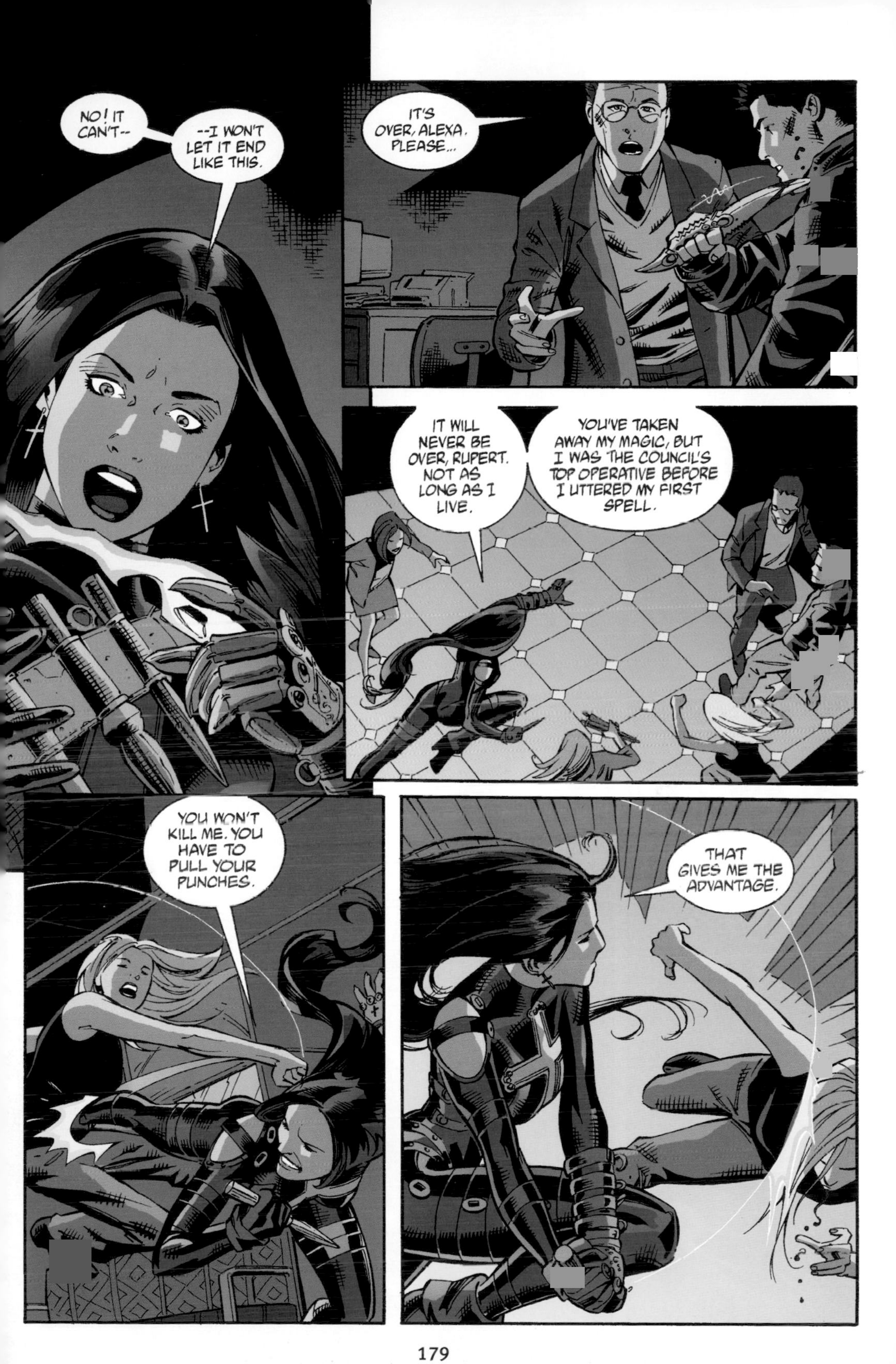
NO! IT CAN'T--
--I WON'T LET IT END LIKE THIS.
IT'S OVER, ALEXA. PLEASE...
IT WILL NEVER BE OVER, RUPERT. NOT AS LONG AS I LIVE.
YOU'VE TAKEN AWAY MY MAGIC, BUT I WAS THE COUNCIL'S TOP OPERATIVE BEFORE I UTTERED MY FIRST SPELL.
YOU WON'T KILL ME. YOU HAVE TO PULL YOUR PUNCHES.
THAT GIVES ME THE ADVANTAGE.

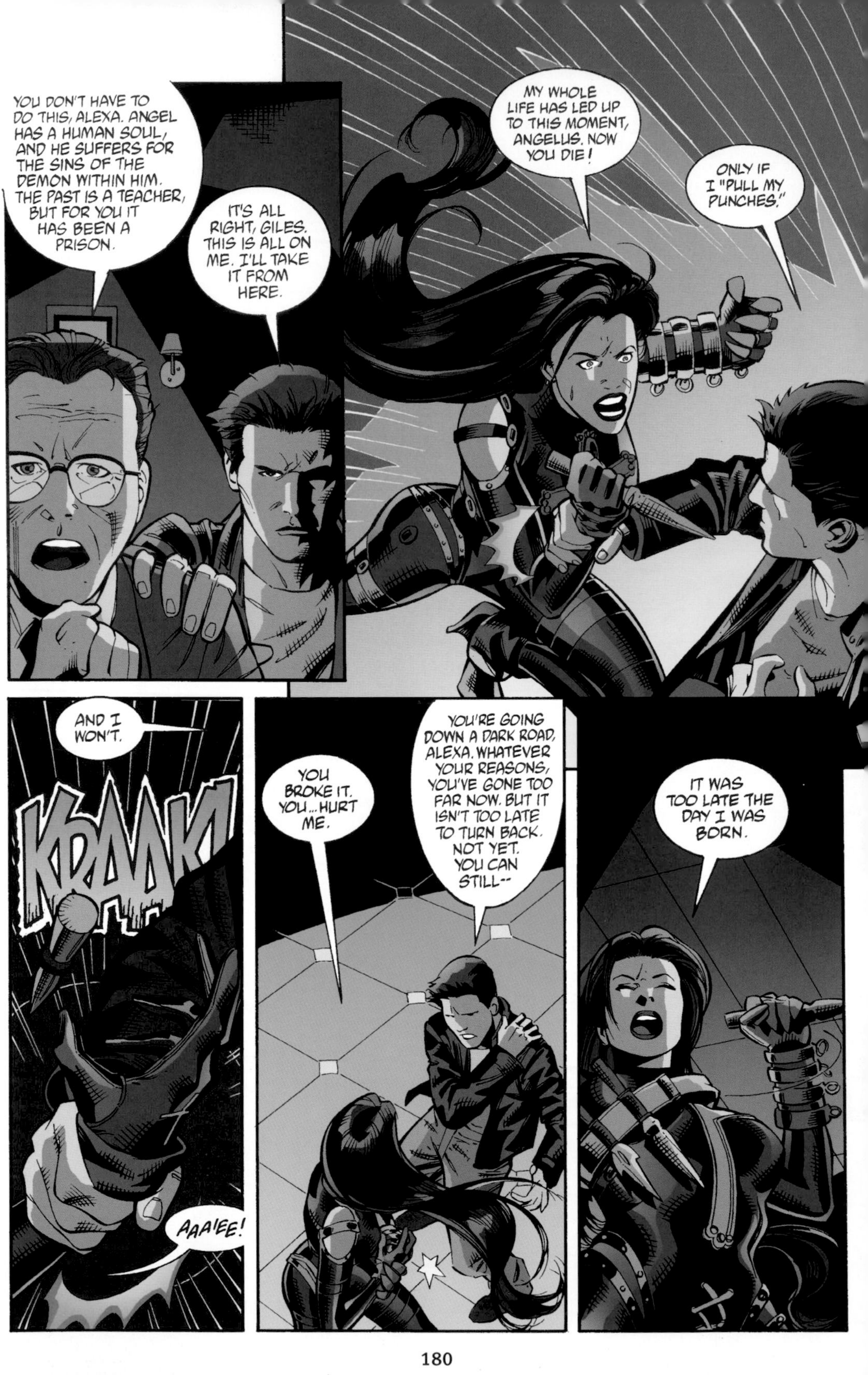
YOU DON'T HAVE TO DO THIS, ALEXA. ANGEL HAS A HUMAN SOUL, AND HE SUFFERS FOR THE SINS OF THE DEMON WITHIN HIM. THE PAST IS A TEACHER, BUT FOR YOU IT HAS BEEN A PRISON.
IT'S ALL RIGHT, GILES. THIS IS ALL ON ME. I'LL TAKE IT FROM HERE.
MY WHOLE LIFE HAS LED UP TO THIS MOMENT, ANGELUS. NOW YOU DIE!
ONLY IF I "PULL MY PUNCHES."
AND I WON'T.
KRAAK!
AAAIEE!
YOU BROKE IT. YOU...HURT ME.
YOU'RE GOING DOWN A DARK ROAD, ALEXA. WHATEVER YOUR REASONS, YOU'VE GONE TOO FAR NOW. BUT IT ISN'T TOO LATE TO TURN BACK. NOT YET. YOU CAN STILL--
IT WAS TOO LATE THE DAY I WAS BORN.

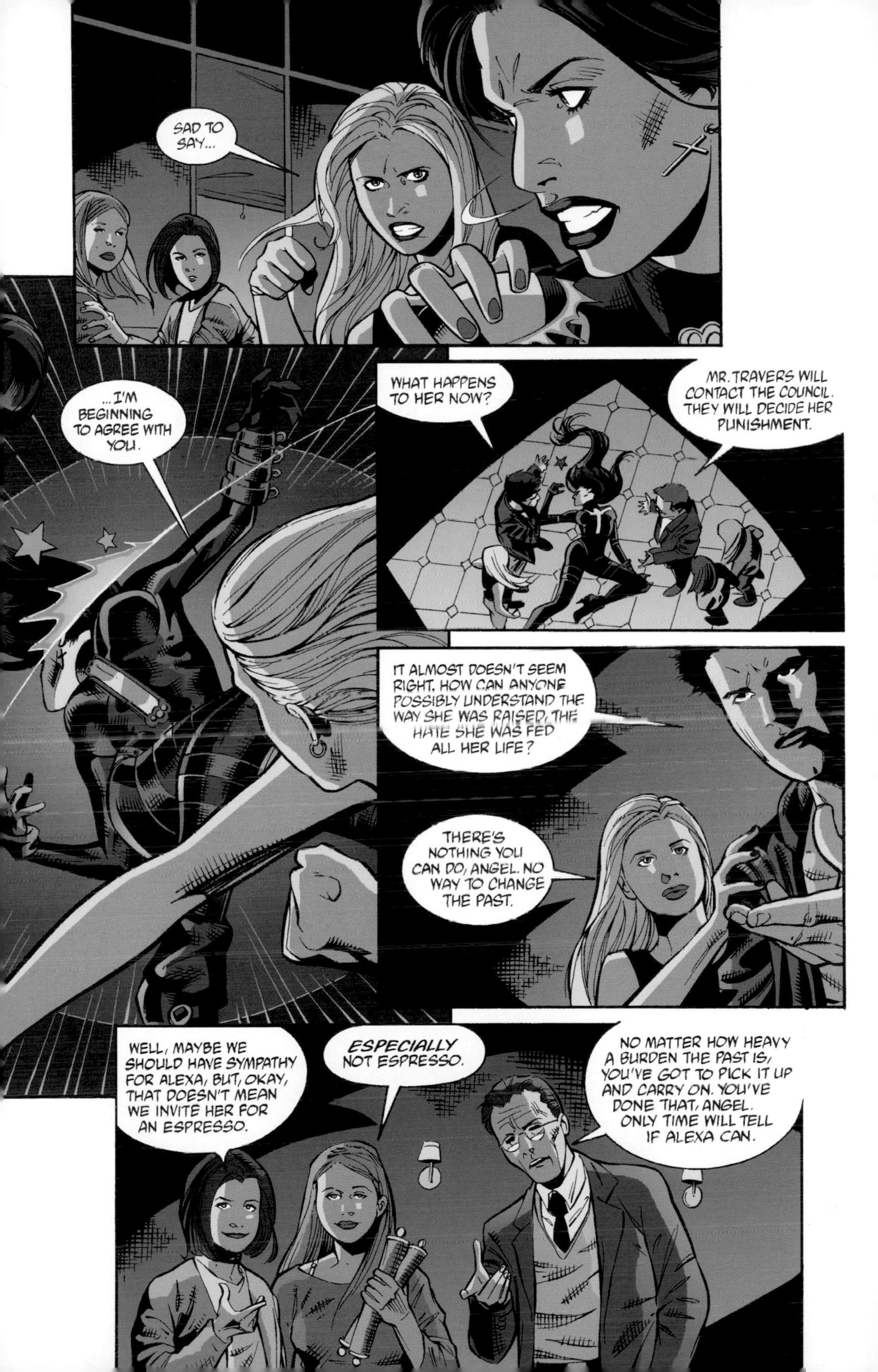
SAD TO SAY...
...I'M BEGINNING TO AGREE WITH YOU.
WHAT HAPPENS TO HER NOW?
MR. TRAVERS WILL CONTACT THE COUNCIL. THEY WILL DECIDE HER PUNISHMENT.
IT ALMOST DOESN'T SEEM RIGHT. HOW CAN ANYONE POSSIBLY UNDERSTAND THE WAY SHE WAS RAISED, THE HATE SHE WAS FED ALL HER LIFE?
THERE'S NOTHING YOU CAN DO, ANGEL. NO WAY TO CHANGE THE PAST.
WELL, MAYBE WE SHOULD HAVE SYMPATHY FOR ALEXA, BUT, OKAY, THAT DOESN'T MEAN WE INVITE HER FOR AN ESPRESSO.
ESPECIALLY NOT ESPRESSO.
NO MATTER HOW HEAVY A BURDEN THE PAST IS, YOU'VE GOT TO PICK IT UP AND CARRY ON. YOU'VE DONE THAT, ANGEL. ONLY TIME WILL TELL IF ALEXA CAN.

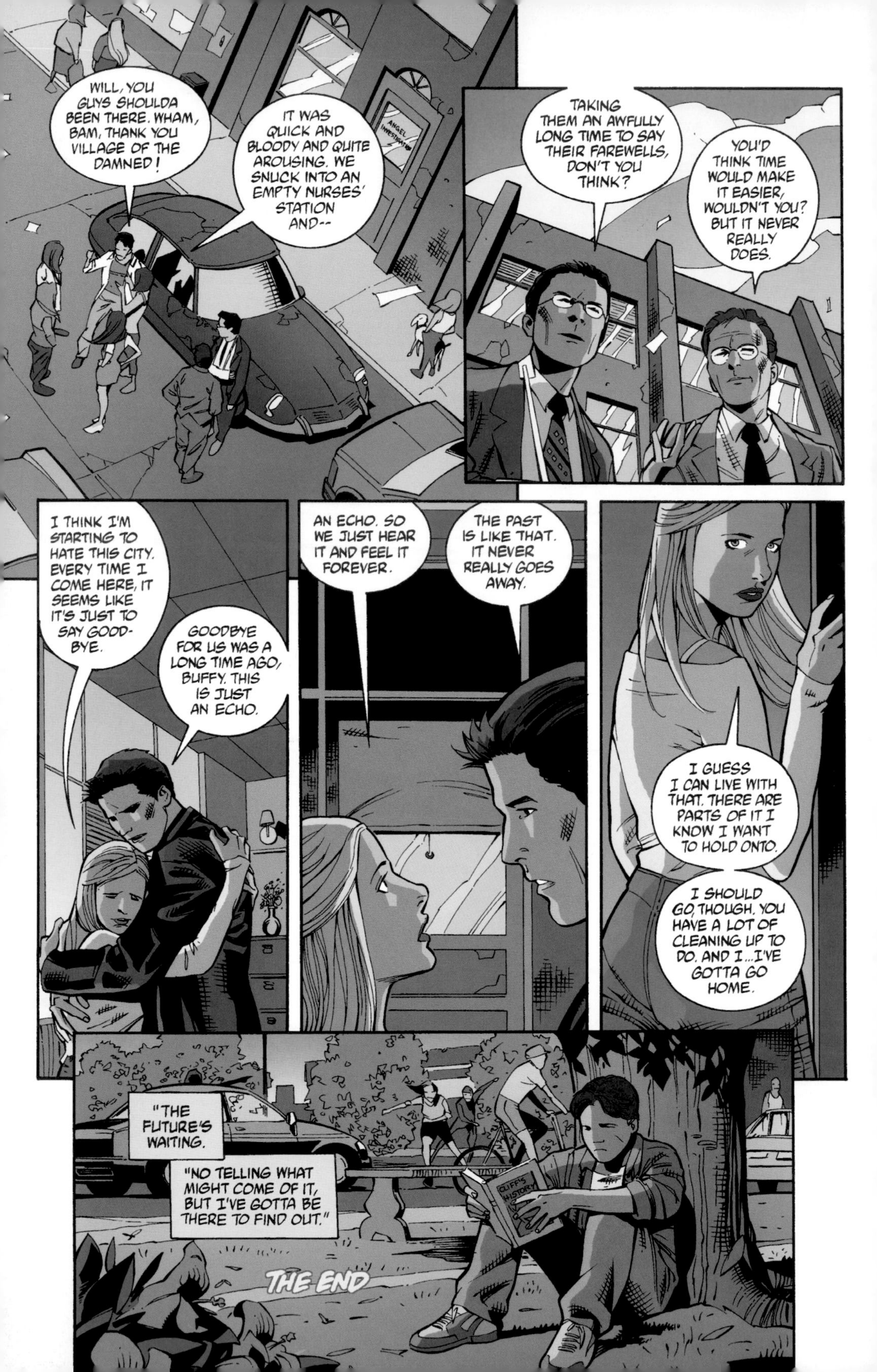
WILL, YOU GUYS SHOULDA BEEN THERE. WHAM, BAM, THANK YOU VILLAGE OF THE DAMNED!
IT WAS QUICK AND BLOODY AND QUITE AROUSING. WE SNUCK INTO AN EMPTY NURSES' STATION AND--
ANGEL INVESTIGATIONS
TAKING THEM AN AWFULLY LONG TIME TO SAY THEIR FAREWELLS, DON'T YOU THINK?
YOU'D THINK TIME WOULD MAKE IT EASIER, WOULDN'T YOU? BUT IT NEVER REALLY DOES.
I THINK I'M STARTING TO HATE THIS CITY. EVERY TIME I COME HERE, IT SEEMS LIKE IT'S JUST TO SAY GOOD-BYE.
GOODBYE FOR US WAS A LONG TIME AGO, BUFFY. THIS IS JUST AN ECHO.
AN ECHO. SO WE JUST HEAR IT AND FEEL IT FOREVER.
THE PAST IS LIKE THAT. IT NEVER REALLY GOES AWAY.
I GUESS I CAN LIVE WITH THAT. THERE ARE PARTS OF IT I KNOW I WANT TO HOLD ONTO.
I SHOULD GO, THOUGH. YOU HAVE A LOT OF CLEANING UP TO DO. AND I...I'VE GOTTA GO HOME.
"THE FUTURE'S WAITING.
"NO TELLING WHAT MIGHT COME OF IT, BUT I'VE GOTTA BE THERE TO FIND OUT."
CLIFF'S HISTORY
THE END

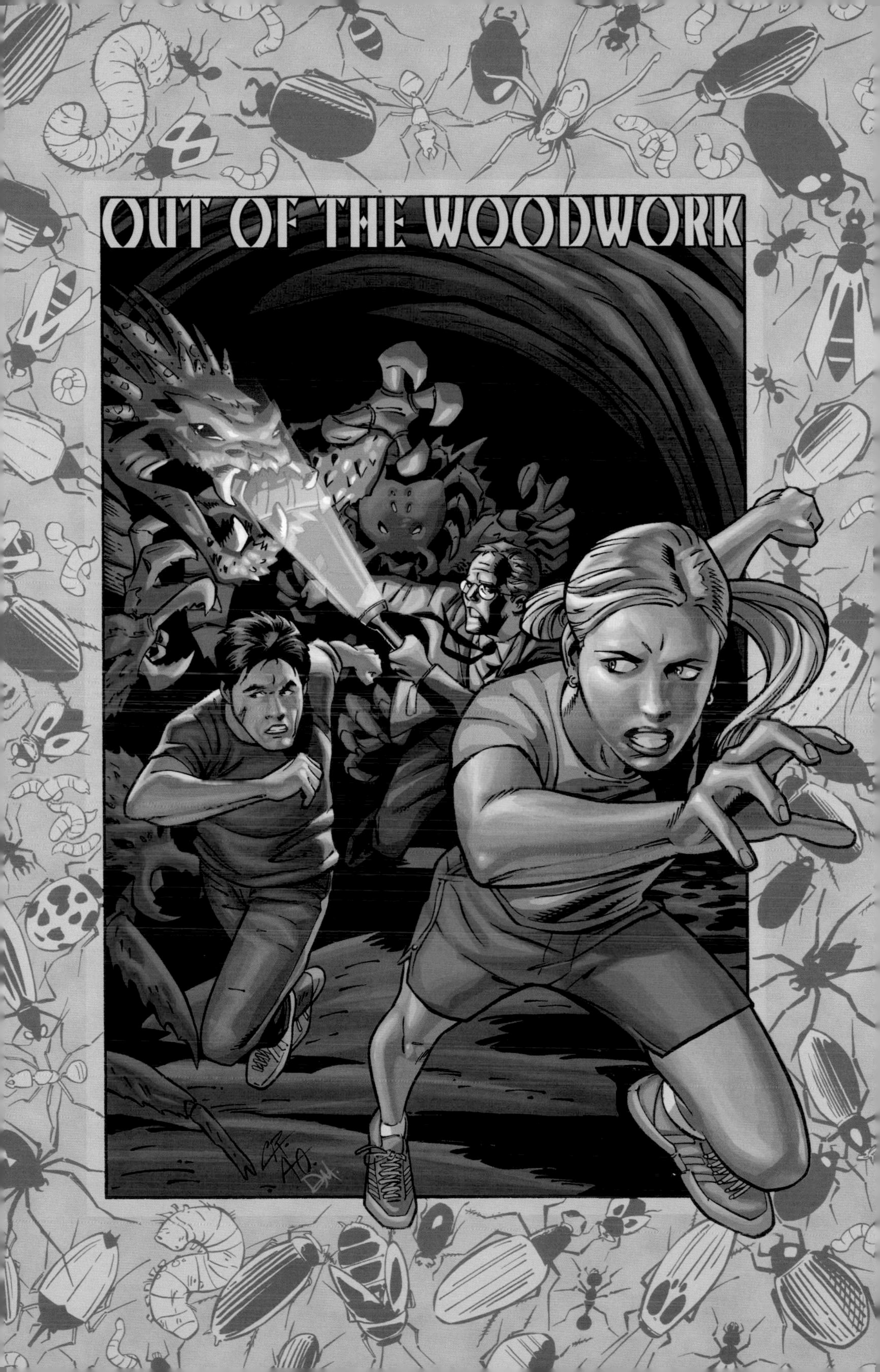
OUT OF THE WOODWORK

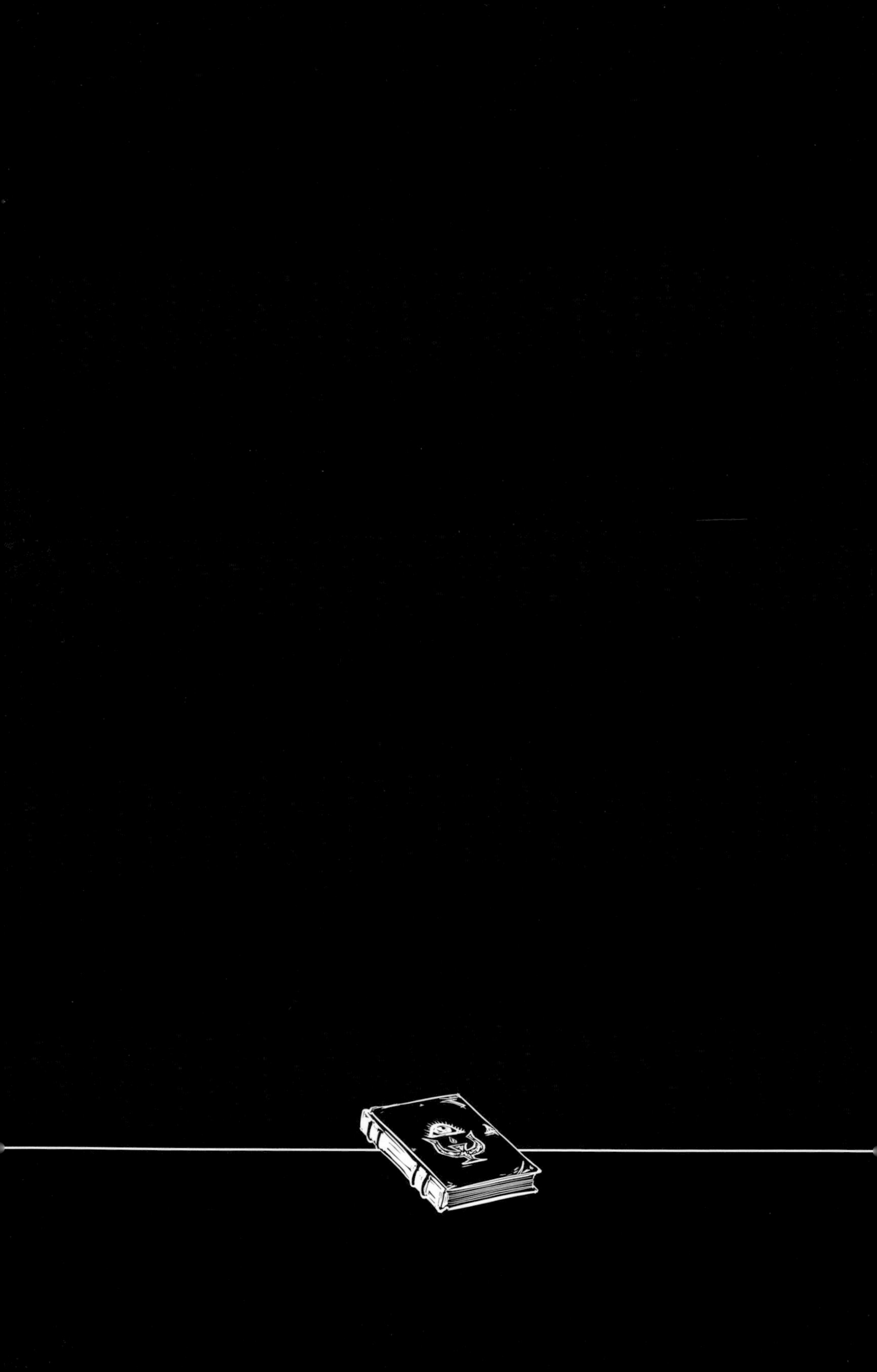

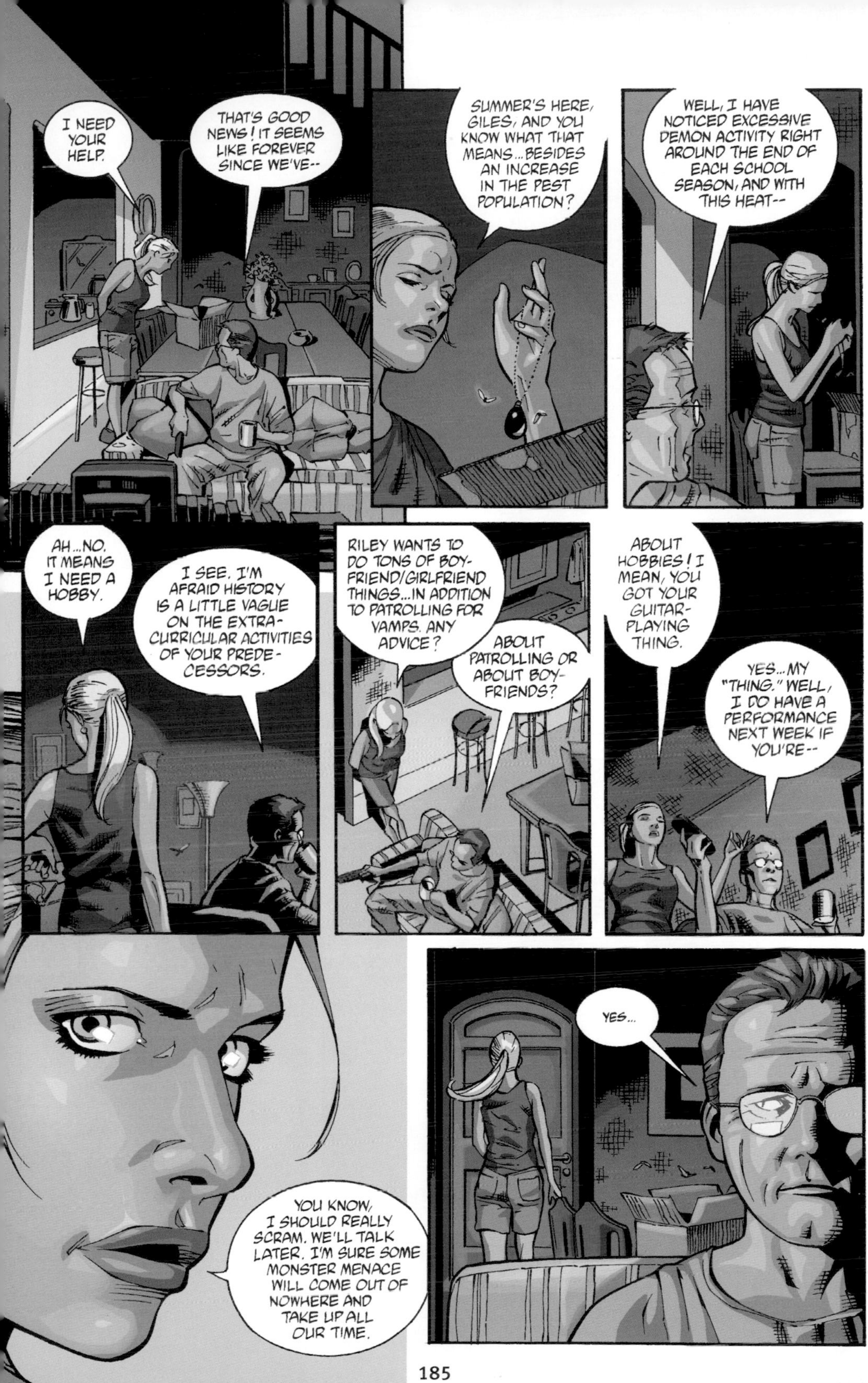
I NEED YOUR HELP.
THAT'S GOOD NEWS! IT SEEMS LIKE FOREVER SINCE WE'VE--
SUMMER'S HERE, GILES, AND YOU KNOW WHAT THAT MEANS...BESIDES AN INCREASE IN THE PEST POPULATION?
WELL, I HAVE NOTICED EXCESSIVE DEMON ACTIVITY RIGHT AROUND THE END OF EACH SCHOOL SEASON, AND WITH THIS HEAT--
AH...NO. IT MEANS I NEED A HOBBY.
I SEE. I'M AFRAID HISTORY IS A LITTLE VAGUE ON THE EXTRA-CURRICULAR ACTIVITIES OF YOUR PREDE-CESSORS.
RILEY WANTS TO DO TONS OF BOY-FRIEND/GIRLFRIEND THINGS...IN ADDITION TO PATROLLING FOR VAMPS. ANY ADVICE?
ABOUT PATROLLING OR ABOUT BOY-FRIENDS?
ABOUT HOBBIES! I MEAN, YOU GOT YOUR GUITAR-PLAYING THING.
YES...MY "THING." WELL, I DO HAVE A PERFORMANCE NEXT WEEK IF YOU'RE--
YOU KNOW, I SHOULD REALLY SCRAM. WE'LL TALK LATER. I'M SURE SOME MONSTER MENACE WILL COME OUT OF NOWHERE AND TAKE UP ALL OUR TIME.
YES...

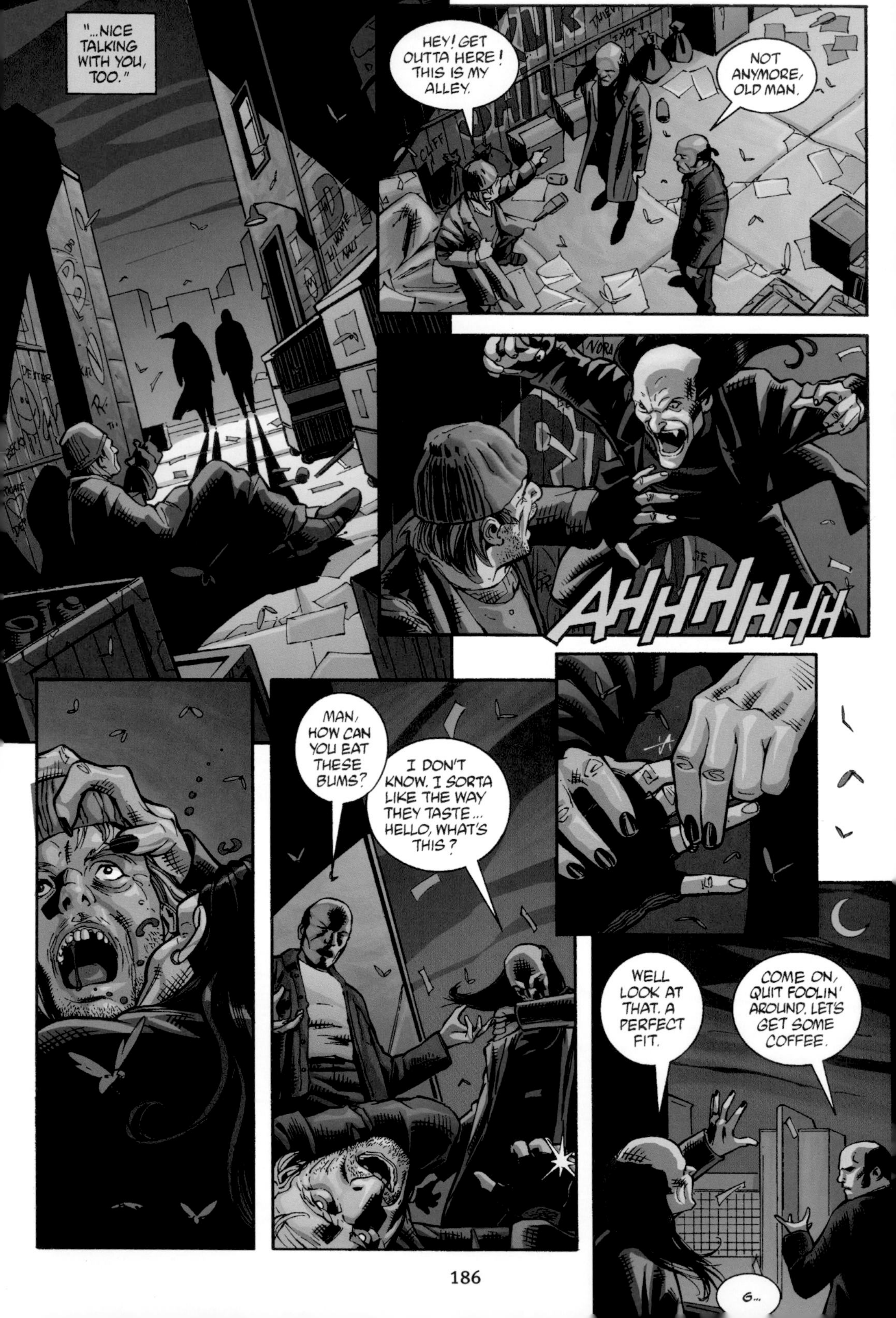
"...NICE TALKING WITH YOU, TOO."
HEY! GET OUTTA HERE! THIS IS MY ALLEY.
NOT ANYMORE, OLD MAN.
AHHHHHH
MAN, HOW CAN YOU EAT THESE BUMS?
I DON'T KNOW. I SORTA LIKE THE WAY THEY TASTE... HELLO, WHAT'S THIS?
WELL LOOK AT THAT. A PERFECT FIT.
COME ON, QUIT FOOLIN' AROUND. LET'S GET SOME COFFEE.
G...

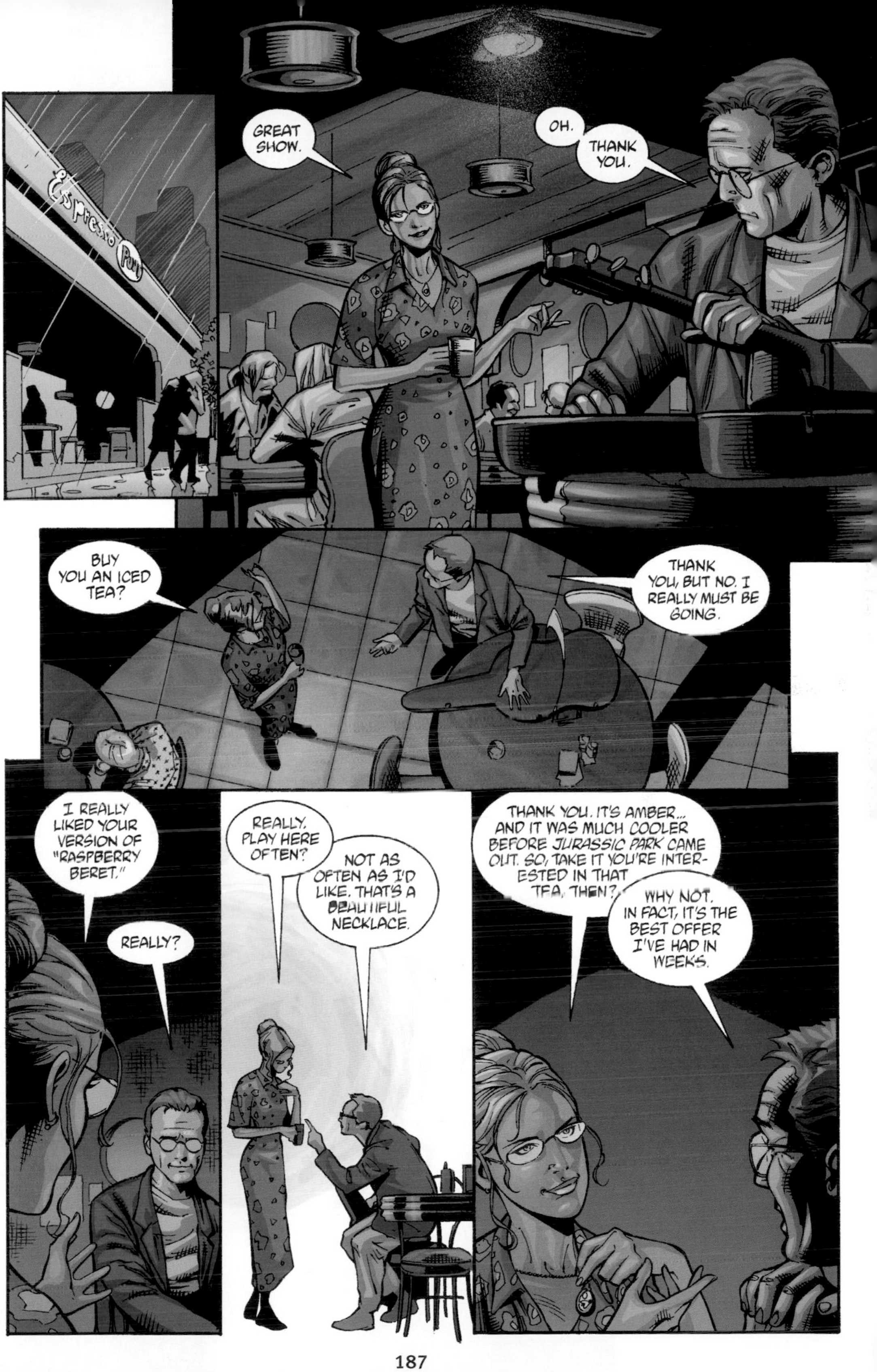
Espresso Pun
GREAT SHOW.
OH.
THANK YOU.
BUY YOU AN ICED TEA?
THANK YOU, BUT NO. I REALLY MUST BE GOING.
I REALLY LIKED YOUR VERSION OF "RASPBERRY BERET."
REALLY?
REALLY. PLAY HERE OFTEN?
NOT AS OFTEN AS I'D LIKE. THAT'S A BEAUTIFUL NECKLACE.
THANK YOU. IT'S AMBER... AND IT WAS MUCH COOLER BEFORE JURASSIC PARK CAME OUT. SO, TAKE IT YOU'RE INTERESTED IN THAT TEA, THEN?
WHY NOT. IN FACT, IT'S THE BEST OFFER I'VE HAD IN WEEKS.

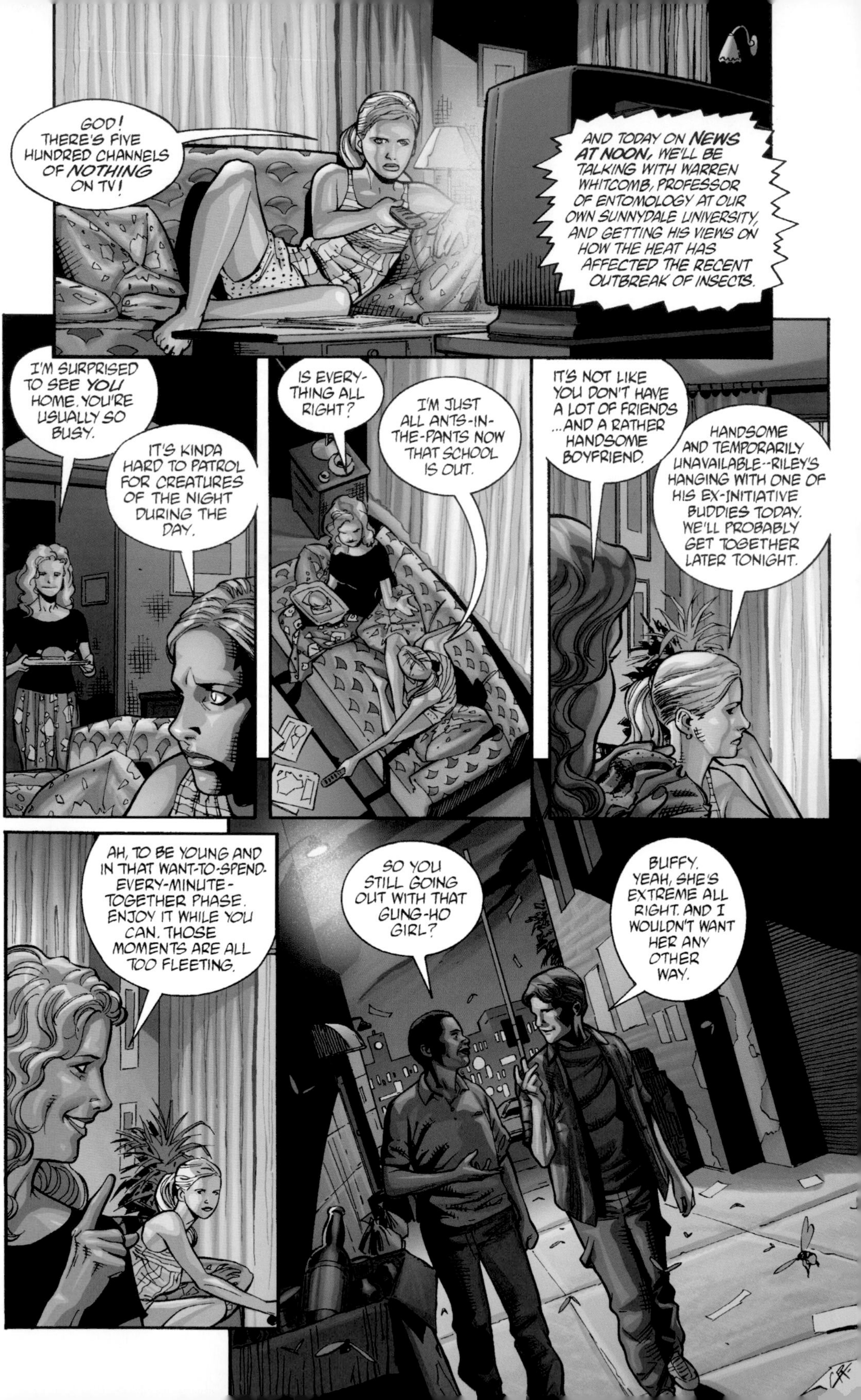
GOD! THERE'S FIVE HUNDRED CHANNELS OF NOTHING ON TV!
AND TODAY ON NEWS AT NOON, WE'LL BE TALKING WITH WARREN WHITCOMB, PROFESSOR OF ENTOMOLOGY AT OUR OWN SUNNYDALE UNIVERSITY, AND GETTING HIS VIEWS ON HOW THE HEAT HAS AFFECTED THE RECENT OUTBREAK OF INSECTS.
I'M SURPRISED TO SEE YOU HOME. YOU'RE USUALLY SO BUSY.
IT'S KINDA HARD TO PATROL FOR CREATURES OF THE NIGHT DURING THE DAY.
IS EVERY-THING ALL RIGHT?
I'M JUST ALL ANTS-IN-THE-PANTS NOW THAT SCHOOL IS OUT.
IT'S NOT LIKE YOU DON'T HAVE A LOT OF FRIENDS ...AND A RATHER HANDSOME BOYFRIEND.
HANDSOME AND TEMPORARILY UNAVAILABLE--RILEY'S HANGING WITH ONE OF HIS EX-INITIATIVE BUDDIES TODAY. WE'LL PROBABLY GET TOGETHER LATER TONIGHT.
AH, TO BE YOUNG AND IN THAT WANT-TO-SPEND-EVERY-MINUTE-TOGETHER PHASE. ENJOY IT WHILE YOU CAN. THOSE MOMENTS ARE ALL TOO FLEETING.
SO YOU STILL GOING OUT WITH THAT GUNG-HO GIRL?
BUFFY. YEAH, SHE'S EXTREME ALL RIGHT. AND I WOULDN'T WANT HER ANY OTHER WAY.

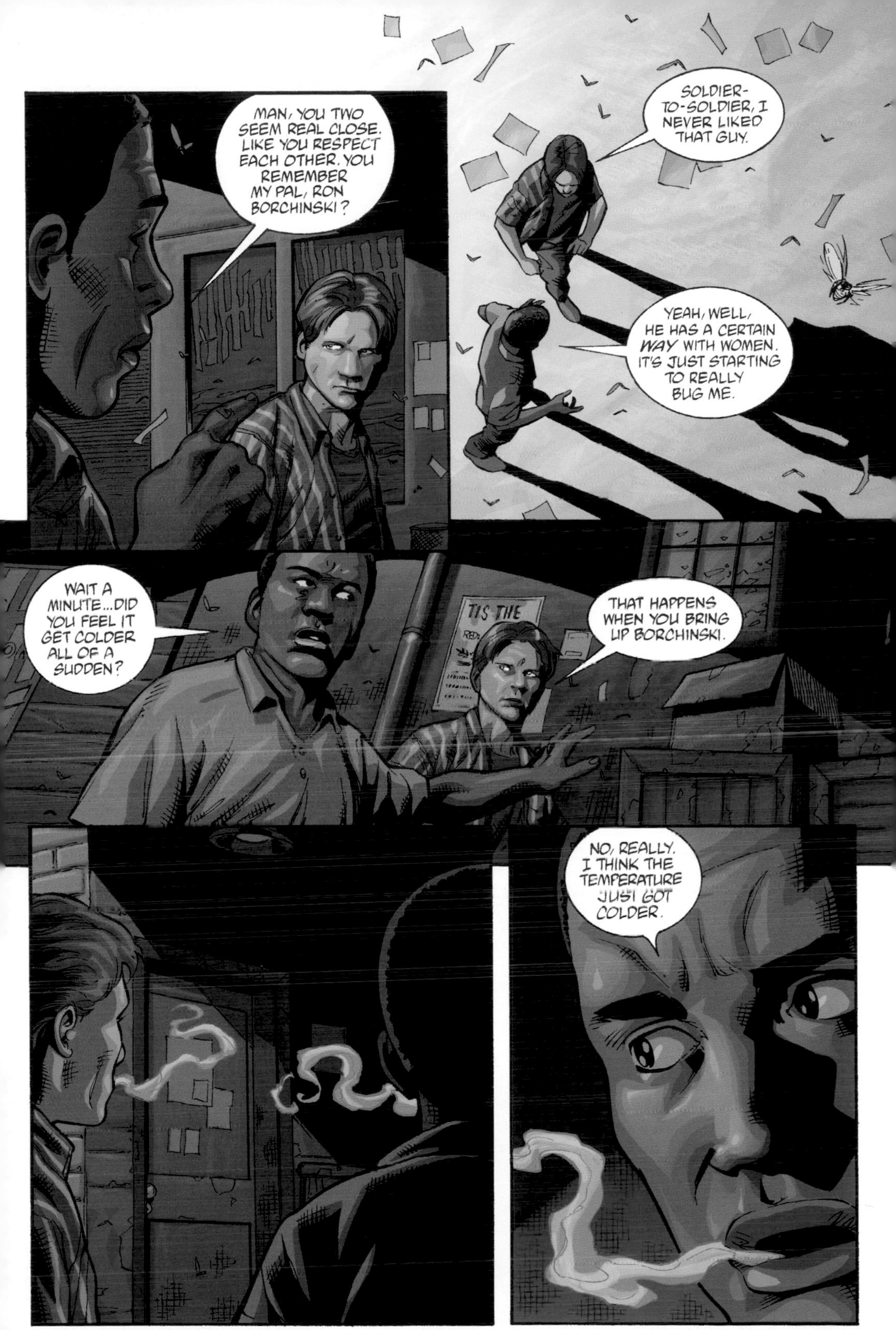
MAN, YOU TWO SEEM REAL CLOSE. LIKE YOU RESPECT EACH OTHER. YOU REMEMBER MY PAL, RON BORCHINSKI?
SOLDIER-TO-SOLDIER, I NEVER LIKED THAT GUY.
YEAH, WELL, HE HAS A CERTAIN WAY WITH WOMEN. IT'S JUST STARTING TO REALLY BUG ME.
WAIT A MINUTE...DID YOU FEEL IT GET COLDER ALL OF A SUDDEN?
THAT HAPPENS WHEN YOU BRING UP BORCHINSKI.
TIS THE
NO, REALLY. I THINK THE TEMPERATURE JUST GOT COLDER.

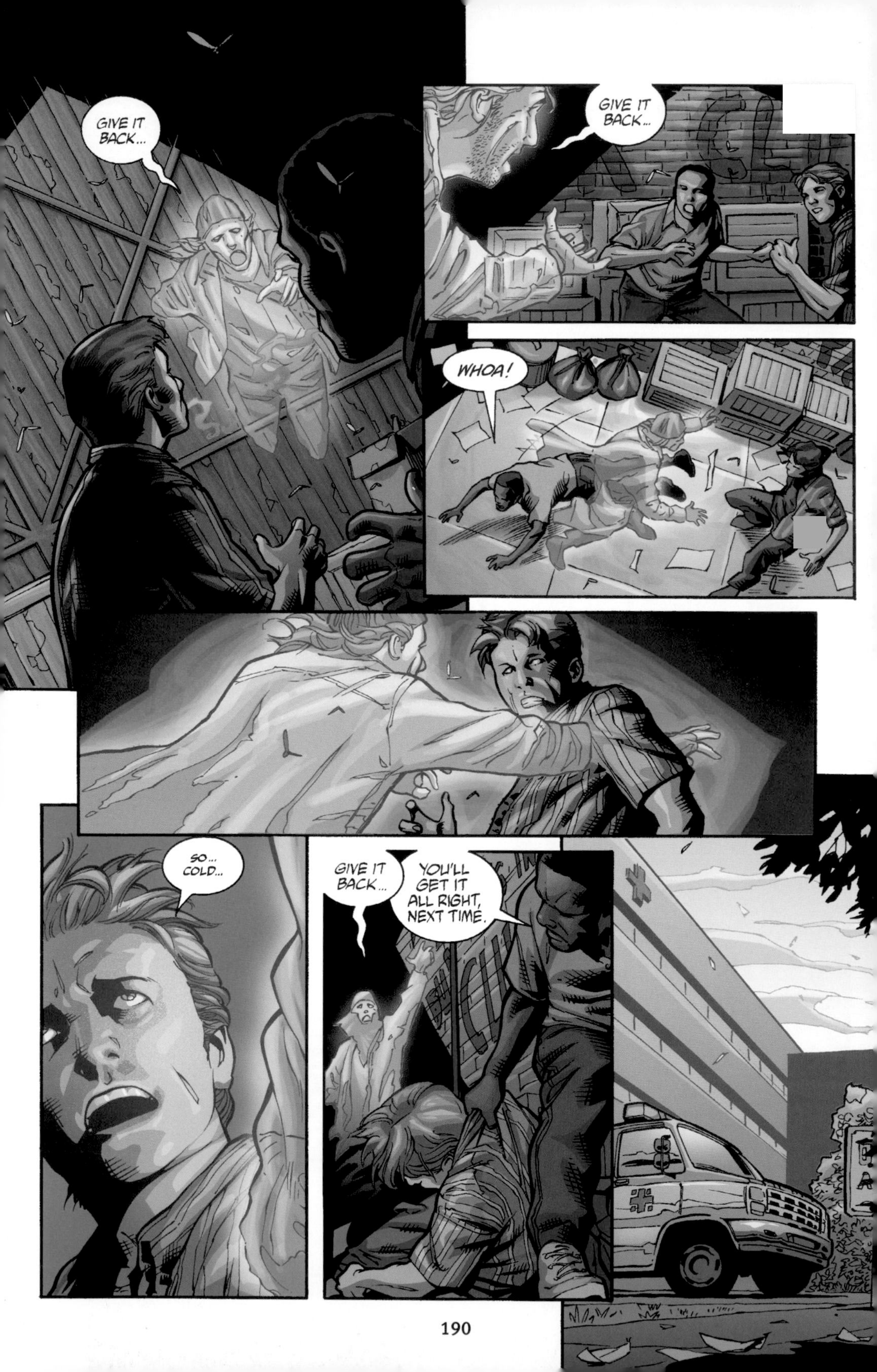
GIVE IT BACK...
GIVE IT BACK...
WHOA!
SO... COLD...
GIVE IT BACK...
YOU'LL GET IT ALL RIGHT, NEXT TIME.

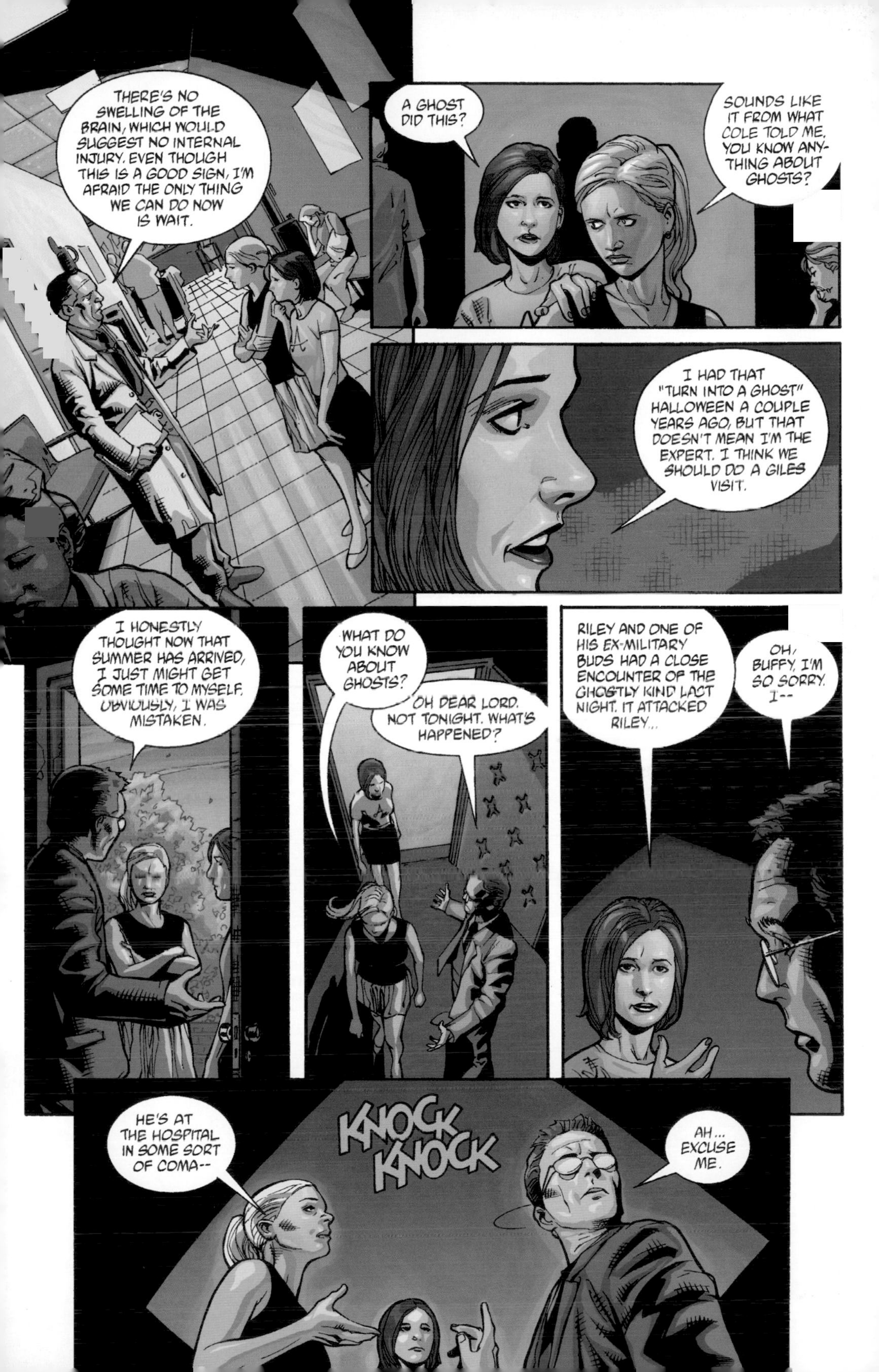
THERE'S NO SWELLING OF THE BRAIN, WHICH WOULD SUGGEST NO INTERNAL INJURY. EVEN THOUGH THIS IS A GOOD SIGN, I'M AFRAID THE ONLY THING WE CAN DO NOW IS WAIT.
A GHOST DID THIS?
SOUNDS LIKE IT FROM WHAT COLE TOLD ME. YOU KNOW ANYTHING ABOUT GHOSTS?
I HAD THAT "TURN INTO A GHOST" HALLOWEEN A COUPLE YEARS AGO, BUT THAT DOESN'T MEAN I'M THE EXPERT. I THINK WE SHOULD DO A GILES VISIT.
I HONESTLY THOUGHT NOW THAT SUMMER HAS ARRIVED, I JUST MIGHT GET SOME TIME TO MYSELF. OBVIOUSLY, I WAS MISTAKEN.
WHAT DO YOU KNOW ABOUT GHOSTS?
OH DEAR LORD. NOT TONIGHT. WHAT'S HAPPENED?
RILEY AND ONE OF HIS EX-MILITARY BUDS HAD A CLOSE ENCOUNTER OF THE GHOSTLY KIND LAST NIGHT. IT ATTACKED RILEY...
OH, BUFFY, I'M SO SORRY. I--
HE'S AT THE HOSPITAL IN SOME SORT OF COMA--
KNOCK KNOCK
AH... EXCUSE ME.

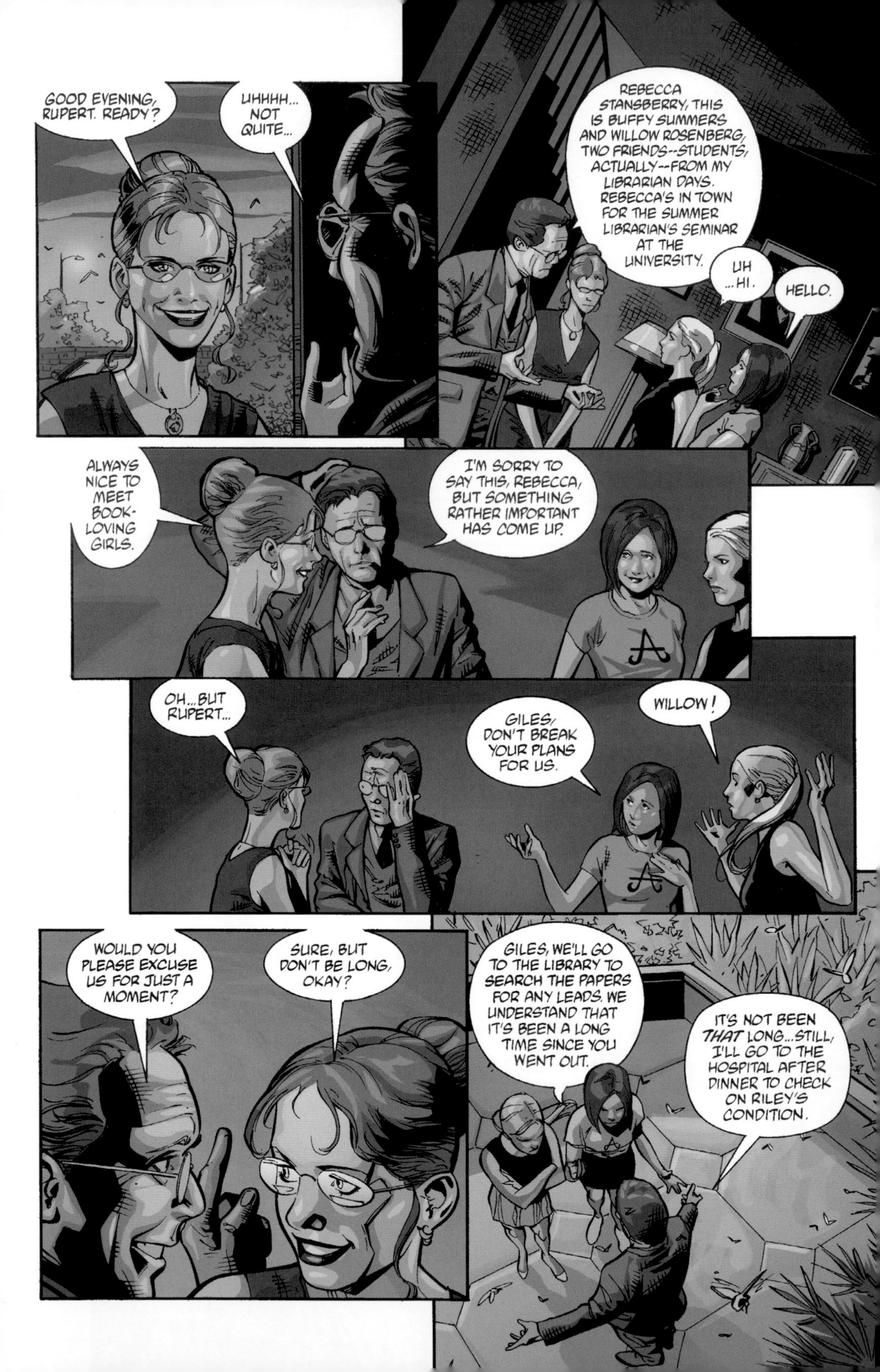
GOOD EVENING, RUPERT. READY?
UHHHH... NOT QUITE...
REBECCA STANSBERRY, THIS IS BUFFY SUMMERS AND WILLOW ROSENBERG, TWO FRIENDS--STUDENTS, ACTUALLY--FROM MY LIBRARIAN DAYS. REBECCA'S IN TOWN FOR THE SUMMER LIBRARIAN'S SEMINAR AT THE UNIVERSITY.
UH ...HI.
HELLO.
ALWAYS NICE TO MEET BOOK-LOVING GIRLS.
I'M SORRY TO SAY THIS, REBECCA, BUT SOMETHING RATHER IMPORTANT HAS COME UP.
OH...BUT RUPERT...
GILES, DON'T BREAK YOUR PLANS FOR US.
WILLOW!
WOULD YOU PLEASE EXCUSE US FOR JUST A MOMENT?
SURE, BUT DON'T BE LONG, OKAY?
GILES, WE'LL GO TO THE LIBRARY TO SEARCH THE PAPERS FOR ANY LEADS. WE UNDERSTAND THAT IT'S BEEN A LONG TIME SINCE YOU WENT OUT.
IT'S NOT BEEN *THAT* LONG...STILL, I'LL GO TO THE HOSPITAL AFTER DINNER TO CHECK ON RILEY'S CONDITION.

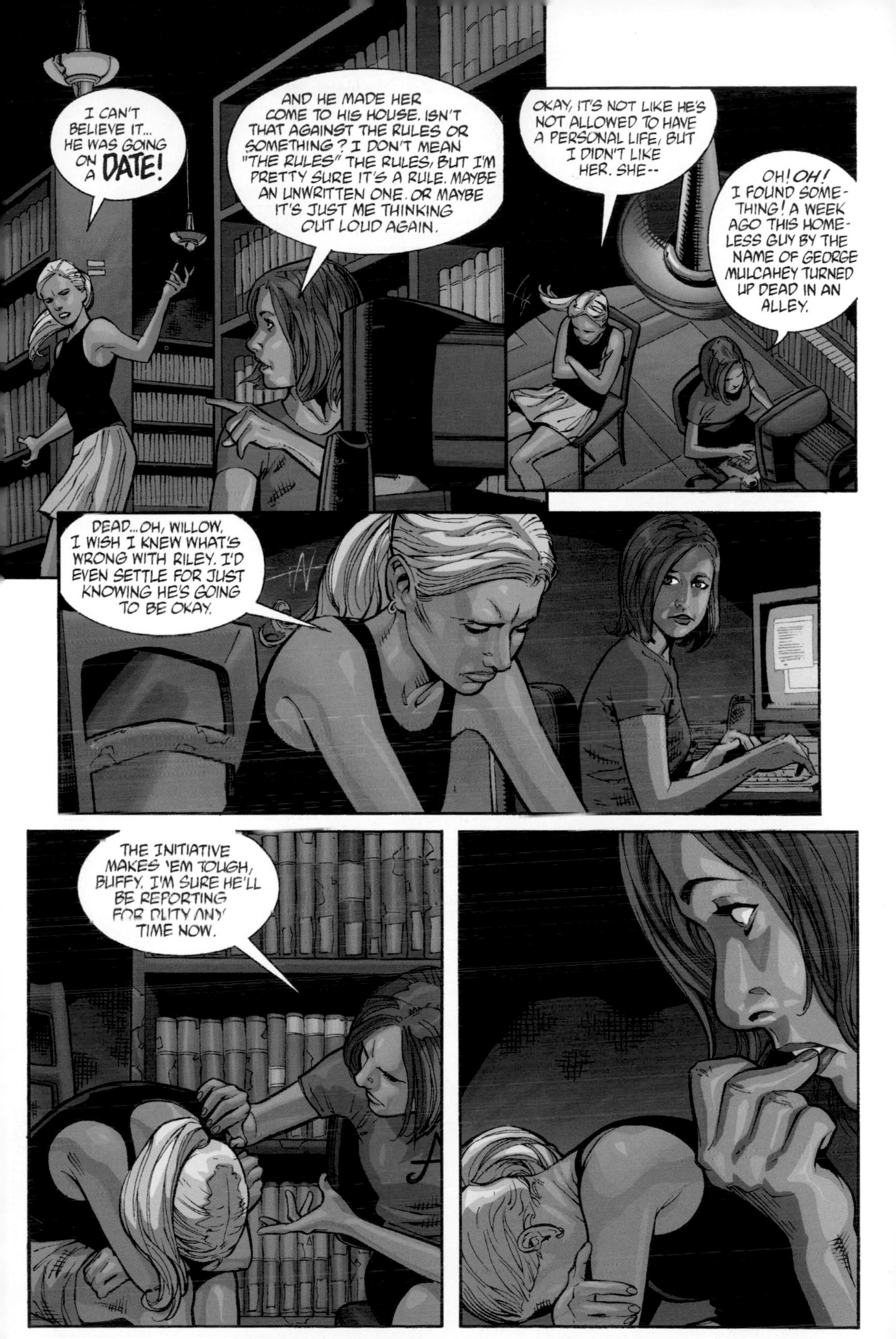
I CAN'T BELIEVE IT... HE WAS GOING ON A DATE!
AND HE MADE HER COME TO HIS HOUSE. ISN'T THAT AGAINST THE RULES OR SOMETHING? I DON'T MEAN "THE RULES" THE RULES, BUT I'M PRETTY SURE IT'S A RULE. MAYBE AN UNWRITTEN ONE. OR MAYBE IT'S JUST ME THINKING OUT LOUD AGAIN.
OKAY, IT'S NOT LIKE HE'S NOT ALLOWED TO HAVE A PERSONAL LIFE, BUT I DIDN'T LIKE HER. SHE--
OH! OH! I FOUND SOMETHING! A WEEK AGO THIS HOMELESS GUY BY THE NAME OF GEORGE MULCAHEY TURNED UP DEAD IN AN ALLEY.
DEAD...OH, WILLOW, I WISH I KNEW WHAT'S WRONG WITH RILEY. I'D EVEN SETTLE FOR JUST KNOWING HE'S GOING TO BE OKAY.
THE INITIATIVE MAKES 'EM TOUGH, BUFFY. I'M SURE HE'LL BE REPORTING FOR DUTY ANY TIME NOW.

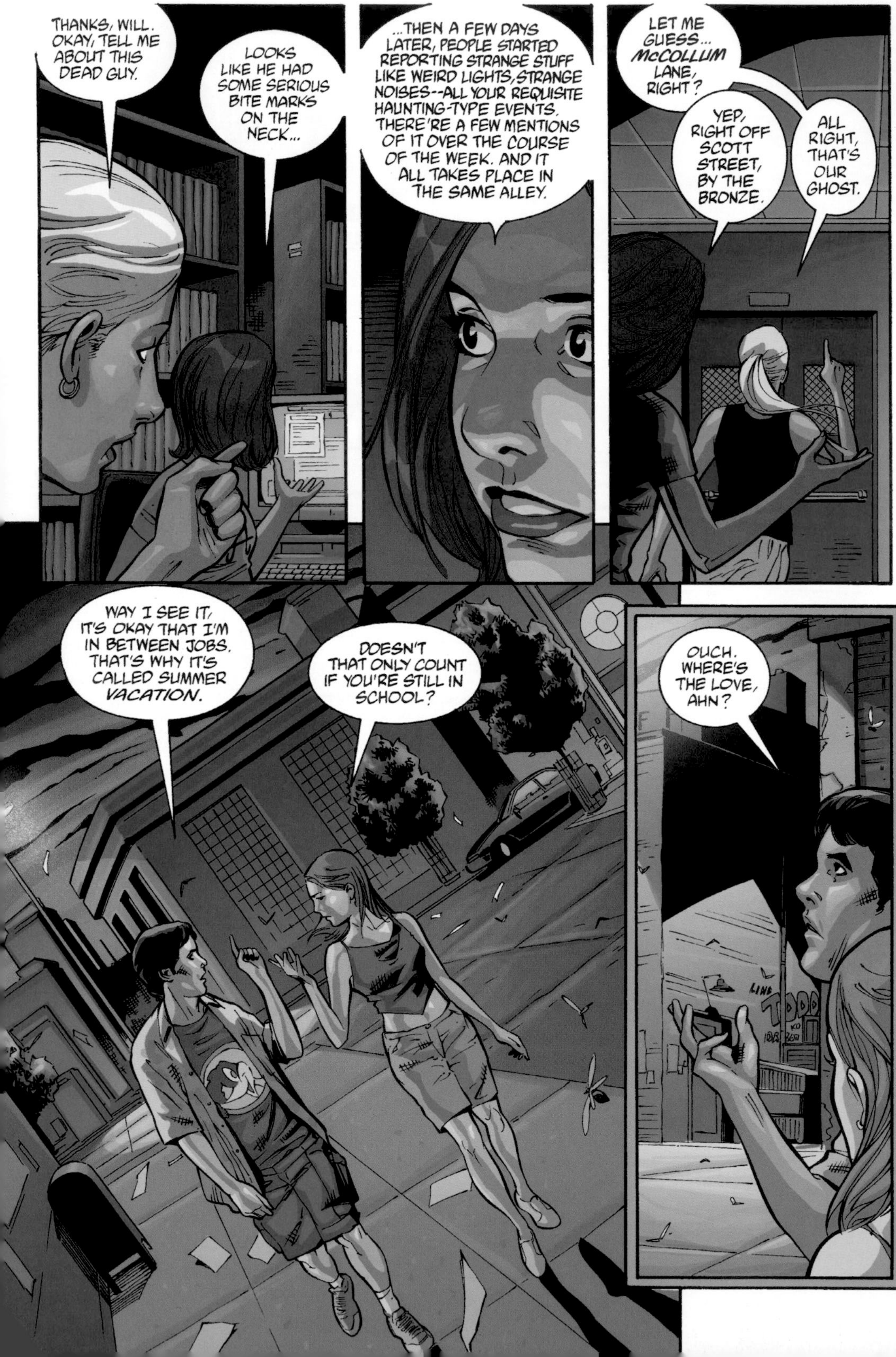
THANKS, WILL. OKAY, TELL ME ABOUT THIS DEAD GUY.
LOOKS LIKE HE HAD SOME SERIOUS BITE MARKS ON THE NECK...
...THEN A FEW DAYS LATER, PEOPLE STARTED REPORTING STRANGE STUFF LIKE WEIRD LIGHTS, STRANGE NOISES--ALL YOUR REQUISITE HAUNTING-TYPE EVENTS. THERE'RE A FEW MENTIONS OF IT OVER THE COURSE OF THE WEEK. AND IT ALL TAKES PLACE IN THE SAME ALLEY.
LET ME GUESS... McCOLLUM LANE, RIGHT?
YEP, RIGHT OFF SCOTT STREET, BY THE BRONZE.
ALL RIGHT, THAT'S OUR GHOST.
WAY I SEE IT, IT'S OKAY THAT I'M IN BETWEEN JOBS. THAT'S WHY IT'S CALLED SUMMER VACATION.
DOESN'T THAT ONLY COUNT IF YOU'RE STILL IN SCHOOL?
OUCH. WHERE'S THE LOVE, AHN?

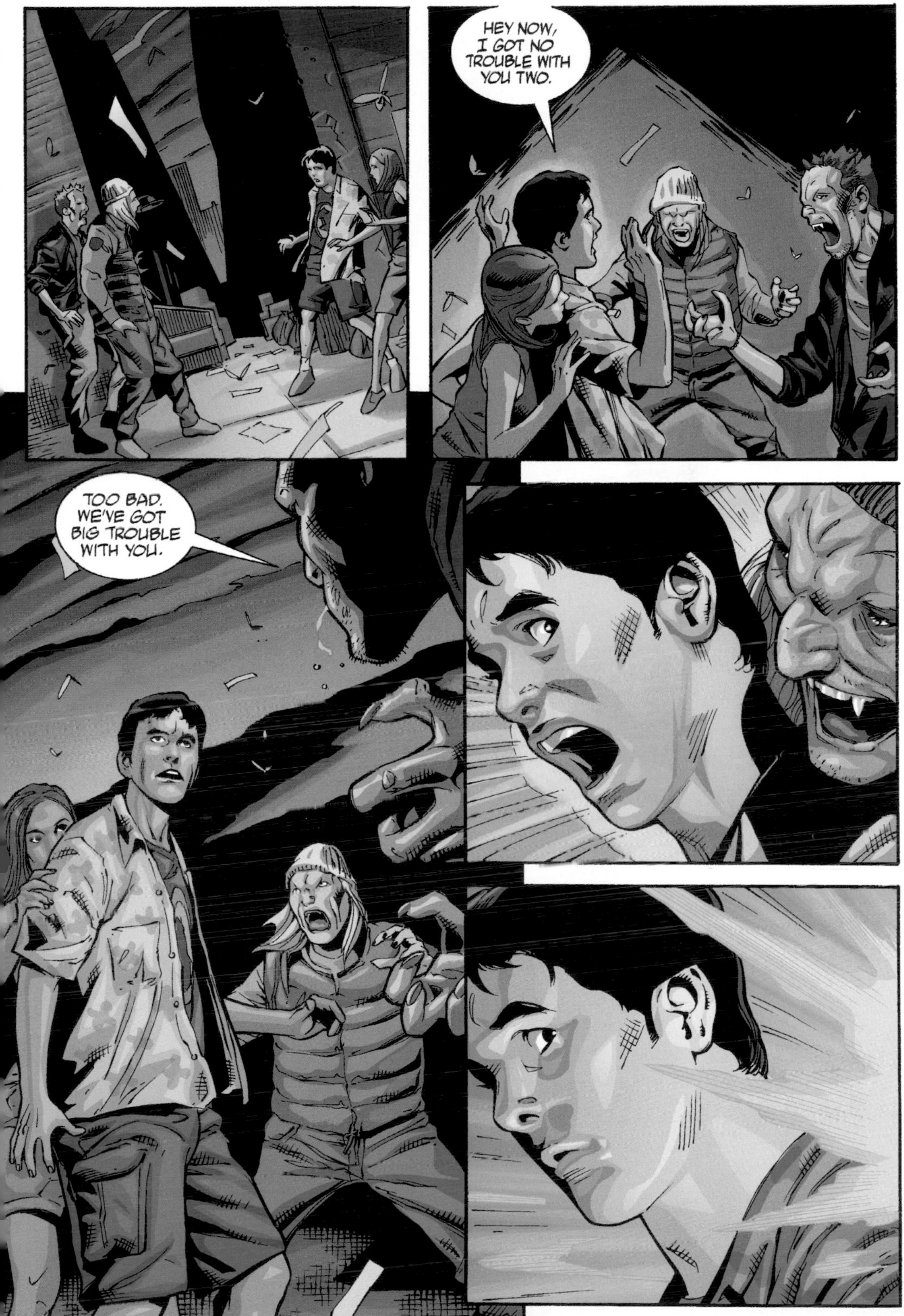

HEY NOW, I GOT NO TROUBLE WITH YOU TWO.
TOO BAD. WE'VE GOT BIG TROUBLE WITH YOU.

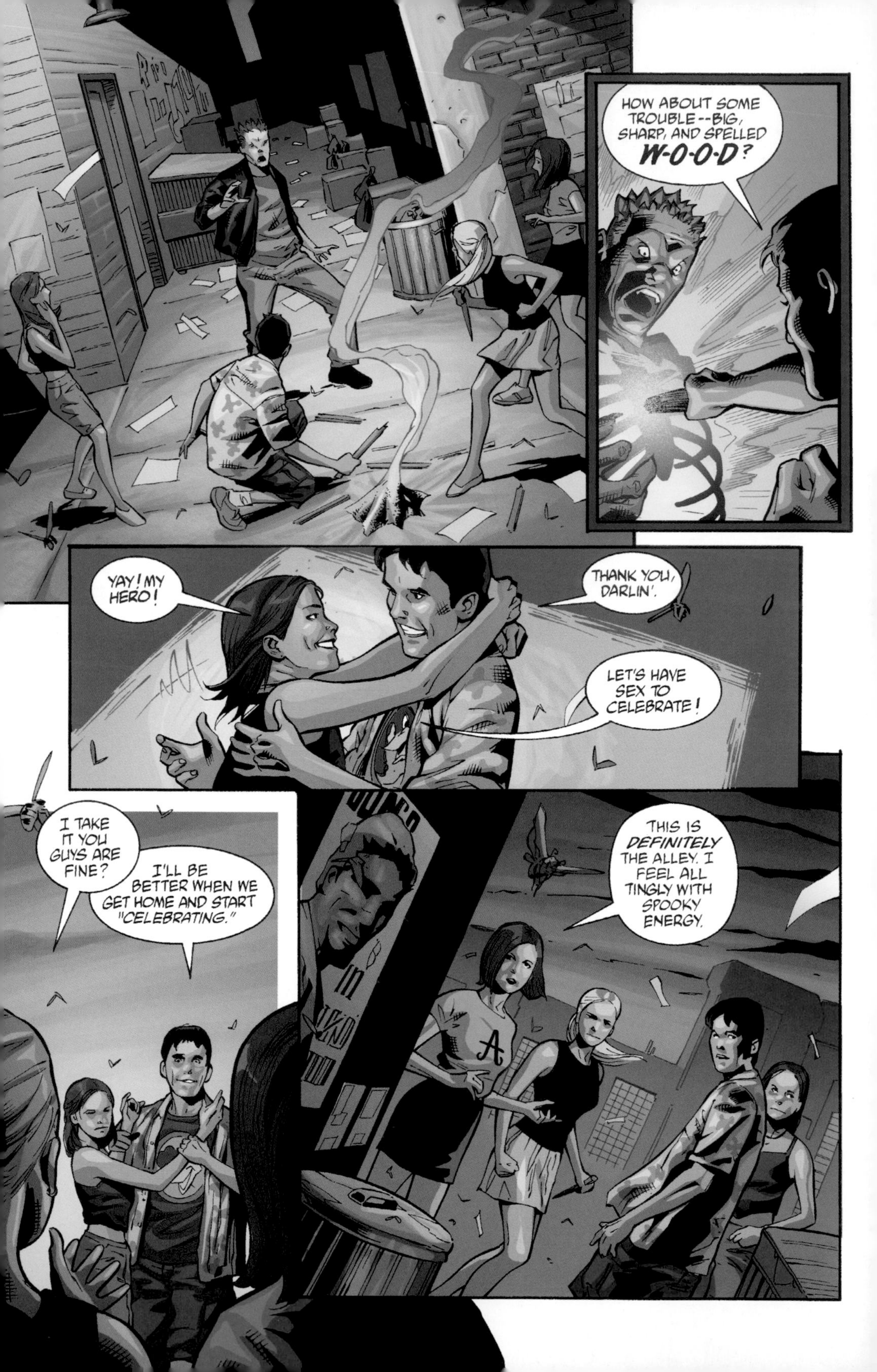
HOW ABOUT SOME TROUBLE--BIG, SHARP, AND SPELLED W-O-O-D?
YAY! MY HERO!
THANK YOU, DARLIN'.
LET'S HAVE SEX TO CELEBRATE!
I TAKE IT YOU GUYS ARE FINE?
I'LL BE BETTER WHEN WE GET HOME AND START "CELEBRATING."
THIS IS DEFINITELY THE ALLEY. I FEEL ALL TINGLY WITH SPOOKY ENERGY.

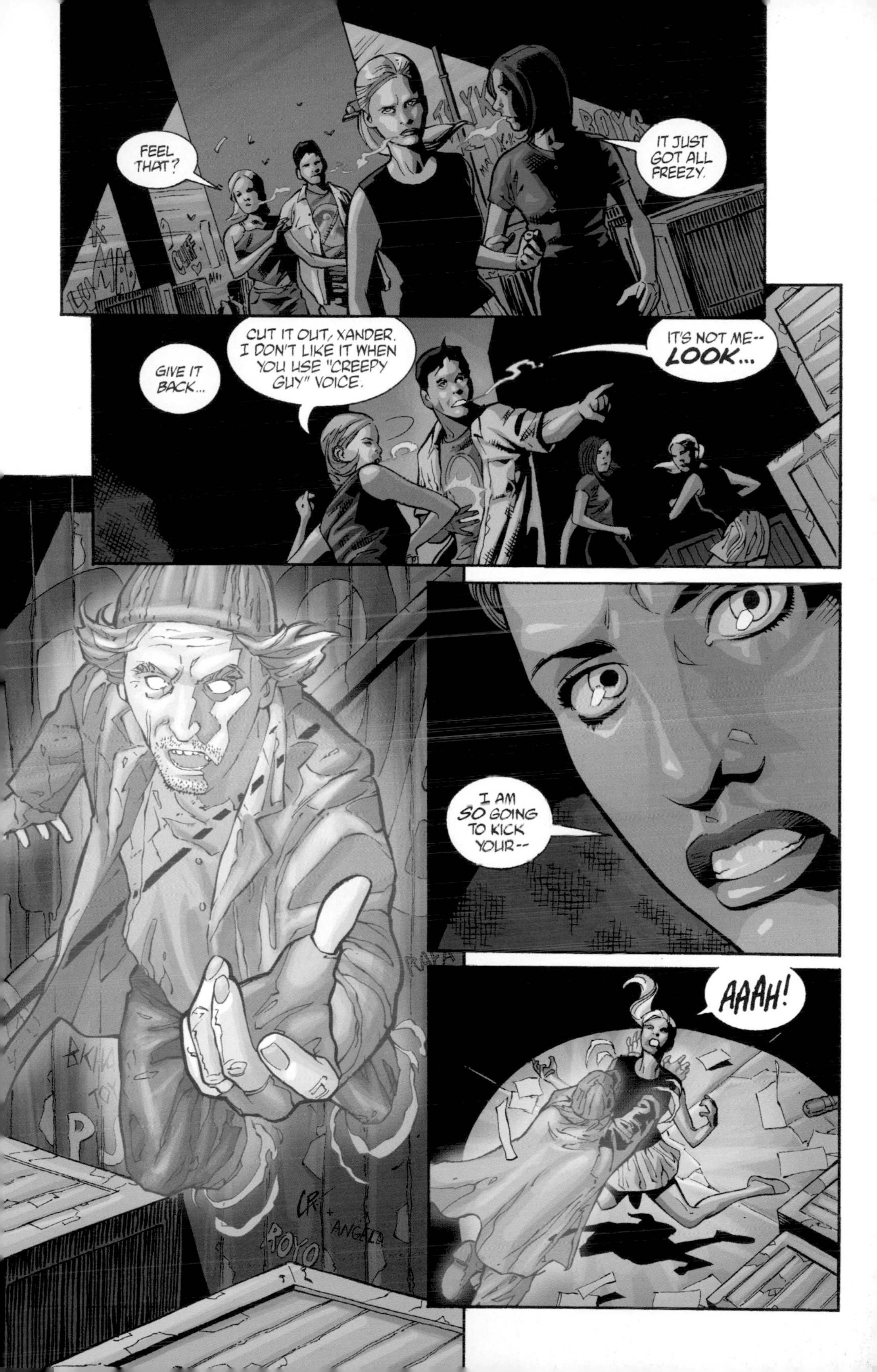

FEEL THAT?
IT JUST GOT ALL FREEZY.
GIVE IT BACK...
CUT IT OUT, XANDER. I DON'T LIKE IT WHEN YOU USE "CREEPY GUY" VOICE.
IT'S NOT ME-- LOOK...
I AM SO GOING TO KICK YOUR--
AAAH!

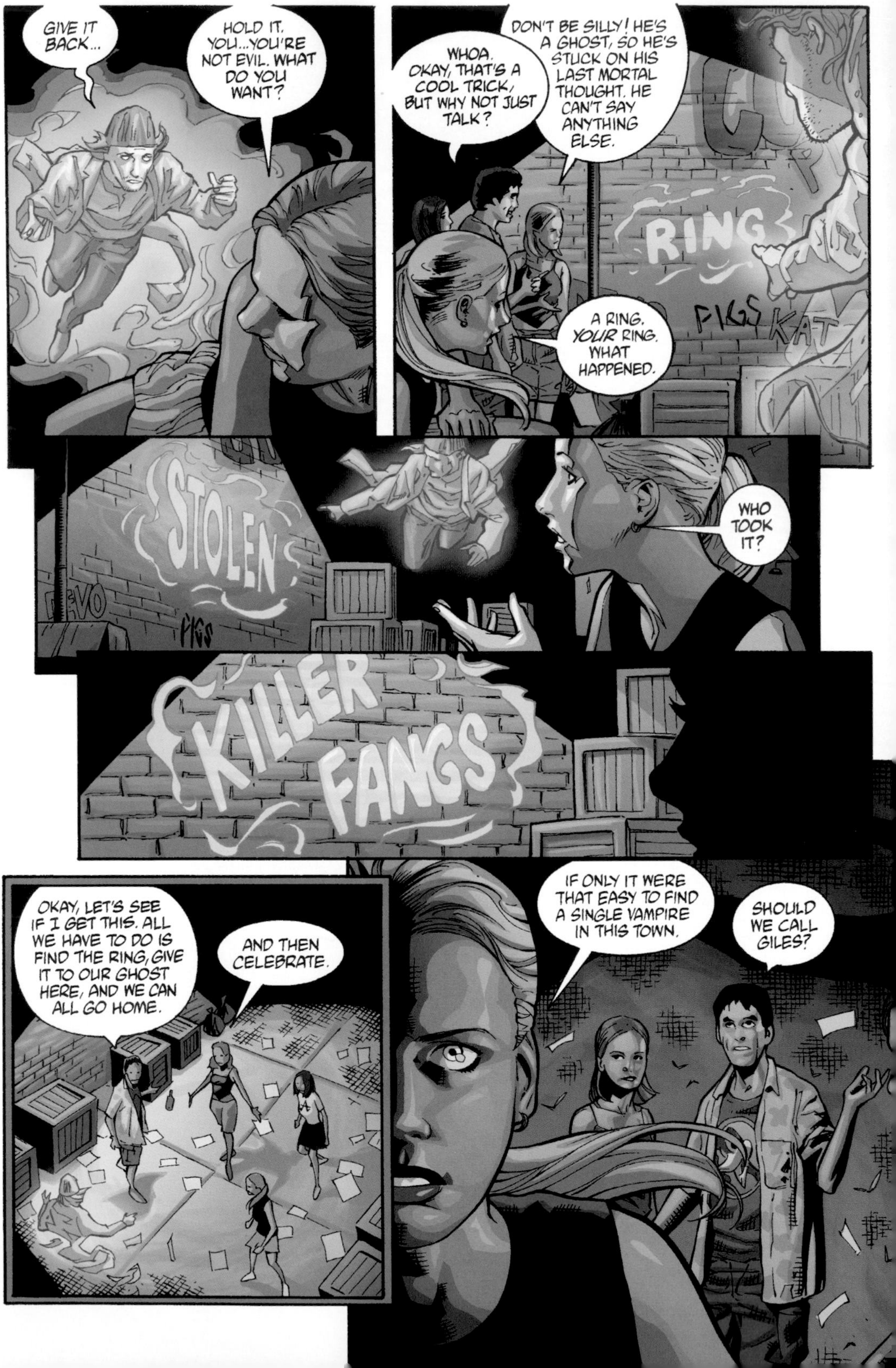
GIVE IT BACK...
HOLD IT. YOU...YOU'RE NOT EVIL. WHAT DO YOU WANT?
WHOA. OKAY, THAT'S A COOL TRICK, BUT WHY NOT JUST TALK?
DON'T BE SILLY! HE'S A GHOST, SO HE'S STUCK ON HIS LAST MORTAL THOUGHT. HE CAN'T SAY ANYTHING ELSE.
RING
FIGS KAT
A RING. *YOUR* RING. WHAT HAPPENED.
STOLEN
DEVO
FIGS
WHO TOOK IT?
KILLER FANGS
OKAY, LET'S SEE IF I GET THIS. ALL WE HAVE TO DO IS FIND THE RING, GIVE IT TO OUR GHOST HERE, AND WE CAN ALL GO HOME.
AND THEN CELEBRATE.
IF ONLY IT WERE THAT EASY TO FIND A SINGLE VAMPIRE IN THIS TOWN.
SHOULD WE CALL GILES?

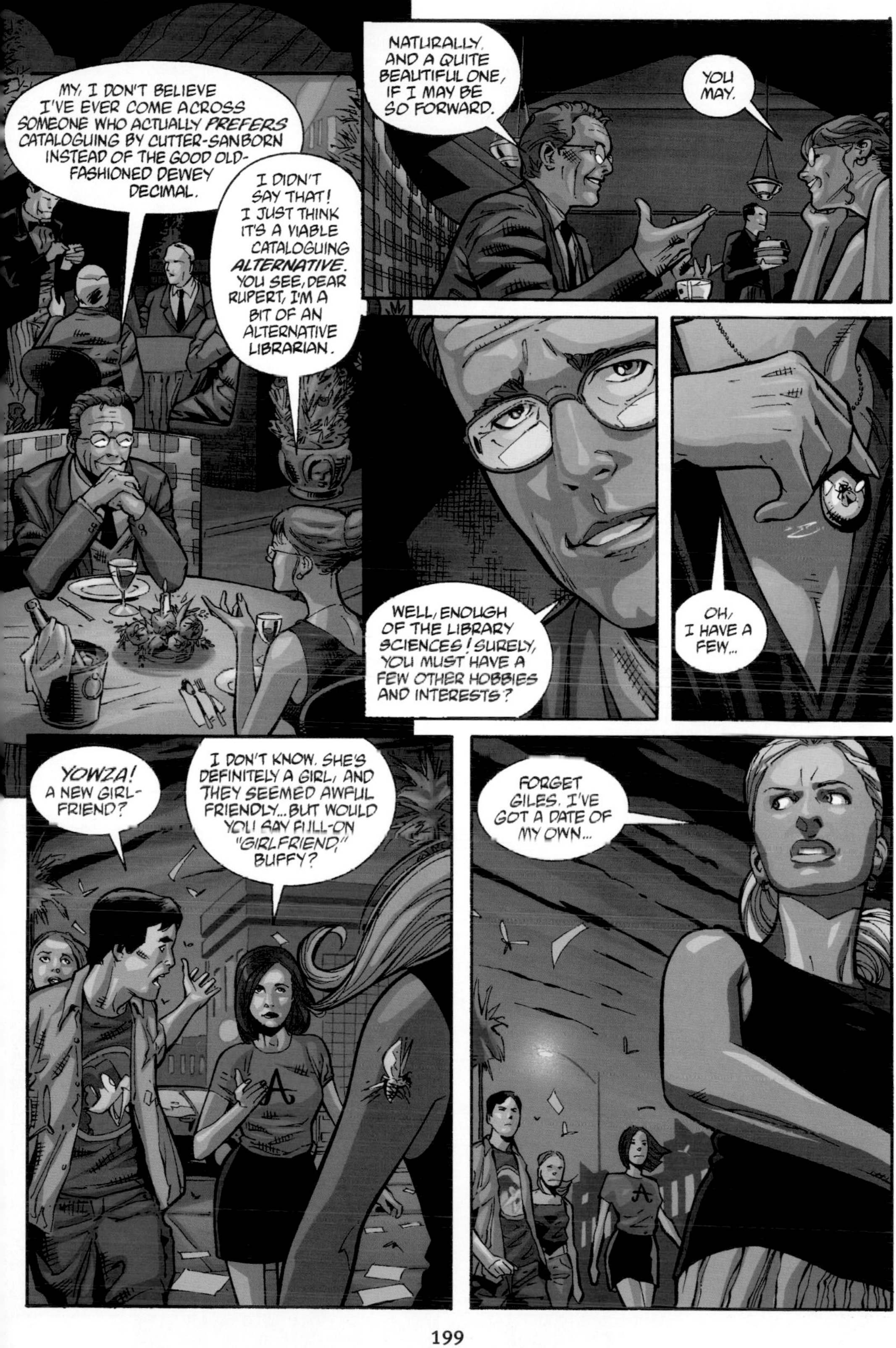
MY, I DON'T BELIEVE I'VE EVER COME ACROSS SOMEONE WHO ACTUALLY *PREFERS* CATALOGUING BY CUTTER-SANBORN INSTEAD OF THE GOOD OLD-FASHIONED DEWEY DECIMAL.
I DIDN'T SAY THAT! I JUST THINK IT'S A VIABLE CATALOGUING *ALTERNATIVE*. YOU SEE, DEAR RUPERT, I'M A BIT OF AN ALTERNATIVE LIBRARIAN.
NATURALLY. AND A QUITE BEAUTIFUL ONE, IF I MAY BE SO FORWARD.
YOU MAY.
WELL, ENOUGH OF THE LIBRARY SCIENCES! SURELY, YOU MUST HAVE A FEW OTHER HOBBIES AND INTERESTS?
OH, I HAVE A FEW...
YOWZA! A NEW GIRL-FRIEND?
I DON'T KNOW. SHE'S DEFINITELY A GIRL, AND THEY SEEMED AWFUL FRIENDLY... BUT WOULD YOU SAY FULL-ON "GIRLFRIEND," BUFFY?
FORGET GILES. I'VE GOT A DATE OF MY OWN...

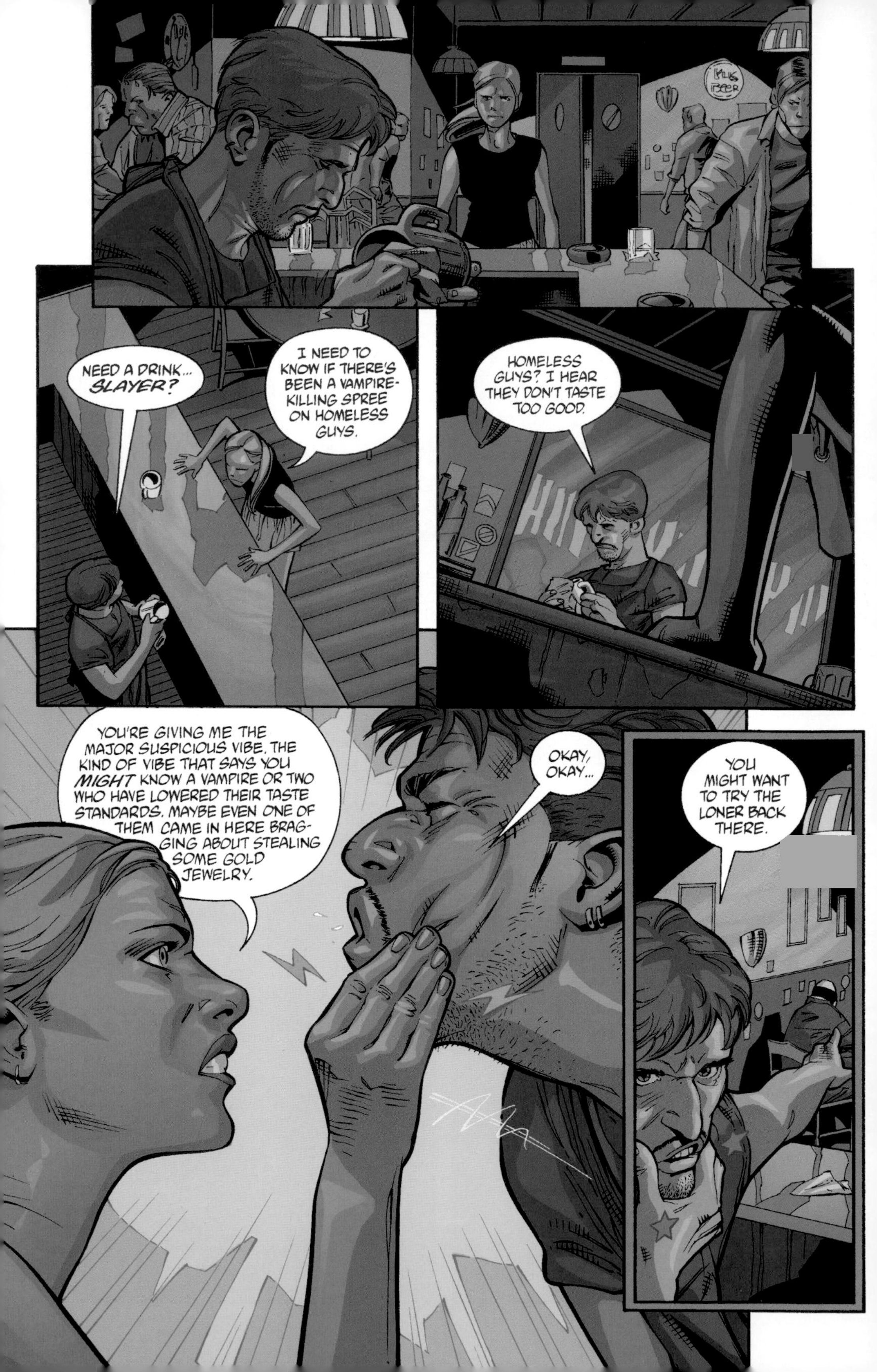
NEED A DRINK... SLAYER?
I NEED TO KNOW IF THERE'S BEEN A VAMPIRE-KILLING SPREE ON HOMELESS GUYS.
HOMELESS GUYS? I HEAR THEY DON'T TASTE TOO GOOD.
YOU'RE GIVING ME THE MAJOR SUSPICIOUS VIBE. THE KIND OF VIBE THAT SAYS YOU MIGHT KNOW A VAMPIRE OR TWO WHO HAVE LOWERED THEIR TASTE STANDARDS. MAYBE EVEN ONE OF THEM CAME IN HERE BRAGGING ABOUT STEALING SOME GOLD JEWELRY.
OKAY, OKAY...
YOU MIGHT WANT TO TRY THE LONER BACK THERE.

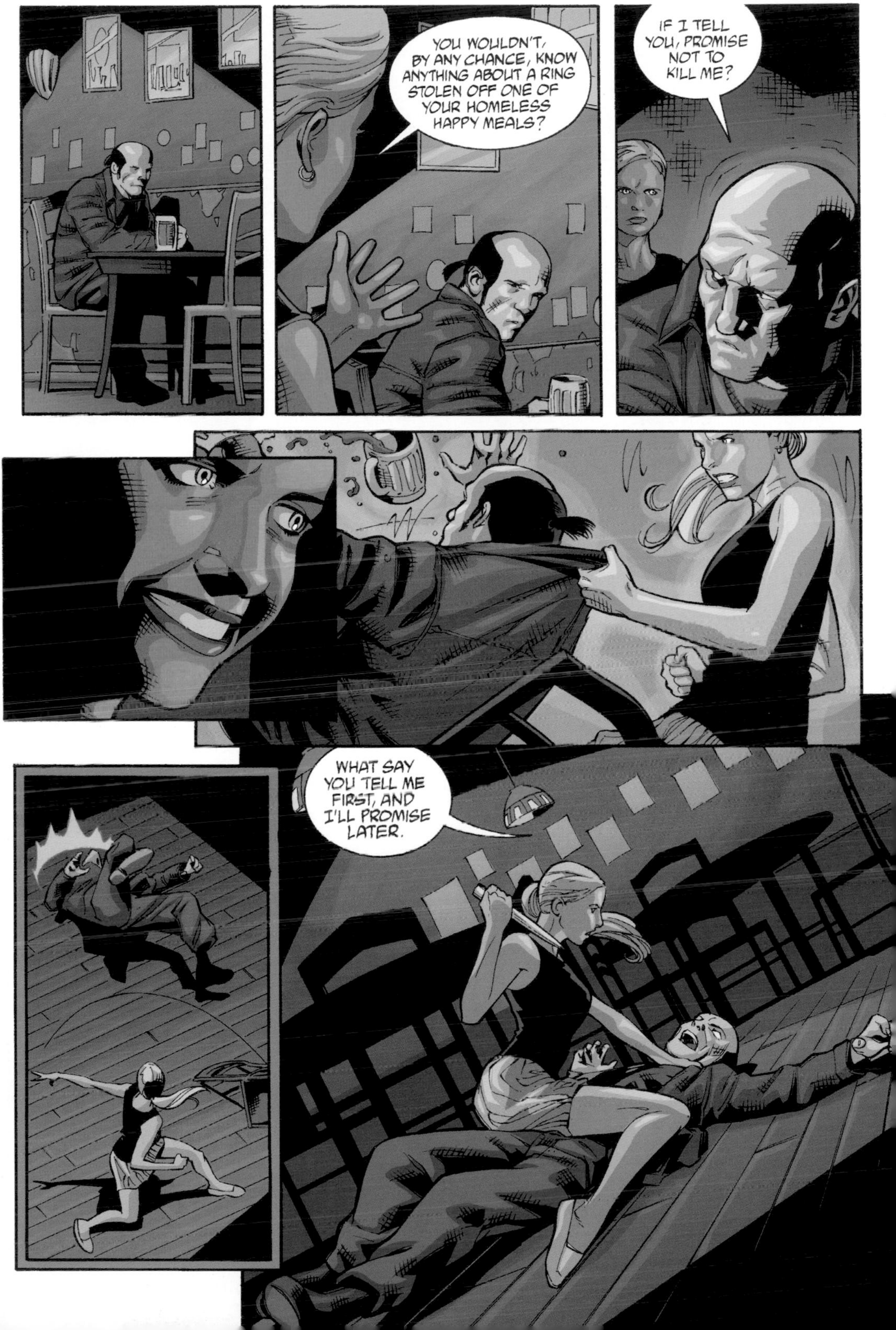
YOU WOULDN'T, BY ANY CHANCE, KNOW ANYTHING ABOUT A RING STOLEN OFF ONE OF YOUR HOMELESS HAPPY MEALS?
IF I TELL YOU, PROMISE NOT TO KILL ME?
WHAT SAY YOU TELL ME FIRST, AND I'LL PROMISE LATER.

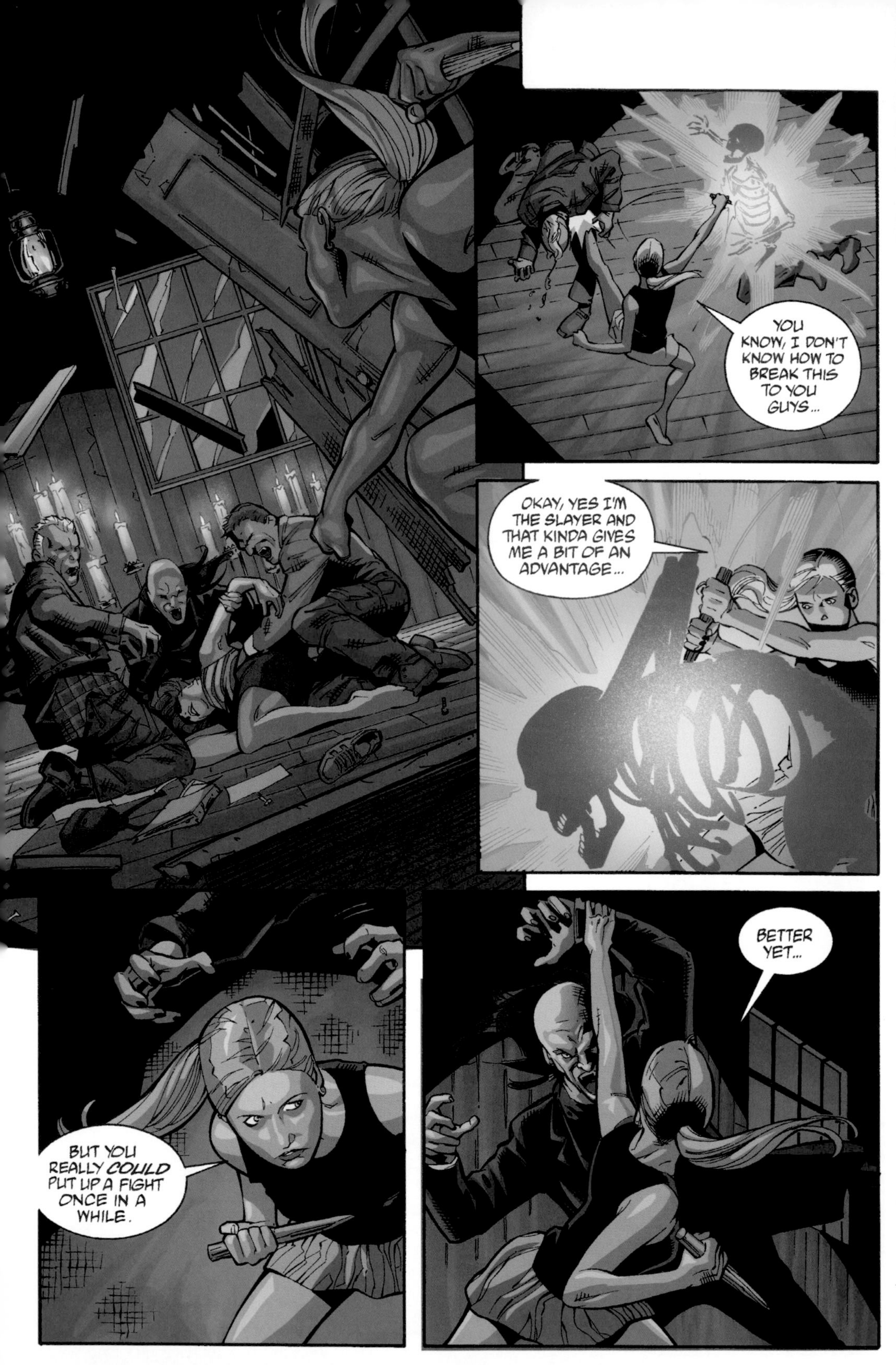
YOU KNOW, I DON'T KNOW HOW TO BREAK THIS TO YOU GUYS...
OKAY, YES I'M THE SLAYER AND THAT KINDA GIVES ME A BIT OF AN ADVANTAGE...
BUT YOU REALLY ***COULD*** PUT UP A FIGHT ONCE IN A WHILE.
BETTER YET...

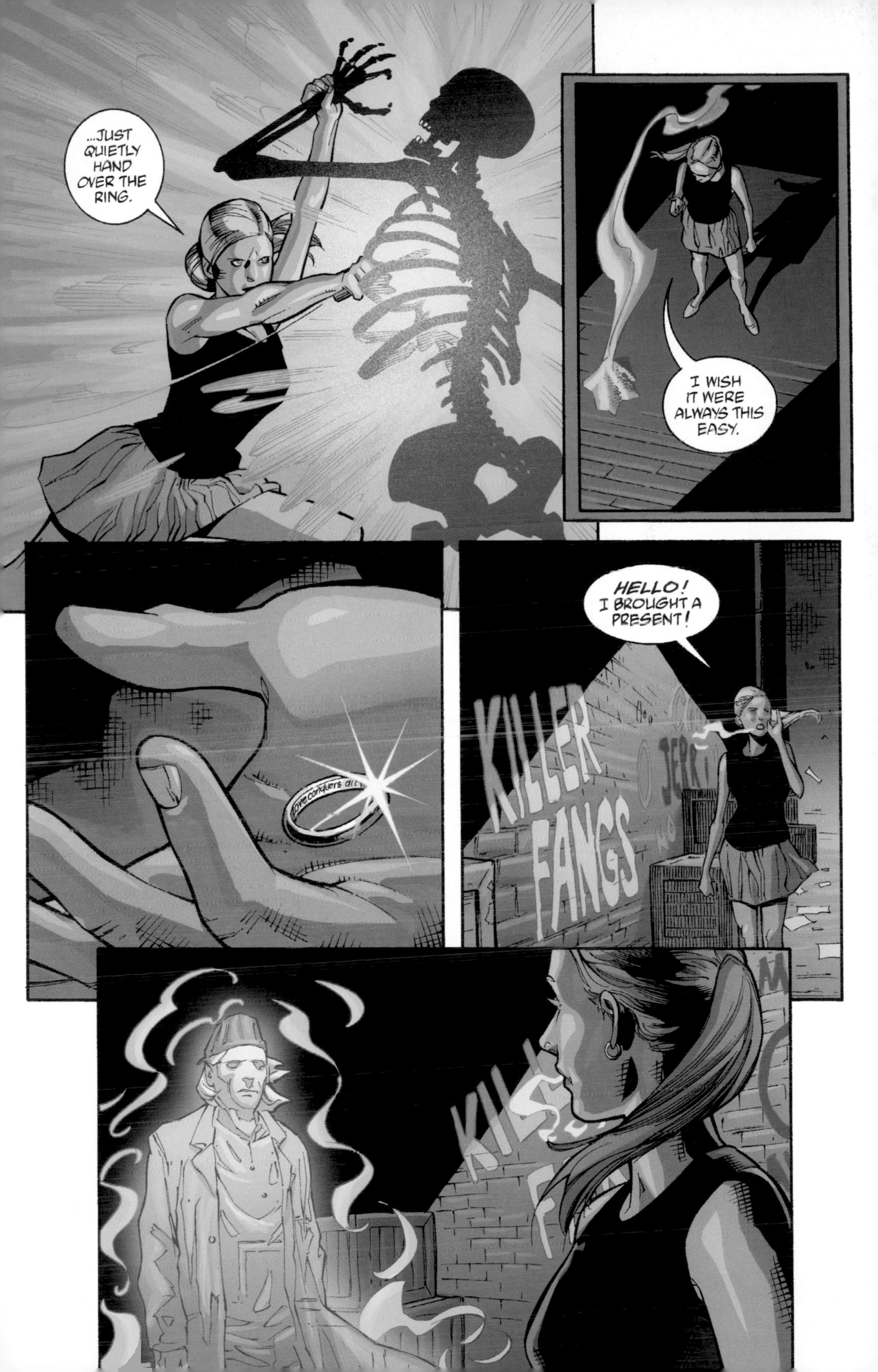
...JUST QUIETLY HAND OVER THE RING.
I WISH IT WERE ALWAYS THIS EASY.
HELLO! I BROUGHT A PRESENT!
KILLER FANGS

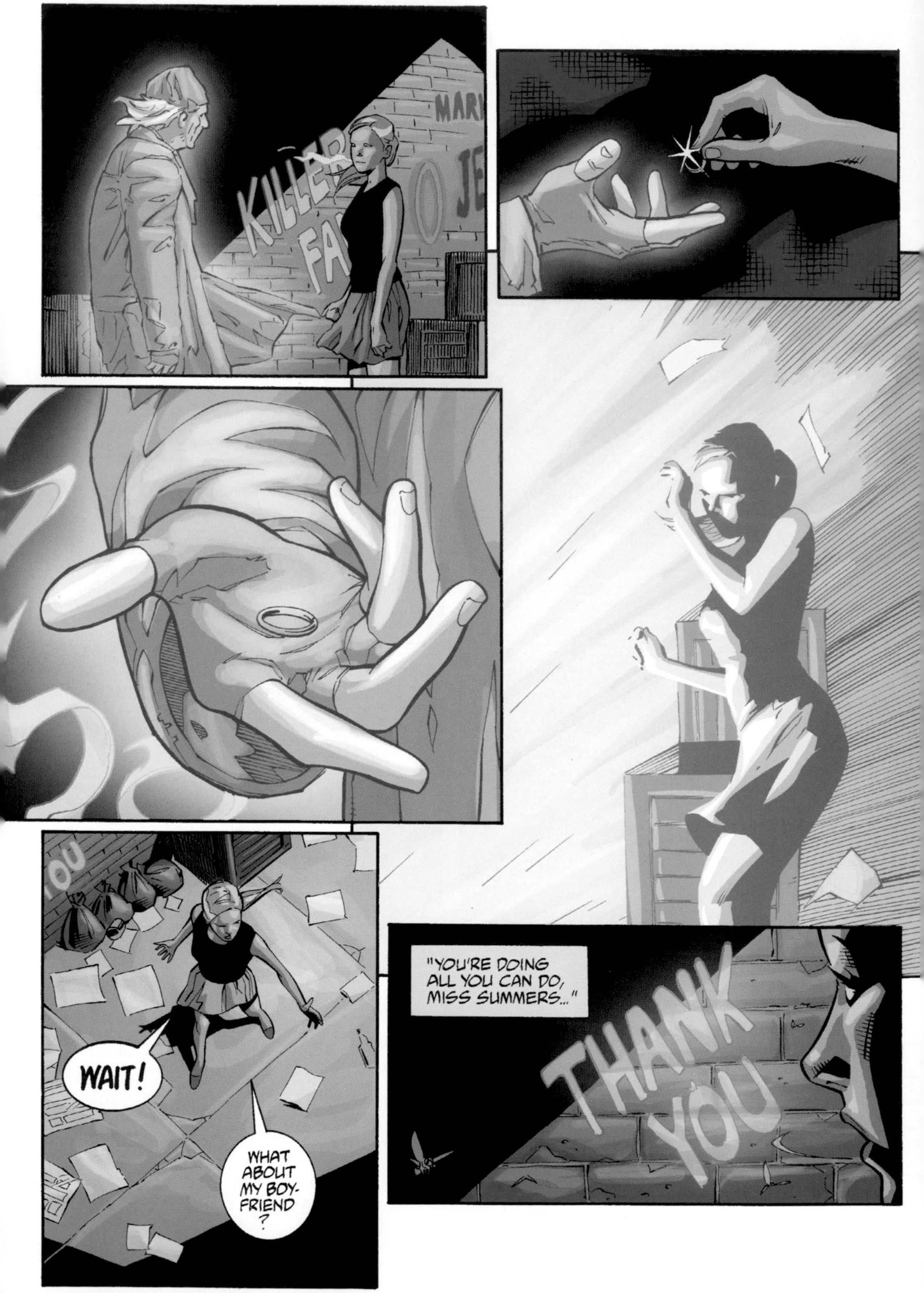
KILLER
"YOU'RE DOING ALL YOU CAN DO, MISS SUMMERS..."
THANK YOU
WAIT!
WHAT ABOUT MY BOY-FRIEND ?

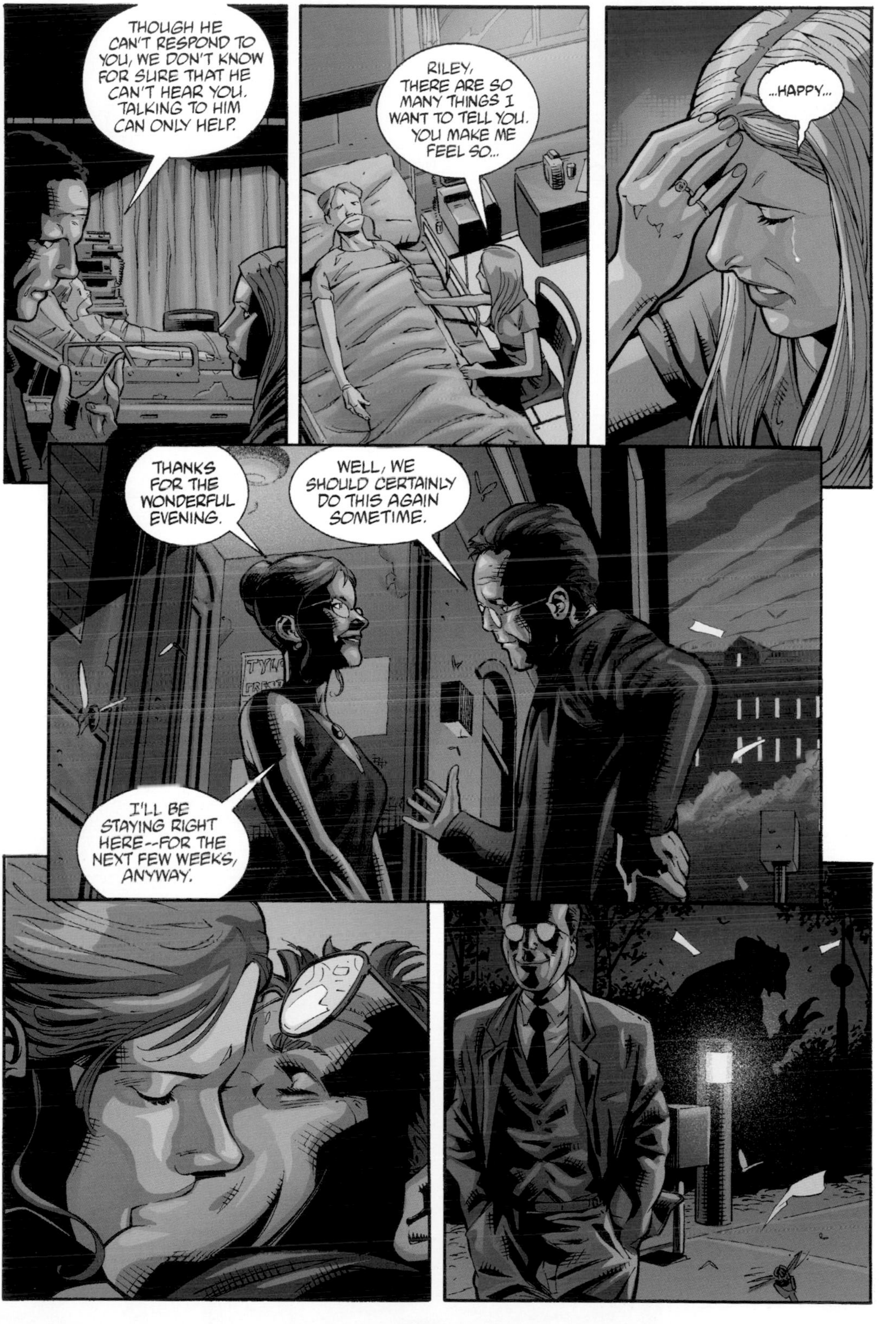
THOUGH HE CAN'T RESPOND TO YOU, WE DON'T KNOW FOR SURE THAT HE CAN'T HEAR YOU. TALKING TO HIM CAN ONLY HELP.
RILEY, THERE ARE SO MANY THINGS I WANT TO TELL YOU. YOU MAKE ME FEEL SO...
...HAPPY...
THANKS FOR THE WONDERFUL EVENING.
WELL, WE SHOULD CERTAINLY DO THIS AGAIN SOMETIME.
I'LL BE STAYING RIGHT HERE--FOR THE NEXT FEW WEEKS, ANYWAY.

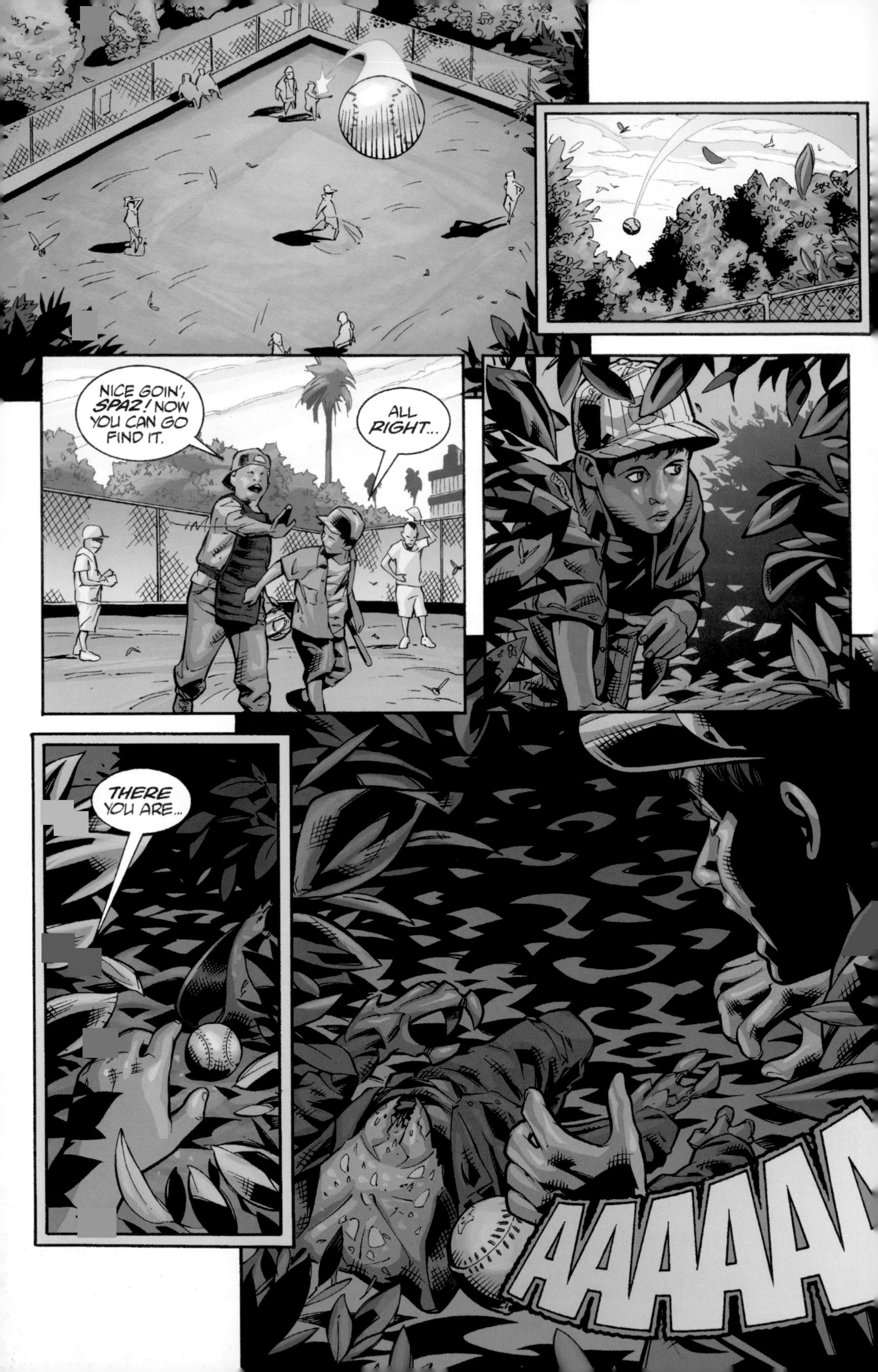

NICE GOIN', SPAZ! NOW YOU CAN GO FIND IT.
ALL RIGHT...
THERE YOU ARE...
AAAAA

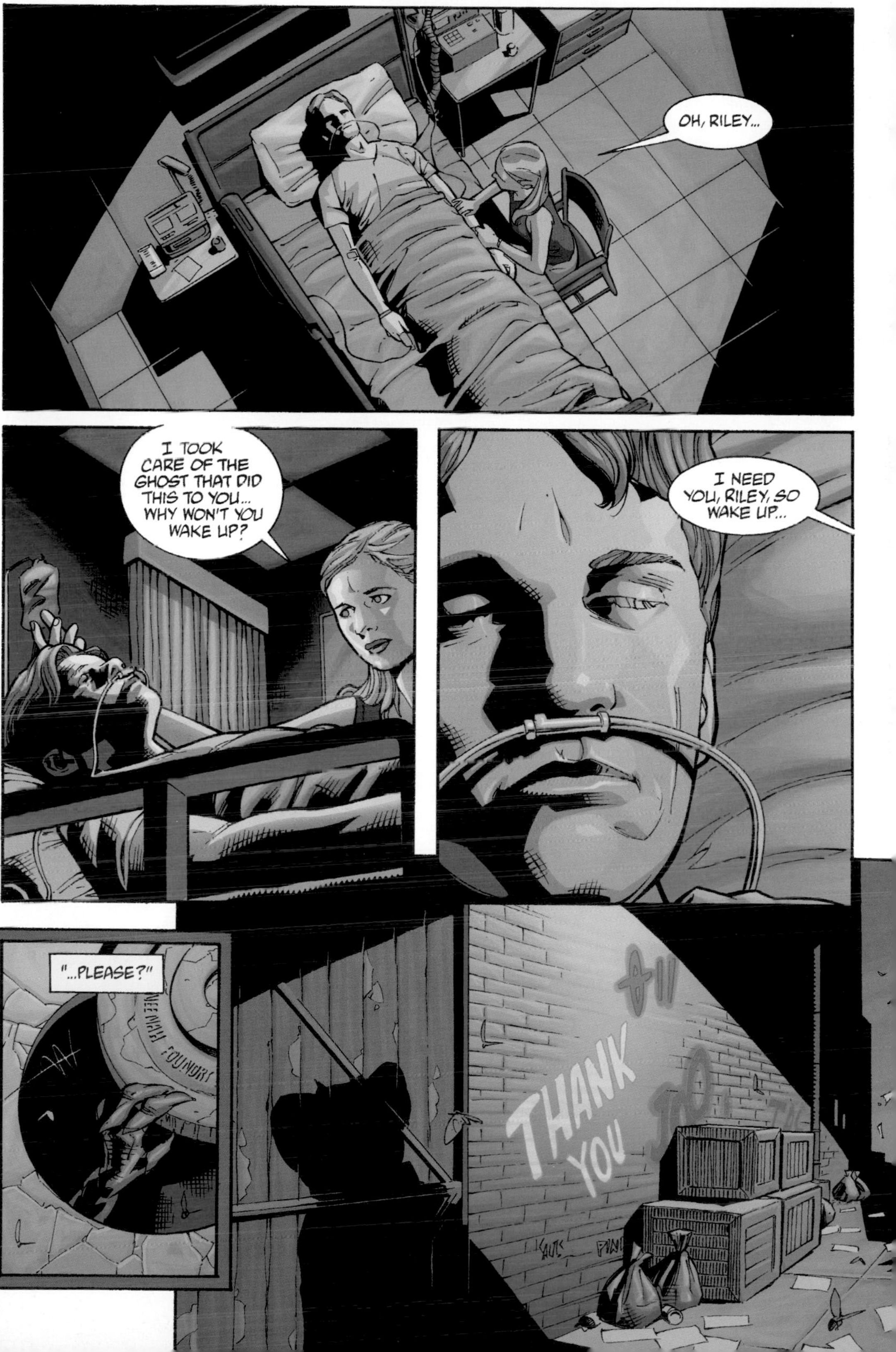
OH, RILEY...
I TOOK CARE OF THE GHOST THAT DID THIS TO YOU... WHY WON'T YOU WAKE UP?
I NEED YOU, RILEY, SO WAKE UP...
"...PLEASE?"
NEENAH FOUNDRY
THANK YOU

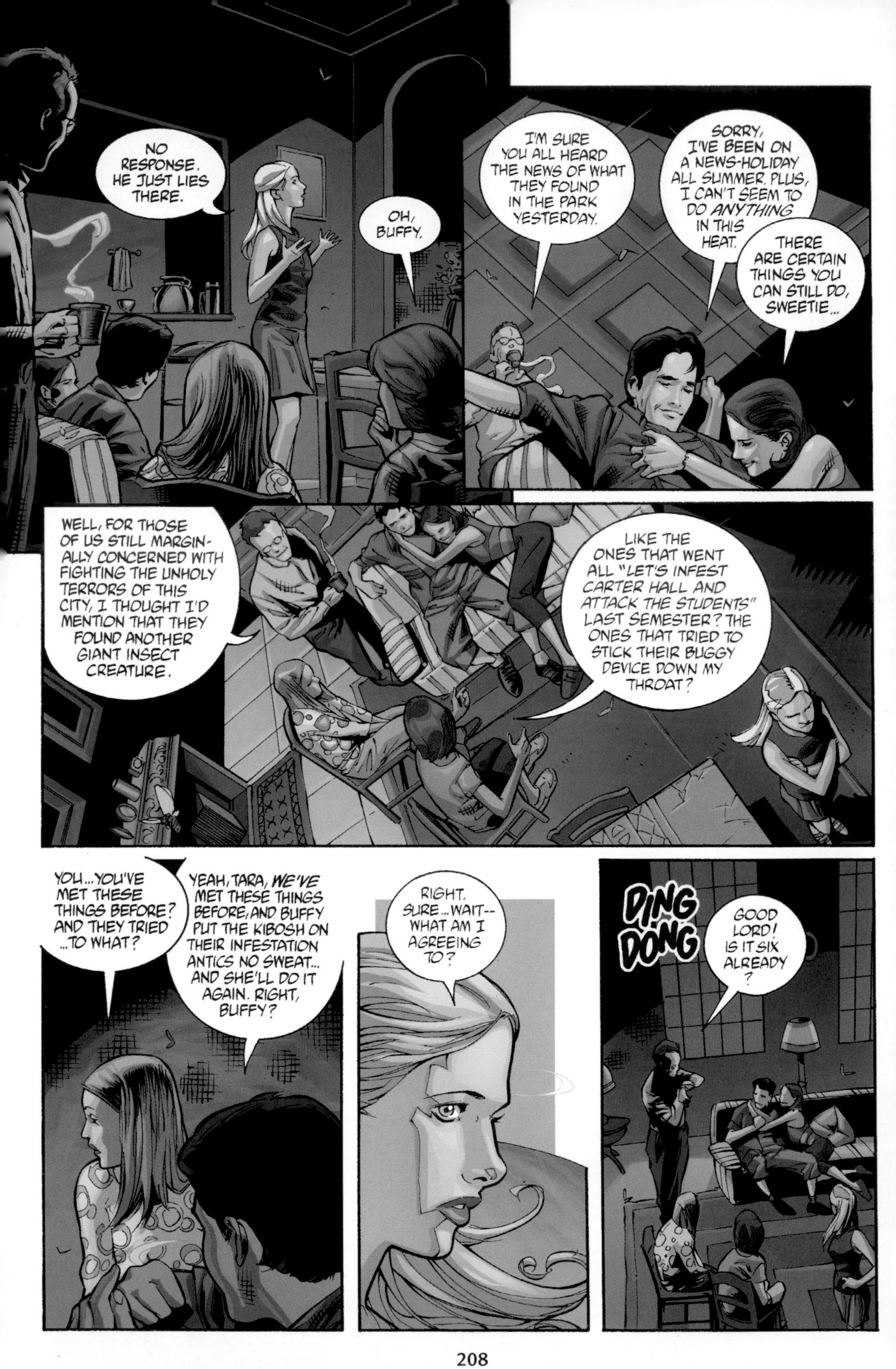
NO RESPONSE. HE JUST LIES THERE.
OH, BUFFY.
I'M SURE YOU ALL HEARD THE NEWS OF WHAT THEY FOUND IN THE PARK YESTERDAY.
SORRY, I'VE BEEN ON A NEWS-HOLIDAY ALL SUMMER. PLUS, I CAN'T SEEM TO DO ANYTHING IN THIS HEAT.
THERE ARE CERTAIN THINGS YOU CAN STILL DO, SWEETIE...
WELL, FOR THOSE OF US STILL MARGINALLY CONCERNED WITH FIGHTING THE UNHOLY TERRORS OF THIS CITY, I THOUGHT I'D MENTION THAT THEY FOUND ANOTHER GIANT INSECT CREATURE.
LIKE THE ONES THAT WENT ALL "LET'S INFEST CARTER HALL AND ATTACK THE STUDENTS" LAST SEMESTER? THE ONES THAT TRIED TO STICK THEIR BUGGY DEVICE DOWN MY THROAT?
YOU...YOU'VE MET THESE THINGS BEFORE? AND THEY TRIED ...TO WHAT?
YEAH, TARA, WE'VE MET THESE THINGS BEFORE, AND BUFFY PUT THE KIBOSH ON THEIR INFESTATION ANTICS NO SWEAT... AND SHE'LL DO IT AGAIN. RIGHT, BUFFY?
RIGHT. SURE...WAIT-- WHAT AM I AGREEING TO?
DING DONG
GOOD LORD! IS IT SIX ALREADY?

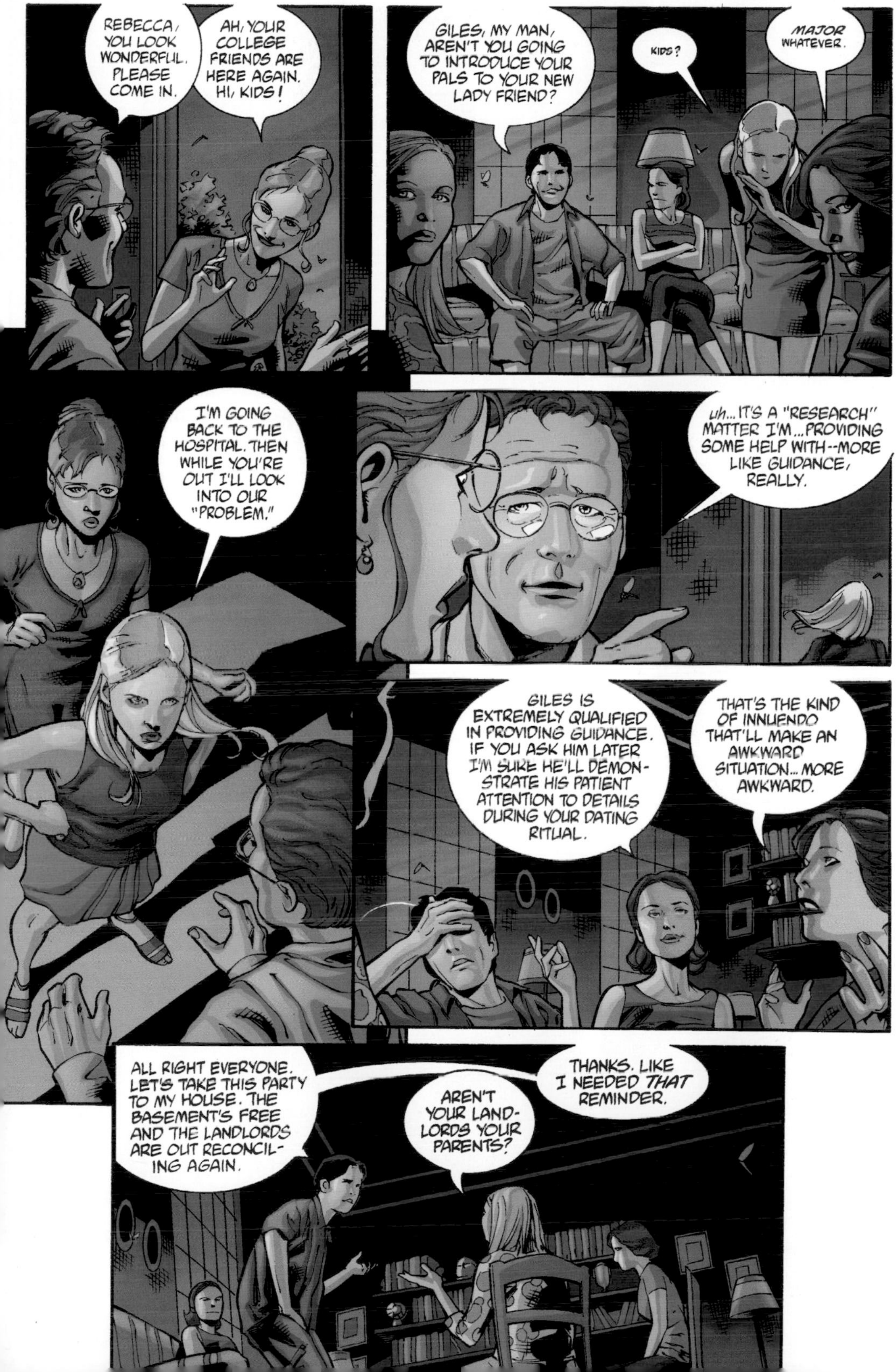
REBECCA, YOU LOOK WONDERFUL. PLEASE COME IN.
AH, YOUR COLLEGE FRIENDS ARE HERE AGAIN. HI, KIDS!
GILES, MY MAN, AREN'T YOU GOING TO INTRODUCE YOUR PALS TO YOUR NEW LADY FRIEND?
KIDS?
MAJOR WHATEVER.
I'M GOING BACK TO THE HOSPITAL. THEN WHILE YOU'RE OUT I'LL LOOK INTO OUR "PROBLEM."
uh... IT'S A "RESEARCH" MATTER I'M... PROVIDING SOME HELP WITH--MORE LIKE GUIDANCE, REALLY.
GILES IS EXTREMELY QUALIFIED IN PROVIDING GUIDANCE. IF YOU ASK HIM LATER I'M SURE HE'LL DEMON-STRATE HIS PATIENT ATTENTION TO DETAILS DURING YOUR DATING RITUAL.
THAT'S THE KIND OF INNUENDO THAT'LL MAKE AN AWKWARD SITUATION... MORE AWKWARD.
ALL RIGHT EVERYONE. LET'S TAKE THIS PARTY TO MY HOUSE. THE BASEMENT'S FREE AND THE LANDLORDS ARE OUT RECONCIL-ING AGAIN.
AREN'T YOUR LAND-LORDS YOUR PARENTS?
THANKS. LIKE I NEEDED THAT REMINDER.

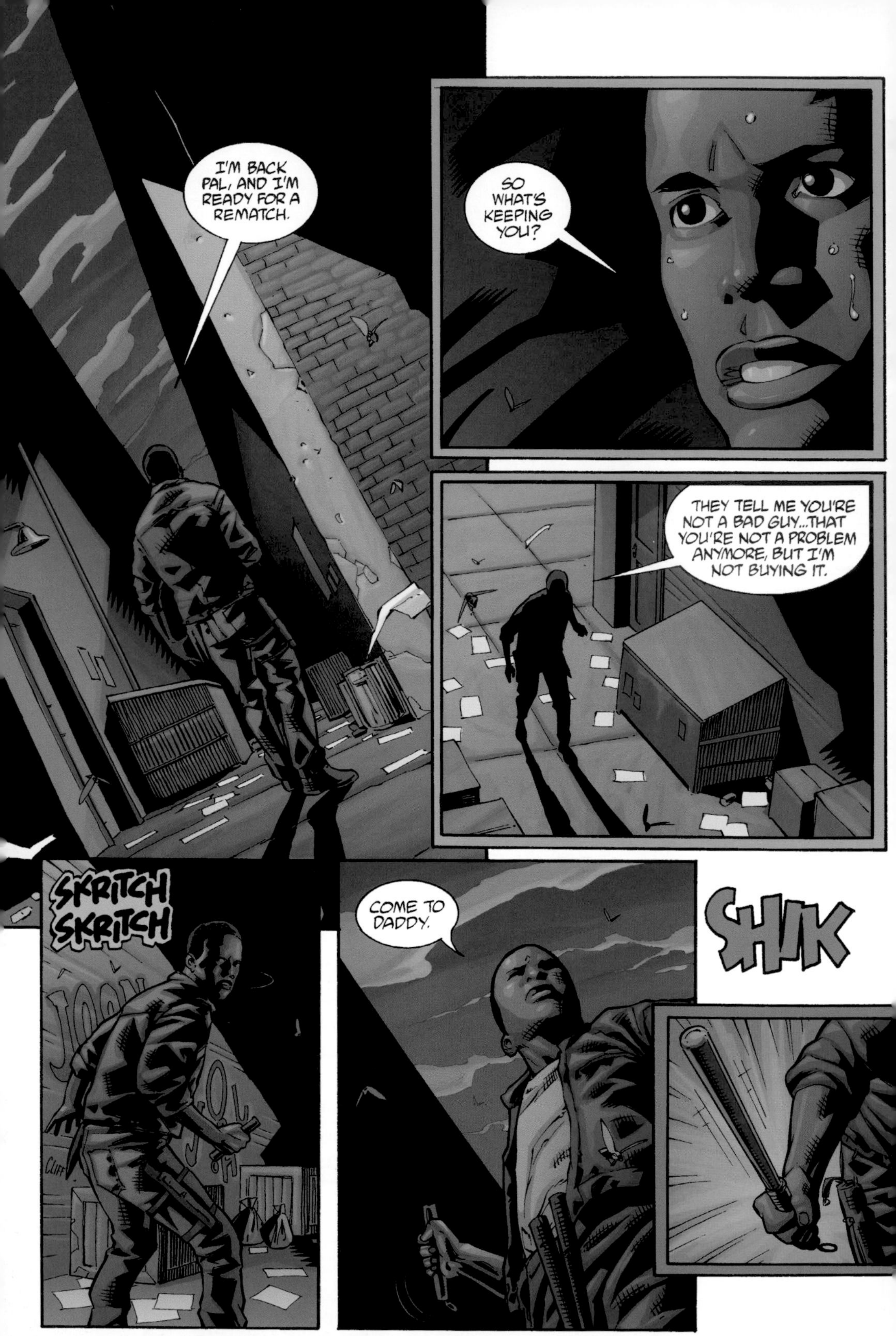
I'M BACK PAL, AND I'M READY FOR A REMATCH.
SO WHAT'S KEEPING YOU?
THEY TELL ME YOU'RE NOT A BAD GUY...THAT YOU'RE NOT A PROBLEM ANYMORE, BUT I'M NOT BUYING IT.
SKRITCH SKRITCH
COME TO DADDY.
SHIK

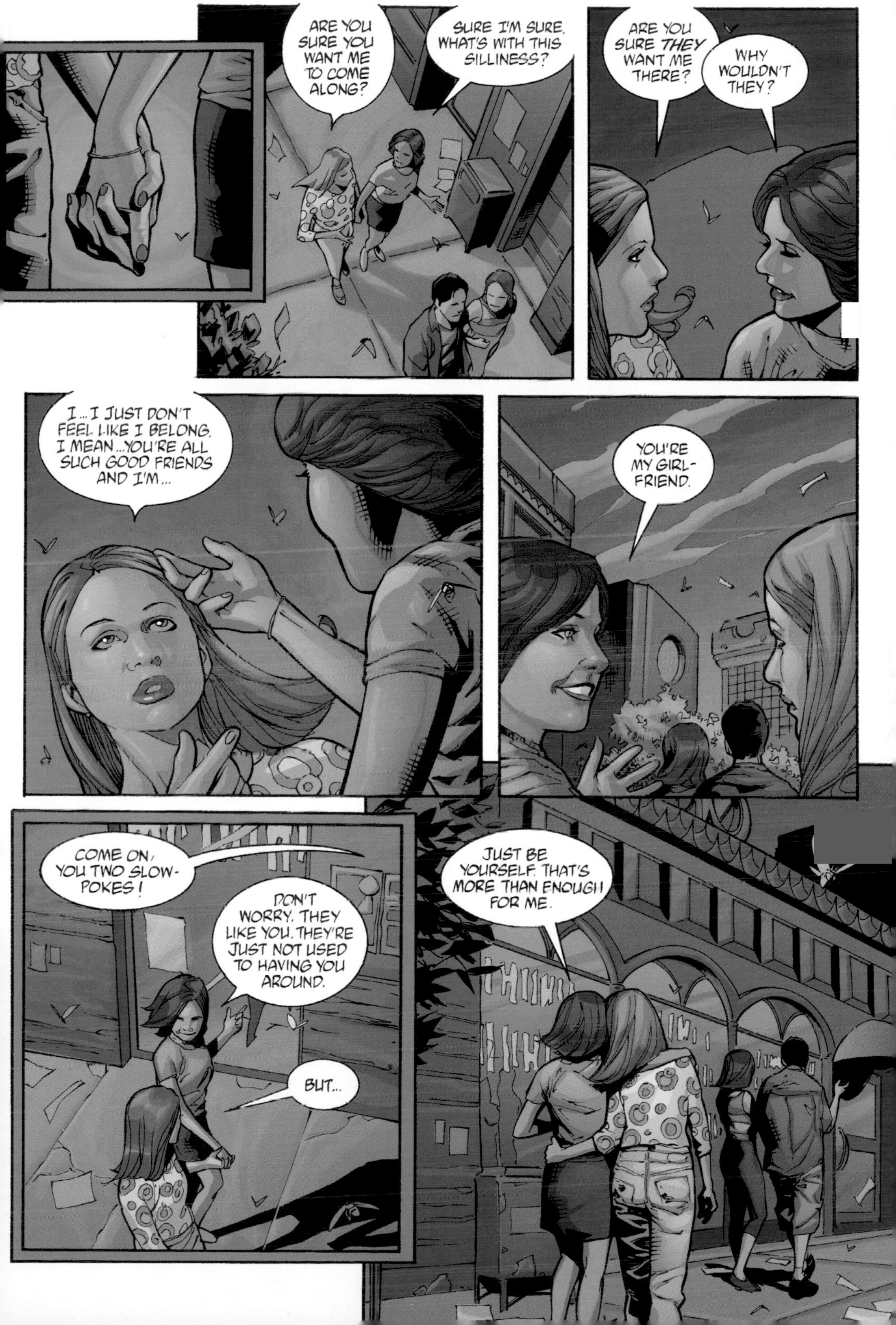
ARE YOU SURE YOU WANT ME TO COME ALONG?
SURE I'M SURE. WHAT'S WITH THIS SILLINESS?
ARE YOU SURE *THEY* WANT ME THERE?
WHY WOULDN'T THEY?
I... I JUST DON'T FEEL LIKE I BELONG. I MEAN... YOU'RE ALL SUCH GOOD FRIENDS AND I'M...
YOU'RE MY GIRL-FRIEND.
COME ON, YOU TWO SLOW-POKES!
DON'T WORRY. THEY LIKE YOU. THEY'RE JUST NOT USED TO HAVING YOU AROUND.
BUT...
JUST BE YOURSELF. THAT'S MORE THAN ENOUGH FOR ME.

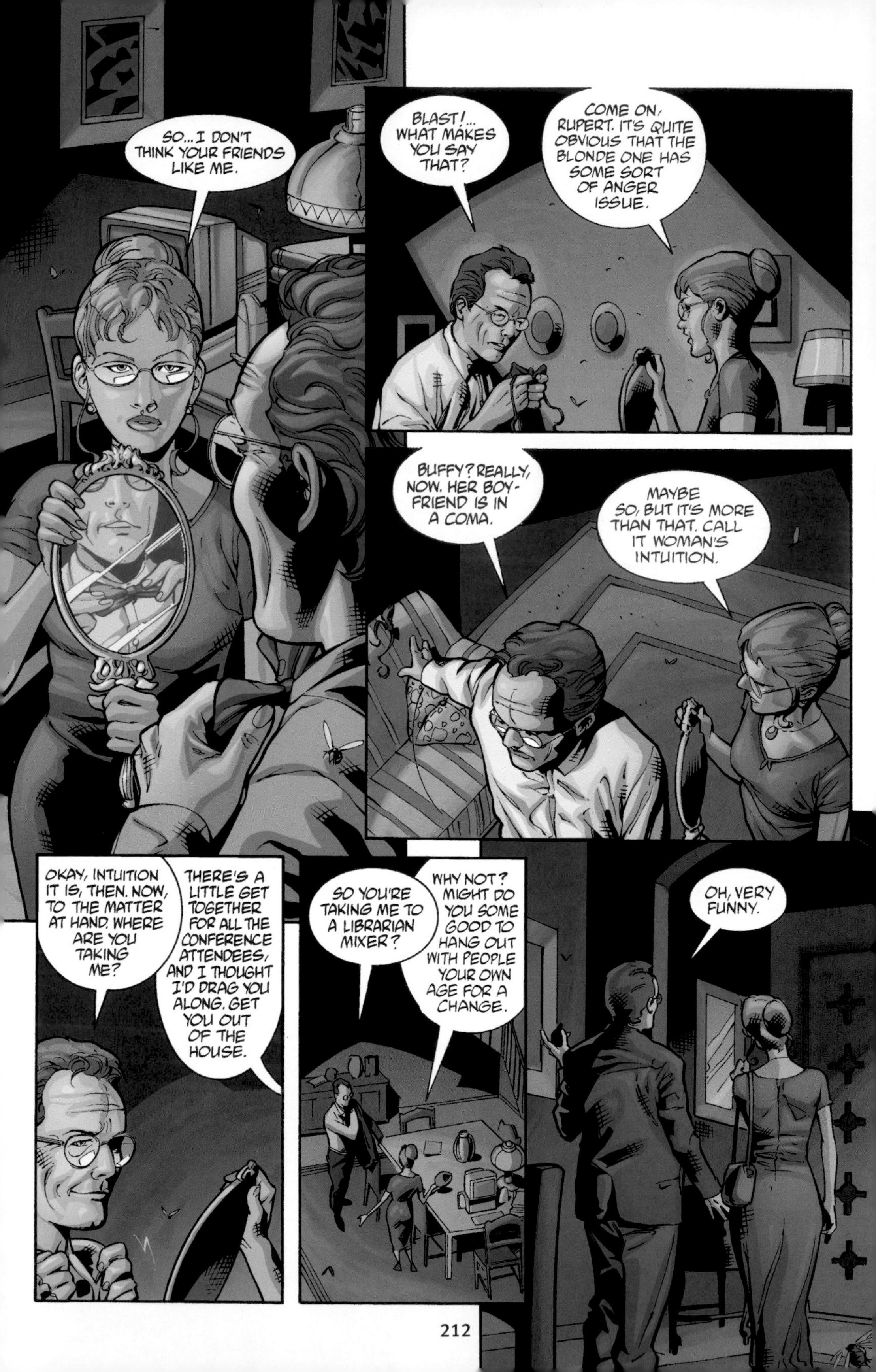
SO... I DON'T THINK YOUR FRIENDS LIKE ME.
BLAST!... WHAT MAKES YOU SAY THAT?
COME ON, RUPERT. IT'S QUITE OBVIOUS THAT THE BLONDE ONE HAS SOME SORT OF ANGER ISSUE.
BUFFY? REALLY, NOW. HER BOY-FRIEND IS IN A COMA.
MAYBE SO, BUT IT'S MORE THAN THAT. CALL IT WOMAN'S INTUITION.
OKAY, INTUITION IT IS, THEN. NOW, TO THE MATTER AT HAND. WHERE ARE YOU TAKING ME?
THERE'S A LITTLE GET TOGETHER FOR ALL THE CONFERENCE ATTENDEES, AND I THOUGHT I'D DRAG YOU ALONG. GET YOU OUT OF THE HOUSE.
SO YOU'RE TAKING ME TO A LIBRARIAN MIXER?
WHY NOT? MIGHT DO YOU SOME GOOD TO HANG OUT WITH PEOPLE YOUR OWN AGE FOR A CHANGE.
OH, VERY FUNNY.

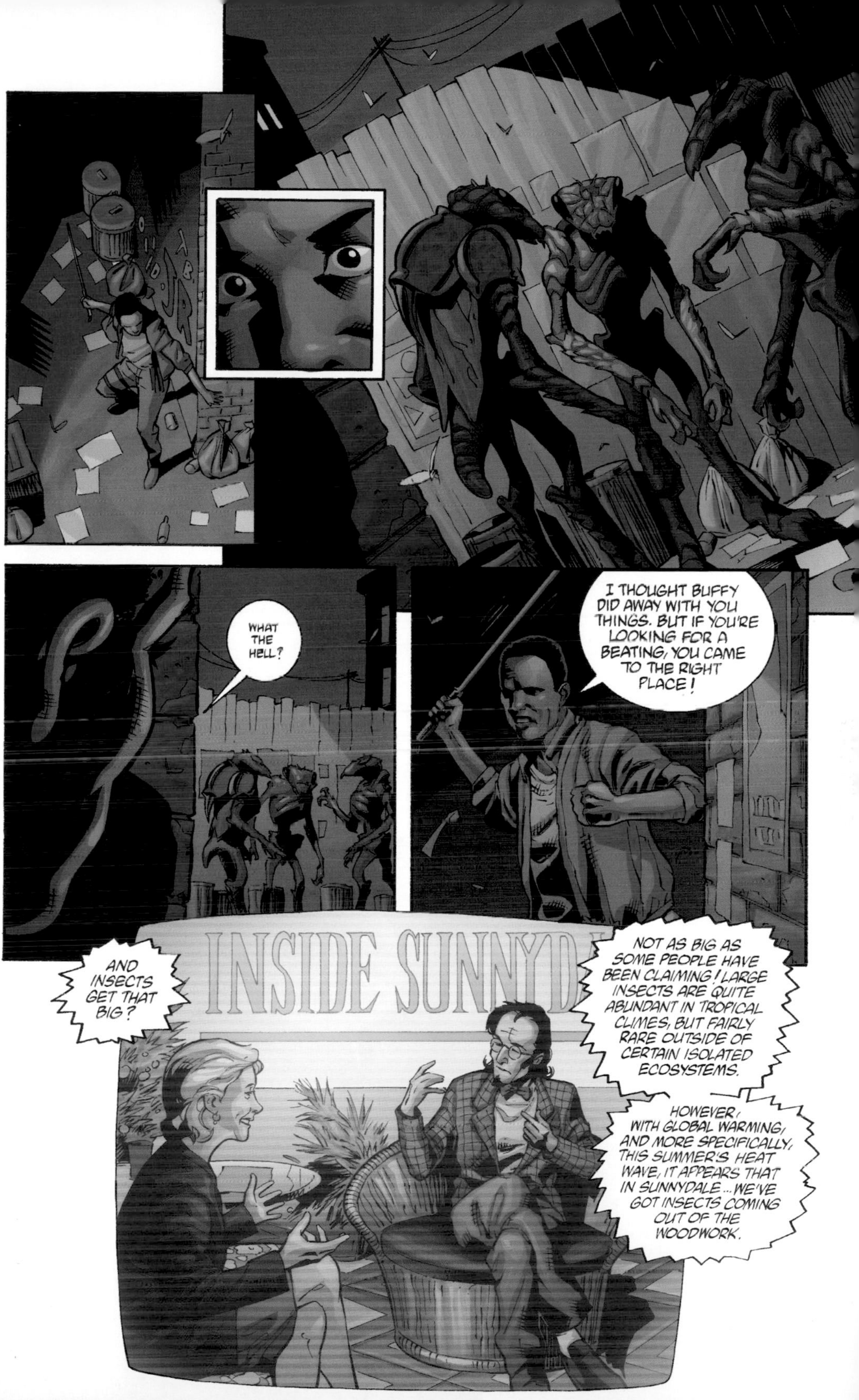
WHAT THE HELL?
I THOUGHT BUFFY DID AWAY WITH YOU THINGS. BUT IF YOU'RE LOOKING FOR A BEATING, YOU CAME TO THE RIGHT PLACE!
INSIDE SUNNYD
AND INSECTS GET THAT BIG?
NOT AS BIG AS SOME PEOPLE HAVE BEEN CLAIMING! LARGE INSECTS ARE QUITE ABUNDANT IN TROPICAL CLIMES, BUT FAIRLY RARE OUTSIDE OF CERTAIN ISOLATED ECOSYSTEMS.
HOWEVER, WITH GLOBAL WARMING, AND MORE SPECIFICALLY, THIS SUMMER'S HEAT WAVE, IT APPEARS THAT IN SUNNYDALE... WE'VE GOT INSECTS COMING OUT OF THE WOODWORK.

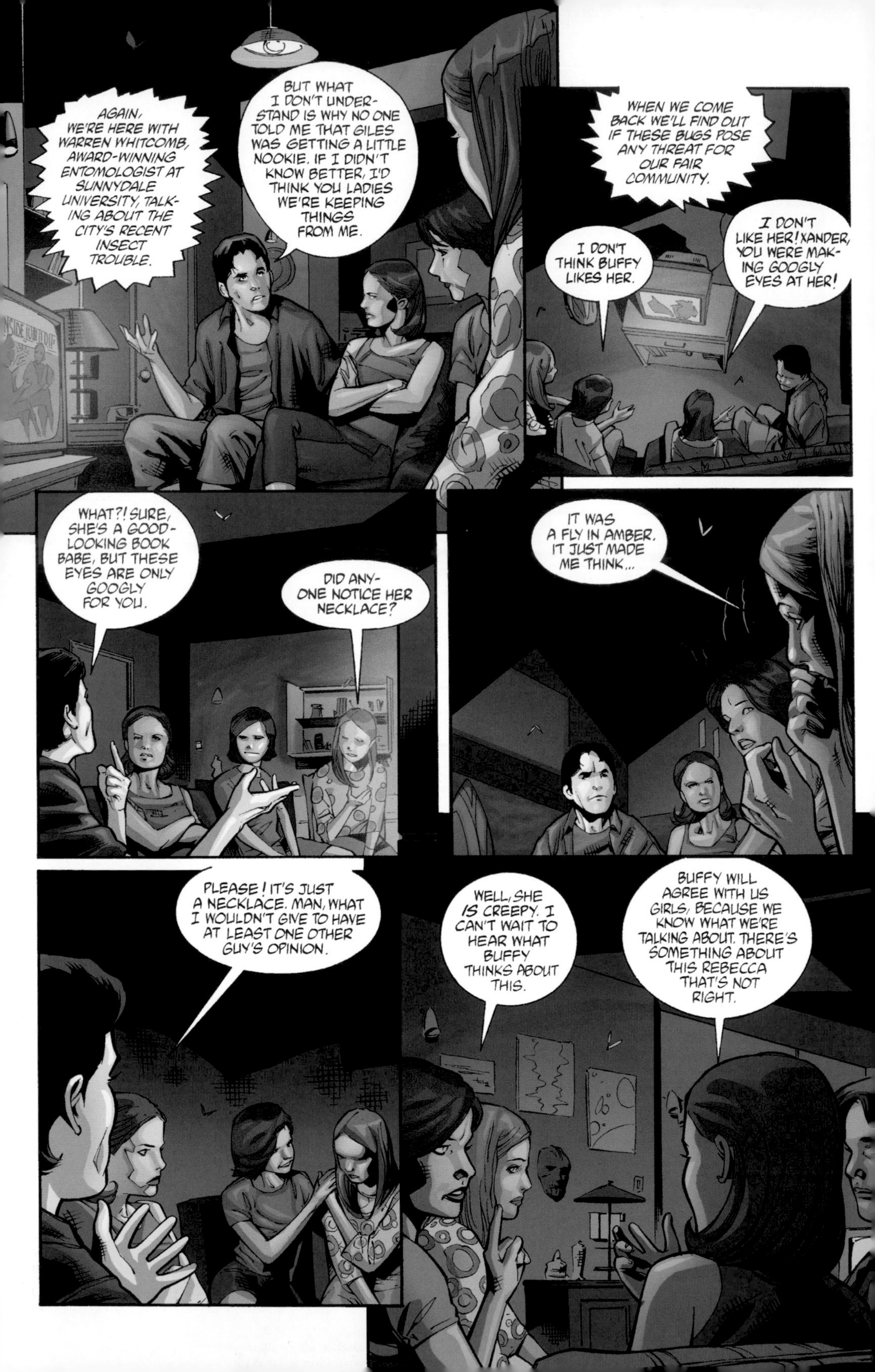
AGAIN, WE'RE HERE WITH WARREN WHITCOMB, AWARD-WINNING ENTOMOLOGIST AT SUNNYDALE UNIVERSITY, TALKING ABOUT THE CITY'S RECENT INSECT TROUBLE.
BUT WHAT I DON'T UNDERSTAND IS WHY NO ONE TOLD ME THAT GILES WAS GETTING A LITTLE NOOKIE. IF I DIDN'T KNOW BETTER, I'D THINK YOU LADIES WE'RE KEEPING THINGS FROM ME.
WHEN WE COME BACK WE'LL FIND OUT IF THESE BUGS POSE ANY THREAT FOR OUR FAIR COMMUNITY.
I DON'T THINK BUFFY LIKES HER.
I DON'T LIKE HER! XANDER, YOU WERE MAKING GOOGLY EYES AT HER!
WHAT?! SURE, SHE'S A GOOD-LOOKING BOOK BABE, BUT THESE EYES ARE ONLY GOOGLY FOR YOU.
DID ANYONE NOTICE HER NECKLACE?
IT WAS A FLY IN AMBER. IT JUST MADE ME THINK...
PLEASE! IT'S JUST A NECKLACE. MAN, WHAT I WOULDN'T GIVE TO HAVE AT LEAST ONE OTHER GUY'S OPINION.
WELL, SHE IS CREEPY. I CAN'T WAIT TO HEAR WHAT BUFFY THINKS ABOUT THIS.
BUFFY WILL AGREE WITH US GIRLS, BECAUSE WE KNOW WHAT WE'RE TALKING ABOUT. THERE'S SOMETHING ABOUT THIS REBECCA THAT'S NOT RIGHT.

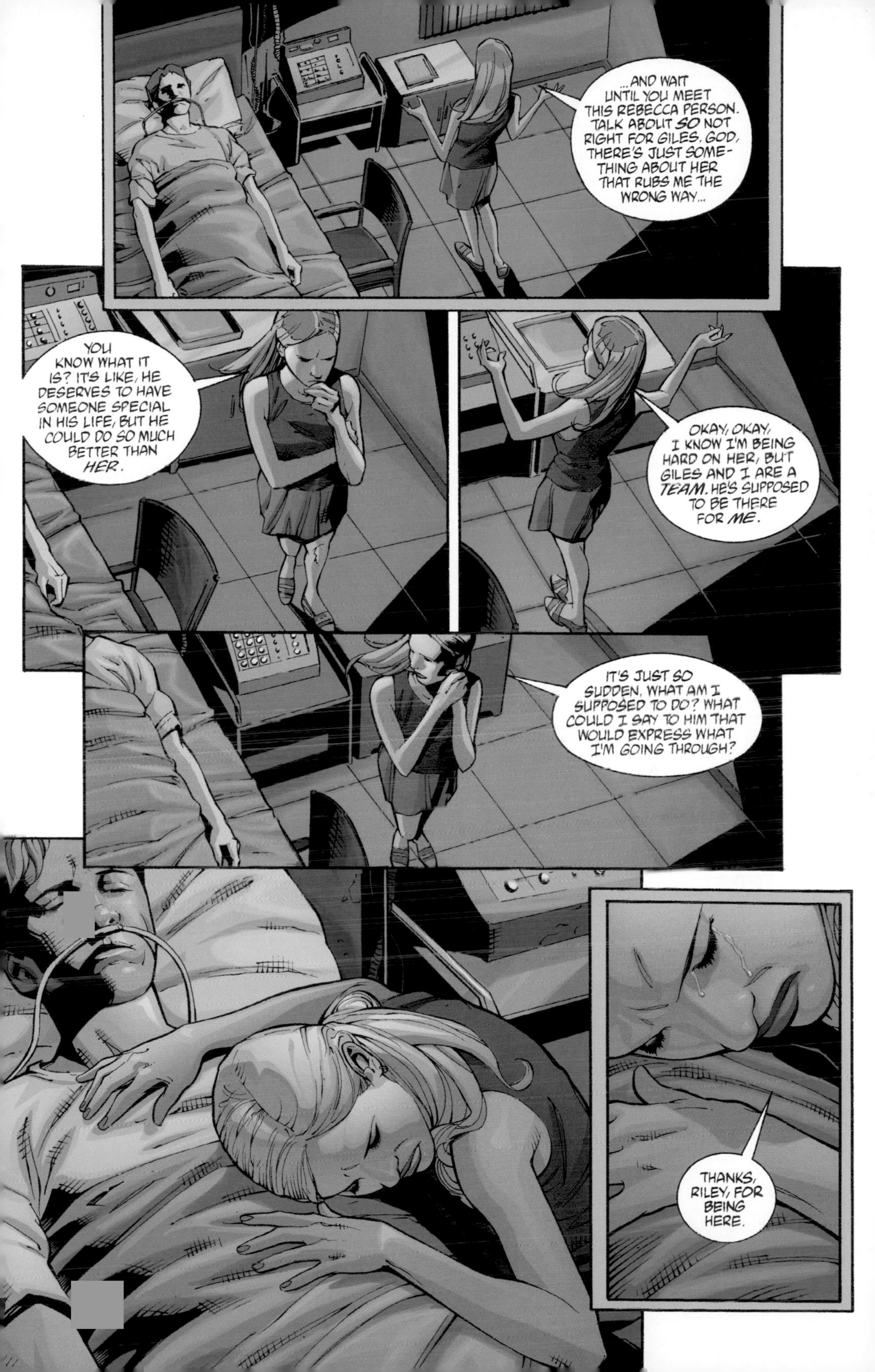

...AND WAIT UNTIL YOU MEET THIS REBECCA PERSON. TALK ABOUT SO NOT RIGHT FOR GILES. GOD, THERE'S JUST SOMETHING ABOUT HER THAT RUBS ME THE WRONG WAY...
YOU KNOW WHAT IT IS? IT'S LIKE, HE DESERVES TO HAVE SOMEONE SPECIAL IN HIS LIFE, BUT HE COULD DO SO MUCH BETTER THAN HER.
OKAY, OKAY, I KNOW I'M BEING HARD ON HER, BUT GILES AND I ARE A TEAM. HE'S SUPPOSED TO BE THERE FOR ME.
IT'S JUST SO SUDDEN. WHAT AM I SUPPOSED TO DO? WHAT COULD I SAY TO HIM THAT WOULD EXPRESS WHAT I'M GOING THROUGH?
THANKS, RILEY, FOR BEING HERE.

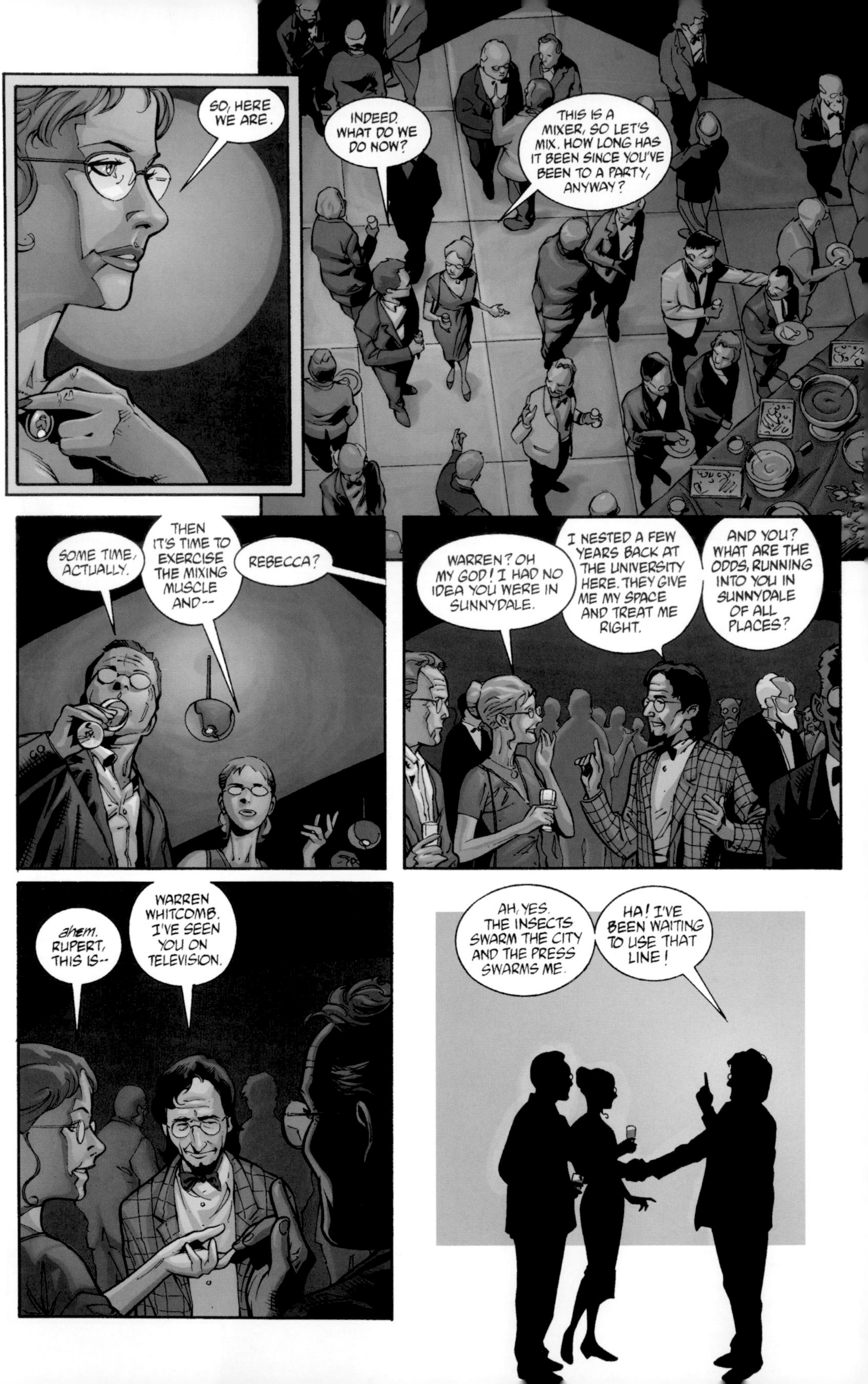
SO, HERE WE ARE.
INDEED. WHAT DO WE DO NOW?
THIS IS A MIXER, SO LET'S MIX. HOW LONG HAS IT BEEN SINCE YOU'VE BEEN TO A PARTY, ANYWAY?
SOME TIME, ACTUALLY.
THEN IT'S TIME TO EXERCISE THE MIXING MUSCLE AND--
REBECCA?
WARREN? OH MY GOD! I HAD NO IDEA YOU WERE IN SUNNYDALE.
I NESTED A FEW YEARS BACK AT THE UNIVERSITY HERE. THEY GIVE ME MY SPACE AND TREAT ME RIGHT.
AND YOU? WHAT ARE THE ODDS, RUNNING INTO YOU IN SUNNYDALE OF ALL PLACES?
ahem. RUPERT, THIS IS--
WARREN WHITCOMB. I'VE SEEN YOU ON TELEVISION.
AH, YES. THE INSECTS SWARM THE CITY AND THE PRESS SWARMS ME.
HA! I'VE BEEN WAITING TO USE THAT LINE!

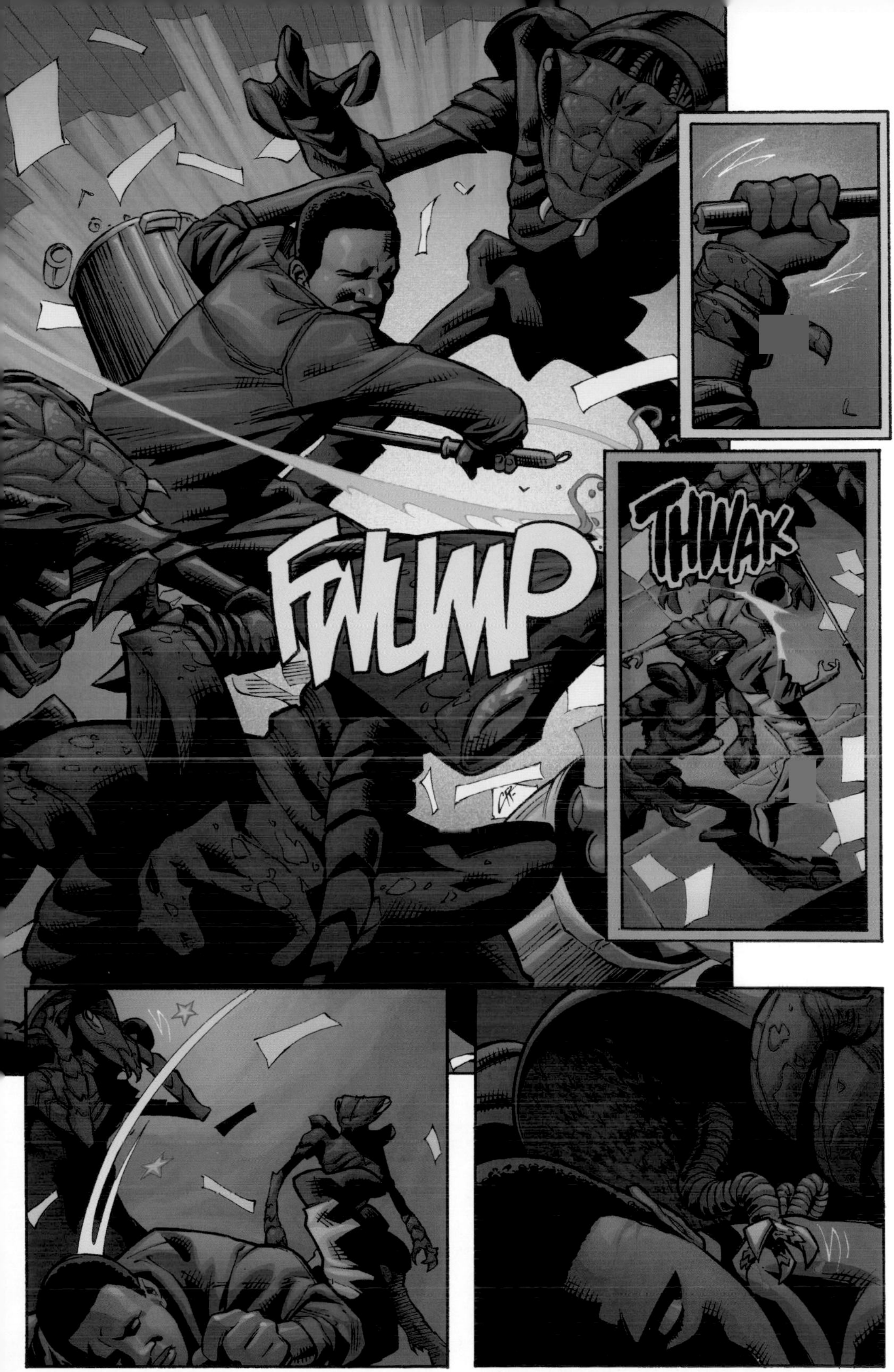
FWUMP
THWAK

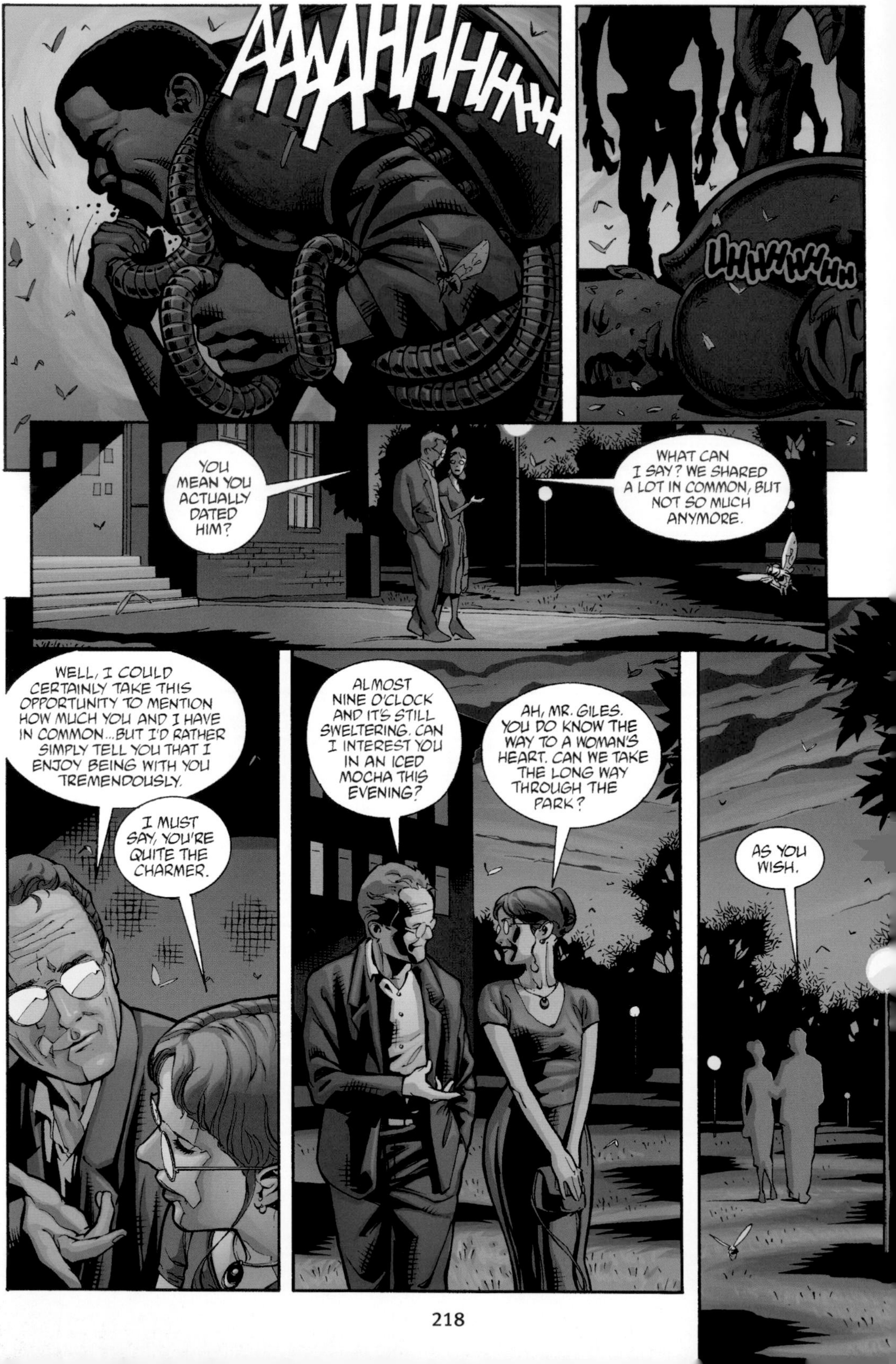
AAAAHHHHHH
UHHHHHHH
YOU MEAN YOU ACTUALLY DATED HIM?
WHAT CAN I SAY? WE SHARED A LOT IN COMMON, BUT NOT SO MUCH ANYMORE.
WELL, I COULD CERTAINLY TAKE THIS OPPORTUNITY TO MENTION HOW MUCH YOU AND I HAVE IN COMMON...BUT I'D RATHER SIMPLY TELL YOU THAT I ENJOY BEING WITH YOU TREMENDOUSLY.
I MUST SAY, YOU'RE QUITE THE CHARMER.
ALMOST NINE O'CLOCK AND IT'S STILL SWELTERING. CAN I INTEREST YOU IN AN ICED MOCHA THIS EVENING?
AH, MR. GILES. YOU DO KNOW THE WAY TO A WOMAN'S HEART. CAN WE TAKE THE LONG WAY THROUGH THE PARK?
AS YOU WISH.

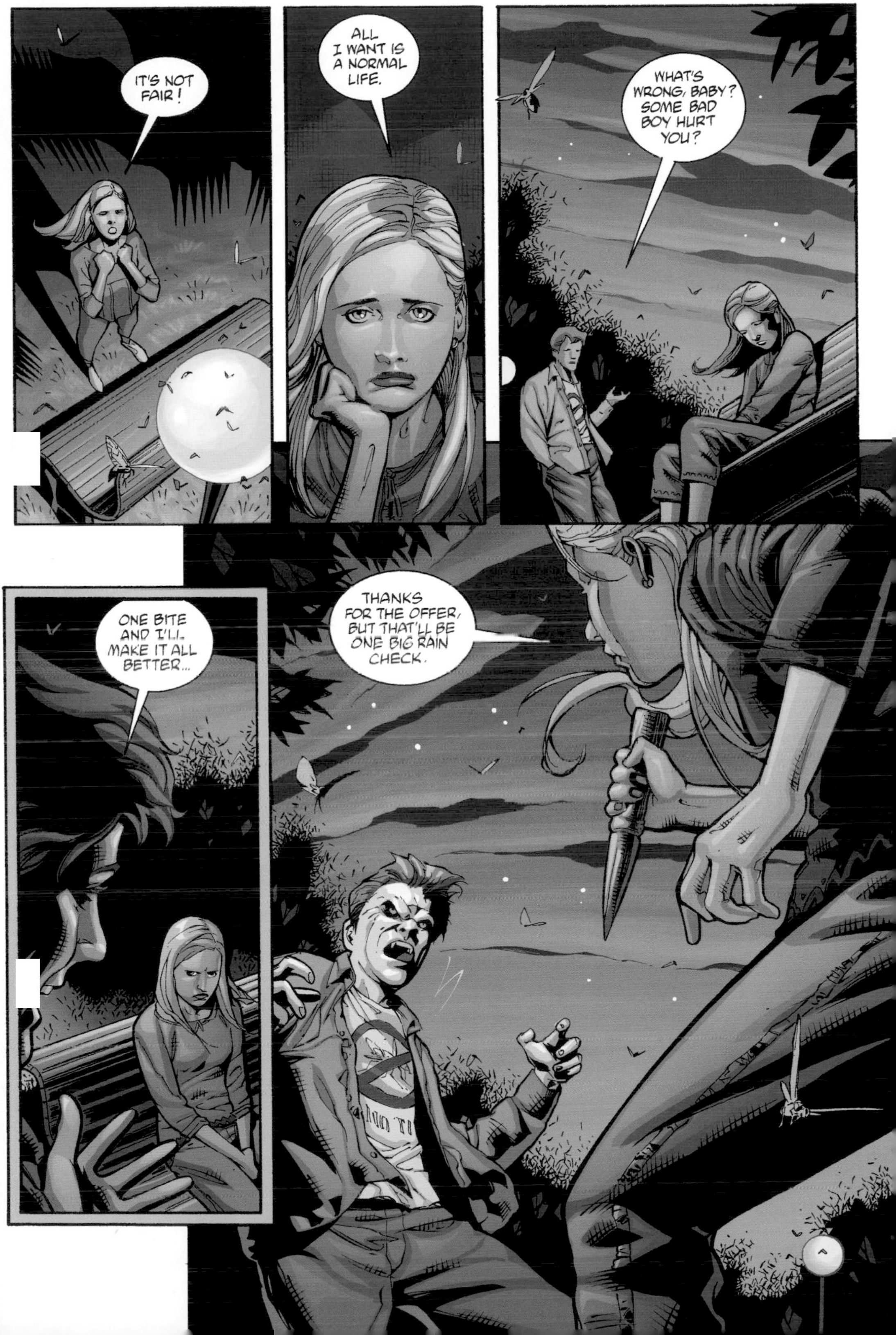
IT'S NOT FAIR!
ALL I WANT IS A NORMAL LIFE.
WHAT'S WRONG, BABY? SOME BAD BOY HURT YOU?
ONE BITE AND I'LL MAKE IT ALL BETTER...
THANKS FOR THE OFFER, BUT THAT'LL BE ONE BIG RAIN CHECK.

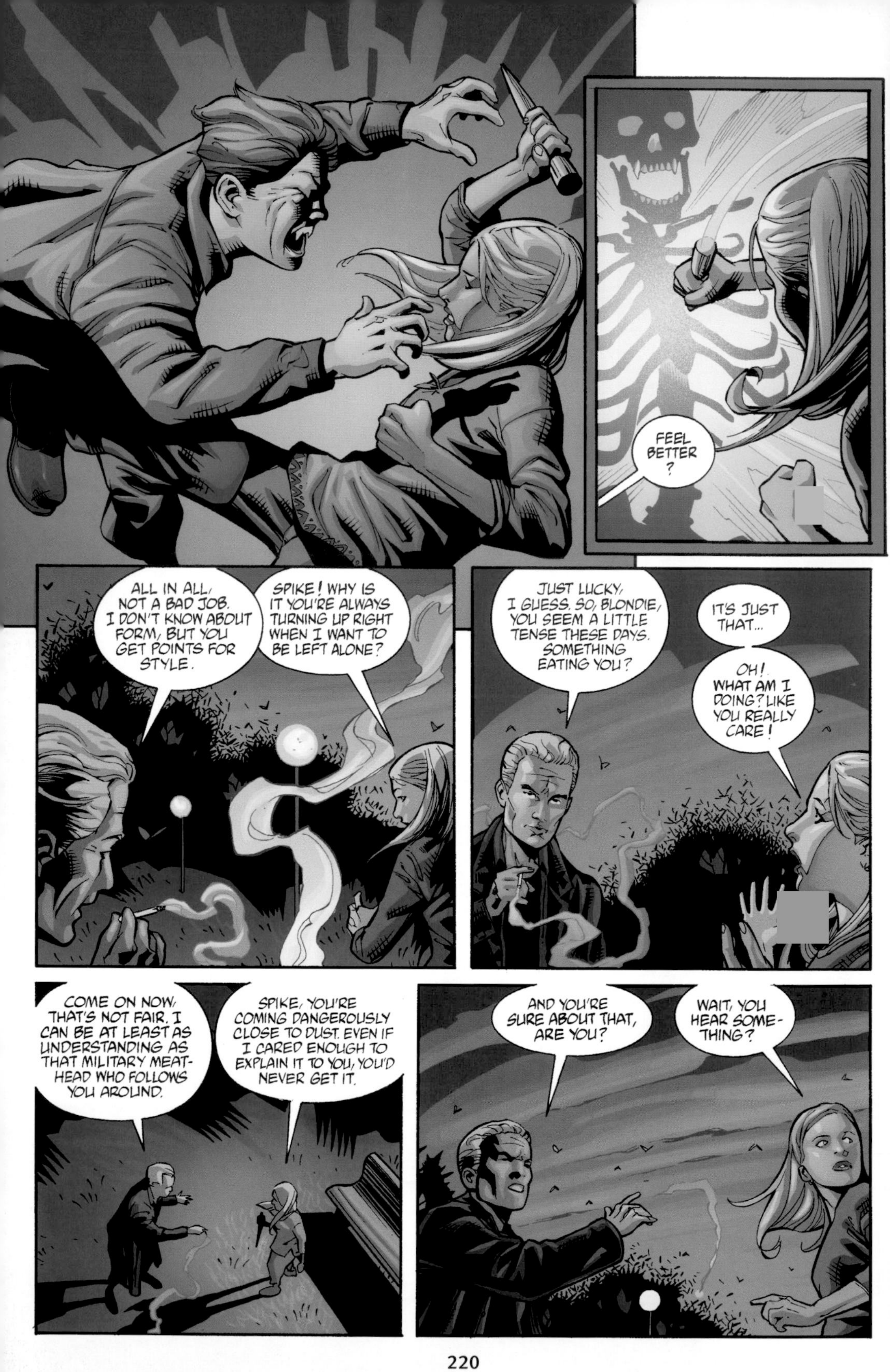
FEEL BETTER?
ALL IN ALL, NOT A BAD JOB. I DON'T KNOW ABOUT FORM, BUT YOU GET POINTS FOR STYLE.
SPIKE! WHY IS IT YOU'RE ALWAYS TURNING UP RIGHT WHEN I WANT TO BE LEFT ALONE?
JUST LUCKY, I GUESS. SO, BLONDIE, YOU SEEM A LITTLE TENSE THESE DAYS. SOMETHING EATING YOU?
IT'S JUST THAT...
OH! WHAT AM I DOING? LIKE YOU REALLY CARE!
COME ON NOW, THAT'S NOT FAIR. I CAN BE AT LEAST AS UNDERSTANDING AS THAT MILITARY MEAT-HEAD WHO FOLLOWS YOU AROUND.
SPIKE, YOU'RE COMING DANGEROUSLY CLOSE TO DUST. EVEN IF I CARED ENOUGH TO EXPLAIN IT TO YOU, YOU'D NEVER GET IT.
AND YOU'RE SURE ABOUT THAT, ARE YOU?
WAIT, YOU HEAR SOME-THING?

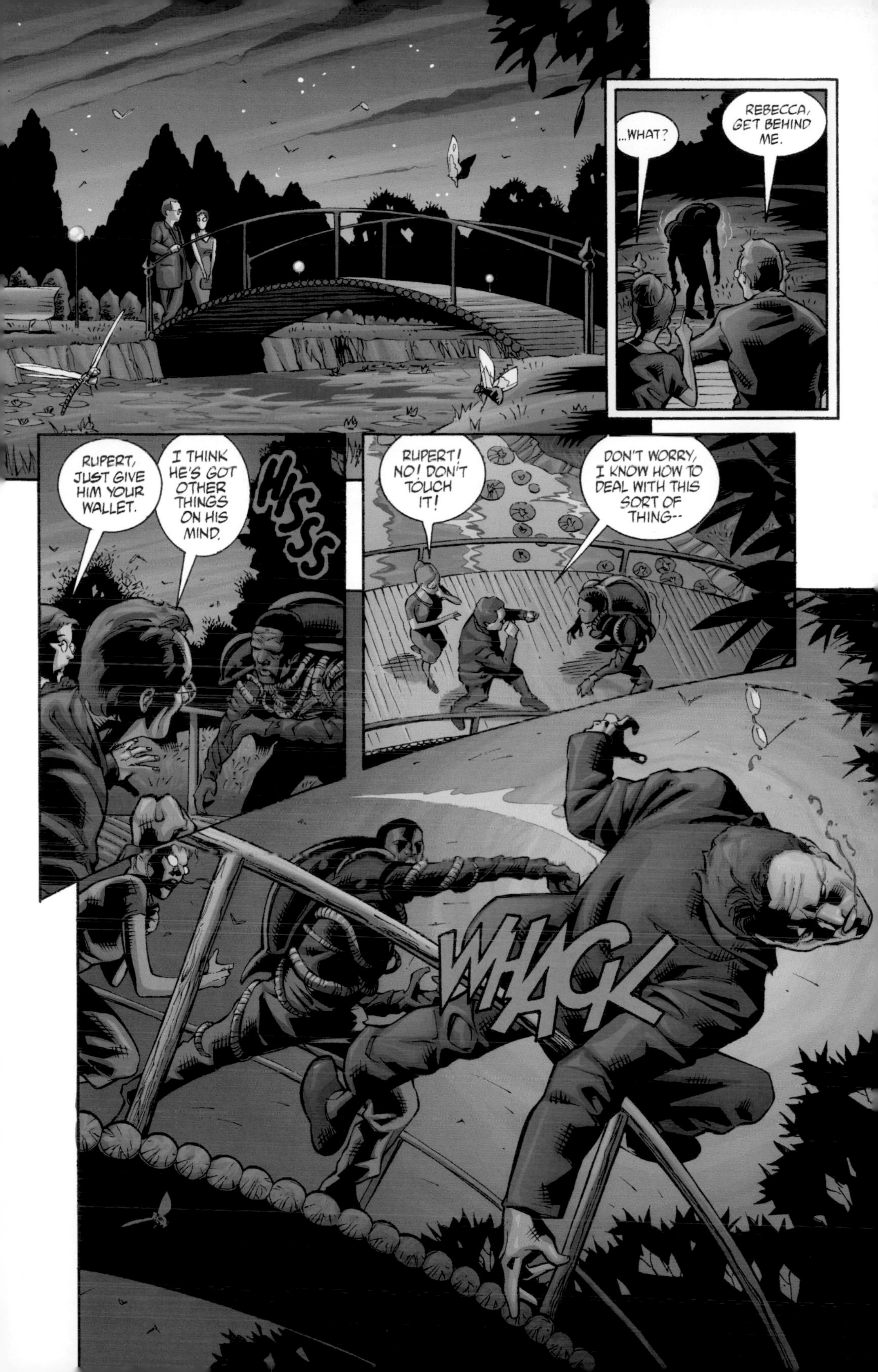
...WHAT?
REBECCA, GET BEHIND ME.
RUPERT, JUST GIVE HIM YOUR WALLET.
I THINK HE'S GOT OTHER THINGS ON HIS MIND.
HISSS
RUPERT! NO! DON'T TOUCH IT!
DON'T WORRY, I KNOW HOW TO DEAL WITH THIS SORT OF THING--
WHACK

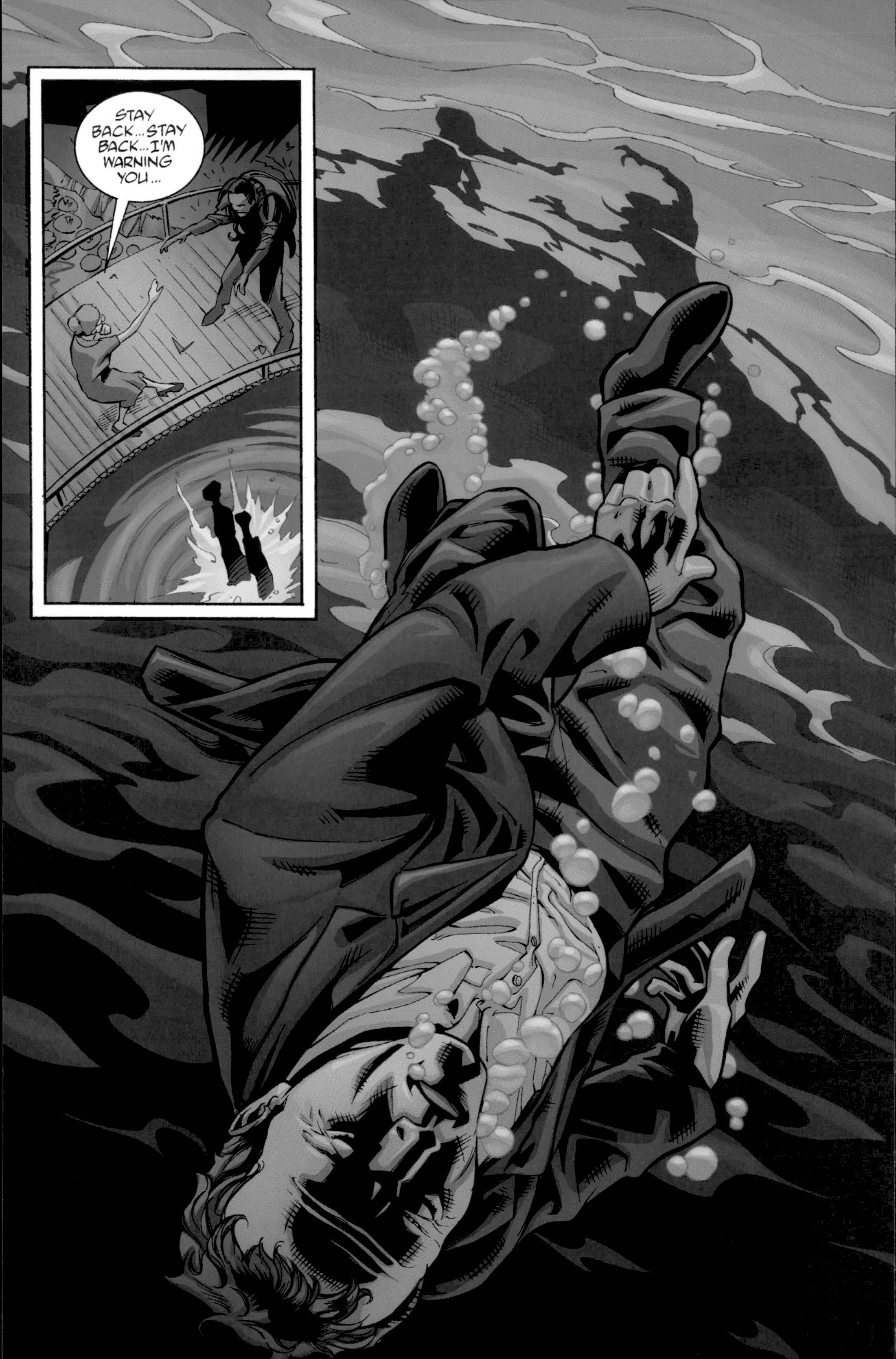
STAY BACK...STAY BACK...I'M WARNING YOU...

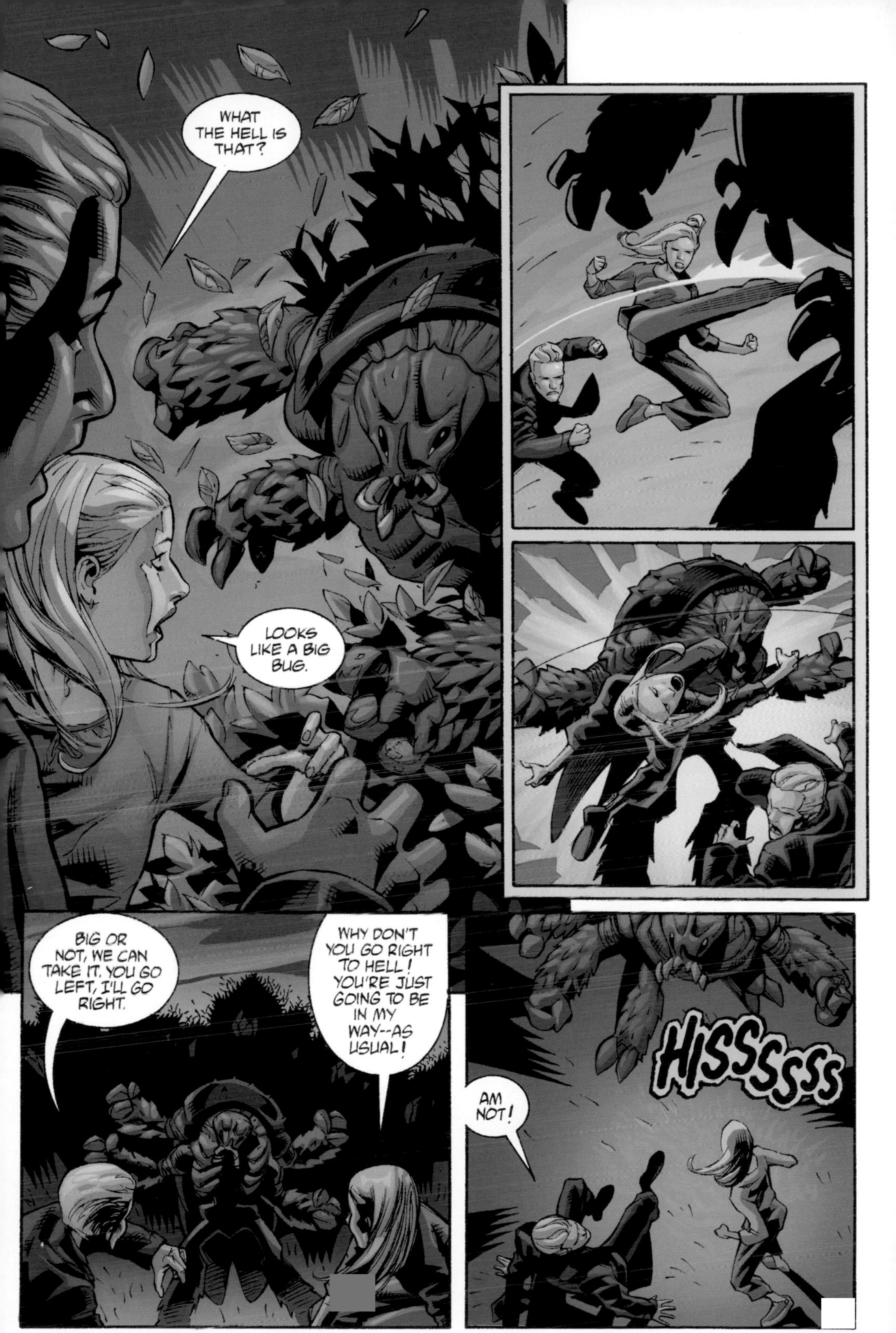

WHAT THE HELL IS THAT?
LOOKS LIKE A BIG BUG.
BIG OR NOT, WE CAN TAKE IT. YOU GO LEFT, I'LL GO RIGHT.
WHY DON'T YOU GO RIGHT TO HELL! YOU'RE JUST GOING TO BE IN MY WAY--AS USUAL!
HISSSSSS
AM NOT!

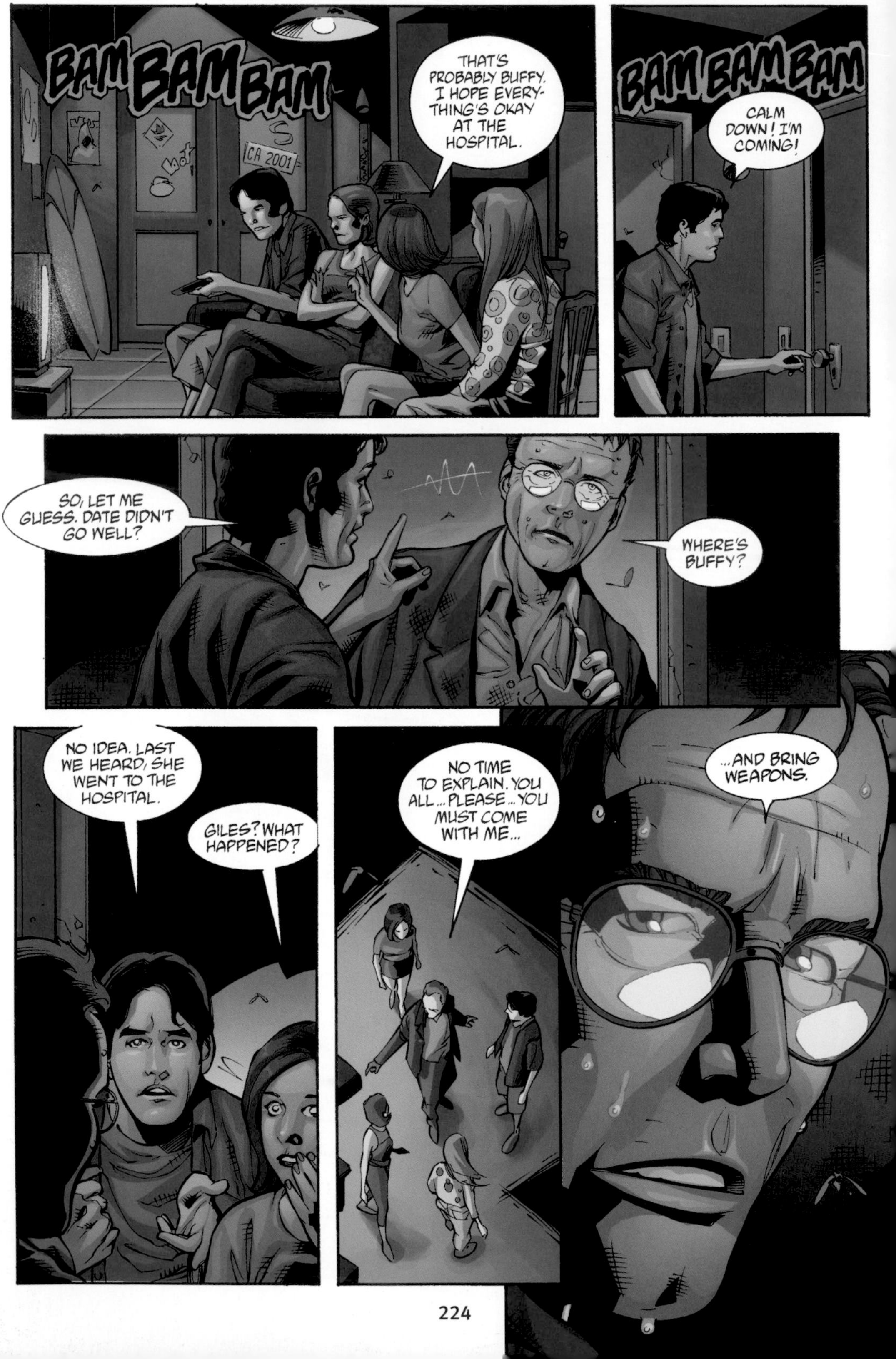
BAM BAM BAM
THAT'S PROBABLY BUFFY. I HOPE EVERYTHING'S OKAY AT THE HOSPITAL.
BAM BAM BAM
CALM DOWN! I'M COMING!
SO, LET ME GUESS. DATE DIDN'T GO WELL?
WHERE'S BUFFY?
NO IDEA. LAST WE HEARD, SHE WENT TO THE HOSPITAL.
GILES? WHAT HAPPENED?
NO TIME TO EXPLAIN. YOU ALL... PLEASE... YOU MUST COME WITH ME...
...AND BRING WEAPONS.

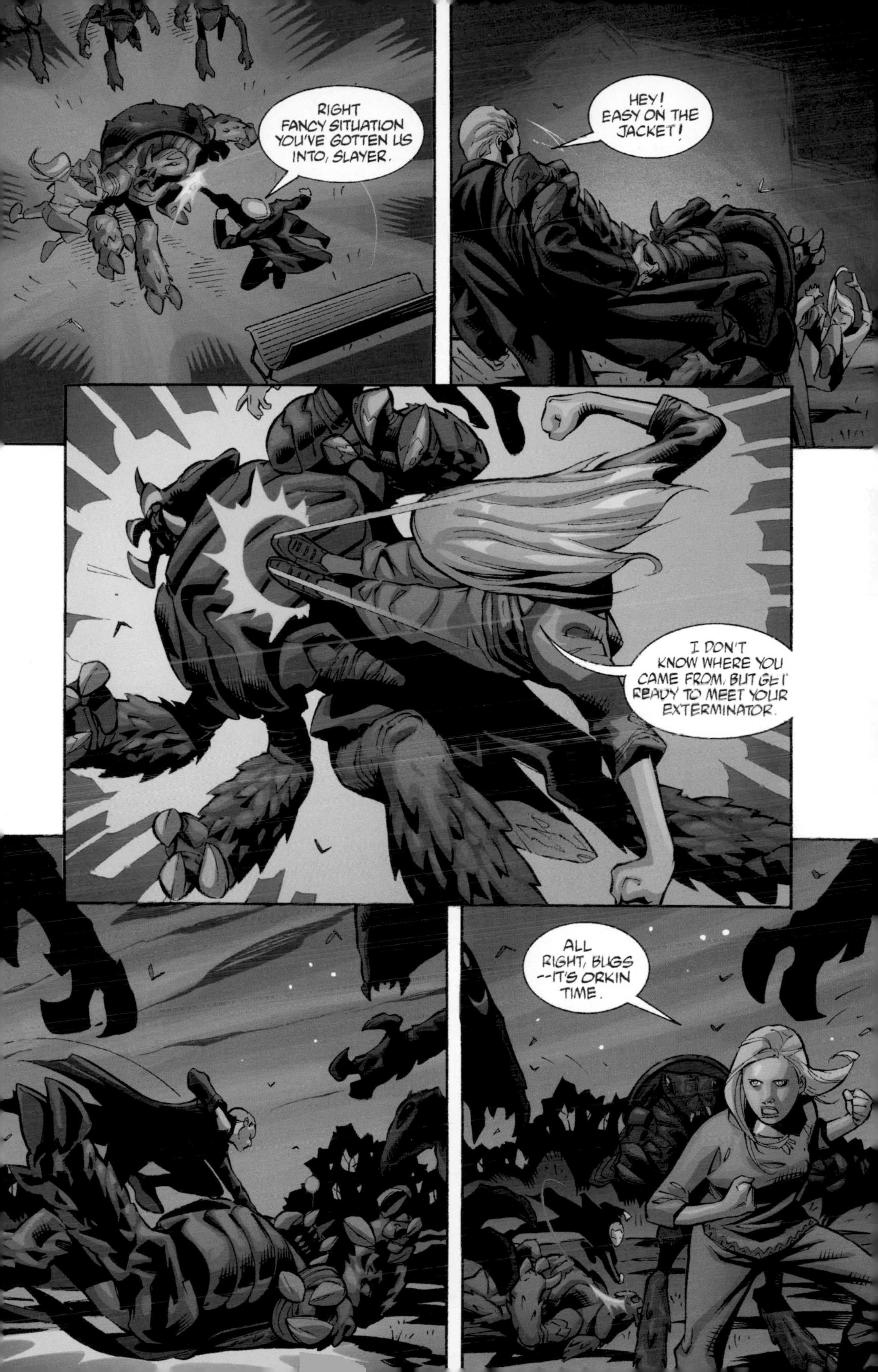
RIGHT FANCY SITUATION YOU'VE GOTTEN US INTO, SLAYER.
HEY! EASY ON THE JACKET!
I DON'T KNOW WHERE YOU CAME FROM, BUT GET READY TO MEET YOUR EXTERMINATOR.
ALL RIGHT, BUGS --IT'S ORKIN TIME.

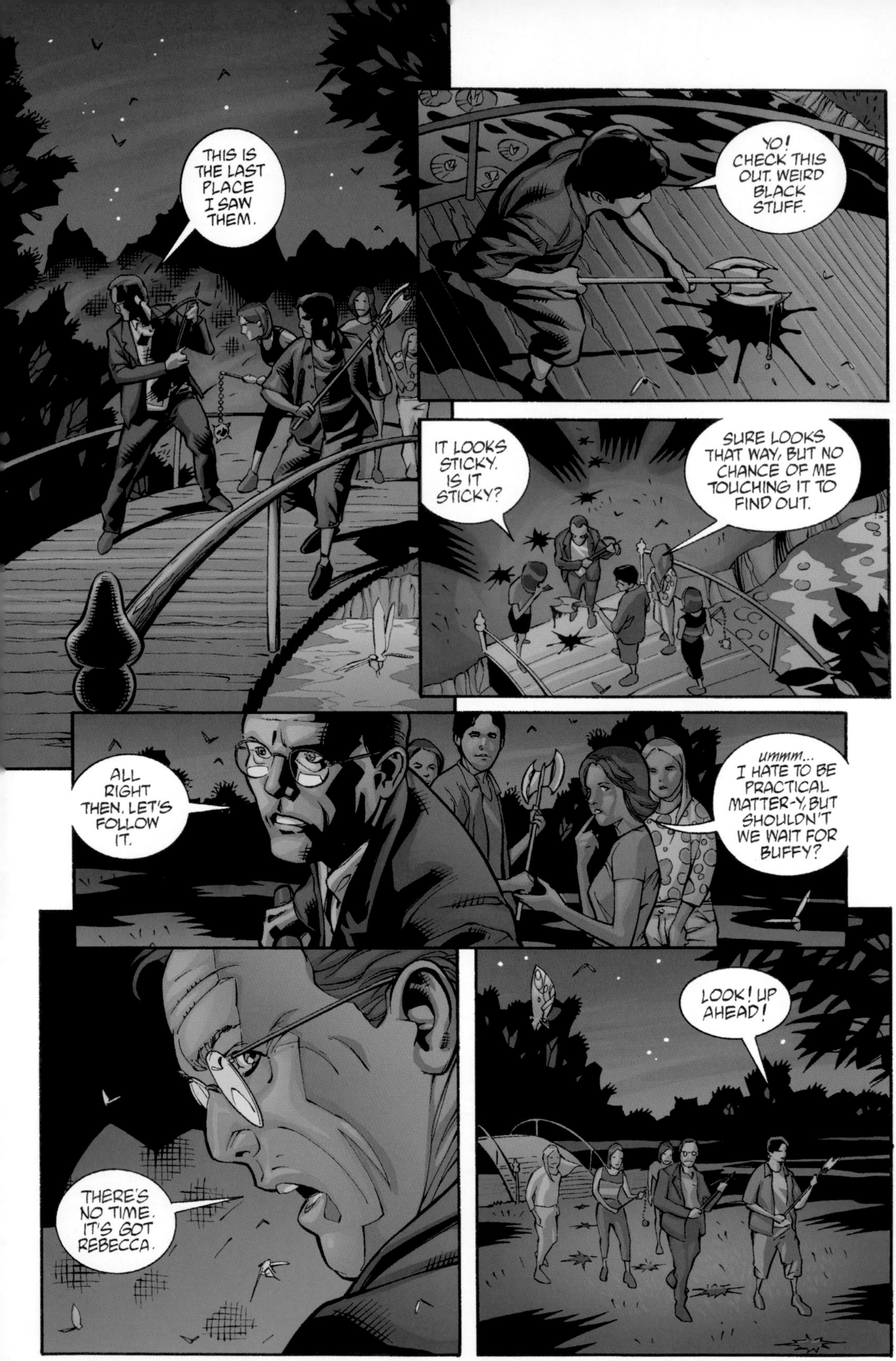
THIS IS THE LAST PLACE I SAW THEM.
YO! CHECK THIS OUT. WEIRD BLACK STUFF.
IT LOOKS STICKY. IS IT STICKY?
SURE LOOKS THAT WAY, BUT NO CHANCE OF ME TOUCHING IT TO FIND OUT.
ALL RIGHT THEN. LET'S FOLLOW IT.
ummm... I HATE TO BE PRACTICAL MATTER-Y, BUT SHOULDN'T WE WAIT FOR BUFFY?
THERE'S NO TIME. IT'S GOT REBECCA.
LOOK! UP AHEAD!

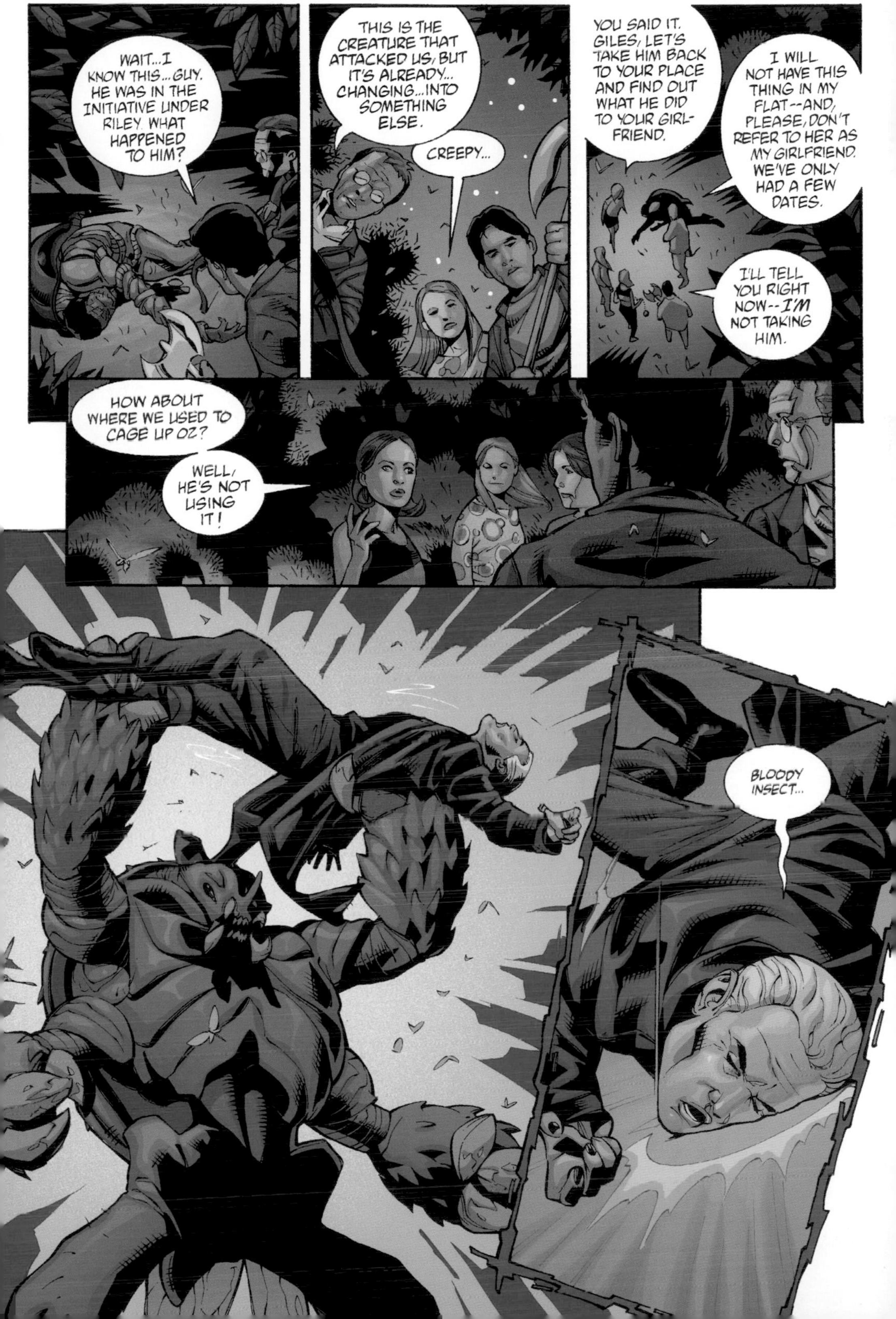
WAIT...I KNOW THIS...GUY. HE WAS IN THE INITIATIVE UNDER RILEY. WHAT HAPPENED TO HIM?
THIS IS THE CREATURE THAT ATTACKED US, BUT IT'S ALREADY... CHANGING...INTO SOMETHING ELSE.
CREEPY...
YOU SAID IT. GILES, LET'S TAKE HIM BACK TO YOUR PLACE AND FIND OUT WHAT HE DID TO YOUR GIRL-FRIEND.
I WILL NOT HAVE THIS THING IN MY FLAT--AND, PLEASE, DON'T REFER TO HER AS MY GIRLFRIEND. WE'VE ONLY HAD A FEW DATES.
I'LL TELL YOU RIGHT NOW--I'M NOT TAKING HIM.
HOW ABOUT WHERE WE USED TO CAGE UP OZ?
WELL, HE'S NOT USING IT!
BLOODY INSECT...

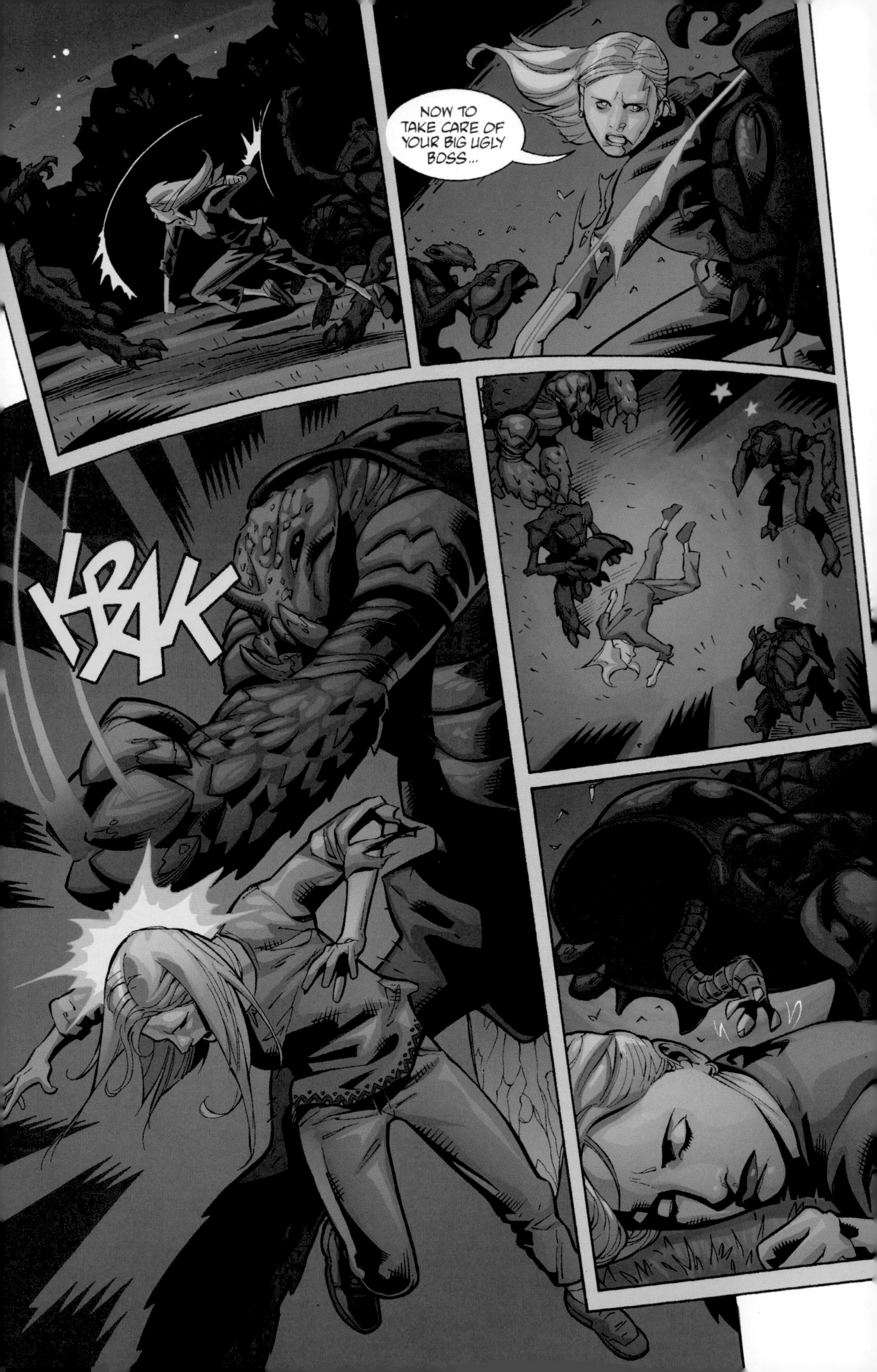
NOW TO TAKE CARE OF YOUR BIG UGLY BOSS...
KRAK

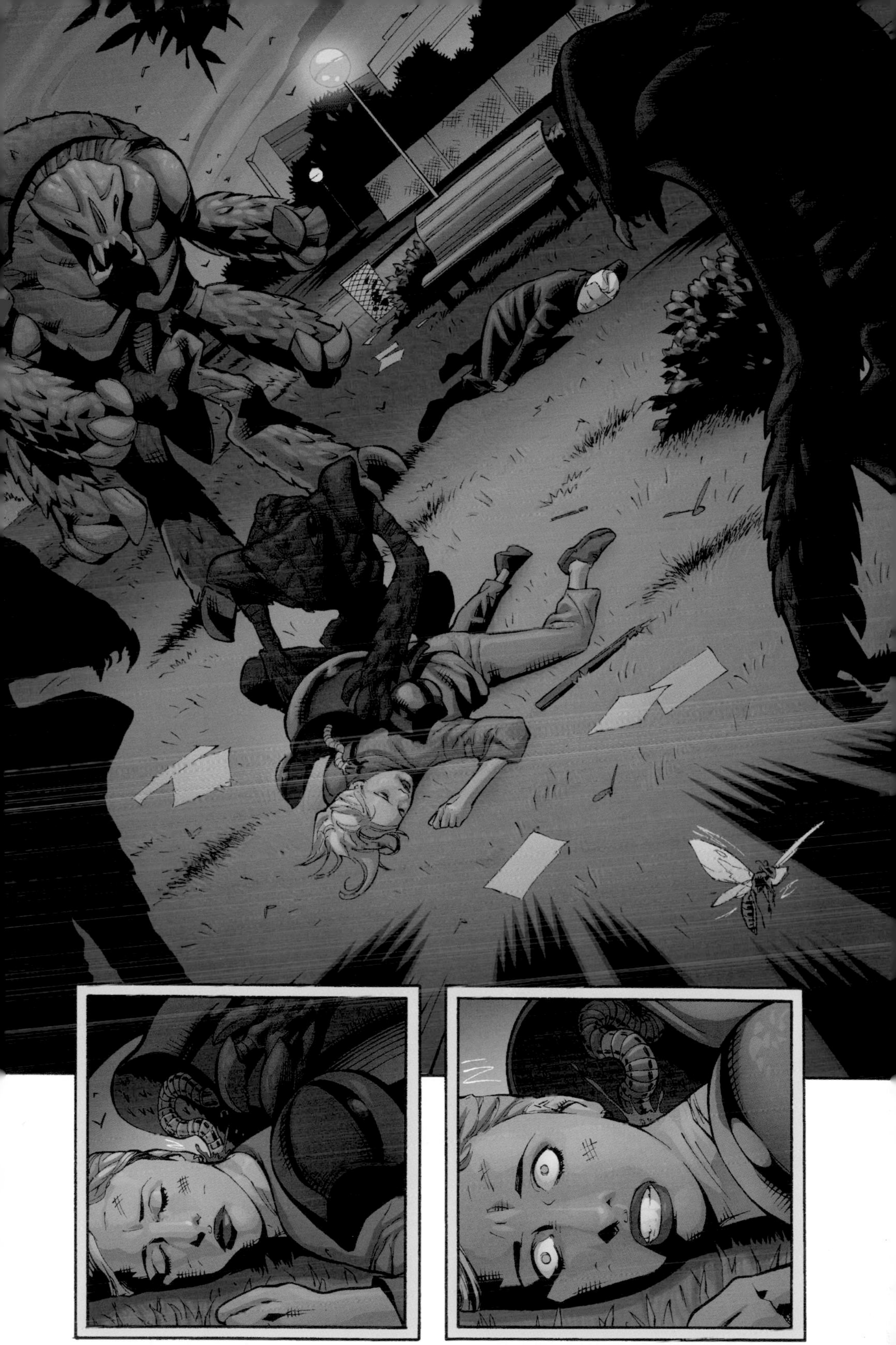

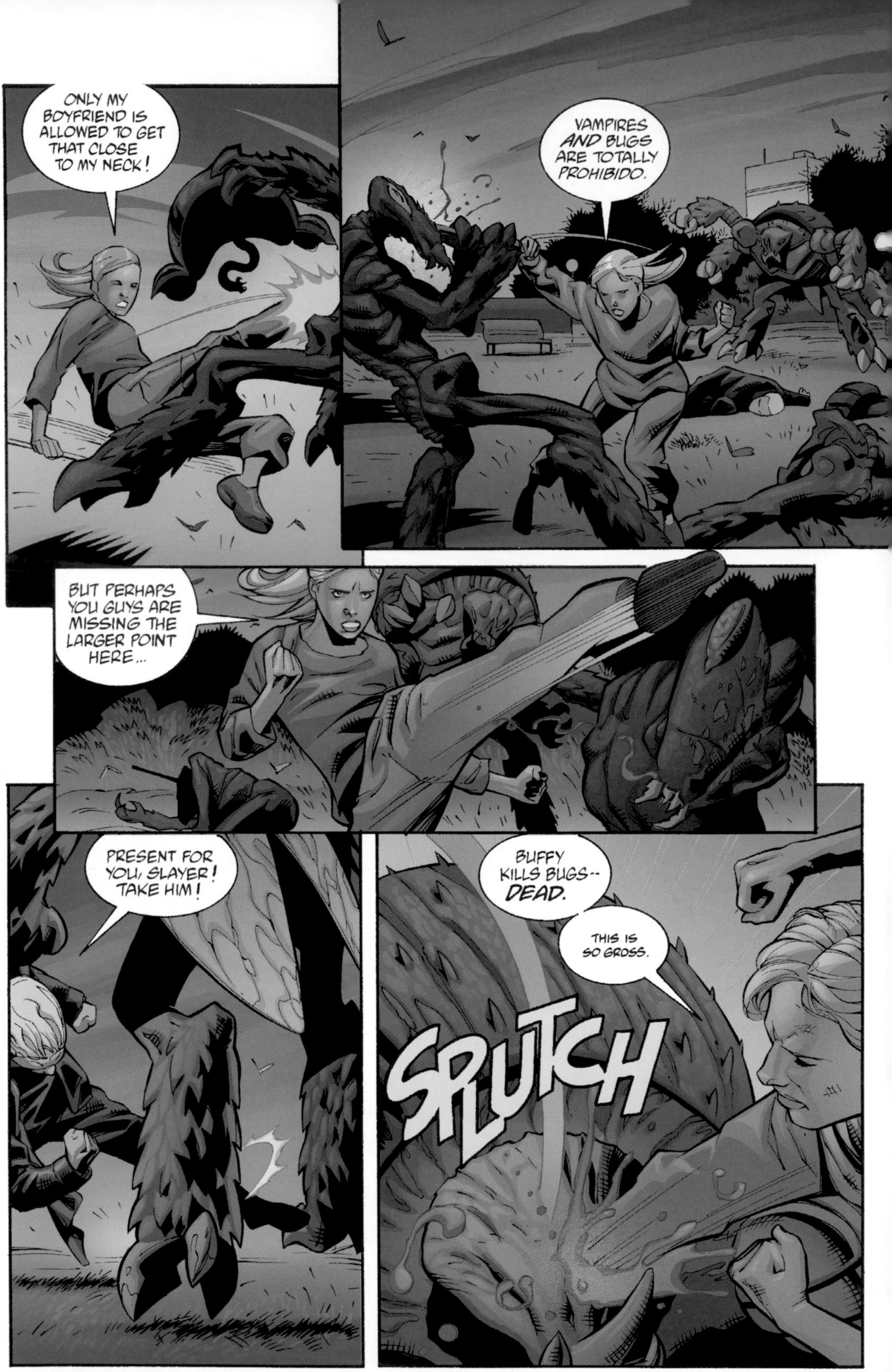
ONLY MY BOYFRIEND IS ALLOWED TO GET THAT CLOSE TO MY NECK!
VAMPIRES AND BUGS ARE TOTALLY PROHIBIDO.
BUT PERHAPS YOU GUYS ARE MISSING THE LARGER POINT HERE...
PRESENT FOR YOU, SLAYER! TAKE HIM!
BUFFY KILLS BUGS-- DEAD.
THIS IS SO GROSS.
SPLUTCH

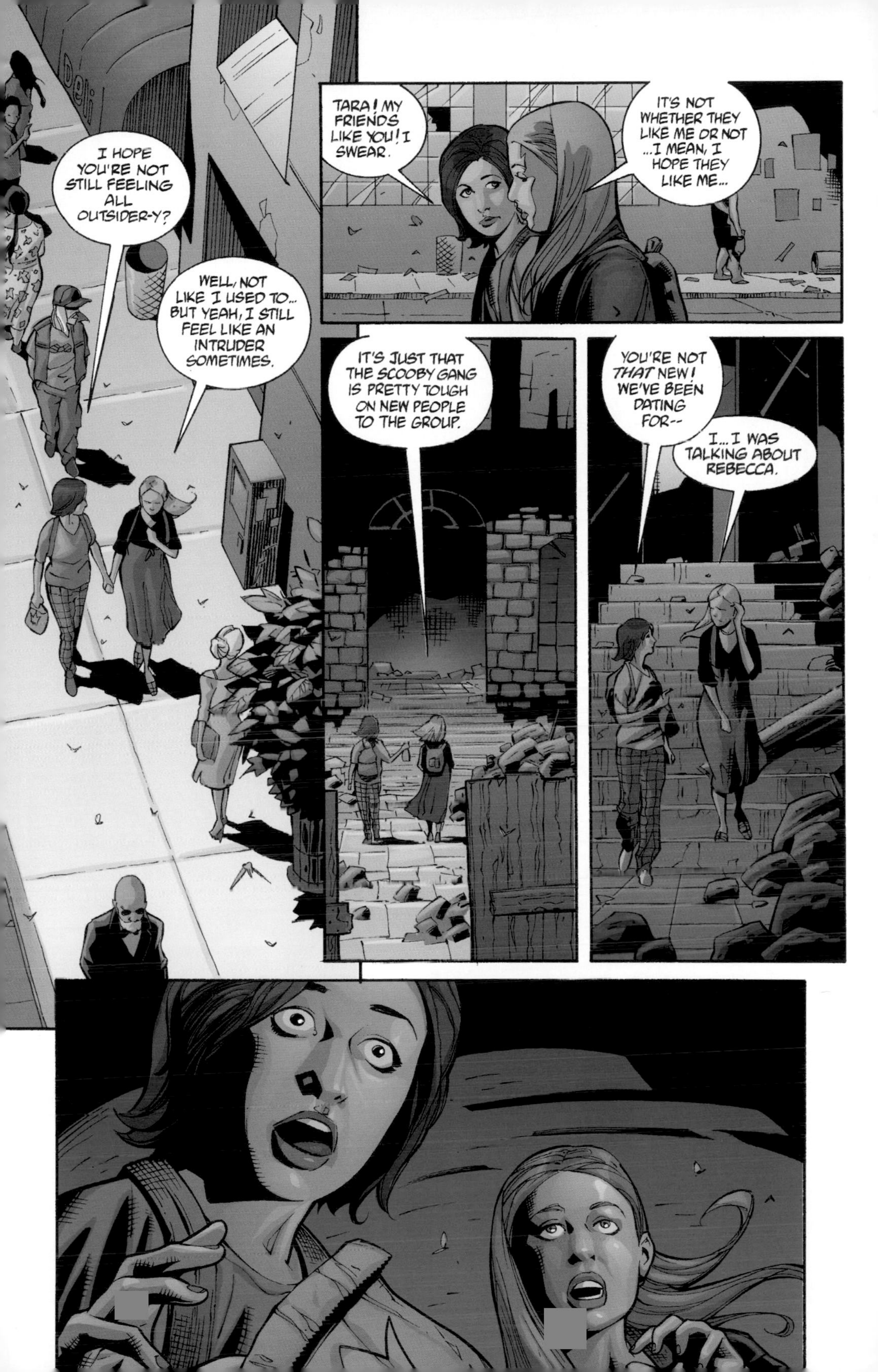
I HOPE YOU'RE NOT STILL FEELING ALL OUTSIDER-Y?
WELL, NOT LIKE I USED TO... BUT YEAH, I STILL FEEL LIKE AN INTRUDER SOMETIMES.
TARA! MY FRIENDS LIKE YOU! I SWEAR.
IT'S NOT WHETHER THEY LIKE ME OR NOT ...I MEAN, I HOPE THEY LIKE ME...
IT'S JUST THAT THE SCOOBY GANG IS PRETTY TOUGH ON NEW PEOPLE TO THE GROUP.
YOU'RE NOT THAT NEW! WE'VE BEEN DATING FOR--
I... I WAS TALKING ABOUT REBECCA.

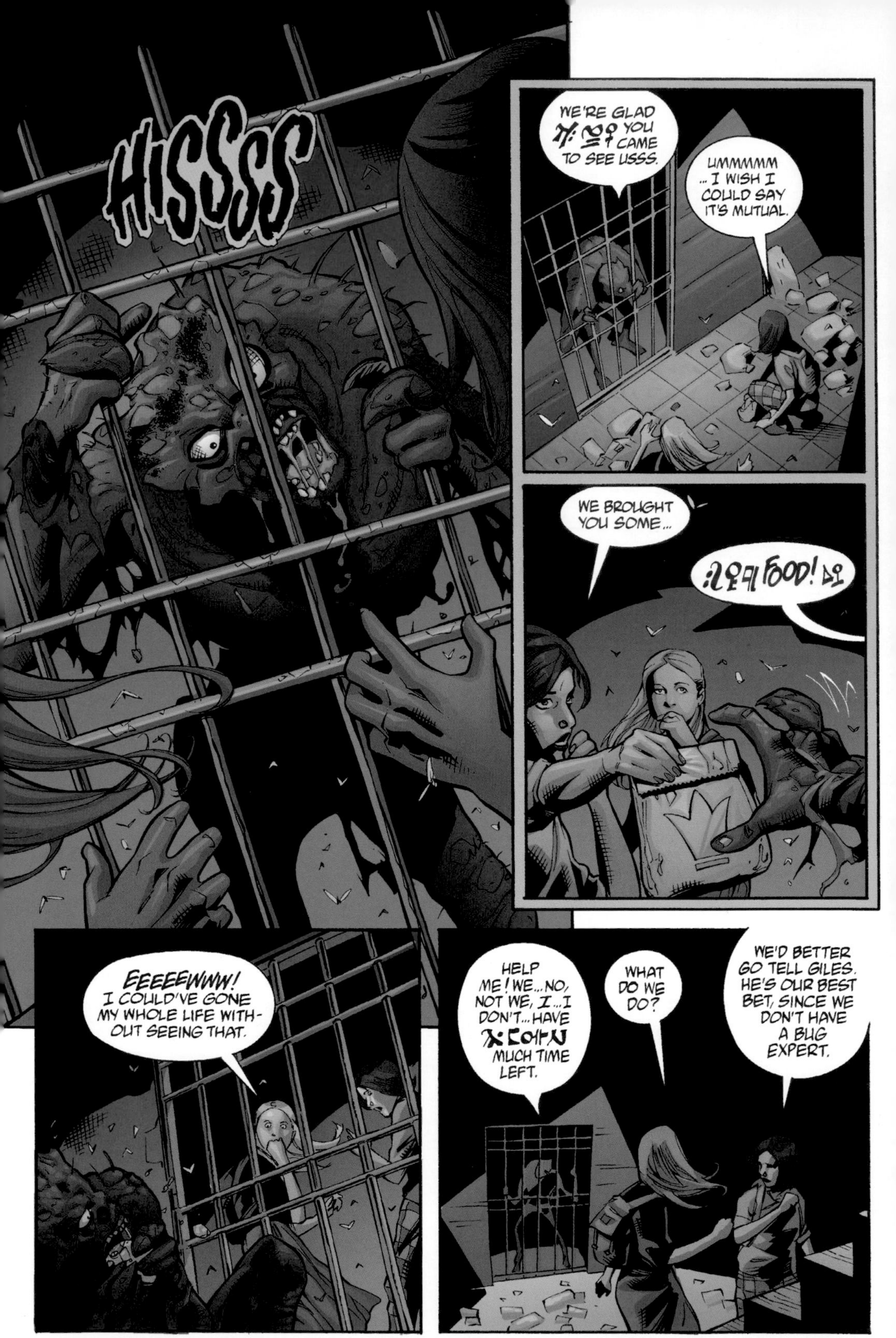
HISSSS
WE'RE GLAD YOU CAME TO SEE USSS.
UMMMMM ... I WISH I COULD SAY IT'S MUTUAL.
WE BROUGHT YOU SOME...
FOOD!
EEEEEWWW! I COULD'VE GONE MY WHOLE LIFE WITH-OUT SEEING THAT.
HELP ME! WE...NO, NOT WE, I...I DON'T...HAVE MUCH TIME LEFT.
WHAT DO WE DO?
WE'D BETTER GO TELL GILES. HE'S OUR BEST BET, SINCE WE DON'T HAVE A BUG EXPERT.

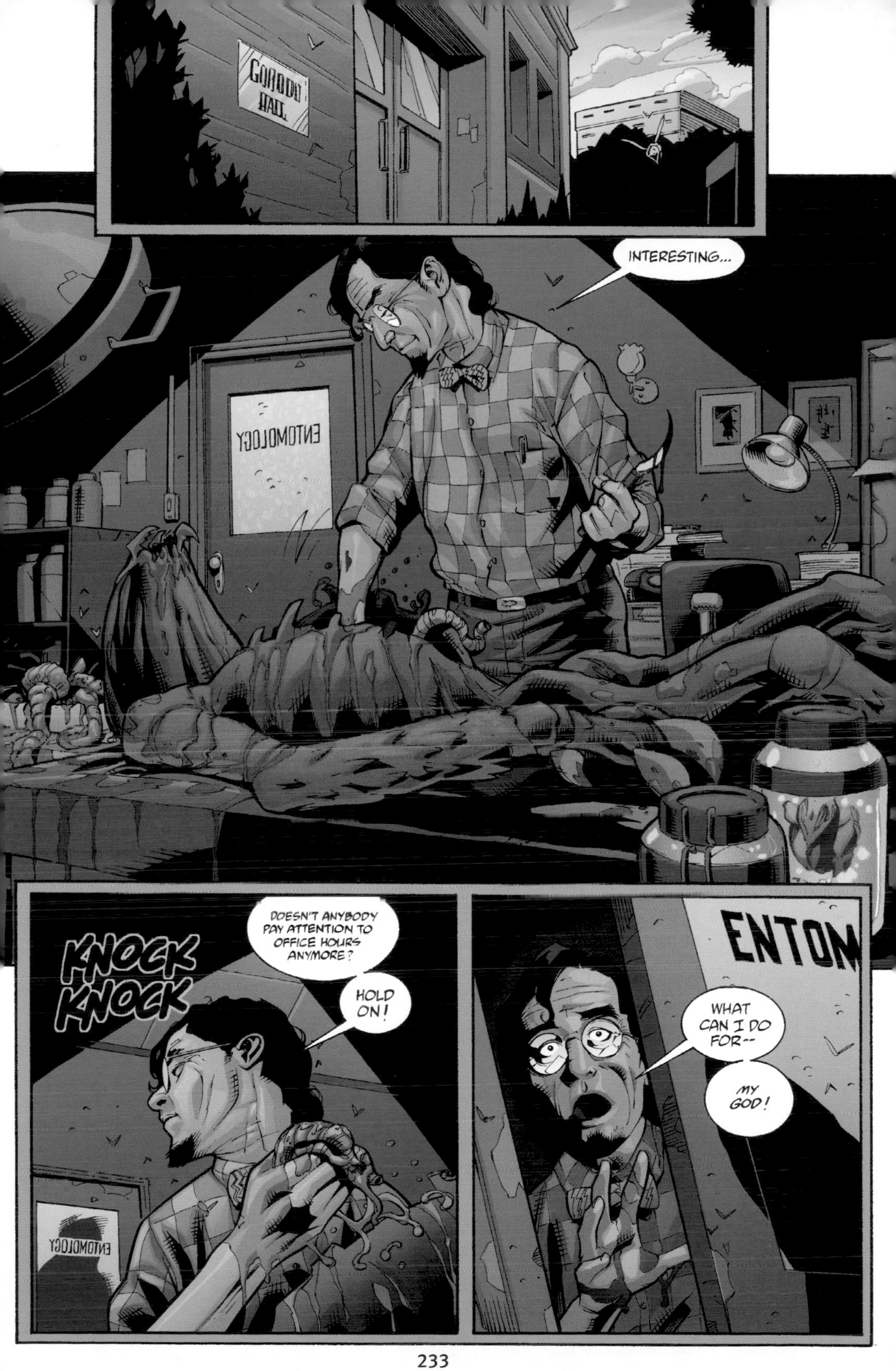
GORDON HALL
INTERESTING...
ENTOMOLOGY
KNOCK KNOCK
DOESN'T ANYBODY PAY ATTENTION TO OFFICE HOURS ANYMORE?
HOLD ON!
ENTOM
WHAT CAN I DO FOR--
MY GOD!

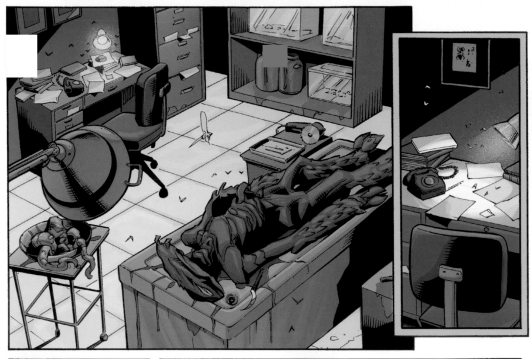

AND WITH THE LOCAL INSECT POPULATION EXPLODING WITH NO APPARENT END IN SIGHT, A DIFFERENT KIND OF INSECT MYSTERY HIT SUNNYDALE THIS MORNING WHEN RENOWNED ENTOMOLOGIST DR. WARREN WHITCOMB DISAPPEARED FROM HIS CAMPUS OFFICE.

MORE ON THAT STORY HERE ON *NEWS AT NOON*, AFTER THESE MESSAGES.

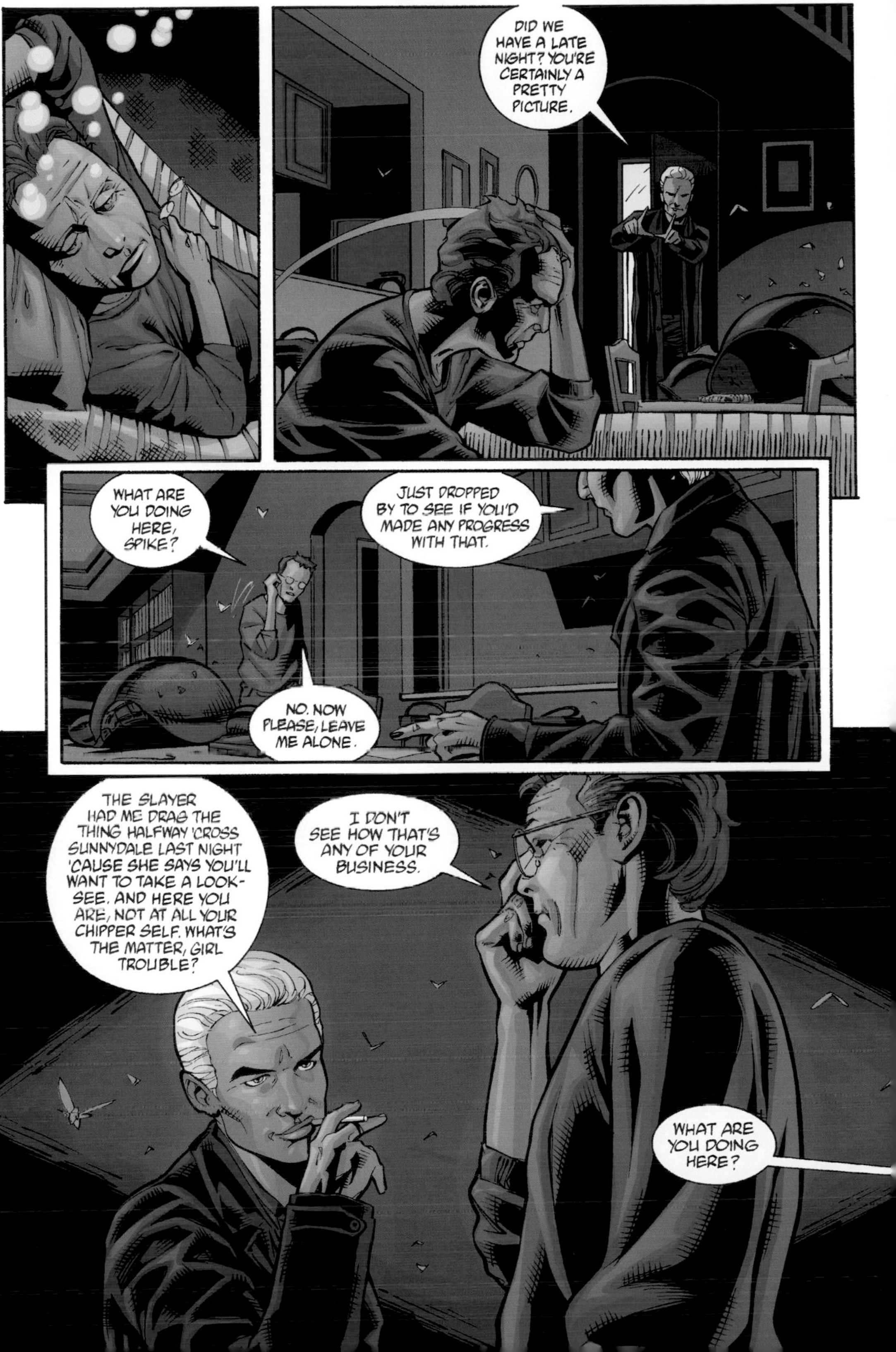
DID WE HAVE A LATE NIGHT? YOU'RE CERTAINLY A PRETTY PICTURE.
WHAT ARE YOU DOING HERE, SPIKE?
JUST DROPPED BY TO SEE IF YOU'D MADE ANY PROGRESS WITH THAT.
NO. NOW PLEASE, LEAVE ME ALONE.
THE SLAYER HAD ME DRAG THE THING HALFWAY 'CROSS SUNNYDALE LAST NIGHT 'CAUSE SHE SAYS YOU'LL WANT TO TAKE A LOOK-SEE. AND HERE YOU ARE, NOT AT ALL YOUR CHIPPER SELF. WHAT'S THE MATTER, GIRL TROUBLE?
I DON'T SEE HOW THAT'S ANY OF YOUR BUSINESS.
WHAT ARE YOU DOING HERE?

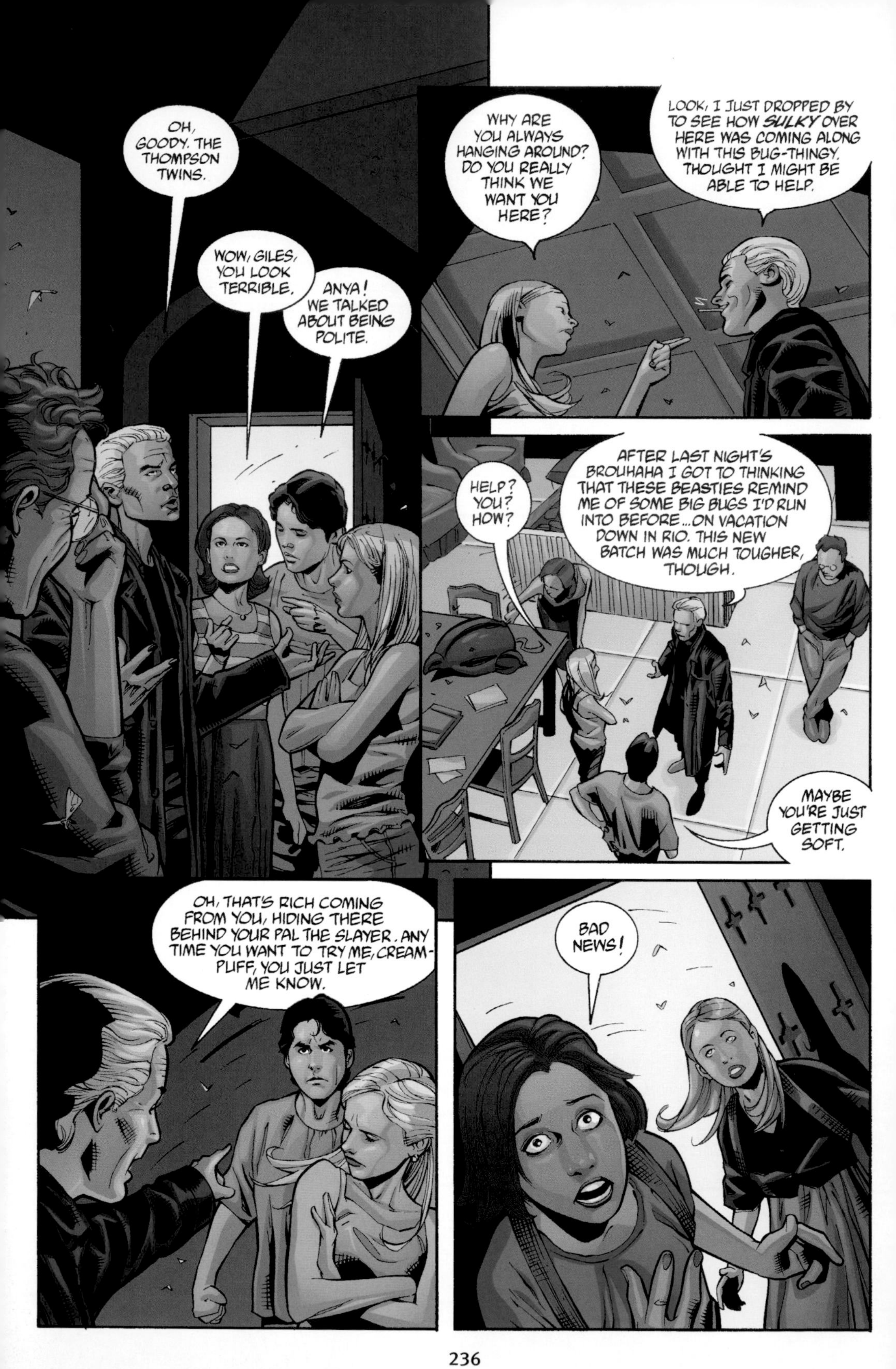
OH, GOODY. THE THOMPSON TWINS.
WOW, GILES, YOU LOOK TERRIBLE.
ANYA! WE TALKED ABOUT BEING POLITE.
WHY ARE YOU ALWAYS HANGING AROUND? DO YOU REALLY THINK WE WANT YOU HERE?
LOOK, I JUST DROPPED BY TO SEE HOW SULKY OVER HERE WAS COMING ALONG WITH THIS BUG-THINGY. THOUGHT I MIGHT BE ABLE TO HELP.
HELP? YOU? HOW?
AFTER LAST NIGHT'S BROUHAHA I GOT TO THINKING THAT THESE BEASTIES REMIND ME OF SOME BIG BUGS I'D RUN INTO BEFORE...ON VACATION DOWN IN RIO. THIS NEW BATCH WAS MUCH TOUGHER, THOUGH.
MAYBE YOU'RE JUST GETTING SOFT.
OH, THAT'S RICH COMING FROM YOU, HIDING THERE BEHIND YOUR PAL THE SLAYER. ANY TIME YOU WANT TO TRY ME, CREAM-PUFF, YOU JUST LET ME KNOW.
BAD NEWS!

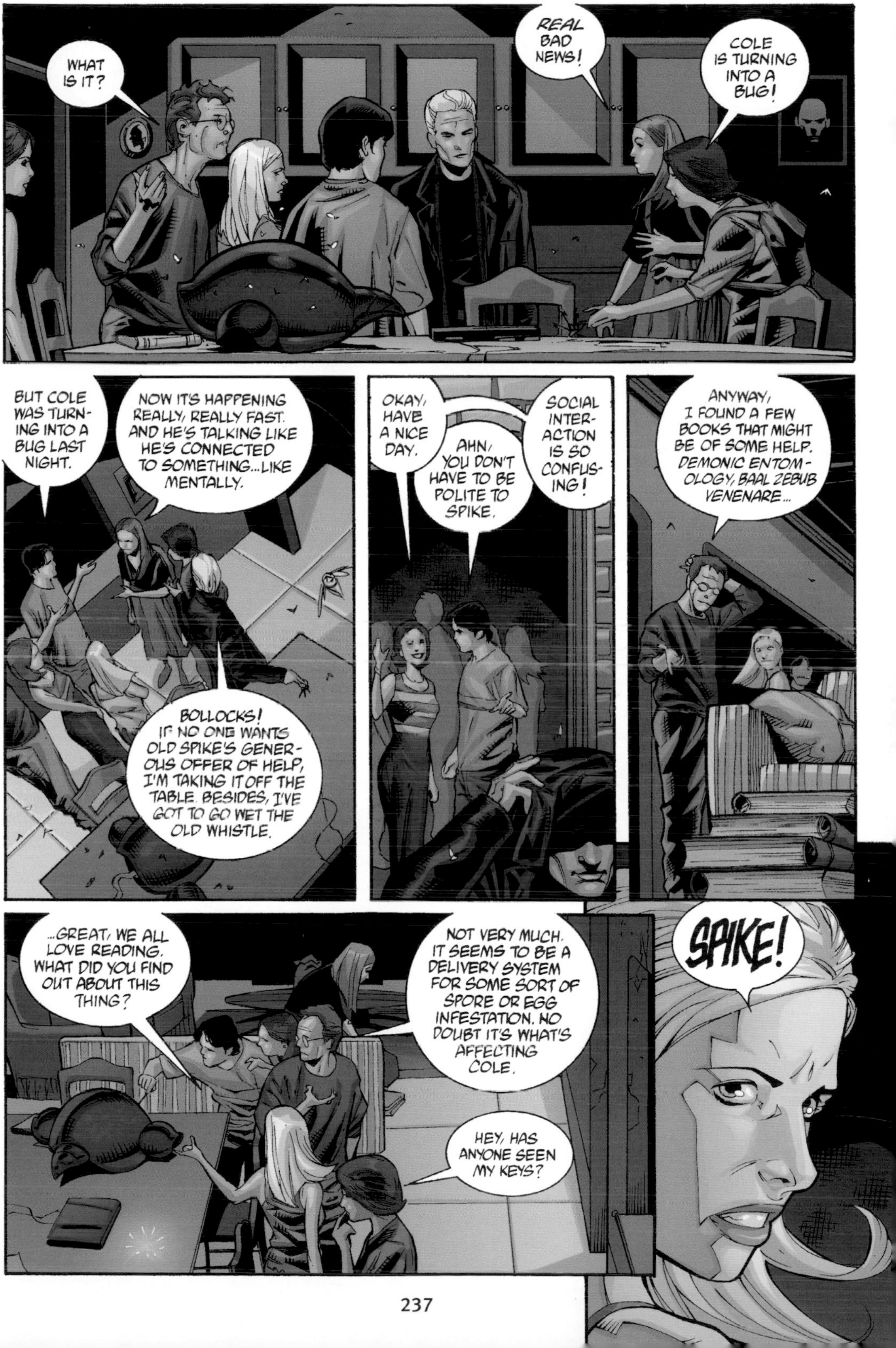
WHAT IS IT?
REAL BAD NEWS!
COLE IS TURNING INTO A BUG!
BUT COLE WAS TURNING INTO A BUG LAST NIGHT.
NOW IT'S HAPPENING REALLY, REALLY FAST. AND HE'S TALKING LIKE HE'S CONNECTED TO SOMETHING...LIKE MENTALLY.
BOLLOCKS! IF NO ONE WANTS OLD SPIKE'S GENEROUS OFFER OF HELP, I'M TAKING IT OFF THE TABLE. BESIDES, I'VE GOT TO GO WET THE OLD WHISTLE.
OKAY, HAVE A NICE DAY.
AHN, YOU DON'T HAVE TO BE POLITE TO SPIKE.
SOCIAL INTERACTION IS SO CONFUSING!
ANYWAY, I FOUND A FEW BOOKS THAT MIGHT BE OF SOME HELP. DEMONIC ENTOMOLOGY, BAAL ZEBUB VENENARE...
...GREAT, WE ALL LOVE READING. WHAT DID YOU FIND OUT ABOUT THIS THING?
NOT VERY MUCH. IT SEEMS TO BE A DELIVERY SYSTEM FOR SOME SORT OF SPORE OR EGG INFESTATION. NO DOUBT IT'S WHAT'S AFFECTING COLE.
HEY, HAS ANYONE SEEN MY KEYS?
SPIKE!

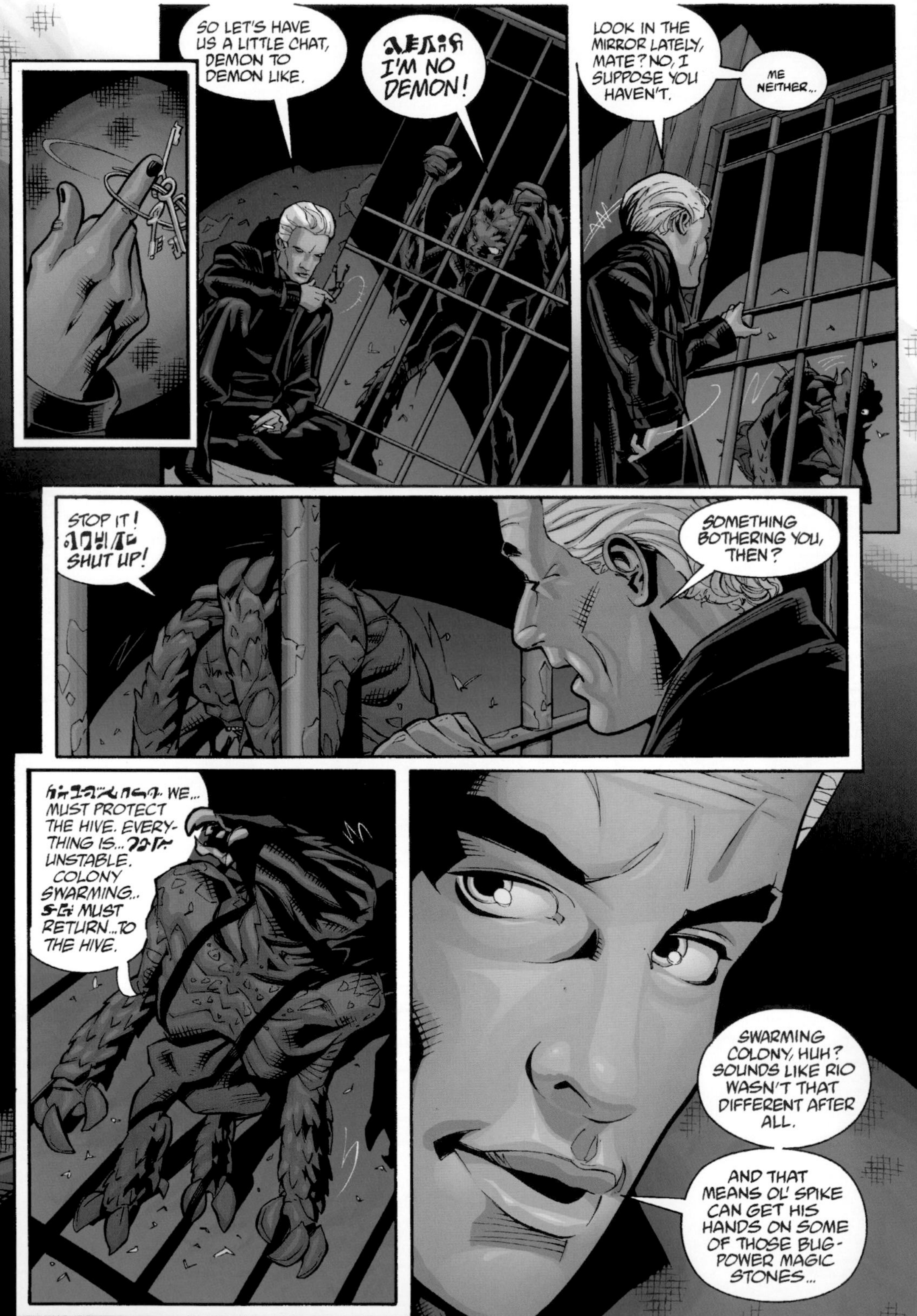
SO LET'S HAVE US A LITTLE CHAT, DEMON TO DEMON LIKE.
I'M NO DEMON!
LOOK IN THE MIRROR LATELY, MATE? NO, I SUPPOSE YOU HAVEN'T.
ME NEITHER...
STOP IT! SHUT UP!
SOMETHING BOTHERING YOU, THEN?
WE... MUST PROTECT THE HIVE. EVERYTHING IS... UNSTABLE. COLONY SWARMING.. MUST RETURN...TO THE HIVE.
SWARMING COLONY, HUH? SOUNDS LIKE RIO WASN'T THAT DIFFERENT AFTER ALL.
AND THAT MEANS OL' SPIKE CAN GET HIS HANDS ON SOME OF THOSE BUG-POWER MAGIC STONES...

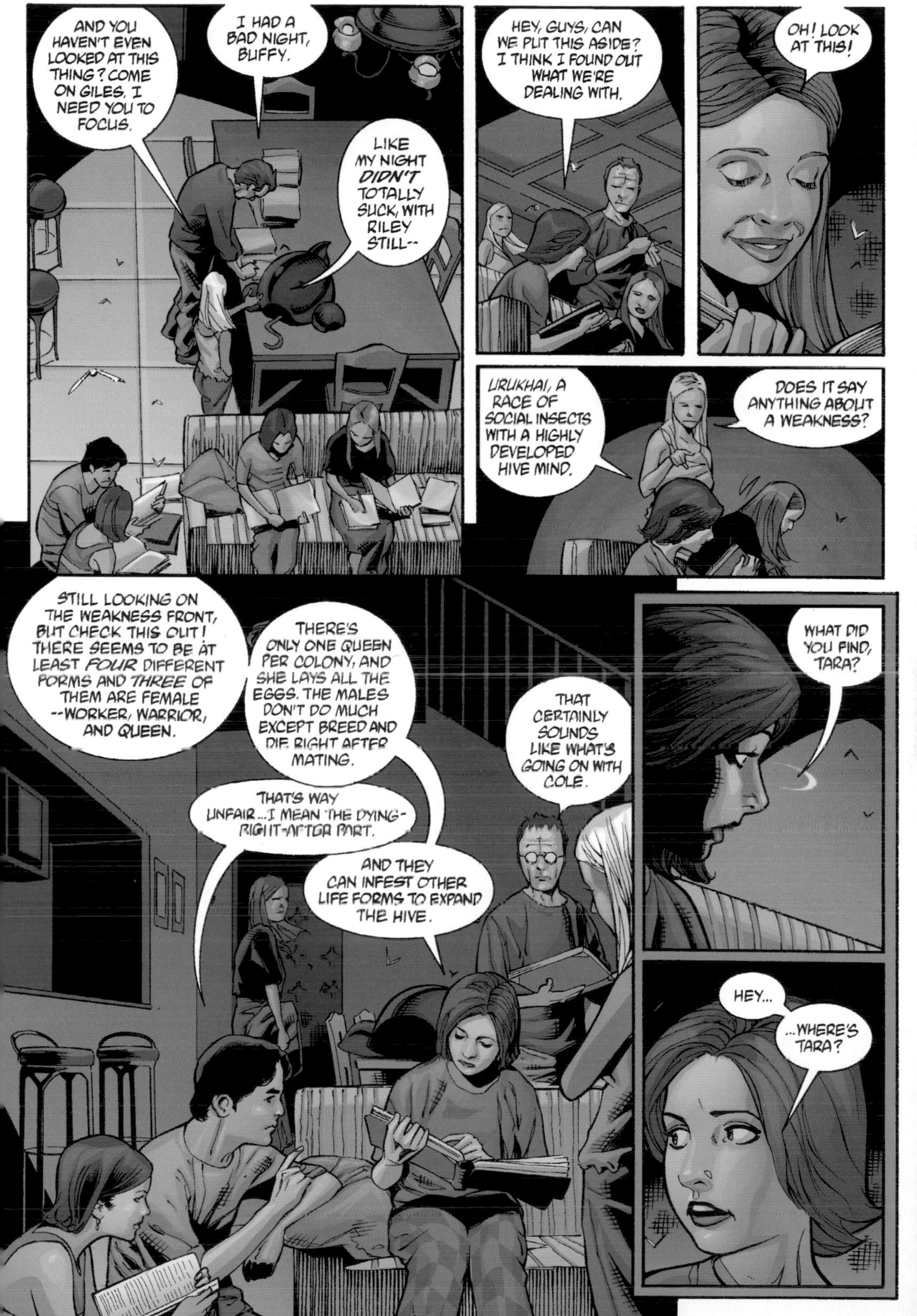
AND YOU HAVEN'T EVEN LOOKED AT THIS THING? COME ON GILES, I NEED YOU TO FOCUS.
I HAD A BAD NIGHT, BUFFY.
LIKE MY NIGHT DIDN'T TOTALLY SUCK, WITH RILEY STILL--
HEY, GUYS, CAN WE PUT THIS ASIDE? I THINK I FOUND OUT WHAT WE'RE DEALING WITH.
OH! LOOK AT THIS!
URUKHAI, A RACE OF SOCIAL INSECTS WITH A HIGHLY DEVELOPED HIVE MIND.
DOES IT SAY ANYTHING ABOUT A WEAKNESS?
STILL LOOKING ON THE WEAKNESS FRONT, BUT CHECK THIS OUT! THERE SEEMS TO BE AT LEAST FOUR DIFFERENT FORMS AND THREE OF THEM ARE FEMALE --WORKER, WARRIOR, AND QUEEN.
THERE'S ONLY ONE QUEEN PER COLONY, AND SHE LAYS ALL THE EGGS. THE MALES DON'T DO MUCH EXCEPT BREED AND DIE RIGHT AFTER MATING.
THAT'S WAY UNFAIR...I MEAN THE DYING-RIGHT-AFTER PART.
AND THEY CAN INFEST OTHER LIFE FORMS TO EXPAND THE HIVE.
THAT CERTAINLY SOUNDS LIKE WHAT'S GOING ON WITH COLE.
WHAT DID YOU FIND, TARA?
HEY...
...WHERE'S TARA?

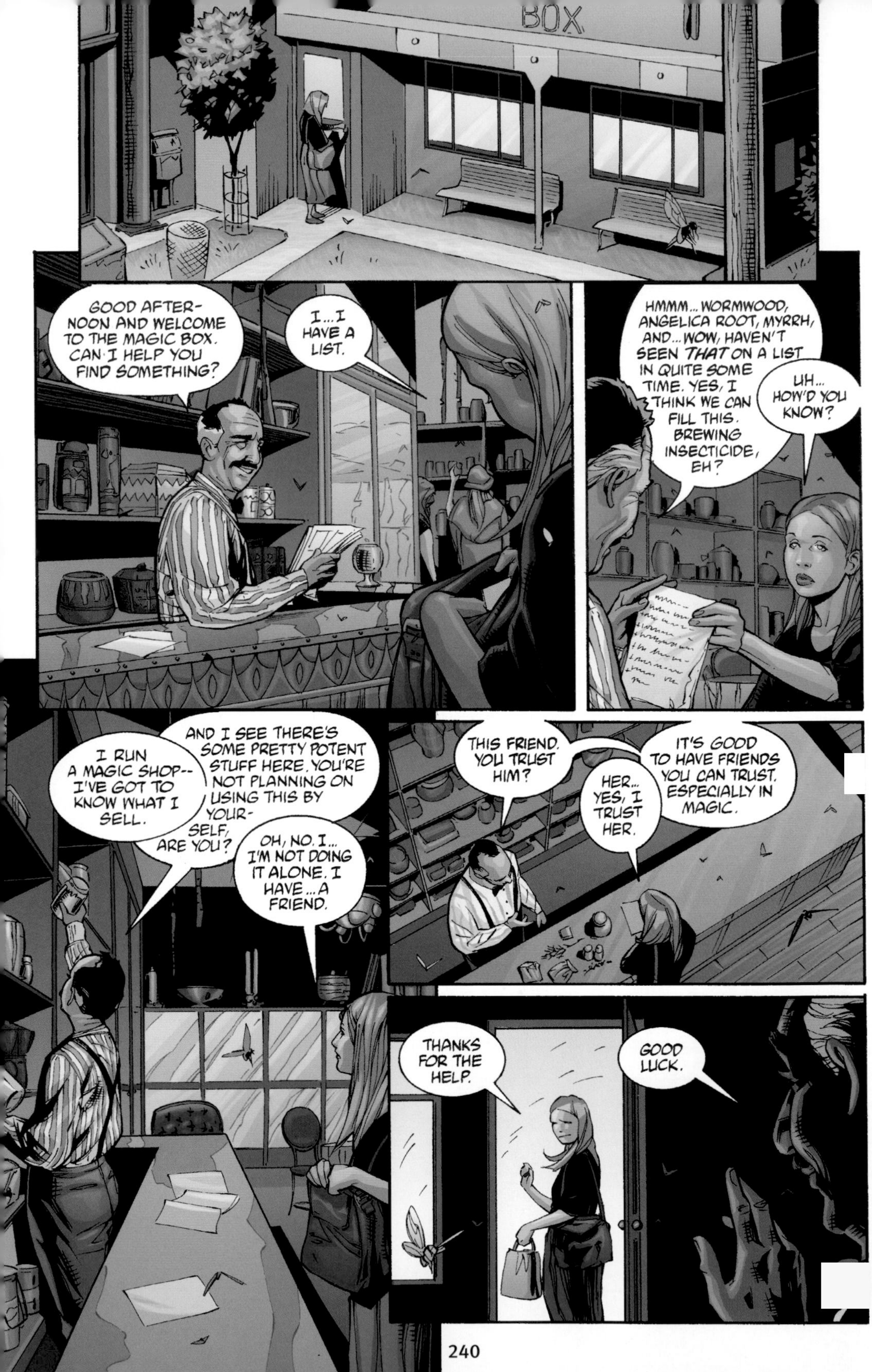
BOX
GOOD AFTER-NOON AND WELCOME TO THE MAGIC BOX. CAN I HELP YOU FIND SOMETHING?
I... I HAVE A LIST.
HMMM... WORMWOOD, ANGELICA ROOT, MYRRH, AND... WOW, HAVEN'T SEEN THAT ON A LIST IN QUITE SOME TIME. YES, I THINK WE CAN FILL THIS. BREWING INSECTICIDE, EH?
UH... HOW'D YOU KNOW?
I RUN A MAGIC SHOP-- I'VE GOT TO KNOW WHAT I SELL.
AND I SEE THERE'S SOME PRETTY POTENT STUFF HERE. YOU'RE NOT PLANNING ON USING THIS BY YOUR-SELF, ARE YOU?
OH, NO. I... I'M NOT DOING IT ALONE. I HAVE... A FRIEND.
THIS FRIEND. YOU TRUST HIM?
HER... YES, I TRUST HER.
IT'S GOOD TO HAVE FRIENDS YOU CAN TRUST. ESPECIALLY IN MAGIC.
THANKS FOR THE HELP.
GOOD LUCK.

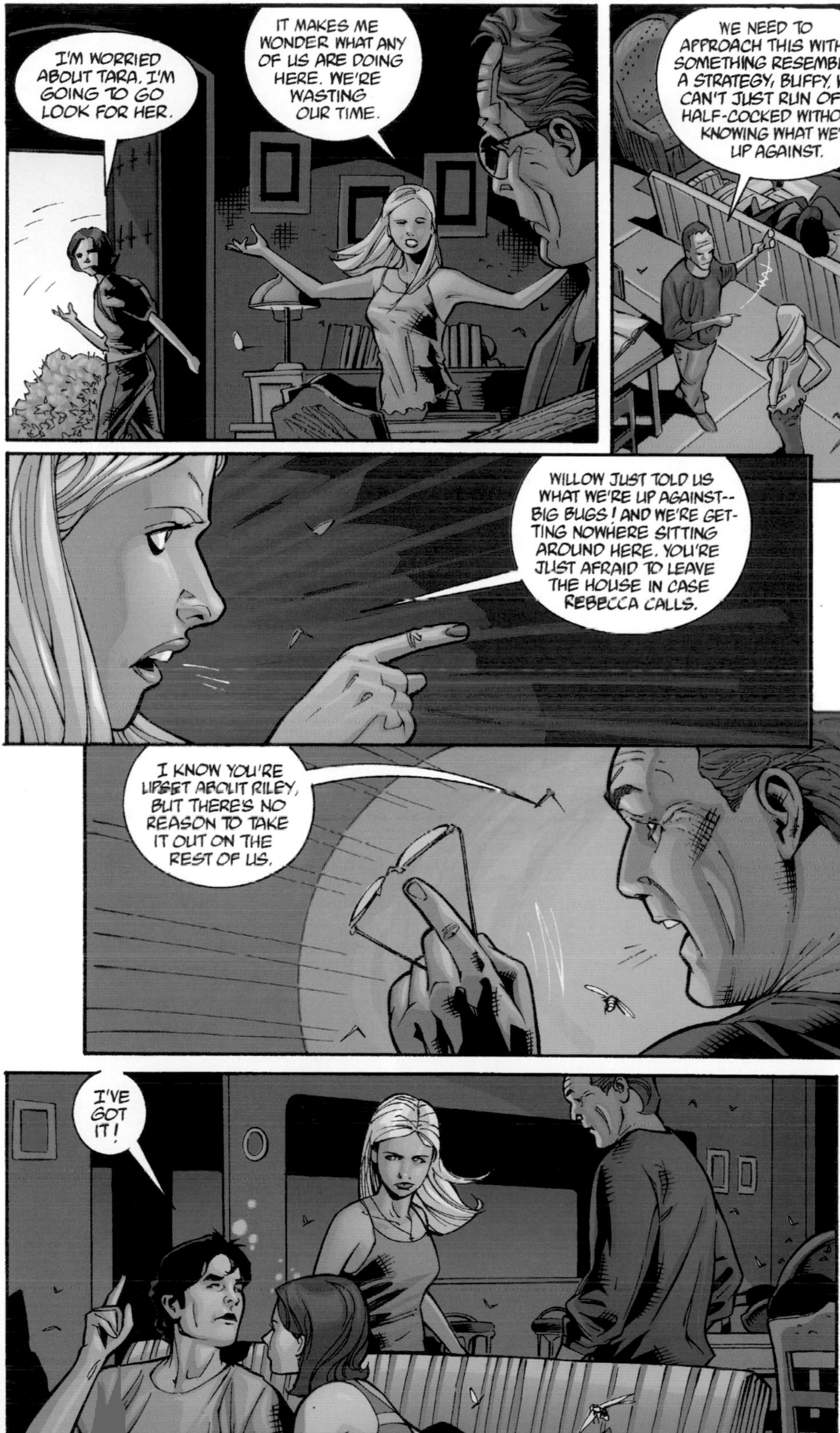
I'M WORRIED ABOUT TARA. I'M GOING TO GO LOOK FOR HER.
IT MAKES ME WONDER WHAT ANY OF US ARE DOING HERE. WE'RE WASTING OUR TIME.
WE NEED TO APPROACH THIS WITH SOMETHING RESEMBLING A STRATEGY, BUFFY. WE CAN'T JUST RUN OFF HALF-COCKED WITHOUT KNOWING WHAT WE'RE UP AGAINST.
WILLOW JUST TOLD US WHAT WE'RE UP AGAINST-- BIG BUGS! AND WE'RE GETTING NOWHERE SITTING AROUND HERE. YOU'RE JUST AFRAID TO LEAVE THE HOUSE IN CASE REBECCA CALLS.
I KNOW YOU'RE UPSET ABOUT RILEY, BUT THERE'S NO REASON TO TAKE IT OUT ON THE REST OF US.
I'VE GOT IT!

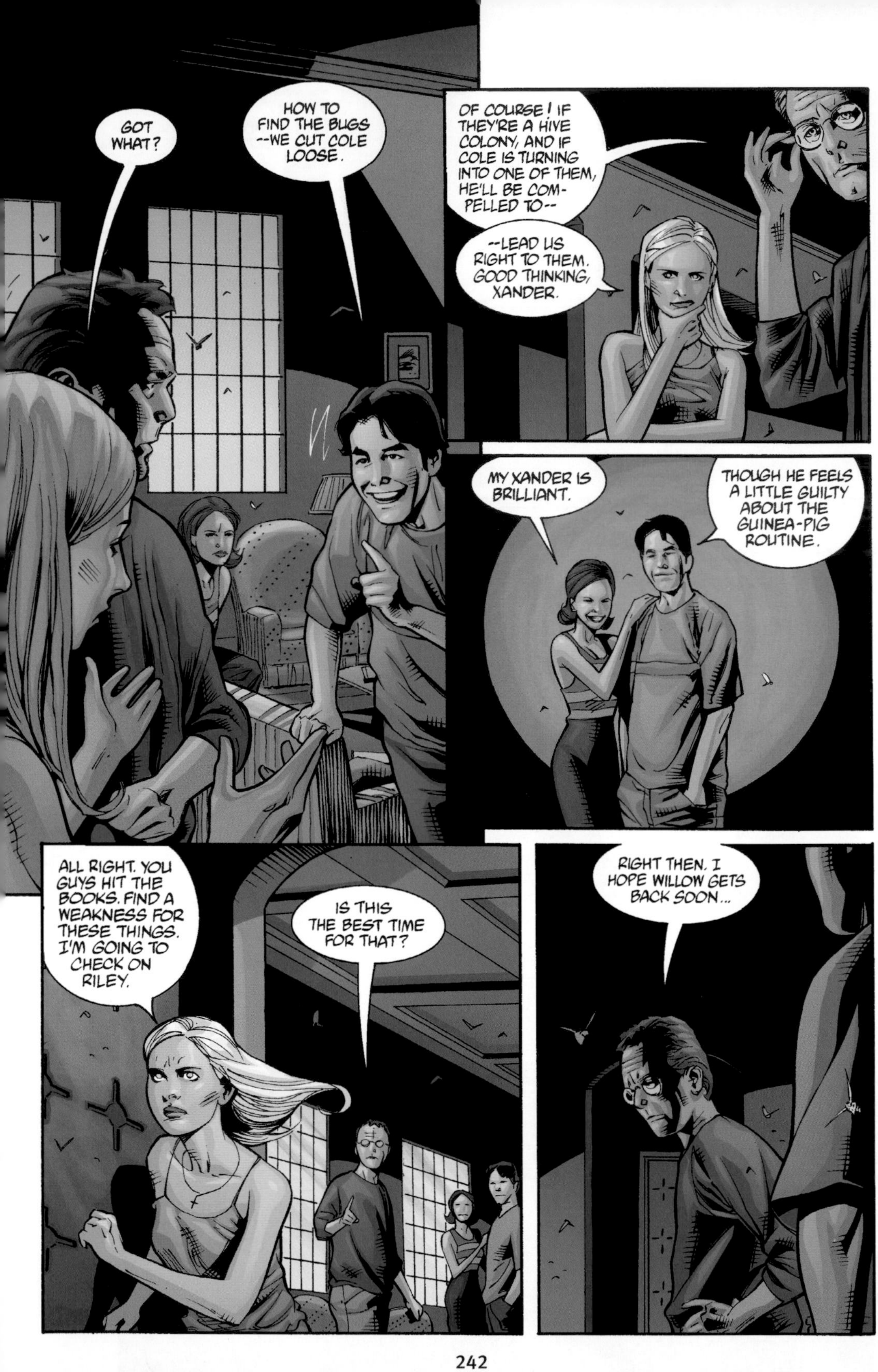
GOT WHAT?
HOW TO FIND THE BUGS --WE CUT COLE LOOSE.
OF COURSE! IF THEY'RE A HIVE COLONY, AND IF COLE IS TURNING INTO ONE OF THEM, HE'LL BE COM-PELLED TO--
--LEAD US RIGHT TO THEM. GOOD THINKING, XANDER.
MY XANDER IS BRILLIANT.
THOUGH HE FEELS A LITTLE GUILTY ABOUT THE GUINEA-PIG ROUTINE.
ALL RIGHT. YOU GUYS HIT THE BOOKS. FIND A WEAKNESS FOR THESE THINGS. I'M GOING TO CHECK ON RILEY.
IS THIS THE BEST TIME FOR THAT?
RIGHT THEN. I HOPE WILLOW GETS BACK SOON...

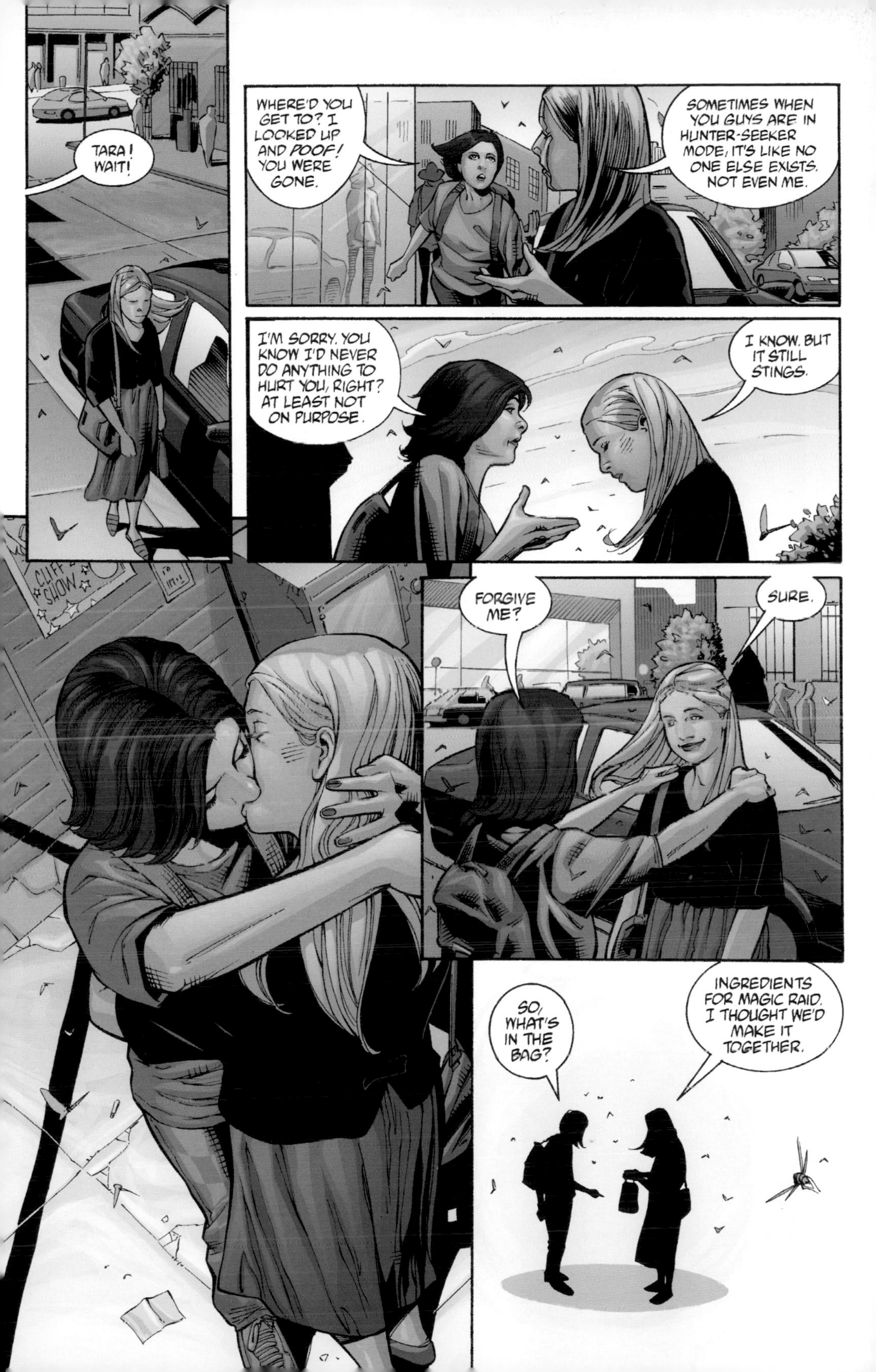
TARA! WAIT!
WHERE'D YOU GET TO? I LOOKED UP AND POOF! YOU WERE GONE.
SOMETIMES WHEN YOU GUYS ARE IN HUNTER-SEEKER MODE, IT'S LIKE NO ONE ELSE EXISTS. NOT EVEN ME.
I'M SORRY. YOU KNOW I'D NEVER DO ANYTHING TO HURT YOU, RIGHT? AT LEAST NOT ON PURPOSE.
I KNOW. BUT IT STILL STINGS.
CLIFF SHOW
FORGIVE ME?
SURE.
SO, WHAT'S IN THE BAG?
INGREDIENTS FOR MAGIC RAID. I THOUGHT WE'D MAKE IT TOGETHER.

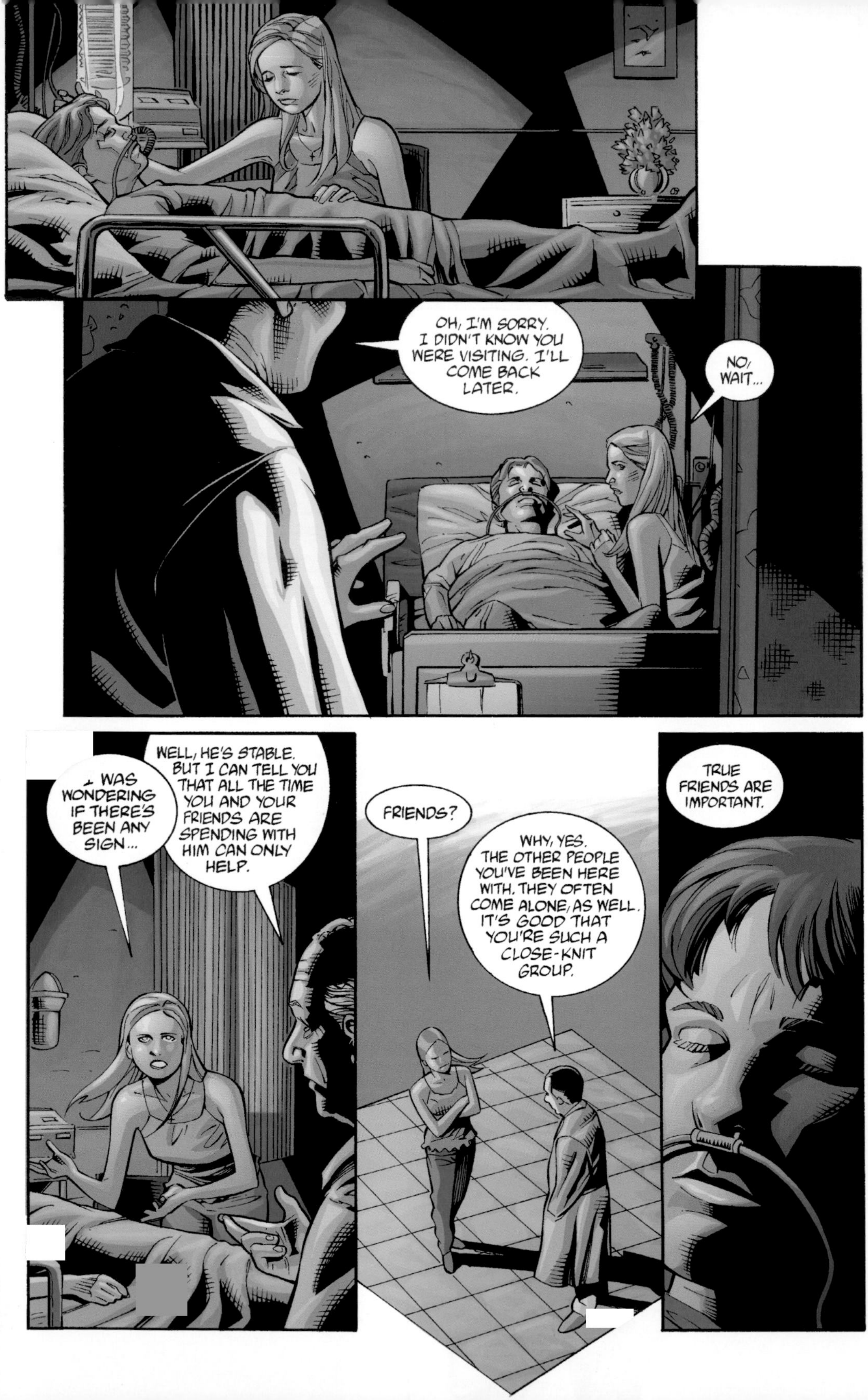
OH, I'M SORRY. I DIDN'T KNOW YOU WERE VISITING. I'LL COME BACK LATER.
NO, WAIT...
I WAS WONDERING IF THERE'S BEEN ANY SIGN...
WELL, HE'S STABLE. BUT I CAN TELL YOU THAT ALL THE TIME YOU AND YOUR FRIENDS ARE SPENDING WITH HIM CAN ONLY HELP.
FRIENDS?
WHY, YES. THE OTHER PEOPLE YOU'VE BEEN HERE WITH, THEY OFTEN COME ALONE, AS WELL. IT'S GOOD THAT YOU'RE SUCH A CLOSE-KNIT GROUP.
TRUE FRIENDS ARE IMPORTANT.

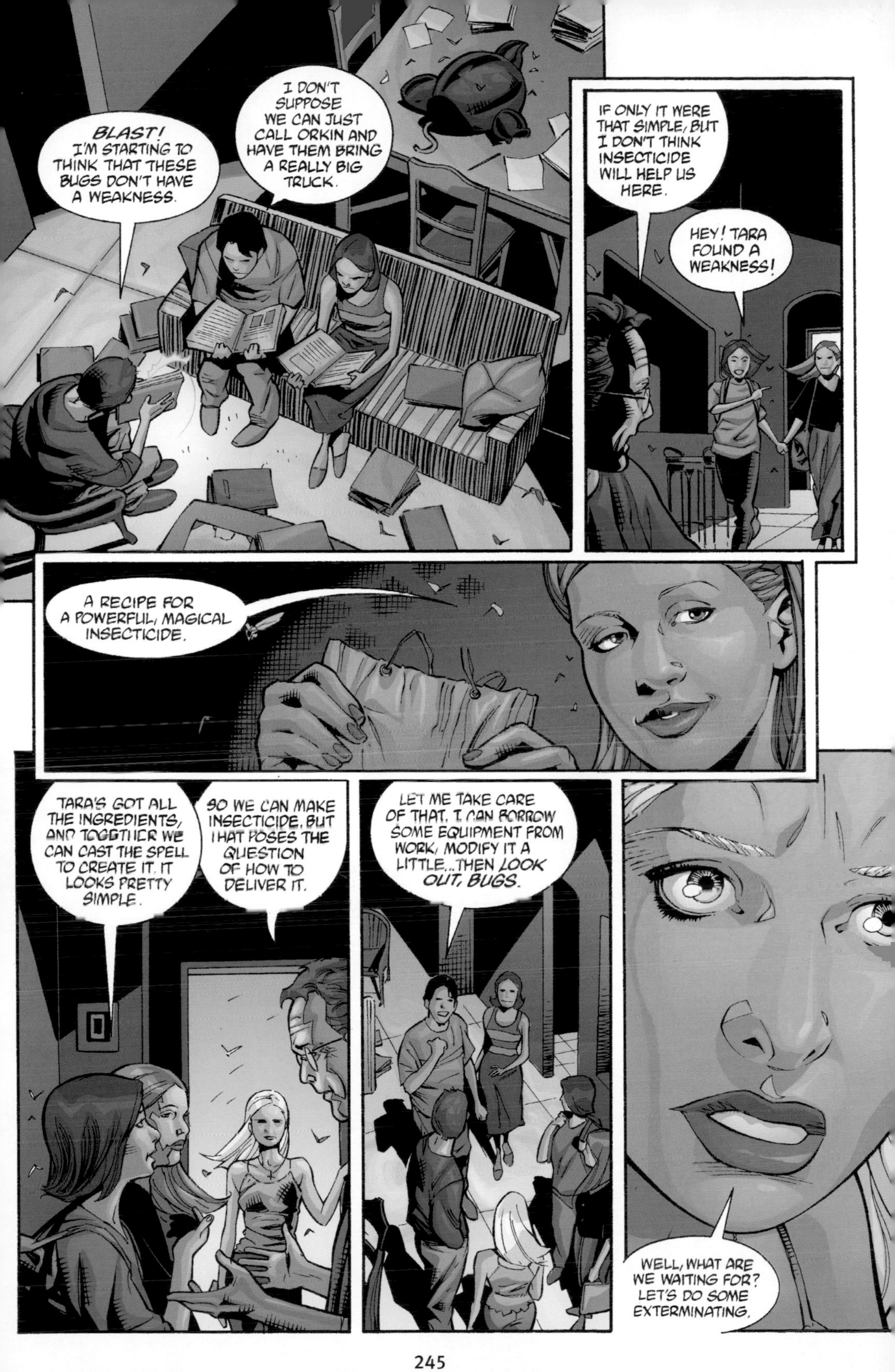
BLAST! I'M STARTING TO THINK THAT THESE BUGS DON'T HAVE A WEAKNESS.
I DON'T SUPPOSE WE CAN JUST CALL ORKIN AND HAVE THEM BRING A REALLY BIG TRUCK.
IF ONLY IT WERE THAT SIMPLE, BUT I DON'T THINK INSECTICIDE WILL HELP US HERE.
HEY! TARA FOUND A WEAKNESS!
A RECIPE FOR A POWERFUL, MAGICAL INSECTICIDE.
TARA'S GOT ALL THE INGREDIENTS, AND TOGETHER WE CAN CAST THE SPELL TO CREATE IT. IT LOOKS PRETTY SIMPLE.
SO WE CAN MAKE INSECTICIDE, BUT THAT POSES THE QUESTION OF HOW TO DELIVER IT.
LET ME TAKE CARE OF THAT. I CAN BORROW SOME EQUIPMENT FROM WORK, MODIFY IT A LITTLE...THEN LOOK OUT, BUGS.
WELL, WHAT ARE WE WAITING FOR? LET'S DO SOME EXTERMINATING.

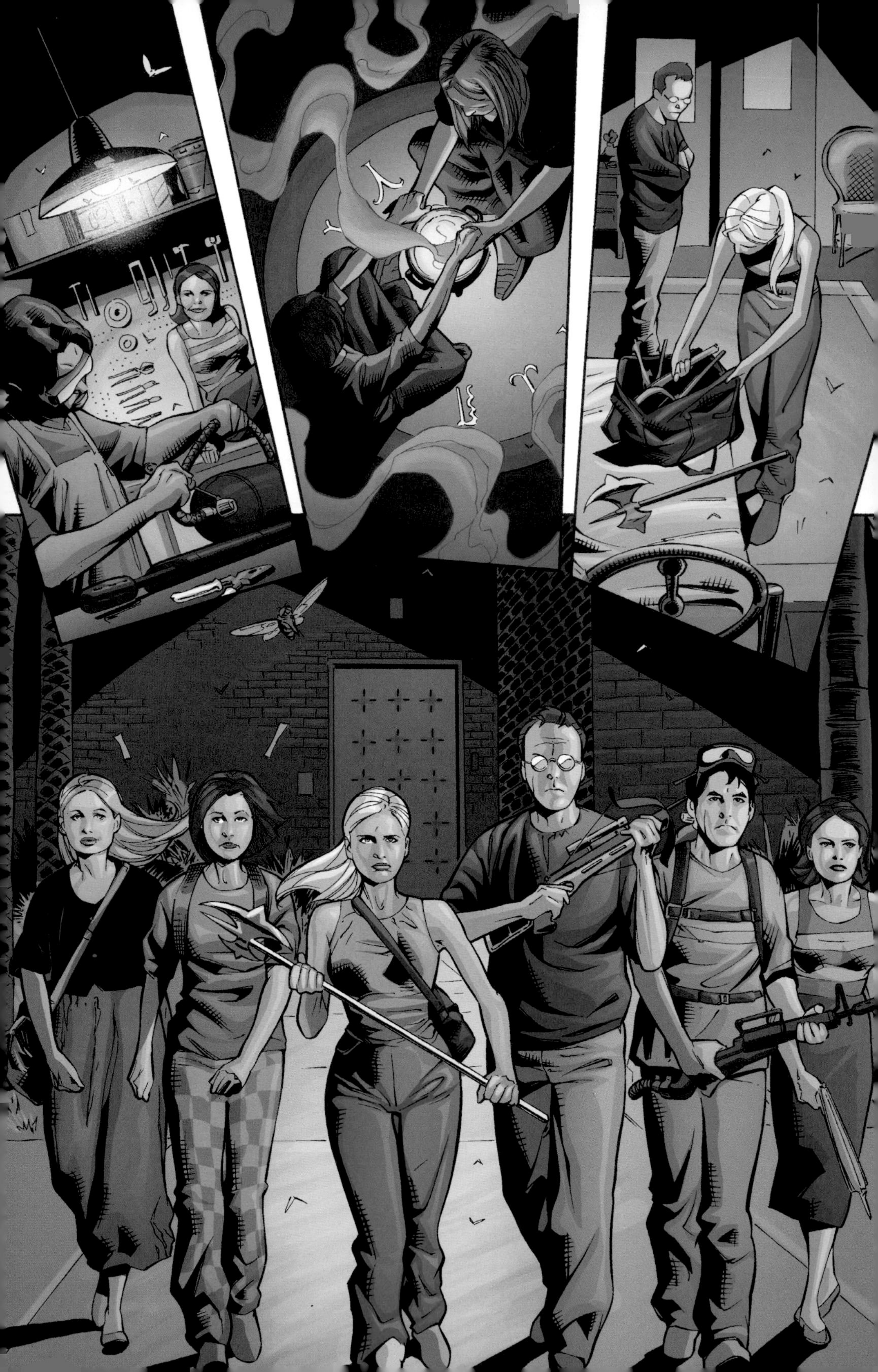

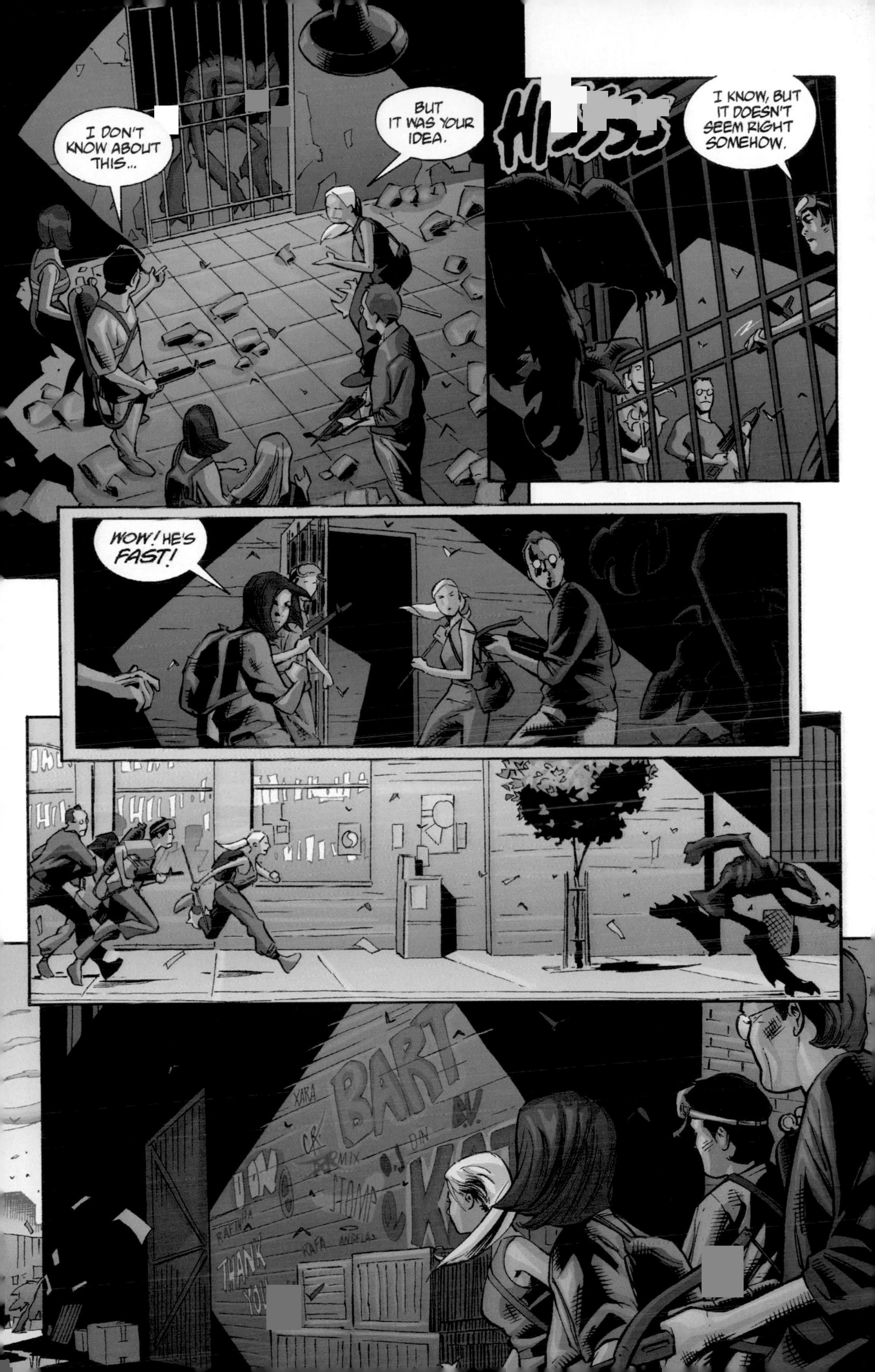
I DON'T KNOW ABOUT THIS...
BUT IT WAS YOUR IDEA.
I KNOW, BUT IT DOESN'T SEEM RIGHT SOMEHOW.
WOW! HE'S FAST!
BART
XARA

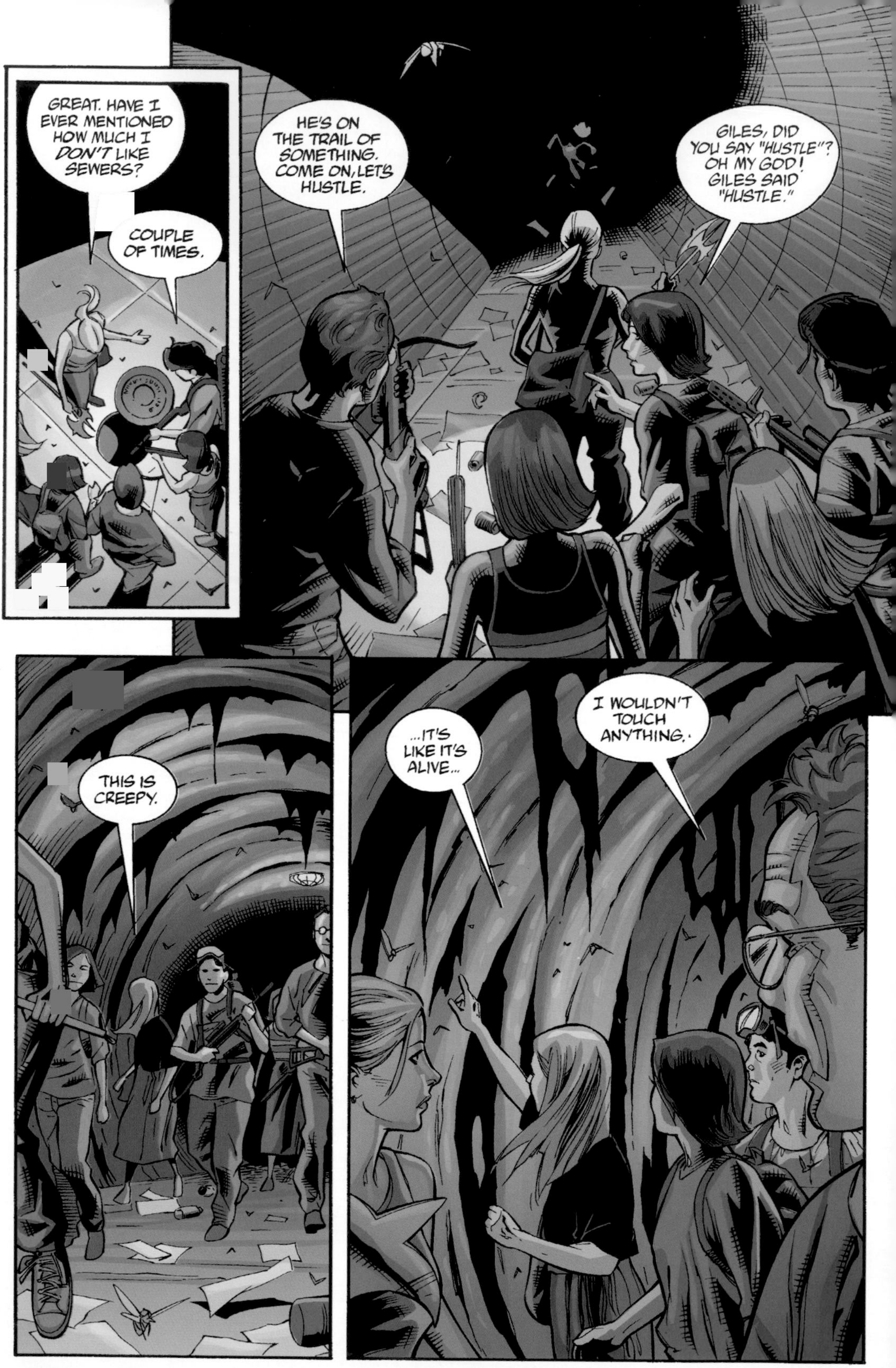
GREAT. HAVE I EVER MENTIONED HOW MUCH I DON'T LIKE SEWERS?
COUPLE OF TIMES.
HE'S ON THE TRAIL OF SOMETHING. COME ON, LET'S HUSTLE.
GILES, DID YOU SAY "HUSTLE"? OH MY GOD! GILES SAID "HUSTLE."
THIS IS CREEPY.
...IT'S LIKE IT'S ALIVE...
I WOULDN'T TOUCH ANYTHING.

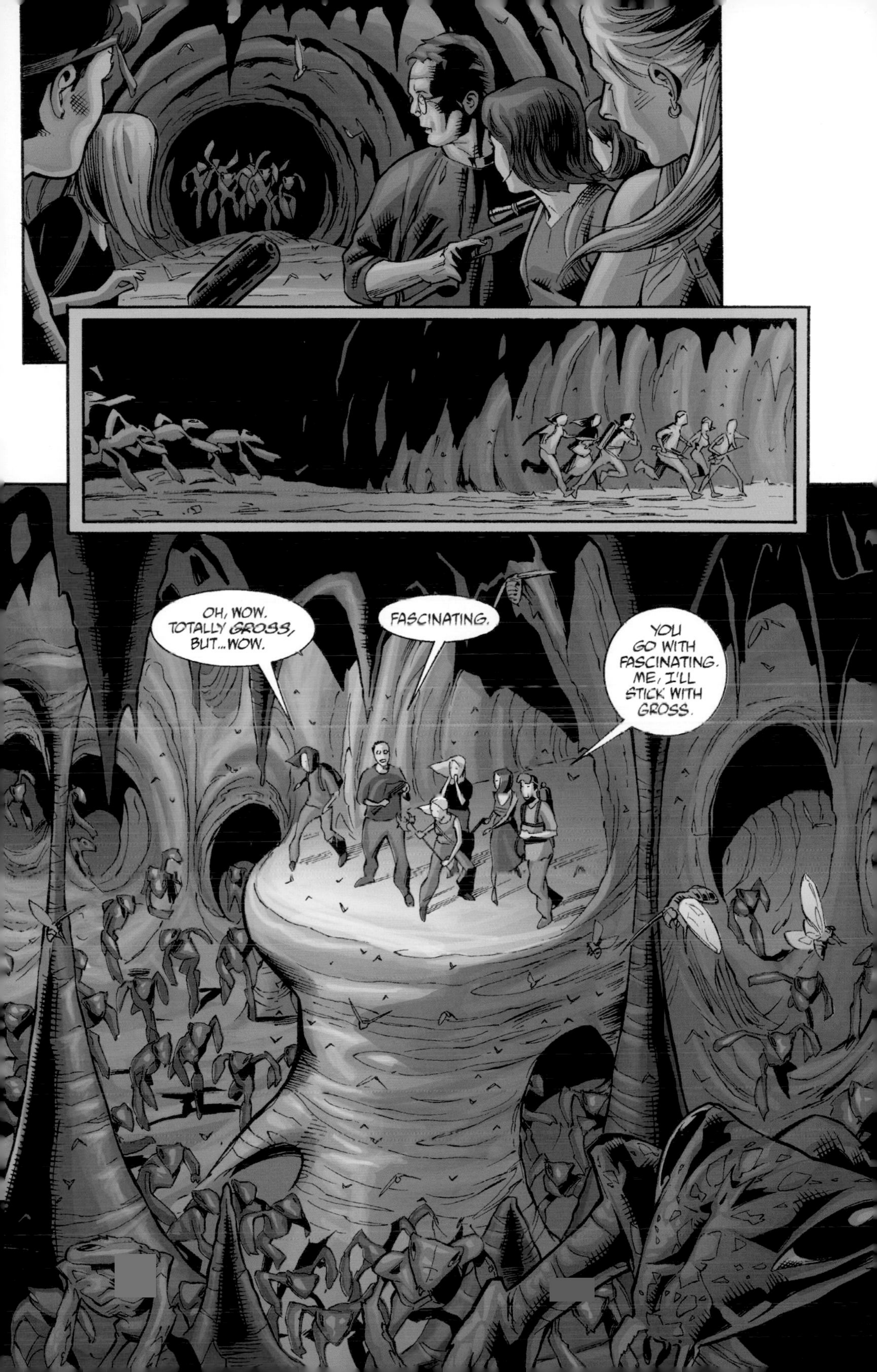
OH, WOW. TOTALLY GROSS, BUT...WOW.
FASCINATING.
YOU GO WITH FASCINATING. ME, I'LL STICK WITH GROSS.

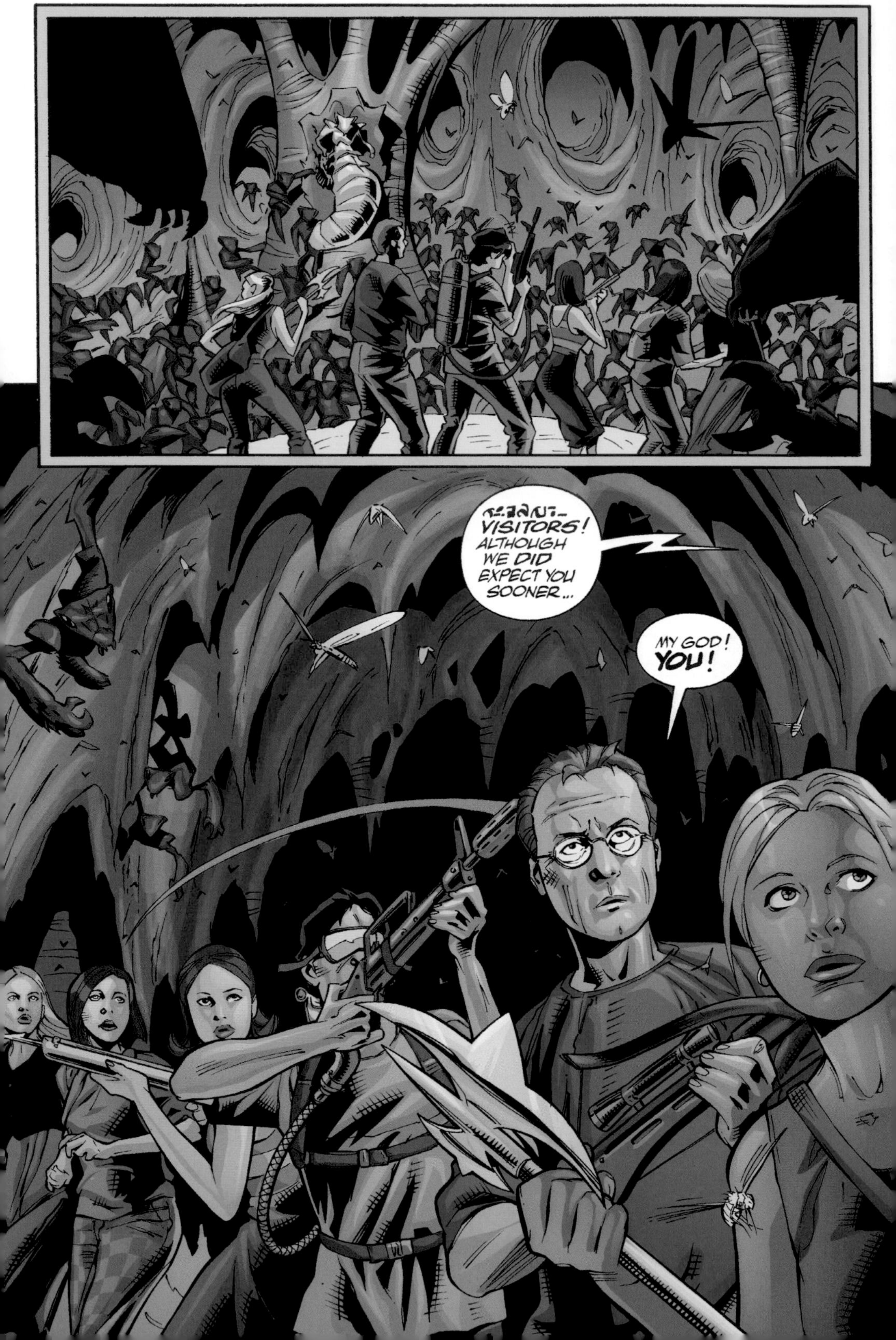
VISITORS! ALTHOUGH WE DID EXPECT YOU SOONER...
MY GOD! YOU!

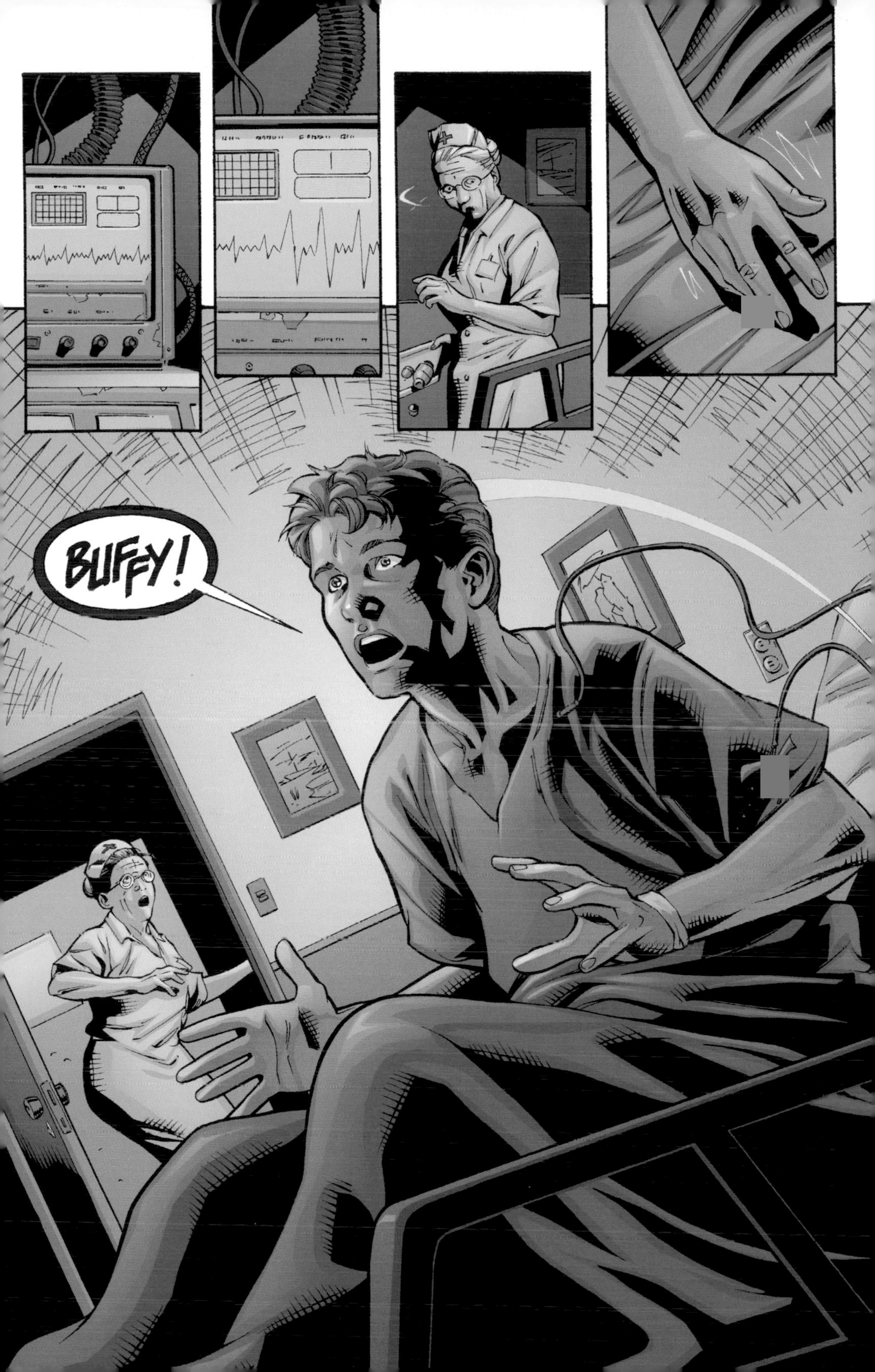
BUFFY!

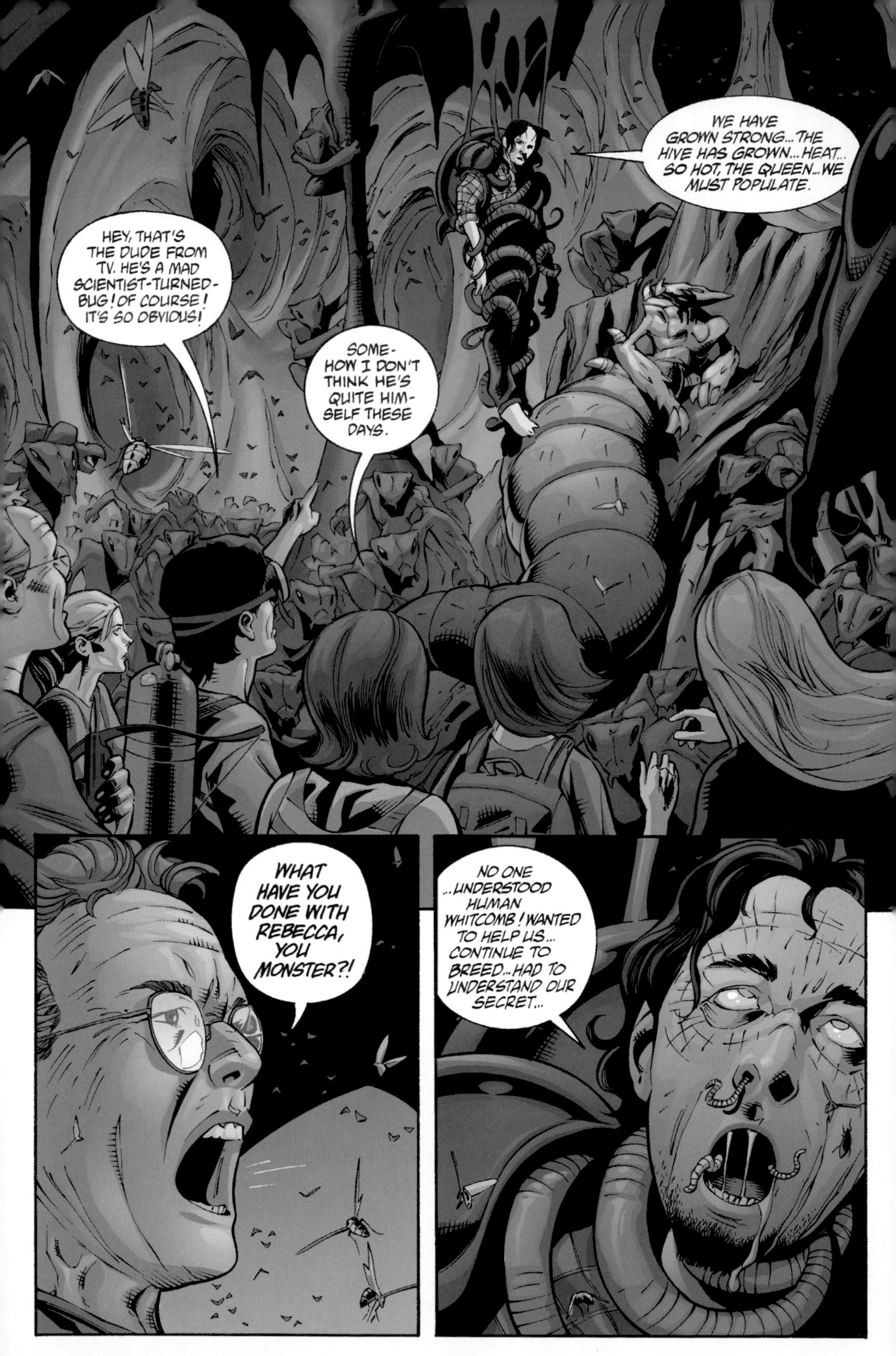
WE HAVE GROWN STRONG... THE HIVE HAS GROWN... HEAT... SO HOT, THE QUEEN... WE MUST POPULATE.
HEY, THAT'S THE DUDE FROM TV. HE'S A MAD SCIENTIST-TURNED-BUG! OF COURSE! IT'S SO OBVIOUS!
SOME-HOW I DON'T THINK HE'S QUITE HIM-SELF THESE DAYS.
WHAT HAVE YOU DONE WITH REBECCA, YOU MONSTER?!
NO ONE ...UNDERSTOOD HUMAN WHITCOMB! WANTED TO HELP US... CONTINUE TO BREED... HAD TO UNDERSTAND OUR SECRET...

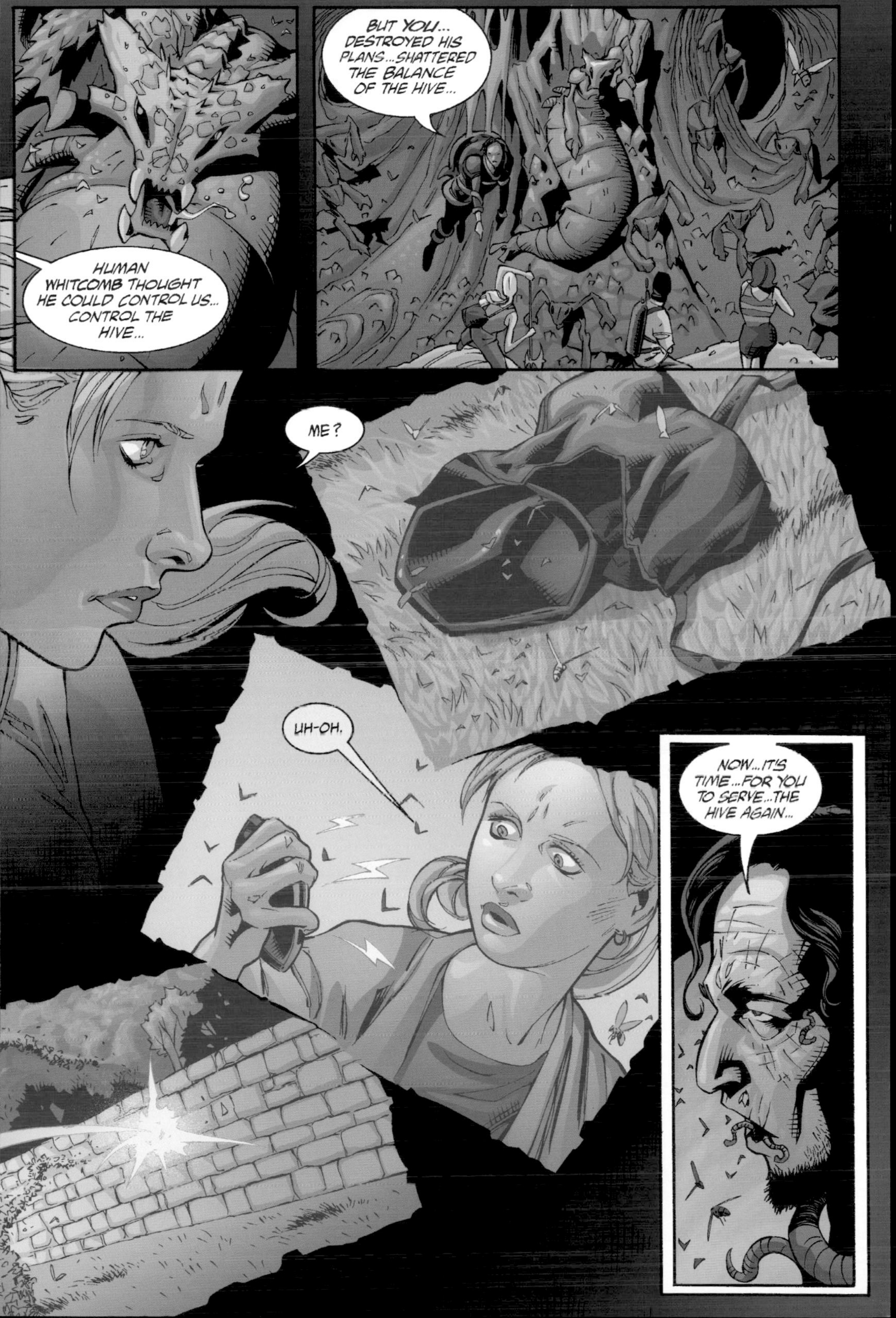
HUMAN WHITCOMB THOUGHT HE COULD CONTROL US... CONTROL THE HIVE...
BUT YOU... DESTROYED HIS PLANS...SHATTERED THE BALANCE OF THE HIVE...
ME?
UH-OH.
NOW...IT'S TIME...FOR YOU TO SERVE...THE HIVE AGAIN...

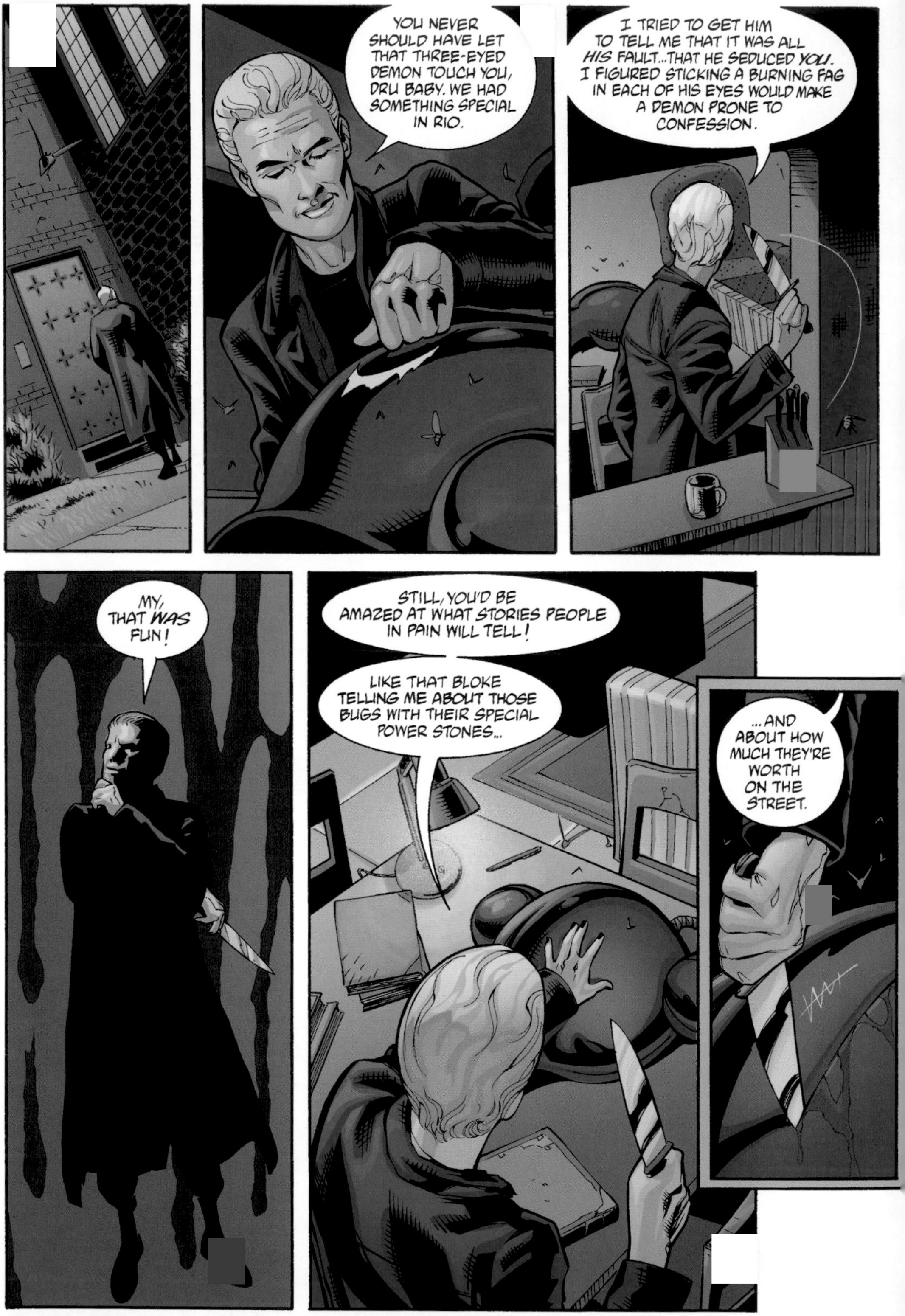
YOU NEVER SHOULD HAVE LET THAT THREE-EYED DEMON TOUCH YOU, DRU BABY. WE HAD SOMETHING SPECIAL IN RIO.
I TRIED TO GET HIM TO TELL ME THAT IT WAS ALL *HIS* FAULT...THAT HE SEDUCED *YOU*. I FIGURED STICKING A BURNING FAG IN EACH OF HIS EYES WOULD MAKE A DEMON PRONE TO CONFESSION.
MY, THAT *WAS* FUN!
STILL, YOU'D BE AMAZED AT WHAT STORIES PEOPLE IN PAIN WILL TELL!
LIKE THAT BLOKE TELLING ME ABOUT THOSE BUGS WITH THEIR SPECIAL POWER STONES...
...AND ABOUT HOW MUCH THEY'RE WORTH ON THE STREET.

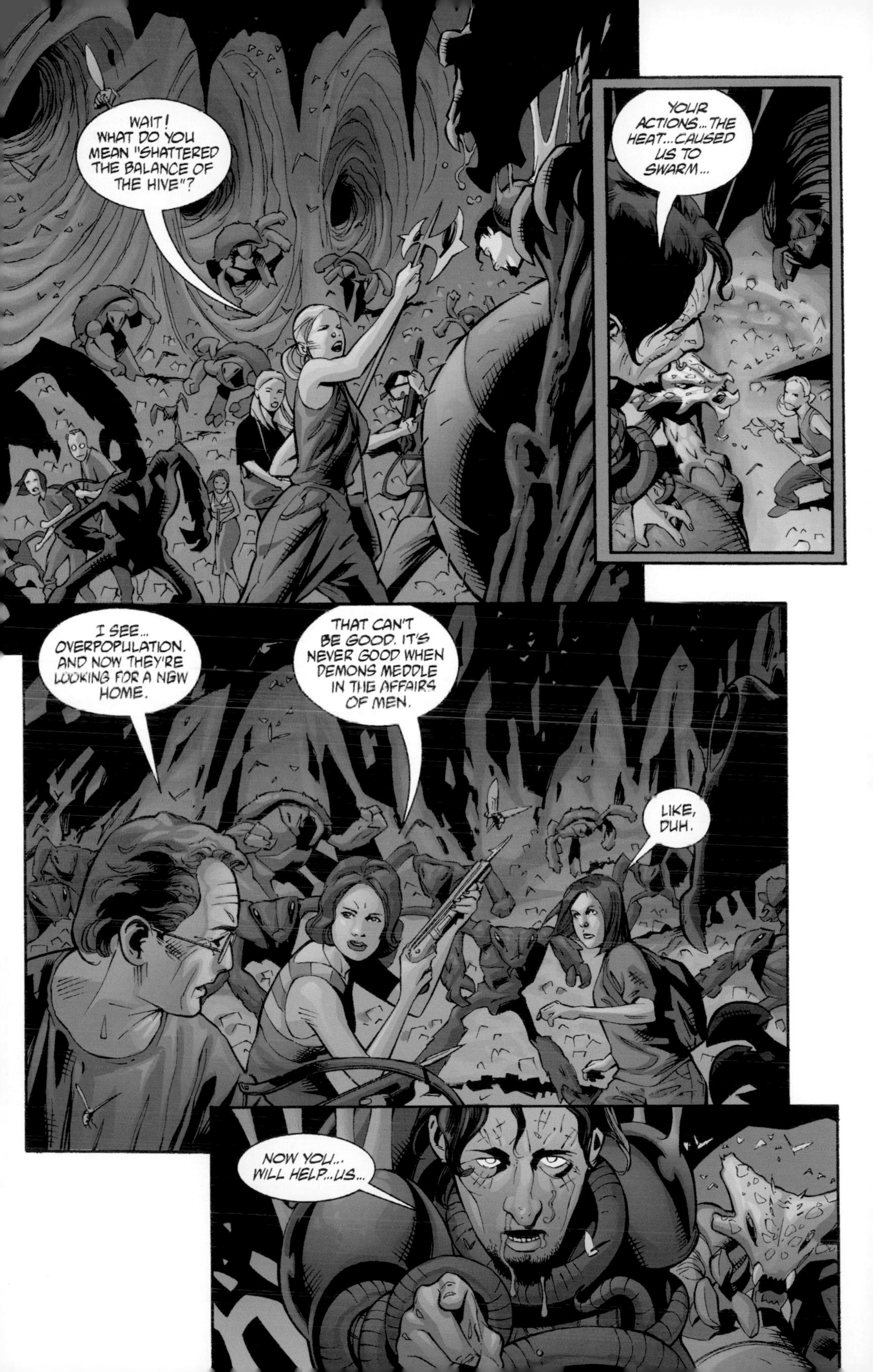
WAIT! WHAT DO YOU MEAN "SHATTERED THE BALANCE OF THE HIVE"?
YOUR ACTIONS... THE HEAT... CAUSED US TO SWARM...
I SEE... OVERPOPULATION. AND NOW THEY'RE LOOKING FOR A NEW HOME.
THAT CAN'T BE GOOD. IT'S NEVER GOOD WHEN DEMONS MEDDLE IN THE AFFAIRS OF MEN.
LIKE, DUH.
NOW YOU... WILL HELP... US...

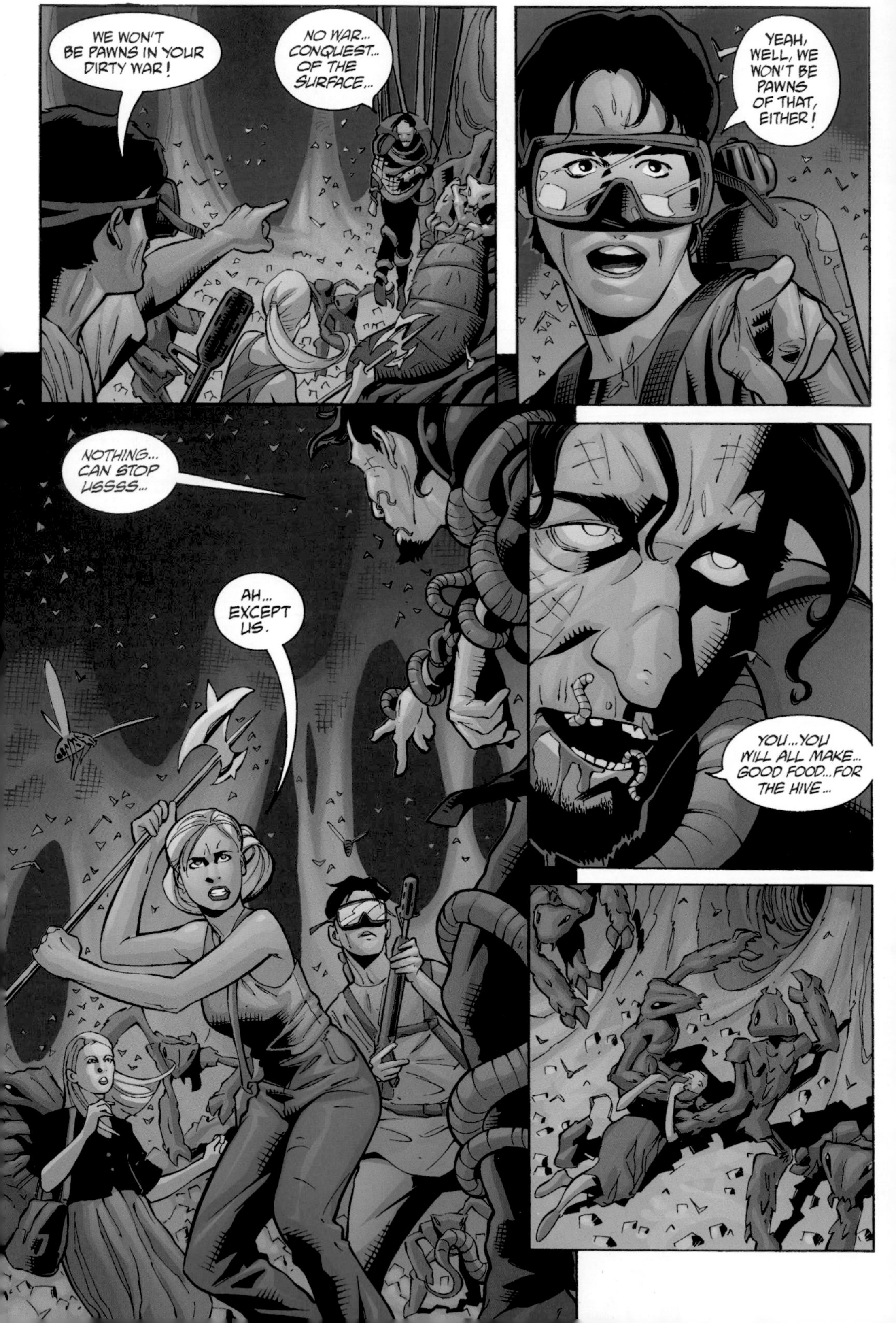
WE WON'T BE PAWNS IN YOUR DIRTY WAR!
NO WAR... CONQUEST... OF THE SURFACE...
YEAH, WELL, WE WON'T BE PAWNS OF THAT, EITHER!
NOTHING... CAN STOP USSSS...
AH... EXCEPT US.
YOU...YOU WILL ALL MAKE... GOOD FOOD...FOR THE HIVE...

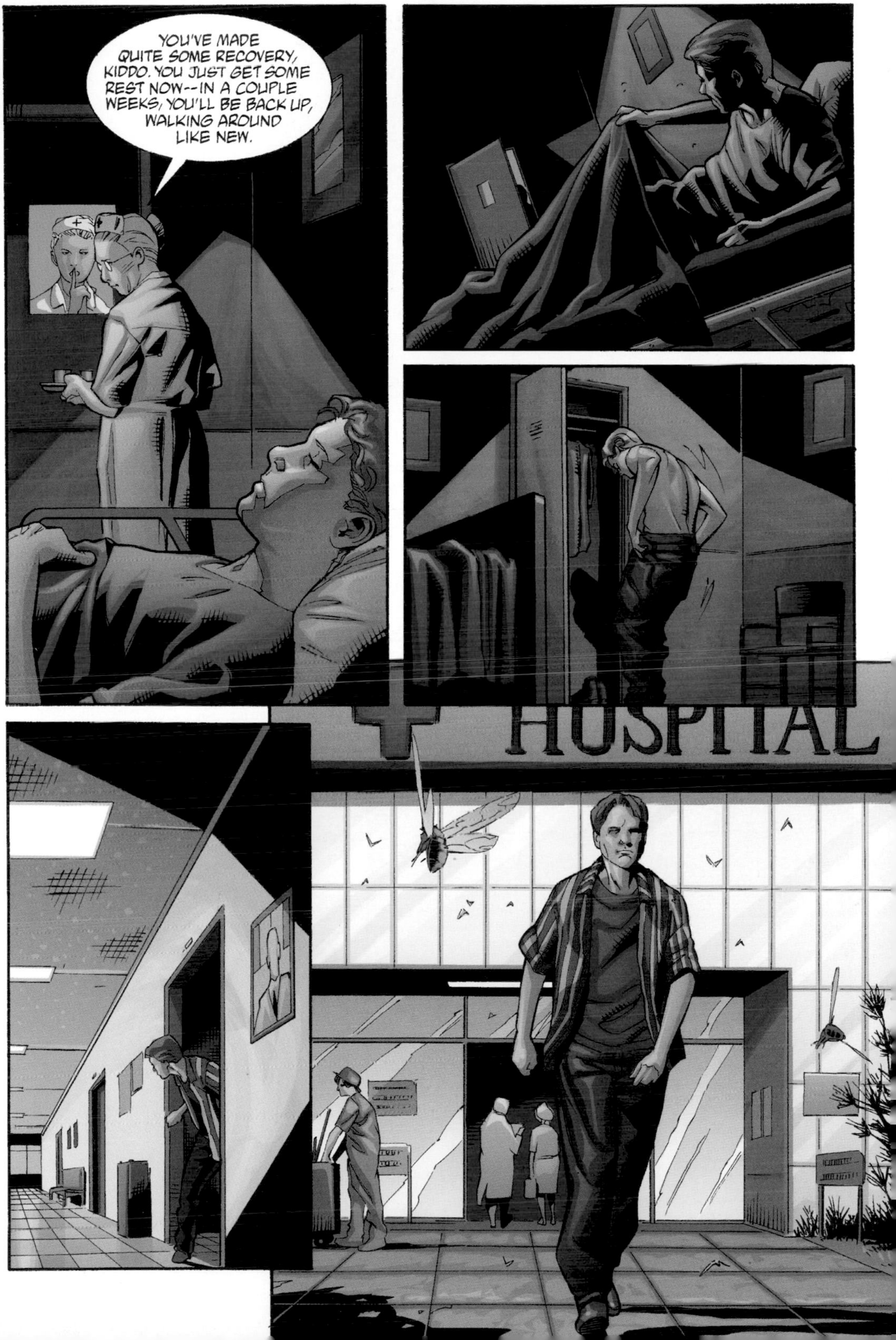
YOU'VE MADE QUITE SOME RECOVERY, KIDDO. YOU JUST GET SOME REST NOW--IN A COUPLE WEEKS, YOU'LL BE BACK UP, WALKING AROUND LIKE NEW.
HOSPITAL

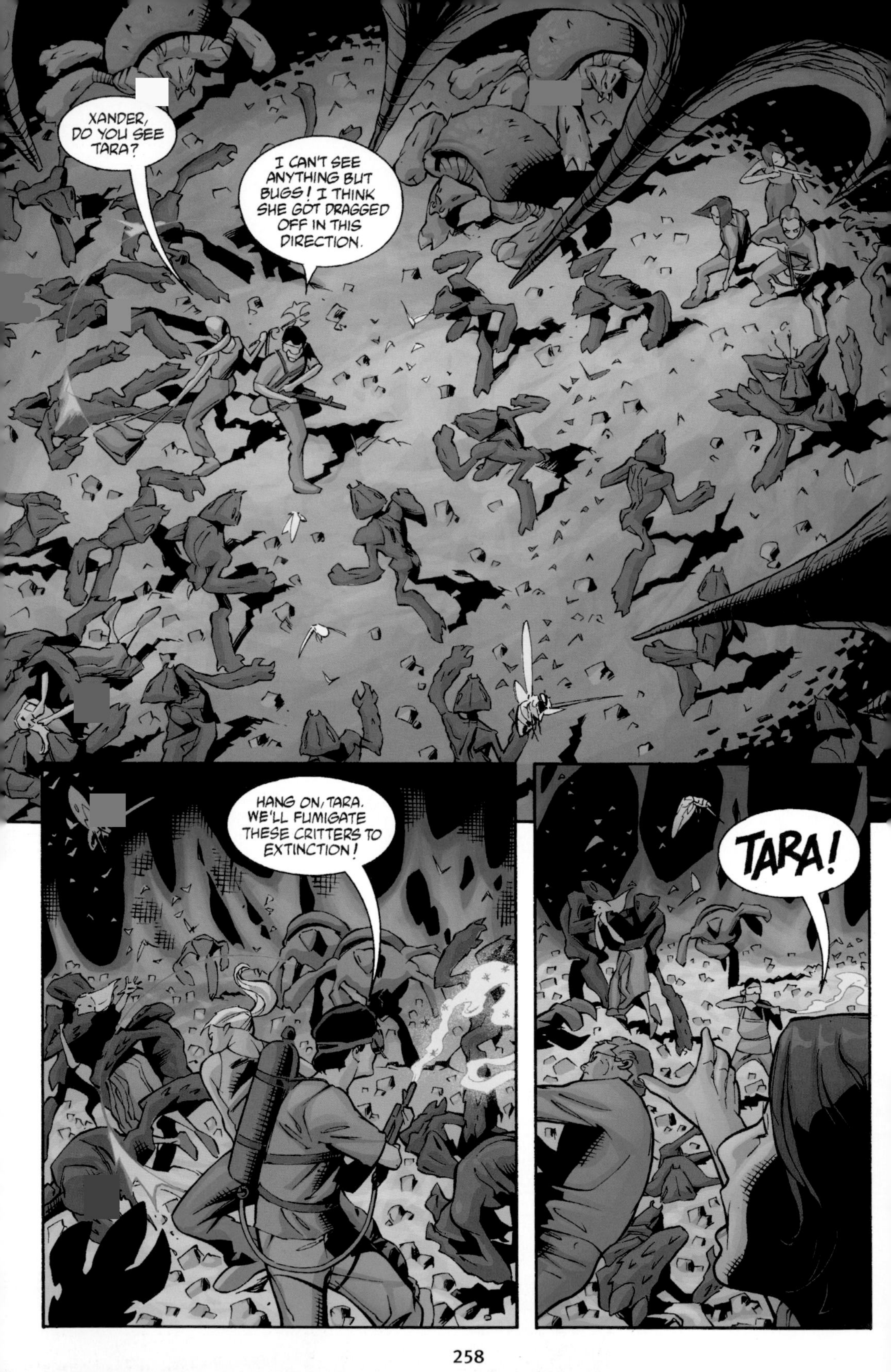
XANDER, DO YOU SEE TARA?
I CAN'T SEE ANYTHING BUT BUGS! I THINK SHE GOT DRAGGED OFF IN THIS DIRECTION.
HANG ON, TARA. WE'LL FUMIGATE THESE CRITTERS TO EXTINCTION!
TARA!

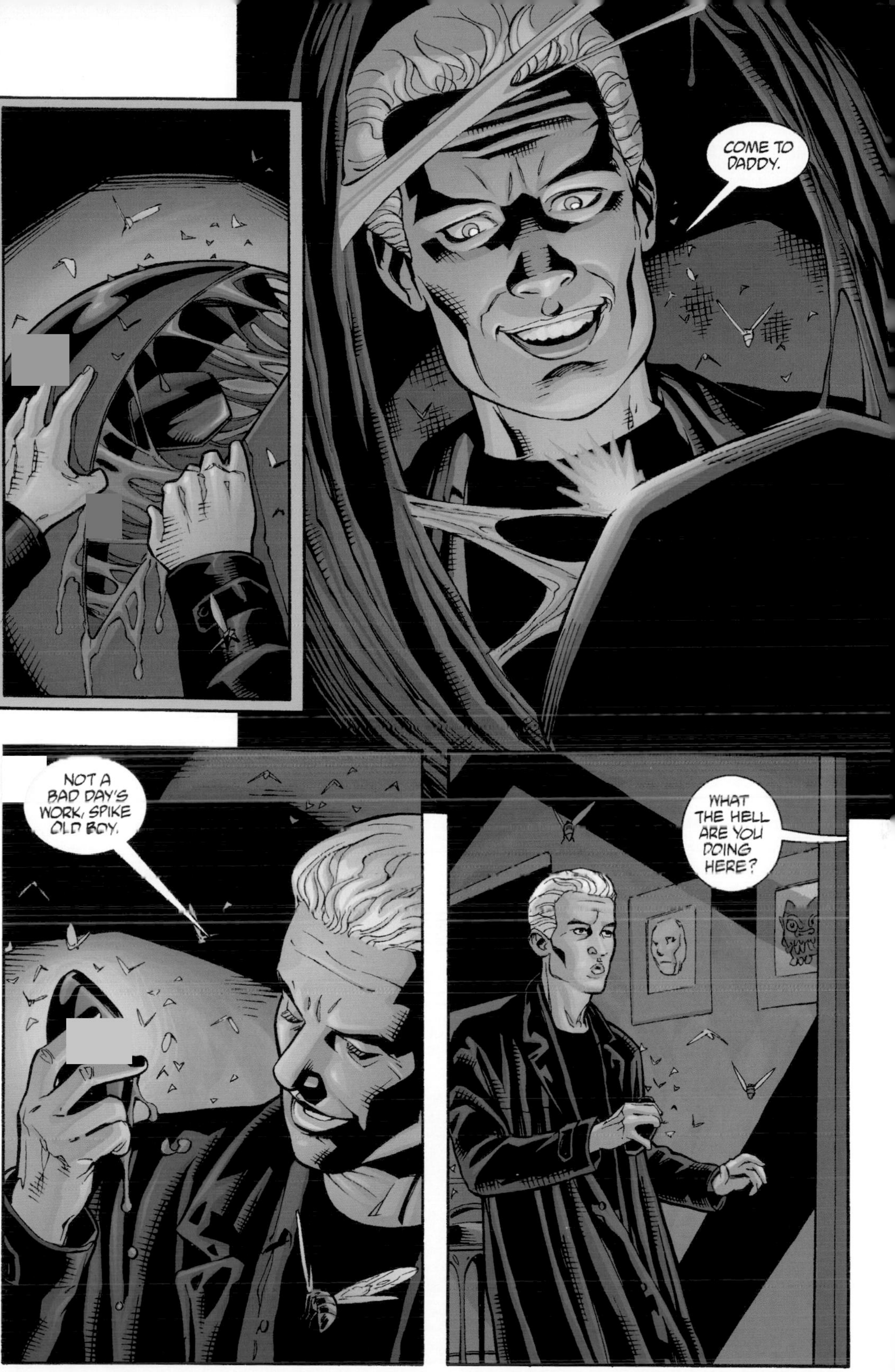
COME TO DADDY.
NOT A BAD DAY'S WORK, SPIKE OLD BOY.
WHAT THE HELL ARE YOU DOING HERE?

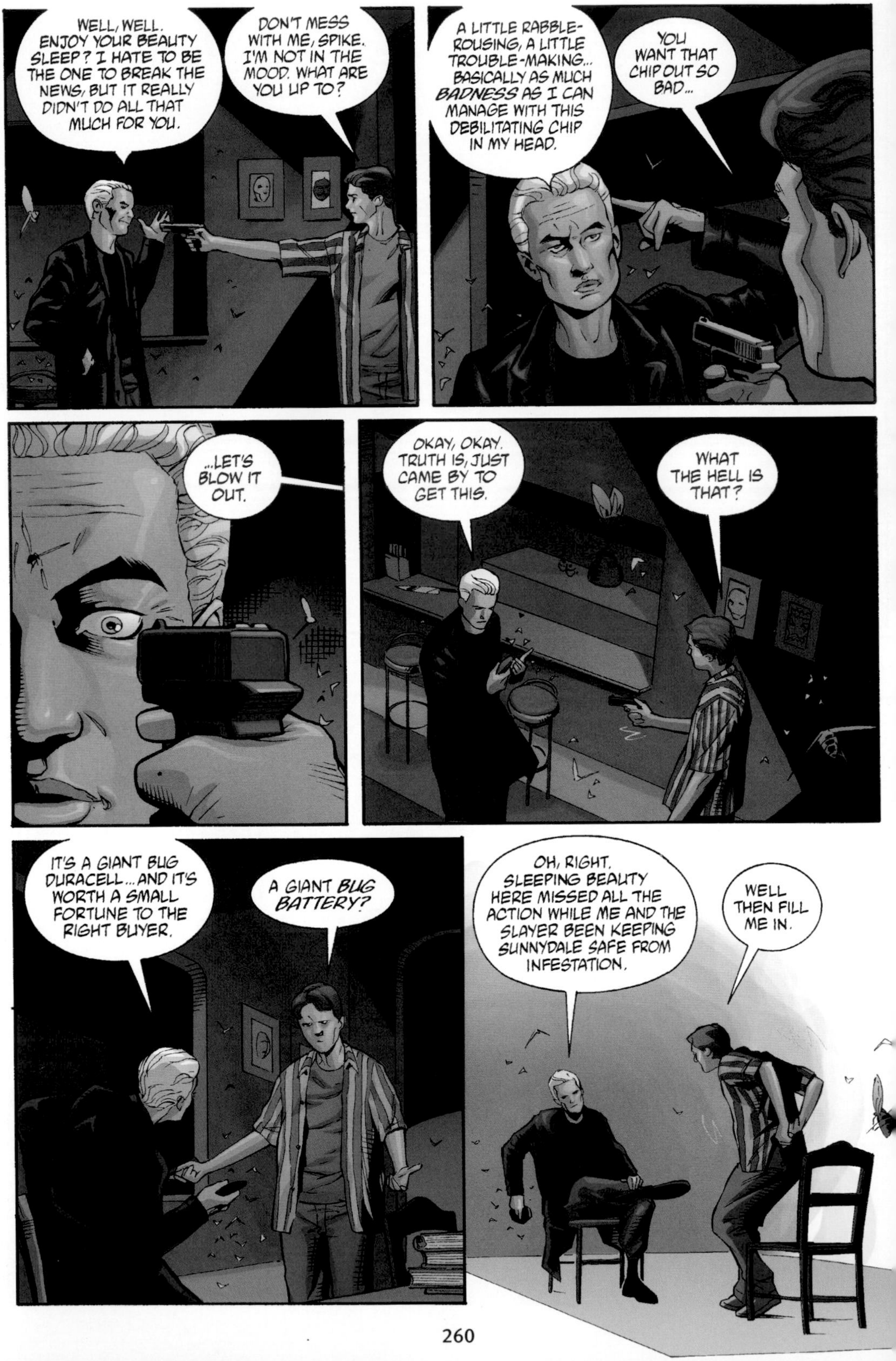

WELL, WELL. ENJOY YOUR BEAUTY SLEEP? I HATE TO BE THE ONE TO BREAK THE NEWS, BUT IT REALLY DIDN'T DO ALL THAT MUCH FOR YOU.
DON'T MESS WITH ME, SPIKE. I'M NOT IN THE MOOD. WHAT ARE YOU UP TO?
A LITTLE RABBLE-ROUSING, A LITTLE TROUBLE-MAKING... BASICALLY AS MUCH *BADNESS* AS I CAN MANAGE WITH THIS DEBILITATING CHIP IN MY HEAD.
YOU WANT THAT CHIP OUT SO BAD...
...LET'S BLOW IT OUT.
OKAY, OKAY. TRUTH IS, JUST CAME BY TO GET THIS.
WHAT THE HELL IS THAT?
IT'S A GIANT BUG DURACELL... AND IT'S WORTH A SMALL FORTUNE TO THE RIGHT BUYER.
A GIANT *BUG BATTERY?*
OH, RIGHT. SLEEPING BEAUTY HERE MISSED ALL THE ACTION WHILE ME AND THE SLAYER BEEN KEEPING SUNNYDALE SAFE FROM INFESTATION.
WELL THEN FILL ME IN.

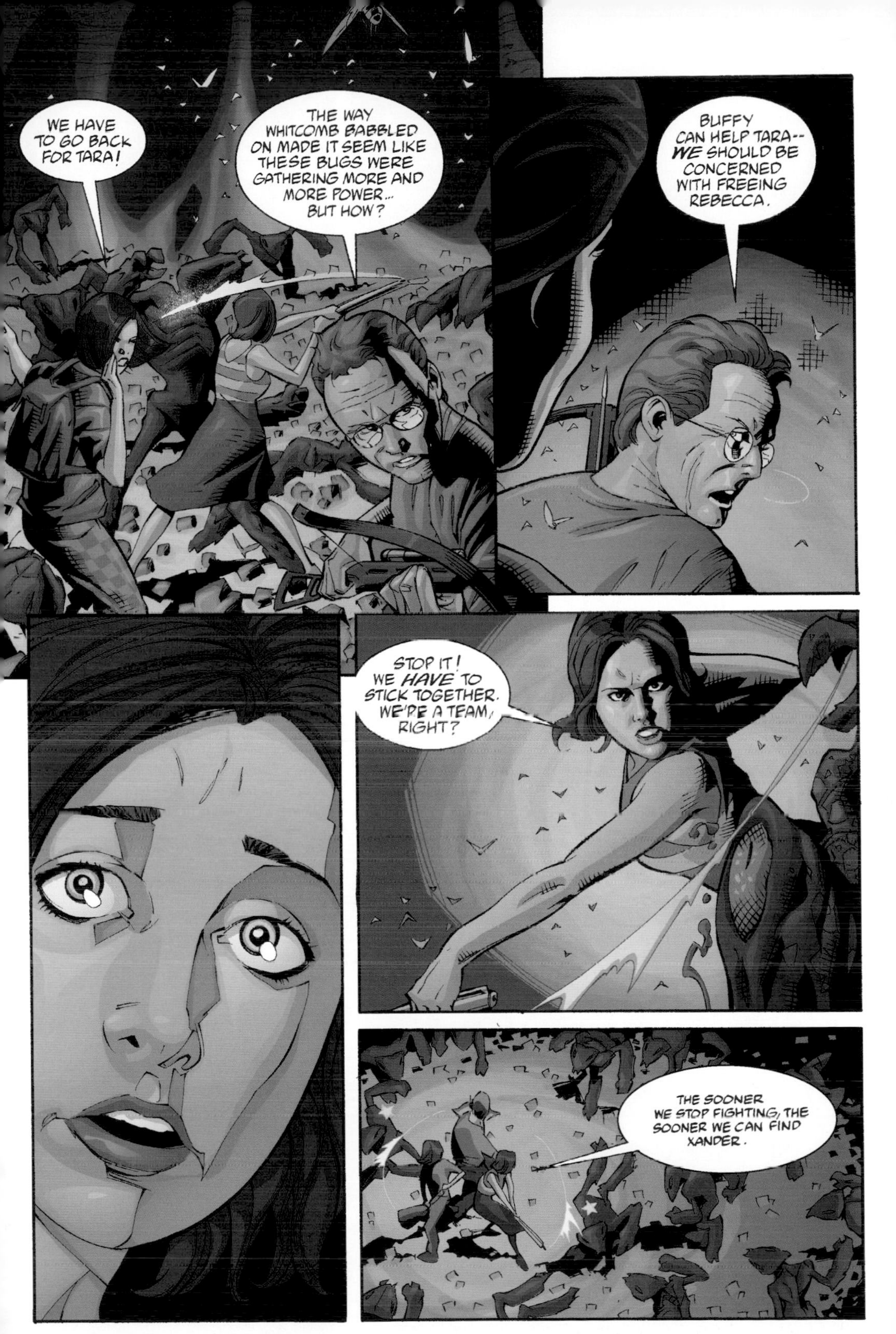
WE HAVE TO GO BACK FOR TARA!
THE WAY WHITCOMB BABBLED ON MADE IT SEEM LIKE THESE BUGS WERE GATHERING MORE AND MORE POWER... BUT HOW?
BUFFY CAN HELP TARA-- WE SHOULD BE CONCERNED WITH FREEING REBECCA.
STOP IT! WE HAVE TO STICK TOGETHER. WE'RE A TEAM, RIGHT?
THE SOONER WE STOP FIGHTING, THE SOONER WE CAN FIND XANDER.

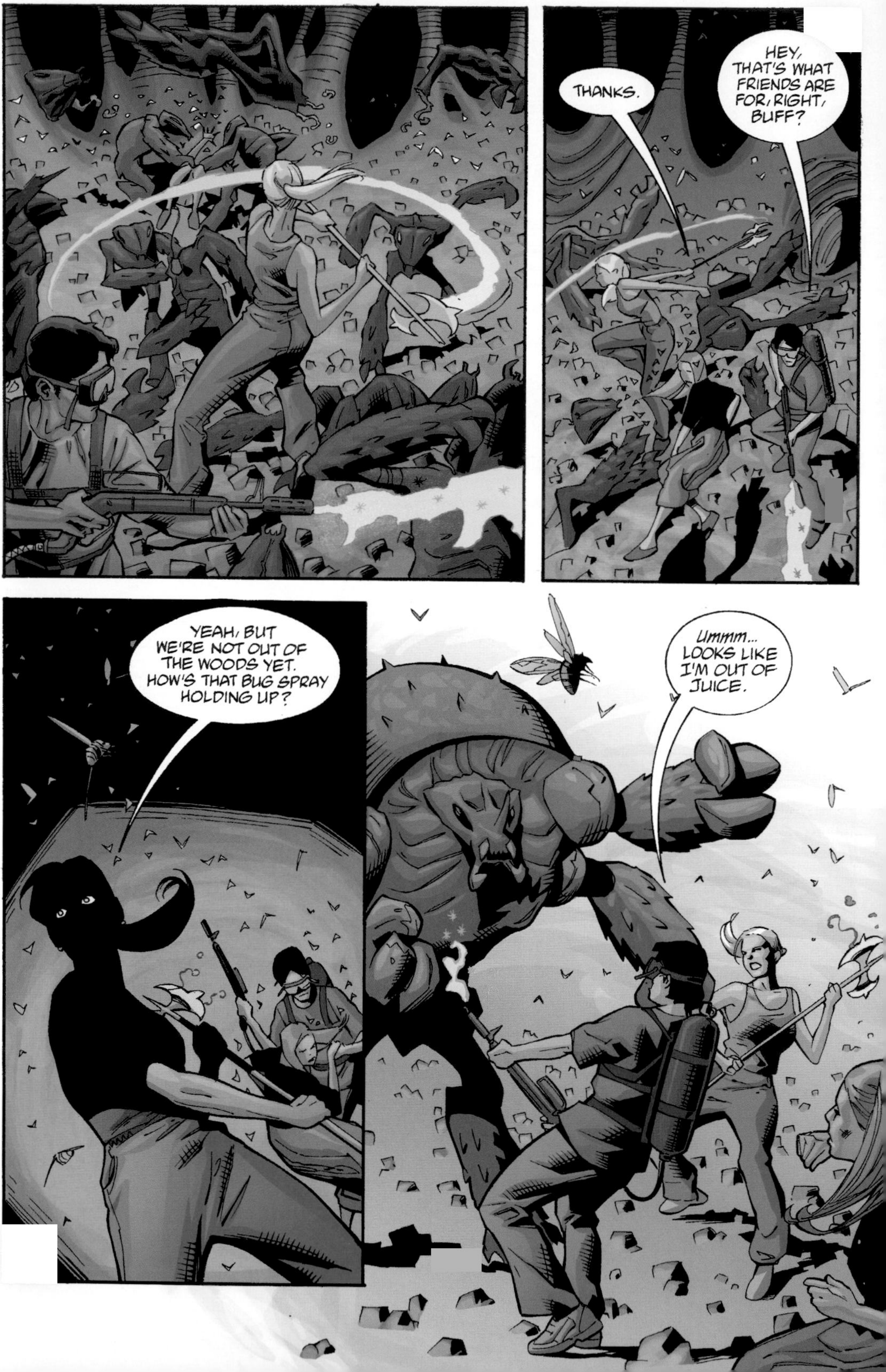
THANKS.
HEY, THAT'S WHAT FRIENDS ARE FOR, RIGHT, BUFF?
YEAH, BUT WE'RE NOT OUT OF THE WOODS YET. HOW'S THAT BUG SPRAY HOLDING UP?
Ummm... LOOKS LIKE I'M OUT OF JUICE.

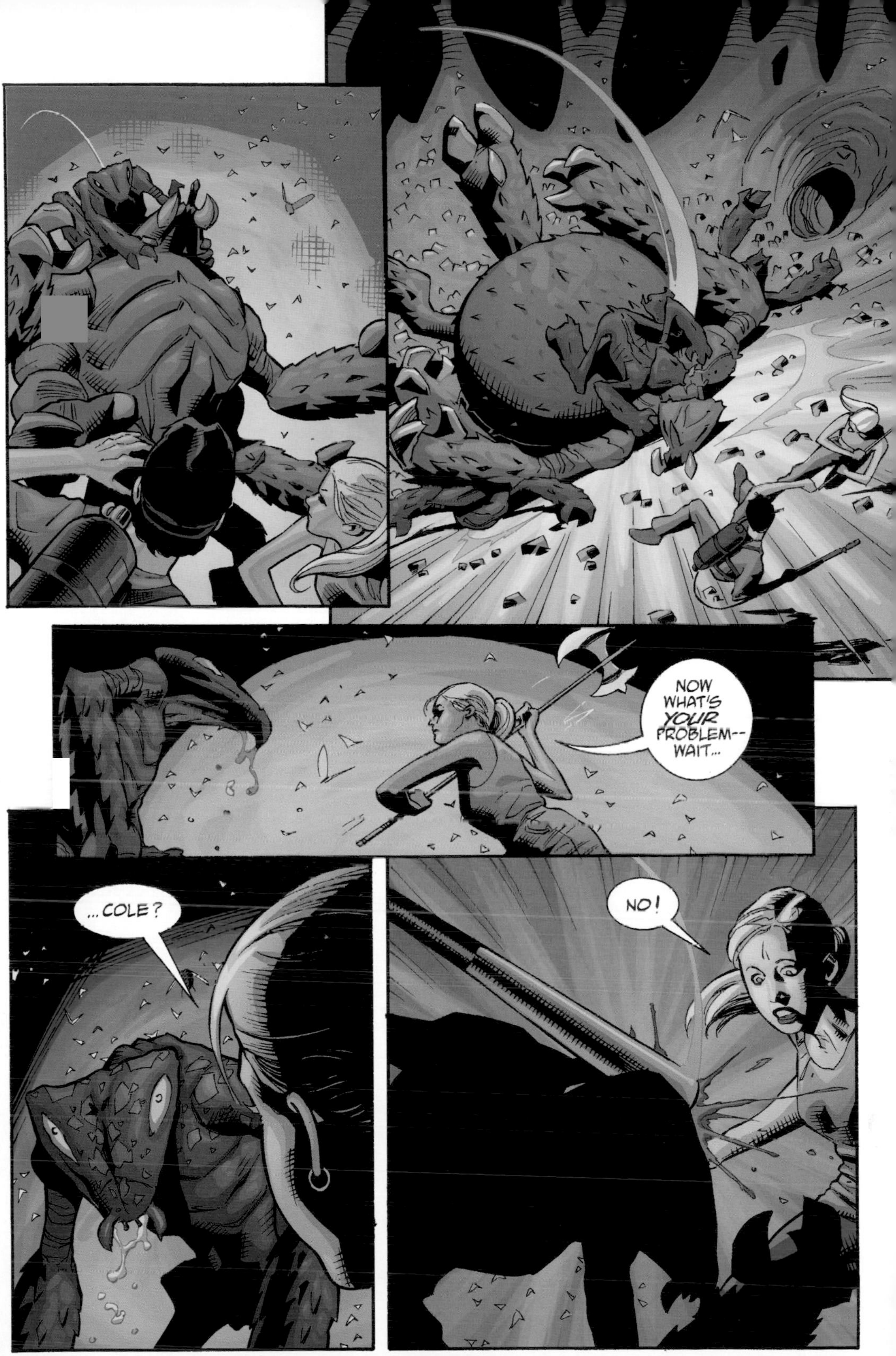
NOW WHAT'S YOUR PROBLEM-- WAIT...
...COLE?
NO!

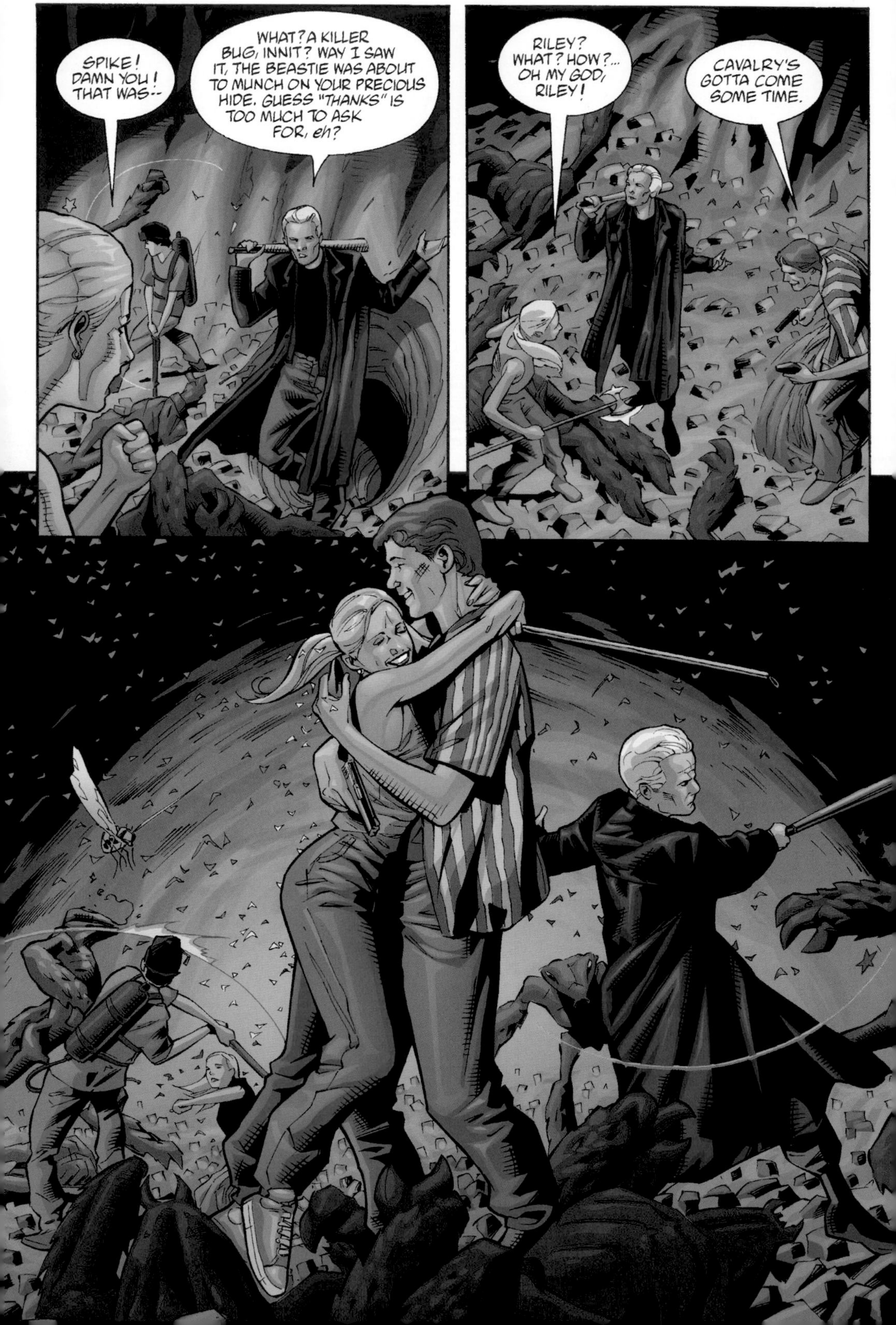
SPIKE! DAMN YOU! THAT WAS--
WHAT? A KILLER BUG, INNIT? WAY I SAW IT, THE BEASTIE WAS ABOUT TO MUNCH ON YOUR PRECIOUS HIDE. GUESS "THANKS" IS TOO MUCH TO ASK FOR, eh?
RILEY? WHAT? HOW?... OH MY GOD, RILEY!
CAVALRY'S GOTTA COME SOME TIME.

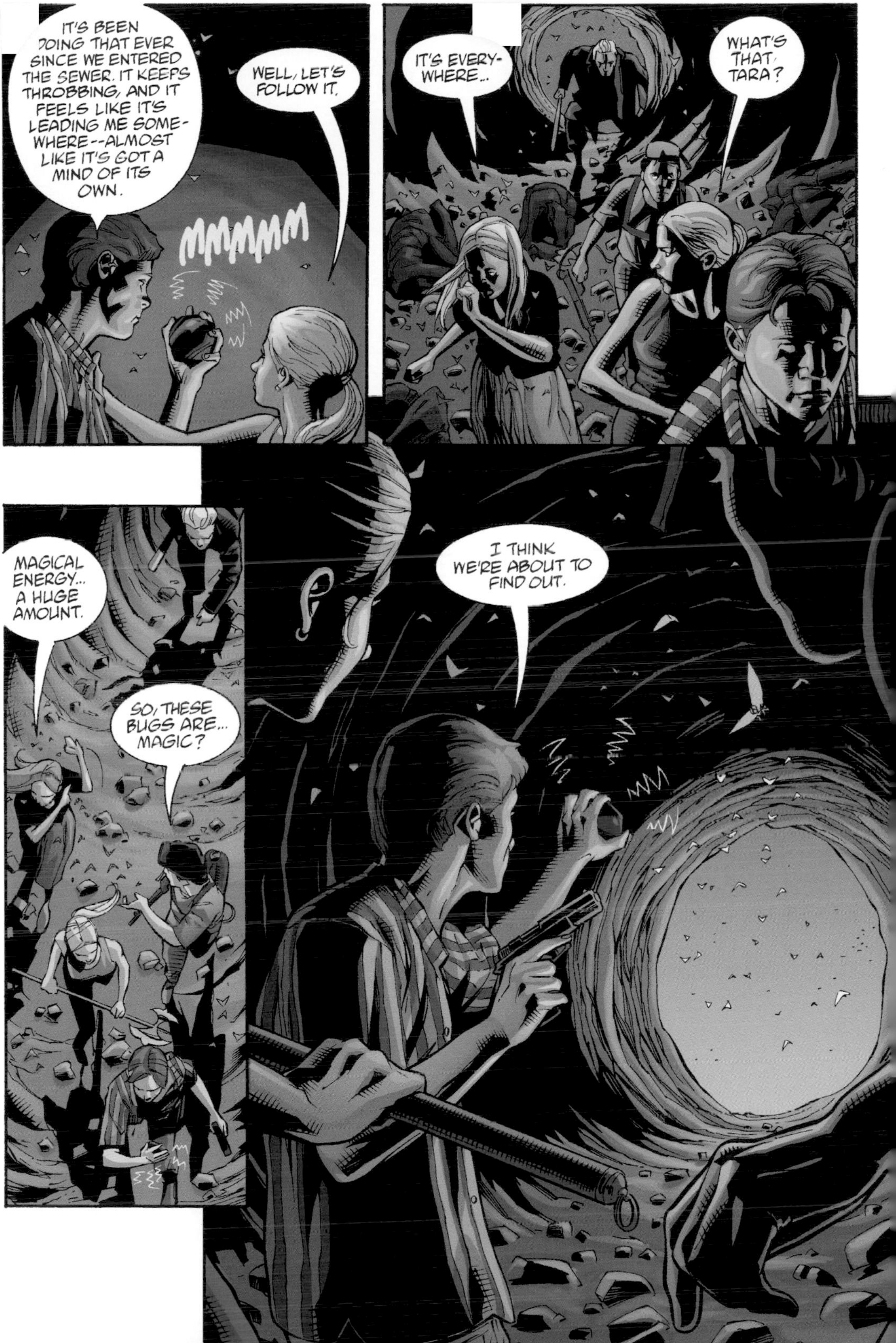
IT'S BEEN DOING THAT EVER SINCE WE ENTERED THE SEWER. IT KEEPS THROBBING, AND IT FEELS LIKE IT'S LEADING ME SOME-WHERE--ALMOST LIKE IT'S GOT A MIND OF ITS OWN.
WELL, LET'S FOLLOW IT.
MMMMMM
IT'S EVERY-WHERE...
WHAT'S THAT, TARA?
MAGICAL ENERGY... A HUGE AMOUNT.
SO, THESE BUGS ARE... MAGIC?
I THINK WE'RE ABOUT TO FIND OUT.

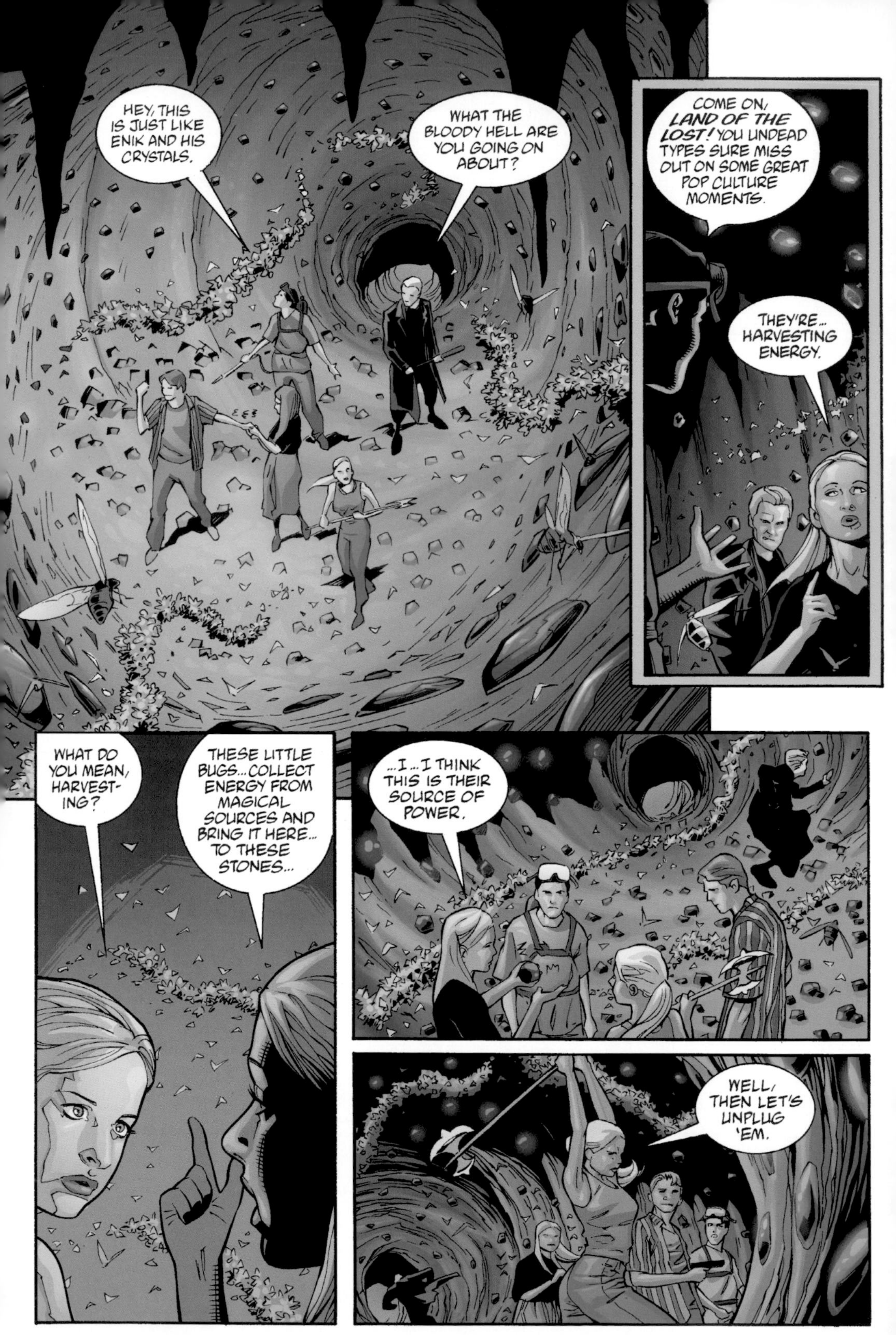

HEY, THIS IS JUST LIKE ENIK AND HIS CRYSTALS.
WHAT THE BLOODY HELL ARE YOU GOING ON ABOUT?
COME ON, LAND OF THE LOST! YOU UNDEAD TYPES SURE MISS OUT ON SOME GREAT POP CULTURE MOMENTS.
THEY'RE... HARVESTING ENERGY.
WHAT DO YOU MEAN, HARVEST-ING?
THESE LITTLE BUGS...COLLECT ENERGY FROM MAGICAL SOURCES AND BRING IT HERE... TO THESE STONES...
...I...I THINK THIS IS THEIR SOURCE OF POWER.
WELL, THEN LET'S UNPLUG 'EM.

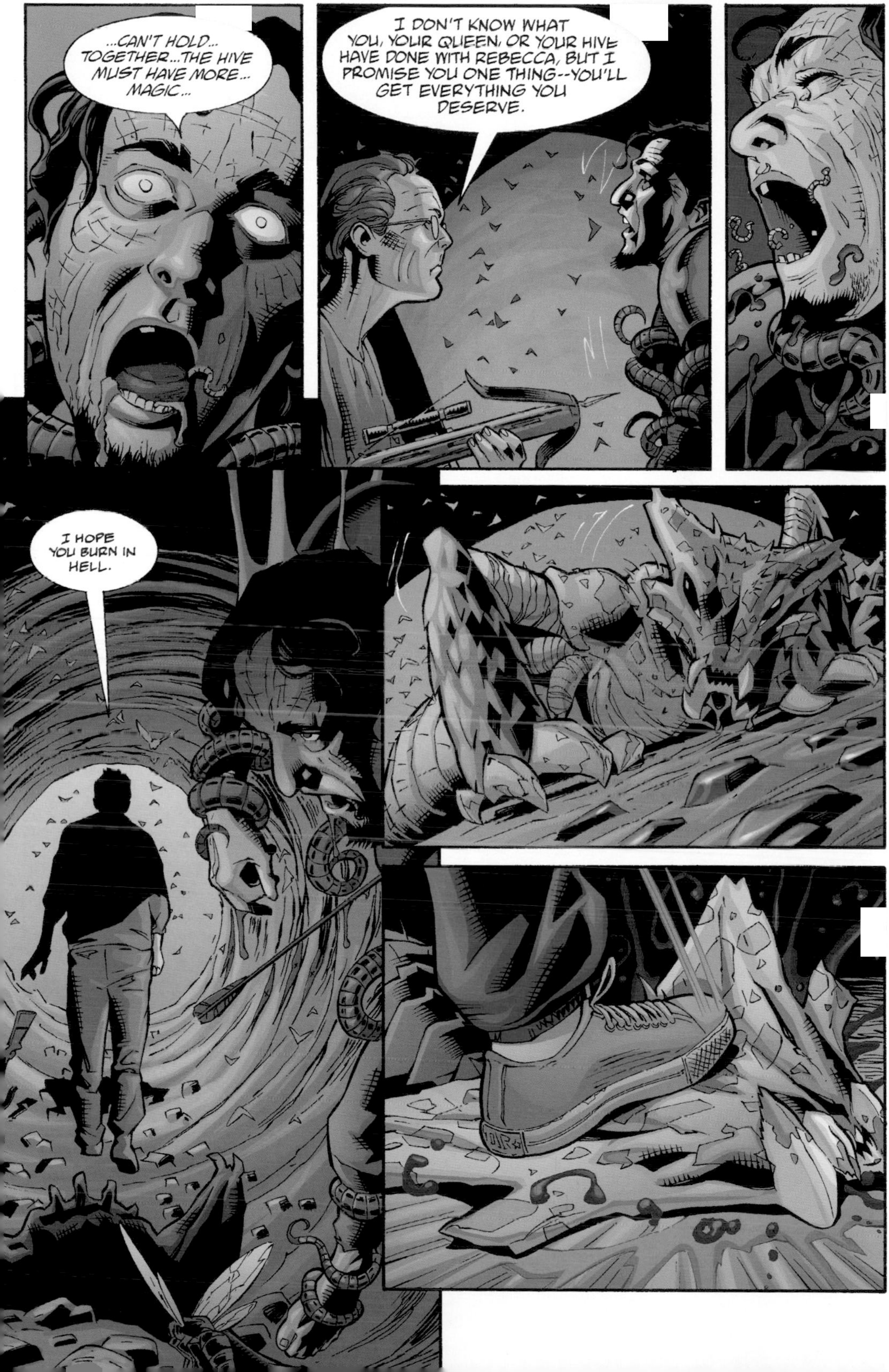
...CAN'T HOLD... TOGETHER...THE HIVE MUST HAVE MORE... MAGIC...
I DON'T KNOW WHAT YOU, YOUR QUEEN, OR YOUR HIVE HAVE DONE WITH REBECCA, BUT I PROMISE YOU ONE THING--YOU'LL GET EVERYTHING YOU DESERVE.
I HOPE YOU BURN IN HELL.

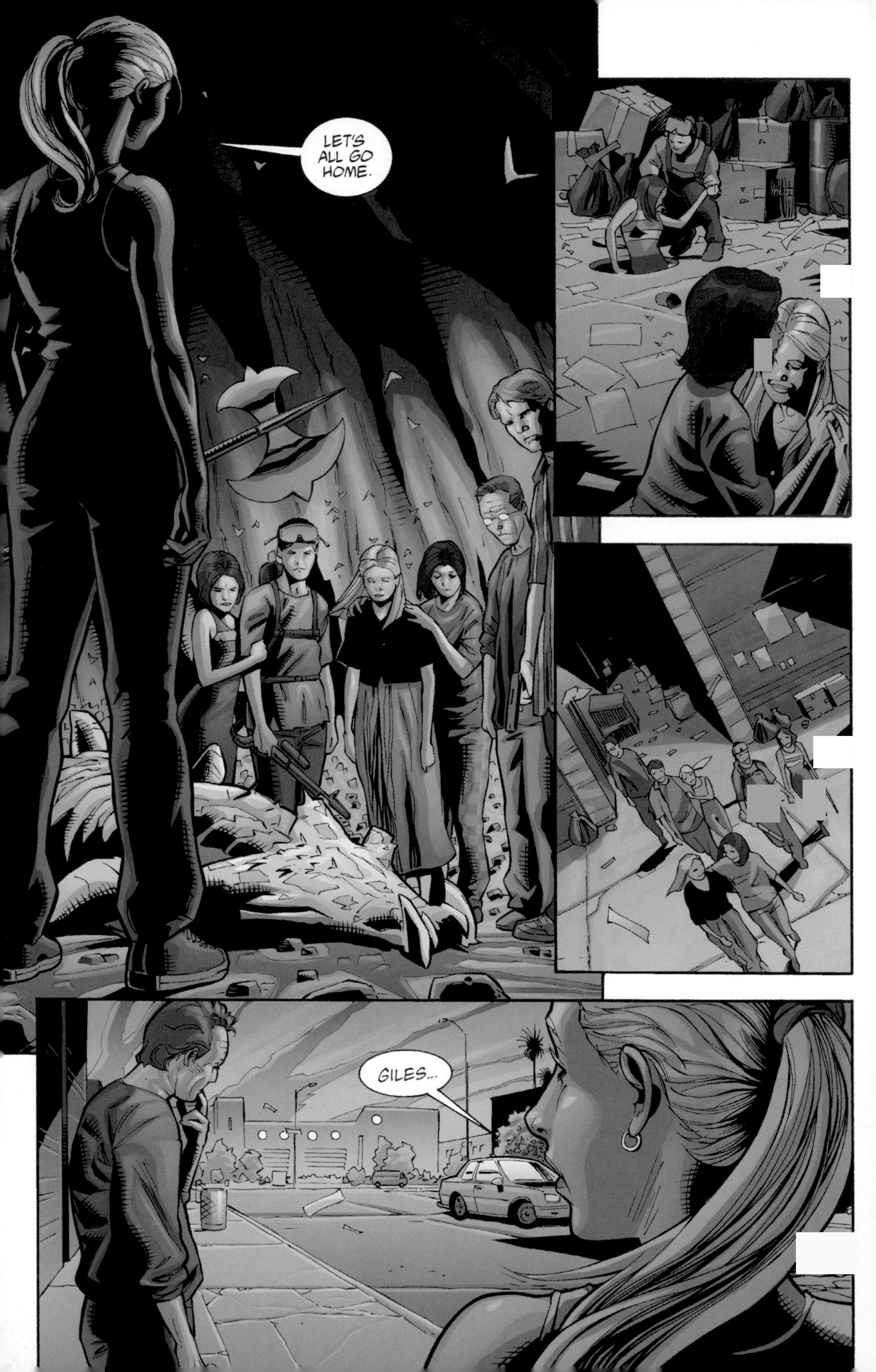
LET'S ALL GO HOME.
GILES...

...I'M SO SORRY.

HEY GILES, YOU NEVER FOUND YOUR GIRLFRIEND, DID YOU?

THAT'S FUNNY, WE THOUGHT SHE WAS THE EVIL BUG MASTERMIND.

ANYA, REMEMBER THAT CONVERSATION WE HAD ABOUT RIGHT TIME, RIGHT PLACE?

THERE ARE A LOT OF UNANSWERED QUESTIONS ABOUT THE *MYSTERIOUOUS REBECCA STANSBERRY*. IT'S NOT LIKE PEOPLE *JUST SHOW UP IN SUNNYDALE*--WITH CREEPY, BUGGY, NECKLACE-Y THINGS--AND AREN'T INVOLVED IN THE BUGGY BADNESS!

I MEAN, COME ON, WHO DIDN'T SEE THAT WHOLE WARREN WHITCOMB THING COMING? AN ENTOMOLOGIST IN SUNNYDALE? O-KAY.

I DIDN'T SEE THAT COMING.

WHAT A MOTLEY CREW *YOU* ARE.

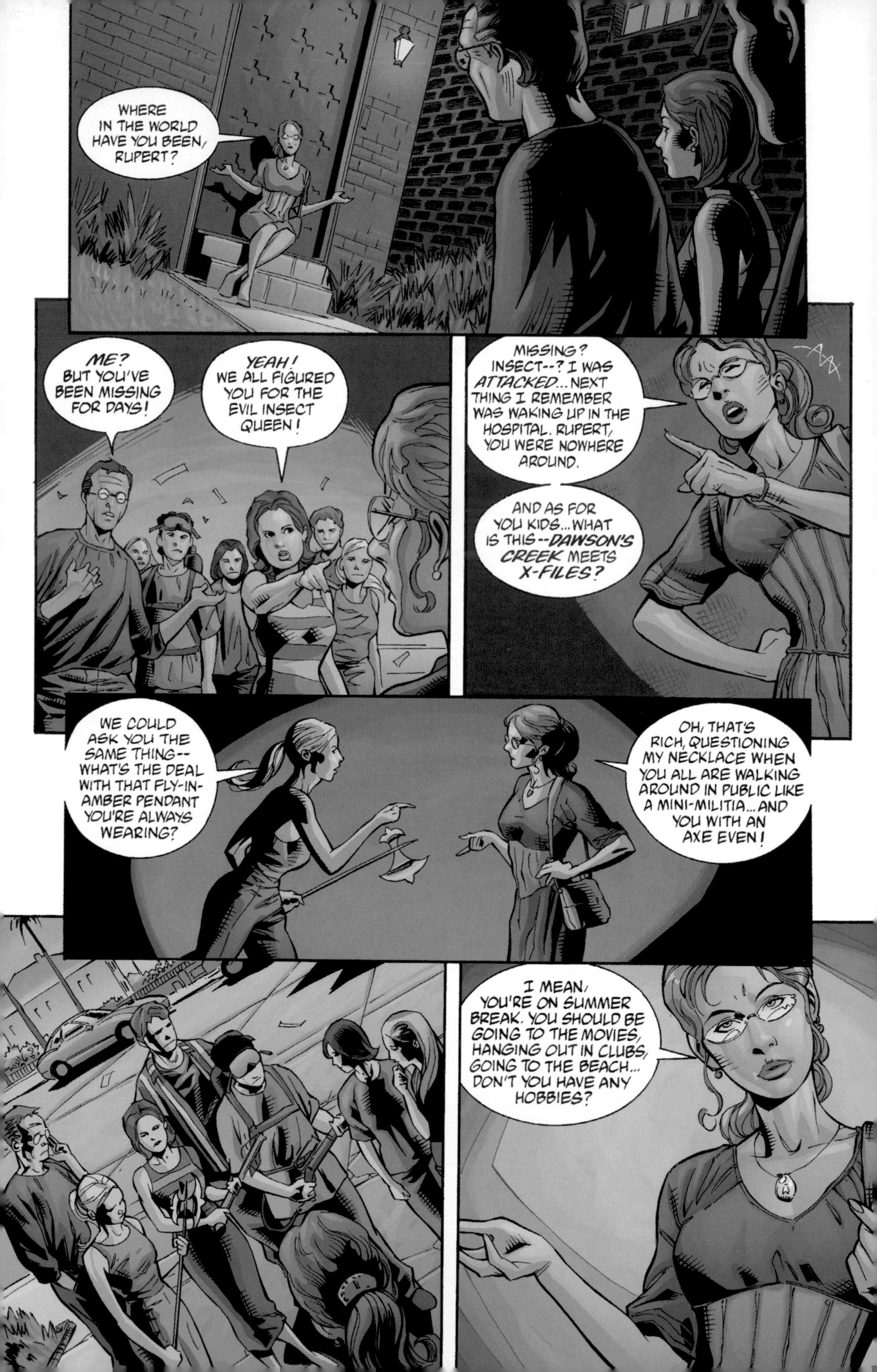
WHERE IN THE WORLD HAVE YOU BEEN, RUPERT?
ME? BUT YOU'VE BEEN MISSING FOR DAYS!
YEAH! WE ALL FIGURED YOU FOR THE EVIL INSECT QUEEN!
MISSING? INSECT--? I WAS ATTACKED... NEXT THING I REMEMBER WAS WAKING UP IN THE HOSPITAL. RUPERT, YOU WERE NOWHERE AROUND.
AND AS FOR YOU KIDS... WHAT IS THIS--DAWSON'S CREEK MEETS X-FILES?
WE COULD ASK YOU THE SAME THING--WHAT'S THE DEAL WITH THAT FLY-IN-AMBER PENDANT YOU'RE ALWAYS WEARING?
OH, THAT'S RICH, QUESTIONING MY NECKLACE WHEN YOU ALL ARE WALKING AROUND IN PUBLIC LIKE A MINI-MILITIA... AND YOU WITH AN AXE EVEN!
I MEAN, YOU'RE ON SUMMER BREAK. YOU SHOULD BE GOING TO THE MOVIES, HANGING OUT IN CLUBS, GOING TO THE BEACH... DON'T YOU HAVE ANY HOBBIES?

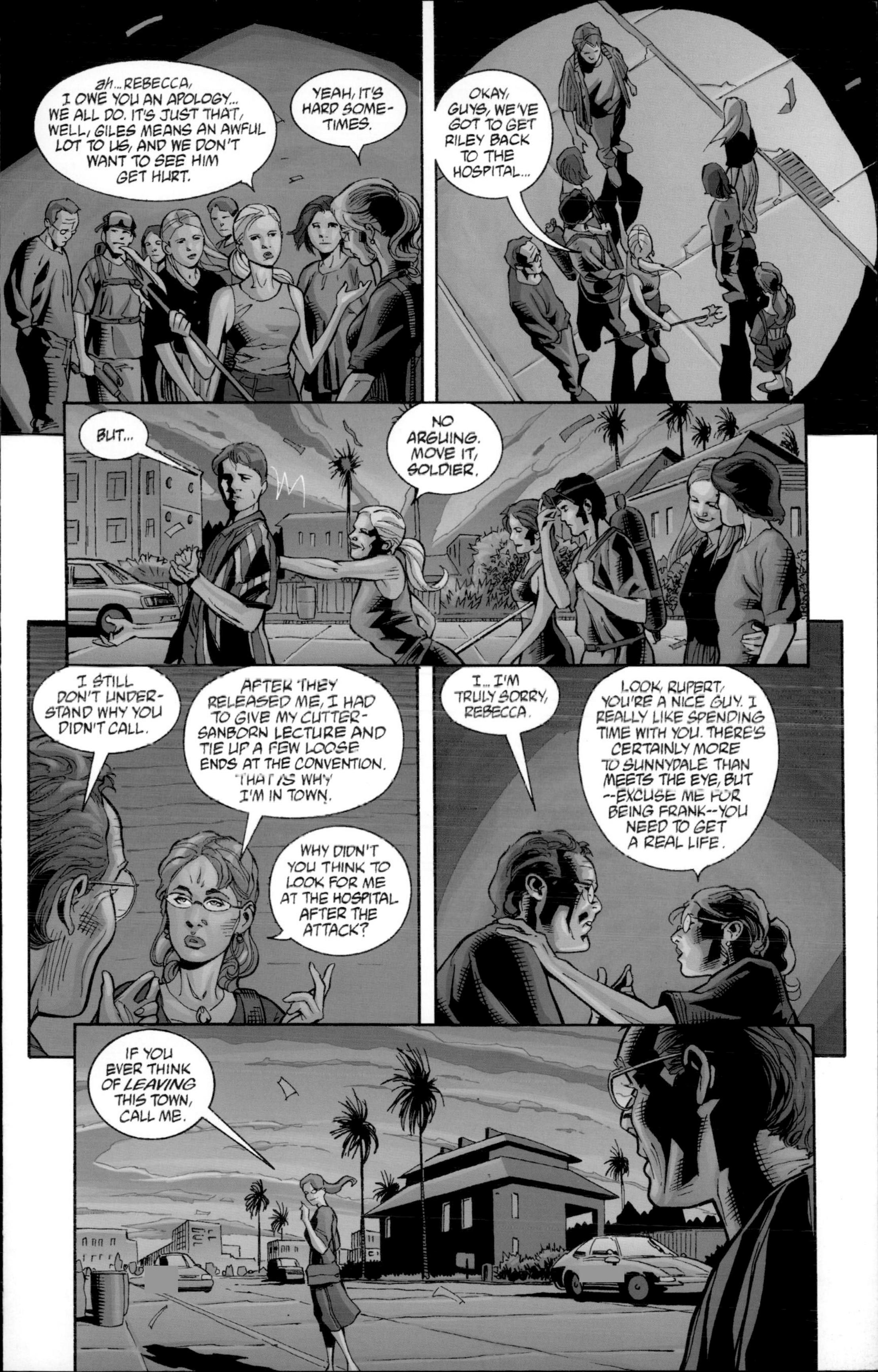
ah... REBECCA, I OWE YOU AN APOLOGY... WE ALL DO. IT'S JUST THAT, WELL, GILES MEANS AN AWFUL LOT TO US, AND WE DON'T WANT TO SEE HIM GET HURT.
YEAH, IT'S HARD SOME-TIMES.
OKAY, GUYS, WE'VE GOT TO GET RILEY BACK TO THE HOSPITAL...
BUT...
NO ARGUING. MOVE IT, SOLDIER.
I STILL DON'T UNDER-STAND WHY YOU DIDN'T CALL.
AFTER THEY RELEASED ME, I HAD TO GIVE MY CUTTER-SANBORN LECTURE AND TIE UP A FEW LOOSE ENDS AT THE CONVENTION. THAT IS WHY I'M IN TOWN.
WHY DIDN'T YOU THINK TO LOOK FOR ME AT THE HOSPITAL AFTER THE ATTACK?
I... I'M TRULY SORRY, REBECCA.
LOOK, RUPERT, YOU'RE A NICE GUY. I REALLY LIKE SPENDING TIME WITH YOU. THERE'S CERTAINLY MORE TO SUNNYDALE THAN MEETS THE EYE, BUT --EXCUSE ME FOR BEING FRANK--YOU NEED TO GET A REAL LIFE.
IF YOU EVER THINK OF LEAVING THIS TOWN, CALL ME.

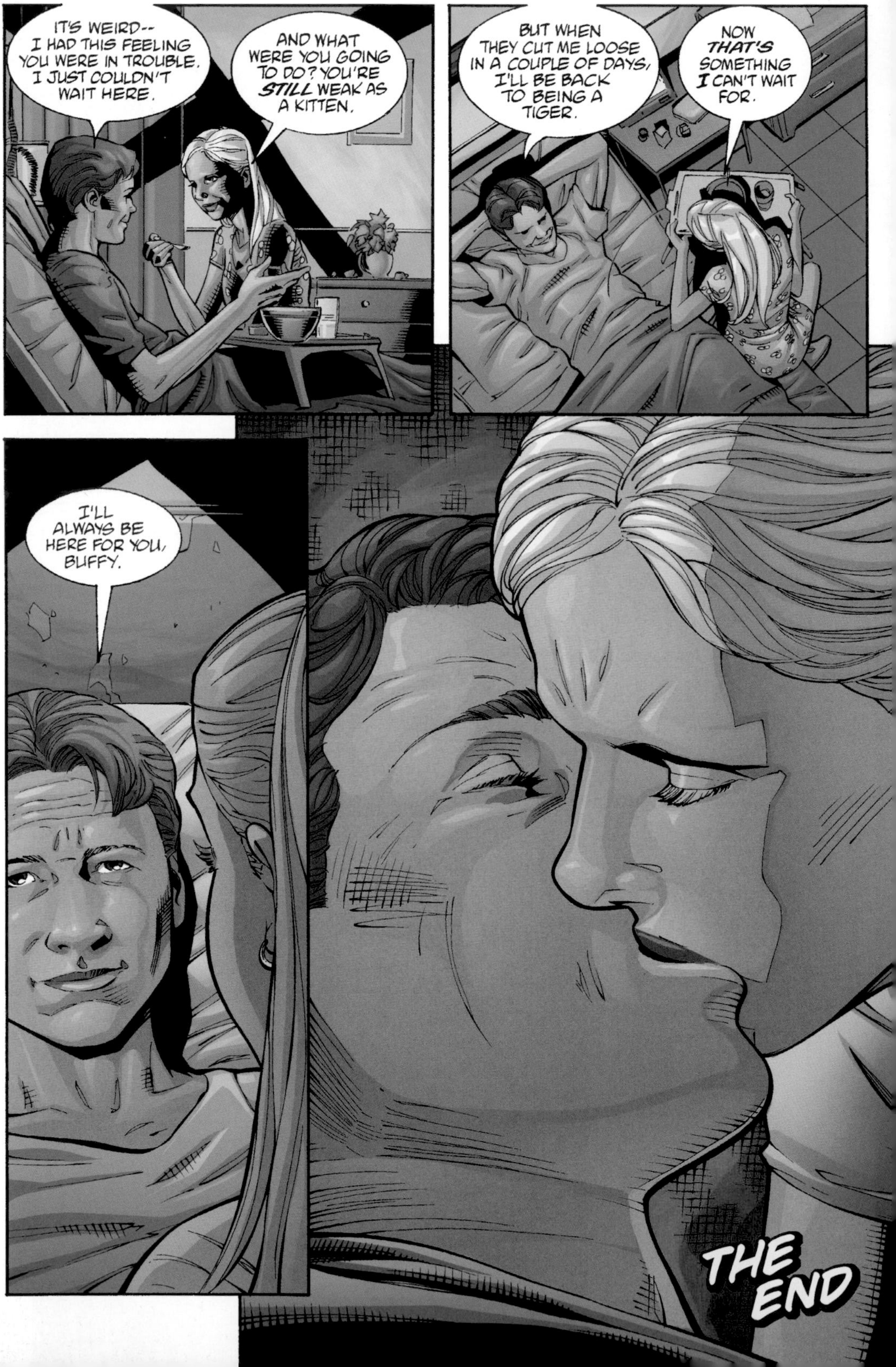
IT'S WEIRD-- I HAD THIS FEELING YOU WERE IN TROUBLE. I JUST COULDN'T WAIT HERE.
AND WHAT WERE YOU GOING TO DO? YOU'RE STILL WEAK AS A KITTEN.
BUT WHEN THEY CUT ME LOOSE IN A COUPLE OF DAYS, I'LL BE BACK TO BEING A TIGER.
NOW THAT'S SOMETHING I CAN'T WAIT FOR.
I'LL ALWAYS BE HERE FOR YOU, BUFFY.
THE END

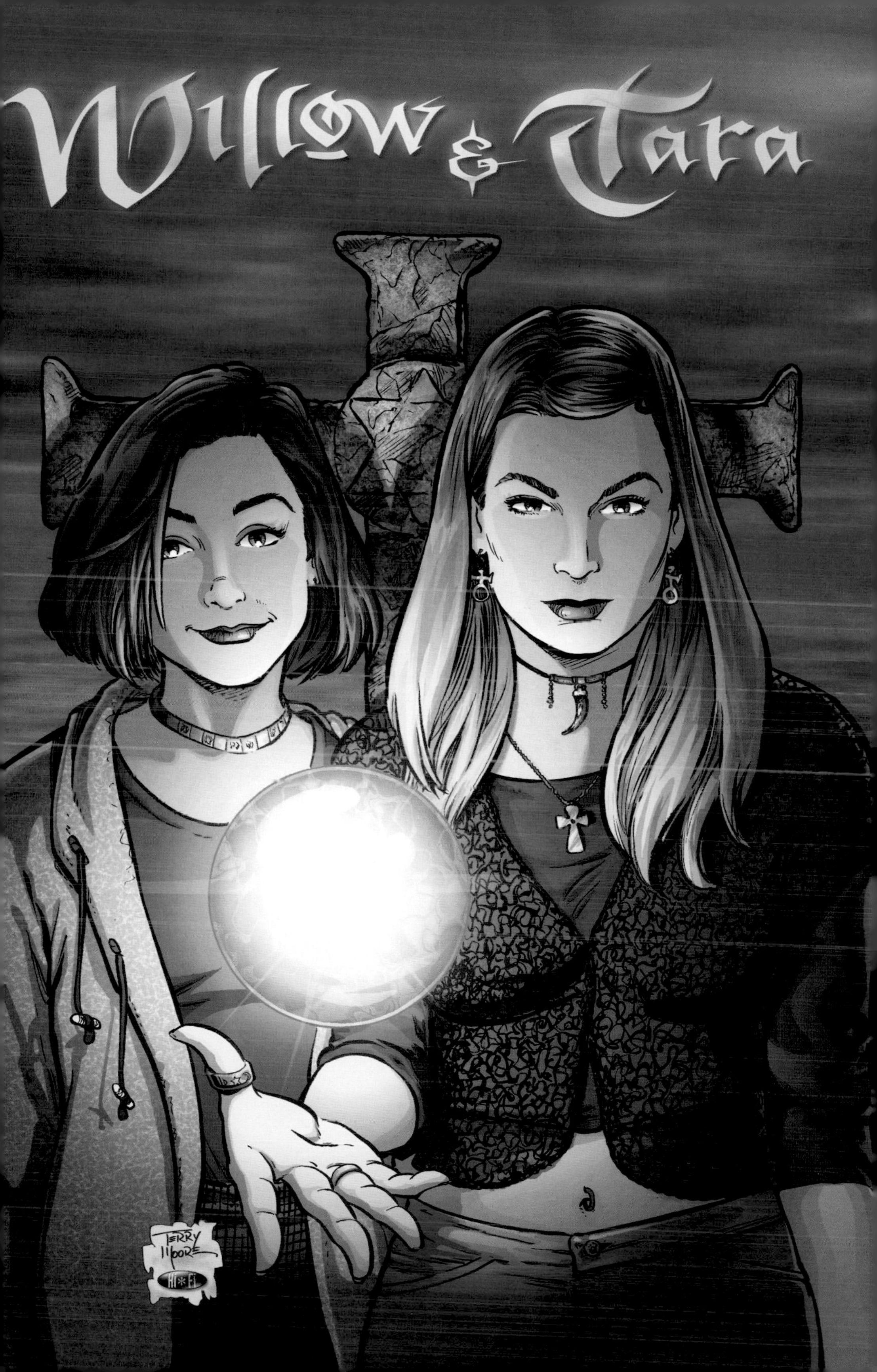
Willow & Tara
TERRY MOORE

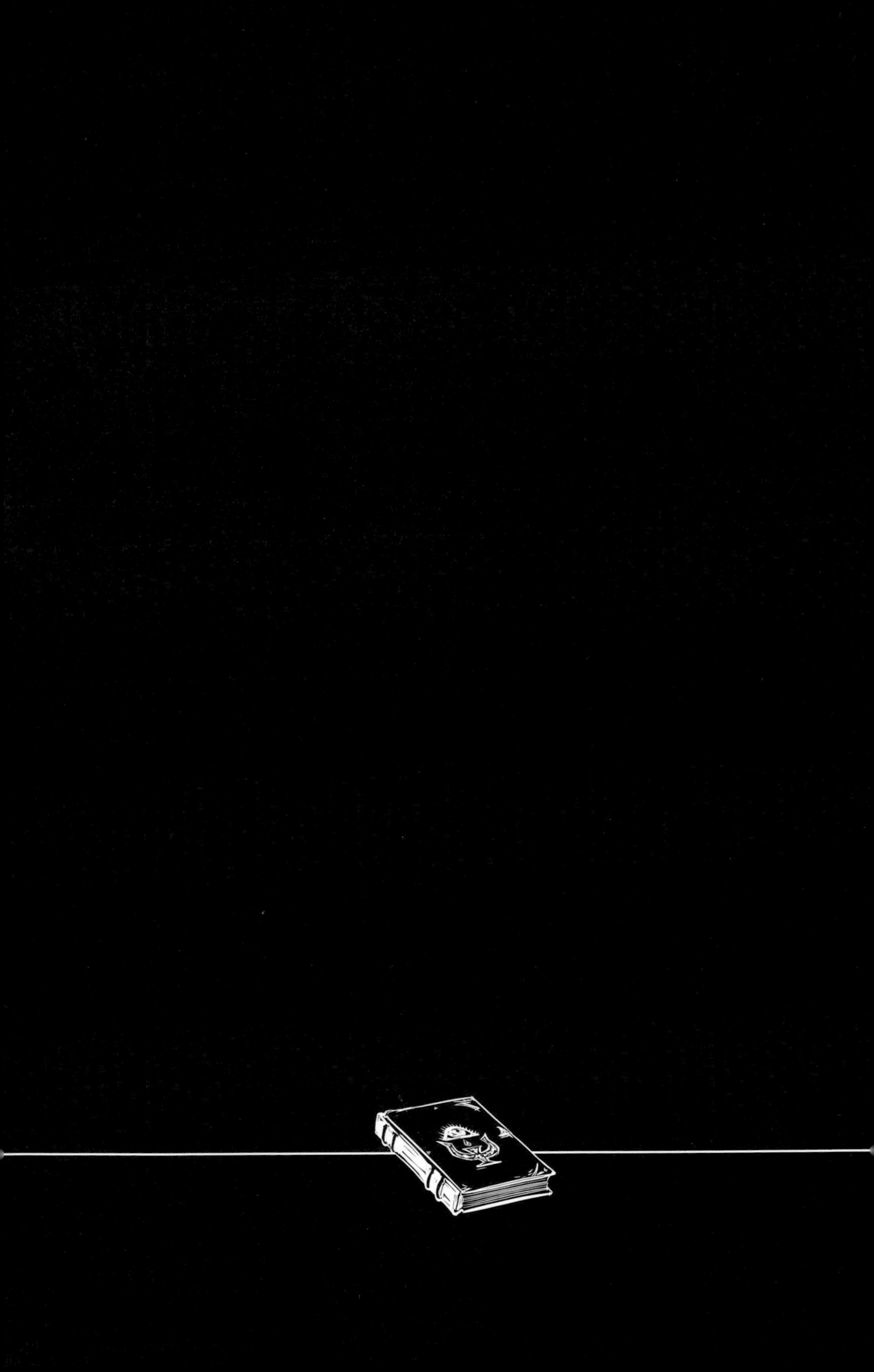

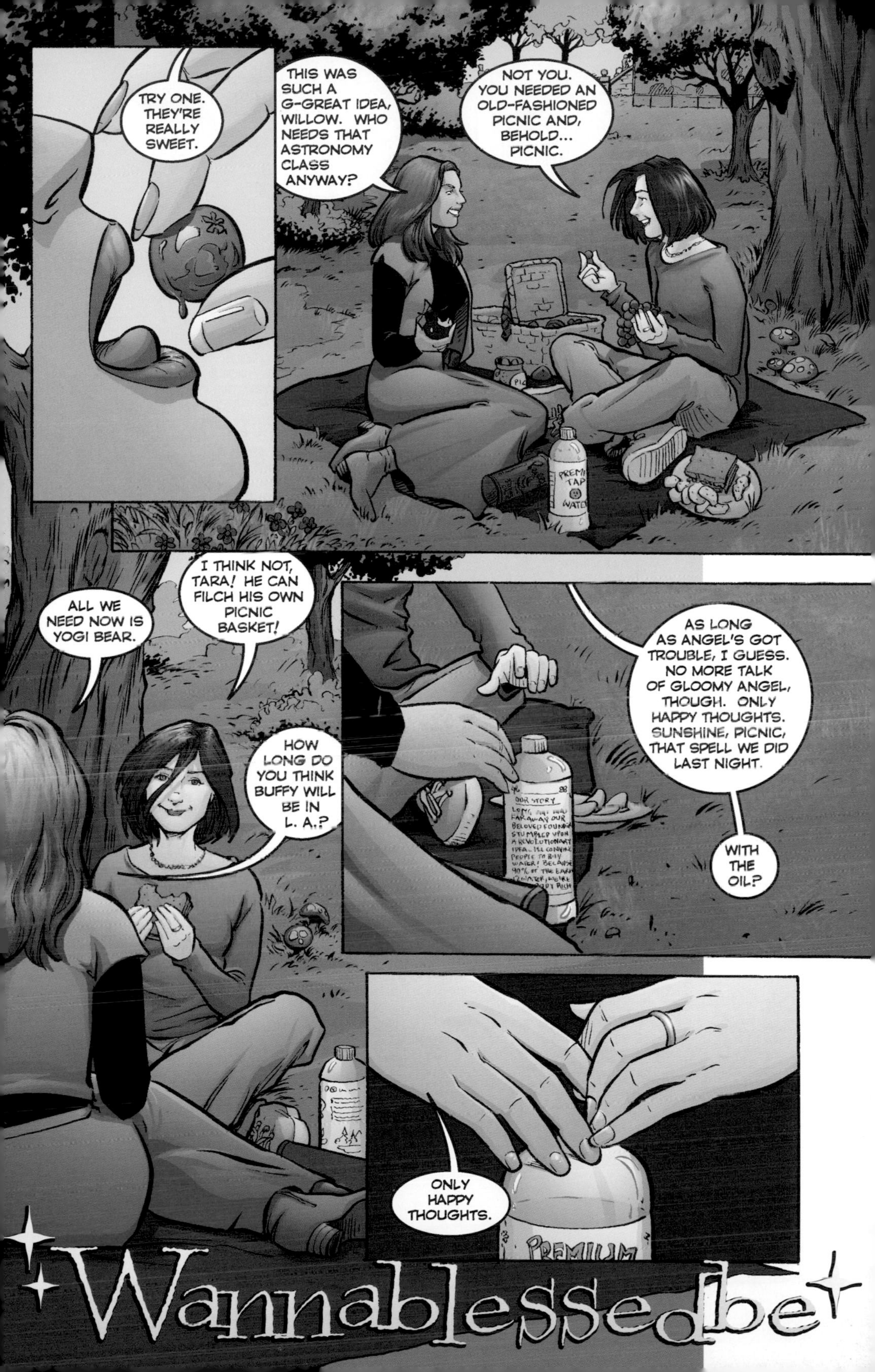
TRY ONE. THEY'RE REALLY SWEET.
THIS WAS SUCH A G-GREAT IDEA, WILLOW. WHO NEEDS THAT ASTRONOMY CLASS ANYWAY?
NOT YOU. YOU NEEDED AN OLD-FASHIONED PICNIC AND, BEHOLD... PICNIC.
ALL WE NEED NOW IS YOGI BEAR.
I THINK NOT, TARA! HE CAN FILCH HIS OWN PICNIC BASKET!
HOW LONG DO YOU THINK BUFFY WILL BE IN L. A.?
AS LONG AS ANGEL'S GOT TROUBLE, I GUESS. NO MORE TALK OF GLOOMY ANGEL, THOUGH. ONLY HAPPY THOUGHTS. SUNSHINE, PICNIC, THAT SPELL WE DID LAST NIGHT.
WITH THE OIL?
ONLY HAPPY THOUGHTS.
PREMIUM
Wannablessedbe

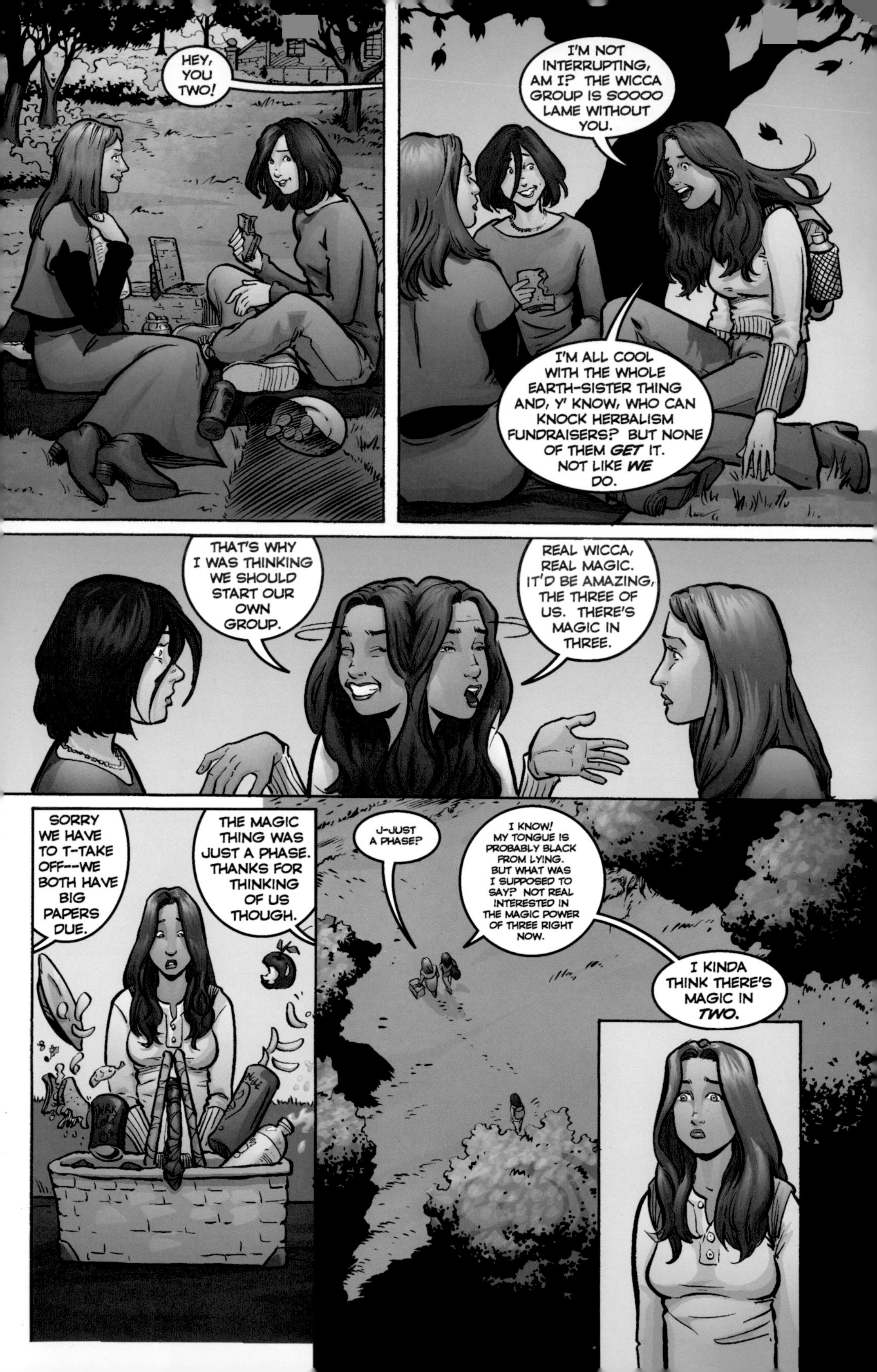
HEY, YOU TWO!
I'M NOT INTERRUPTING, AM I? THE WICCA GROUP IS SOOOO LAME WITHOUT YOU.
I'M ALL COOL WITH THE WHOLE EARTH-SISTER THING AND, Y' KNOW, WHO CAN KNOCK HERBALISM FUNDRAISERS? BUT NONE OF THEM GET IT. NOT LIKE WE DO.
THAT'S WHY I WAS THINKING WE SHOULD START OUR OWN GROUP.
REAL WICCA, REAL MAGIC. IT'D BE AMAZING, THE THREE OF US. THERE'S MAGIC IN THREE.
SORRY WE HAVE TO T-TAKE OFF--WE BOTH HAVE BIG PAPERS DUE.
THE MAGIC THING WAS JUST A PHASE. THANKS FOR THINKING OF US THOUGH.
J-JUST A PHASE?
I KNOW! MY TONGUE IS PROBABLY BLACK FROM LYING. BUT WHAT WAS I SUPPOSED TO SAY? NOT REAL INTERESTED IN THE MAGIC POWER OF THREE RIGHT NOW.
I KINDA THINK THERE'S MAGIC IN TWO.

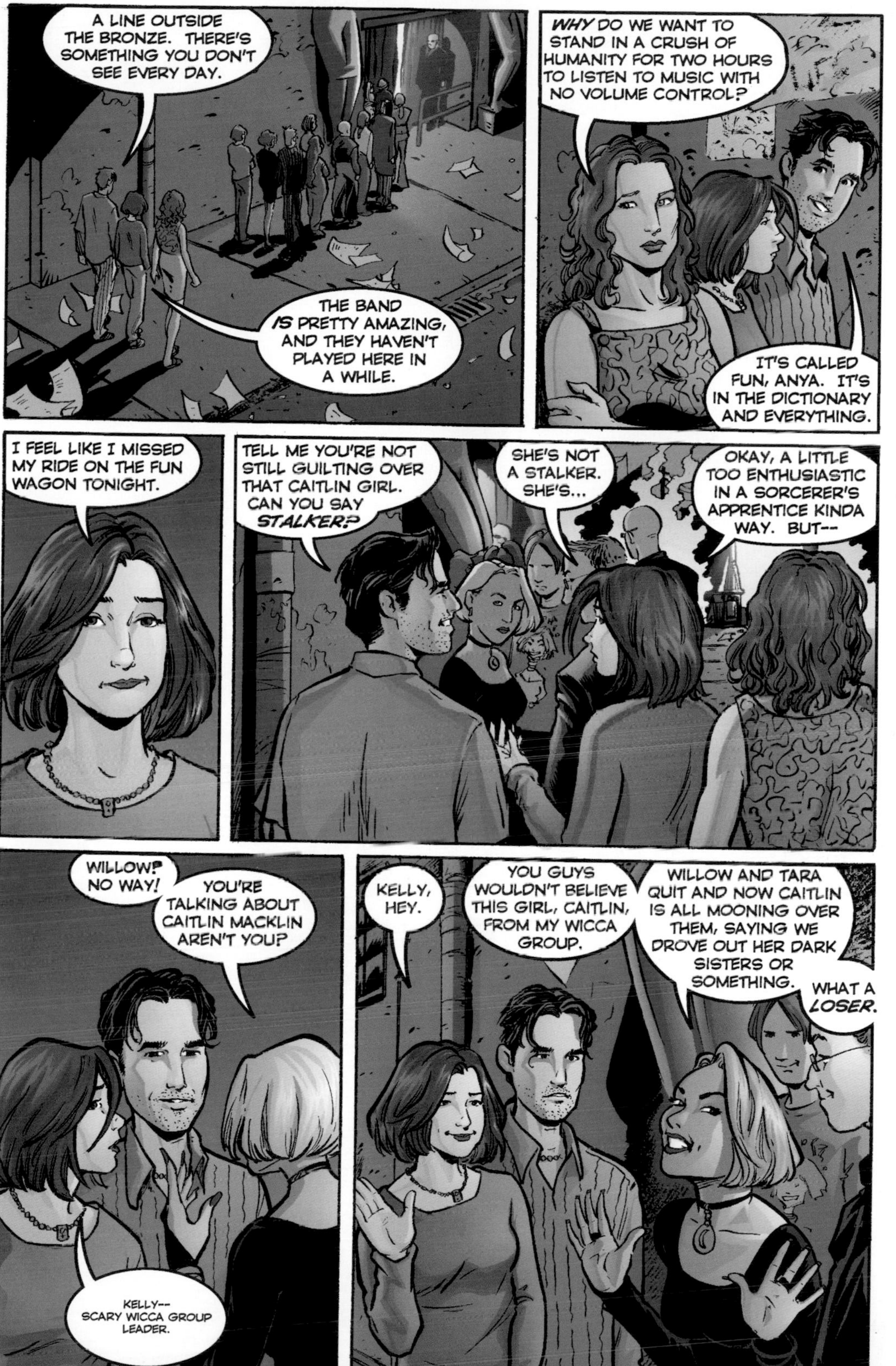
A LINE OUTSIDE THE BRONZE. THERE'S SOMETHING YOU DON'T SEE EVERY DAY.
THE BAND *IS* PRETTY AMAZING, AND THEY HAVEN'T PLAYED HERE IN A WHILE.
WHY DO WE WANT TO STAND IN A CRUSH OF HUMANITY FOR TWO HOURS TO LISTEN TO MUSIC WITH NO VOLUME CONTROL?
IT'S CALLED FUN, ANYA. IT'S IN THE DICTIONARY AND EVERYTHING.
I FEEL LIKE I MISSED MY RIDE ON THE FUN WAGON TONIGHT.
TELL ME YOU'RE NOT STILL GUILTING OVER THAT CAITLIN GIRL. CAN YOU SAY *STALKER?*
SHE'S NOT A STALKER. SHE'S...
OKAY, A LITTLE TOO ENTHUSIASTIC IN A SORCERER'S APPRENTICE KINDA WAY. BUT--
WILLOW! NO WAY!
YOU'RE TALKING ABOUT CAITLIN MACKLIN AREN'T YOU?
KELLY-- SCARY WICCA GROUP LEADER.
KELLY, HEY.
YOU GUYS WOULDN'T BELIEVE THIS GIRL, CAITLIN, FROM MY WICCA GROUP.
WILLOW AND TARA QUIT AND NOW CAITLIN IS ALL MOONING OVER THEM, SAYING WE DROVE OUT HER DARK SISTERS OR SOMETHING.
WHAT A *LOSER*.

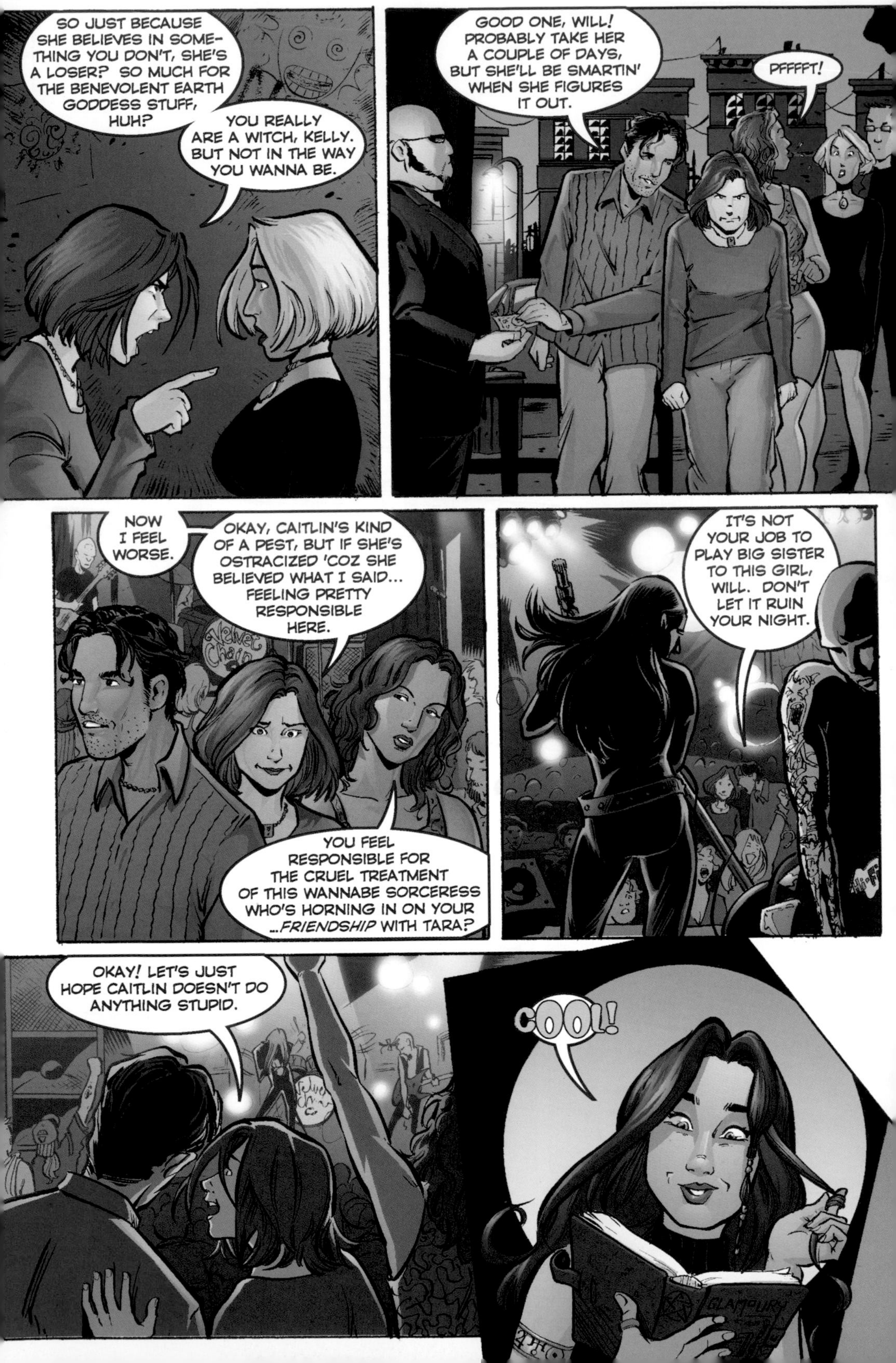
SO JUST BECAUSE SHE BELIEVES IN SOMETHING YOU DON'T, SHE'S A LOSER? SO MUCH FOR THE BENEVOLENT EARTH GODDESS STUFF, HUH?
YOU REALLY ARE A WITCH, KELLY. BUT NOT IN THE WAY YOU WANNA BE.
GOOD ONE, WILL! PROBABLY TAKE HER A COUPLE OF DAYS, BUT SHE'LL BE SMARTIN' WHEN SHE FIGURES IT OUT.
PFFFFT!
NOW I FEEL WORSE.
OKAY, CAITLIN'S KIND OF A PEST, BUT IF SHE'S OSTRACIZED 'COZ SHE BELIEVED WHAT I SAID... FEELING PRETTY RESPONSIBLE HERE.
YOU FEEL RESPONSIBLE FOR THE CRUEL TREATMENT OF THIS WANNABE SORCERESS WHO'S HORNING IN ON YOUR ...*FRIENDSHIP* WITH TARA?
IT'S NOT YOUR JOB TO PLAY BIG SISTER TO THIS GIRL, WILL. DON'T LET IT RUIN YOUR NIGHT.
OKAY! LET'S JUST HOPE CAITLIN DOESN'T DO ANYTHING STUPID.
COOL!
GLAMOURY

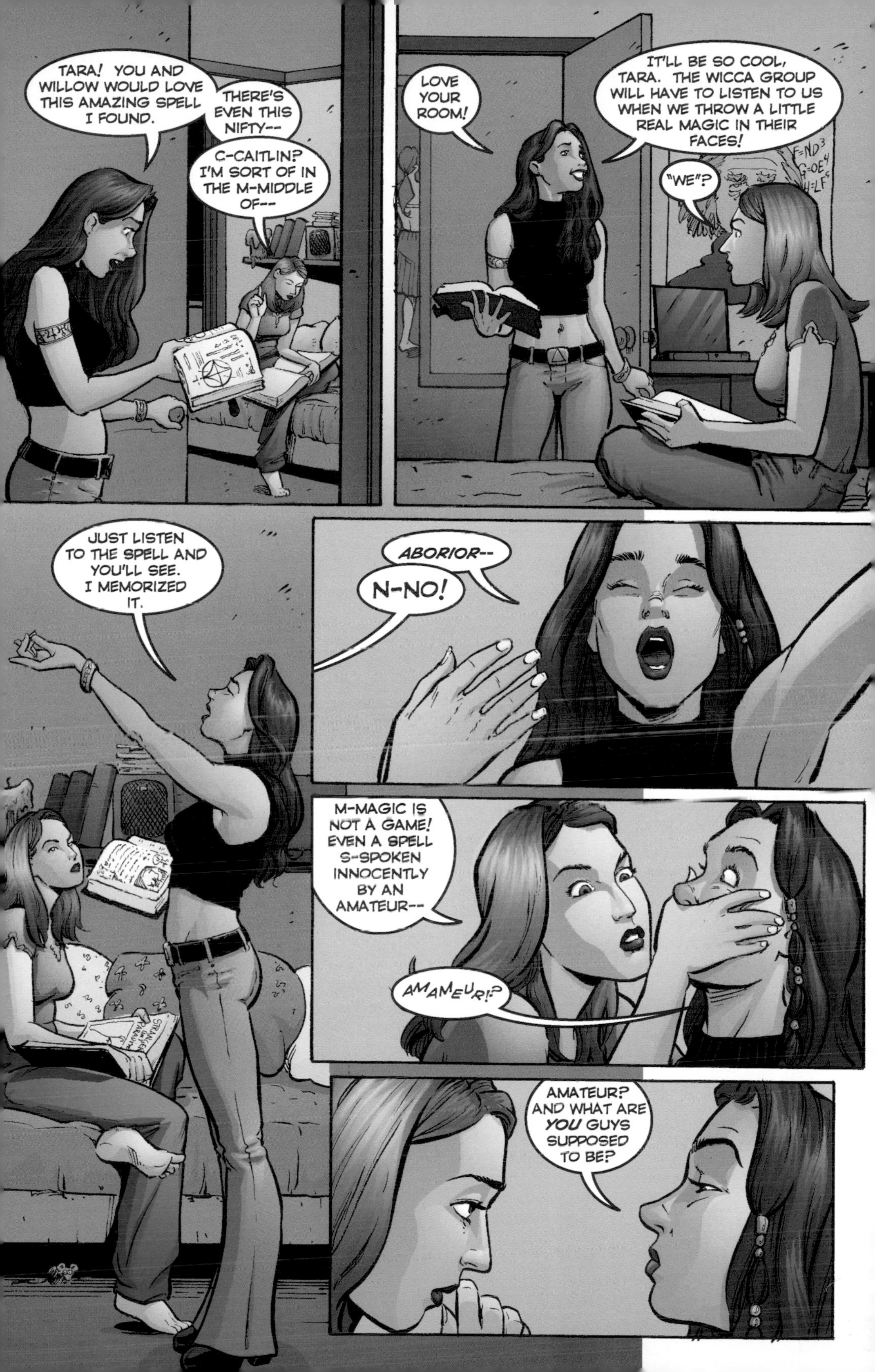
TARA! YOU AND WILLOW WOULD LOVE THIS AMAZING SPELL I FOUND.
THERE'S EVEN THIS NIFTY--
C-CAITLIN? I'M SORT OF IN THE M-MIDDLE OF--
LOVE YOUR ROOM!
IT'LL BE SO COOL, TARA. THE WICCA GROUP WILL HAVE TO LISTEN TO US WHEN WE THROW A LITTLE REAL MAGIC IN THEIR FACES!
"WE"?
JUST LISTEN TO THE SPELL AND YOU'LL SEE. I MEMORIZED IT.
ABORIOR--
N-NO!
M-MAGIC IS NOT A GAME! EVEN A SPELL S-SPOKEN INNOCENTLY BY AN AMATEUR--
AMAMEUR!?
AMATEUR? AND WHAT ARE YOU GUYS SUPPOSED TO BE?

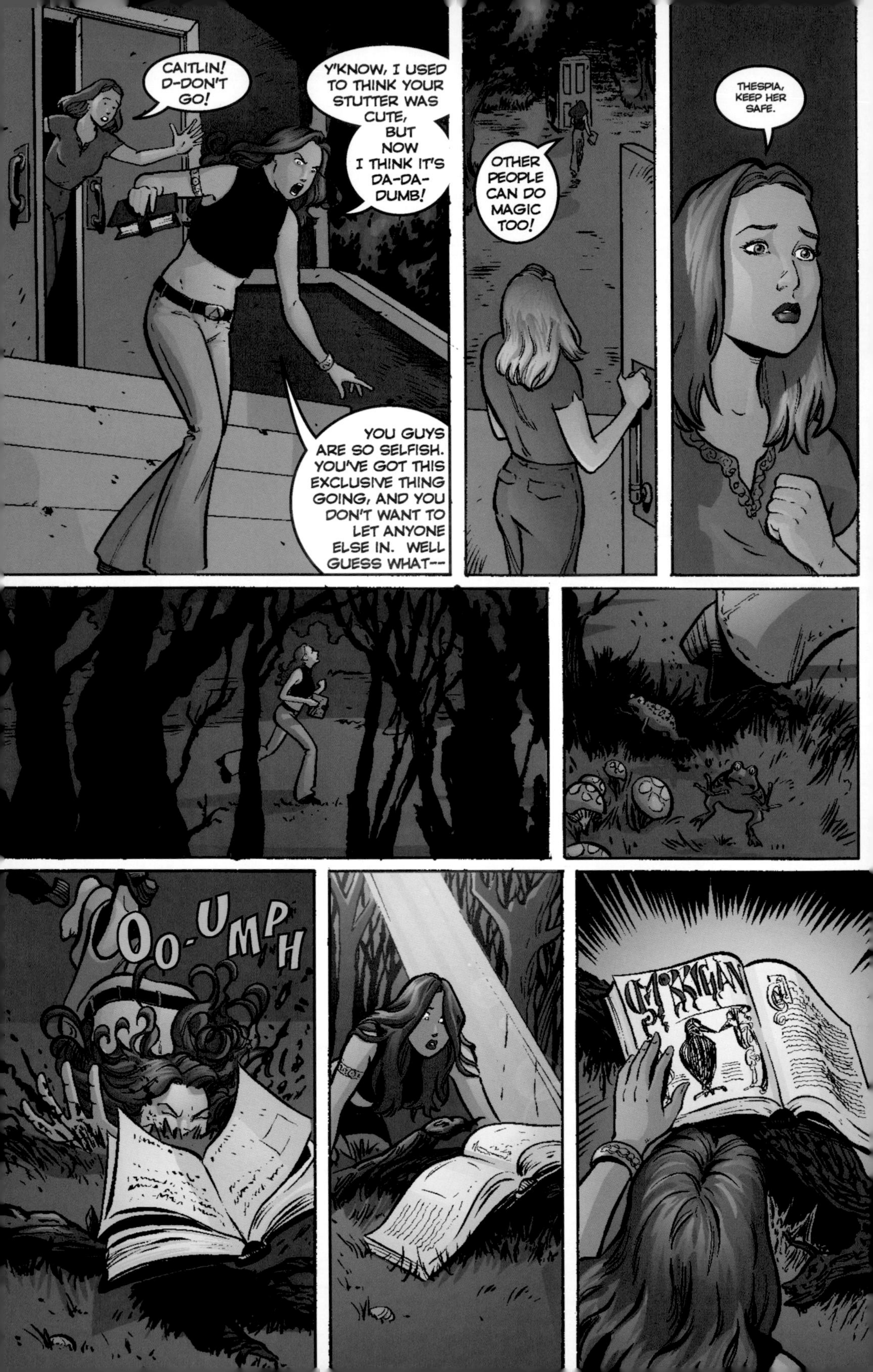
CAITLIN! D-DON'T GO!
Y'KNOW, I USED TO THINK YOUR STUTTER WAS CUTE,
BUT NOW I THINK IT'S DA-DA-DUMB!
YOU GUYS ARE SO SELFISH. YOU'VE GOT THIS EXCLUSIVE THING GOING, AND YOU DON'T WANT TO LET ANYONE ELSE IN. WELL GUESS WHAT--
OTHER PEOPLE CAN DO MAGIC TOO!
THESPIA, KEEP HER SAFE.
OO-UMPH

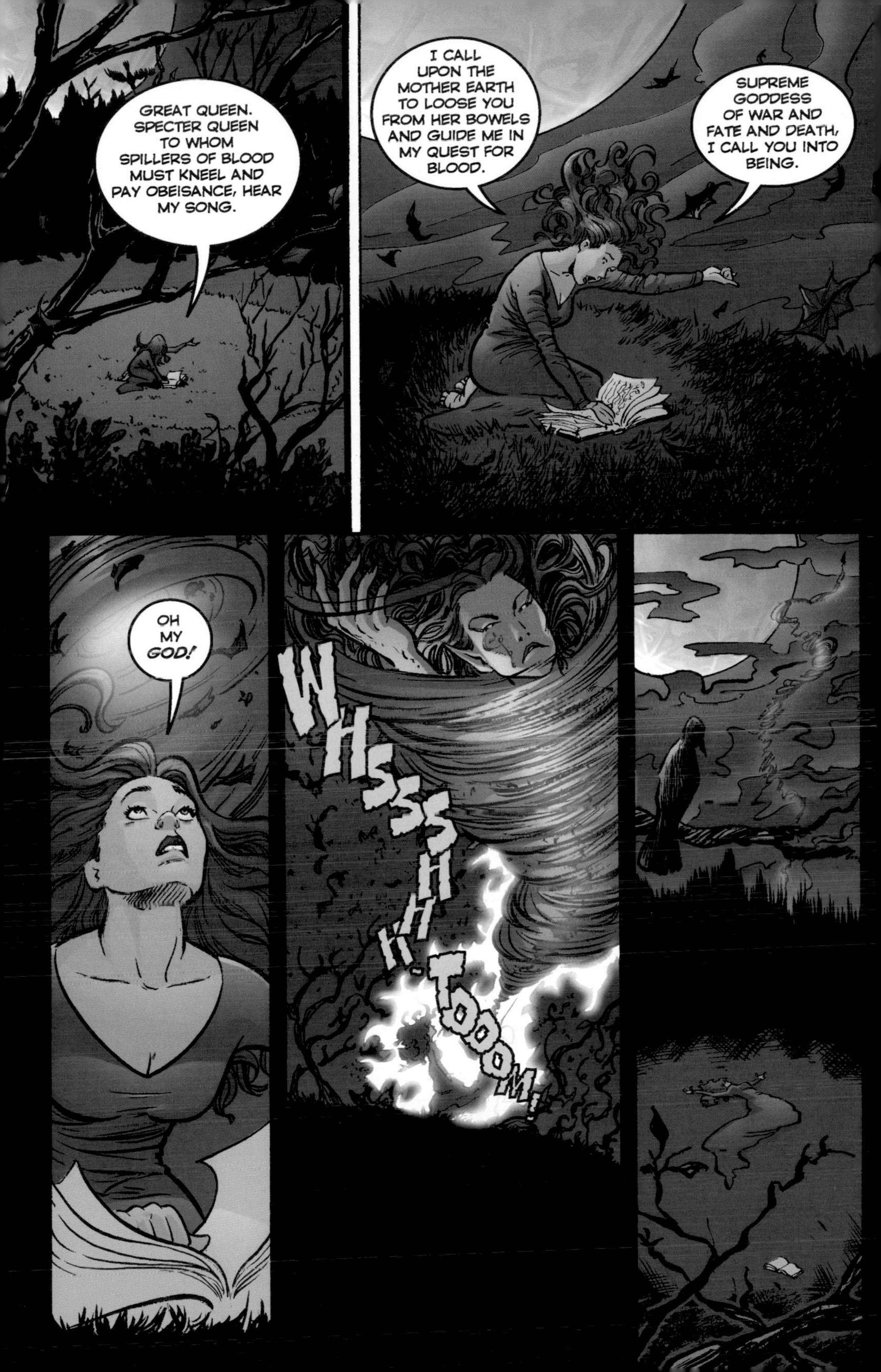
GREAT QUEEN. SPECTER QUEEN TO WHOM SPILLERS OF BLOOD MUST KNEEL AND PAY OBEISANCE, HEAR MY SONG.
I CALL UPON THE MOTHER EARTH TO LOOSE YOU FROM HER BOWELS AND GUIDE ME IN MY QUEST FOR BLOOD.
SUPREME GODDESS OF WAR AND FATE AND DEATH, I CALL YOU INTO BEING.
OH MY GOD!
WHSSSHHHH-TOOOM!

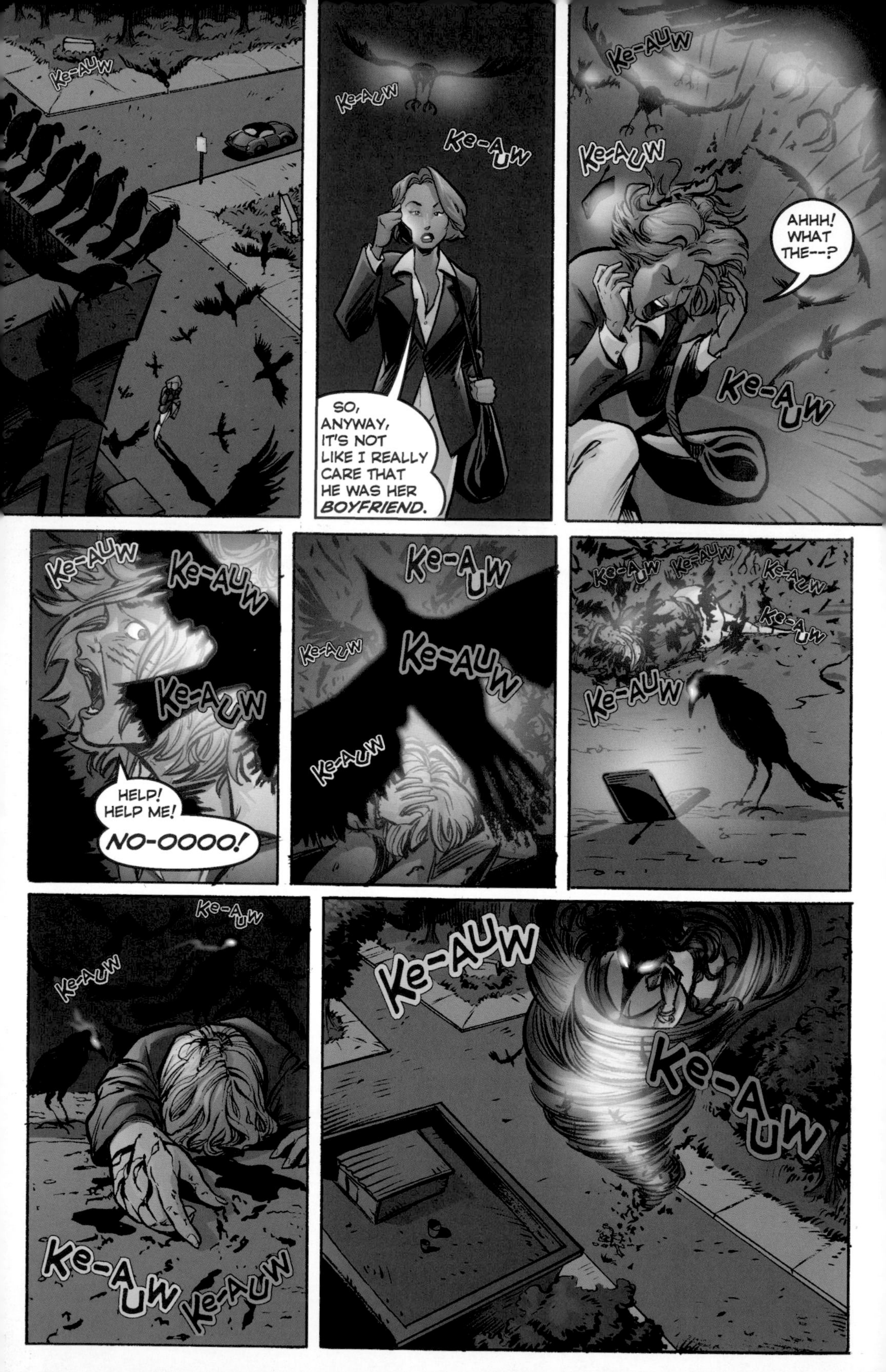
KE-AUW
KE-AUW
KE-AUW
SO, ANYWAY, IT'S NOT LIKE I REALLY CARE THAT HE WAS HER BOYFRIEND.
KE-AUW
KE-AUW
AHHH! WHAT THE--?
KE-AUW
KE-AUW
KE-AUW
KE-AUW
HELP! HELP ME!
NO-OOOO!
KE-AUW
KE-AUW
KE-AUW
KE-AUW
KE-AUW
KE-AUW
KE-AUW
KE-AUW
KE-AUW
KE-AUW
KE-AUW
KE-AUW
KE-AUW
KE-AUW
KE-AUW

SEE YOU AT FEM PSYCH.

LATER.

NORTH CAMPUS

KE-AUW

KE-AUW

KE-AUW

AAGGHHHH!

AIIEEE--!

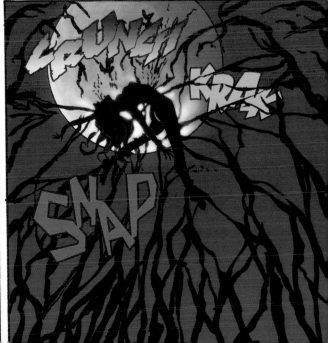

CRUNCH

KRA

SMAP

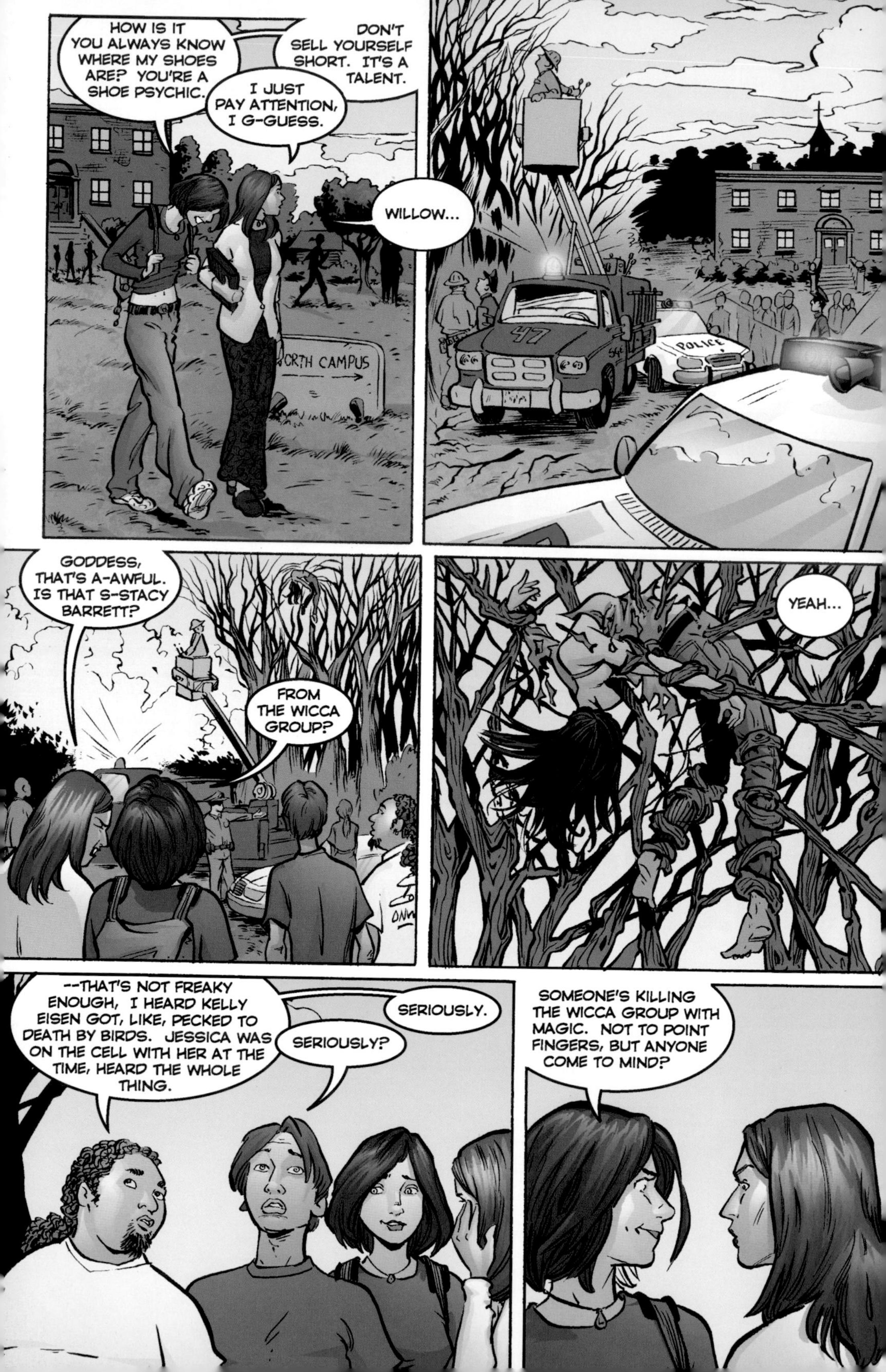
HOW IS IT YOU ALWAYS KNOW WHERE MY SHOES ARE? YOU'RE A SHOE PSYCHIC.
I JUST PAY ATTENTION, I G-GUESS.
DON'T SELL YOURSELF SHORT. IT'S A TALENT.
ORTH CAMPUS
WILLOW...
POLICE
GODDESS, THAT'S A-AWFUL. IS THAT S-STACY BARRETT?
FROM THE WICCA GROUP?
YEAH...
--THAT'S NOT FREAKY ENOUGH, I HEARD KELLY EISEN GOT, LIKE, PECKED TO DEATH BY BIRDS. JESSICA WAS ON THE CELL WITH HER AT THE TIME, HEARD THE WHOLE THING.
SERIOUSLY?
SERIOUSLY.
SOMEONE'S KILLING THE WICCA GROUP WITH MAGIC. NOT TO POINT FINGERS, BUT ANYONE COME TO MIND?

CAITLIN...?

YOU THINK WE SHOULD COME BACK LATER?

SNiff, UFFF-Uhh

I THINK NOT.

CAITLIN, WE KNOW SOMETHING HAPPENED.

SOMETHING BAD.

I DIDN'T... I NEVER MEANT FOR... *HER* TO COME...

IT WAS JUST...

...AN ACCIDENT.

OH, CAITLIN...

NOT MORRIGAN.

PLEASE DON'T TELL ME YOU DID THAT SPELL WITHOUT ANY CHARMS OR PROTECTIVE WARDS?

UM... WHAT'S A WARD?

OH MY GODDESS.

WE SHOULD TALK. OUT HERE. MUCH MORE... SPACIOUS IN THE HALLWAY.

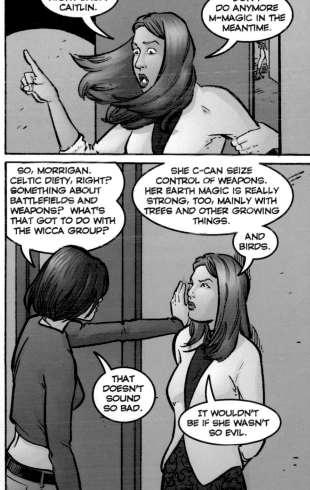

WE'LL BE RIGHT BACK, CAITLIN.

DON'T DO ANYMORE M-MAGIC IN THE MEANTIME.

SO, MORRIGAN. CELTIC DIETY, RIGHT? SOMETHING ABOUT BATTLEFIELDS AND WEAPONS? WHAT'S THAT GOT TO DO WITH THE WICCA GROUP?

SHE C-CAN SEIZE CONTROL OF WEAPONS. HER EARTH MAGIC IS REALLY STRONG, TOO, MAINLY WITH TREES AND OTHER GROWING THINGS.

AND BIRDS.

THAT DOESN'T SOUND SO BAD.

IT WOULDN'T BE IF SHE WASN'T SO EVIL.

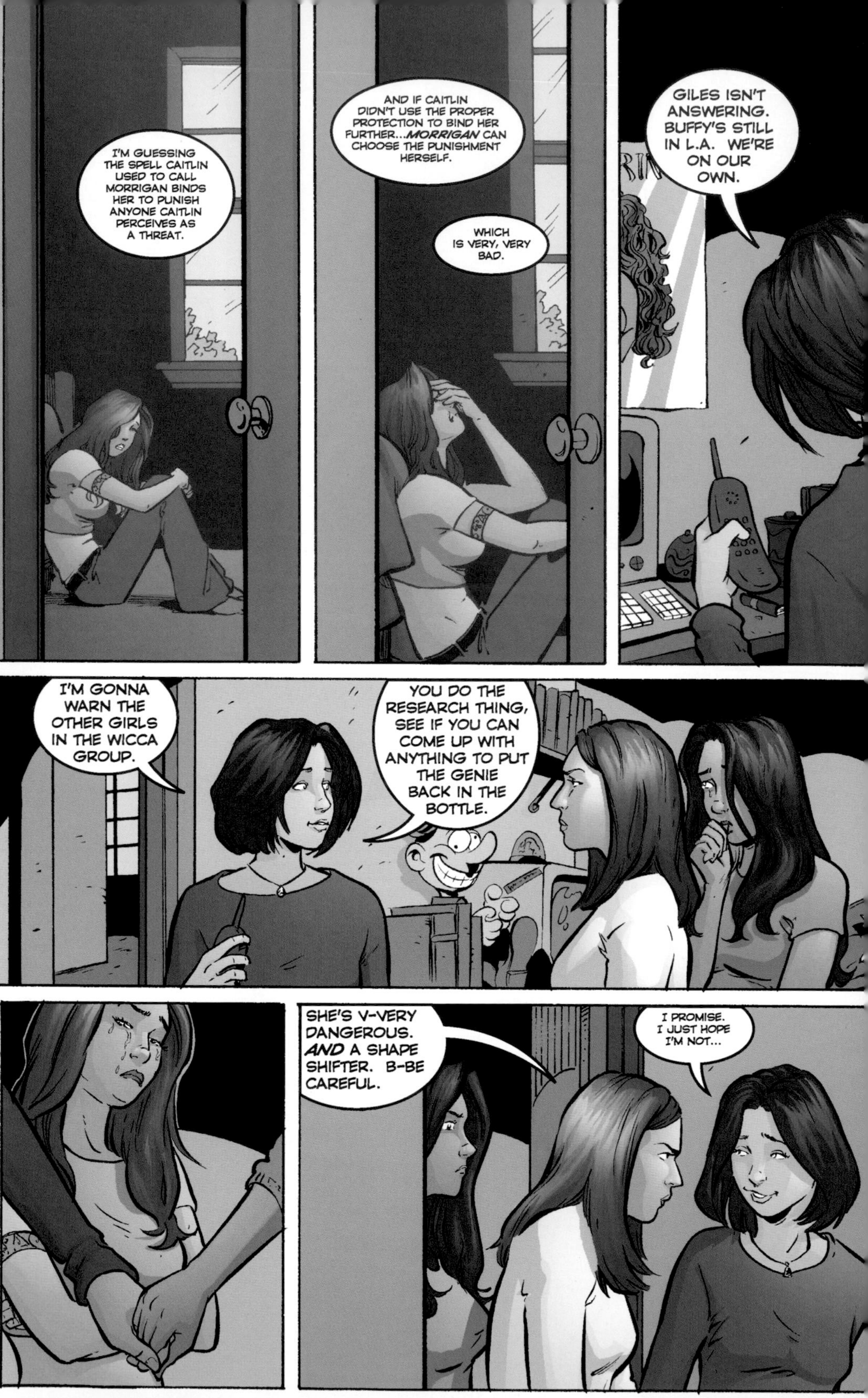
I'M GUESSING THE SPELL CAITLIN USED TO CALL MORRIGAN BINDS HER TO PUNISH ANYONE CAITLIN PERCEIVES AS A THREAT.
AND IF CAITLIN DIDN'T USE THE PROPER PROTECTION TO BIND HER FURTHER...MORRIGAN CAN CHOOSE THE PUNISHMENT HERSELF.
WHICH IS VERY, VERY BAD.
GILES ISN'T ANSWERING. BUFFY'S STILL IN L.A. WE'RE ON OUR OWN.
I'M GONNA WARN THE OTHER GIRLS IN THE WICCA GROUP.
YOU DO THE RESEARCH THING, SEE IF YOU CAN COME UP WITH ANYTHING TO PUT THE GENIE BACK IN THE BOTTLE.
SHE'S V-VERY DANGEROUS. AND A SHAPE SHIFTER. B-BE CAREFUL.
I PROMISE. I JUST HOPE I'M NOT...

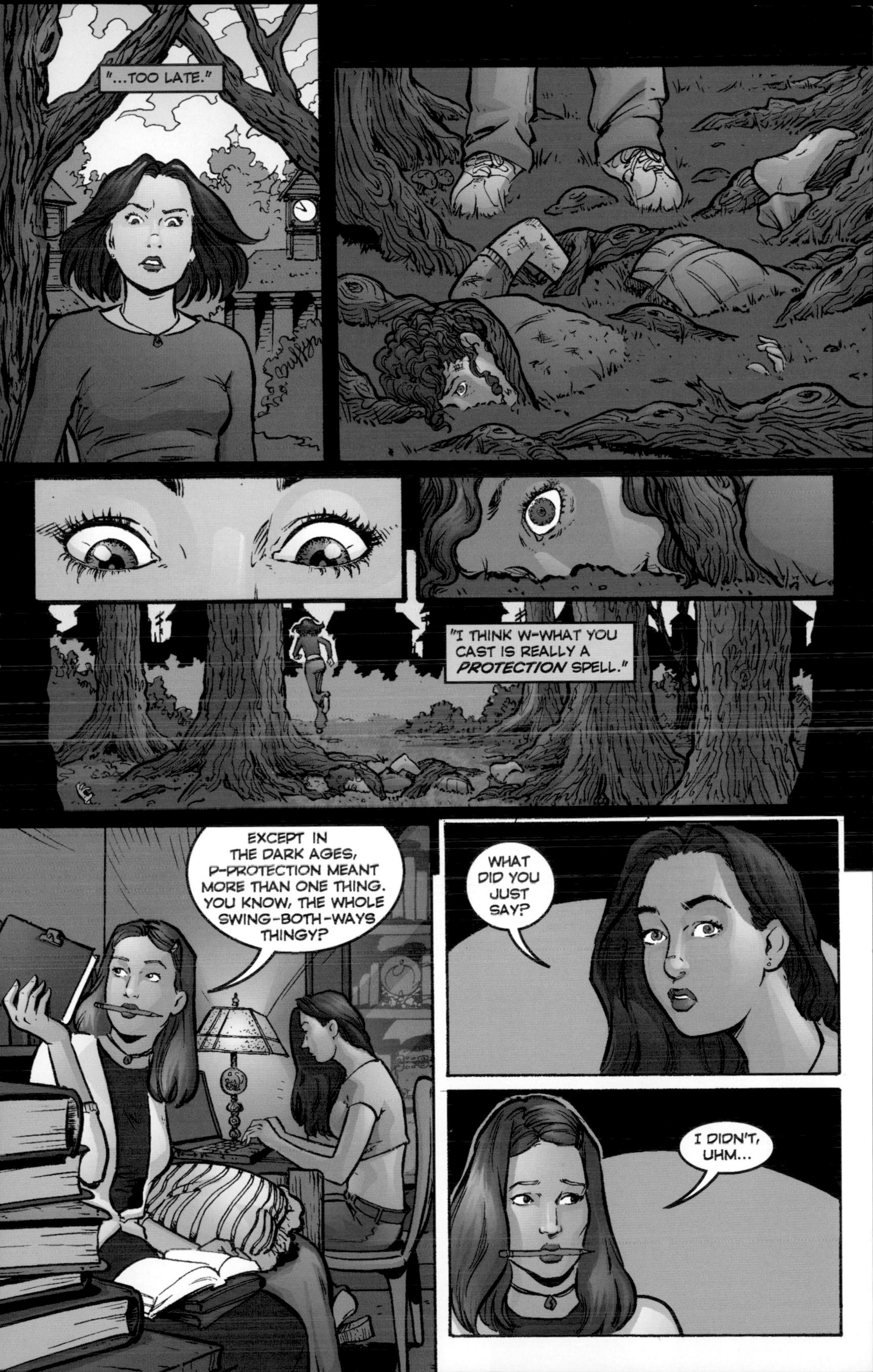
"...TOO LATE."
"I THINK W-WHAT YOU CAST IS REALLY A *PROTECTION* SPELL."
EXCEPT IN THE DARK AGES, P-PROTECTION MEANT MORE THAN ONE THING. YOU KNOW, THE WHOLE SWING-BOTH-WAYS THINGY?
WHAT DID YOU JUST SAY?
I DIDN'T, UHM...

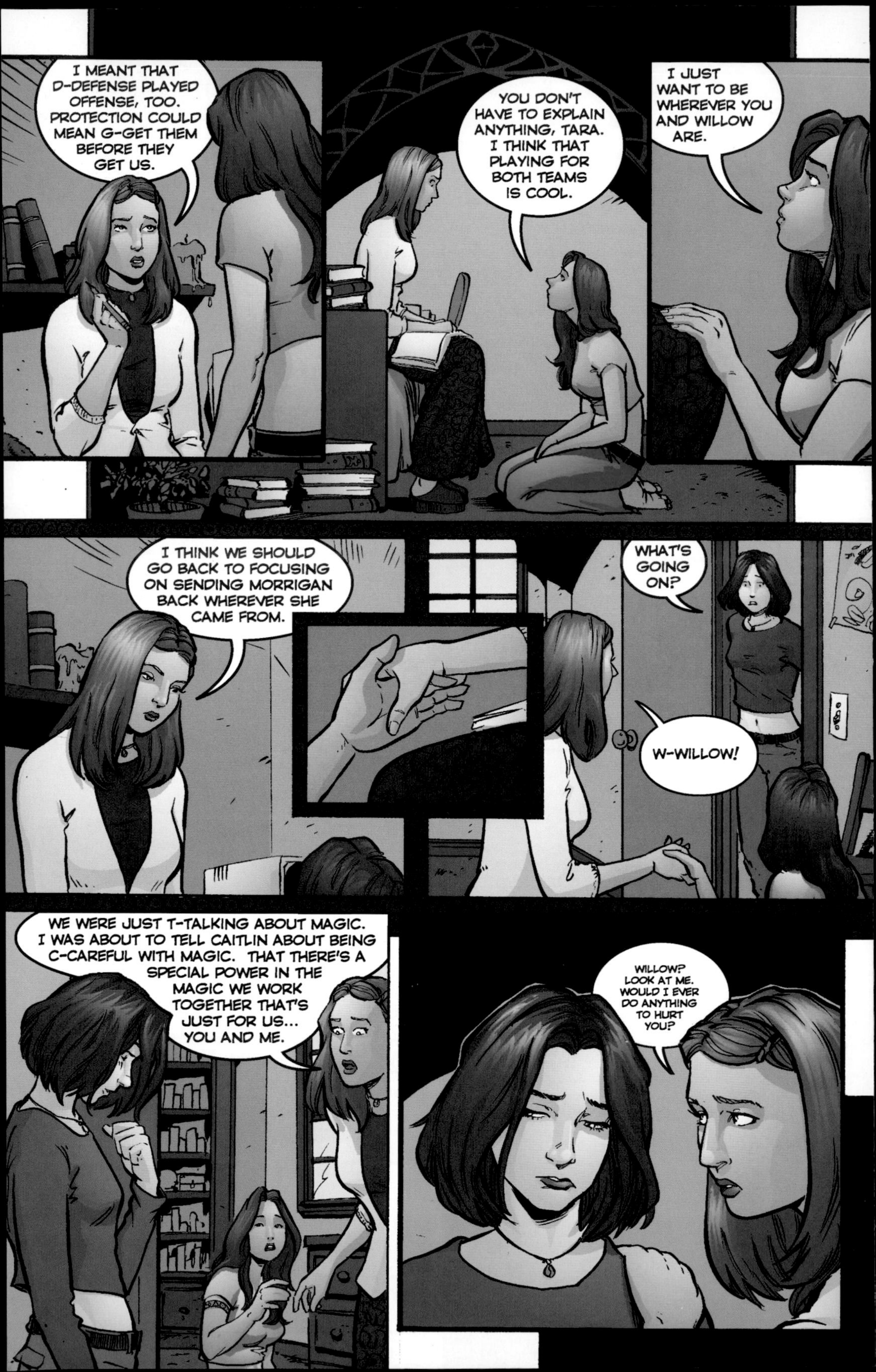
I MEANT THAT D-DEFENSE PLAYED OFFENSE, TOO. PROTECTION COULD MEAN G-GET THEM BEFORE THEY GET US.
YOU DON'T HAVE TO EXPLAIN ANYTHING, TARA. I THINK THAT PLAYING FOR BOTH TEAMS IS COOL.
I JUST WANT TO BE WHEREVER YOU AND WILLOW ARE.
I THINK WE SHOULD GO BACK TO FOCUSING ON SENDING MORRIGAN BACK WHEREVER SHE CAME FROM.
WHAT'S GOING ON?
W-WILLOW!
WE WERE JUST T-TALKING ABOUT MAGIC. I WAS ABOUT TO TELL CAITLIN ABOUT BEING C-CAREFUL WITH MAGIC. THAT THERE'S A SPECIAL POWER IN THE MAGIC WE WORK TOGETHER THAT'S JUST FOR US... YOU AND ME.
WILLOW? LOOK AT ME. WOULD I EVER DO ANYTHING TO HURT YOU?

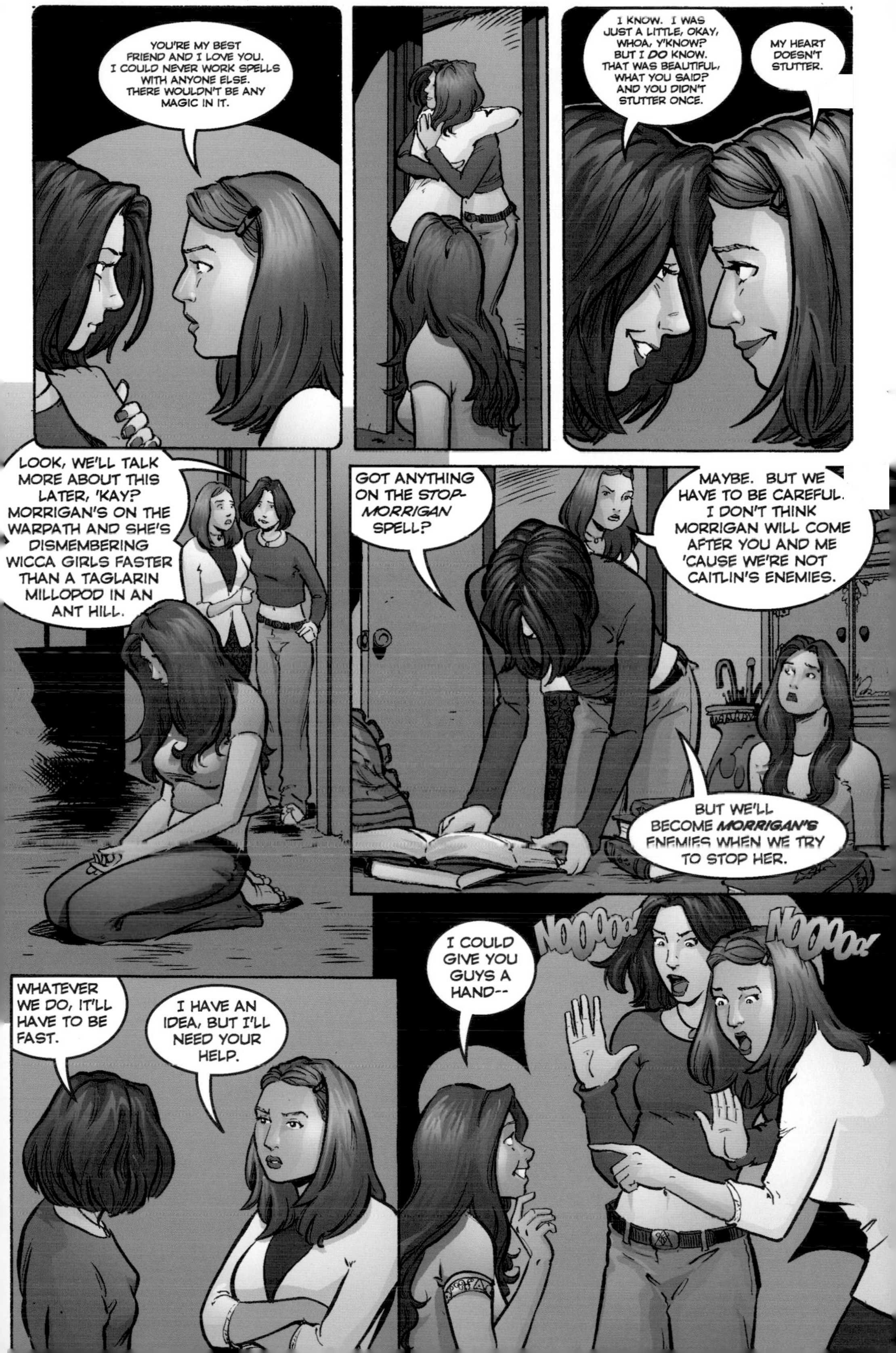
YOU'RE MY BEST FRIEND AND I LOVE YOU. I COULD NEVER WORK SPELLS WITH ANYONE ELSE. THERE WOULDN'T BE ANY MAGIC IN IT.
I KNOW. I WAS JUST A LITTLE, OKAY, WHOA, Y'KNOW? BUT I DO KNOW. THAT WAS BEAUTIFUL, WHAT YOU SAID? AND YOU DIDN'T STUTTER ONCE.
MY HEART DOESN'T STUTTER.
LOOK, WE'LL TALK MORE ABOUT THIS LATER, 'KAY? MORRIGAN'S ON THE WARPATH AND SHE'S DISMEMBERING WICCA GIRLS FASTER THAN A TAGLARIN MILLOPOD IN AN ANT HILL.
GOT ANYTHING ON THE STOP-MORRIGAN SPELL?
MAYBE. BUT WE HAVE TO BE CAREFUL. I DON'T THINK MORRIGAN WILL COME AFTER YOU AND ME 'CAUSE WE'RE NOT CAITLIN'S ENEMIES.
BUT WE'LL BECOME MORRIGAN'S ENEMIES WHEN WE TRY TO STOP HER.
WHATEVER WE DO, IT'LL HAVE TO BE FAST.
I HAVE AN IDEA, BUT I'LL NEED YOUR HELP.
I COULD GIVE YOU GUYS A HAND--
NOOOOO!
NOOOOO!

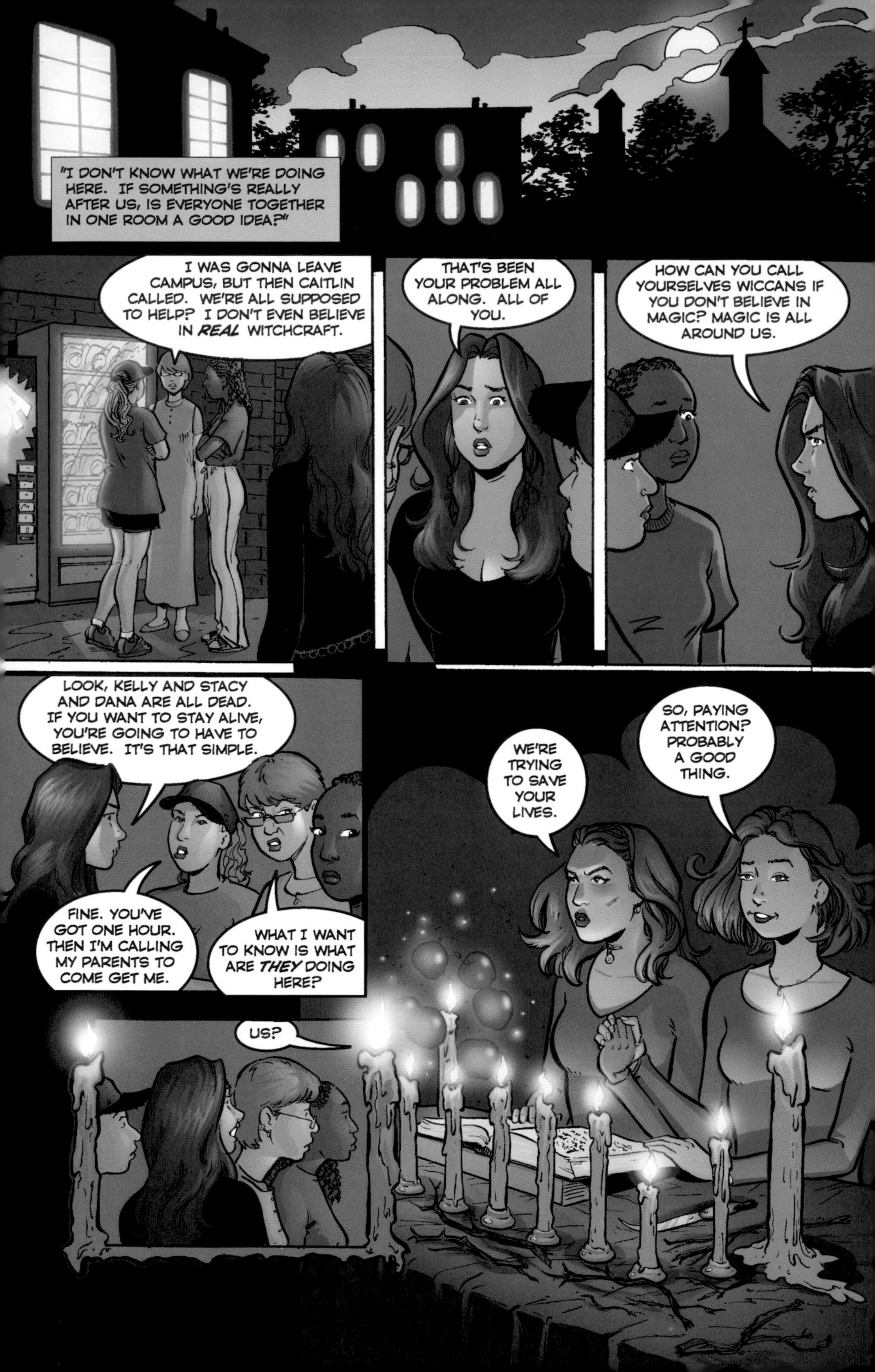
"I DON'T KNOW WHAT WE'RE DOING HERE. IF SOMETHING'S REALLY AFTER US, IS EVERYONE TOGETHER IN ONE ROOM A GOOD IDEA?"
I WAS GONNA LEAVE CAMPUS, BUT THEN CAITLIN CALLED. WE'RE ALL SUPPOSED TO HELP? I DON'T EVEN BELIEVE IN *REAL* WITCHCRAFT.
THAT'S BEEN YOUR PROBLEM ALL ALONG. ALL OF YOU.
HOW CAN YOU CALL YOURSELVES WICCANS IF YOU DON'T BELIEVE IN MAGIC? MAGIC IS ALL AROUND US.
LOOK, KELLY AND STACY AND DANA ARE ALL DEAD. IF YOU WANT TO STAY ALIVE, YOU'RE GOING TO HAVE TO BELIEVE. IT'S THAT SIMPLE.
FINE. YOU'VE GOT ONE HOUR. THEN I'M CALLING MY PARENTS TO COME GET ME.
WHAT I WANT TO KNOW IS WHAT ARE *THEY* DOING HERE?
US?
WE'RE TRYING TO SAVE YOUR LIVES.
SO, PAYING ATTENTION? PROBABLY A GOOD THING.

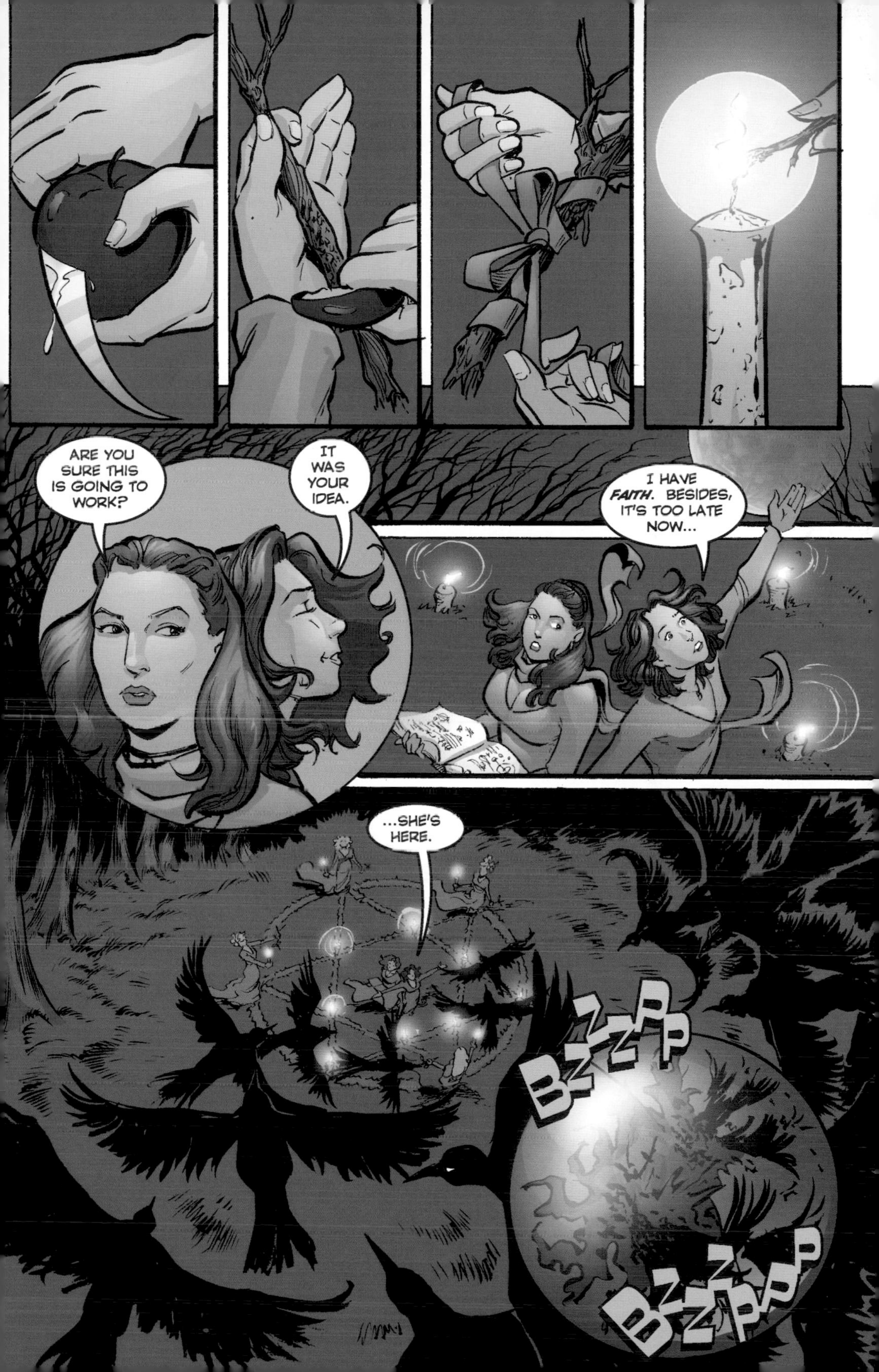

ARE YOU SURE THIS IS GOING TO WORK?
IT WAS YOUR IDEA.
I HAVE *FAITH*. BESIDES, IT'S TOO LATE NOW...
...SHE'S HERE.
BZZZPP
BZZZPPP

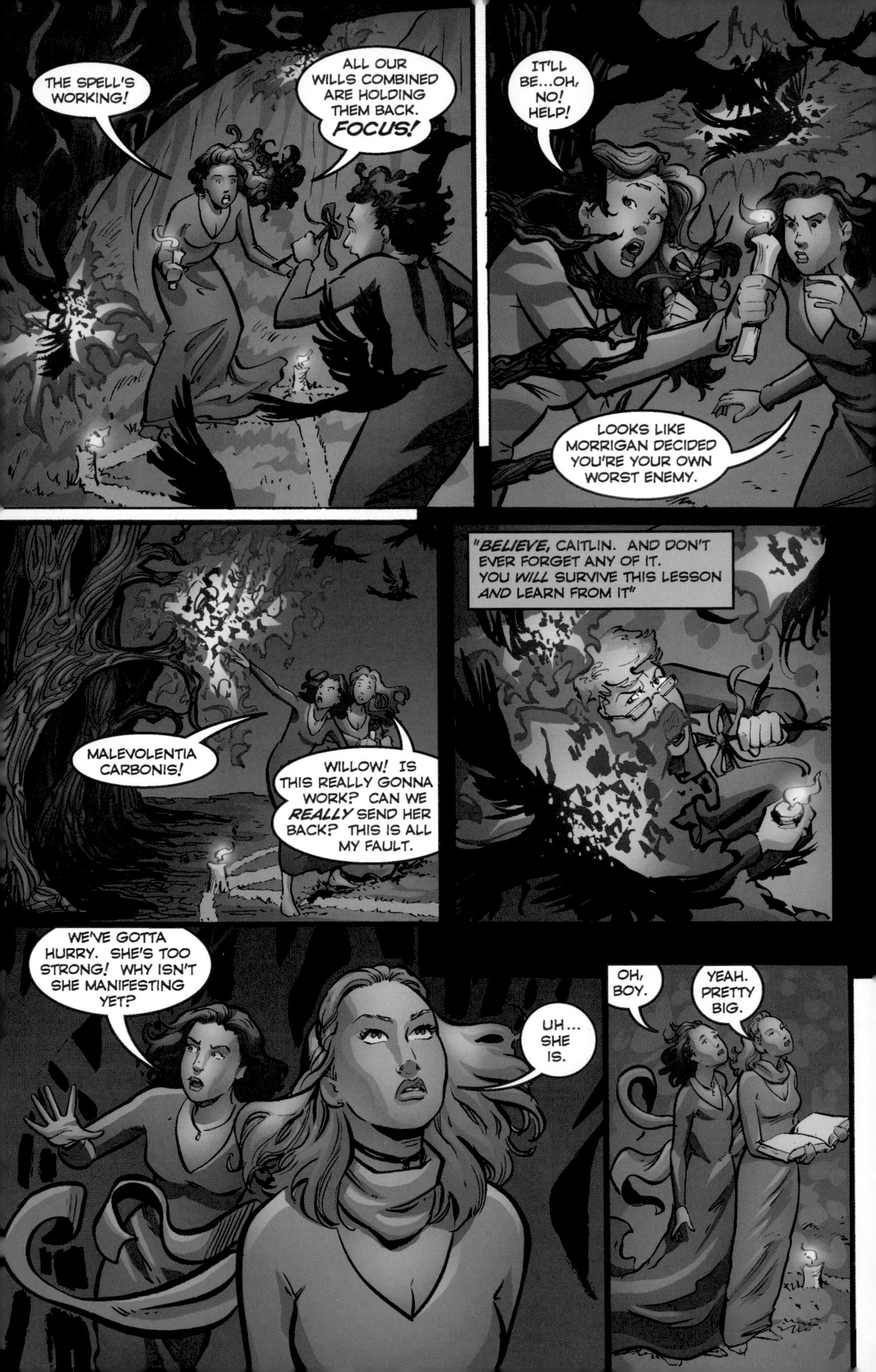
THE SPELL'S WORKING!
ALL OUR WILLS COMBINED ARE HOLDING THEM BACK. *FOCUS!*
IT'LL BE...OH, NO! HELP!
LOOKS LIKE MORRIGAN DECIDED YOU'RE YOUR OWN WORST ENEMY.
MALEVOLENTIA CARBONIS!
WILLOW! IS THIS REALLY GONNA WORK? CAN WE *REALLY* SEND HER BACK? THIS IS ALL MY FAULT.
"*BELIEVE,* CAITLIN. AND DON'T EVER FORGET ANY OF IT. YOU *WILL* SURVIVE THIS LESSON *AND* LEARN FROM IT"
WE'VE GOTTA HURRY. SHE'S TOO STRONG! WHY ISN'T SHE MANIFESTING YET?
UH... SHE IS.
OH, BOY.
YEAH. PRETTY BIG.

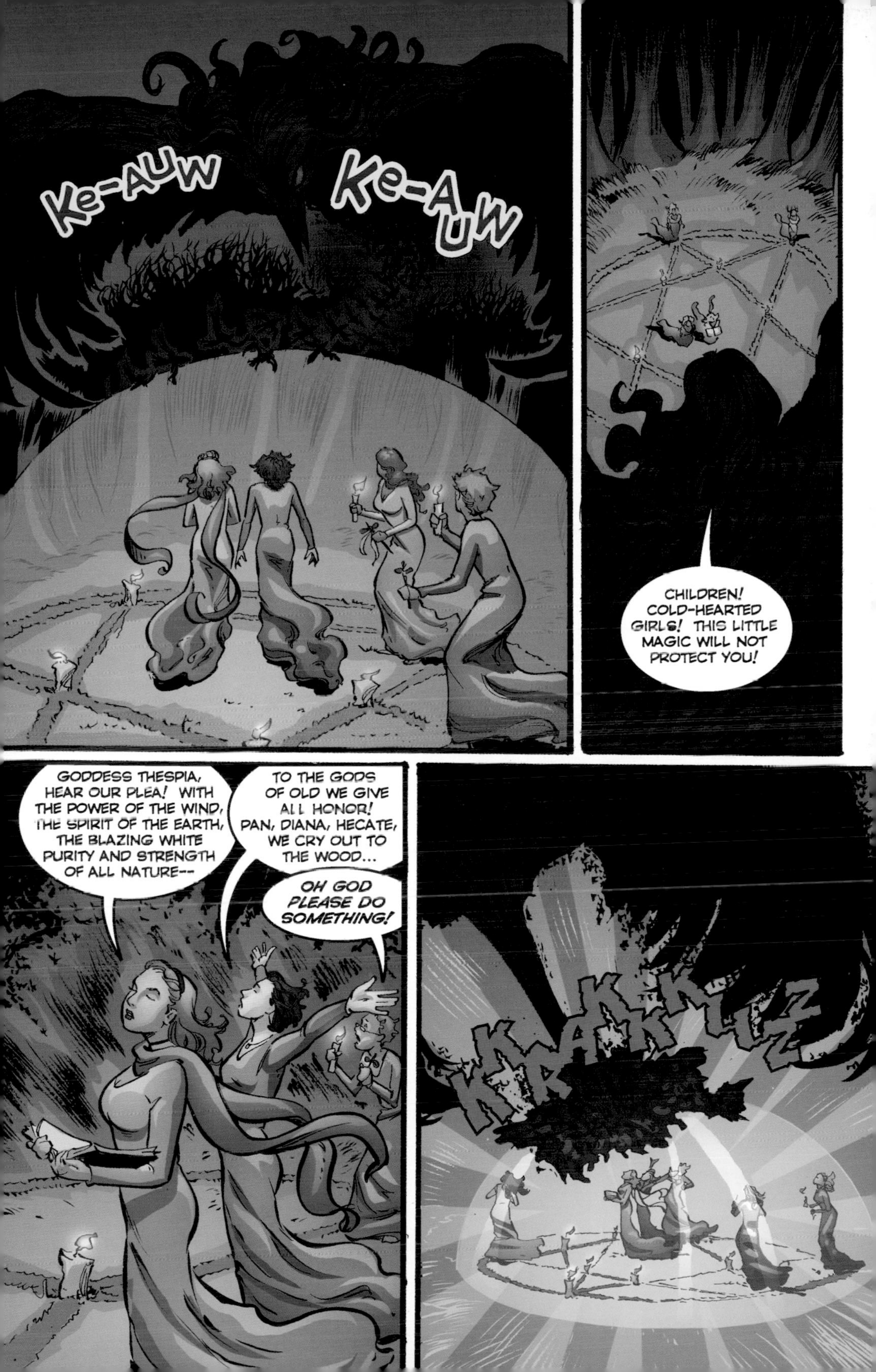

KE-AUW
KE-AUW
CHILDREN! COLD-HEARTED GIRLS! THIS LITTLE MAGIC WILL NOT PROTECT YOU!
GODDESS THESPIA, HEAR OUR PLEA! WITH THE POWER OF THE WIND, THE SPIRIT OF THE EARTH, THE BLAZING WHITE PURITY AND STRENGTH OF ALL NATURE--
TO THE GODS OF OLD WE GIVE ALL HONOR! PAN, DIANA, HECATE, WE CRY OUT TO THE WOOD...
OH GOD PLEASE DO SOMETHING!
KRAKKKUZ

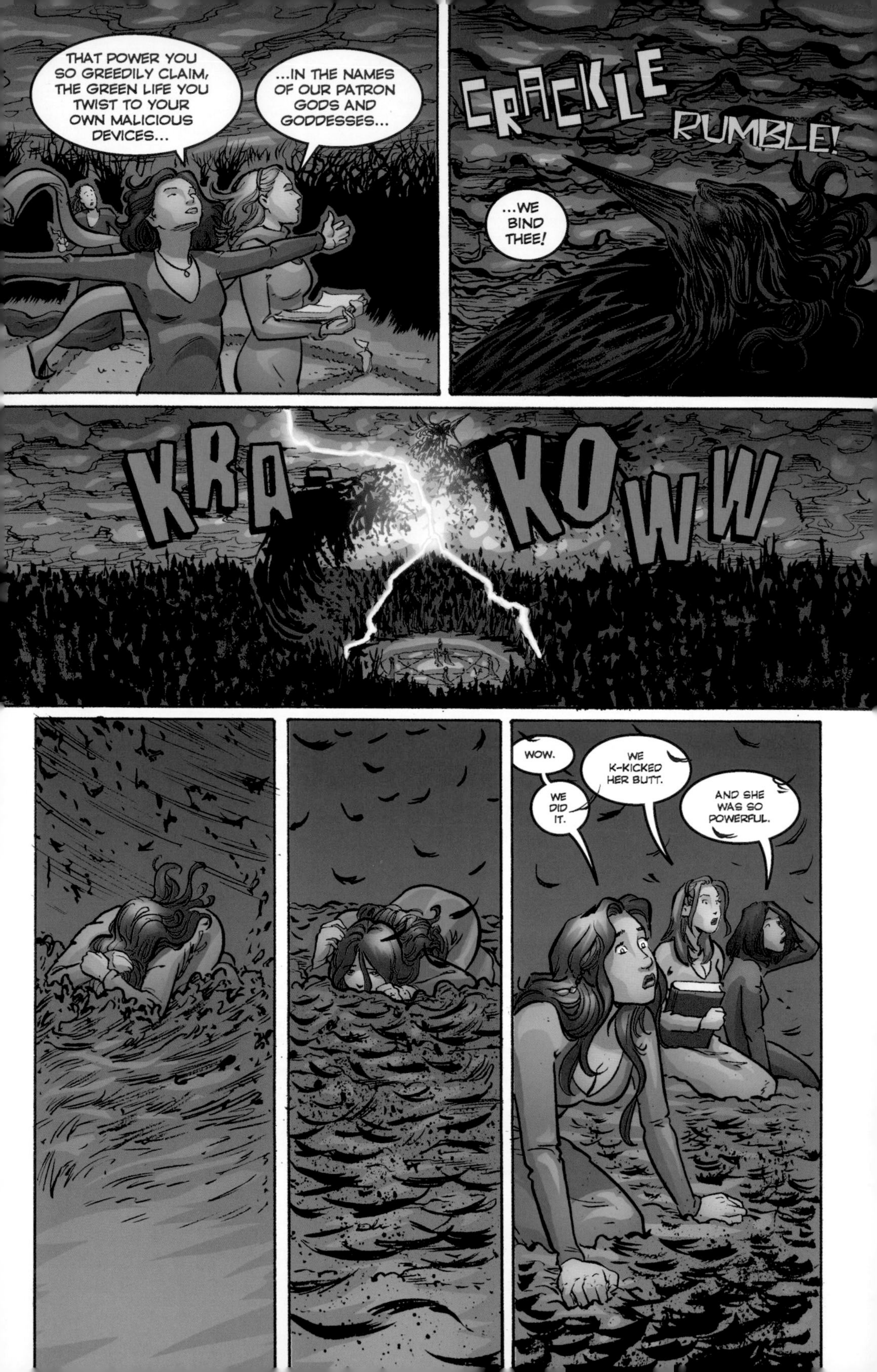

THAT POWER YOU SO GREEDILY CLAIM, THE GREEN LIFE YOU TWIST TO YOUR OWN MALICIOUS DEVICES...
...IN THE NAMES OF OUR PATRON GODS AND GODDESSES...
CRACKLE
RUMBLE!
...WE BIND THEE!
KRA-KOWW
WOW.
WE DID IT.
WE K-KICKED HER BUTT.
AND SHE WAS SO POWERFUL.

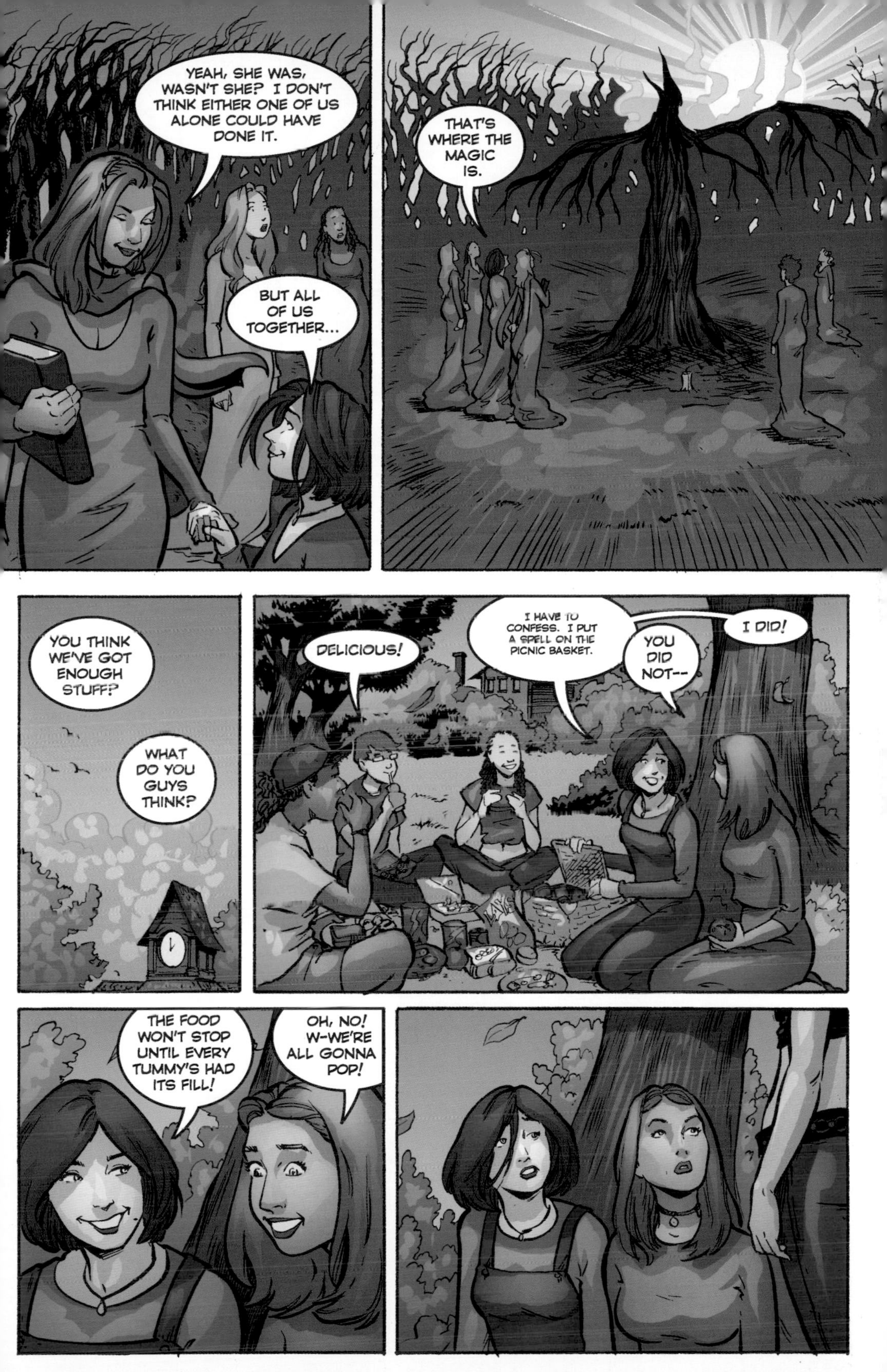
YEAH, SHE WAS, WASN'T SHE? I DON'T THINK EITHER ONE OF US ALONE COULD HAVE DONE IT.
BUT ALL OF US TOGETHER...
THAT'S WHERE THE MAGIC IS.
YOU THINK WE'VE GOT ENOUGH STUFF?
WHAT DO YOU GUYS THINK?
DELICIOUS!
I HAVE TO CONFESS. I PUT A SPELL ON THE PICNIC BASKET.
YOU DID NOT--
I DID!
THE FOOD WON'T STOP UNTIL EVERY TUMMY'S HAD ITS FILL!
OH, NO! W-WE'RE ALL GONNA POP!

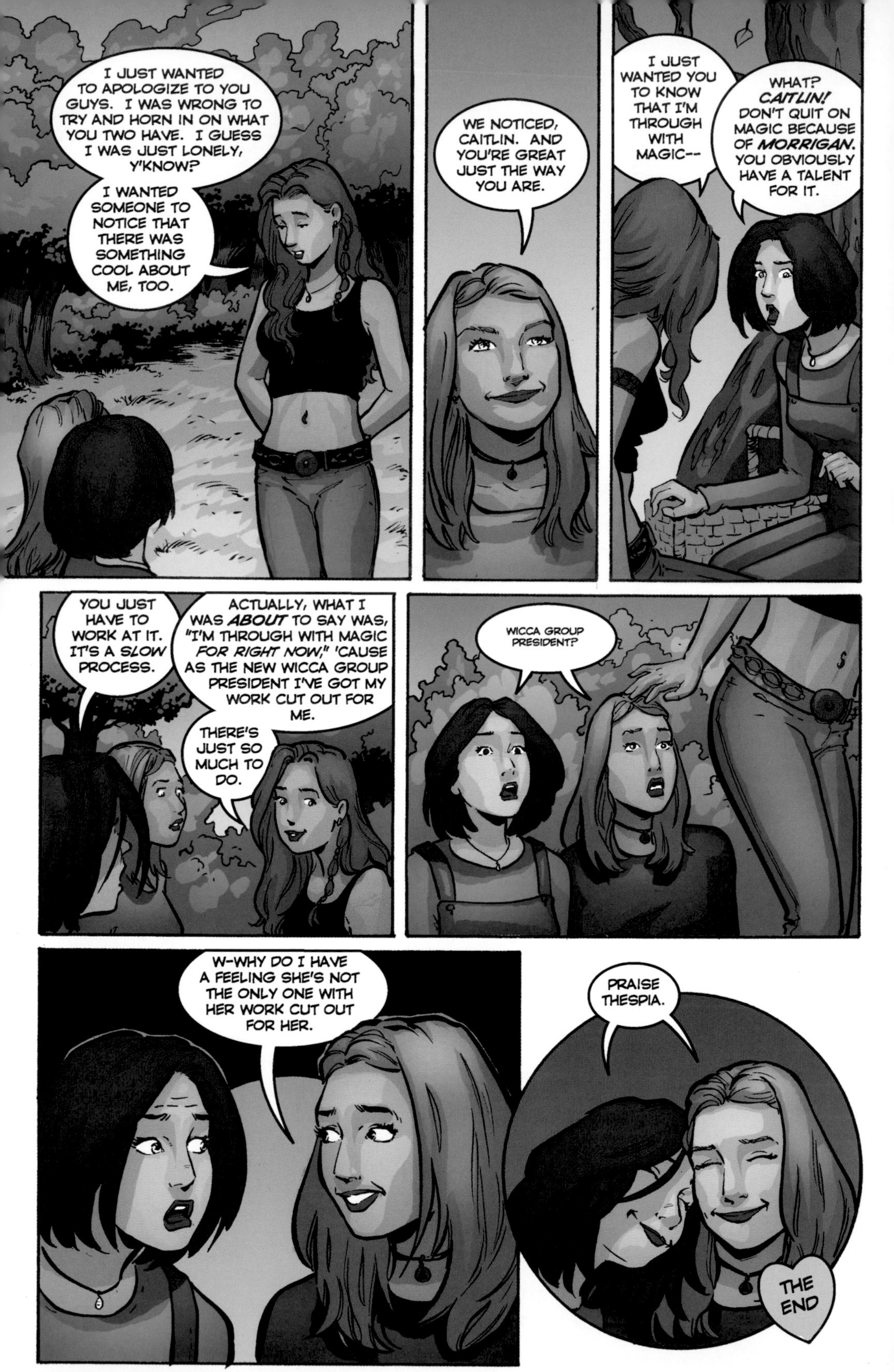
I JUST WANTED TO APOLOGIZE TO YOU GUYS. I WAS WRONG TO TRY AND HORN IN ON WHAT YOU TWO HAVE. I GUESS I WAS JUST LONELY, Y'KNOW?
I WANTED SOMEONE TO NOTICE THAT THERE WAS SOMETHING COOL ABOUT ME, TOO.
WE NOTICED, CAITLIN. AND YOU'RE GREAT JUST THE WAY YOU ARE.
I JUST WANTED YOU TO KNOW THAT I'M THROUGH WITH MAGIC--
WHAT? *CAITLIN!* DON'T QUIT ON MAGIC BECAUSE OF *MORRIGAN.* YOU OBVIOUSLY HAVE A TALENT FOR IT.
YOU JUST HAVE TO WORK AT IT. IT'S A *SLOW* PROCESS.
ACTUALLY, WHAT I WAS *ABOUT* TO SAY WAS, "I'M THROUGH WITH MAGIC *FOR RIGHT NOW,*" 'CAUSE AS THE NEW WICCA GROUP PRESIDENT I'VE GOT MY WORK CUT OUT FOR ME.
THERE'S JUST SO MUCH TO DO.
WICCA GROUP PRESIDENT?
W-WHY DO I HAVE A FEELING SHE'S NOT THE ONLY ONE WITH HER WORK CUT OUT FOR HER.
PRAISE THESPIA.
THE END

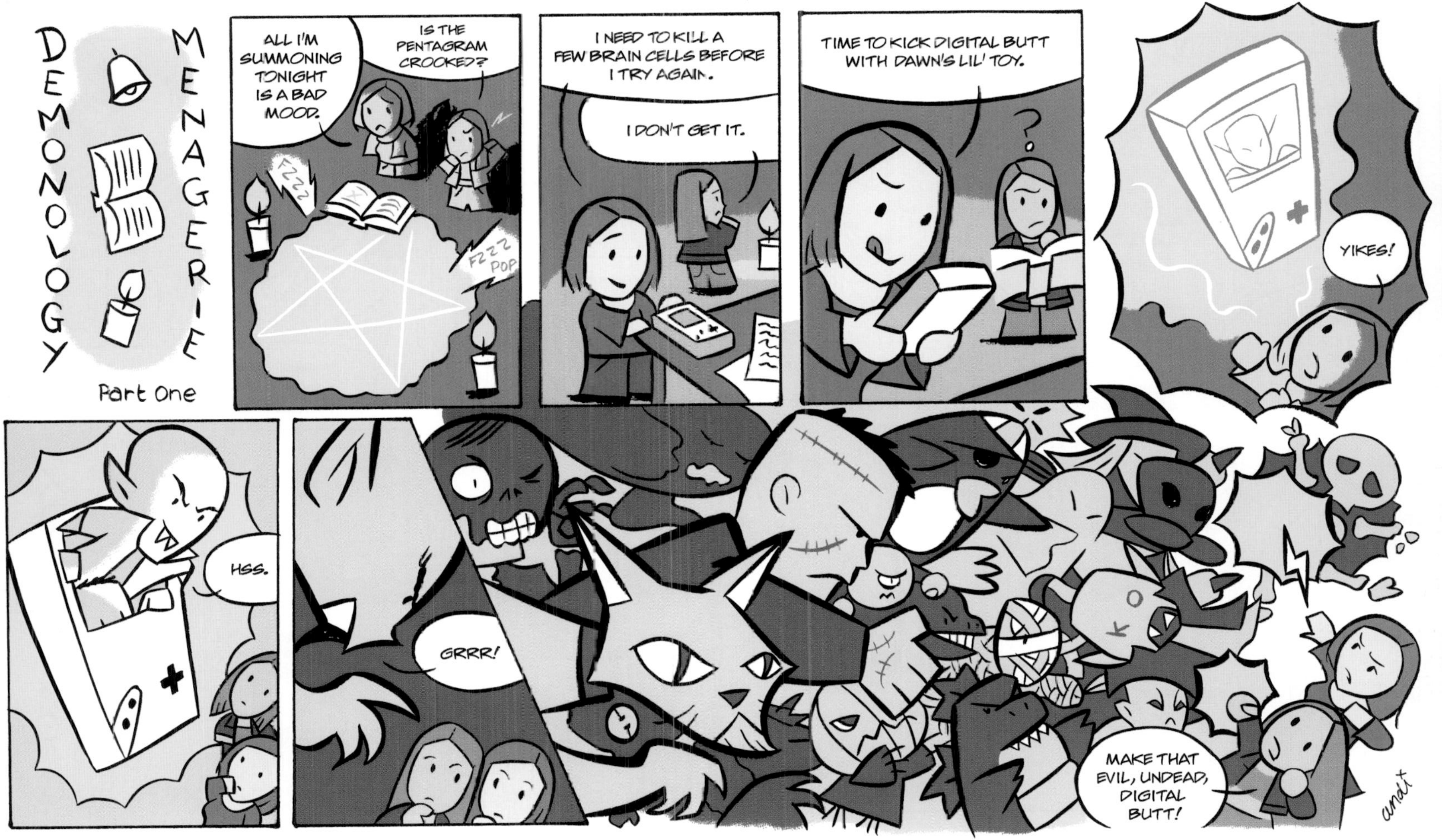
DEMONOLOGY MENAGERIE
Part One
ALL I'M SUMMONING TONIGHT IS A BAD MOOD.
IS THE PENTAGRAM CROOKED?
FZZZ
FZZZ POP
I NEED TO KILL A FEW BRAIN CELLS BEFORE I TRY AGAIN.
I DON'T GET IT.
TIME TO KICK DIGITAL BUTT WITH DAWN'S LIL' TOY.
?
YIKES!
HSS.
GRRR!
MAKE THAT EVIL, UNDEAD, DIGITAL BUTT!
andi

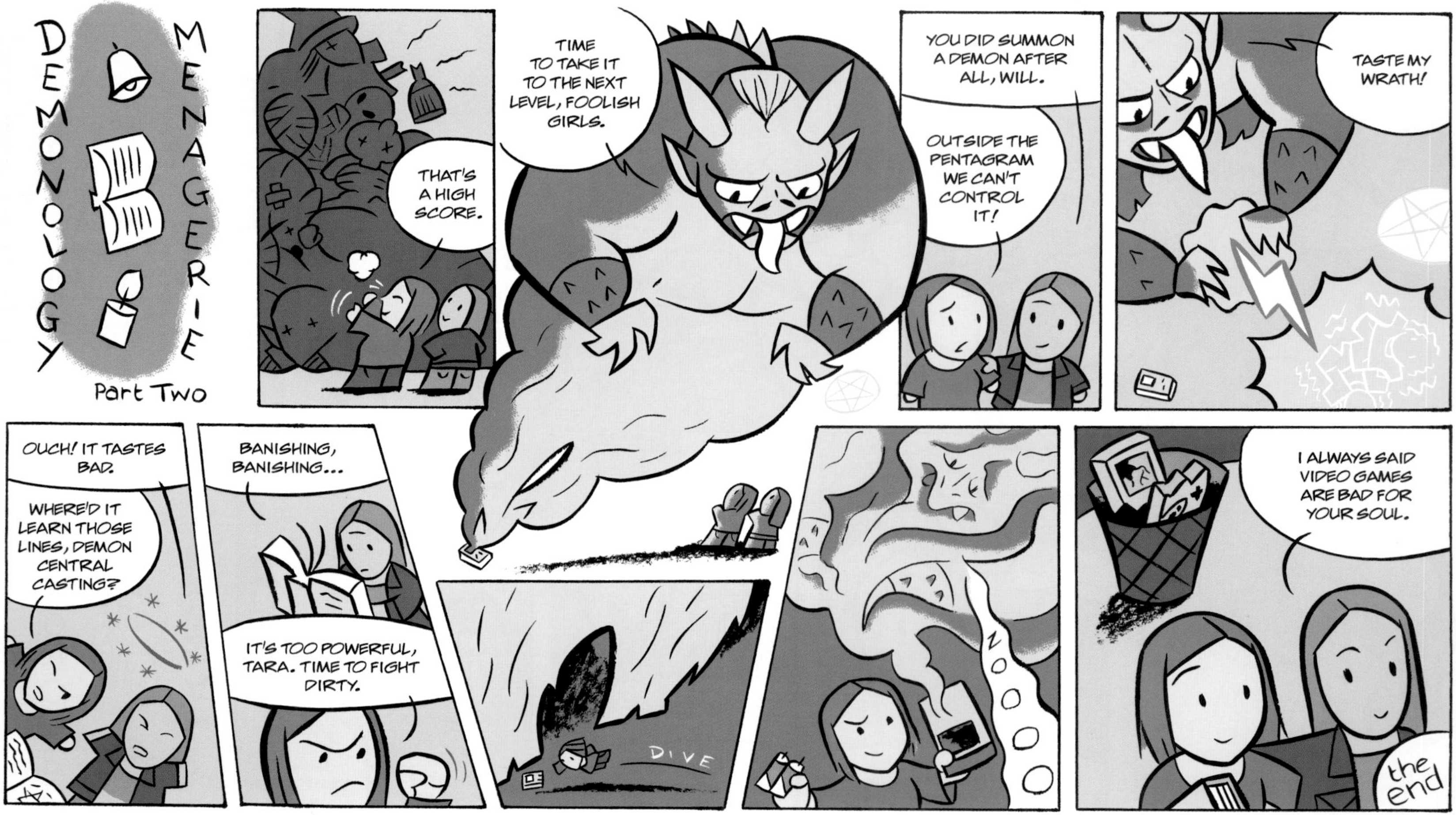
DEMONOLOGY MENAGERIE
Part Two
THAT'S A HIGH SCORE.
TIME TO TAKE IT TO THE NEXT LEVEL, FOOLISH GIRLS.
YOU DID SUMMON A DEMON AFTER ALL, WILL.
OUTSIDE THE PENTAGRAM WE CAN'T CONTROL IT!
TASTE MY WRATH!
OUCH! IT TASTES BAD.
WHERE'D IT LEARN THOSE LINES, DEMON CENTRAL CASTING?
BANISHING, BANISHING...
IT'S TOO POWERFUL, TARA. TIME TO FIGHT DIRTY.
DIVE
ZOOOOO
I ALWAYS SAID VIDEO GAMES ARE BAD FOR YOUR SOUL.
the end

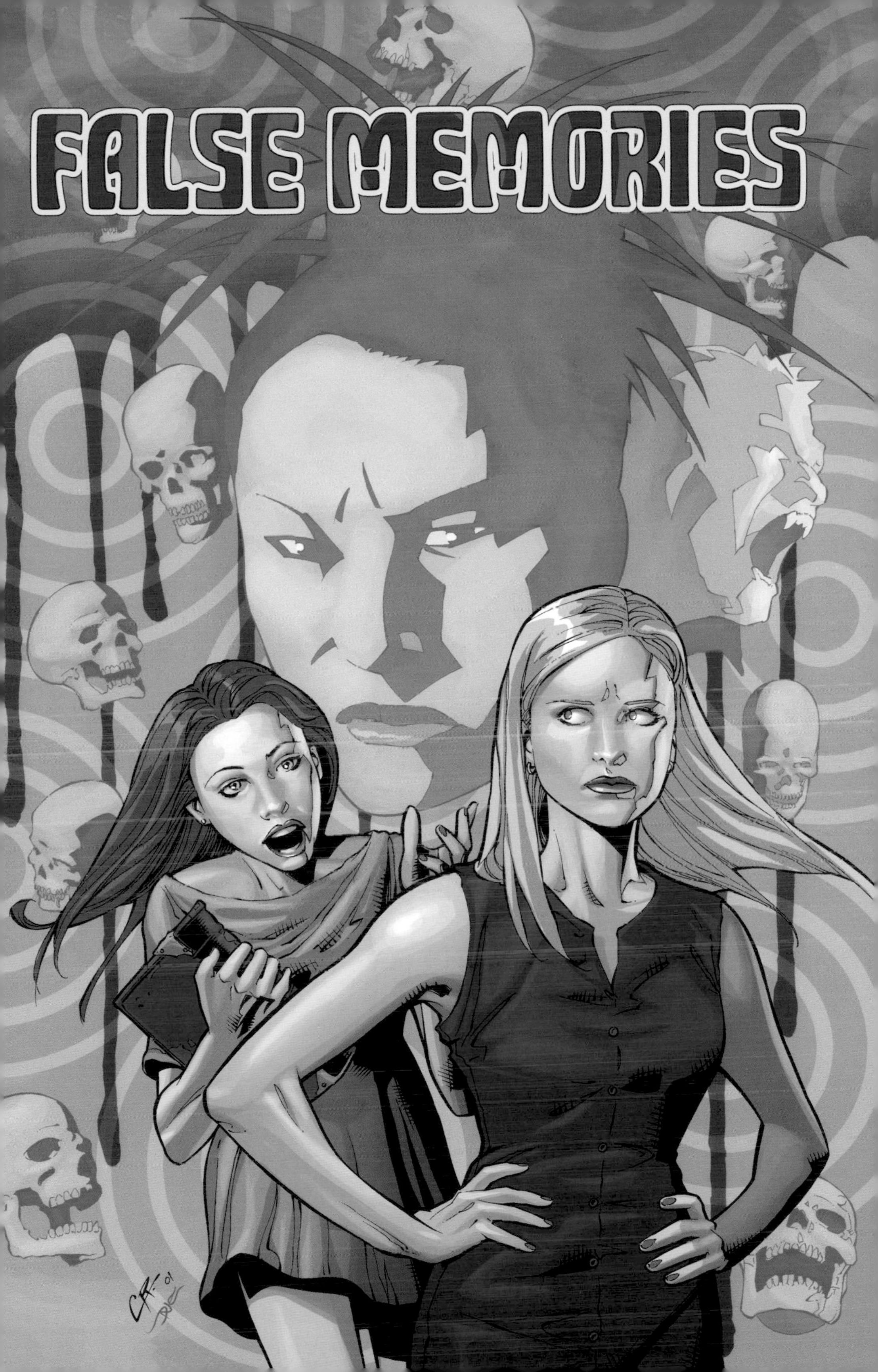
FALSE MEMORIES

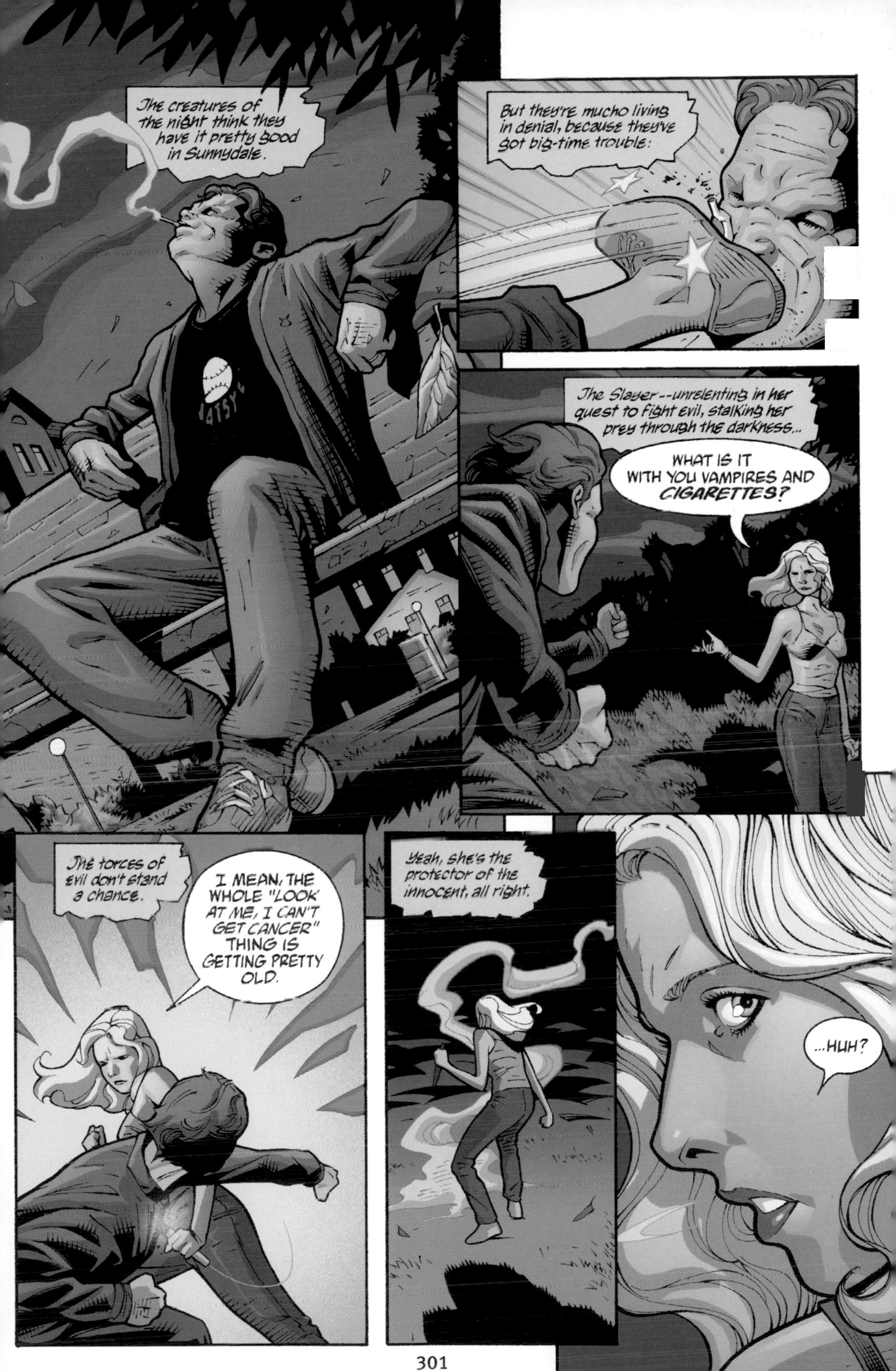
The creatures of the night think they have it pretty good in Sunnydale.
But they're mucho living in denial, because they've got big-time trouble:
The Slayer--unrelenting in her quest to fight evil, stalking her prey through the darkness...
WHAT IS IT WITH YOU VAMPIRES AND CIGARETTES?
The forces of evil don't stand a chance.
I MEAN, THE WHOLE "LOOK AT ME, I CAN'T GET CANCER" THING IS GETTING PRETTY OLD.
Yeah, she's the protector of the innocent, all right.
...HUH?

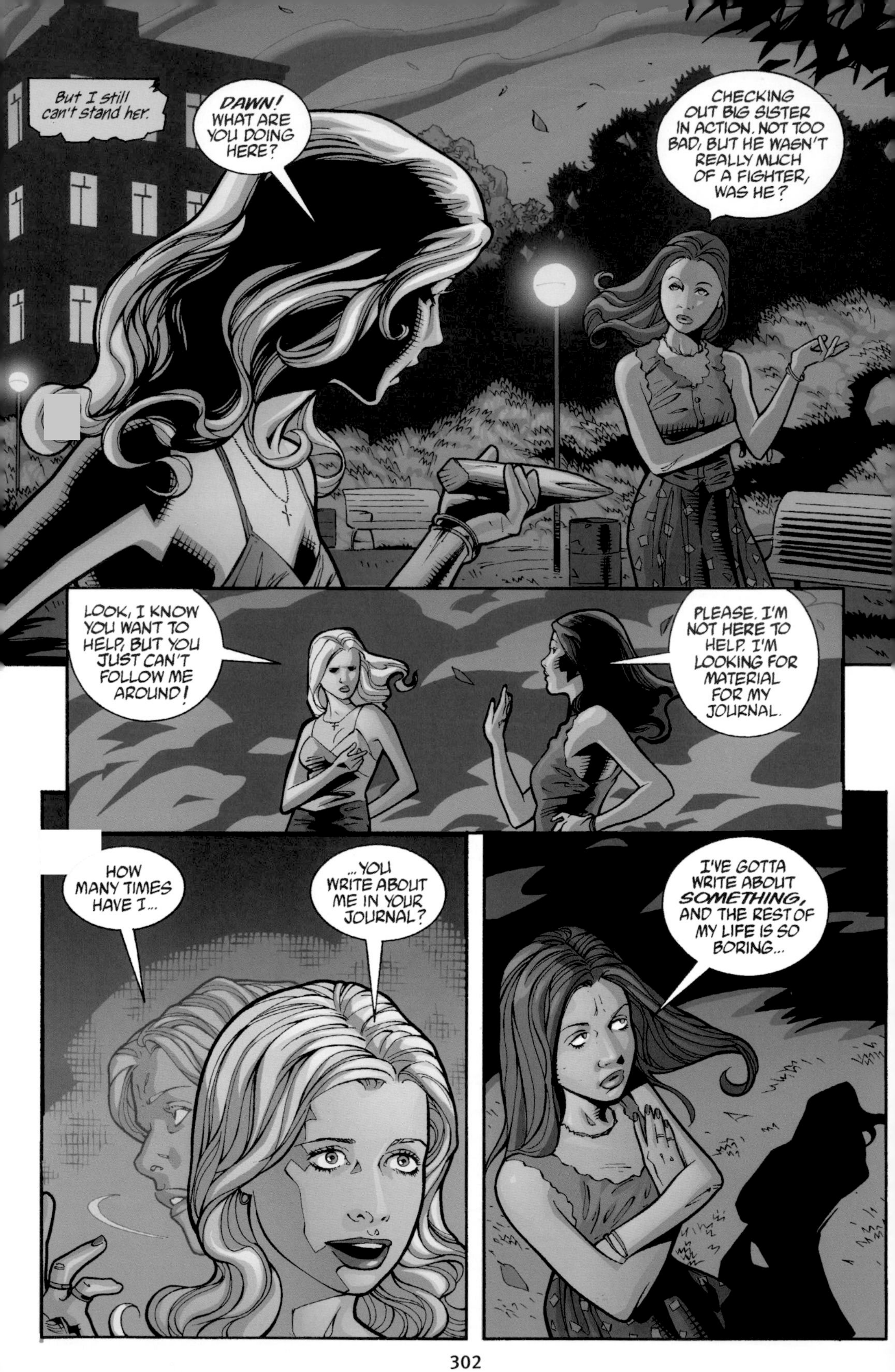
But I still can't stand her.
DAWN! WHAT ARE YOU DOING HERE?
CHECKING OUT BIG SISTER IN ACTION. NOT TOO BAD, BUT HE WASN'T REALLY MUCH OF A FIGHTER, WAS HE?
LOOK, I KNOW YOU WANT TO HELP, BUT YOU JUST CAN'T FOLLOW ME AROUND!
PLEASE. I'M NOT HERE TO HELP. I'M LOOKING FOR MATERIAL FOR MY JOURNAL.
HOW MANY TIMES HAVE I...
...YOU WRITE ABOUT ME IN YOUR JOURNAL?
I'VE GOTTA WRITE ABOUT SOMETHING, AND THE REST OF MY LIFE IS SO BORING...

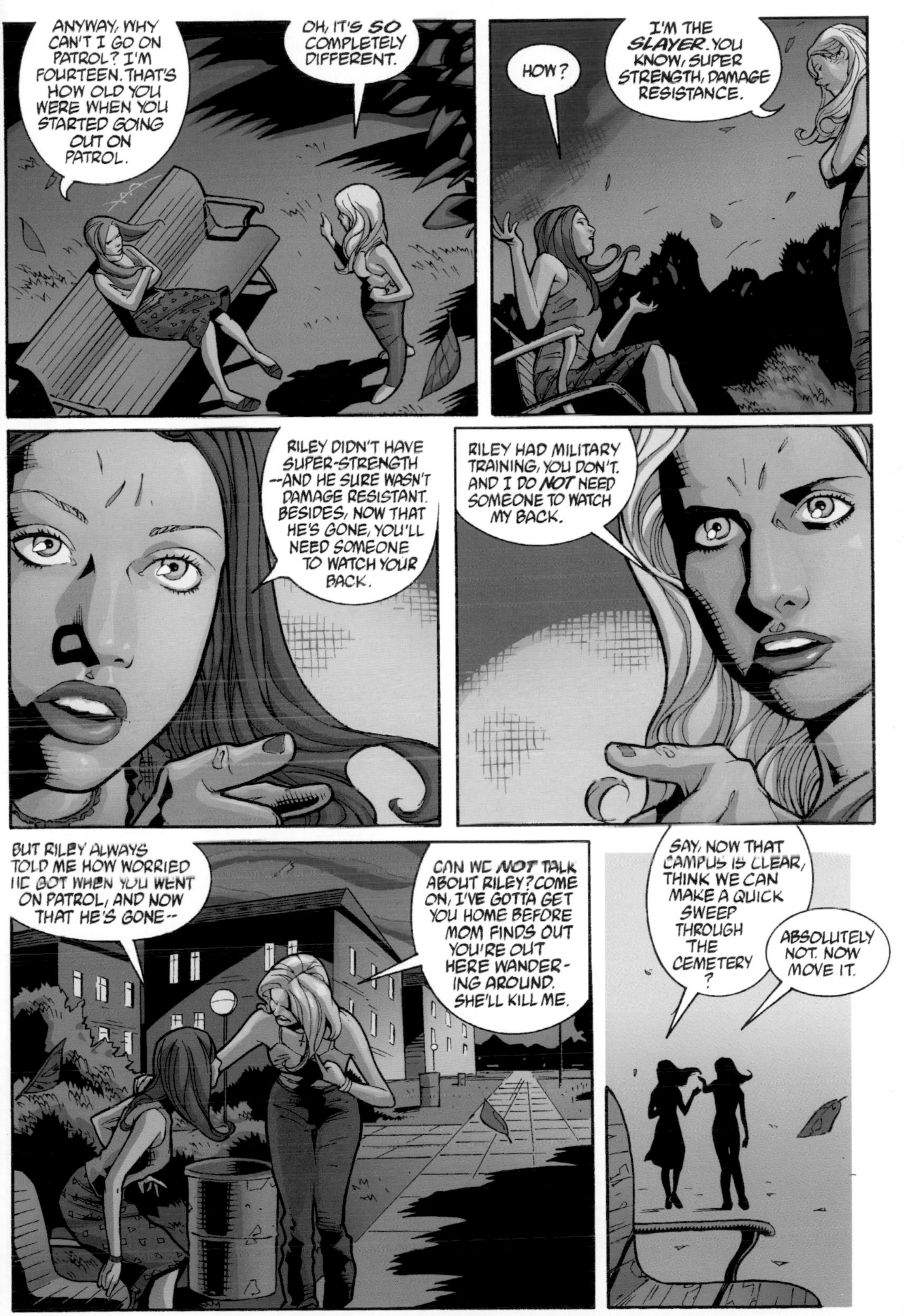
ANYWAY, WHY CAN'T I GO ON PATROL? I'M FOURTEEN. THAT'S HOW OLD YOU WERE WHEN YOU STARTED GOING OUT ON PATROL.
OH, IT'S SO COMPLETELY DIFFERENT.
HOW?
I'M THE SLAYER. YOU KNOW, SUPER STRENGTH, DAMAGE RESISTANCE.
RILEY DIDN'T HAVE SUPER-STRENGTH --AND HE SURE WASN'T DAMAGE RESISTANT. BESIDES, NOW THAT HE'S GONE, YOU'LL NEED SOMEONE TO WATCH YOUR BACK.
RILEY HAD MILITARY TRAINING, YOU DON'T. AND I DO NOT NEED SOMEONE TO WATCH MY BACK.
BUT RILEY ALWAYS TOLD ME HOW WORRIED HE GOT WHEN YOU WENT ON PATROL, AND NOW THAT HE'S GONE--
CAN WE NOT TALK ABOUT RILEY? COME ON, I'VE GOTTA GET YOU HOME BEFORE MOM FINDS OUT YOU'RE OUT HERE WANDERING AROUND. SHE'LL KILL ME.
SAY, NOW THAT CAMPUS IS CLEAR, THINK WE CAN MAKE A QUICK SWEEP THROUGH THE CEMETERY?
ABSOLUTELY NOT. NOW MOVE IT.

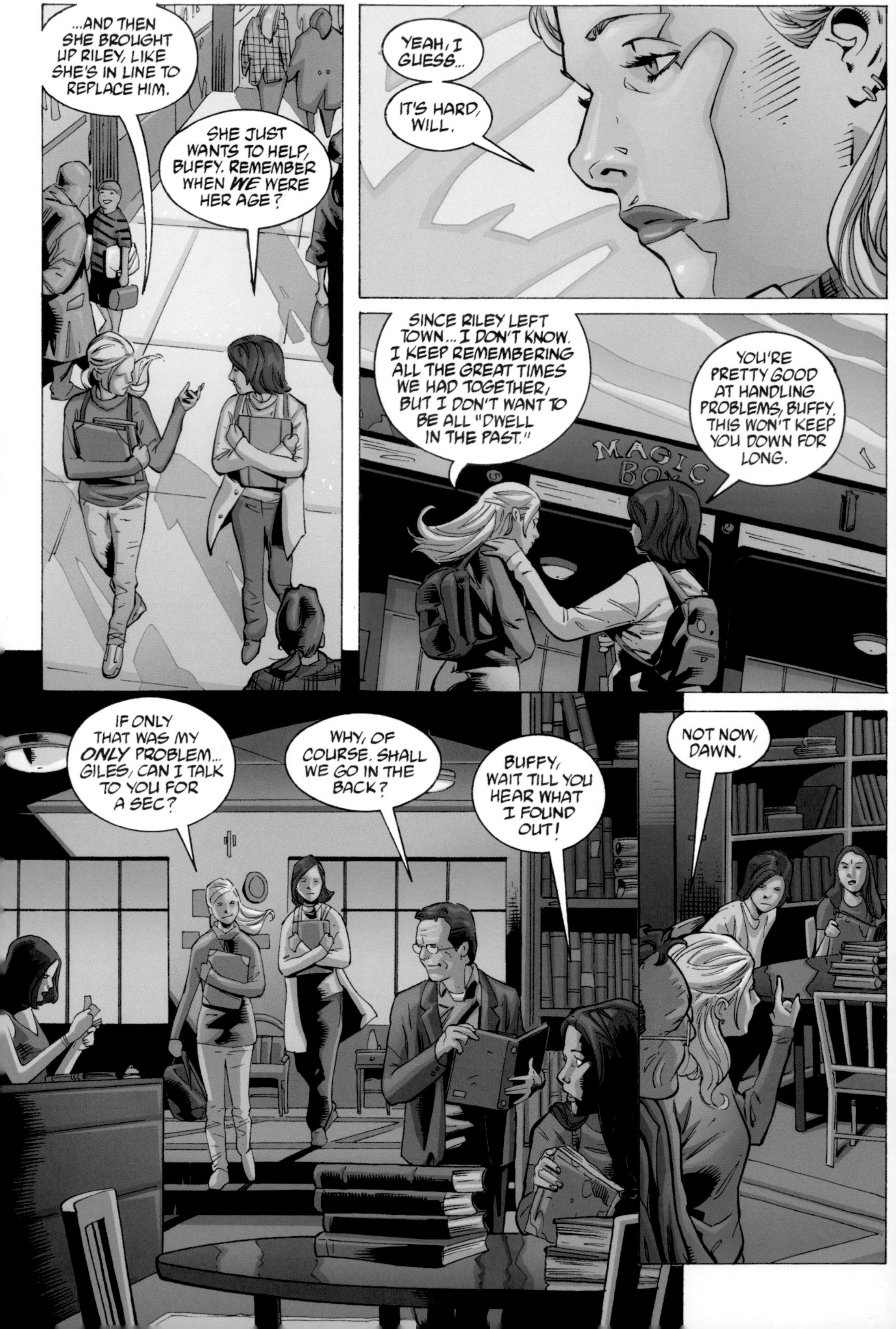
...AND THEN SHE BROUGHT UP RILEY, LIKE SHE'S IN LINE TO REPLACE HIM.
SHE JUST WANTS TO HELP, BUFFY. REMEMBER WHEN WE WERE HER AGE?
YEAH, I GUESS...
IT'S HARD, WILL.
SINCE RILEY LEFT TOWN... I DON'T KNOW. I KEEP REMEMBERING ALL THE GREAT TIMES WE HAD TOGETHER, BUT I DON'T WANT TO BE ALL "DWELL IN THE PAST."
YOU'RE PRETTY GOOD AT HANDLING PROBLEMS, BUFFY. THIS WON'T KEEP YOU DOWN FOR LONG.
MAGIC BOX
IF ONLY THAT WAS MY ONLY PROBLEM... GILES, CAN I TALK TO YOU FOR A SEC?
WHY, OF COURSE. SHALL WE GO IN THE BACK?
BUFFY, WAIT TILL YOU HEAR WHAT I FOUND OUT!
NOT NOW, DAWN.

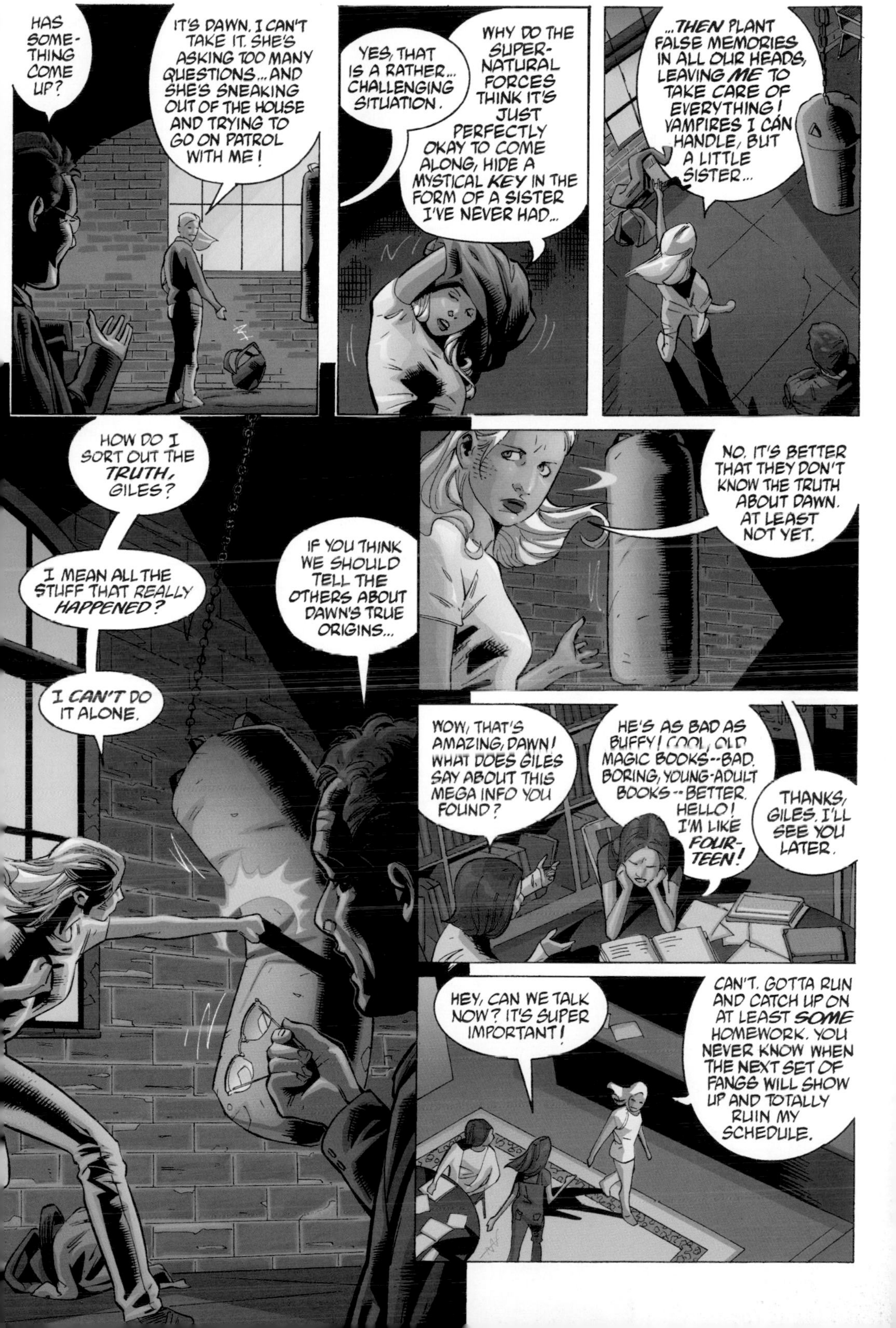
HAS SOMETHING COME UP?
IT'S DAWN. I CAN'T TAKE IT. SHE'S ASKING TOO MANY QUESTIONS... AND SHE'S SNEAKING OUT OF THE HOUSE AND TRYING TO GO ON PATROL WITH ME!
YES, THAT IS A RATHER... CHALLENGING SITUATION.
WHY DO THE SUPERNATURAL FORCES THINK IT'S JUST PERFECTLY OKAY TO COME ALONG, HIDE A MYSTICAL KEY IN THE FORM OF A SISTER I'VE NEVER HAD...
...THEN PLANT FALSE MEMORIES IN ALL OUR HEADS, LEAVING ME TO TAKE CARE OF EVERYTHING! VAMPIRES I CAN HANDLE, BUT A LITTLE SISTER...
HOW DO I SORT OUT THE TRUTH, GILES?
I MEAN ALL THE STUFF THAT REALLY HAPPENED?
I CAN'T DO IT ALONE.
IF YOU THINK WE SHOULD TELL THE OTHERS ABOUT DAWN'S TRUE ORIGINS...
NO. IT'S BETTER THAT THEY DON'T KNOW THE TRUTH ABOUT DAWN. AT LEAST NOT YET.
WOW, THAT'S AMAZING, DAWN! WHAT DOES GILES SAY ABOUT THIS MEGA INFO YOU FOUND?
HE'S AS BAD AS BUFFY! COOL, OLD MAGIC BOOKS--BAD. BORING, YOUNG-ADULT BOOKS--BETTER. HELLO! I'M LIKE FOURTEEN!
THANKS, GILES. I'LL SEE YOU LATER.
HEY, CAN WE TALK NOW? IT'S SUPER IMPORTANT!
CAN'T. GOTTA RUN AND CATCH UP ON AT LEAST SOME HOMEWORK. YOU NEVER KNOW WHEN THE NEXT SET OF FANGS WILL SHOW UP AND TOTALLY RUIN MY SCHEDULE.

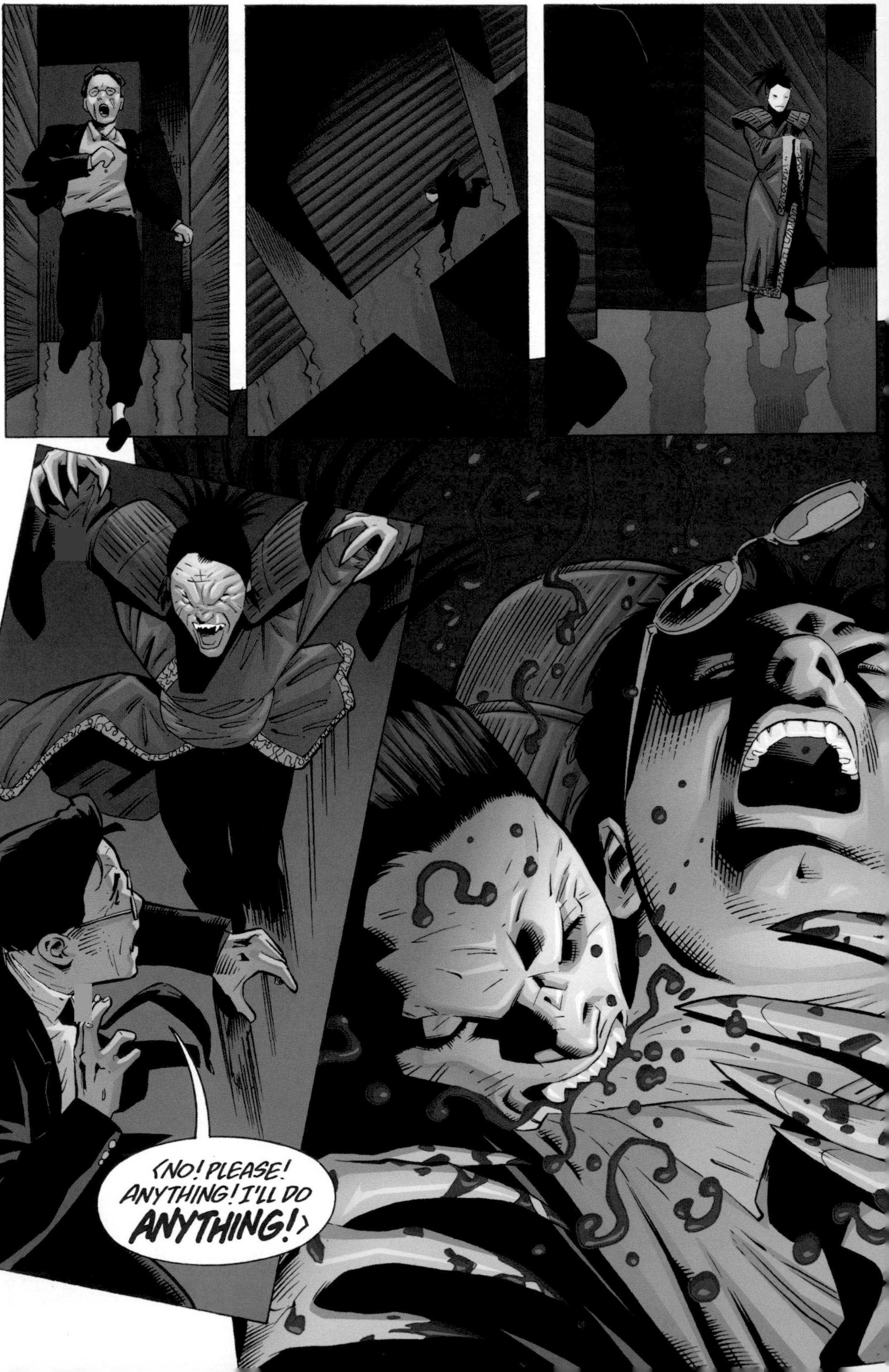
⟨NO! PLEASE! ANYTHING! I'LL DO ANYTHING!⟩

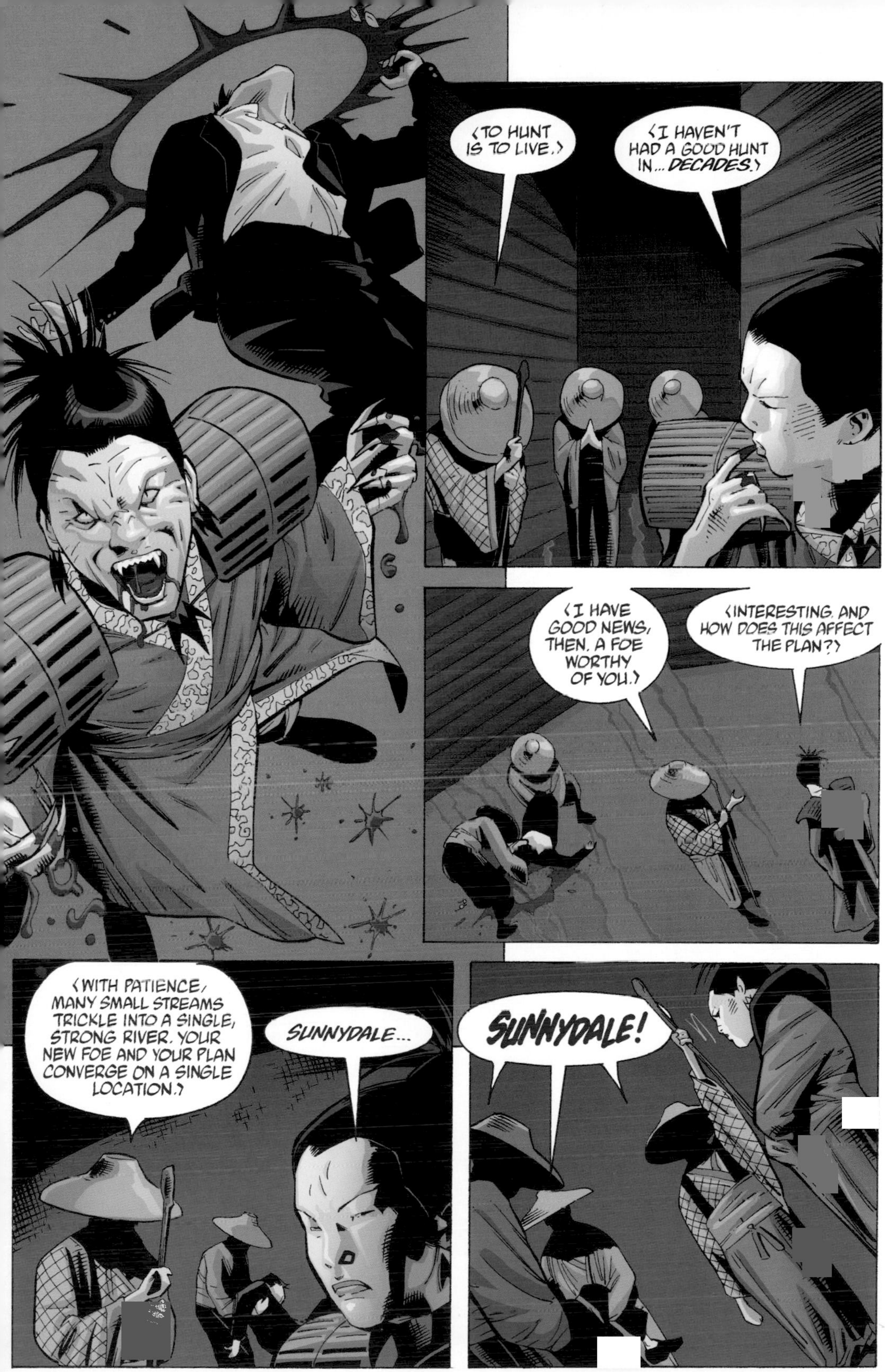

‹TO HUNT IS TO LIVE.›
‹I HAVEN'T HAD A GOOD HUNT IN... DECADES.›
‹I HAVE GOOD NEWS, THEN. A FOE WORTHY OF YOU.›
‹INTERESTING. AND HOW DOES THIS AFFECT THE PLAN?›
‹WITH PATIENCE, MANY SMALL STREAMS TRICKLE INTO A SINGLE, STRONG RIVER. YOUR NEW FOE AND YOUR PLAN CONVERGE ON A SINGLE LOCATION.›
SUNNYDALE...
SUNNYDALE!

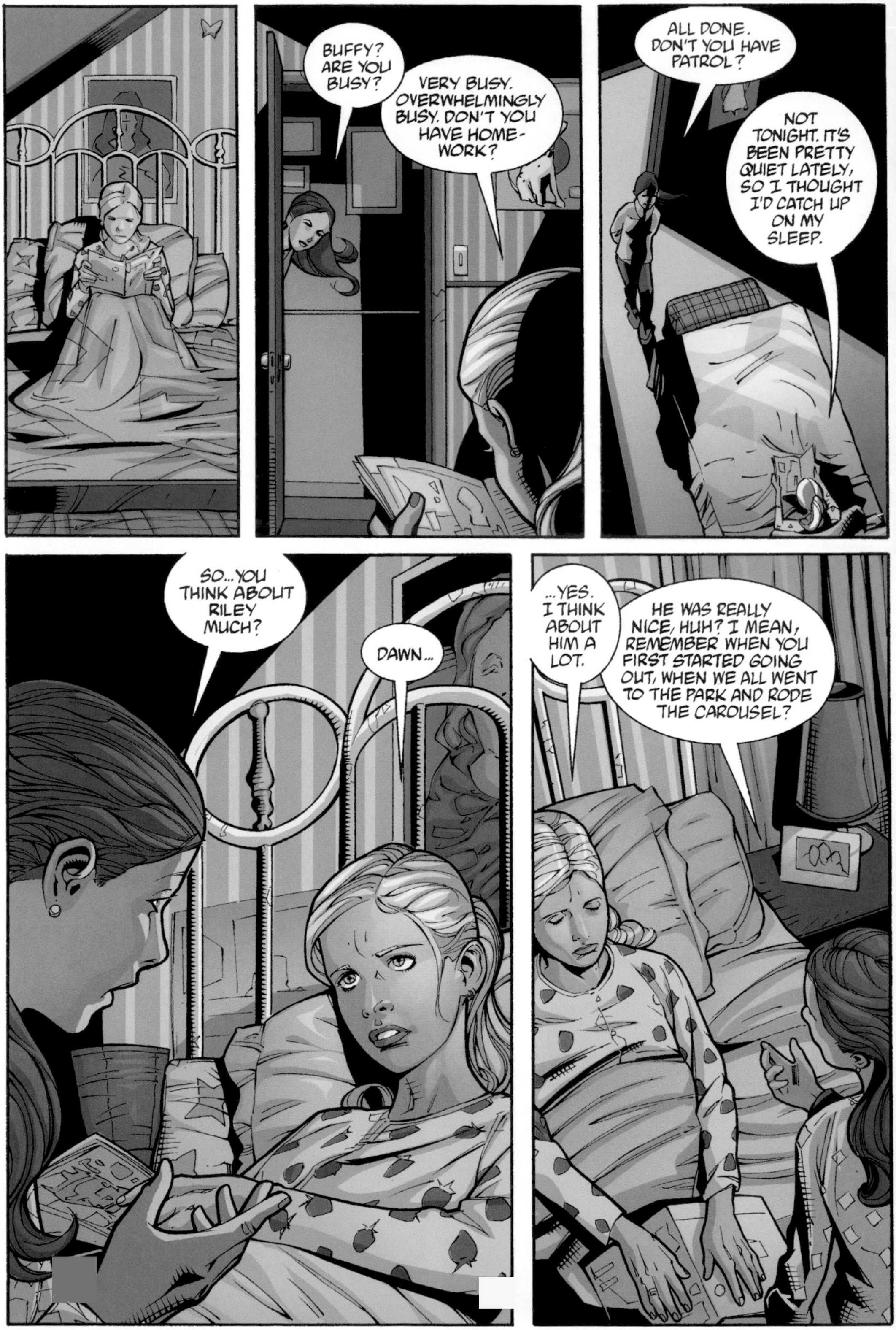
BUFFY? ARE YOU BUSY?
VERY BUSY. OVERWHELMINGLY BUSY. DON'T YOU HAVE HOME-WORK?
ALL DONE. DON'T YOU HAVE PATROL?
NOT TONIGHT. IT'S BEEN PRETTY QUIET LATELY, SO I THOUGHT I'D CATCH UP ON MY SLEEP.
SO...YOU THINK ABOUT RILEY MUCH?
DAWN...
...YES. I THINK ABOUT HIM A LOT.
HE WAS REALLY NICE, HUH? I MEAN, REMEMBER WHEN YOU FIRST STARTED GOING OUT, WHEN WE ALL WENT TO THE PARK AND RODE THE CAROUSEL?

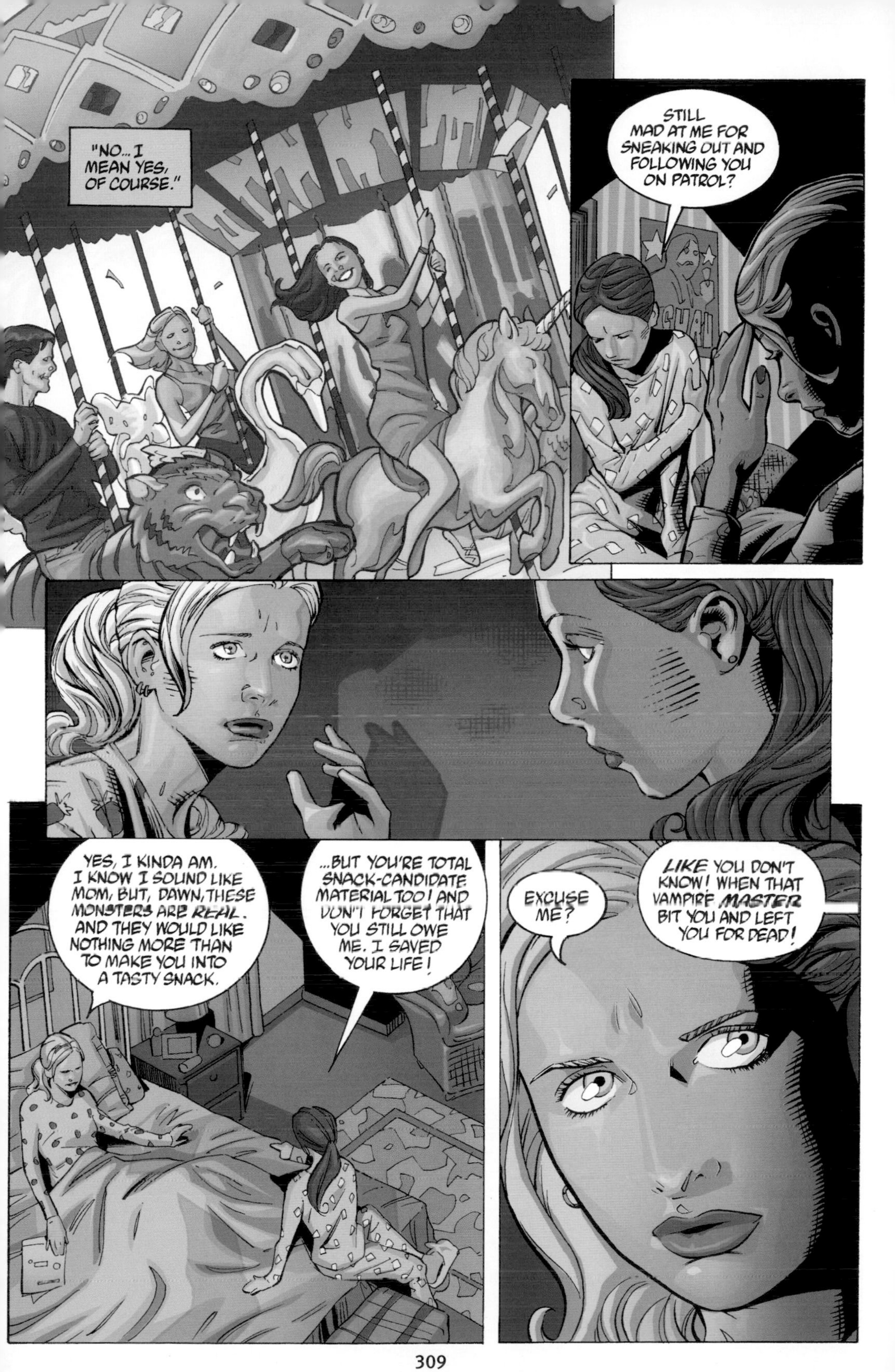
"NO... I MEAN YES, OF COURSE."
STILL MAD AT ME FOR SNEAKING OUT AND FOLLOWING YOU ON PATROL?
YES, I KINDA AM. I KNOW I SOUND LIKE MOM, BUT, DAWN, THESE MONSTERS ARE REAL. AND THEY WOULD LIKE NOTHING MORE THAN TO MAKE YOU INTO A TASTY SNACK.
...BUT YOU'RE TOTAL SNACK-CANDIDATE MATERIAL TOO! AND DON'T FORGET THAT YOU STILL OWE ME. I SAVED YOUR LIFE!
EXCUSE ME?
LIKE YOU DON'T KNOW! WHEN THAT VAMPIRE MASTER BIT YOU AND LEFT YOU FOR DEAD!

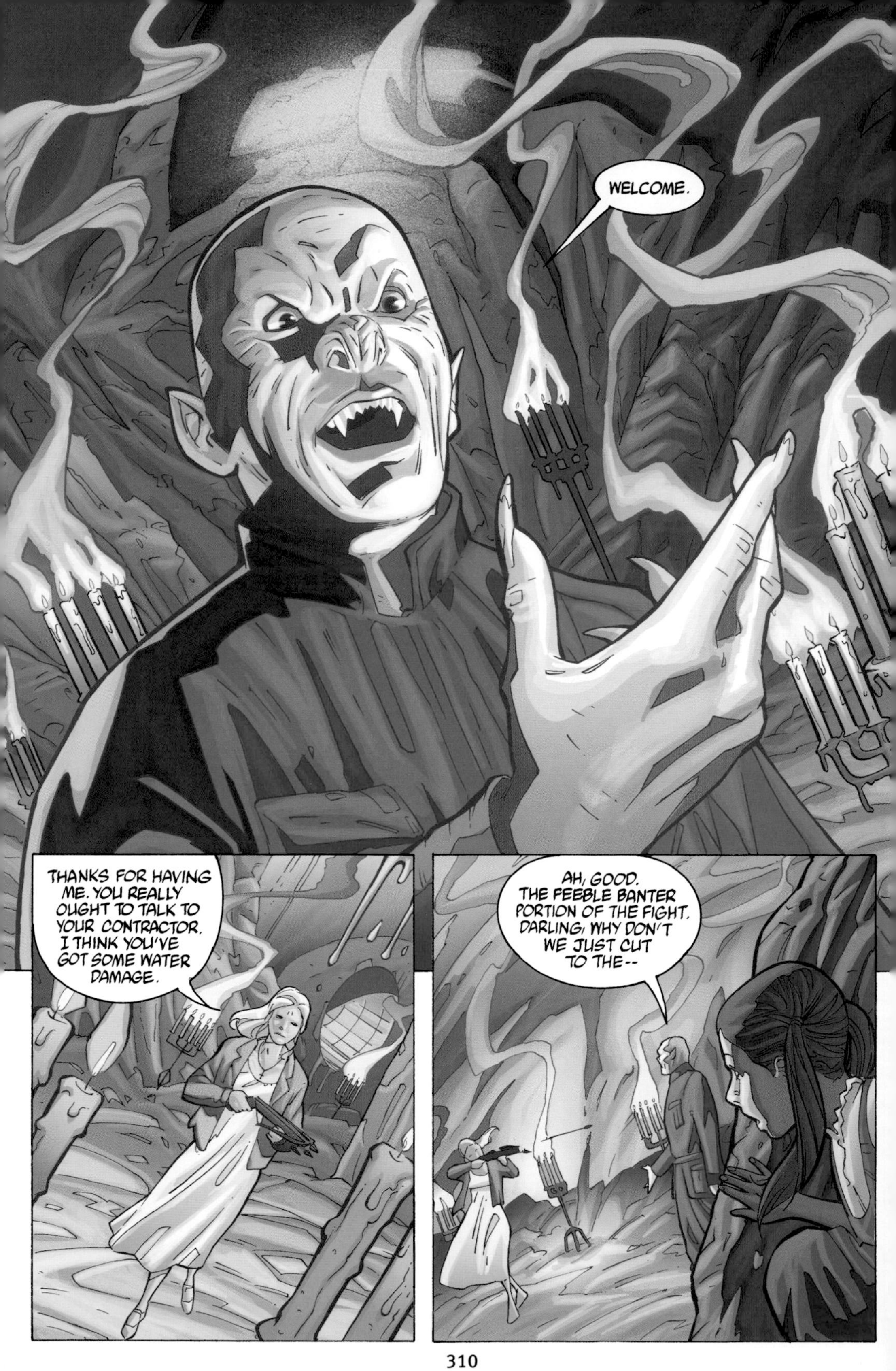
WELCOME.
THANKS FOR HAVING ME. YOU REALLY OUGHT TO TALK TO YOUR CONTRACTOR. I THINK YOU'VE GOT SOME WATER DAMAGE.
AH, GOOD. THE FEEBLE BANTER PORTION OF THE FIGHT. DARLING, WHY DON'T WE JUST CUT TO THE--

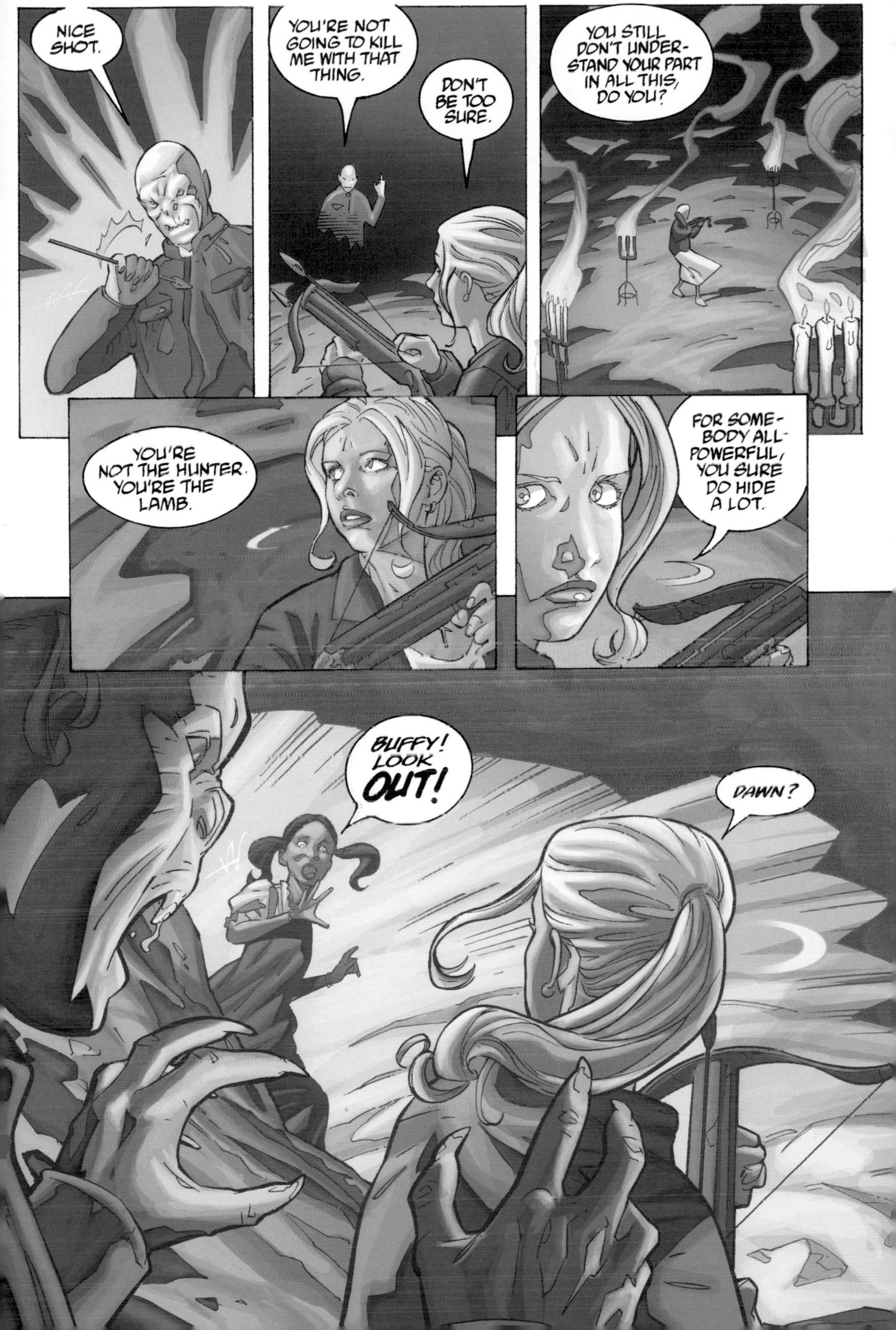
NICE SHOT.
YOU'RE NOT GOING TO KILL ME WITH THAT THING.
DON'T BE TOO SURE.
YOU STILL DON'T UNDER-STAND YOUR PART IN ALL THIS, DO YOU?
YOU'RE NOT THE HUNTER. YOU'RE THE LAMB.
FOR SOME-BODY ALL-POWERFUL, YOU SURE DO HIDE A LOT.
BUFFY! LOOK OUT!
DAWN?

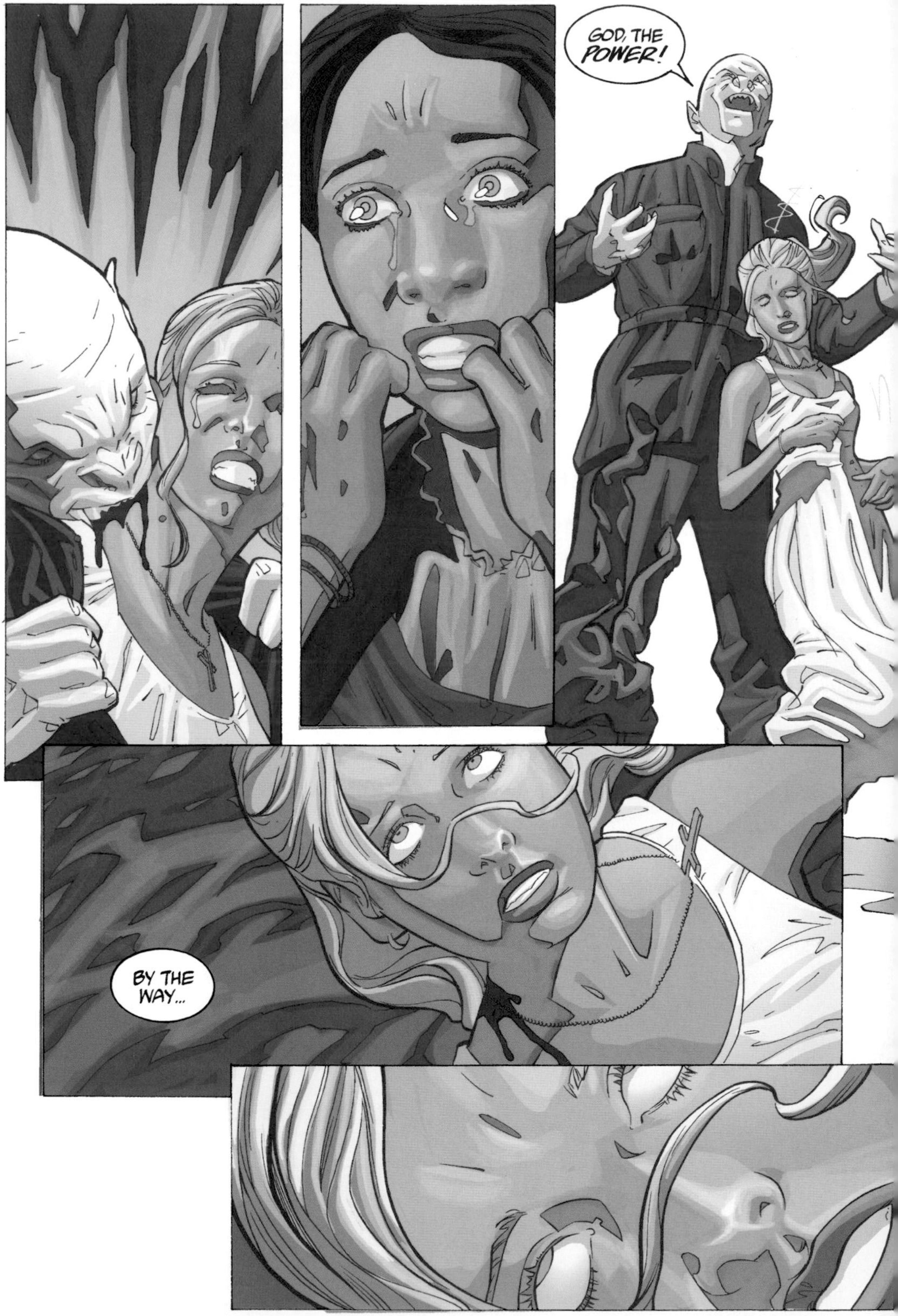
GOD, THE POWER!
BY THE WAY...

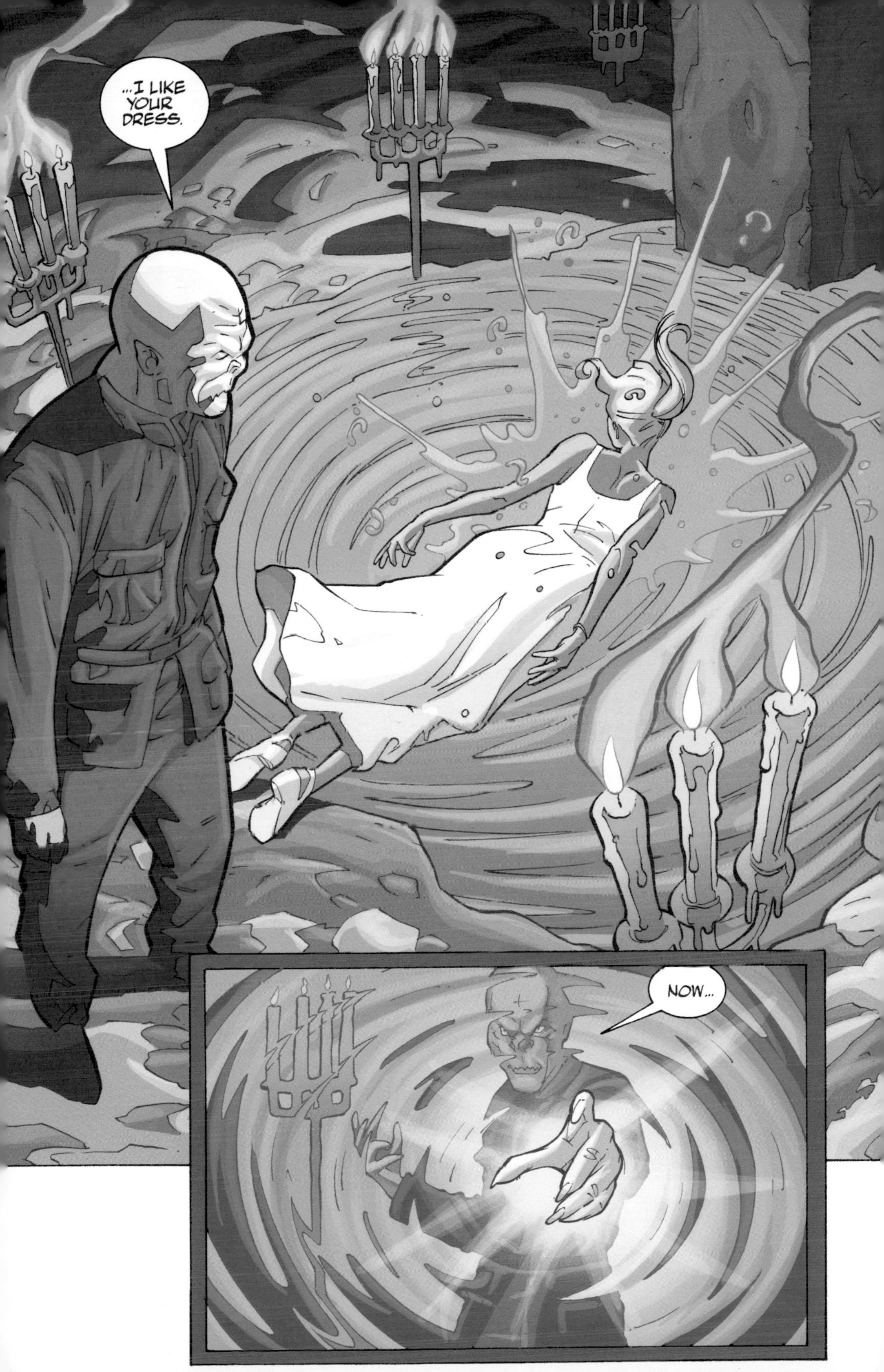
...I LIKE YOUR DRESS.
NOW...

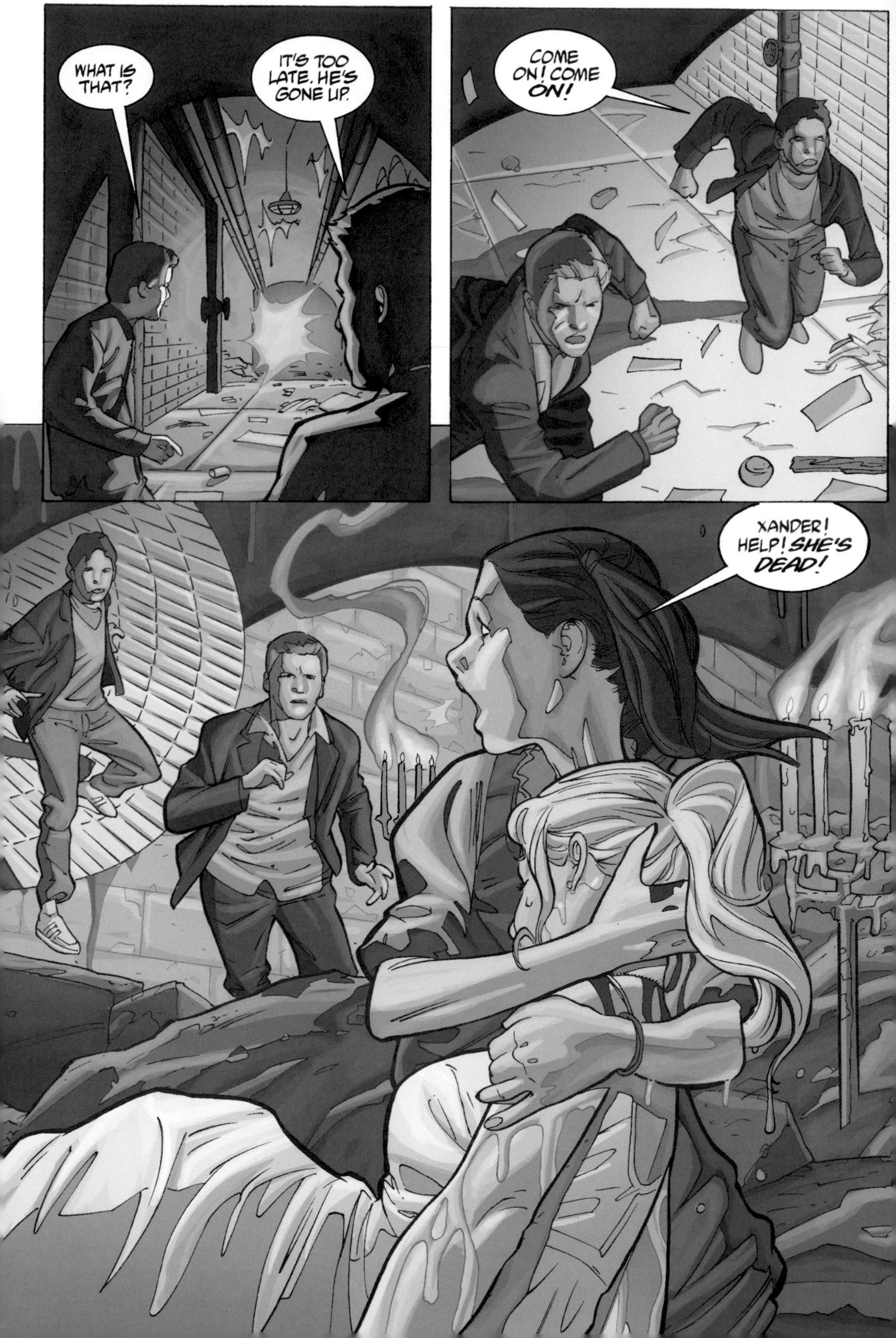
WHAT IS THAT?
IT'S TOO LATE. HE'S GONE UP.
COME ON! COME ON!
XANDER! HELP! SHE'S DEAD!

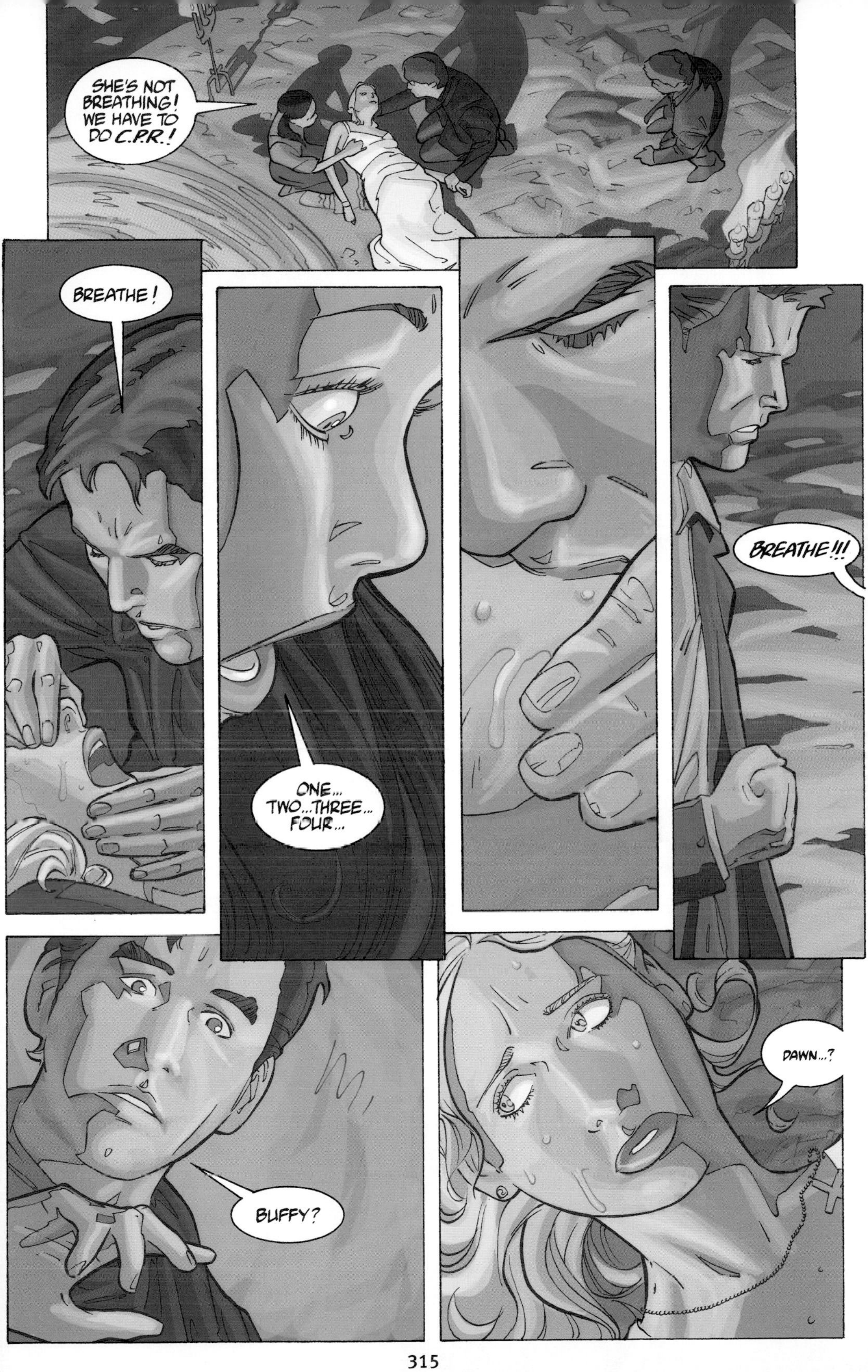
SHE'S NOT BREATHING! WE HAVE TO DO C.P.R.!
BREATHE!
ONE... TWO...THREE... FOUR...
BREATHE!!!
BUFFY?
DAWN...?

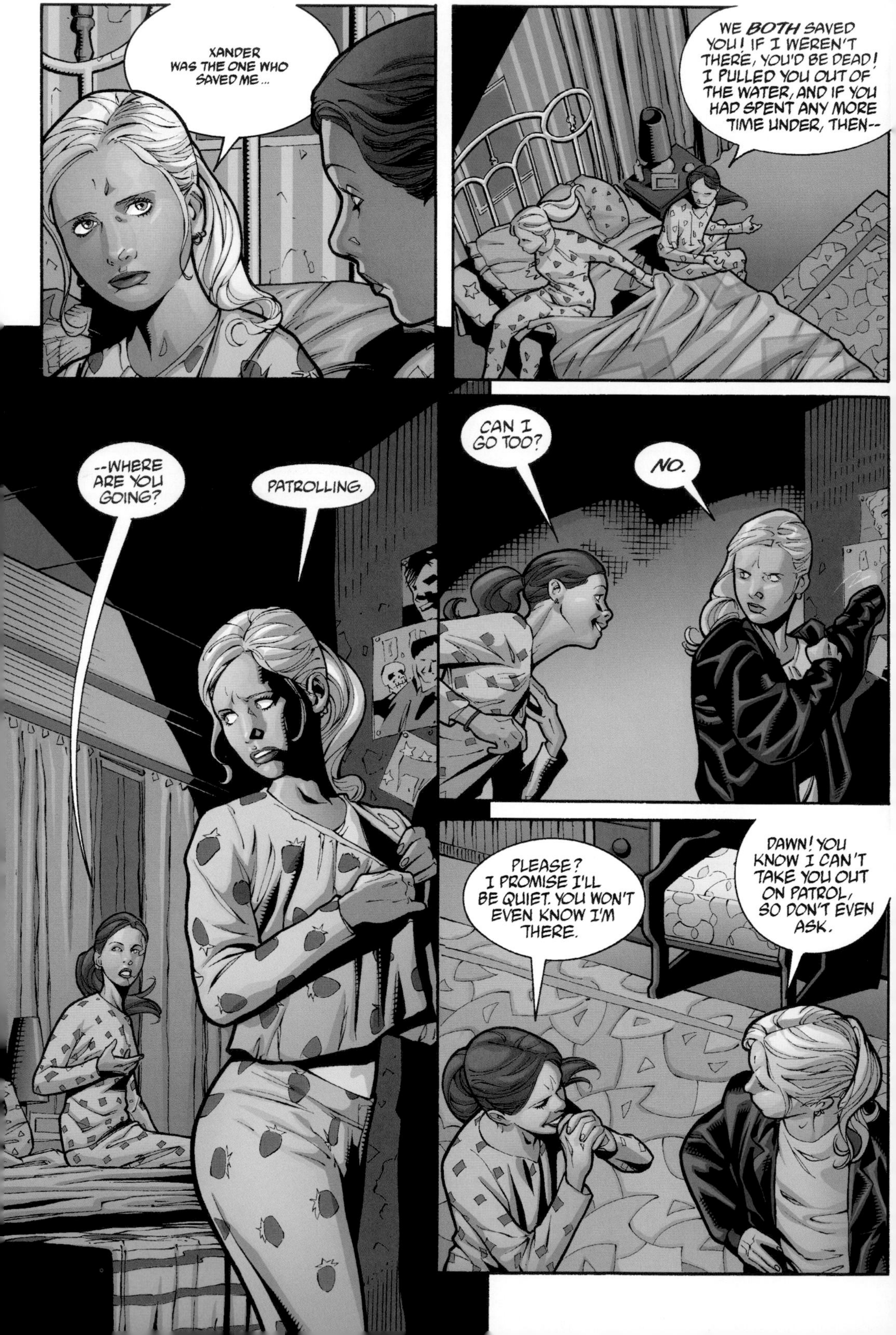
XANDER WAS THE ONE WHO SAVED ME...
WE BOTH SAVED YOU! IF I WEREN'T THERE, YOU'D BE DEAD! I PULLED YOU OUT OF THE WATER, AND IF YOU HAD SPENT ANY MORE TIME UNDER, THEN--
--WHERE ARE YOU GOING?
PATROLLING.
CAN I GO TOO?
NO.
PLEASE? I PROMISE I'LL BE QUIET. YOU WON'T EVEN KNOW I'M THERE.
DAWN! YOU KNOW I CAN'T TAKE YOU OUT ON PATROL, SO DON'T EVEN ASK.

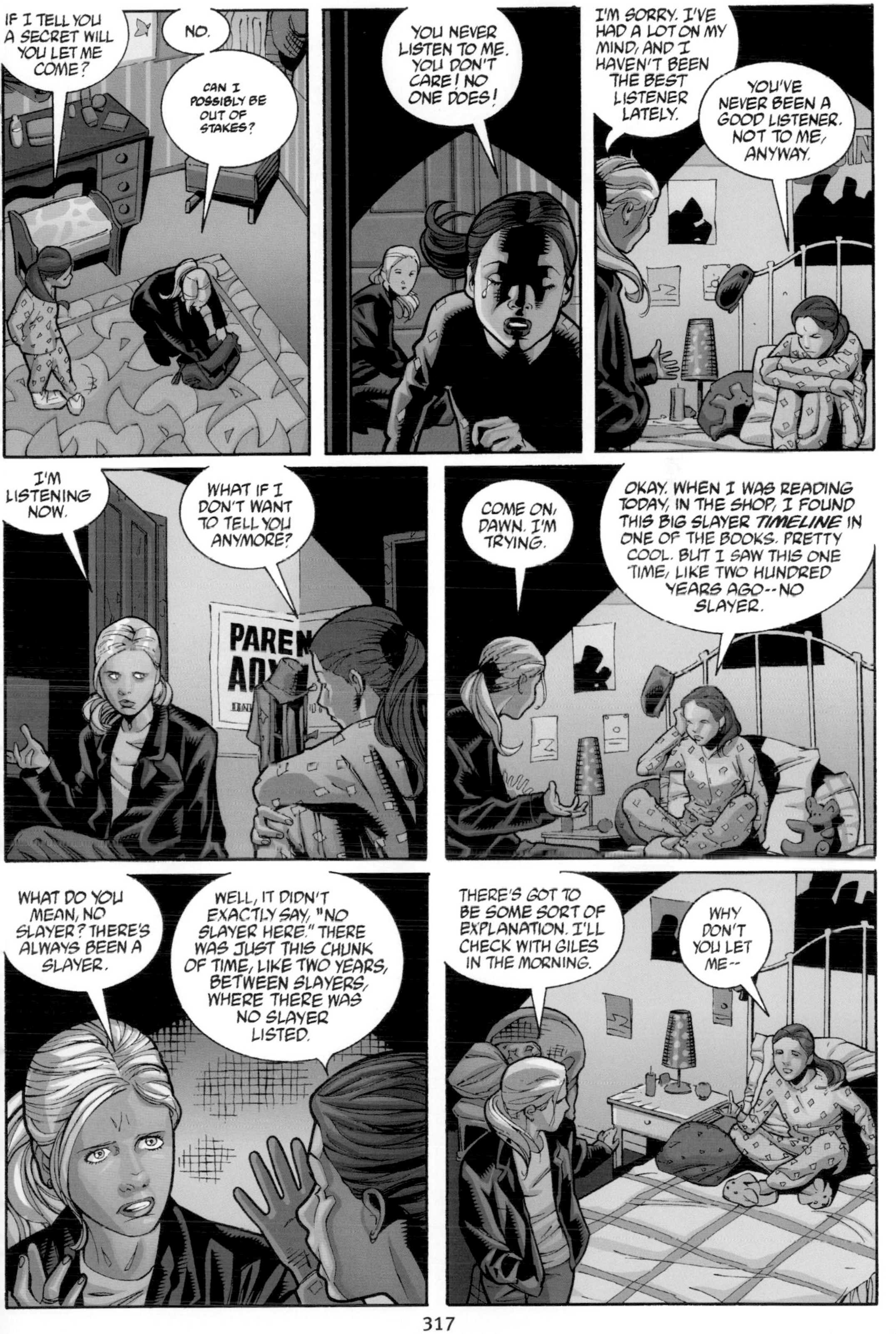
IF I TELL YOU A SECRET WILL YOU LET ME COME?
NO.
CAN I POSSIBLY BE OUT OF STAKES?
YOU NEVER LISTEN TO ME. YOU DON'T CARE! NO ONE DOES!
I'M SORRY. I'VE HAD A LOT ON MY MIND, AND I HAVEN'T BEEN THE BEST LISTENER LATELY.
YOU'VE NEVER BEEN A GOOD LISTENER. NOT TO ME, ANYWAY.
I'M LISTENING NOW.
WHAT IF I DON'T WANT TO TELL YOU ANYMORE?
PAREN
ADV
COME ON, DAWN. I'M TRYING.
OKAY. WHEN I WAS READING TODAY, IN THE SHOP, I FOUND THIS BIG SLAYER *TIMELINE* IN ONE OF THE BOOKS. PRETTY COOL. BUT I SAW THIS ONE TIME, LIKE TWO HUNDRED YEARS AGO--NO SLAYER.
WHAT DO YOU MEAN, NO SLAYER? THERE'S ALWAYS BEEN A SLAYER.
WELL, IT DIDN'T EXACTLY SAY, "NO SLAYER HERE." THERE WAS JUST THIS CHUNK OF TIME, LIKE TWO YEARS, BETWEEN SLAYERS, WHERE THERE WAS NO SLAYER LISTED.
THERE'S GOT TO BE SOME SORT OF EXPLANATION. I'LL CHECK WITH GILES IN THE MORNING.
WHY DON'T YOU LET ME--

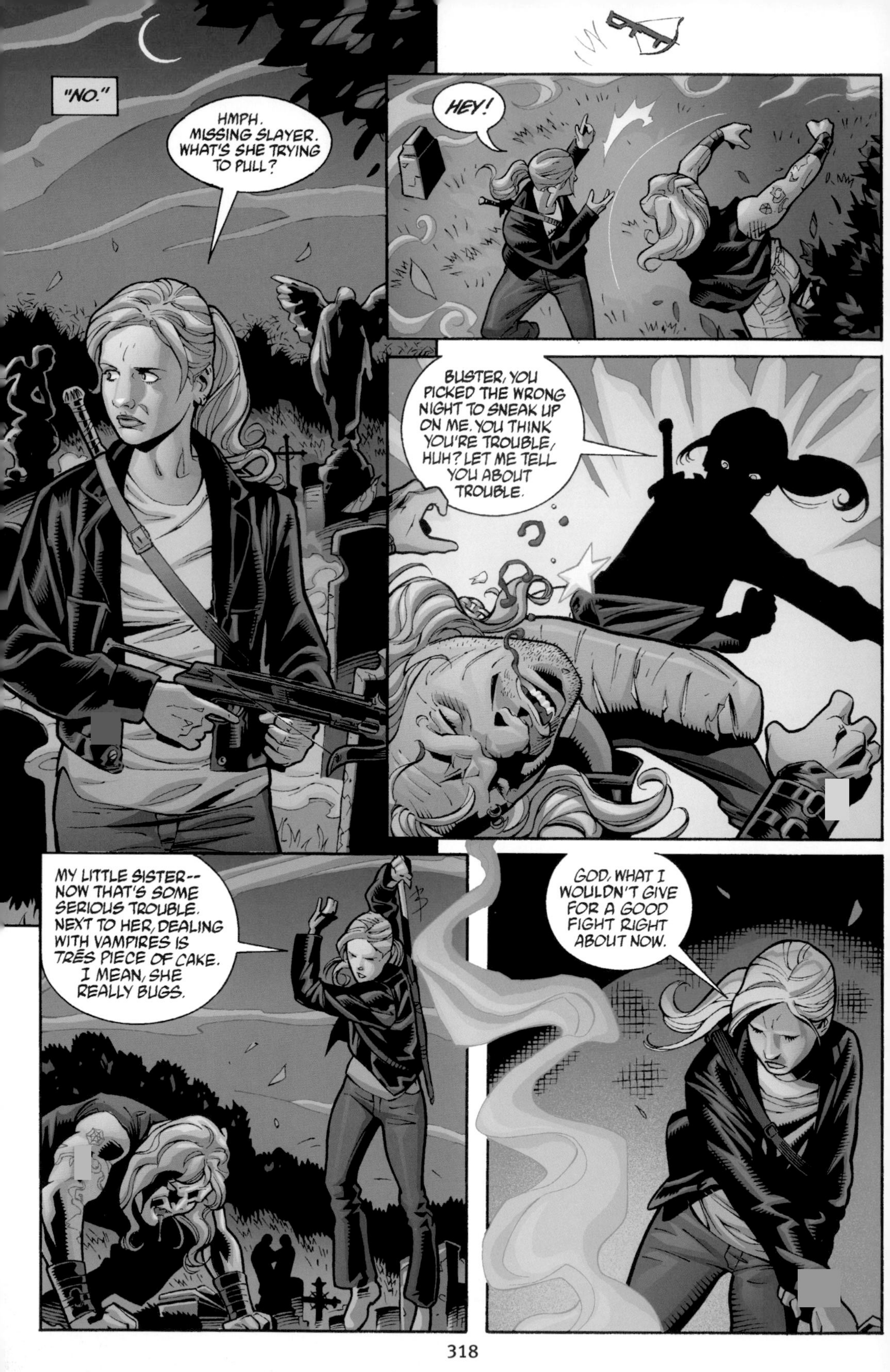
"NO."
HMPH. MISSING SLAYER. WHAT'S SHE TRYING TO PULL?
HEY!
BUSTER, YOU PICKED THE WRONG NIGHT TO SNEAK UP ON ME. YOU THINK YOU'RE TROUBLE, HUH? LET ME TELL YOU ABOUT TROUBLE.
MY LITTLE SISTER-- NOW THAT'S SOME SERIOUS TROUBLE. NEXT TO HER, DEALING WITH VAMPIRES IS TRÉS PIECE OF CAKE. I MEAN, SHE REALLY BUGS.
GOD, WHAT I WOULDN'T GIVE FOR A GOOD FIGHT RIGHT ABOUT NOW.

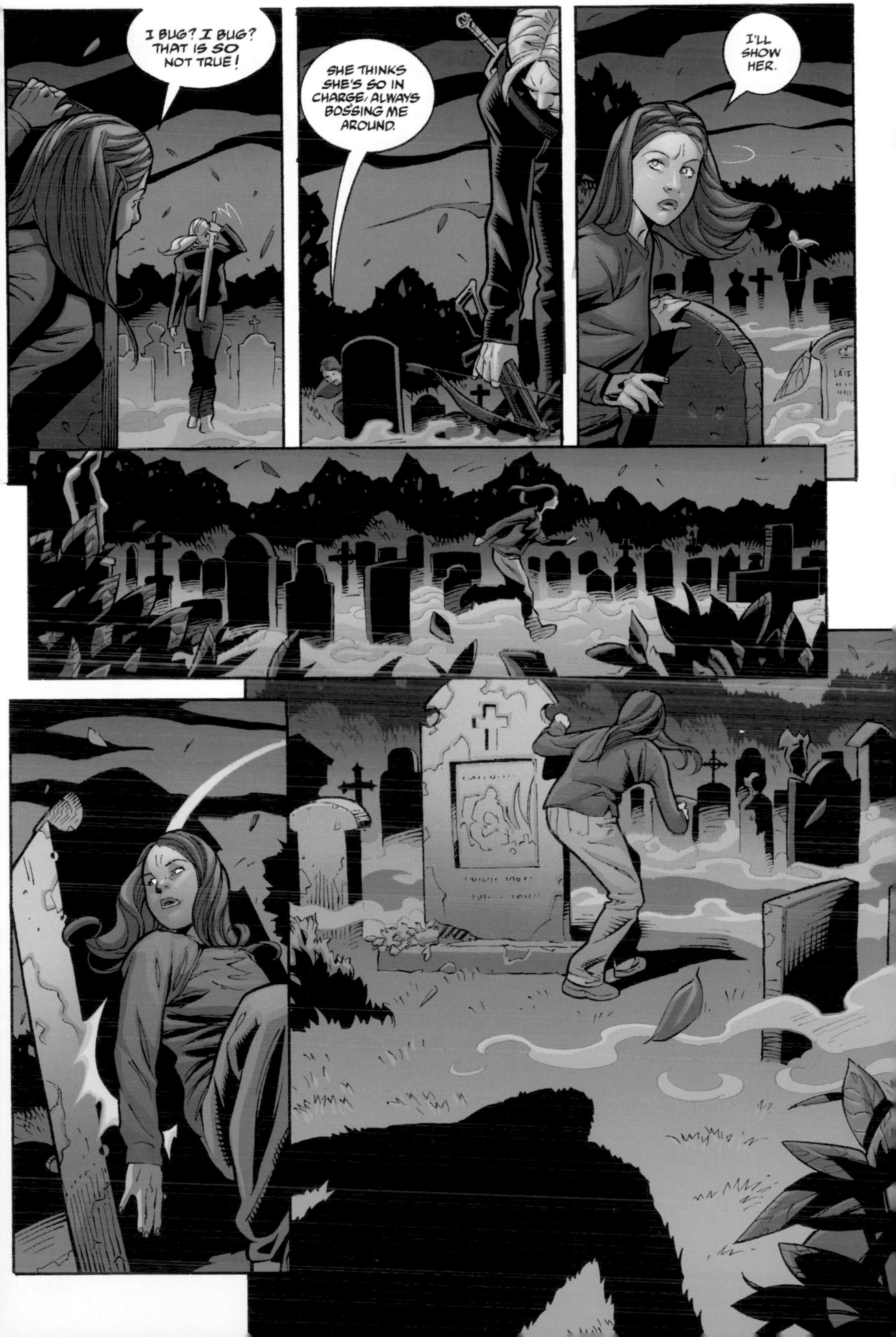
I BUG? I BUG? THAT IS SO NOT TRUE!
SHE THINKS SHE'S SO IN CHARGE, ALWAYS BOSSING ME AROUND.
I'LL SHOW HER.

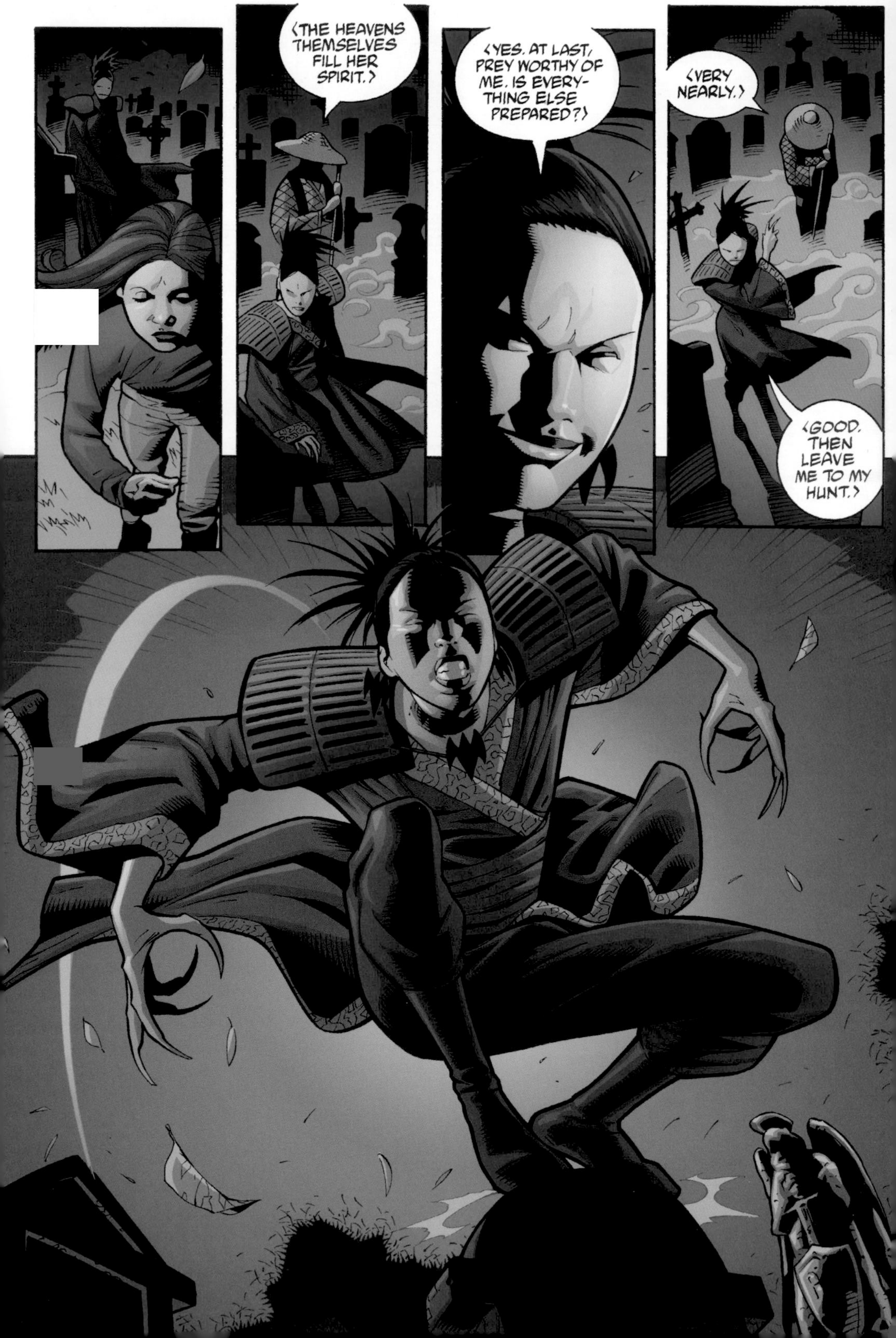
‹THE HEAVENS THEMSELVES FILL HER SPIRIT.›
‹YES. AT LAST, PREY WORTHY OF ME. IS EVERY-THING ELSE PREPARED?›
‹VERY NEARLY.›
‹GOOD. THEN LEAVE ME TO MY HUNT.›

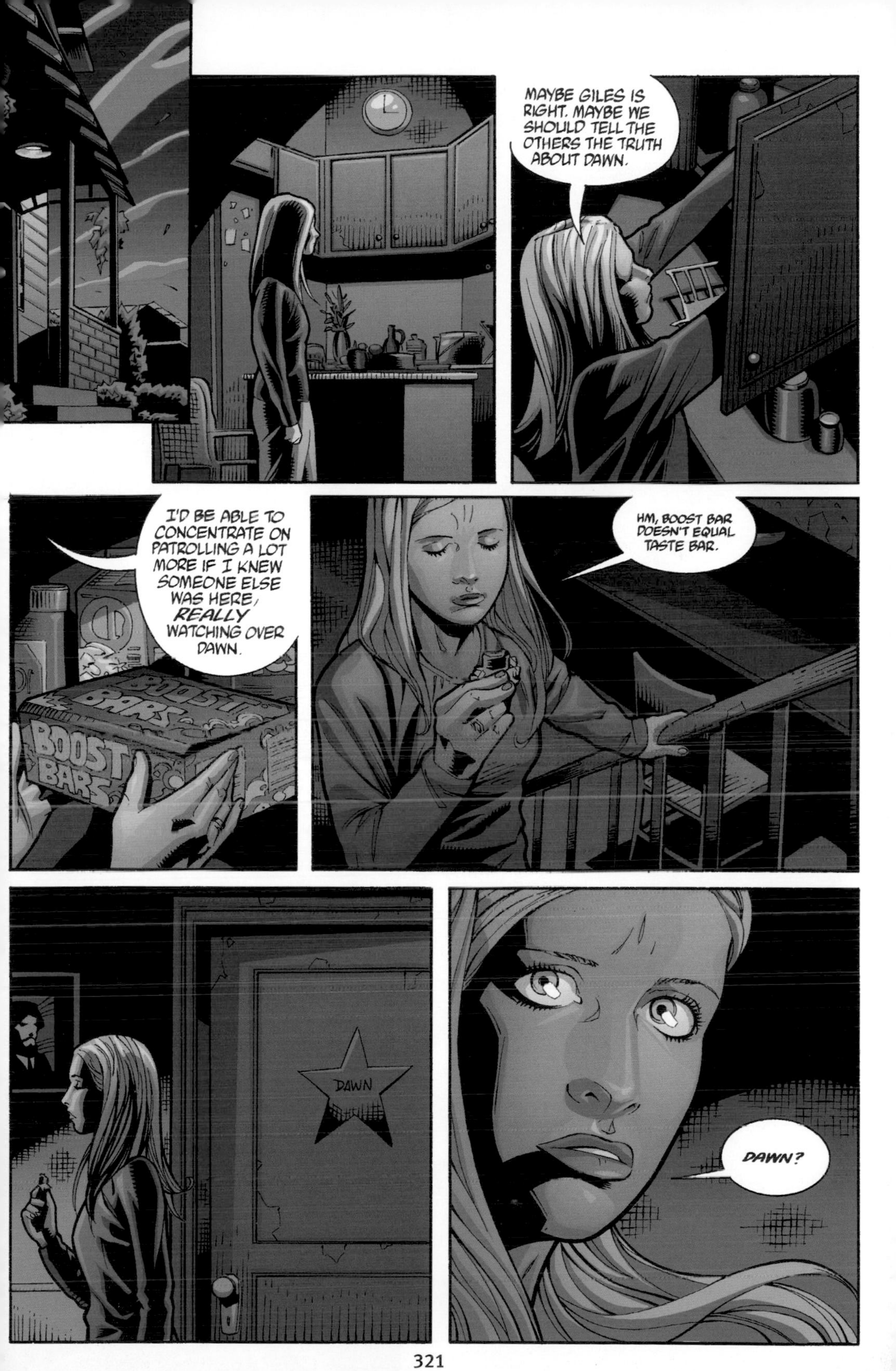
MAYBE GILES IS RIGHT. MAYBE WE SHOULD TELL THE OTHERS THE TRUTH ABOUT DAWN.
I'D BE ABLE TO CONCENTRATE ON PATROLLING A LOT MORE IF I KNEW SOMEONE ELSE WAS HERE, *REALLY* WATCHING OVER DAWN.
BOOST BARS
HM, BOOST BAR DOESN'T EQUAL TASTE BAR.
DAWN
DAWN?

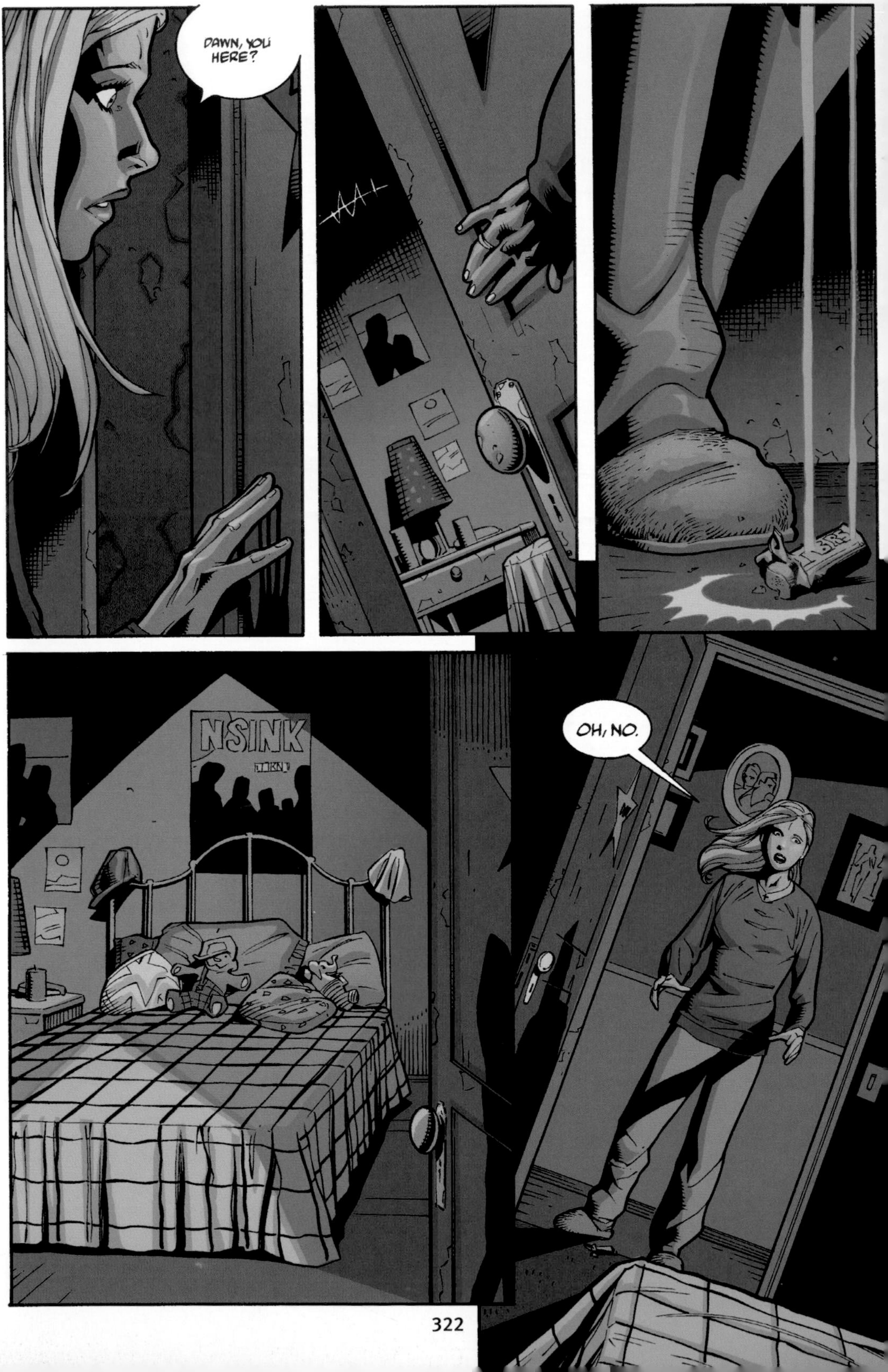
DAWN, YOU HERE?
NSINK
OH, NO.

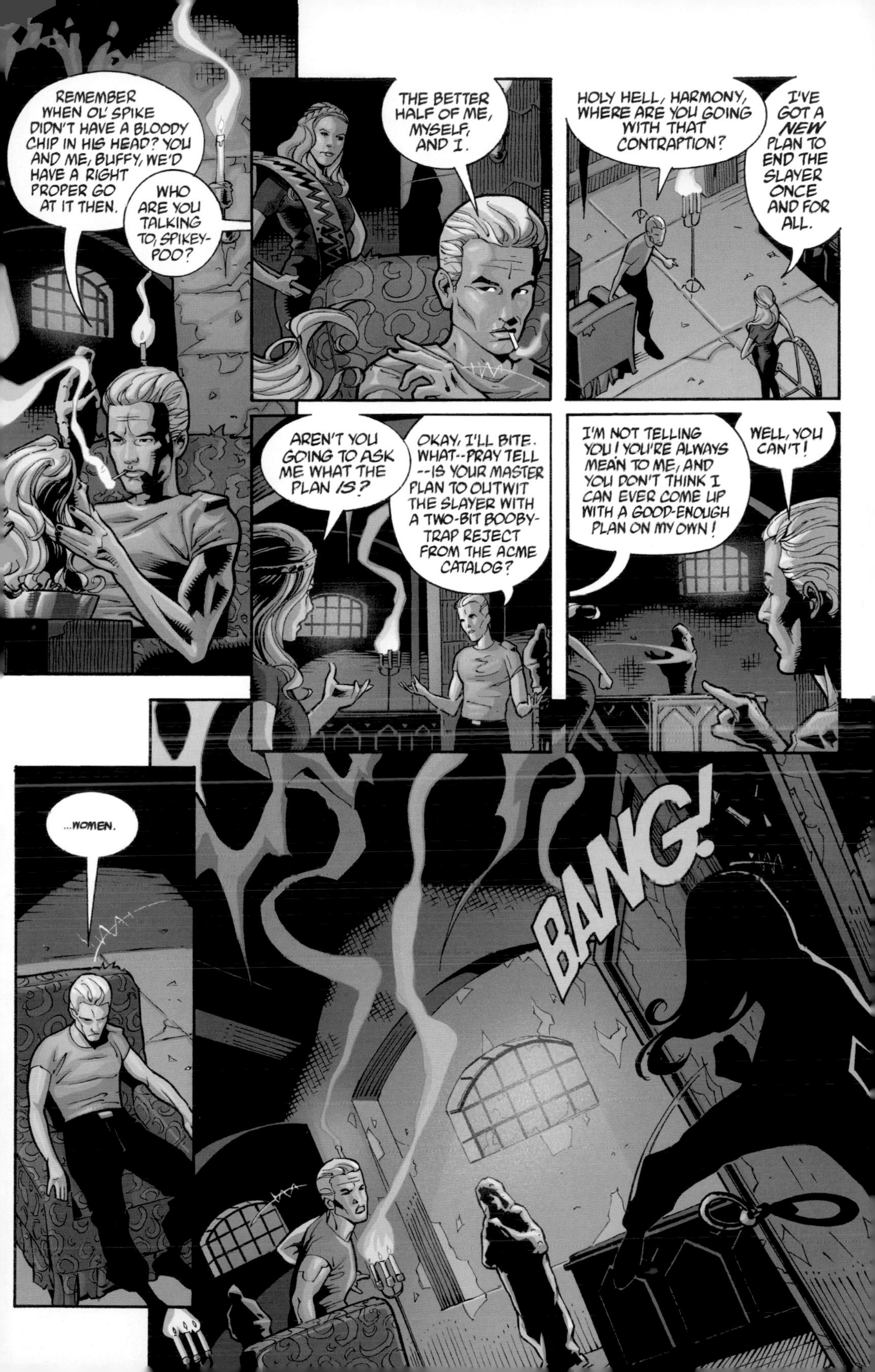
REMEMBER WHEN OL' SPIKE DIDN'T HAVE A BLOODY CHIP IN HIS HEAD? YOU AND ME, BUFFY, WE'D HAVE A RIGHT PROPER GO AT IT THEN.
WHO ARE YOU TALKING TO, SPIKEY-POO?
THE BETTER HALF OF ME, MYSELF, AND I.
HOLY HELL, HARMONY, WHERE ARE YOU GOING WITH THAT CONTRAPTION?
I'VE GOT A NEW PLAN TO END THE SLAYER ONCE AND FOR ALL.
AREN'T YOU GOING TO ASK ME WHAT THE PLAN IS?
OKAY, I'LL BITE. WHAT--PRAY TELL--IS YOUR MASTER PLAN TO OUTWIT THE SLAYER WITH A TWO-BIT BOOBY-TRAP REJECT FROM THE ACME CATALOG?
I'M NOT TELLING YOU! YOU'RE ALWAYS MEAN TO ME, AND YOU DON'T THINK I CAN EVER COME UP WITH A GOOD-ENOUGH PLAN ON MY OWN!
WELL, YOU CAN'T!
...WOMEN.
BANG!

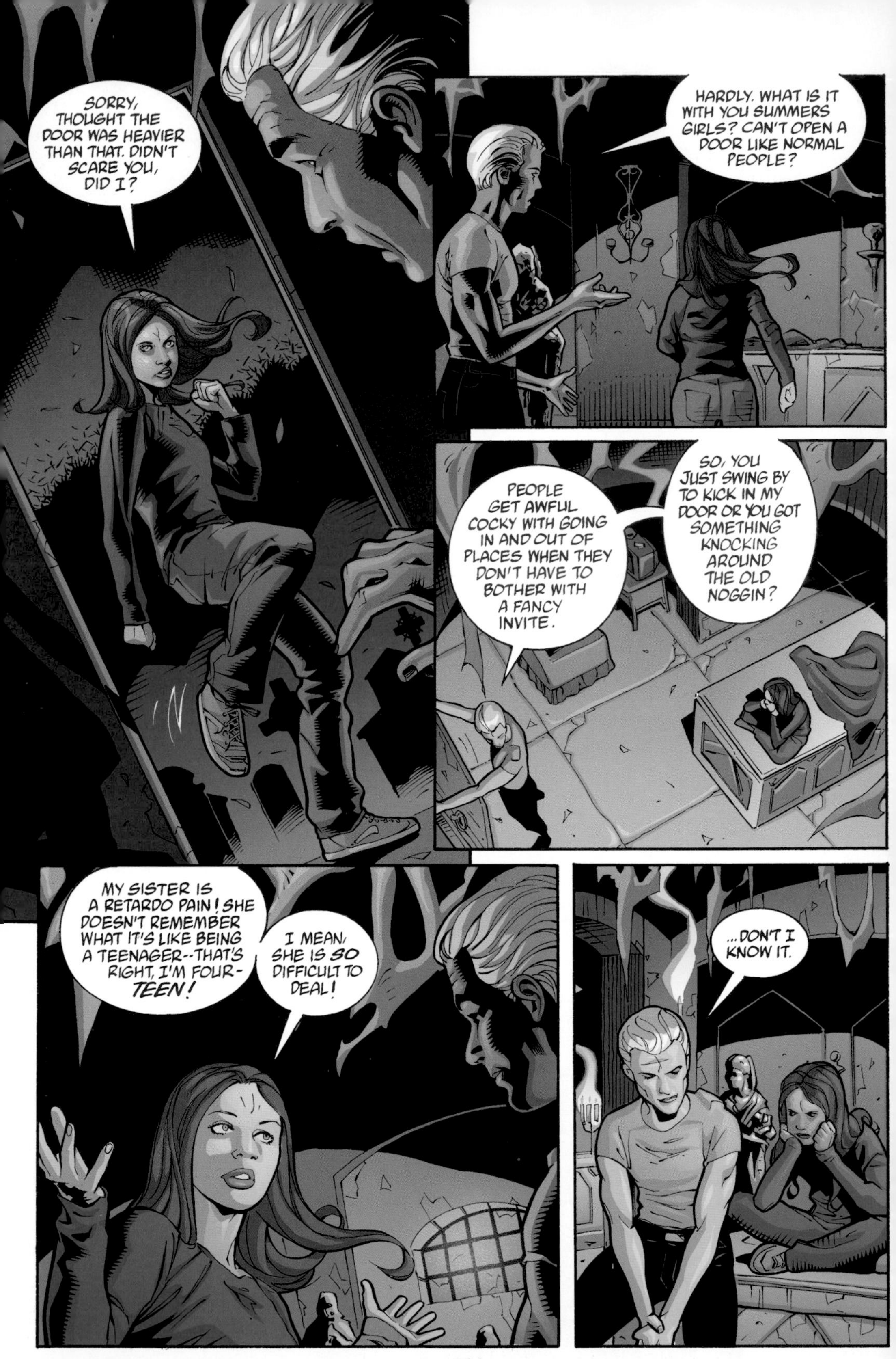
SORRY, THOUGHT THE DOOR WAS HEAVIER THAN THAT. DIDN'T SCARE YOU, DID I?
HARDLY. WHAT IS IT WITH YOU SUMMERS GIRLS? CAN'T OPEN A DOOR LIKE NORMAL PEOPLE?
PEOPLE GET AWFUL COCKY WITH GOING IN AND OUT OF PLACES WHEN THEY DON'T HAVE TO BOTHER WITH A FANCY INVITE.
SO, YOU JUST SWING BY TO KICK IN MY DOOR OR YOU GOT SOMETHING KNOCKING AROUND THE OLD NOGGIN?
MY SISTER IS A RETARDO PAIN! SHE DOESN'T REMEMBER WHAT IT'S LIKE BEING A TEENAGER--THAT'S RIGHT, I'M FOUR-TEEN!
I MEAN, SHE IS SO DIFFICULT TO DEAL!
...DON'T I KNOW IT.

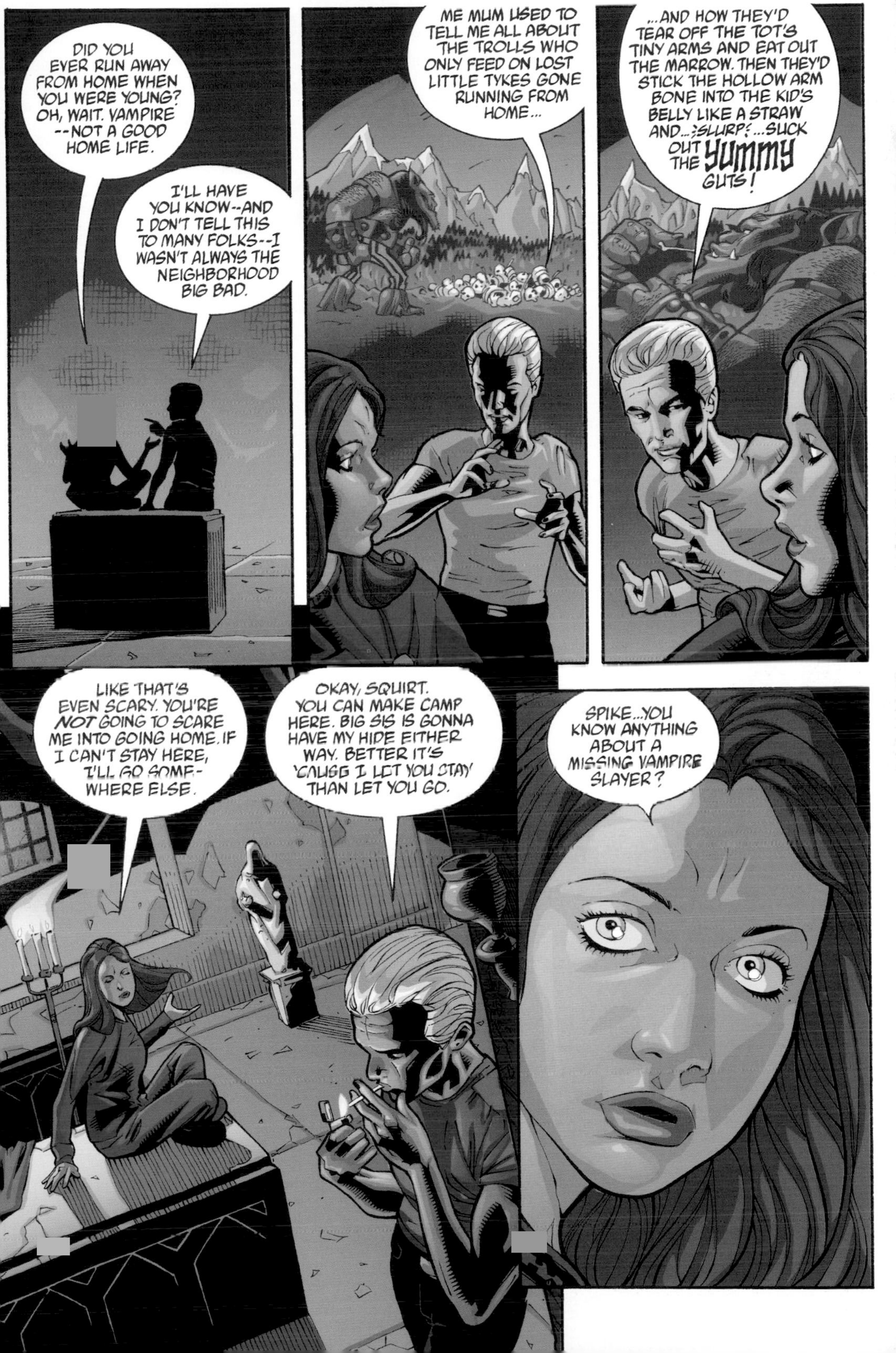
DID YOU EVER RUN AWAY FROM HOME WHEN YOU WERE YOUNG? OH, WAIT. VAMPIRE --NOT A GOOD HOME LIFE.
I'LL HAVE YOU KNOW--AND I DON'T TELL THIS TO MANY FOLKS--I WASN'T ALWAYS THE NEIGHBORHOOD BIG BAD.
ME MUM USED TO TELL ME ALL ABOUT THE TROLLS WHO ONLY FEED ON LOST LITTLE TYKES GONE RUNNING FROM HOME...
...AND HOW THEY'D TEAR OFF THE TOT'S TINY ARMS AND EAT OUT THE MARROW. THEN THEY'D STICK THE HOLLOW ARM BONE INTO THE KID'S BELLY LIKE A STRAW AND... SLURP ...SUCK OUT THE YUMMY GUTS!
LIKE THAT'S EVEN SCARY. YOU'RE NOT GOING TO SCARE ME INTO GOING HOME. IF I CAN'T STAY HERE, I'LL GO SOMEWHERE ELSE.
OKAY, SQUIRT. YOU CAN MAKE CAMP HERE. BIG SIS IS GONNA HAVE MY HIDE EITHER WAY. BETTER IT'S 'CAUSE I LET YOU STAY THAN LET YOU GO.
SPIKE...YOU KNOW ANYTHING ABOUT A MISSING VAMPIRE SLAYER?

...A MISSING SLAYER, YOU SAY? THAT'S... PREPOSTEROUS...

WHATEVER. I'M NOT WORRIED ABOUT A SLAYER THAT MAY OR MAY NOT HAVE DISAPPEARED OFF THE BOOKS A CENTURY AGO. I'M WORRIED ABOUT DAWN DISAPPEARING IN REAL LIFE, RIGHT NOW.

YES, THAT IS GREATER CAUSE FOR ALARM. TELL ME AGAIN, WHEN WAS THE LAST TIME YOU SAW HER?

HOW MANY TIMES DO I HAVE TO GO OVER IT? I WENT ON PATROL LAST NIGHT, AND WHEN I CAME BACK HOME--NO DAWN. HER BED WAS STILL MADE, EVEN.

HER BED WAS MADE... WOW, THAT IS TOTALLY WEIRD.

WILL! I NEED YOU ON MY SIDE!

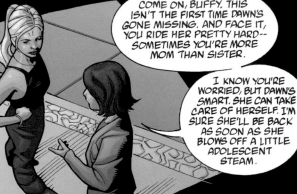

COME ON, BUFFY. THIS ISN'T THE FIRST TIME DAWN'S GONE MISSING. AND FACE IT, YOU RIDE HER PRETTY HARD-- SOMETIMES YOU'RE MORE MOM THAN SISTER.

I KNOW YOU'RE WORRIED, BUT DAWN'S SMART. SHE CAN TAKE CARE OF HERSELF. I'M SURE SHE'LL BE BACK AS SOON AS SHE BLOWS OFF A LITTLE ADOLESCENT STEAM.

I SUSPECT WE SHOULD ORGANIZE A SEARCH--

HAVE YOU LOOKED AT SCHOOL? I HEARD THAT WHEN YOU LOSE SOMETHING, YOU'RE SUPPOSED TO LOOK IN THE PLACE YOU'D MOST EXPECT...

OR IS IT THE PLACE YOU'D LEAST EXPECT?

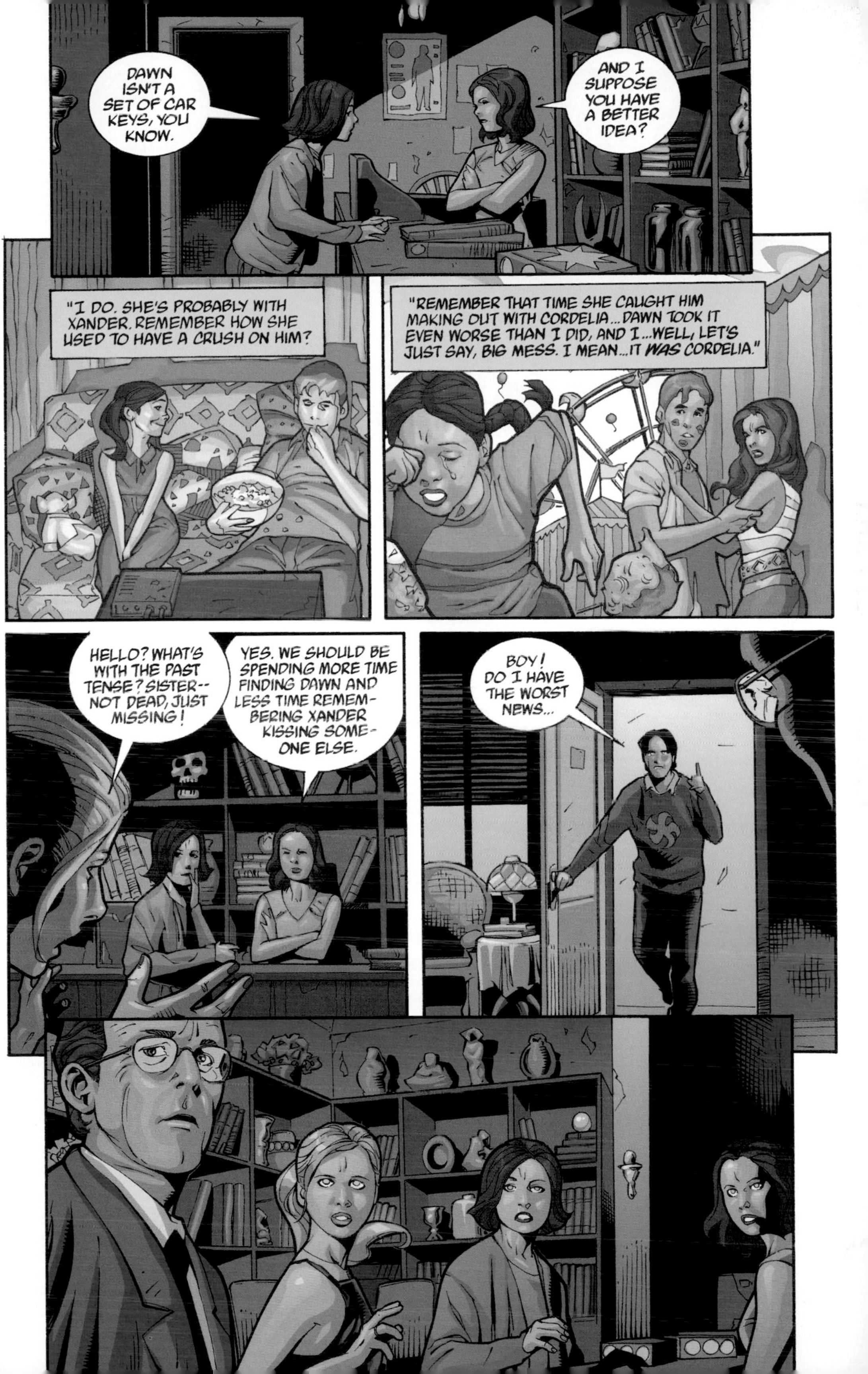
DAWN ISN'T A SET OF CAR KEYS, YOU KNOW.
AND I SUPPOSE YOU HAVE A BETTER IDEA?
"I DO. SHE'S PROBABLY WITH XANDER. REMEMBER HOW SHE USED TO HAVE A CRUSH ON HIM?
"REMEMBER THAT TIME SHE CAUGHT HIM MAKING OUT WITH CORDELIA... DAWN TOOK IT EVEN WORSE THAN I DID, AND I... WELL, LET'S JUST SAY, BIG MESS. I MEAN... IT *WAS* CORDELIA."
HELLO? WHAT'S WITH THE PAST TENSE? SISTER-- NOT DEAD, JUST MISSING!
YES. WE SHOULD BE SPENDING MORE TIME FINDING DAWN AND LESS TIME REMEMBERING XANDER KISSING SOMEONE ELSE.
BOY! DO I HAVE THE WORST NEWS...

WORK SUCKS!

XANDER! WAY TO DRIVE US ALL TO SCARED CITY!

WHAT? WHAT'D I SAY?

WE'VE LOST DAWN!

LOST AS IN MISSING? OR LOST AS IN--

SHE'S MISSING.

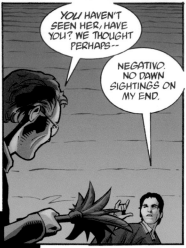

YOU HAVEN'T SEEN HER, HAVE YOU? WE THOUGHT PERHAPS--

NEGATIVO. NO DAWN SIGHTINGS ON MY END.

I DON'T SUPPOSE ANYONE CHECKED SCHOOL?

I'M THINKING SHE'S PUTTING ON A LITTLE RUNAWAY ACT ...YOU KNOW, TO GET OUT FROM UNDER BUFFY'S THUMB.

SHE'S NOT UNDER MY THUMB!

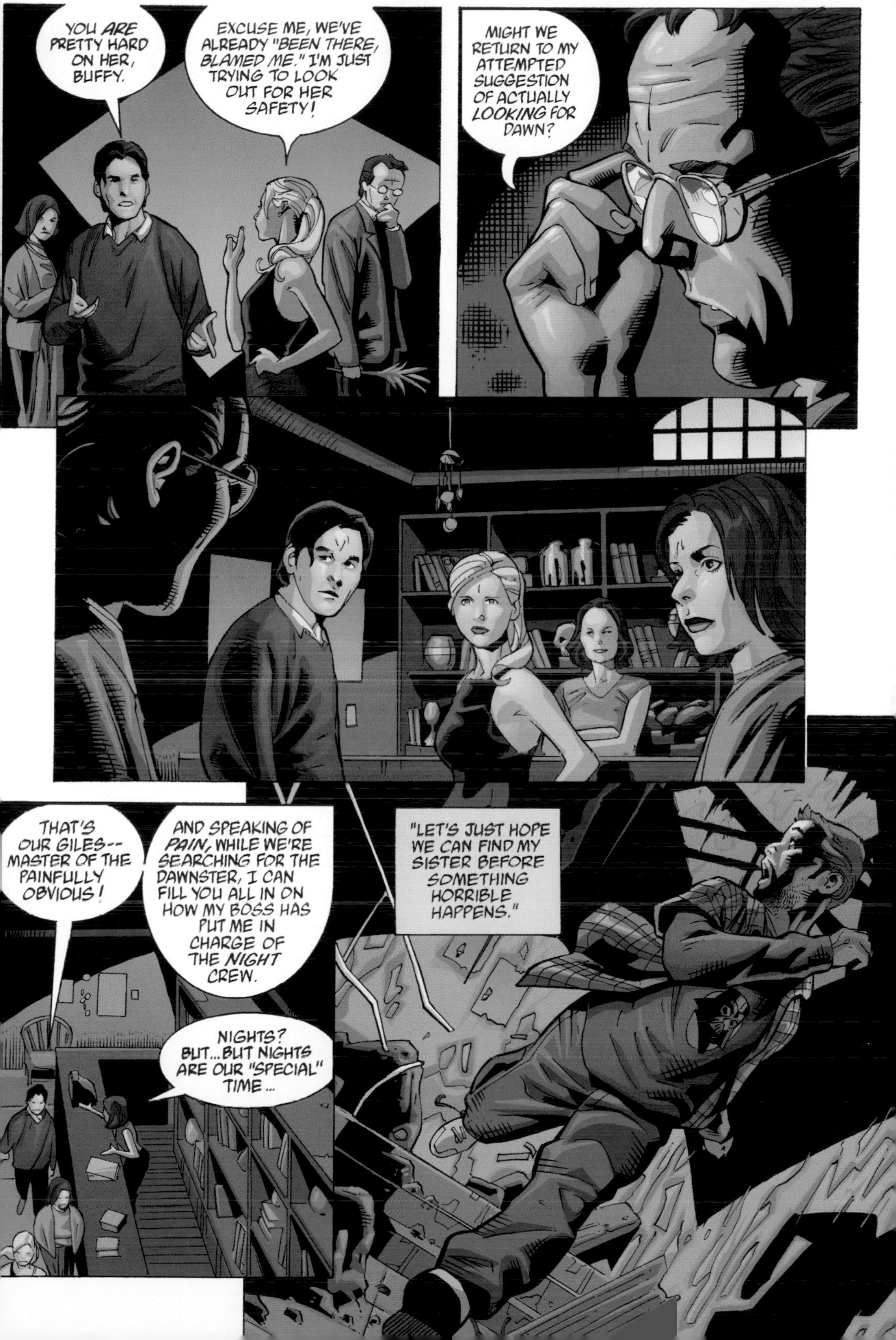
YOU ARE PRETTY HARD ON HER, BUFFY.
EXCUSE ME, WE'VE ALREADY "BEEN THERE, BLAMED ME." I'M JUST TRYING TO LOOK OUT FOR HER SAFETY!
MIGHT WE RETURN TO MY ATTEMPTED SUGGESTION OF ACTUALLY LOOKING FOR DAWN?
THAT'S OUR GILES-- MASTER OF THE PAINFULLY OBVIOUS!
AND SPEAKING OF PAIN, WHILE WE'RE SEARCHING FOR THE DAWNSTER, I CAN FILL YOU ALL IN ON HOW MY BOSS HAS PUT ME IN CHARGE OF THE NIGHT CREW.
NIGHTS? BUT...BUT NIGHTS ARE OUR "SPECIAL" TIME...
"LET'S JUST HOPE WE CAN FIND MY SISTER BEFORE SOMETHING HORRIBLE HAPPENS."

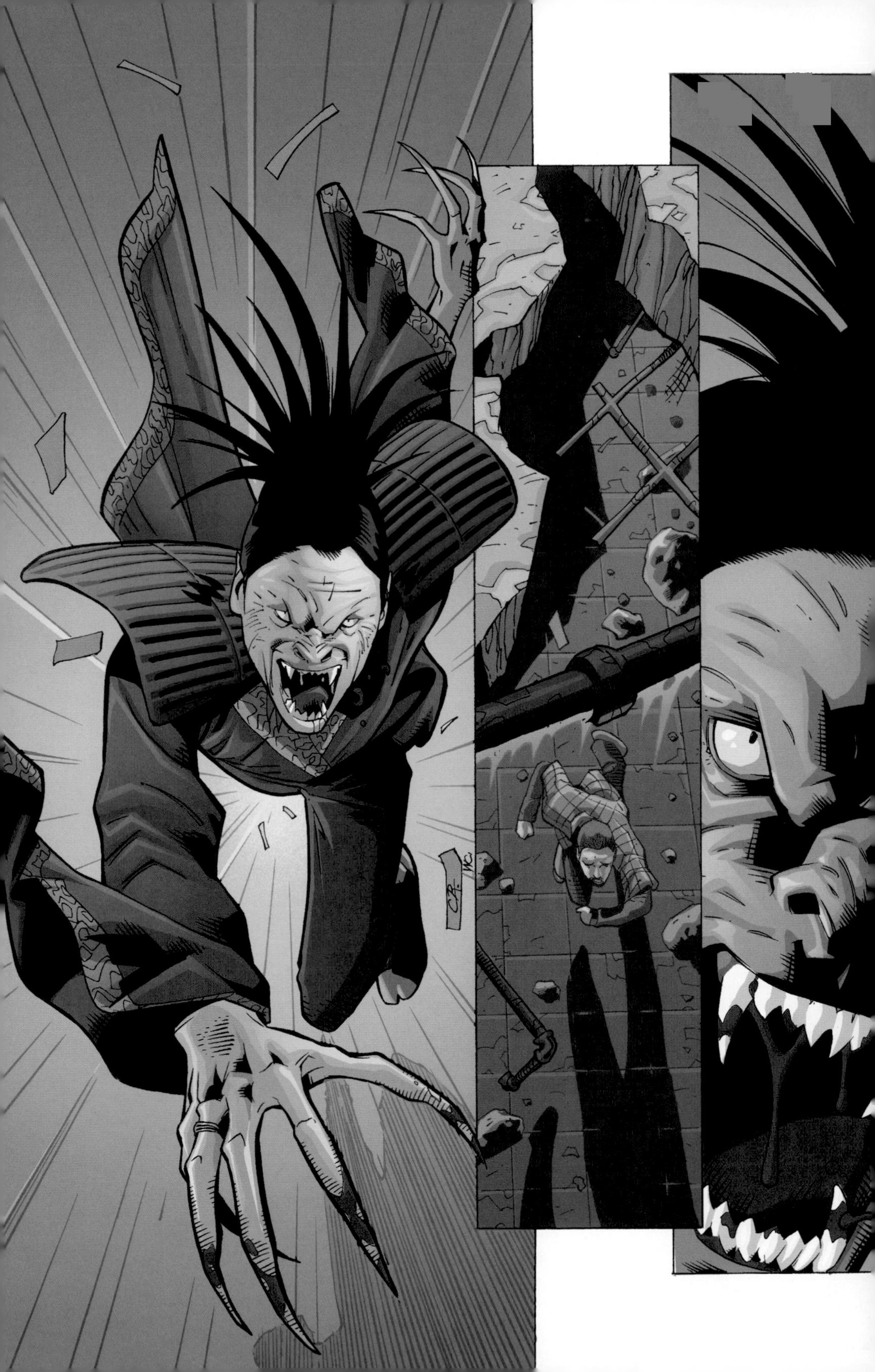

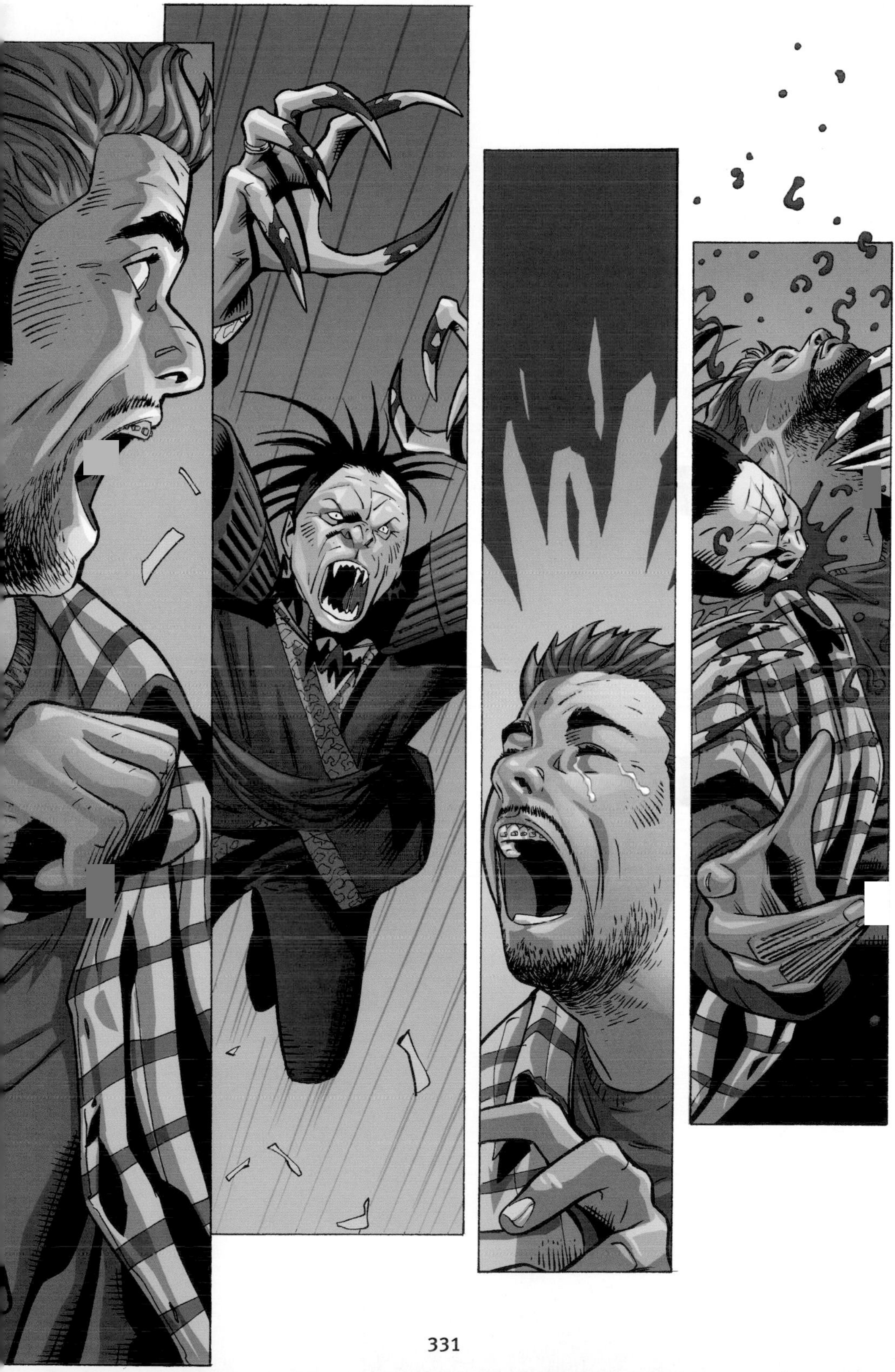

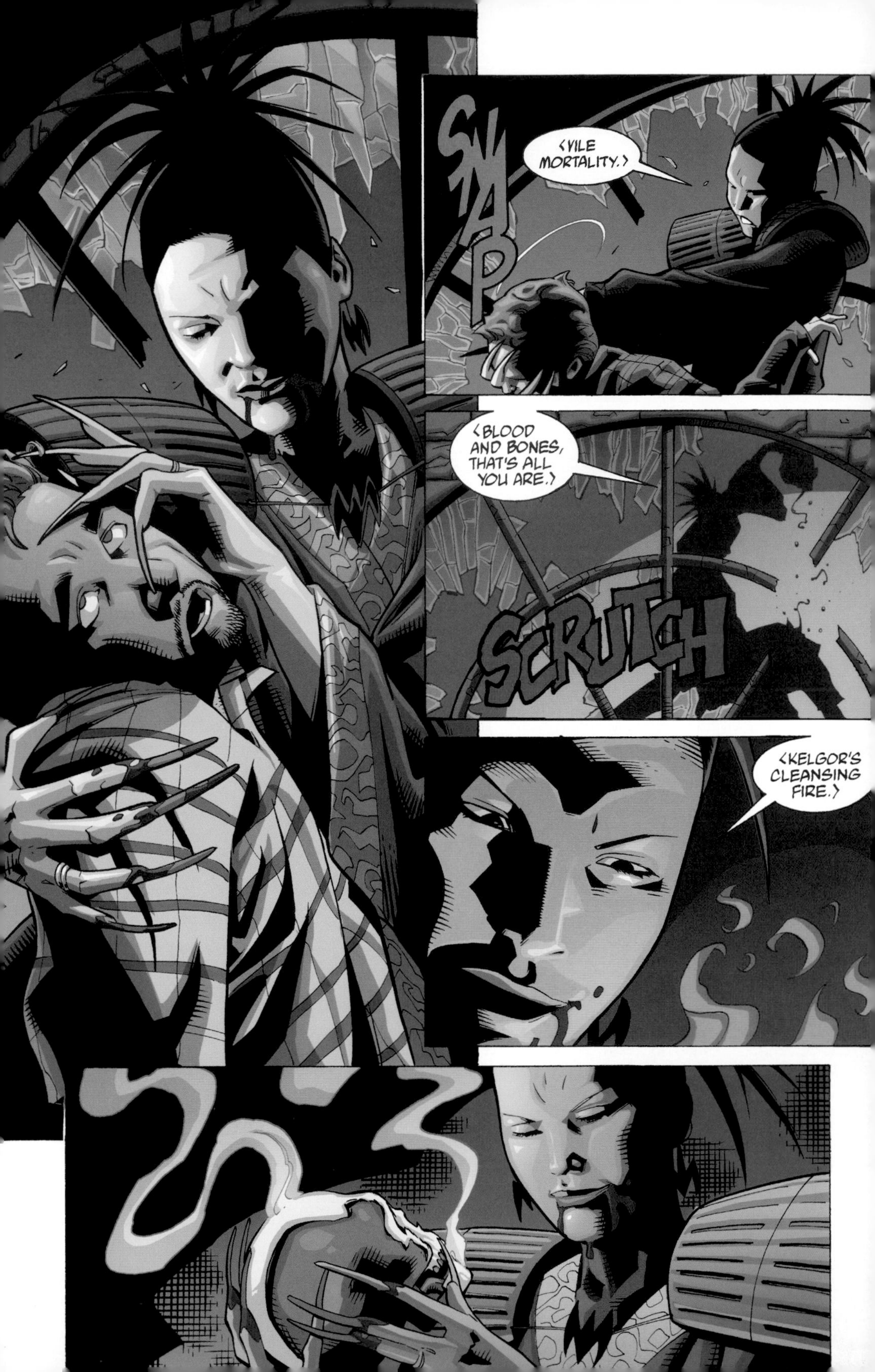

SNAP
<VILE MORTALITY.>
<BLOOD AND BONES, THAT'S ALL YOU ARE.>
SCRUTCH
<KELGOR'S CLEANSING FIRE.>

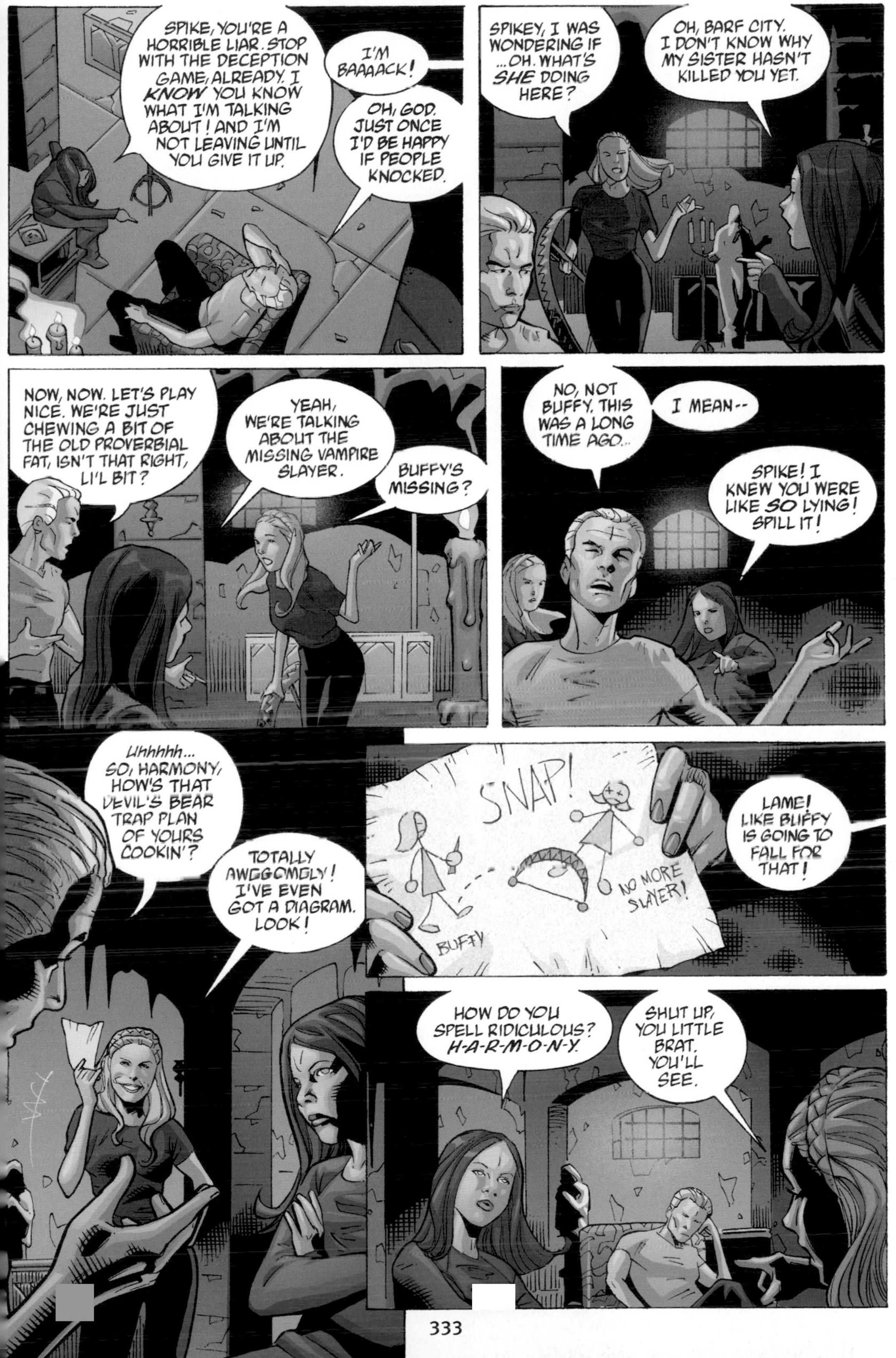
SPIKE, YOU'RE A HORRIBLE LIAR. STOP WITH THE DECEPTION GAME, ALREADY. I KNOW YOU KNOW WHAT I'M TALKING ABOUT! AND I'M NOT LEAVING UNTIL YOU GIVE IT UP.
I'M BAAAACK!
OH, GOD. JUST ONCE I'D BE HAPPY IF PEOPLE KNOCKED.
SPIKEY, I WAS WONDERING IF ...OH. WHAT'S SHE DOING HERE?
OH, BARF CITY. I DON'T KNOW WHY MY SISTER HASN'T KILLED YOU YET.
NOW, NOW. LET'S PLAY NICE. WE'RE JUST CHEWING A BIT OF THE OLD PROVERBIAL FAT, ISN'T THAT RIGHT, LI'L BIT?
YEAH, WE'RE TALKING ABOUT THE MISSING VAMPIRE SLAYER.
BUFFY'S MISSING?
NO, NOT BUFFY. THIS WAS A LONG TIME AGO...
I MEAN--
SPIKE! I KNEW YOU WERE LIKE SO LYING! SPILL IT!
Uhhhhh... SO, HARMONY, HOW'S THAT DEVIL'S BEAR TRAP PLAN OF YOURS COOKIN'?
TOTALLY AWESOMELY! I'VE EVEN GOT A DIAGRAM. LOOK!
SNAP!
BUFFY
NO MORE SLAYER!
LAME! LIKE BUFFY IS GOING TO FALL FOR THAT!
HOW DO YOU SPELL RIDICULOUS? H-A-R-M-O-N-Y.
SHUT UP, YOU LITTLE BRAT. YOU'LL SEE.

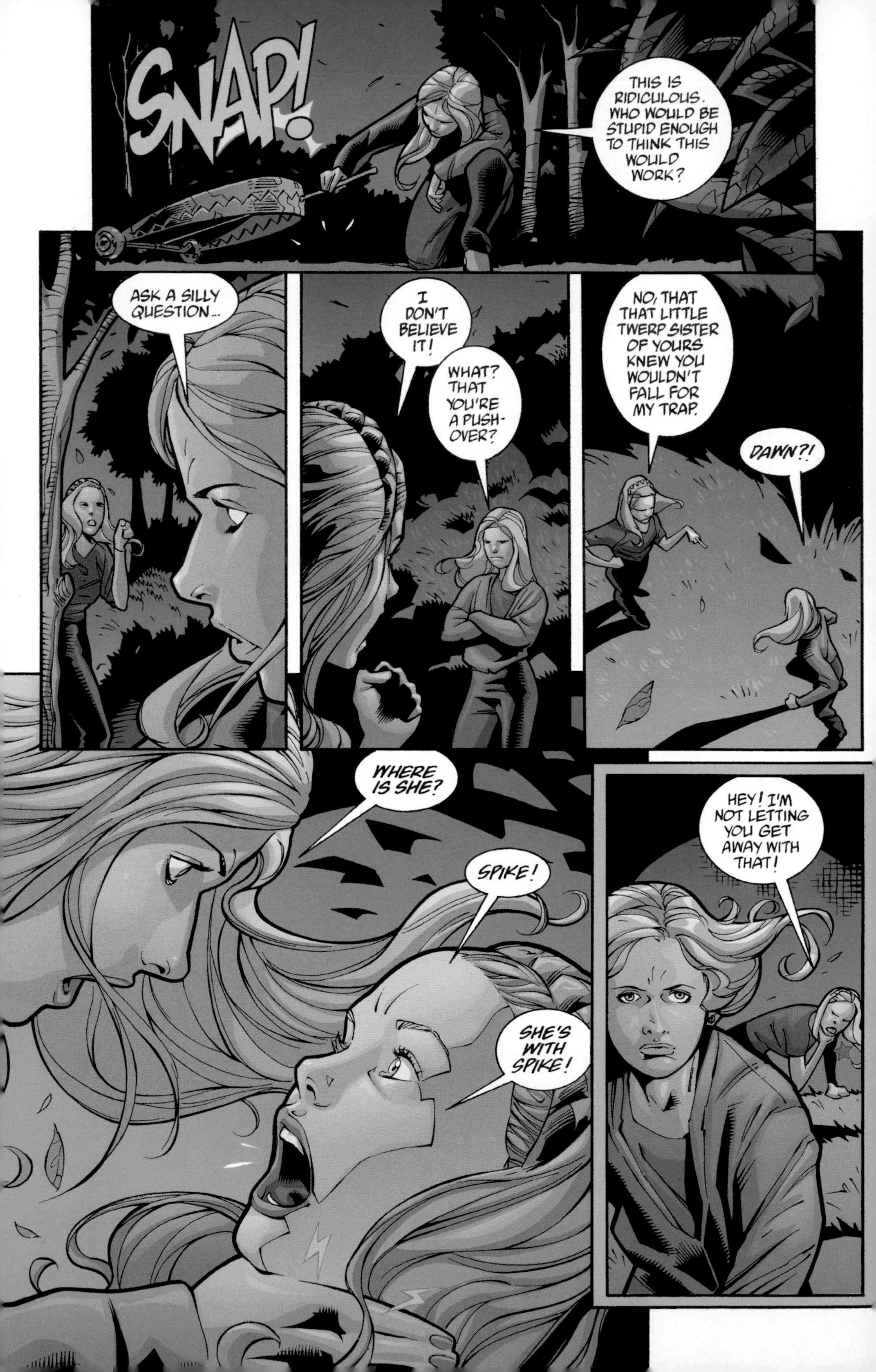
SNAP!
THIS IS RIDICULOUS. WHO WOULD BE STUPID ENOUGH TO THINK THIS WOULD WORK?
ASK A SILLY QUESTION...
I DON'T BELIEVE IT!
WHAT? THAT YOU'RE A PUSH-OVER?
NO, THAT THAT LITTLE TWERP SISTER OF YOURS KNEW YOU WOULDN'T FALL FOR MY TRAP.
DAWN?!
WHERE IS SHE?
SPIKE!
SHE'S WITH SPIKE!
HEY! I'M NOT LETTING YOU GET AWAY WITH THAT!

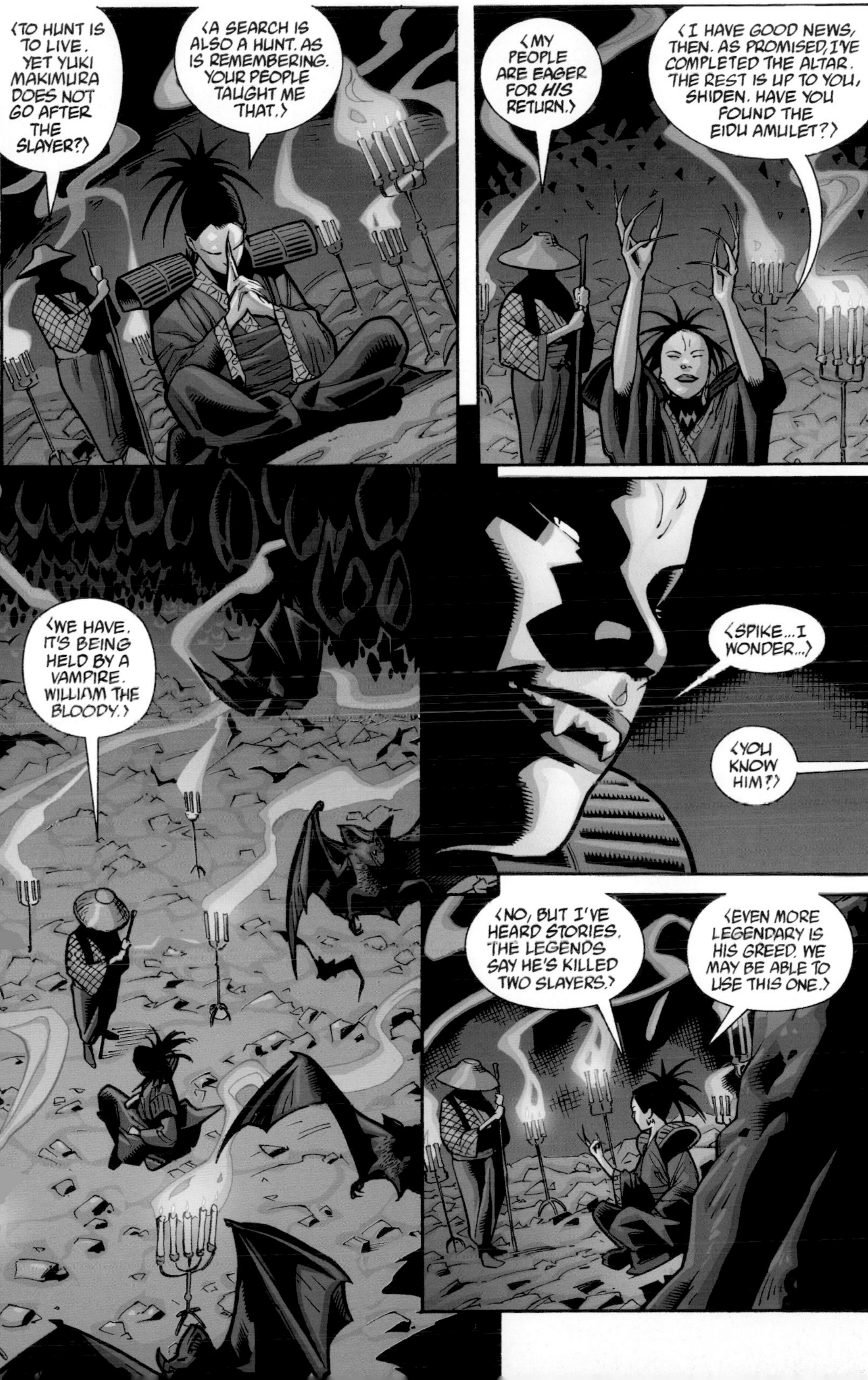

‹TO HUNT IS TO LIVE. YET YUKI MAKIMURA DOES NOT GO AFTER THE SLAYER?›
‹A SEARCH IS ALSO A HUNT. AS IS REMEMBERING. YOUR PEOPLE TAUGHT ME THAT.›
‹MY PEOPLE ARE EAGER FOR HIS RETURN.›
‹I HAVE GOOD NEWS, THEN. AS PROMISED, I'VE COMPLETED THE ALTAR. THE REST IS UP TO YOU, SHIDEN. HAVE YOU FOUND THE EIDU AMULET?›
‹WE HAVE. IT'S BEING HELD BY A VAMPIRE. WILLIAM THE BLOODY.›
‹SPIKE...I WONDER...›
‹YOU KNOW HIM?›
‹NO, BUT I'VE HEARD STORIES. THE LEGENDS SAY HE'S KILLED TWO SLAYERS.›
‹EVEN MORE LEGENDARY IS HIS GREED. WE MAY BE ABLE TO USE THIS ONE.›

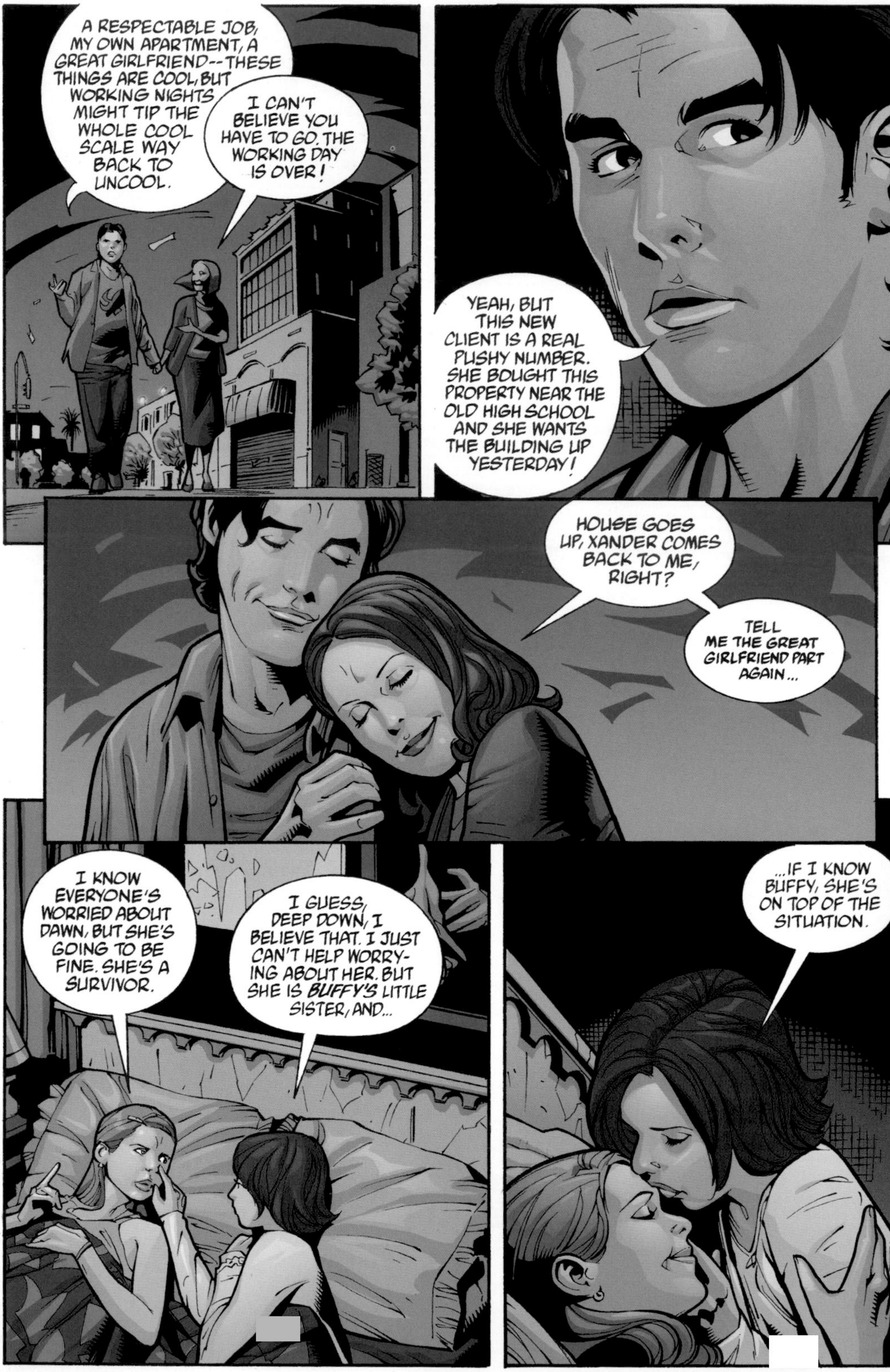
A RESPECTABLE JOB, MY OWN APARTMENT, A GREAT GIRLFRIEND--THESE THINGS ARE COOL, BUT WORKING NIGHTS MIGHT TIP THE WHOLE COOL SCALE WAY BACK TO UNCOOL.
I CAN'T BELIEVE YOU HAVE TO GO. THE WORKING DAY IS OVER!
YEAH, BUT THIS NEW CLIENT IS A REAL PUSHY NUMBER. SHE BOUGHT THIS PROPERTY NEAR THE OLD HIGH SCHOOL AND SHE WANTS THE BUILDING UP YESTERDAY!
HOUSE GOES UP, XANDER COMES BACK TO ME, RIGHT?
TELL ME THE GREAT GIRLFRIEND PART AGAIN...
I KNOW EVERYONE'S WORRIED ABOUT DAWN, BUT SHE'S GOING TO BE FINE. SHE'S A SURVIVOR.
I GUESS, DEEP DOWN, I BELIEVE THAT. I JUST CAN'T HELP WORRYING ABOUT HER. BUT SHE IS BUFFY'S LITTLE SISTER, AND...
...IF I KNOW BUFFY, SHE'S ON TOP OF THE SITUATION.

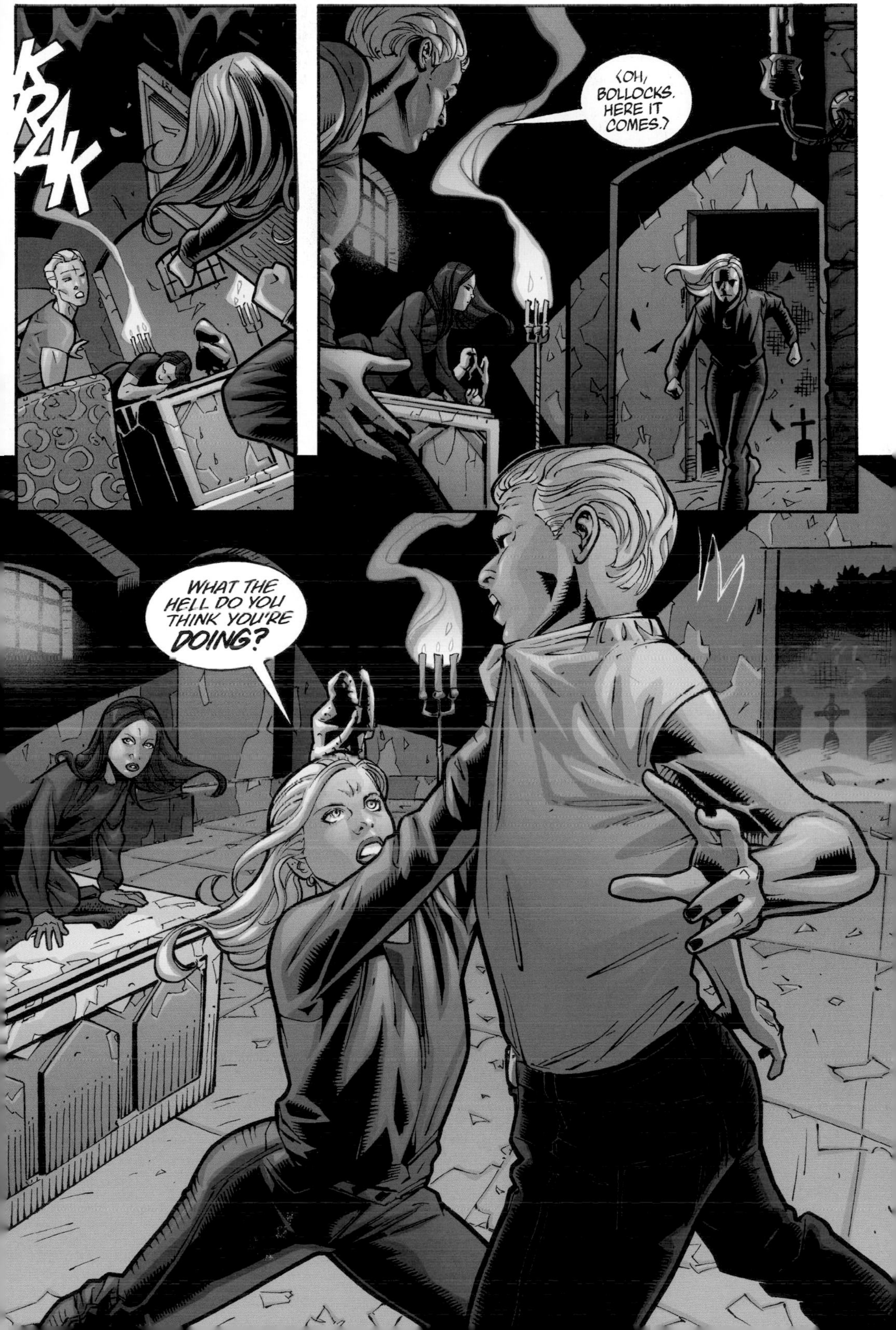
KRAK
<OH, BOLLOCKS. HERE IT COMES.>
WHAT THE HELL DO YOU THINK YOU'RE DOING?

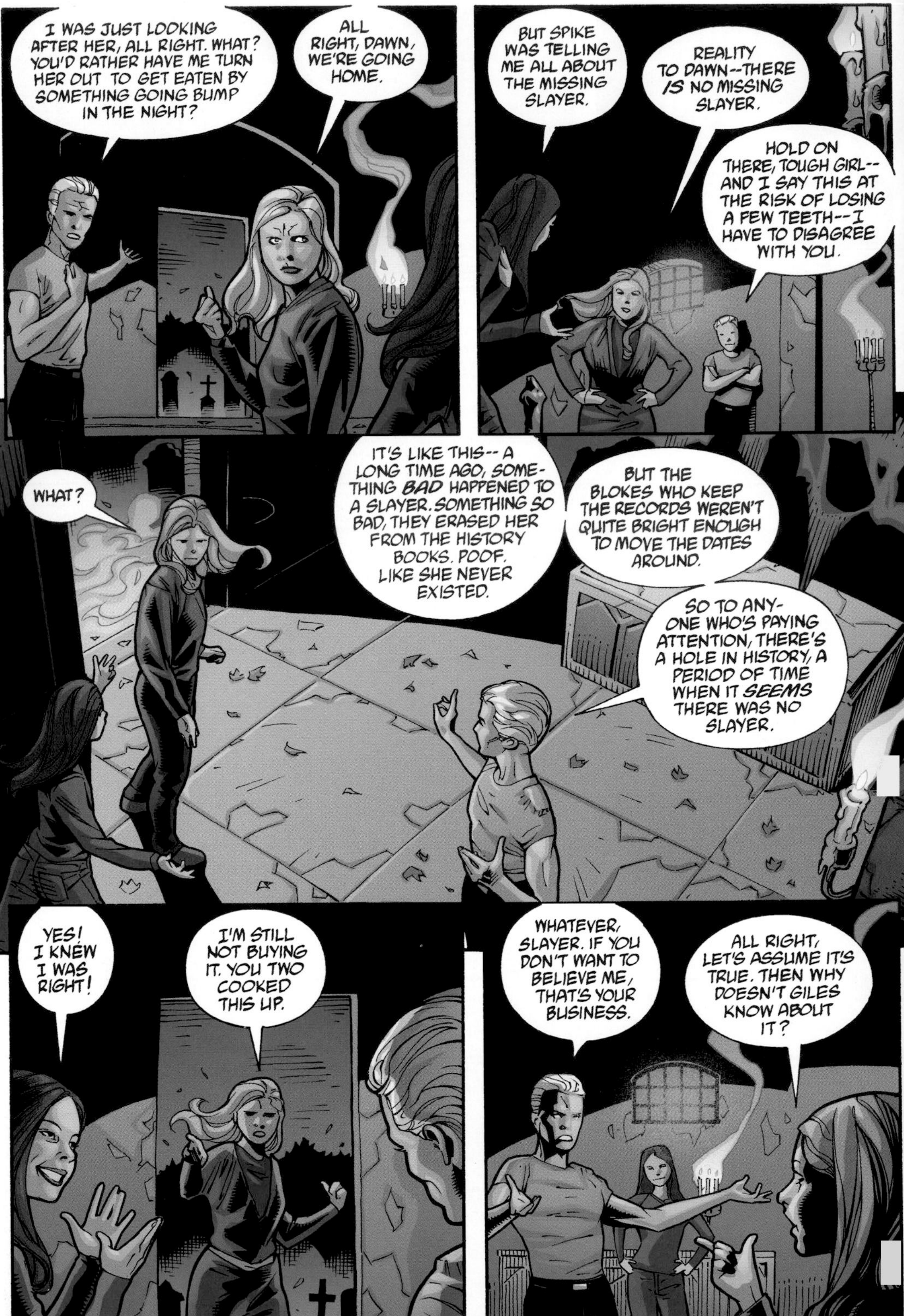
I WAS JUST LOOKING AFTER HER, ALL RIGHT. WHAT? YOU'D RATHER HAVE ME TURN HER OUT TO GET EATEN BY SOMETHING GOING BUMP IN THE NIGHT?
ALL RIGHT, DAWN, WE'RE GOING HOME.
BUT SPIKE WAS TELLING ME ALL ABOUT THE MISSING SLAYER.
REALITY TO DAWN--THERE *IS* NO MISSING SLAYER.
HOLD ON THERE, TOUGH GIRL--AND I SAY THIS AT THE RISK OF LOSING A FEW TEETH--I HAVE TO DISAGREE WITH YOU.
WHAT?
IT'S LIKE THIS-- A LONG TIME AGO, SOMETHING *BAD* HAPPENED TO A SLAYER. SOMETHING SO BAD, THEY ERASED HER FROM THE HISTORY BOOKS. POOF. LIKE SHE NEVER EXISTED.
BUT THE BLOKES WHO KEEP THE RECORDS WEREN'T QUITE BRIGHT ENOUGH TO MOVE THE DATES AROUND.
SO TO ANYONE WHO'S PAYING ATTENTION, THERE'S A HOLE IN HISTORY, A PERIOD OF TIME WHEN IT *SEEMS* THERE WAS NO SLAYER.
YES! I KNEW I WAS RIGHT!
I'M STILL NOT BUYING IT. YOU TWO COOKED THIS UP.
WHATEVER, SLAYER. IF YOU DON'T WANT TO BELIEVE ME, THAT'S YOUR BUSINESS.
ALL RIGHT, LET'S ASSUME IT'S TRUE. THEN WHY DOESN'T GILES KNOW ABOUT IT?

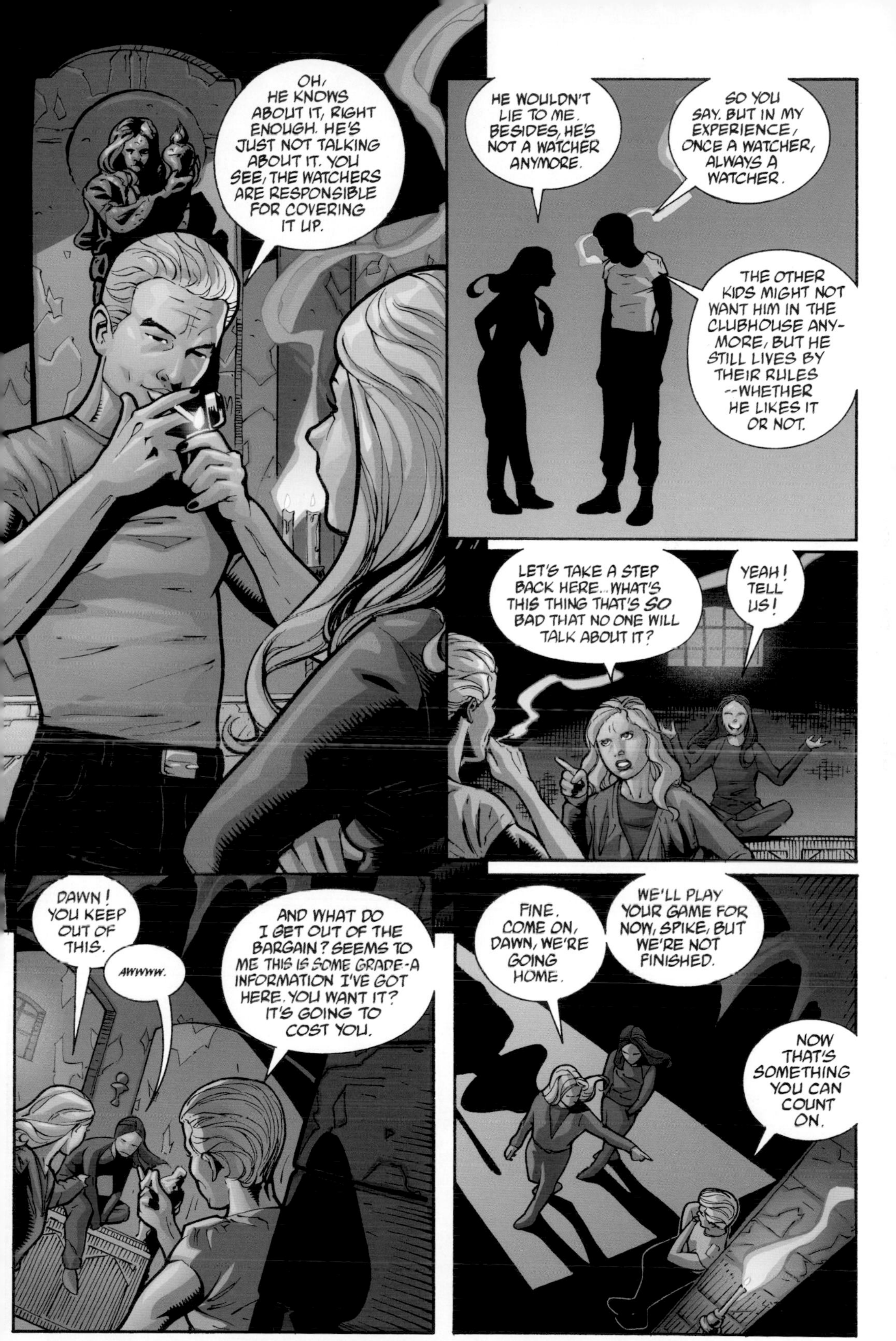
OH, HE KNOWS ABOUT IT, RIGHT ENOUGH. HE'S JUST NOT TALKING ABOUT IT. YOU SEE, THE WATCHERS ARE RESPONSIBLE FOR COVERING IT UP.
HE WOULDN'T LIE TO ME. BESIDES, HE'S NOT A WATCHER ANYMORE.
SO YOU SAY. BUT IN MY EXPERIENCE, ONCE A WATCHER, ALWAYS A WATCHER.
THE OTHER KIDS MIGHT NOT WANT HIM IN THE CLUBHOUSE ANY-MORE, BUT HE STILL LIVES BY THEIR RULES --WHETHER HE LIKES IT OR NOT.
LET'S TAKE A STEP BACK HERE... WHAT'S THIS THING THAT'S SO BAD THAT NO ONE WILL TALK ABOUT IT?
YEAH! TELL US!
DAWN! YOU KEEP OUT OF THIS.
AWWWW.
AND WHAT DO I GET OUT OF THE BARGAIN? SEEMS TO ME THIS IS SOME GRADE-A INFORMATION I'VE GOT HERE. YOU WANT IT? IT'S GOING TO COST YOU.
FINE. COME ON, DAWN, WE'RE GOING HOME.
WE'LL PLAY YOUR GAME FOR NOW, SPIKE, BUT WE'RE NOT FINISHED.
NOW THAT'S SOMETHING YOU CAN COUNT ON.

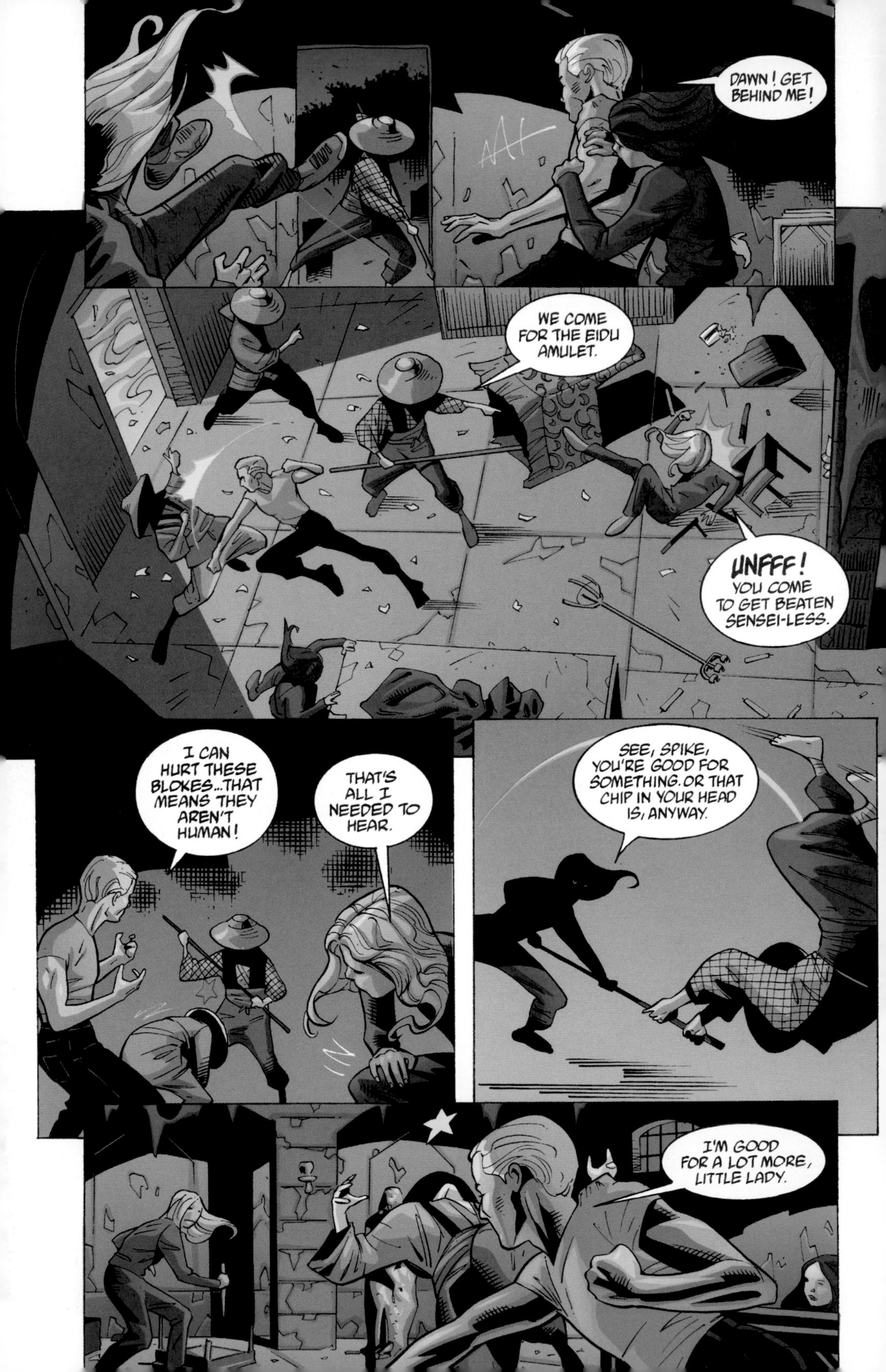
DAWN! GET BEHIND ME!
WE COME FOR THE EIDU AMULET.
UNFFF! YOU COME TO GET BEATEN SENSEI-LESS.
I CAN HURT THESE BLOKES...THAT MEANS THEY AREN'T HUMAN!
THAT'S ALL I NEEDED TO HEAR.
SEE, SPIKE, YOU'RE GOOD FOR SOMETHING. OR THAT CHIP IN YOUR HEAD IS, ANYWAY.
I'M GOOD FOR A LOT MORE, LITTLE LADY.

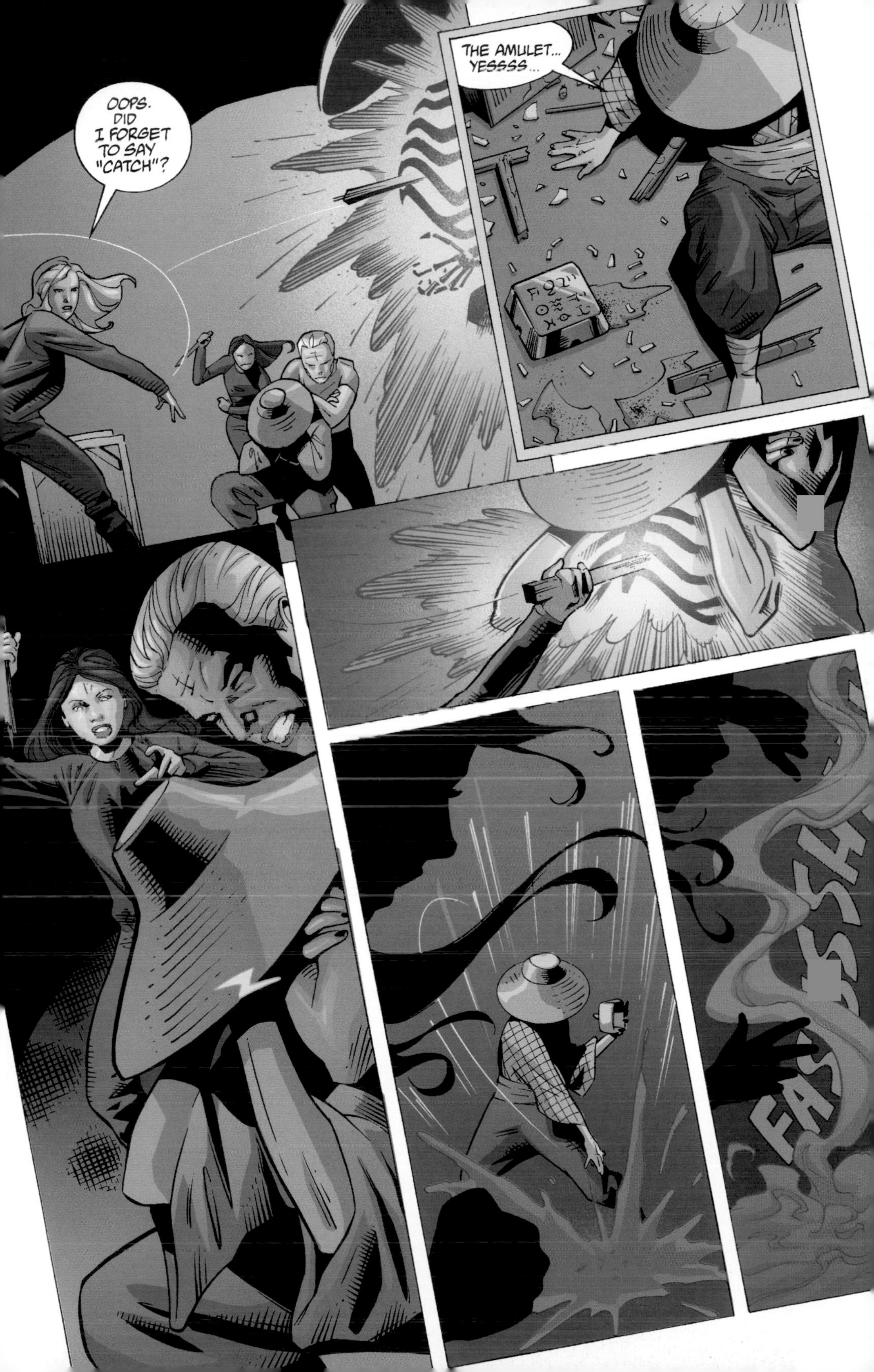
OOPS. DID I FORGET TO SAY "CATCH"?
THE AMULET... YESSSS...
FASSSH

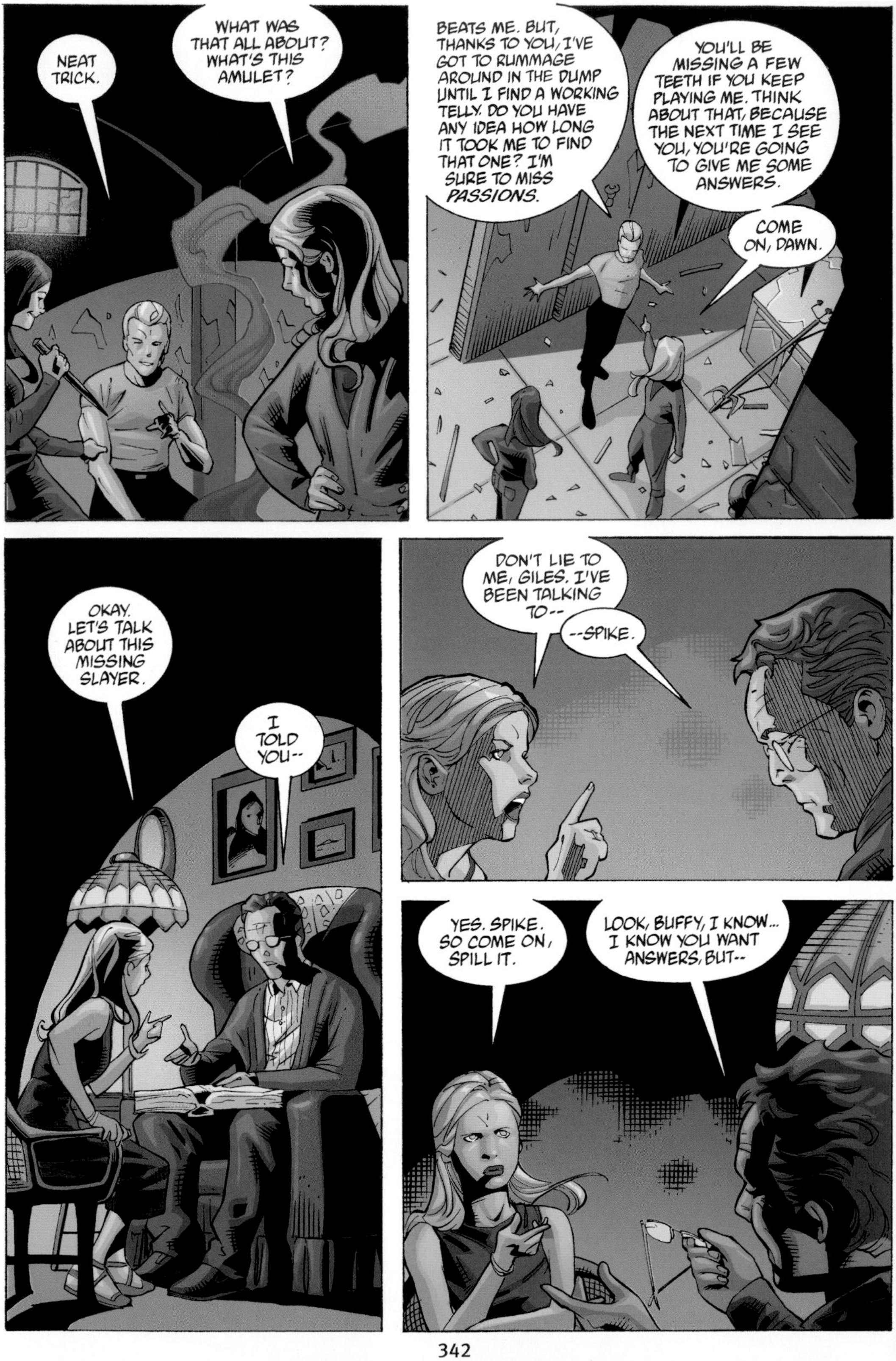
NEAT TRICK.
WHAT WAS THAT ALL ABOUT? WHAT'S THIS AMULET?
BEATS ME. BUT, THANKS TO YOU, I'VE GOT TO RUMMAGE AROUND IN THE DUMP UNTIL I FIND A WORKING TELLY. DO YOU HAVE ANY IDEA HOW LONG IT TOOK ME TO FIND THAT ONE? I'M SURE TO MISS *PASSIONS*.
YOU'LL BE MISSING A FEW TEETH IF YOU KEEP PLAYING ME. THINK ABOUT THAT, BECAUSE THE NEXT TIME I SEE YOU, YOU'RE GOING TO GIVE ME SOME ANSWERS.
COME ON, DAWN.
OKAY. LET'S TALK ABOUT THIS MISSING SLAYER.
I TOLD YOU--
DON'T LIE TO ME, GILES. I'VE BEEN TALKING TO--
--SPIKE.
YES. SPIKE. SO COME ON, SPILL IT.
LOOK, BUFFY, I KNOW... I KNOW YOU WANT ANSWERS, BUT--

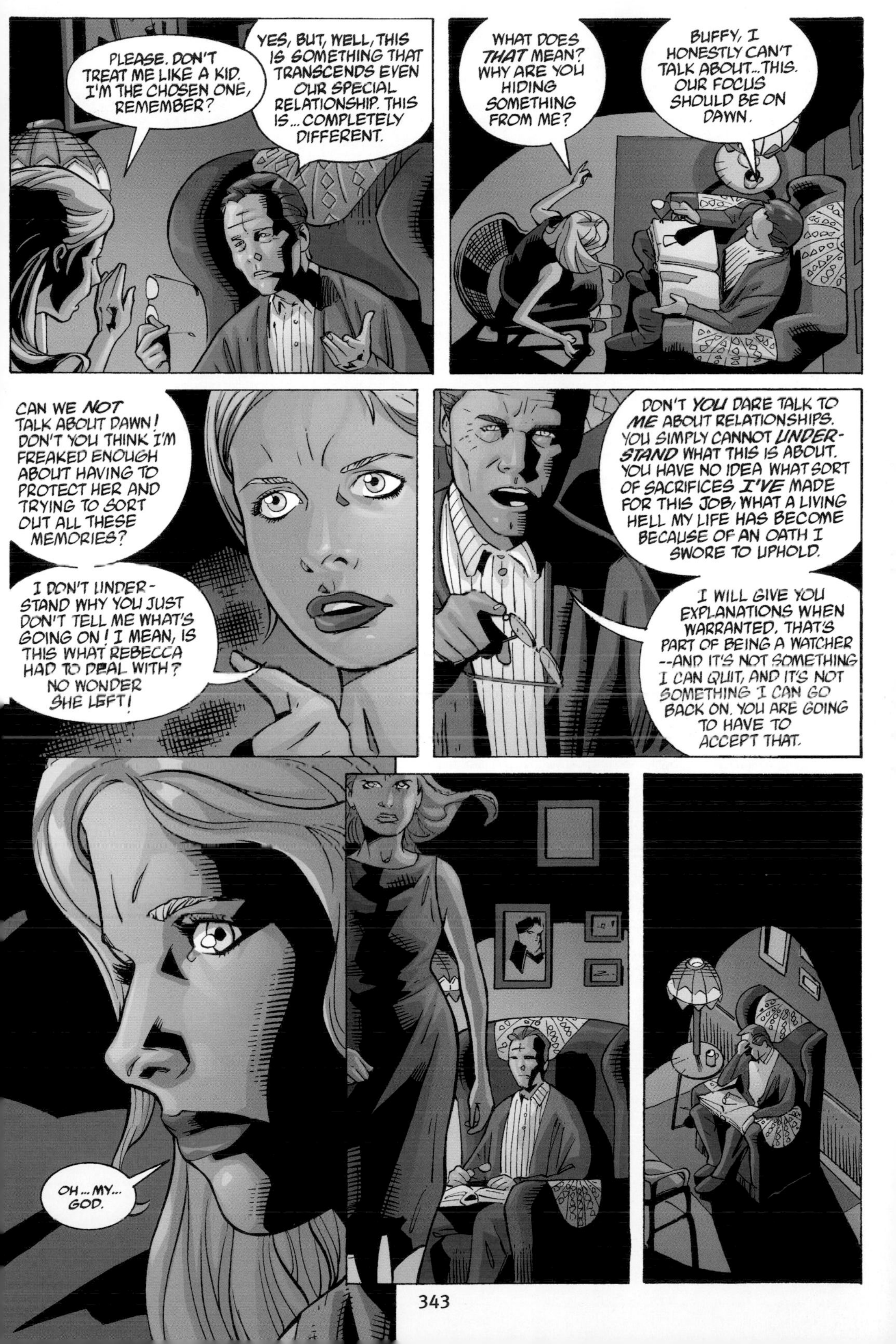
PLEASE. DON'T TREAT ME LIKE A KID. I'M THE CHOSEN ONE, REMEMBER?
YES, BUT, WELL, THIS IS SOMETHING THAT TRANSCENDS EVEN OUR SPECIAL RELATIONSHIP. THIS IS... COMPLETELY DIFFERENT.
WHAT DOES THAT MEAN? WHY ARE YOU HIDING SOMETHING FROM ME?
BUFFY, I HONESTLY CAN'T TALK ABOUT... THIS. OUR FOCUS SHOULD BE ON DAWN.
CAN WE NOT TALK ABOUT DAWN! DON'T YOU THINK I'M FREAKED ENOUGH ABOUT HAVING TO PROTECT HER AND TRYING TO SORT OUT ALL THESE MEMORIES?
I DON'T UNDER-STAND WHY YOU JUST DON'T TELL ME WHAT'S GOING ON! I MEAN, IS THIS WHAT REBECCA HAD TO DEAL WITH? NO WONDER SHE LEFT!
DON'T YOU DARE TALK TO ME ABOUT RELATIONSHIPS. YOU SIMPLY CANNOT UNDER-STAND WHAT THIS IS ABOUT. YOU HAVE NO IDEA WHAT SORT OF SACRIFICES I'VE MADE FOR THIS JOB, WHAT A LIVING HELL MY LIFE HAS BECOME BECAUSE OF AN OATH I SWORE TO UPHOLD.
I WILL GIVE YOU EXPLANATIONS WHEN WARRANTED. THAT'S PART OF BEING A WATCHER --AND IT'S NOT SOMETHING I CAN QUIT, AND IT'S NOT SOMETHING I CAN GO BACK ON. YOU ARE GOING TO HAVE TO ACCEPT THAT.
OH... MY... GOD.

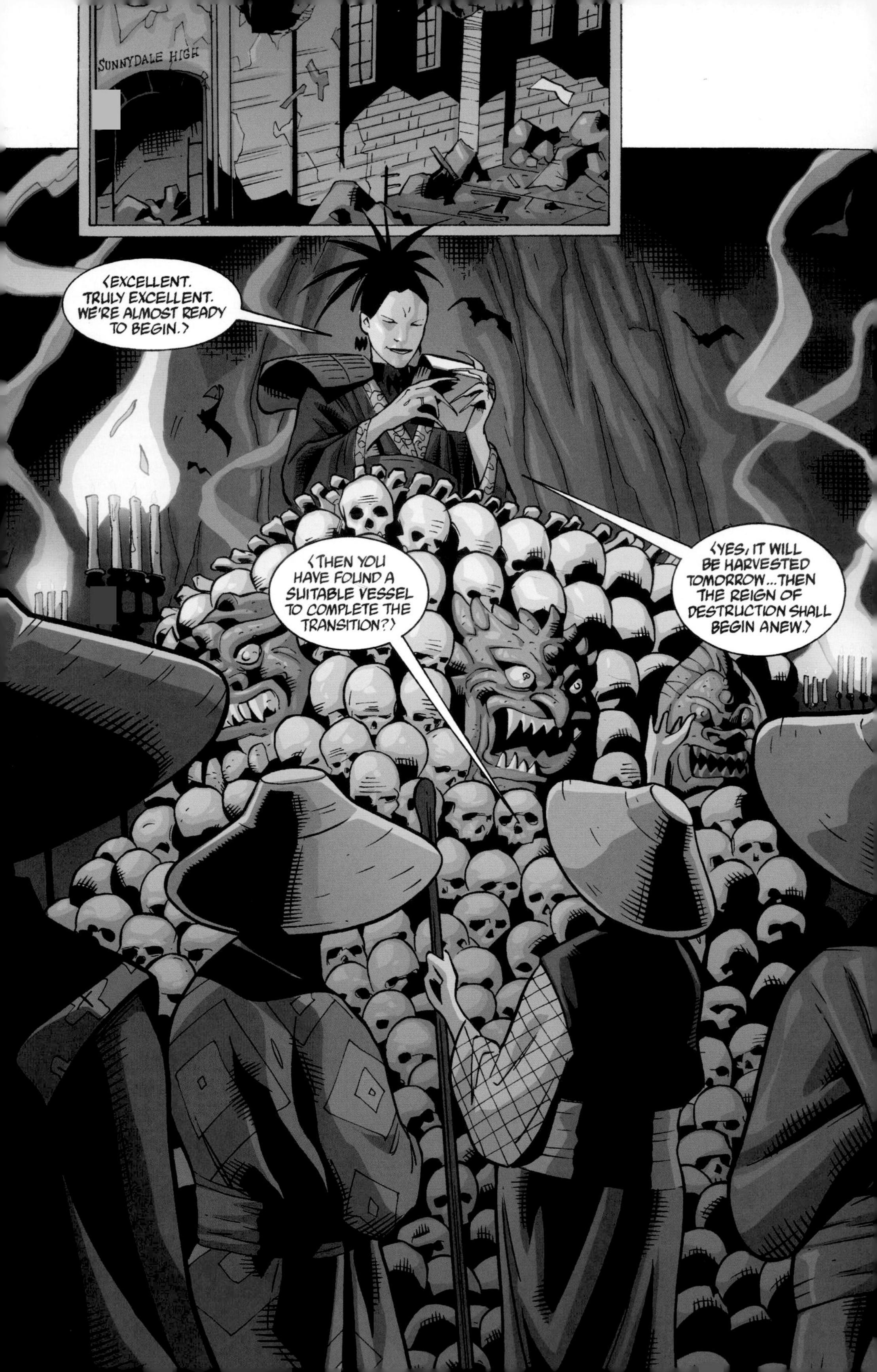
SUNNYDALE HIGH
‹EXCELLENT. TRULY EXCELLENT. WE'RE ALMOST READY TO BEGIN.›
‹THEN YOU HAVE FOUND A SUITABLE VESSEL TO COMPLETE THE TRANSITION?›
‹YES, IT WILL BE HARVESTED TOMORROW...THEN THE REIGN OF DESTRUCTION SHALL BEGIN ANEW.›

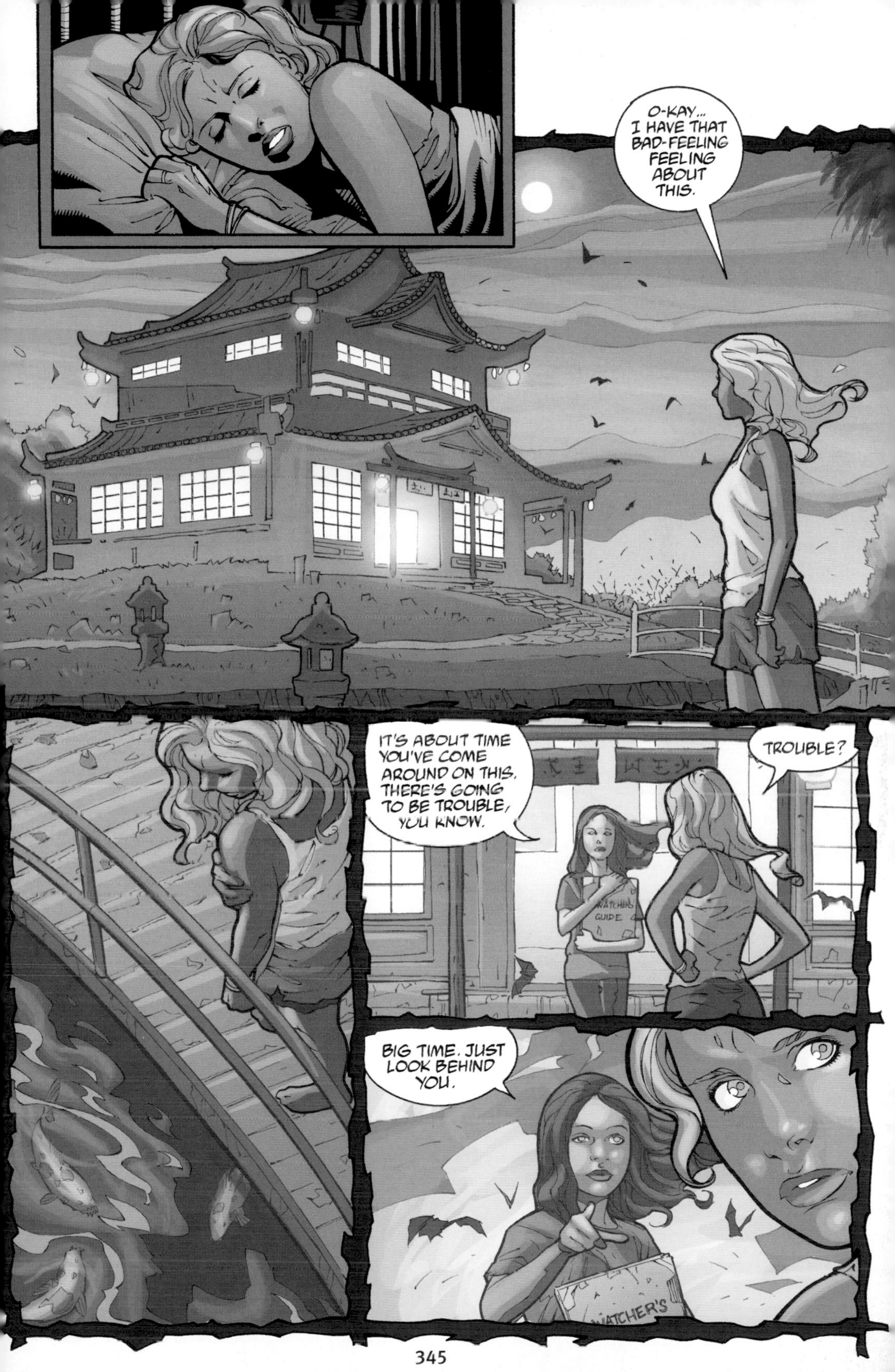
O-KAY... I HAVE THAT BAD-FEELING FEELING ABOUT THIS.
IT'S ABOUT TIME YOU'VE COME AROUND ON THIS. THERE'S GOING TO BE TROUBLE, YOU KNOW.
TROUBLE?
WATCHER'S GUIDE
BIG TIME. JUST LOOK BEHIND YOU.
WATCHER'S

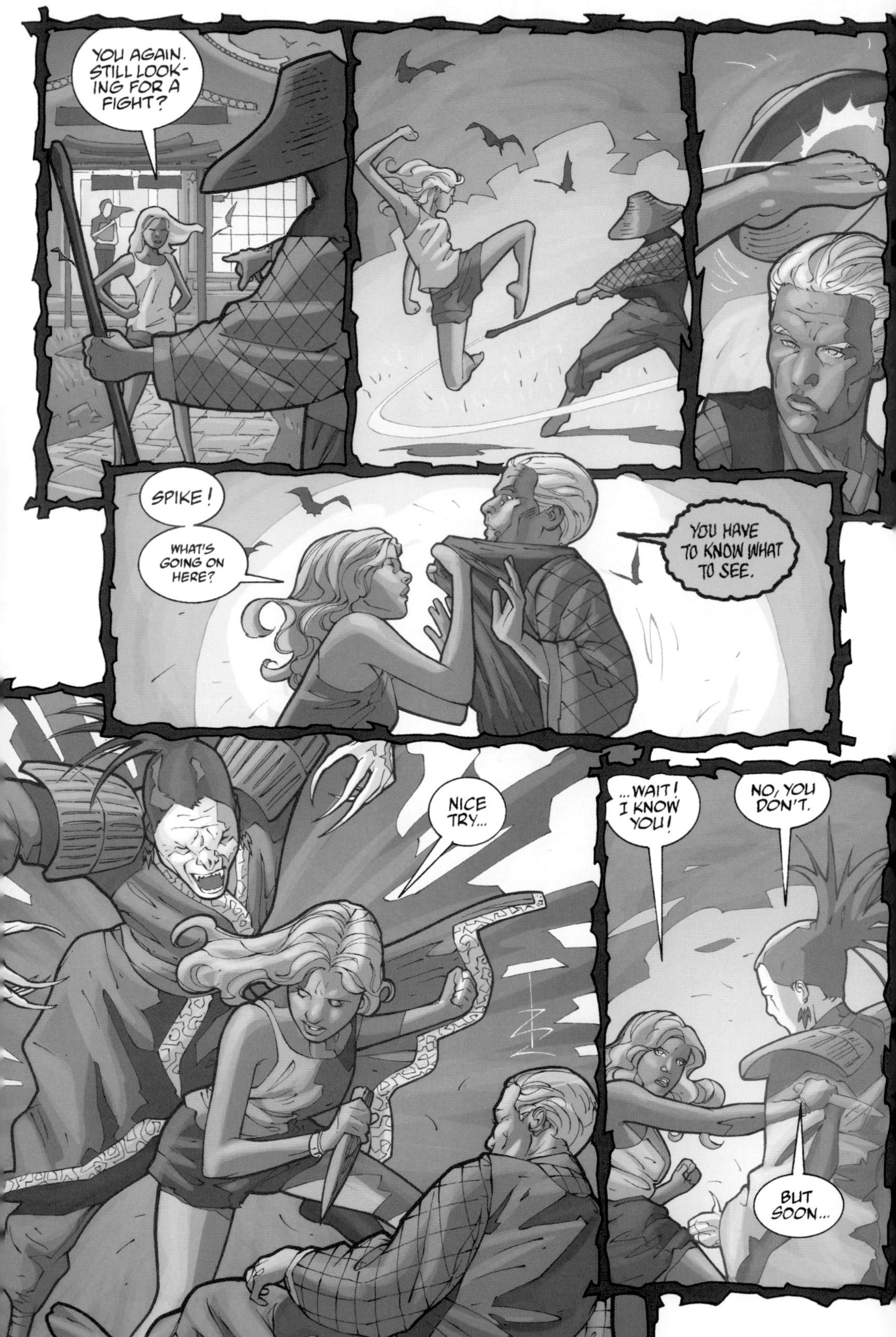
YOU AGAIN. STILL LOOKING FOR A FIGHT?
SPIKE!
WHAT'S GOING ON HERE?
YOU HAVE TO KNOW WHAT TO SEE.
NICE TRY...
...WAIT! I KNOW YOU!
NO, YOU DON'T.
BUT SOON...

OH!

DAWN...WHAT ARE YOU DOING?

I HEARD VOICES...I WANTED TO SEE IF YOU'RE OKAY.

AND YOU CAME IN TO CHECK ON ME? I DON'T THINK SO. WHAT'S THE REAL DEAL?

UM... WELL... I KNOW YOU'RE STILL MAD AT ME FOR RUNNING AWAY...

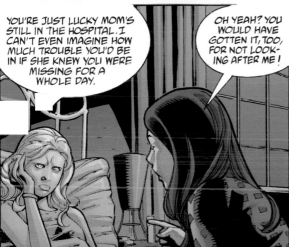

YOU'RE JUST LUCKY MOM'S STILL IN THE HOSPITAL. I CAN'T EVEN IMAGINE HOW MUCH TROUBLE YOU'D BE IN IF SHE KNEW YOU WERE MISSING FOR A WHOLE DAY.

OH YEAH? YOU WOULD HAVE GOTTEN IT, TOO, FOR NOT LOOK-ING AFTER ME!

DON'T YOU TRY TO MAKE THIS ABOUT ME. YOU'RE THE ONE WHO RAN OFF --AND INTO SPIKE'S LAIR, EVEN! WHAT WERE YOU THINKING?

HE'S FUN TO HANG OUT WITH. HE DOESN'T TREAT ME LIKE A KID, LIKE EVERYONE ELSE DOES. BESIDES, I DON'T CARE WHAT YOU SAY--THERE'S GOOD IN HIM.

VAMPIRE EQUALS EVIL CREATURE OF THE UNDEAD. SPIKE DOESN'T HAVE A SOUL...AND EVEN WHEN HE DID, I BET YOU COULDN'T TRUST HIM.

AND WHAT MAKES YOU THINK I WON'T DOUBLE-CROSS YOU?

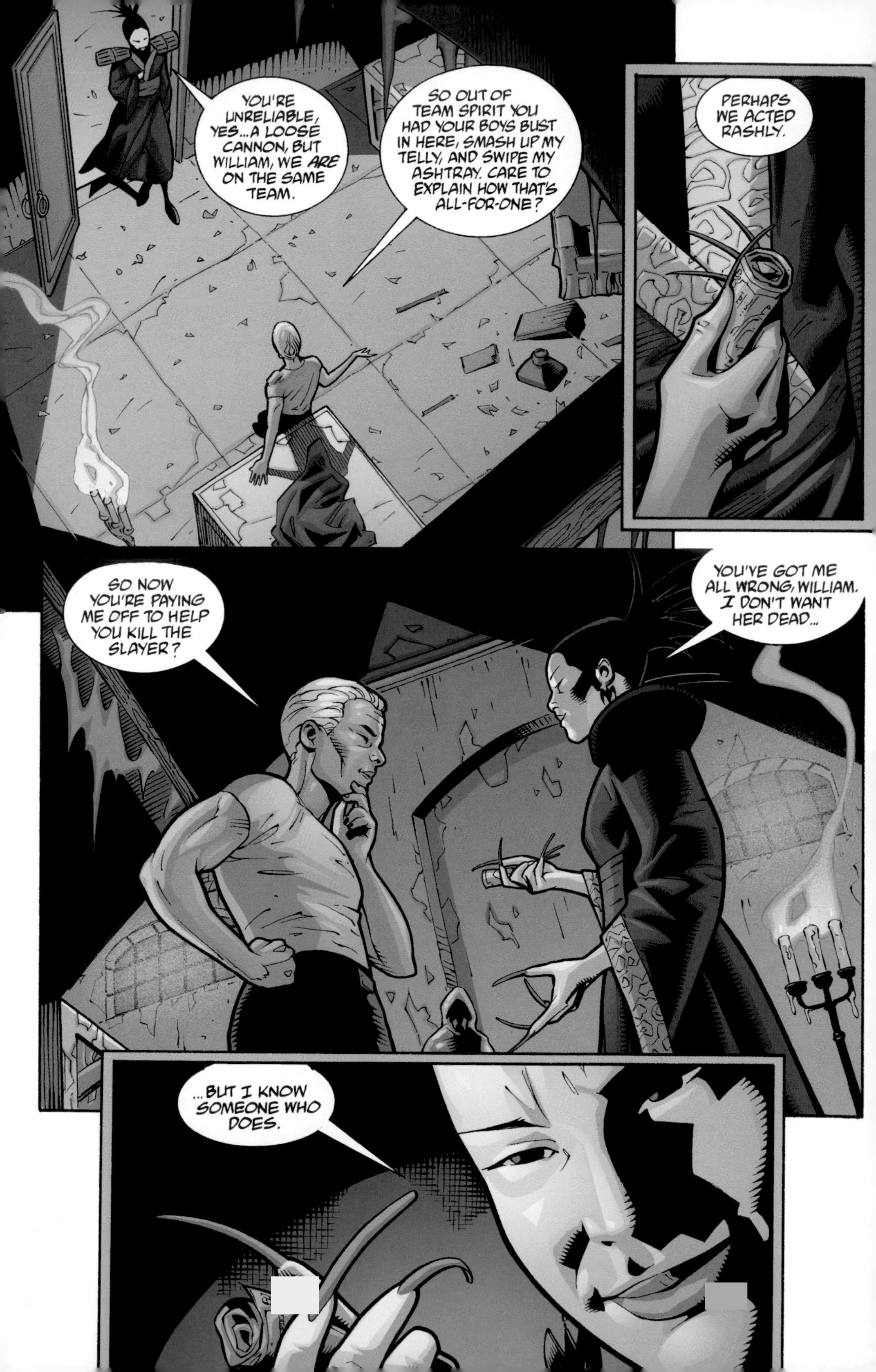
YOU'RE UNRELIABLE, YES...A LOOSE CANNON, BUT WILLIAM, WE *ARE* ON THE SAME TEAM.
SO OUT OF TEAM SPIRIT YOU HAD YOUR BOYS BUST IN HERE, SMASH UP MY TELLY, AND SWIPE MY ASHTRAY. CARE TO EXPLAIN HOW THAT'S ALL-FOR-ONE?
PERHAPS WE ACTED RASHLY.
SO NOW YOU'RE PAYING ME OFF TO HELP YOU KILL THE SLAYER?
YOU'VE GOT ME ALL WRONG, WILLIAM. I DON'T WANT HER DEAD...
...BUT I KNOW SOMEONE WHO DOES.

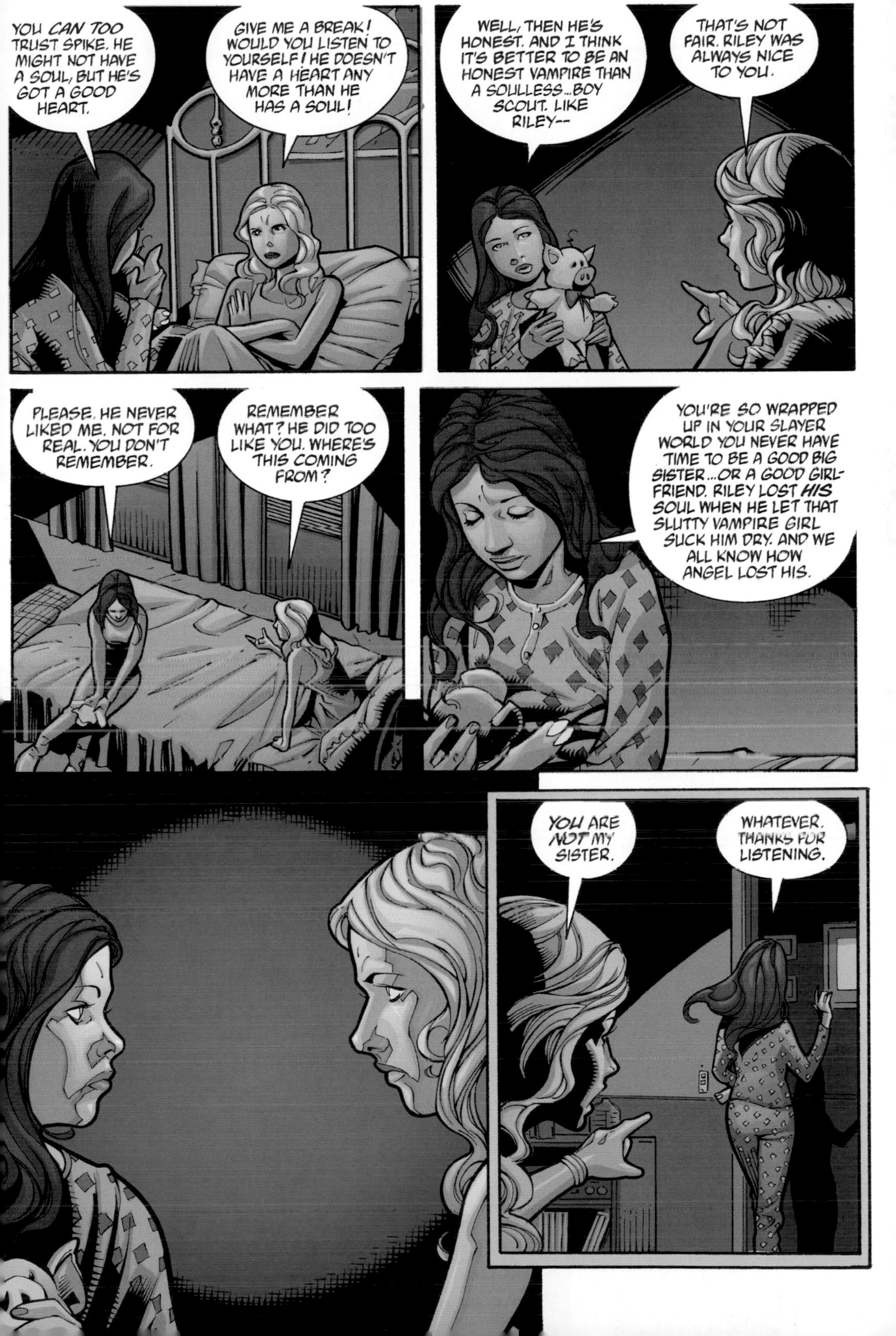
YOU CAN TOO TRUST SPIKE. HE MIGHT NOT HAVE A SOUL, BUT HE'S GOT A GOOD HEART.
GIVE ME A BREAK! WOULD YOU LISTEN TO YOURSELF! HE DOESN'T HAVE A HEART ANY MORE THAN HE HAS A SOUL!
WELL, THEN HE'S HONEST. AND I THINK IT'S BETTER TO BE AN HONEST VAMPIRE THAN A SOULLESS...BOY SCOUT. LIKE RILEY--
THAT'S NOT FAIR. RILEY WAS ALWAYS NICE TO YOU.
PLEASE. HE NEVER LIKED ME. NOT FOR REAL. YOU DON'T REMEMBER.
REMEMBER WHAT? HE DID TOO LIKE YOU. WHERE'S THIS COMING FROM?
YOU'RE SO WRAPPED UP IN YOUR SLAYER WORLD YOU NEVER HAVE TIME TO BE A GOOD BIG SISTER...OR A GOOD GIRL-FRIEND. RILEY LOST HIS SOUL WHEN HE LET THAT SLUTTY VAMPIRE GIRL SUCK HIM DRY. AND WE ALL KNOW HOW ANGEL LOST HIS.
YOU ARE NOT MY SISTER.
WHATEVER. THANKS FOR LISTENING.

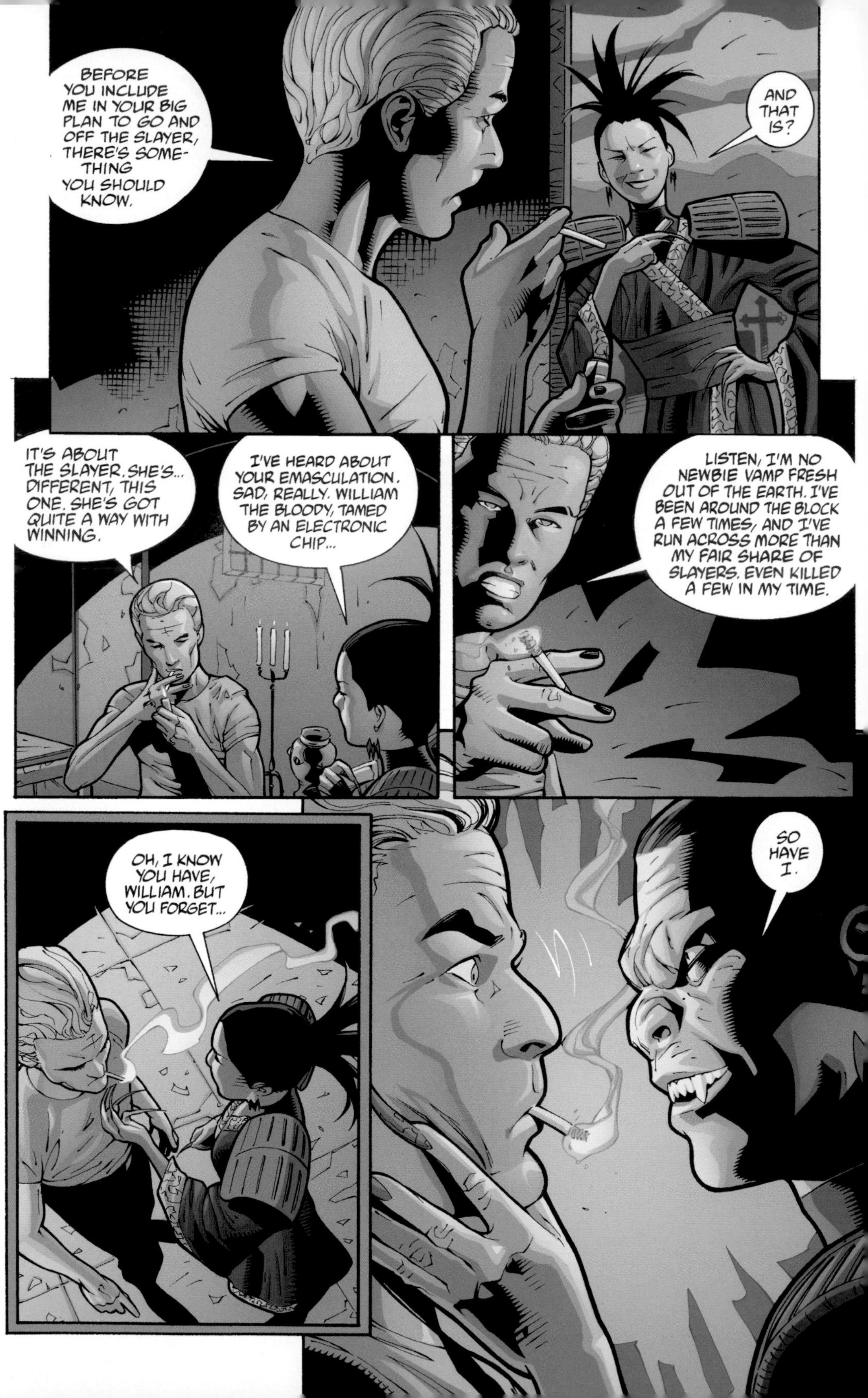
BEFORE YOU INCLUDE ME IN YOUR BIG PLAN TO GO AND OFF THE SLAYER, THERE'S SOMETHING YOU SHOULD KNOW.
AND THAT IS?
IT'S ABOUT THE SLAYER. SHE'S... DIFFERENT, THIS ONE. SHE'S GOT QUITE A WAY WITH WINNING.
I'VE HEARD ABOUT YOUR EMASCULATION. SAD, REALLY. WILLIAM THE BLOODY, TAMED BY AN ELECTRONIC CHIP...
LISTEN, I'M NO NEWBIE VAMP FRESH OUT OF THE EARTH. I'VE BEEN AROUND THE BLOCK A FEW TIMES, AND I'VE RUN ACROSS MORE THAN MY FAIR SHARE OF SLAYERS. EVEN KILLED A FEW IN MY TIME.
OH, I KNOW YOU HAVE, WILLIAM. BUT YOU FORGET...
SO HAVE I.

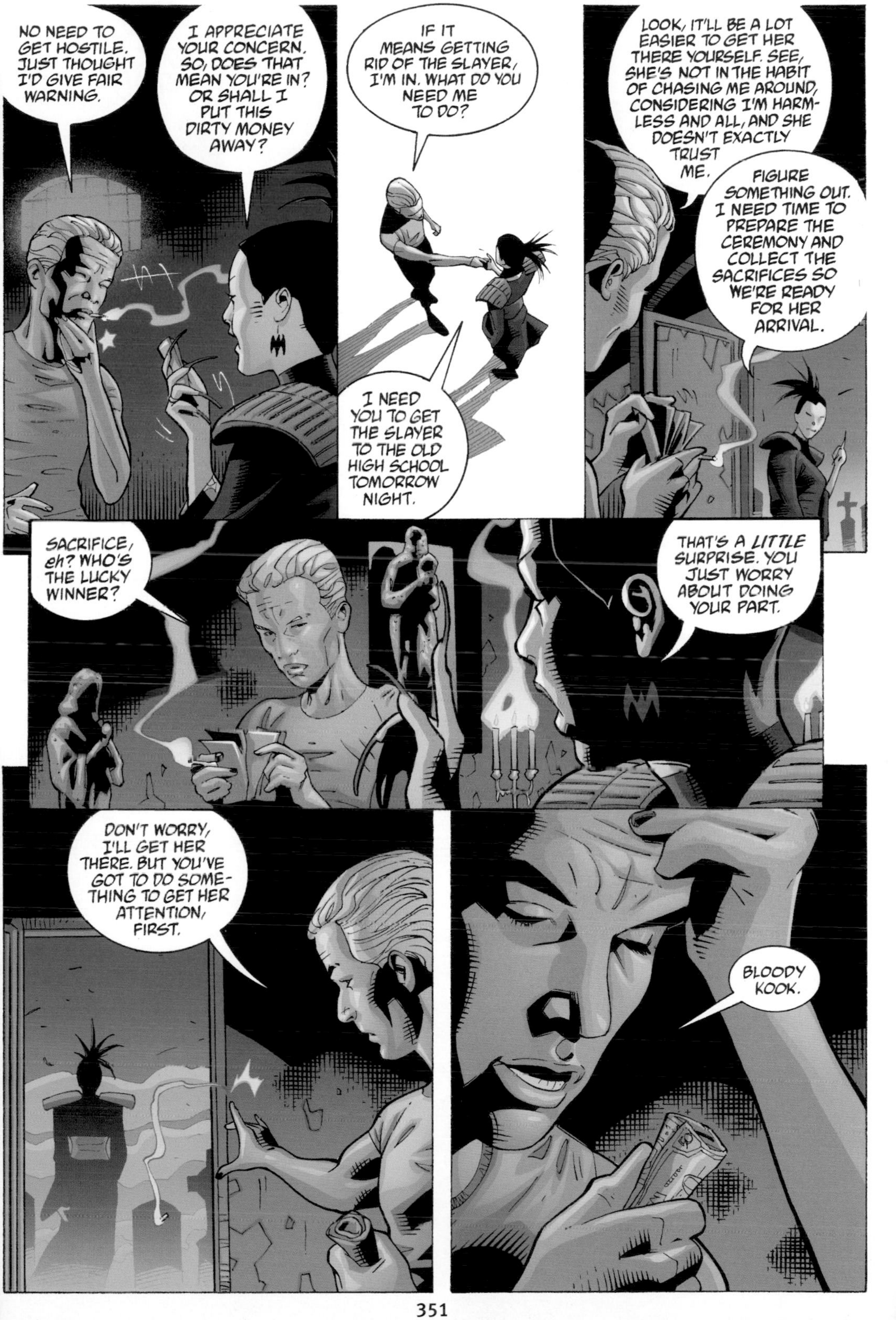

NO NEED TO GET HOSTILE. JUST THOUGHT I'D GIVE FAIR WARNING.
I APPRECIATE YOUR CONCERN. SO, DOES THAT MEAN YOU'RE IN? OR SHALL I PUT THIS DIRTY MONEY AWAY?
IF IT MEANS GETTING RID OF THE SLAYER, I'M IN. WHAT DO YOU NEED ME TO DO?
I NEED YOU TO GET THE SLAYER TO THE OLD HIGH SCHOOL TOMORROW NIGHT.
LOOK, IT'LL BE A LOT EASIER TO GET HER THERE YOURSELF. SEE, SHE'S NOT IN THE HABIT OF CHASING ME AROUND, CONSIDERING I'M HARMLESS AND ALL, AND SHE DOESN'T EXACTLY TRUST ME.
FIGURE SOMETHING OUT. I NEED TIME TO PREPARE THE CEREMONY AND COLLECT THE SACRIFICES SO WE'RE READY FOR HER ARRIVAL.
SACRIFICE, eh? WHO'S THE LUCKY WINNER?
THAT'S A *LITTLE* SURPRISE. YOU JUST WORRY ABOUT DOING YOUR PART.
DON'T WORRY, I'LL GET HER THERE. BUT YOU'VE GOT TO DO SOMETHING TO GET HER ATTENTION, FIRST.
BLOODY KOOK.

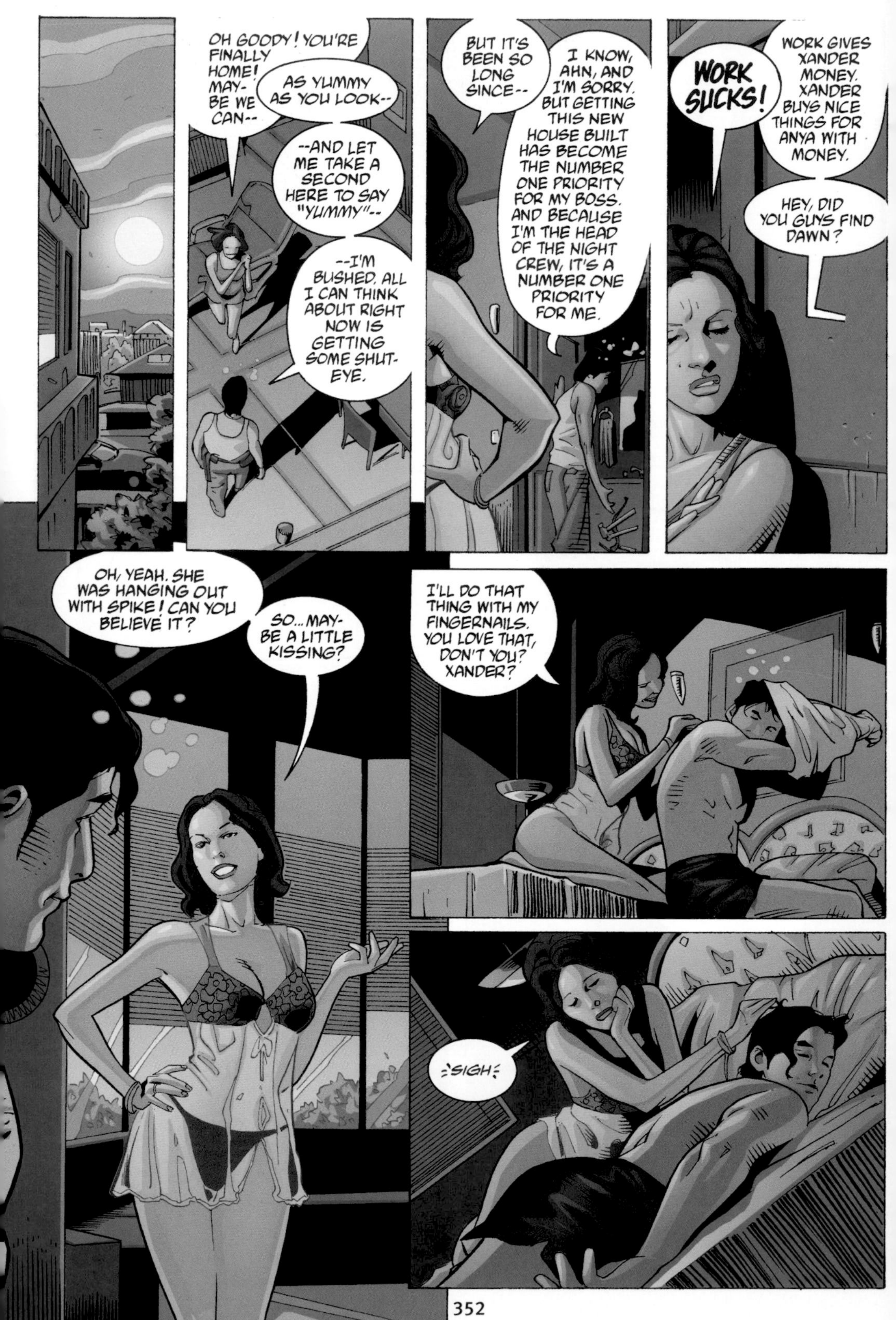
OH GOODY! YOU'RE FINALLY HOME! MAY-BE WE CAN--
AS YUMMY AS YOU LOOK--
--AND LET ME TAKE A SECOND HERE TO SAY "YUMMY"--
--I'M BUSHED. ALL I CAN THINK ABOUT RIGHT NOW IS GETTING SOME SHUT-EYE.
BUT IT'S BEEN SO LONG SINCE--
I KNOW, AHN, AND I'M SORRY. BUT GETTING THIS NEW HOUSE BUILT HAS BECOME THE NUMBER ONE PRIORITY FOR MY BOSS. AND BECAUSE I'M THE HEAD OF THE NIGHT CREW, IT'S A NUMBER ONE PRIORITY FOR ME.
WORK SUCKS!
WORK GIVES XANDER MONEY. XANDER BUYS NICE THINGS FOR ANYA WITH MONEY.
HEY, DID YOU GUYS FIND DAWN?
OH, YEAH. SHE WAS HANGING OUT WITH SPIKE! CAN YOU BELIEVE IT?
SO... MAY-BE A LITTLE KISSING?
I'LL DO THAT THING WITH MY FINGERNAILS. YOU LOVE THAT, DON'T YOU? XANDER?
SIGH

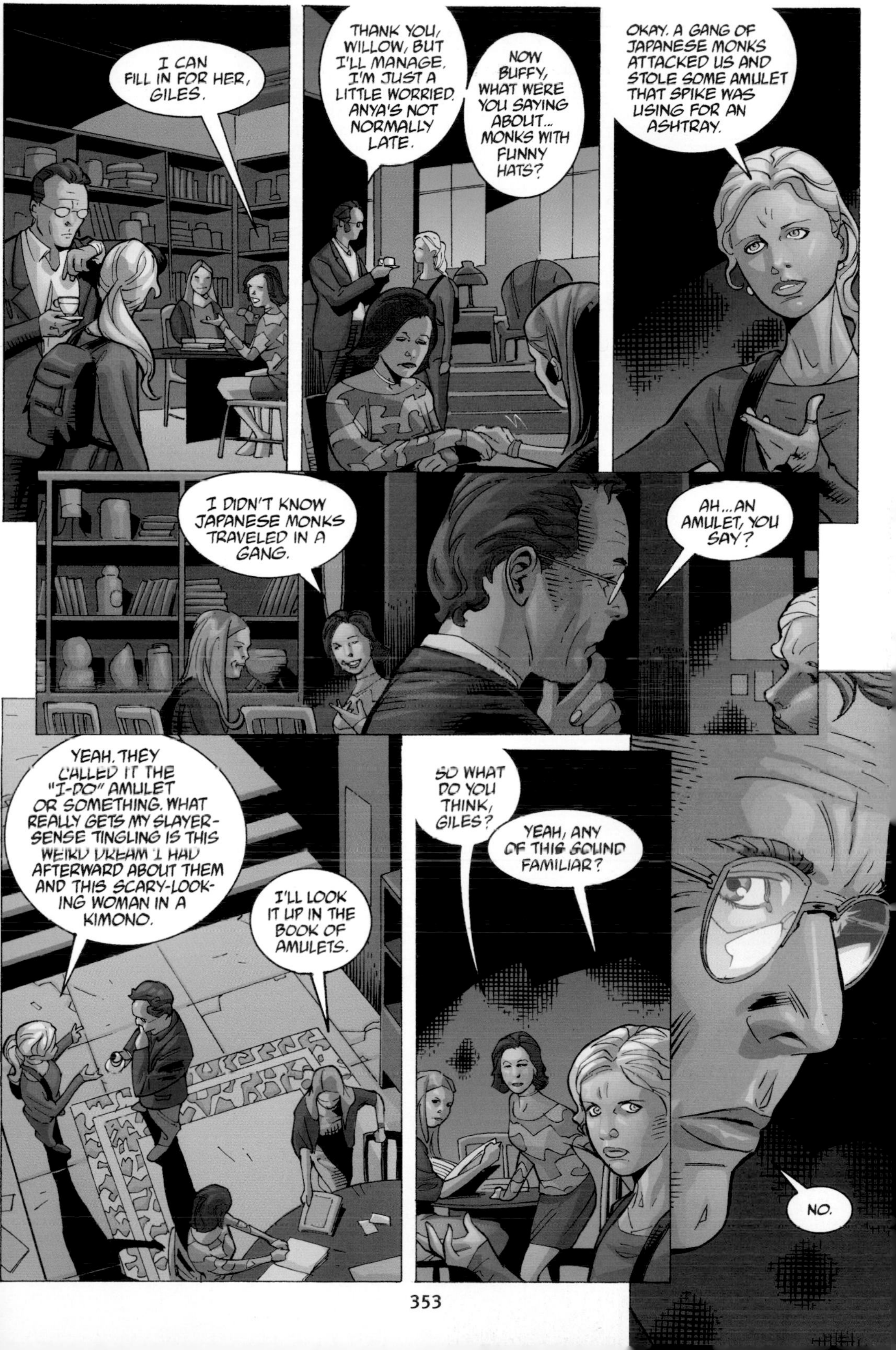

I CAN FILL IN FOR HER, GILES.
THANK YOU, WILLOW, BUT I'LL MANAGE. I'M JUST A LITTLE WORRIED. ANYA'S NOT NORMALLY LATE.
NOW BUFFY, WHAT WERE YOU SAYING ABOUT... MONKS WITH FUNNY HATS?
OKAY. A GANG OF JAPANESE MONKS ATTACKED US AND STOLE SOME AMULET THAT SPIKE WAS USING FOR AN ASHTRAY.
I DIDN'T KNOW JAPANESE MONKS TRAVELED IN A GANG.
AH...AN AMULET, YOU SAY?
YEAH. THEY CALLED IT THE "I-DO" AMULET OR SOMETHING. WHAT REALLY GETS MY SLAYER-SENSE TINGLING IS THIS WEIRD DREAM I HAD AFTERWARD ABOUT THEM AND THIS SCARY-LOOKING WOMAN IN A KIMONO.
I'LL LOOK IT UP IN THE BOOK OF AMULETS.
SO WHAT DO YOU THINK, GILES?
YEAH, ANY OF THIS SOUND FAMILIAR?
NO.

WHAT?

I MEAN... NOT REALLY.

LET'S TAKE A LOOK AND SEE WHAT WE HAVE. BUT FIRST, WAS THERE ANYTHING ELSE IN YOUR DREAM THAT MIGHT TELL US MORE OF WHAT WE'RE DEALING WITH?

I DON'T THINK SO. RIGHT AFTER I WOKE UP, DAWN WAS THERE, HARSHING ON MY TASTE IN BOYFRIENDS.

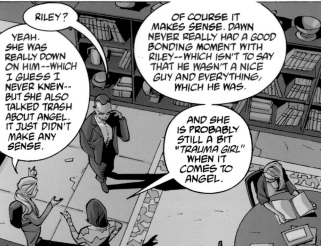

RILEY?

YEAH. SHE WAS REALLY DOWN ON HIM--WHICH I GUESS I NEVER KNEW-- BUT SHE ALSO TALKED TRASH ABOUT ANGEL. IT JUST DIDN'T MAKE ANY SENSE.

OF COURSE IT MAKES SENSE. DAWN NEVER REALLY HAD A GOOD BONDING MOMENT WITH RILEY--WHICH ISN'T TO SAY THAT HE WASN'T A NICE GUY AND EVERYTHING, WHICH HE WAS.

AND SHE IS PROBABLY STILL A BIT "TRAUMA GIRL" WHEN IT COMES TO ANGEL.

WHAT? ANGEL TRAUMATIZED SOME- ONE?

BUFFY, YOU REMEMBER THAT TIME WHEN ANGEL ALMOST KILLED HER BECAUSE HE WENT BAD AFTER... WELL, YOU KNOW WHY HE WENT BAD.

ANGEL! THANK GOD YOU'RE OKAY. I WAS WORRIED ABOUT YOU.

WE'VE ALL BEEN WORRIED ABOUT YOU. DID YOU SEE BUFFY?

YEAH... WHAT'S UP WITH THE LIGHTS?

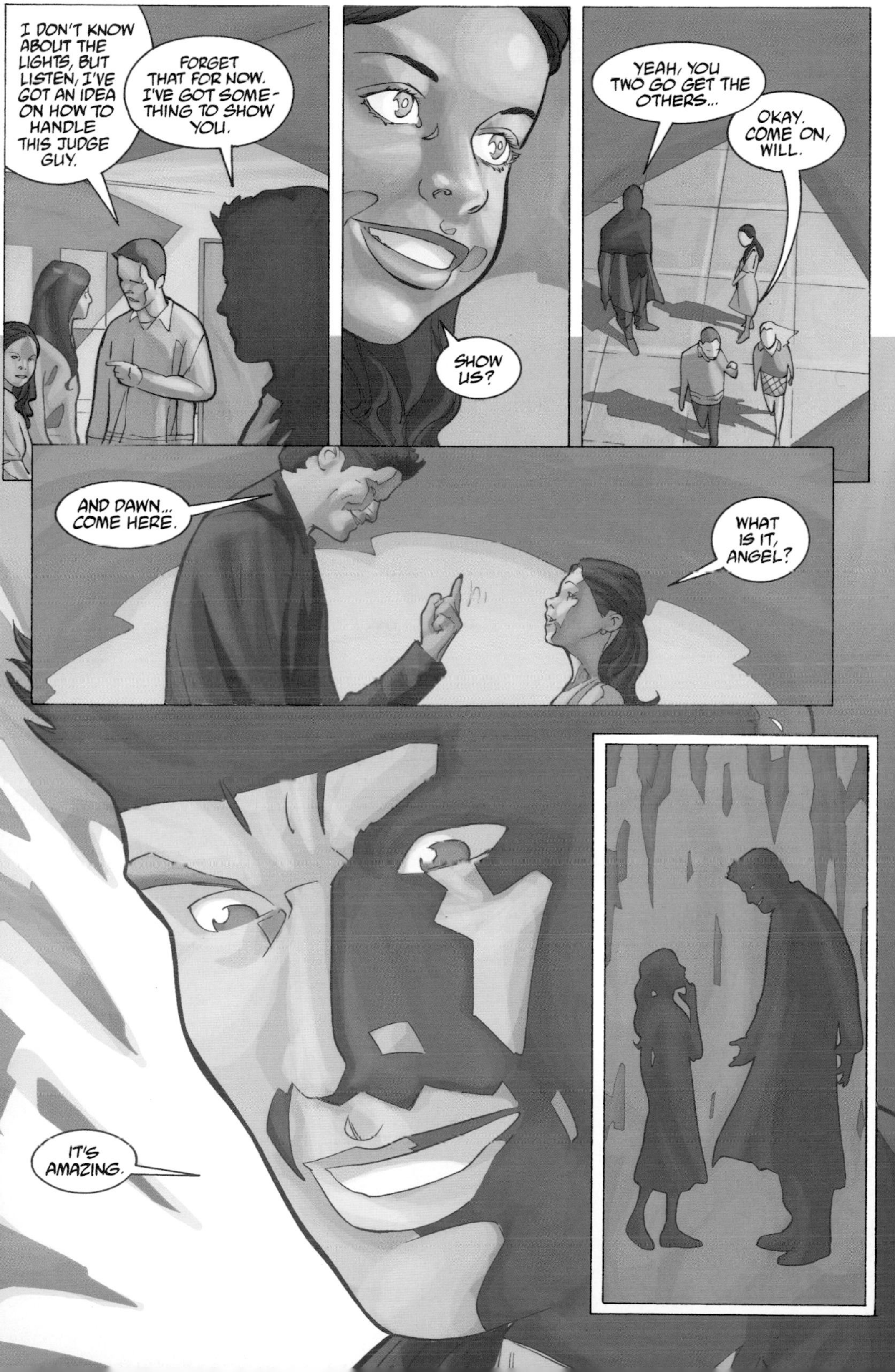

I DON'T KNOW ABOUT THE LIGHTS, BUT LISTEN, I'VE GOT AN IDEA ON HOW TO HANDLE THIS JUDGE GUY.
FORGET THAT FOR NOW. I'VE GOT SOME-THING TO SHOW YOU.
SHOW US?
YEAH, YOU TWO GO GET THE OTHERS...
OKAY. COME ON, WILL.
AND DAWN... COME HERE.
WHAT IS IT, ANGEL?
IT'S AMAZING.

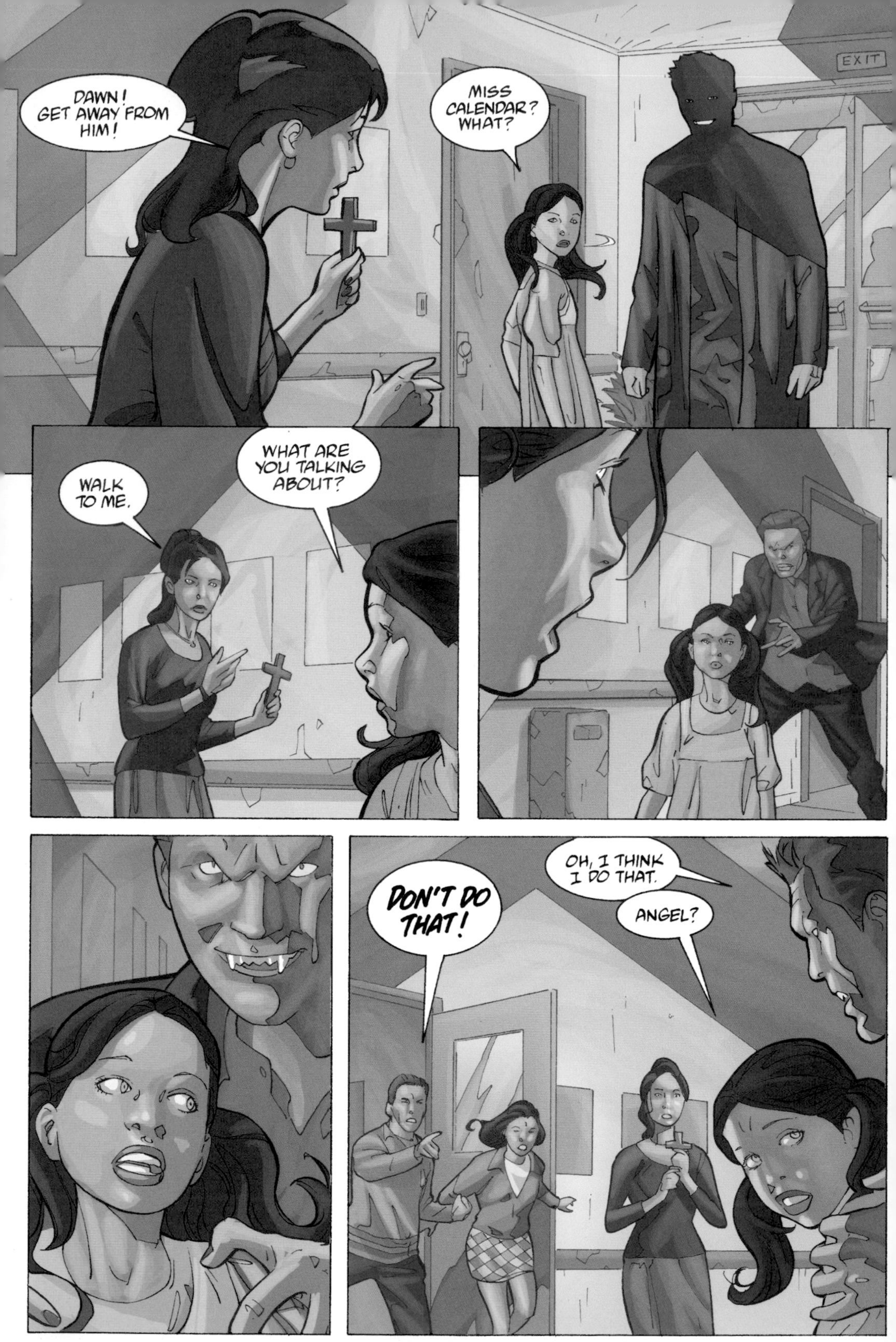
DAWN! GET AWAY FROM HIM!
MISS CALENDAR? WHAT?
EXIT
WALK TO ME.
WHAT ARE YOU TALKING ABOUT?
DON'T DO THAT!
OH, I THINK I DO THAT.
ANGEL?

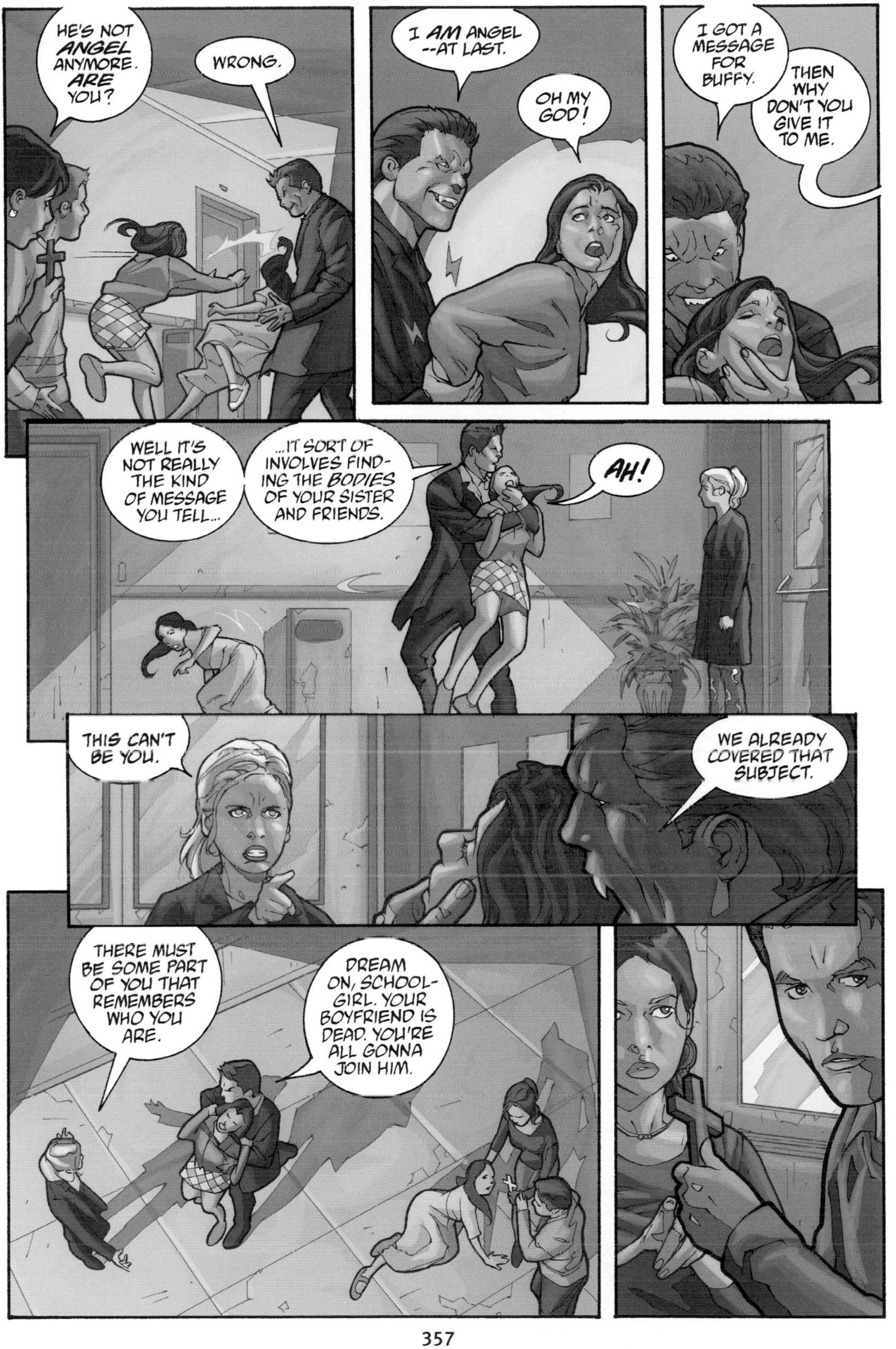
HE'S NOT ANGEL ANYMORE. ARE YOU?
WRONG.
I AM ANGEL --AT LAST.
OH MY GOD!
I GOT A MESSAGE FOR BUFFY.
THEN WHY DON'T YOU GIVE IT TO ME.
WELL IT'S NOT REALLY THE KIND OF MESSAGE YOU TELL...
...IT SORT OF INVOLVES FINDING THE BODIES OF YOUR SISTER AND FRIENDS.
AH!
THIS CAN'T BE YOU.
WE ALREADY COVERED THAT SUBJECT.
THERE MUST BE SOME PART OF YOU THAT REMEMBERS WHO YOU ARE.
DREAM ON, SCHOOLGIRL. YOUR BOYFRIEND IS DEAD. YOU'RE ALL GONNA JOIN HIM.

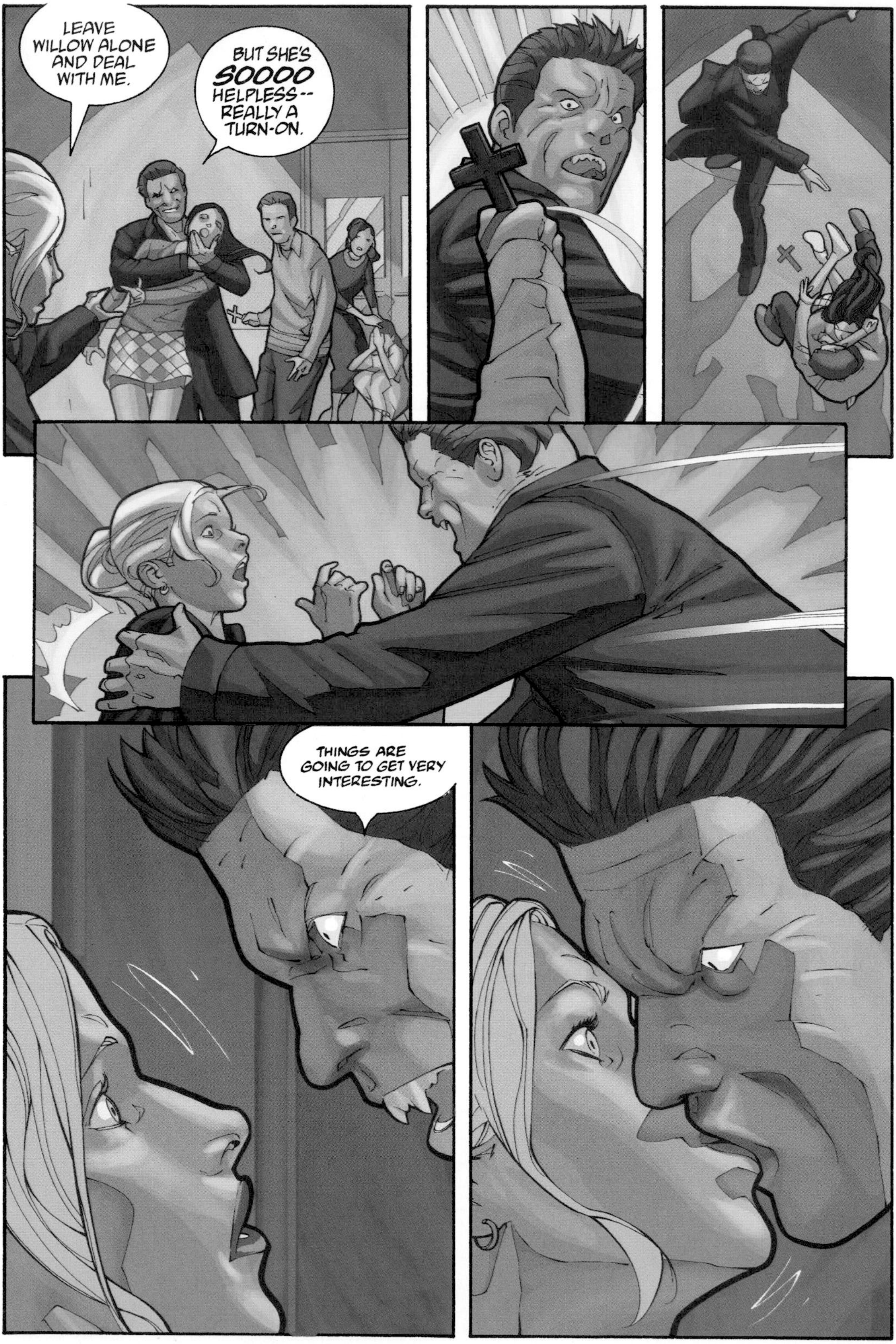
LEAVE WILLOW ALONE AND DEAL WITH ME.
BUT SHE'S SOOOO HELPLESS-- REALLY A TURN-ON.
THINGS ARE GOING TO GET VERY INTERESTING.

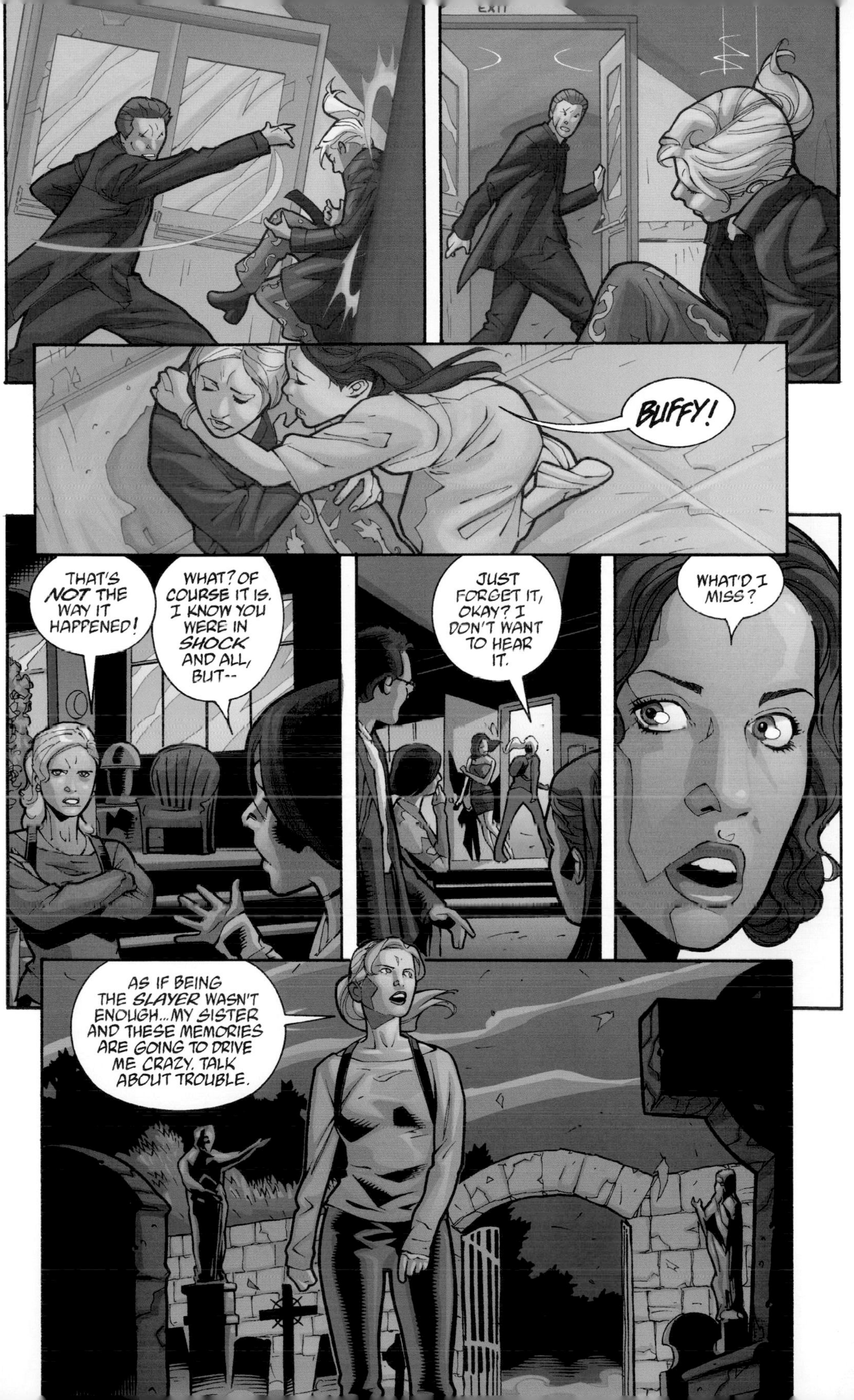

EXIT
BUFFY!
THAT'S NOT THE WAY IT HAPPENED!
WHAT? OF COURSE IT IS. I KNOW YOU WERE IN SHOCK AND ALL, BUT--
JUST FORGET IT, OKAY? I DON'T WANT TO HEAR IT.
WHAT'D I MISS?
AS IF BEING THE SLAYER WASN'T ENOUGH...MY SISTER AND THESE MEMORIES ARE GOING TO DRIVE ME CRAZY. TALK ABOUT TROUBLE.

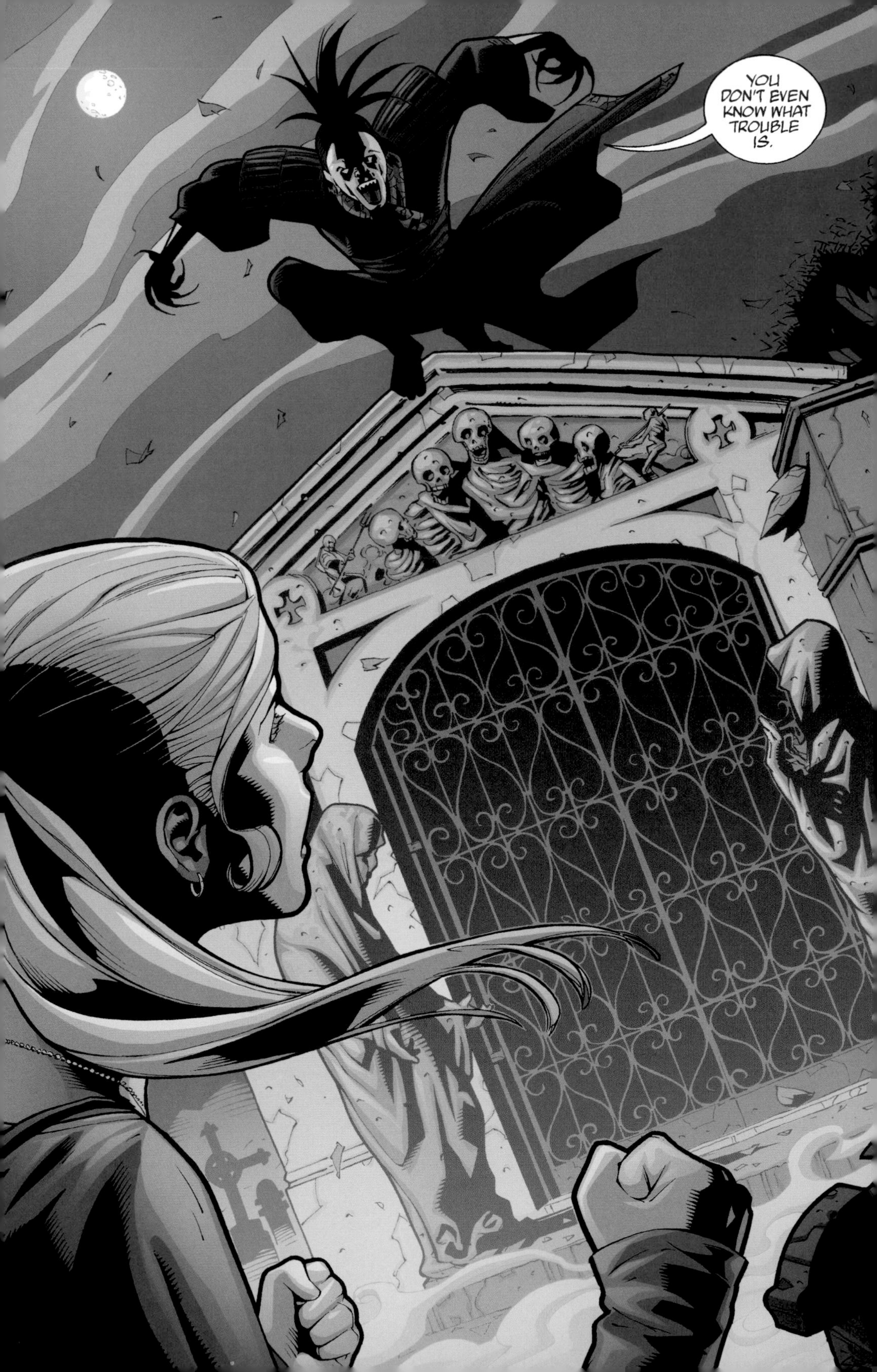
YOU DON'T EVEN KNOW WHAT TROUBLE IS.

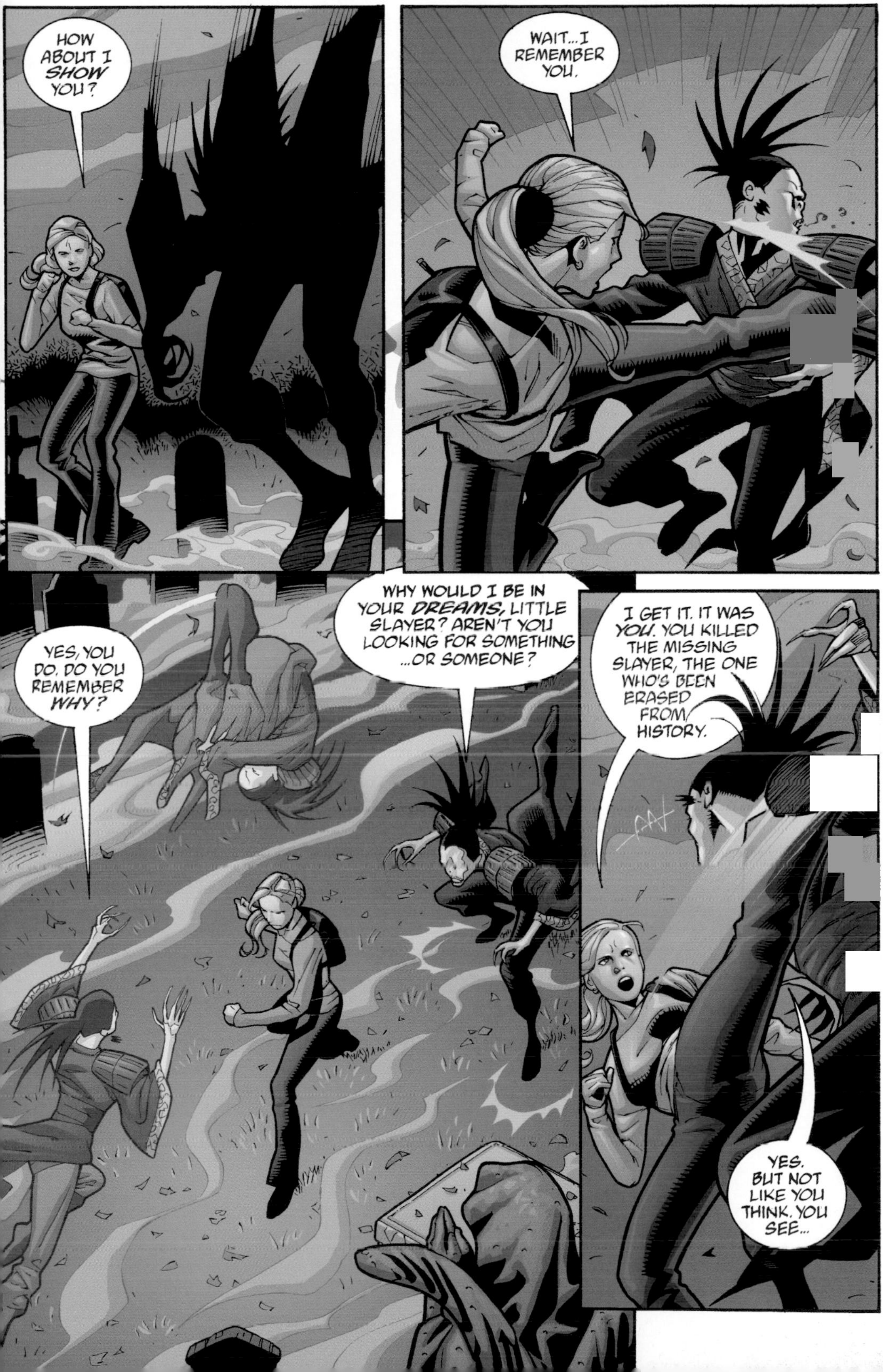

HOW ABOUT I *SHOW* YOU?
WAIT... I REMEMBER YOU.
YES, YOU DO. DO YOU REMEMBER *WHY*?
WHY WOULD I BE IN YOUR *DREAMS,* LITTLE SLAYER? AREN'T YOU LOOKING FOR SOMETHING ...OR SOMEONE?
I GET IT. IT WAS *YOU*. YOU KILLED THE MISSING SLAYER, THE ONE WHO'S BEEN ERASED FROM HISTORY.
YES. BUT NOT LIKE YOU THINK. YOU SEE...

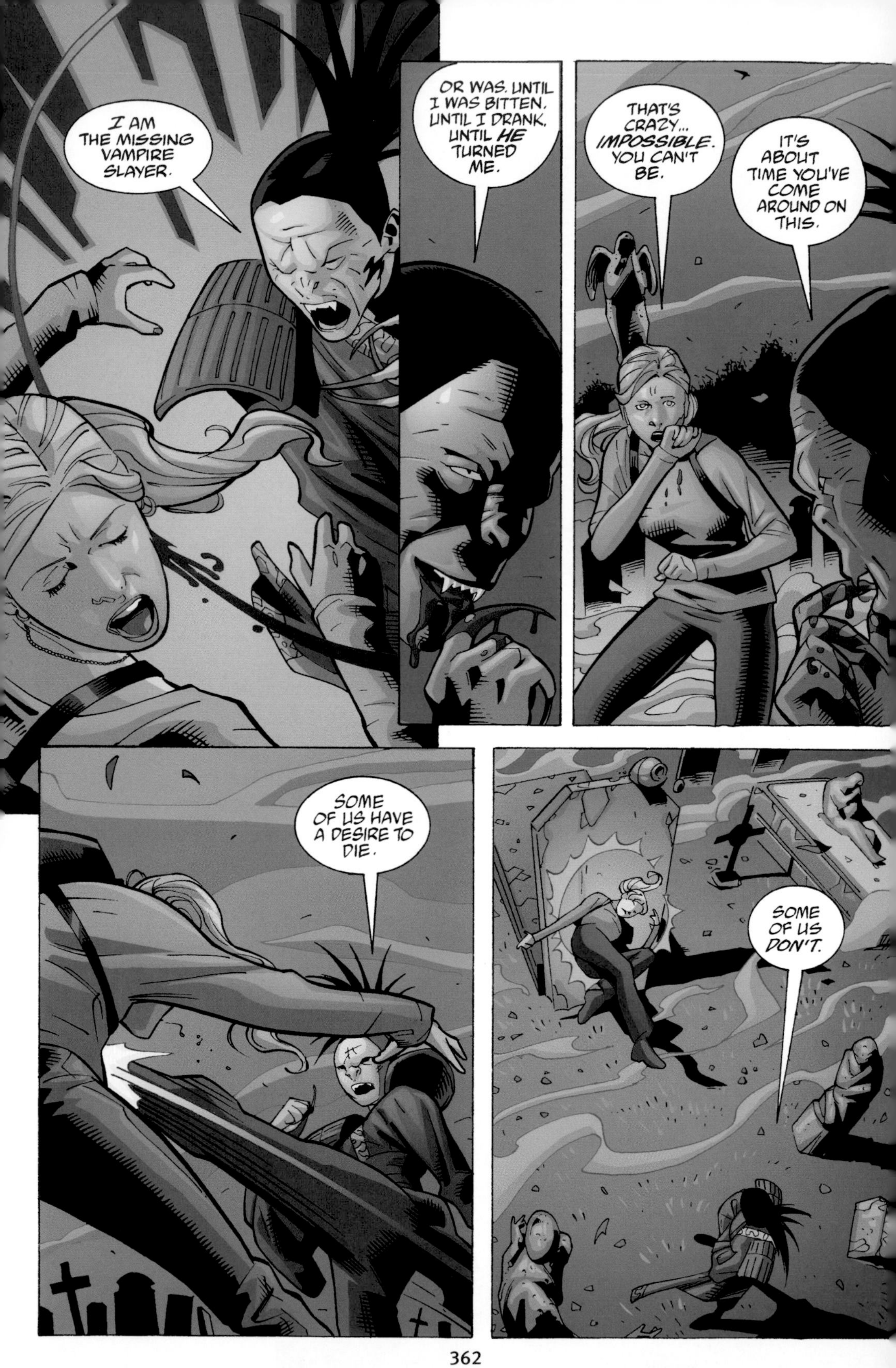
I AM THE MISSING VAMPIRE SLAYER.
OR WAS. UNTIL I WAS BITTEN. UNTIL I DRANK. UNTIL HE TURNED ME.
THAT'S CRAZY... IMPOSSIBLE. YOU CAN'T BE.
IT'S ABOUT TIME YOU'VE COME AROUND ON THIS.
SOME OF US HAVE A DESIRE TO DIE.
SOME OF US DON'T.

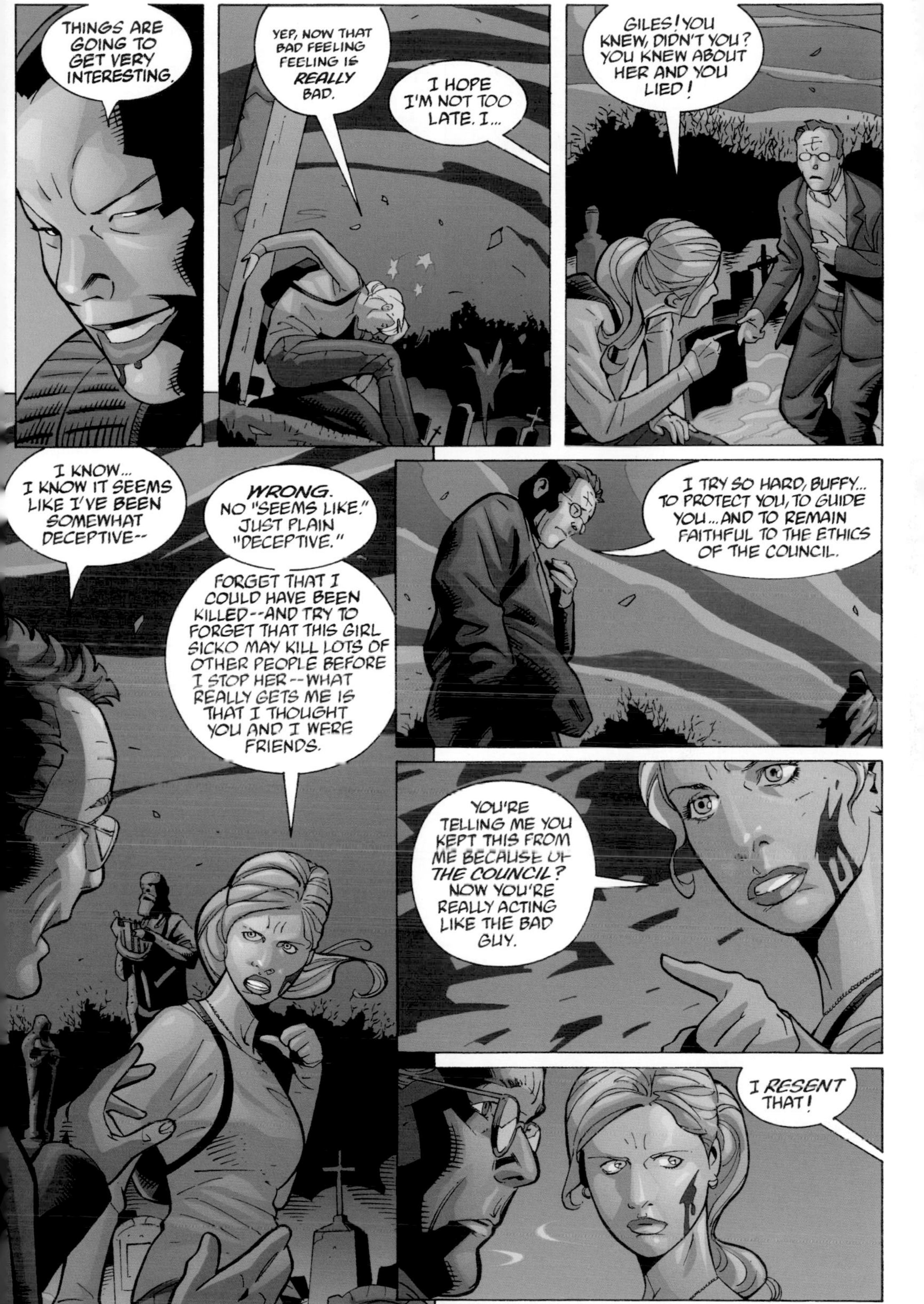
THINGS ARE GOING TO GET VERY INTERESTING.
YEP, NOW THAT BAD FEELING FEELING IS REALLY BAD.
I HOPE I'M NOT TOO LATE. I...
GILES! YOU KNEW, DIDN'T YOU? YOU KNEW ABOUT HER AND YOU LIED!
I KNOW... I KNOW IT SEEMS LIKE I'VE BEEN SOMEWHAT DECEPTIVE--
WRONG. NO "SEEMS LIKE." JUST PLAIN "DECEPTIVE."
FORGET THAT I COULD HAVE BEEN KILLED--AND TRY TO FORGET THAT THIS GIRL SICKO MAY KILL LOTS OF OTHER PEOPLE BEFORE I STOP HER--WHAT REALLY GETS ME IS THAT I THOUGHT YOU AND I WERE FRIENDS.
I TRY SO HARD, BUFFY... TO PROTECT YOU, TO GUIDE YOU...AND TO REMAIN FAITHFUL TO THE ETHICS OF THE COUNCIL.
YOU'RE TELLING ME YOU KEPT THIS FROM ME BECAUSE OF THE COUNCIL? NOW YOU'RE REALLY ACTING LIKE THE BAD GUY.
I RESENT THAT!

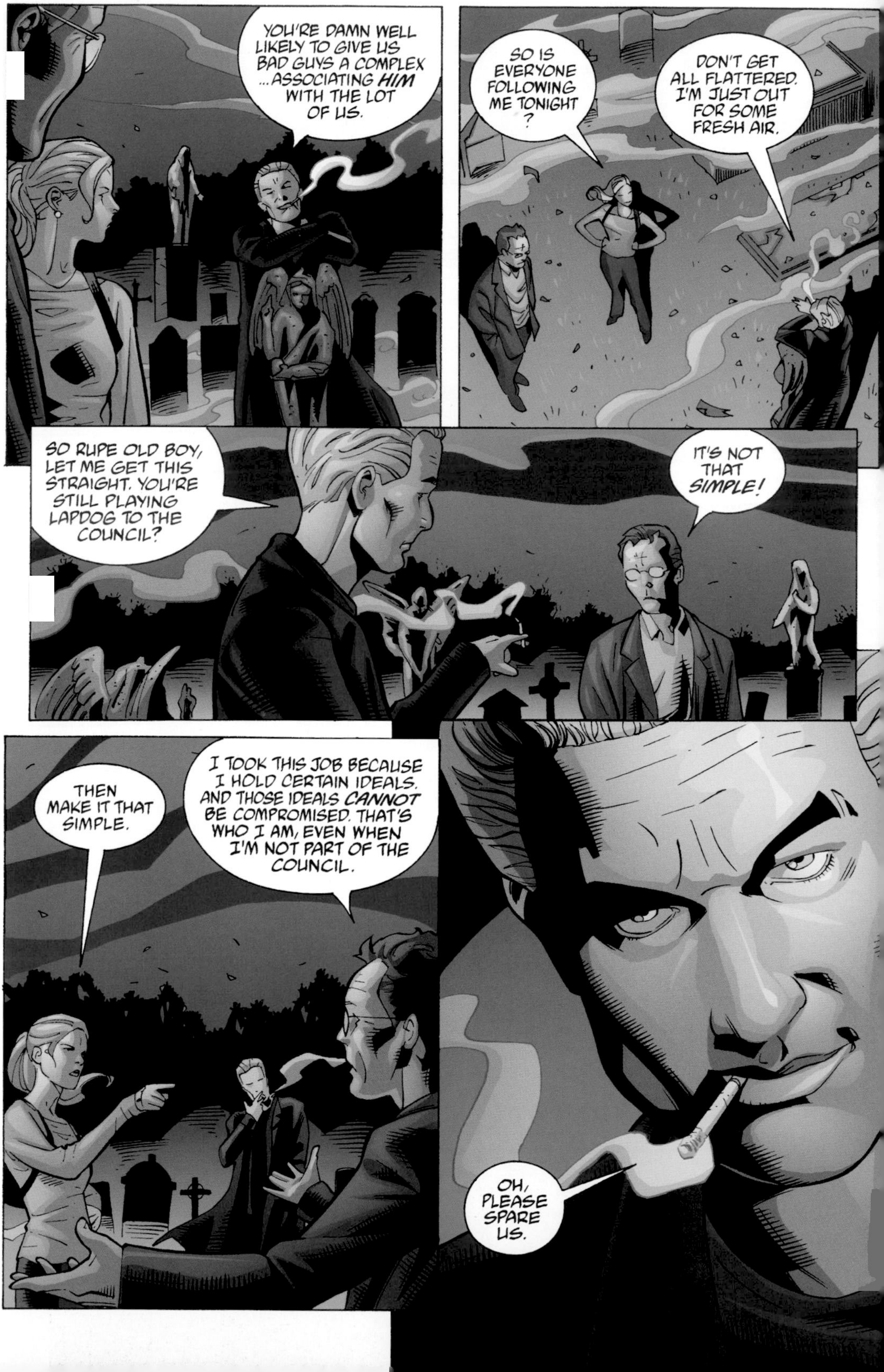
YOU'RE DAMN WELL LIKELY TO GIVE US BAD GUYS A COMPLEX ...ASSOCIATING HIM WITH THE LOT OF US.
SO IS EVERYONE FOLLOWING ME TONIGHT ?
DON'T GET ALL FLATTERED. I'M JUST OUT FOR SOME FRESH AIR.
SO RUPE OLD BOY, LET ME GET THIS STRAIGHT. YOU'RE STILL PLAYING LAPDOG TO THE COUNCIL?
IT'S NOT THAT SIMPLE!
THEN MAKE IT THAT SIMPLE.
I TOOK THIS JOB BECAUSE I HOLD CERTAIN IDEALS. AND THOSE IDEALS CANNOT BE COMPROMISED. THAT'S WHO I AM, EVEN WHEN I'M NOT PART OF THE COUNCIL.
OH, PLEASE SPARE US.

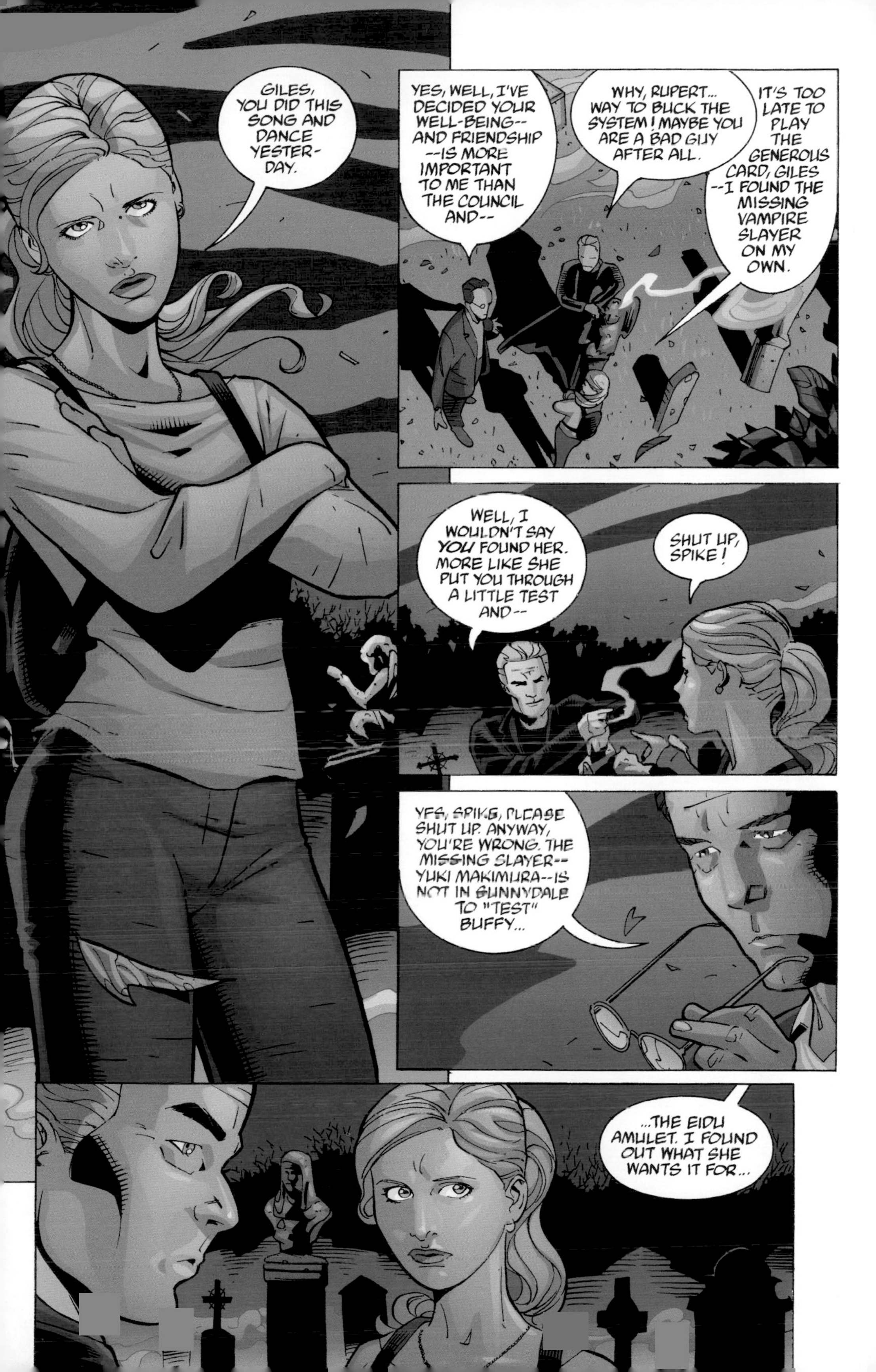
GILES, YOU DID THIS SONG AND DANCE YESTER-DAY.
YES, WELL, I'VE DECIDED YOUR WELL-BEING-- AND FRIENDSHIP --IS MORE IMPORTANT TO ME THAN THE COUNCIL AND--
WHY, RUPERT... WAY TO BUCK THE SYSTEM! MAYBE YOU ARE A BAD GUY AFTER ALL.
IT'S TOO LATE TO PLAY THE GENEROUS CARD, GILES --I FOUND THE MISSING VAMPIRE SLAYER ON MY OWN.
WELL, I WOULDN'T SAY YOU FOUND HER. MORE LIKE SHE PUT YOU THROUGH A LITTLE TEST AND--
SHUT UP, SPIKE!
YES, SPIKE, PLEASE SHUT UP. ANYWAY, YOU'RE WRONG. THE MISSING SLAYER-- YUKI MAKIMURA--IS NOT IN SUNNYDALE TO "TEST" BUFFY...
...THE EIDU AMULET. I FOUND OUT WHAT SHE WANTS IT FOR...

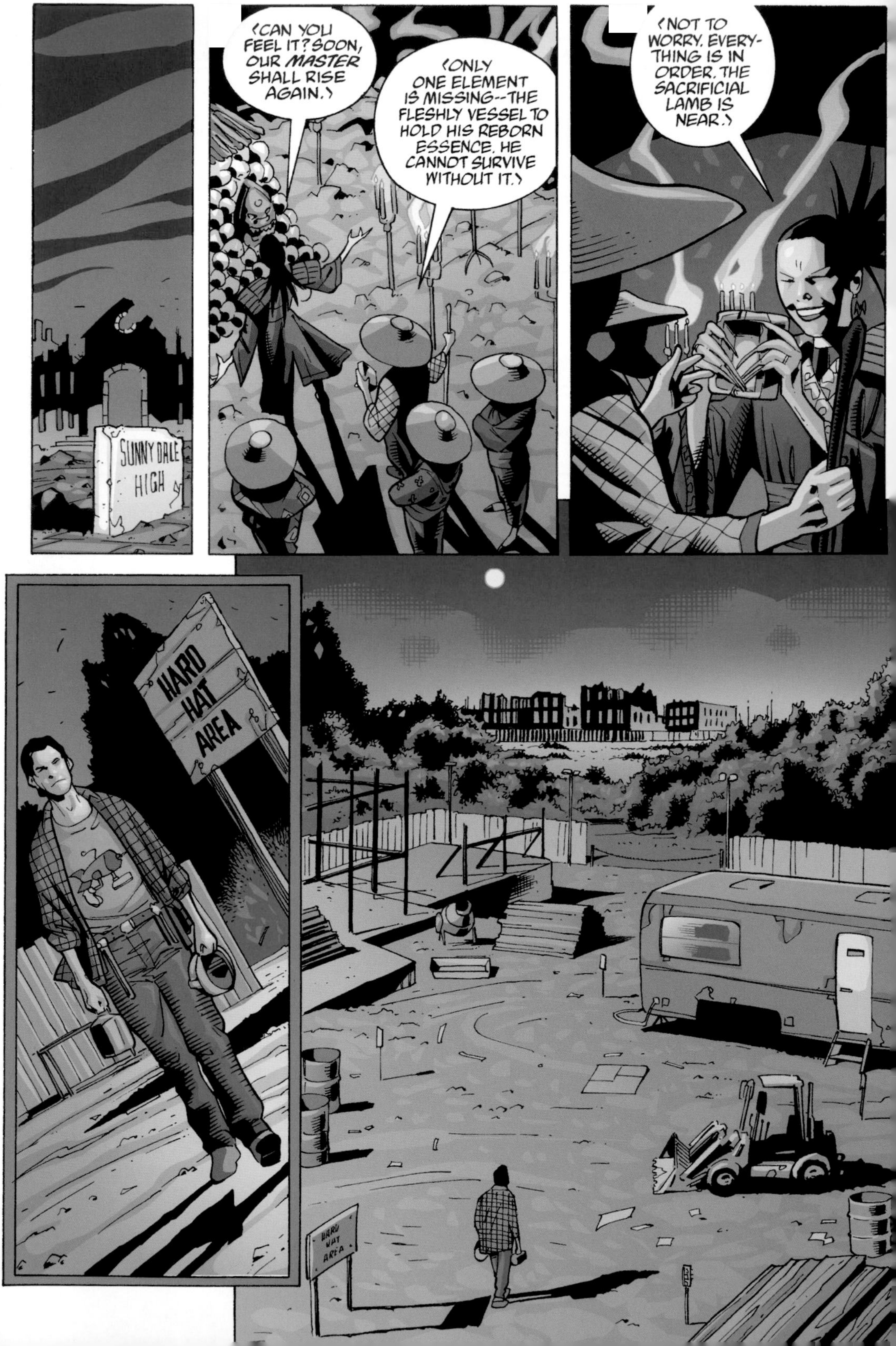
SUNNY DALE HIGH
<CAN YOU FEEL IT? SOON, OUR *MASTER* SHALL RISE AGAIN.>
<ONLY ONE ELEMENT IS MISSING--THE FLESHLY VESSEL TO HOLD HIS REBORN ESSENCE. HE CANNOT SURVIVE WITHOUT IT.>
<NOT TO WORRY. EVERYTHING IS IN ORDER. THE SACRIFICIAL LAMB IS NEAR.>
HARD HAT AREA
HARD HAT AREA

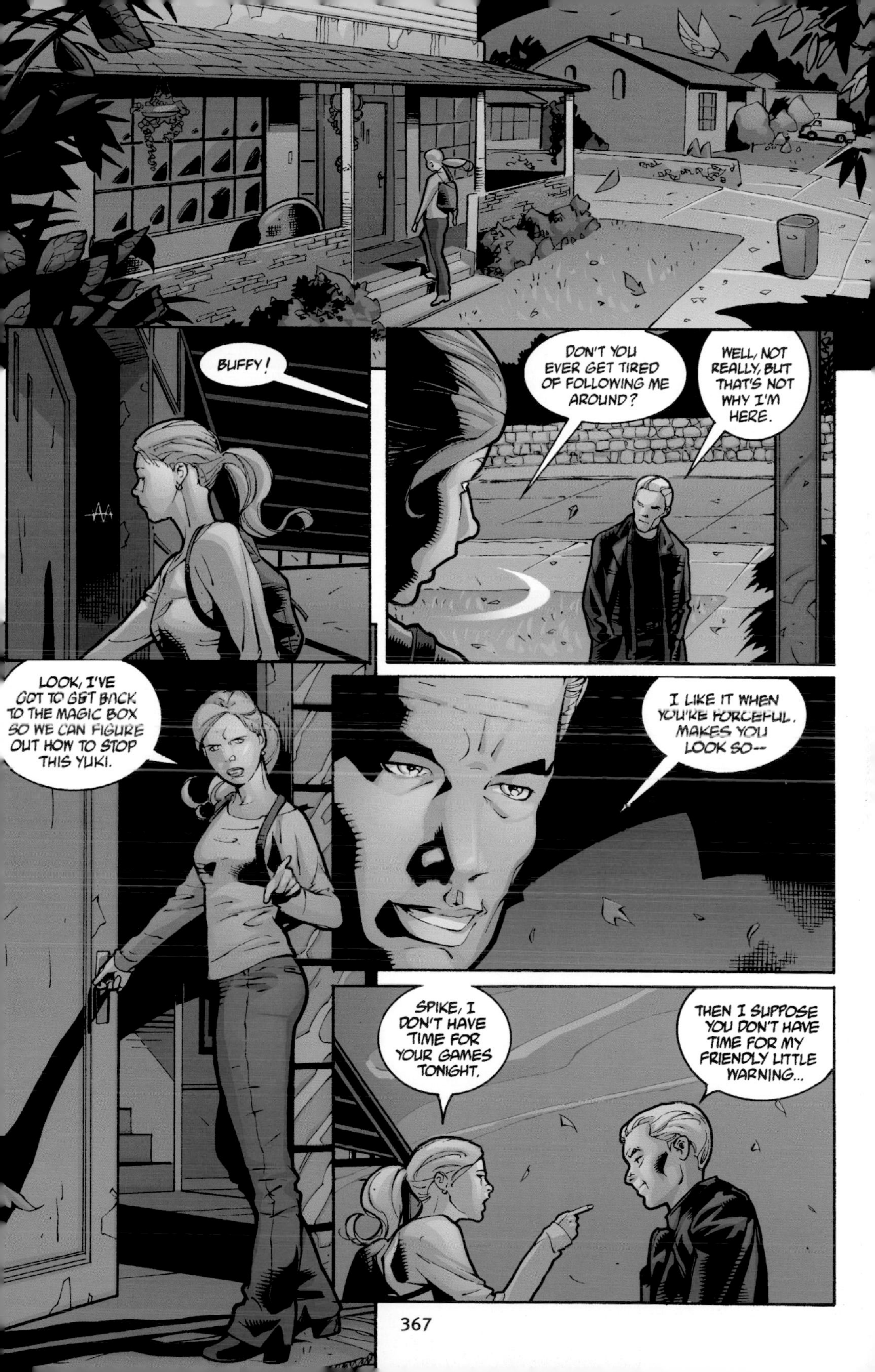
BUFFY!
DON'T YOU EVER GET TIRED OF FOLLOWING ME AROUND?
WELL, NOT REALLY, BUT THAT'S NOT WHY I'M HERE.
LOOK, I'VE GOT TO GET BACK TO THE MAGIC BOX SO WE CAN FIGURE OUT HOW TO STOP THIS YUKI.
I LIKE IT WHEN YOU'RE FORCEFUL. MAKES YOU LOOK SO--
SPIKE, I DON'T HAVE TIME FOR YOUR GAMES TONIGHT.
THEN I SUPPOSE YOU DON'T HAVE TIME FOR MY FRIENDLY LITTLE WARNING...

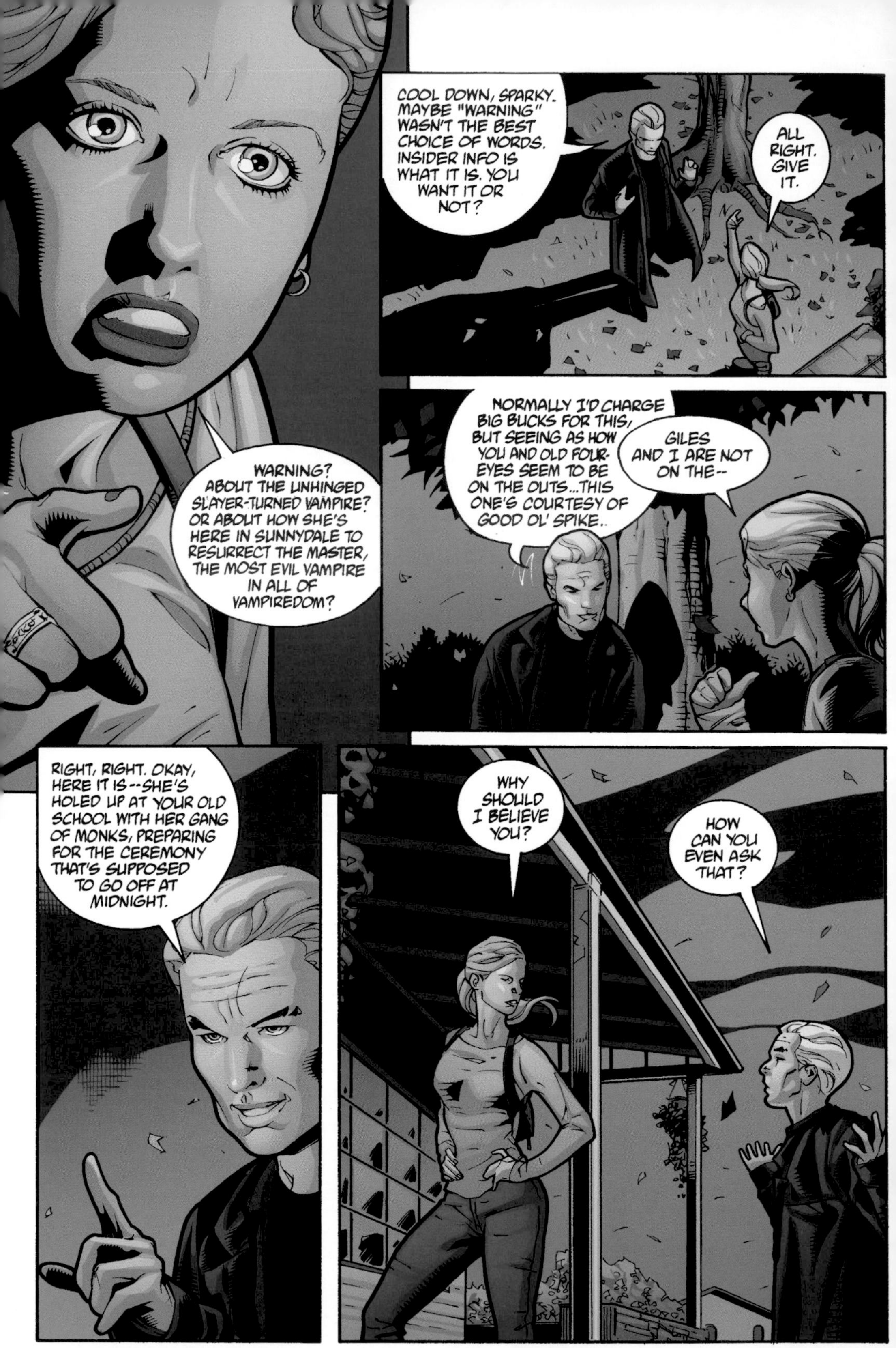
COOL DOWN, SPARKY. MAYBE "WARNING" WASN'T THE BEST CHOICE OF WORDS. INSIDER INFO IS WHAT IT IS. YOU WANT IT OR NOT?
ALL RIGHT. GIVE IT.
WARNING? ABOUT THE UNHINGED SLAYER-TURNED VAMPIRE? OR ABOUT HOW SHE'S HERE IN SUNNYDALE TO RESURRECT THE MASTER, THE MOST EVIL VAMPIRE IN ALL OF VAMPIREDOM?
NORMALLY I'D CHARGE BIG BUCKS FOR THIS, BUT SEEING AS HOW YOU AND OLD FOUR-EYES SEEM TO BE ON THE OUTS...THIS ONE'S COURTESY OF GOOD OL' SPIKE..
GILES AND I ARE NOT ON THE--
RIGHT, RIGHT. OKAY, HERE IT IS--SHE'S HOLED UP AT YOUR OLD SCHOOL WITH HER GANG OF MONKS, PREPARING FOR THE CEREMONY THAT'S SUPPOSED TO GO OFF AT MIDNIGHT.
WHY SHOULD I BELIEVE YOU?
HOW CAN YOU EVEN ASK THAT?

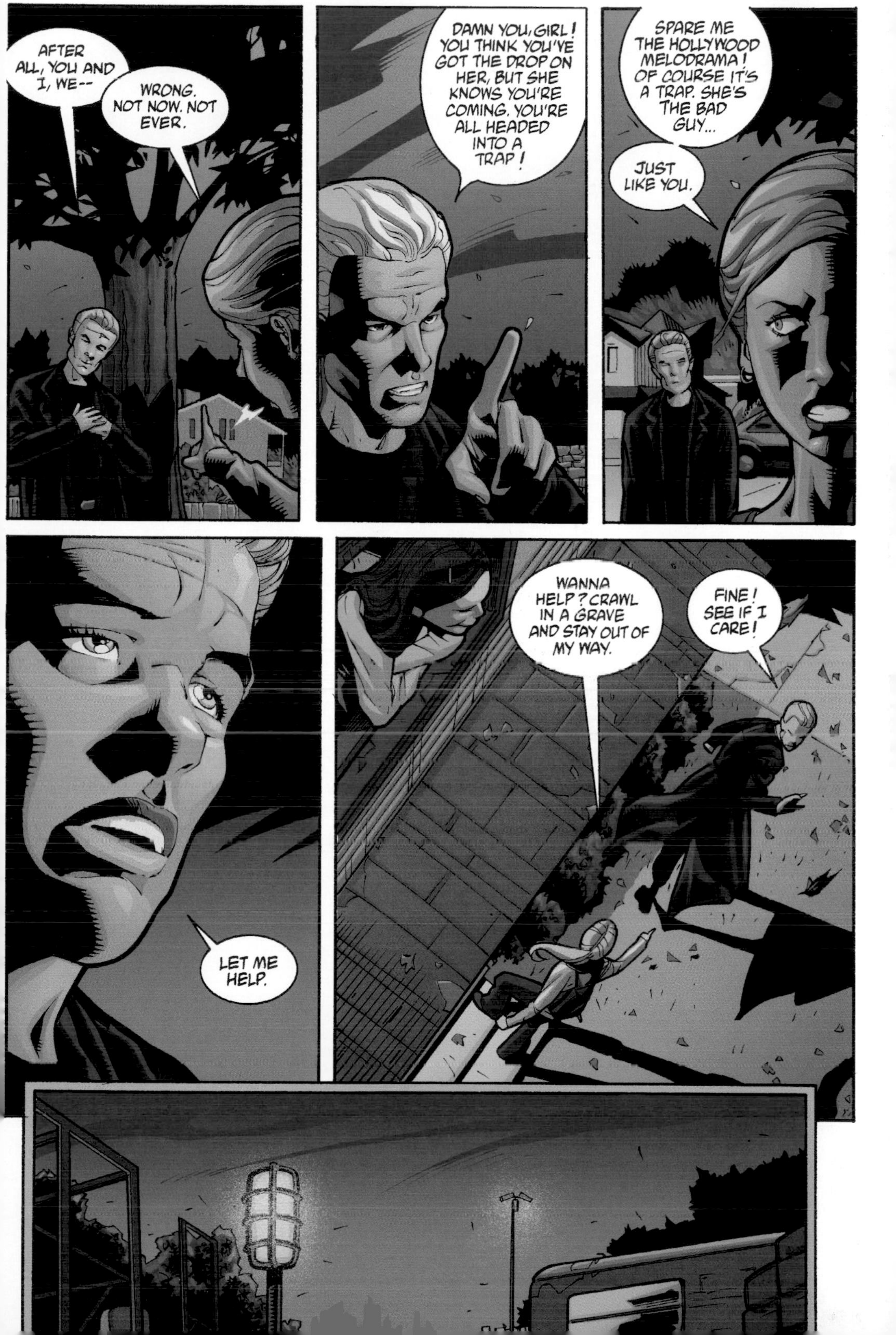
AFTER ALL, YOU AND I, WE--
WRONG. NOT NOW. NOT EVER.
DAMN YOU, GIRL! YOU THINK YOU'VE GOT THE DROP ON HER, BUT SHE KNOWS YOU'RE COMING. YOU'RE ALL HEADED INTO A TRAP!
SPARE ME THE HOLLYWOOD MELODRAMA! OF COURSE IT'S A TRAP. SHE'S THE BAD GUY...
JUST LIKE YOU.
LET ME HELP.
WANNA HELP? CRAWL IN A GRAVE AND STAY OUT OF MY WAY.
FINE! SEE IF I CARE!

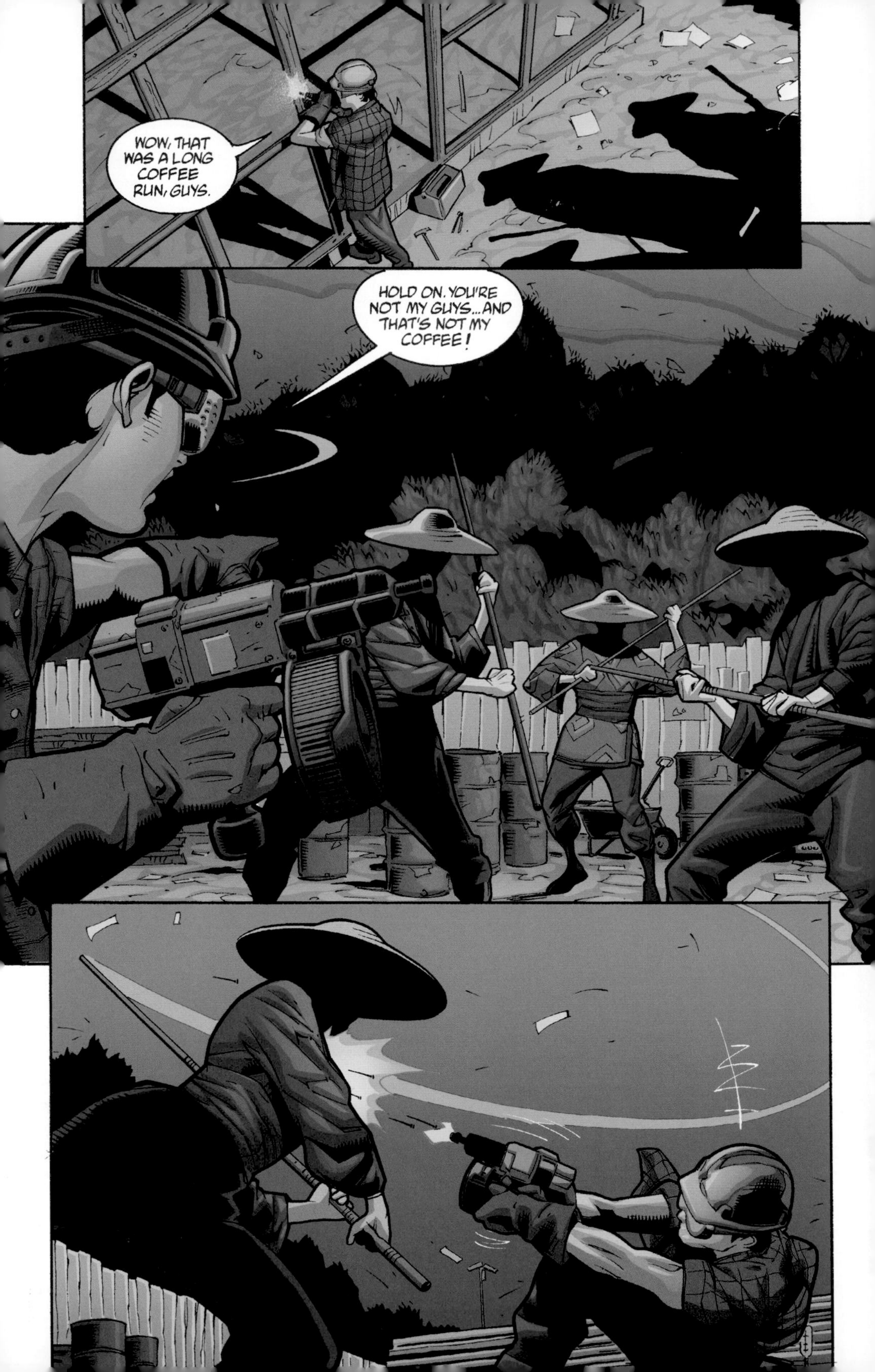
WOW, THAT WAS A LONG COFFEE RUN, GUYS.
HOLD ON. YOU'RE NOT MY GUYS...AND THAT'S NOT MY COFFEE!

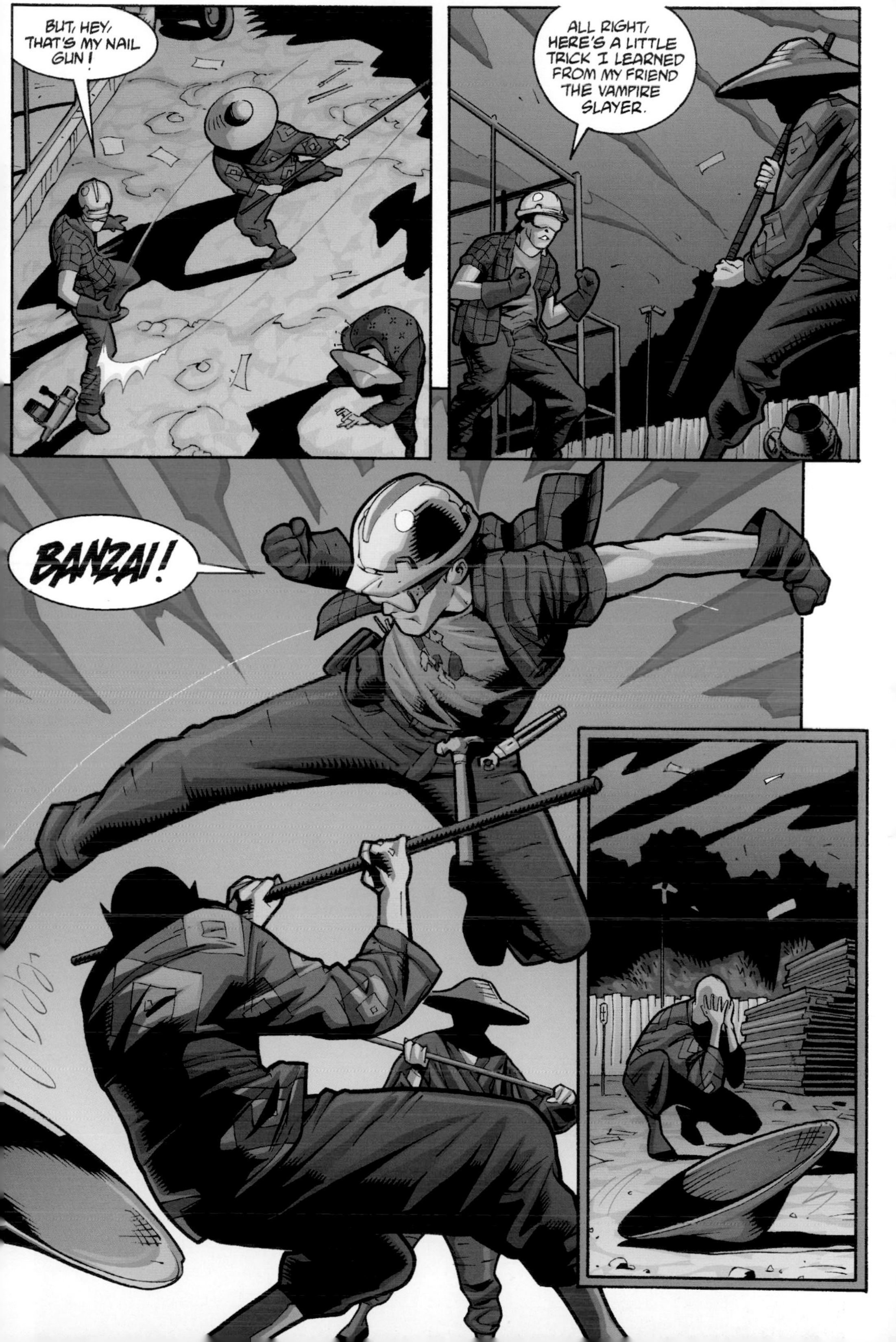
BUT, HEY, THAT'S MY NAIL GUN!
ALL RIGHT, HERE'S A LITTLE TRICK I LEARNED FROM MY FRIEND THE VAMPIRE SLAYER.
BANZAI!

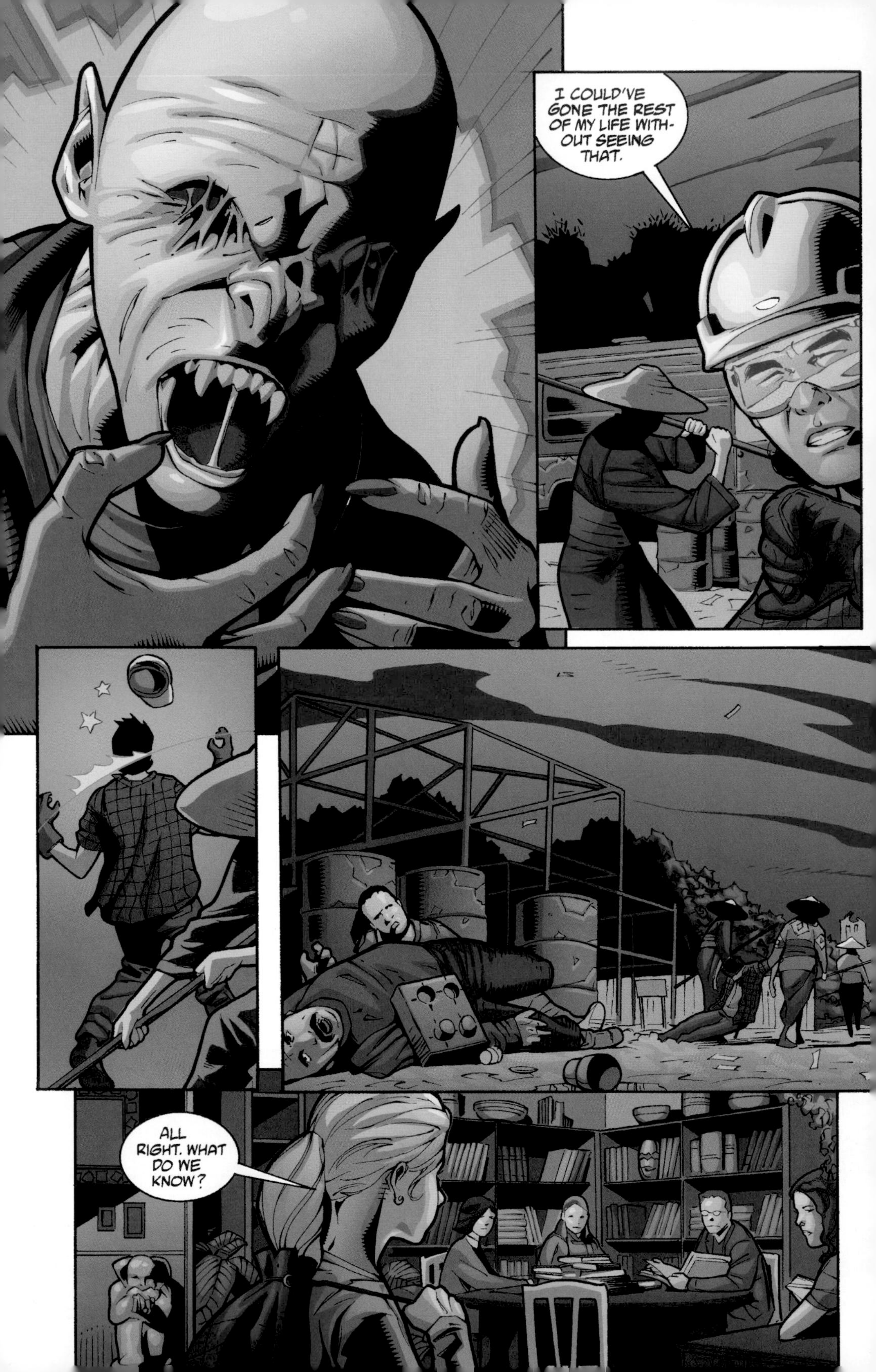
I COULD'VE GONE THE REST OF MY LIFE WITH-OUT SEEING THAT.
ALL RIGHT. WHAT DO WE KNOW?

WELL, AS WE MIGHT HAVE SUSPECTED, AGES AGO WHEN YUKI WAS A VAMPIRE SLAYER, SHE WENT UP AGAINST THE MASTER. HE WAS SOMEHOW ABLE TO GET TO HER MIND. IT WAS HE THAT TURNED HER.

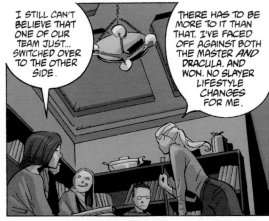

I STILL CAN'T BELIEVE THAT ONE OF OUR TEAM JUST... SWITCHED OVER TO THE OTHER SIDE.

THERE HAS TO BE MORE TO IT THAN THAT. I'VE FACED OFF AGAINST BOTH THE MASTER *AND* DRACULA. AND WON. NO SLAYER LIFESTYLE CHANGES FOR ME.

BUFFY, I REALLY WOULD HAVE TOLD YOU SOONER IF I THOUGHT THERE WAS... DANGER. YUKI WAS TURNED IN JAPAN, AND THERE SHE STAYED. HER ACTIVITY HAS BEEN RATHER MINIMAL.

BUT YOU *WERE* BEING A LITTLE OVER-PROTECTIVE.

AND I TOTALLY UNDER-ESTIMATED THE EIDU.

AS IN AMULET?

AS IN EVIL SECT OF MONK-LIKE VAMPIRES WHO WORSHIP THE MASTER.

THEIR PERVERSION OF RELIGION IS ONLY EXCEEDED BY THEIR PERVERSION OF THEIR OWN SELVES. THEY BELIEVE THE MASTER HAS GIVEN THEM THE LEGACY OF SECOND SIGHT.

TO BECOME EIDU, YOUNG ACOLYTES, STILL HUMAN, ARE BROUGHT TO THE MONKS AND TORTURED. THEY ARE MADE TO BEG FOR THE BLOOD OF EVERLASTING LIFE.

THE FINAL IGNOMINY IS THAT ONCE THEY HAVE BEGGED FOR LIFE IN DEATH, THEY MUST BURN THEIR OWN EYES OUT. ONLY THEN ARE THEY BITTEN AND TURNED.

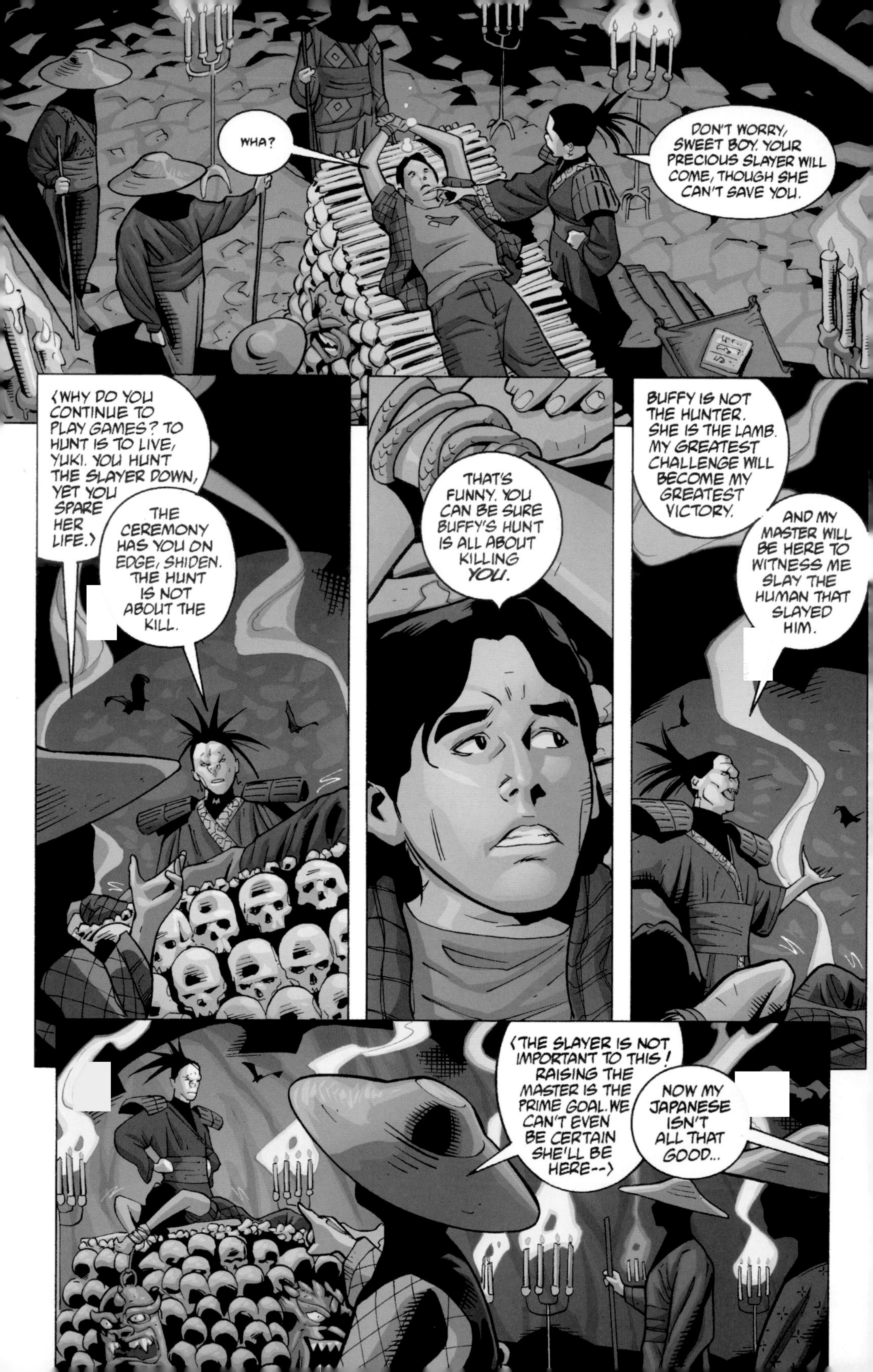
WHA?
DON'T WORRY, SWEET BOY. YOUR PRECIOUS SLAYER WILL COME, THOUGH SHE CAN'T SAVE YOU.
‹WHY DO YOU CONTINUE TO PLAY GAMES? TO HUNT IS TO LIVE, YUKI. YOU HUNT THE SLAYER DOWN, YET YOU SPARE HER LIFE.›
THE CEREMONY HAS YOU ON EDGE, SHIDEN. THE HUNT IS NOT ABOUT THE KILL.
THAT'S FUNNY. YOU CAN BE SURE BUFFY'S HUNT IS ALL ABOUT KILLING *YOU*.
BUFFY IS NOT THE HUNTER. SHE IS THE LAMB. MY GREATEST CHALLENGE WILL BECOME MY GREATEST VICTORY.
AND MY MASTER WILL BE HERE TO WITNESS ME SLAY THE HUMAN THAT SLAYED HIM.
‹THE SLAYER IS NOT IMPORTANT TO THIS! RAISING THE MASTER IS THE PRIME GOAL. WE CAN'T EVEN BE CERTAIN SHE'LL BE HERE--›
NOW MY JAPANESE ISN'T ALL THAT GOOD...

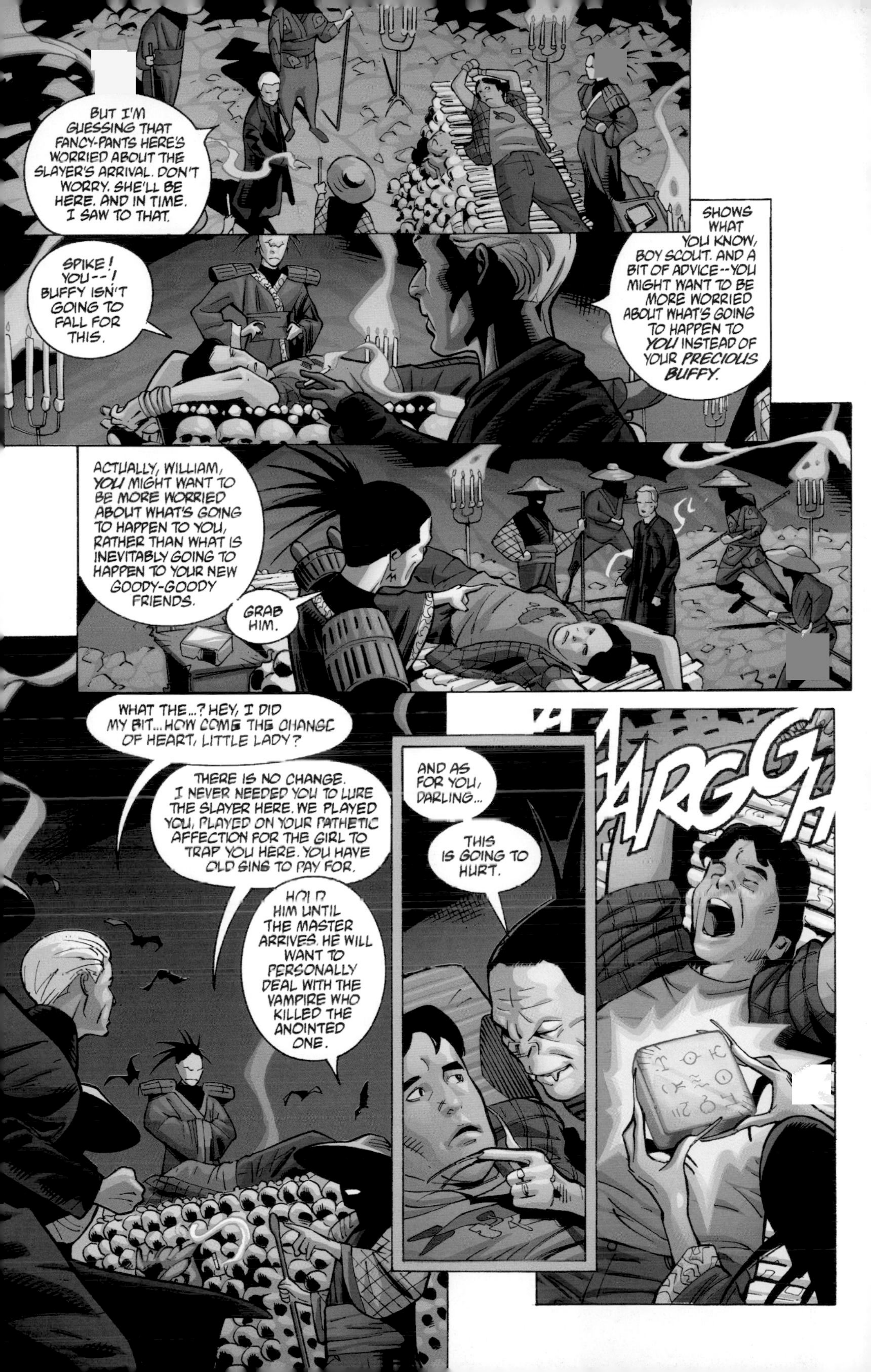

BUT I'M GUESSING THAT FANCY-PANTS HERE'S WORRIED ABOUT THE SLAYER'S ARRIVAL. DON'T WORRY. SHE'LL BE HERE. AND IN TIME. I SAW TO THAT.
SPIKE! YOU--! BUFFY ISN'T GOING TO FALL FOR THIS.
SHOWS WHAT YOU KNOW, BOY SCOUT. AND A BIT OF ADVICE--YOU MIGHT WANT TO BE MORE WORRIED ABOUT WHAT'S GOING TO HAPPEN TO YOU INSTEAD OF YOUR PRECIOUS BUFFY.
ACTUALLY, WILLIAM, YOU MIGHT WANT TO BE MORE WORRIED ABOUT WHAT'S GOING TO HAPPEN TO YOU, RATHER THAN WHAT IS INEVITABLY GOING TO HAPPEN TO YOUR NEW GOODY-GOODY FRIENDS.
GRAB HIM.
WHAT THE...? HEY, I DID MY BIT...HOW COME THE CHANGE OF HEART, LITTLE LADY?
THERE IS NO CHANGE. I NEVER NEEDED YOU TO LURE THE SLAYER HERE. WE PLAYED YOU, PLAYED ON YOUR PATHETIC AFFECTION FOR THE GIRL TO TRAP YOU HERE. YOU HAVE OLD SINS TO PAY FOR.
HOLD HIM UNTIL THE MASTER ARRIVES. HE WILL WANT TO PERSONALLY DEAL WITH THE VAMPIRE WHO KILLED THE ANOINTED ONE.
AND AS FOR YOU, DARLING...
THIS IS GOING TO HURT.
ARGGH

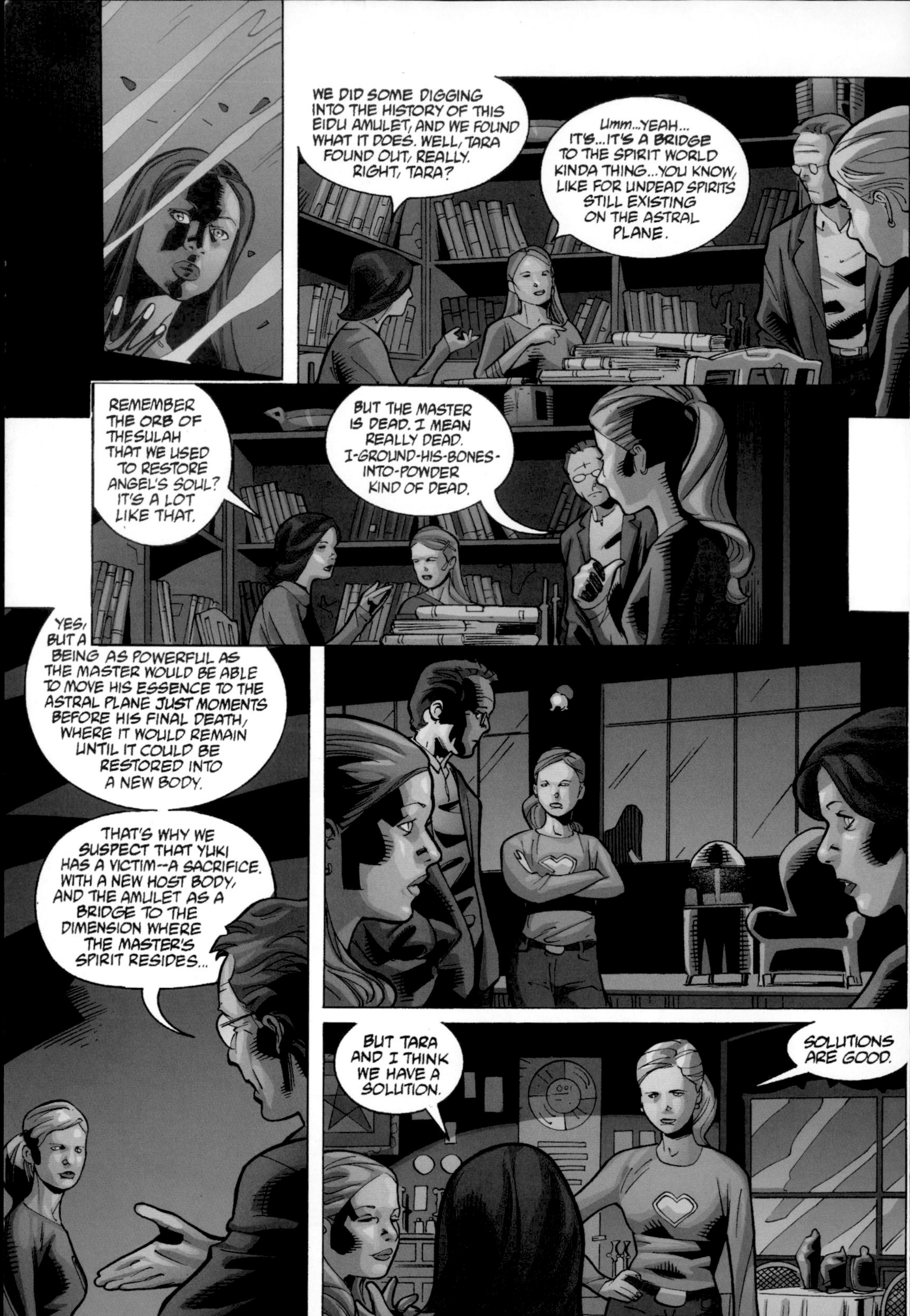
WE DID SOME DIGGING INTO THE HISTORY OF THIS EIDU AMULET, AND WE FOUND WHAT IT DOES. WELL, TARA FOUND OUT, REALLY. RIGHT, TARA?
Umm... YEAH... IT'S... IT'S A BRIDGE TO THE SPIRIT WORLD KINDA THING... YOU KNOW, LIKE FOR UNDEAD SPIRITS STILL EXISTING ON THE ASTRAL PLANE.
REMEMBER THE ORB OF THESULAH THAT WE USED TO RESTORE ANGEL'S SOUL? IT'S A LOT LIKE THAT.
BUT THE MASTER IS DEAD. I MEAN REALLY DEAD. I-GROUND-HIS-BONES-INTO-POWDER KIND OF DEAD.
YES, BUT A BEING AS POWERFUL AS THE MASTER WOULD BE ABLE TO MOVE HIS ESSENCE TO THE ASTRAL PLANE JUST MOMENTS BEFORE HIS FINAL DEATH, WHERE IT WOULD REMAIN UNTIL IT COULD BE RESTORED INTO A NEW BODY.
THAT'S WHY WE SUSPECT THAT YUKI HAS A VICTIM--A SACRIFICE. WITH A NEW HOST BODY, AND THE AMULET AS A BRIDGE TO THE DIMENSION WHERE THE MASTER'S SPIRIT RESIDES...
BUT TARA AND I THINK WE HAVE A SOLUTION.
SOLUTIONS ARE GOOD.

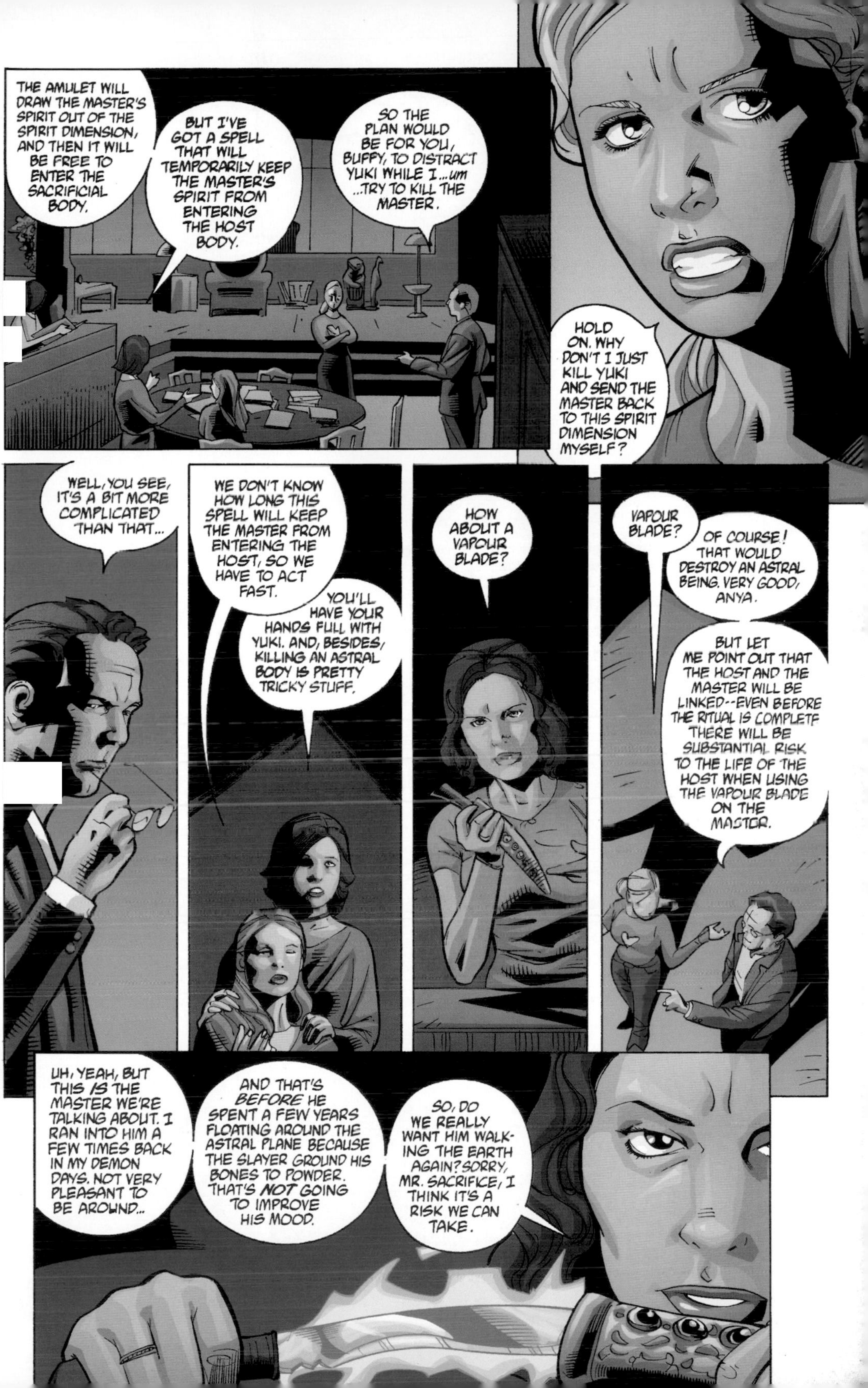
THE AMULET WILL DRAW THE MASTER'S SPIRIT OUT OF THE SPIRIT DIMENSION, AND THEN IT WILL BE FREE TO ENTER THE SACRIFICIAL BODY.
BUT I'VE GOT A SPELL THAT WILL TEMPORARILY KEEP THE MASTER'S SPIRIT FROM ENTERING THE HOST BODY.
SO THE PLAN WOULD BE FOR YOU, BUFFY, TO DISTRACT YUKI WHILE I ...*um* ...TRY TO KILL THE MASTER.
HOLD ON. WHY DON'T I JUST KILL YUKI AND SEND THE MASTER BACK TO THIS SPIRIT DIMENSION MYSELF?
WELL, YOU SEE, IT'S A BIT MORE COMPLICATED THAN THAT...
WE DON'T KNOW HOW LONG THIS SPELL WILL KEEP THE MASTER FROM ENTERING THE HOST, SO WE HAVE TO ACT FAST.
YOU'LL HAVE YOUR HANDS FULL WITH YUKI. AND, BESIDES, KILLING AN ASTRAL BODY IS PRETTY TRICKY STUFF.
HOW ABOUT A VAPOUR BLADE?
VAPOUR BLADE?
OF COURSE! THAT WOULD DESTROY AN ASTRAL BEING. VERY GOOD, ANYA.
BUT LET ME POINT OUT THAT THE HOST AND THE MASTER WILL BE LINKED--EVEN BEFORE THE RITUAL IS COMPLETE THERE WILL BE SUBSTANTIAL RISK TO THE LIFE OF THE HOST WHEN USING THE VAPOUR BLADE ON THE MASTER.
UH, YEAH, BUT THIS *IS* THE MASTER WE'RE TALKING ABOUT. I RAN INTO HIM A FEW TIMES BACK IN MY DEMON DAYS. NOT VERY PLEASANT TO BE AROUND...
AND THAT'S *BEFORE* HE SPENT A FEW YEARS FLOATING AROUND THE ASTRAL PLANE BECAUSE THE SLAYER GROUND HIS BONES TO POWDER. THAT'S *NOT* GOING TO IMPROVE HIS MOOD.
SO, DO WE REALLY WANT HIM WALKING THE EARTH AGAIN? SORRY, MR. SACRIFICE, I THINK IT'S A RISK WE CAN TAKE.

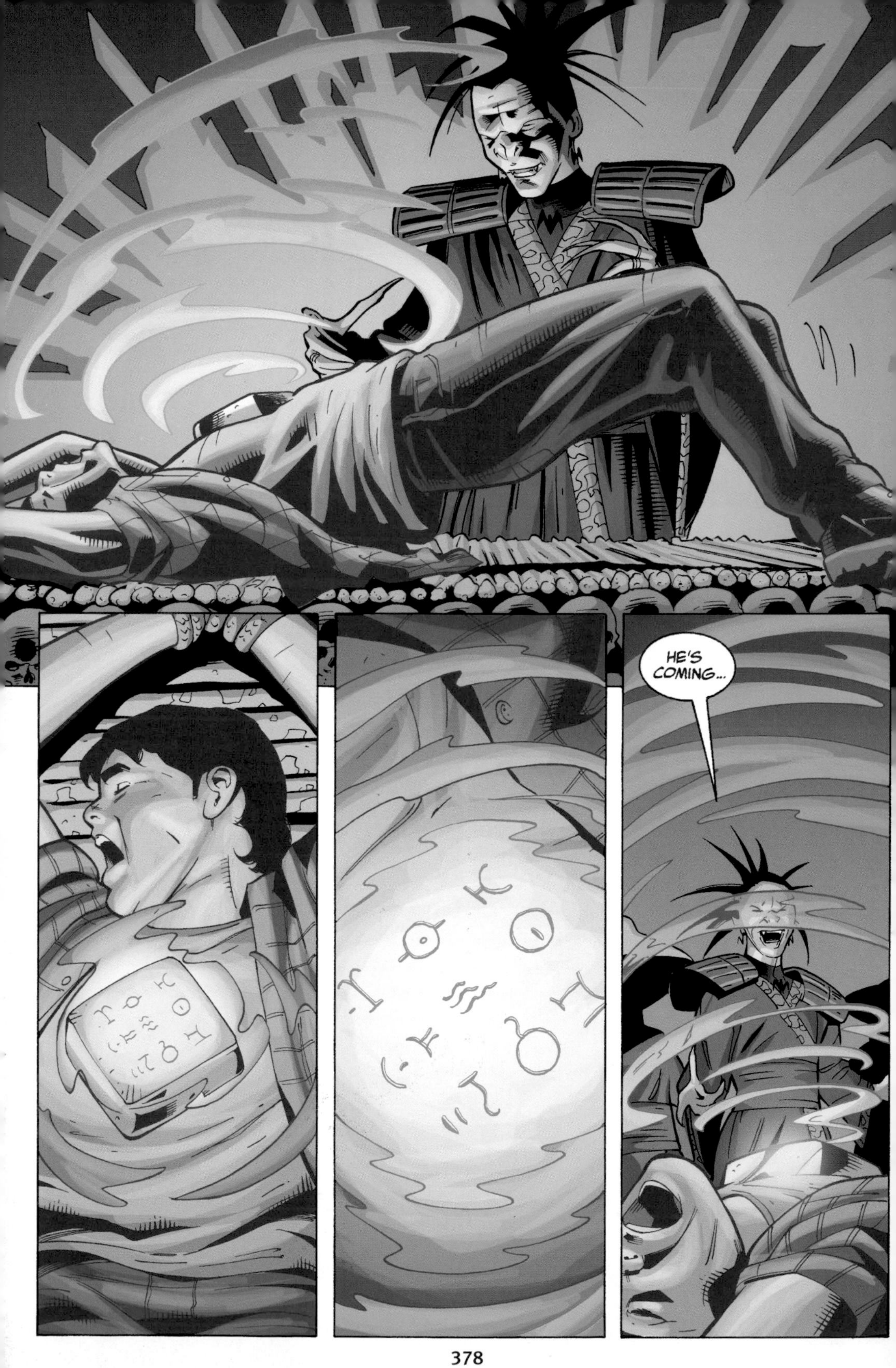
HE'S COMING...

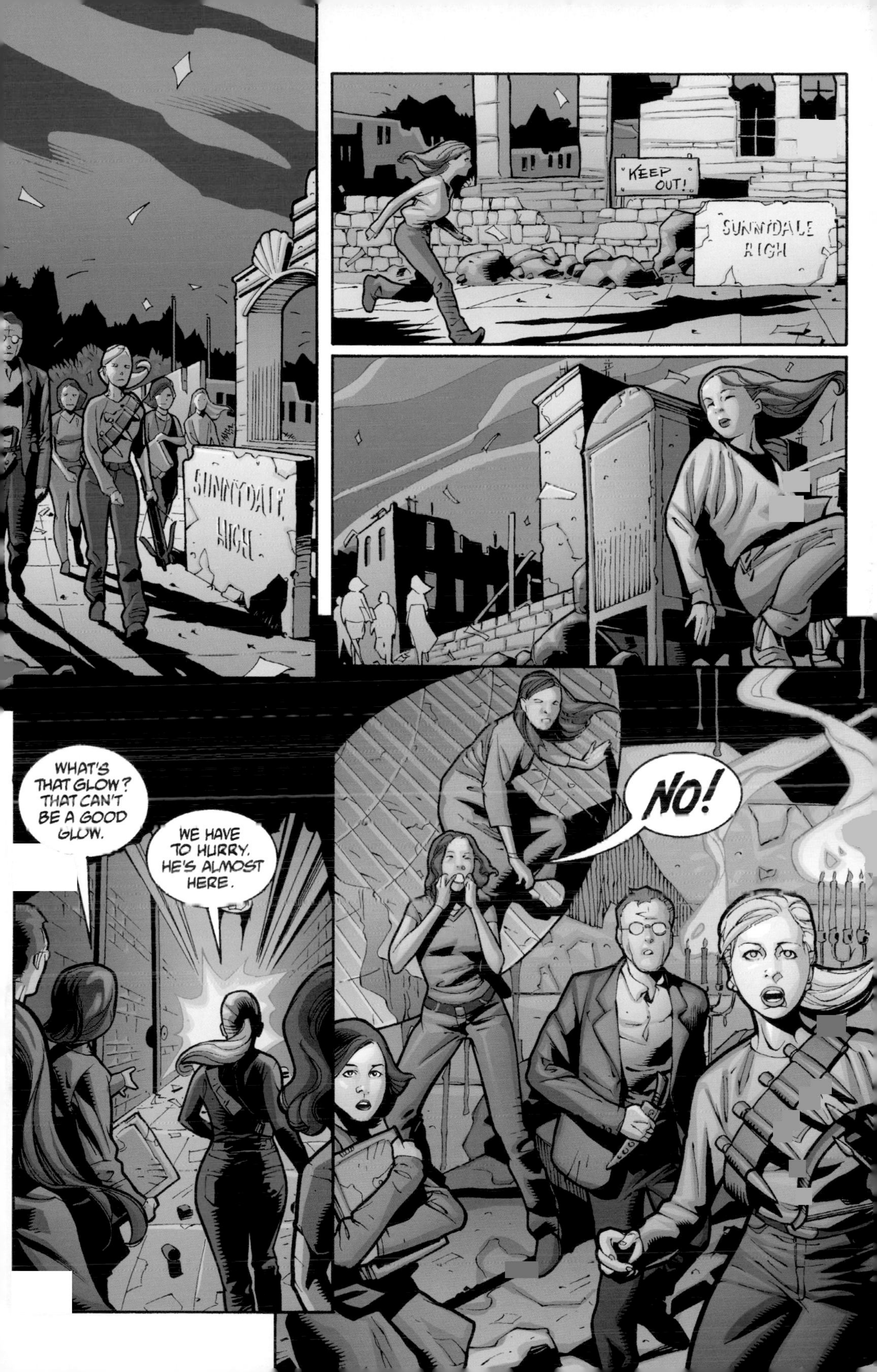

SUNNYDALE HIGH
KEEP OUT!
SUNNYDALE HIGH
WHAT'S THAT GLOW? THAT CAN'T BE A GOOD GLOW.
WE HAVE TO HURRY. HE'S ALMOST HERE.
NO!

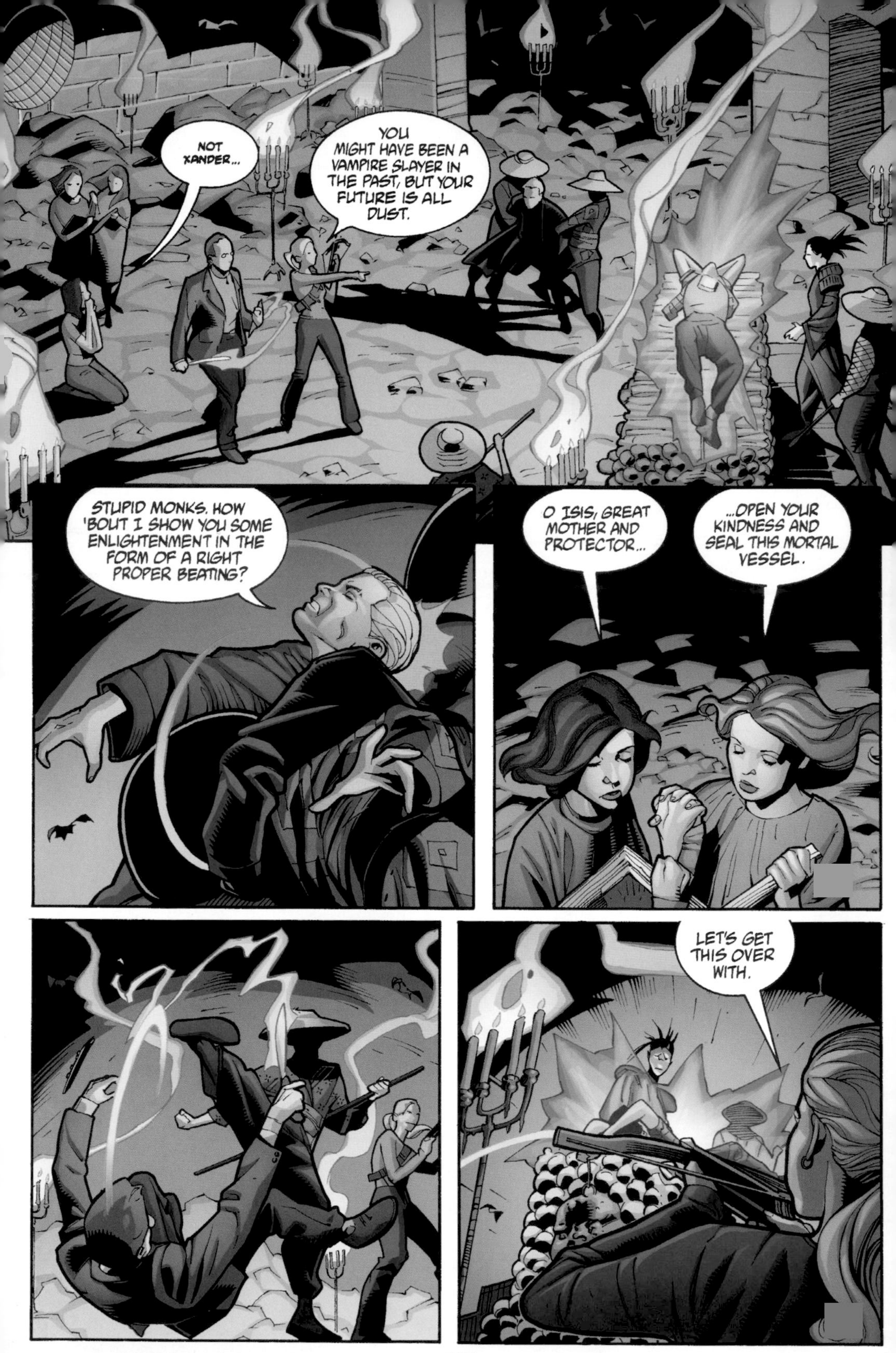
NOT XANDER...
YOU MIGHT HAVE BEEN A VAMPIRE SLAYER IN THE PAST, BUT YOUR FUTURE IS ALL DUST.
STUPID MONKS. HOW 'BOUT I SHOW YOU SOME ENLIGHTENMENT IN THE FORM OF A RIGHT PROPER BEATING?
O ISIS, GREAT MOTHER AND PROTECTOR...
...OPEN YOUR KINDNESS AND SEAL THIS MORTAL VESSEL.
LET'S GET THIS OVER WITH.

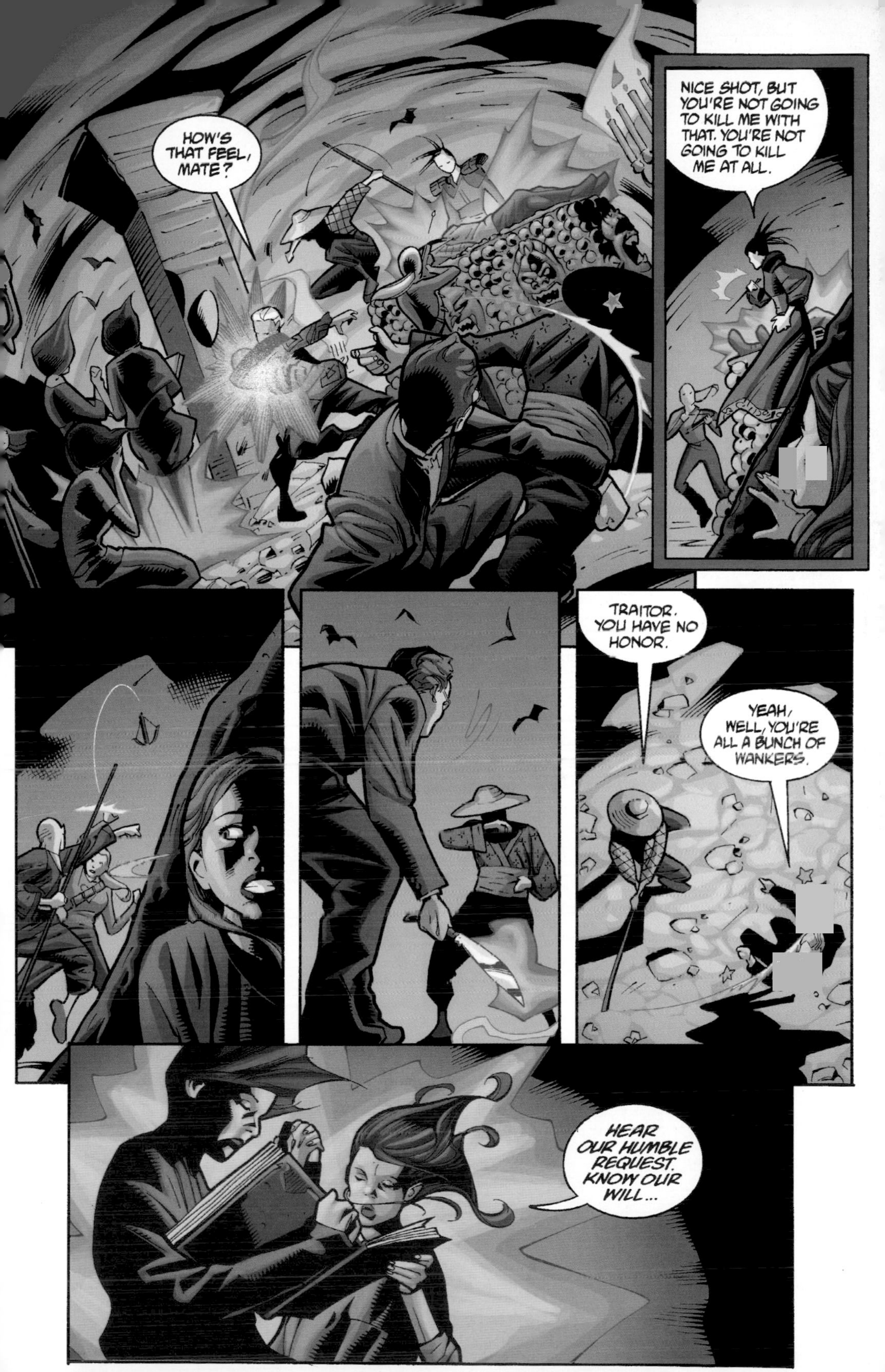
HOW'S THAT FEEL, MATE?
NICE SHOT, BUT YOU'RE NOT GOING TO KILL ME WITH THAT. YOU'RE NOT GOING TO KILL ME AT ALL.
TRAITOR. YOU HAVE NO HONOR.
YEAH, WELL, YOU'RE ALL A BUNCH OF WANKERS.
HEAR OUR HUMBLE REQUEST. KNOW OUR WILL...

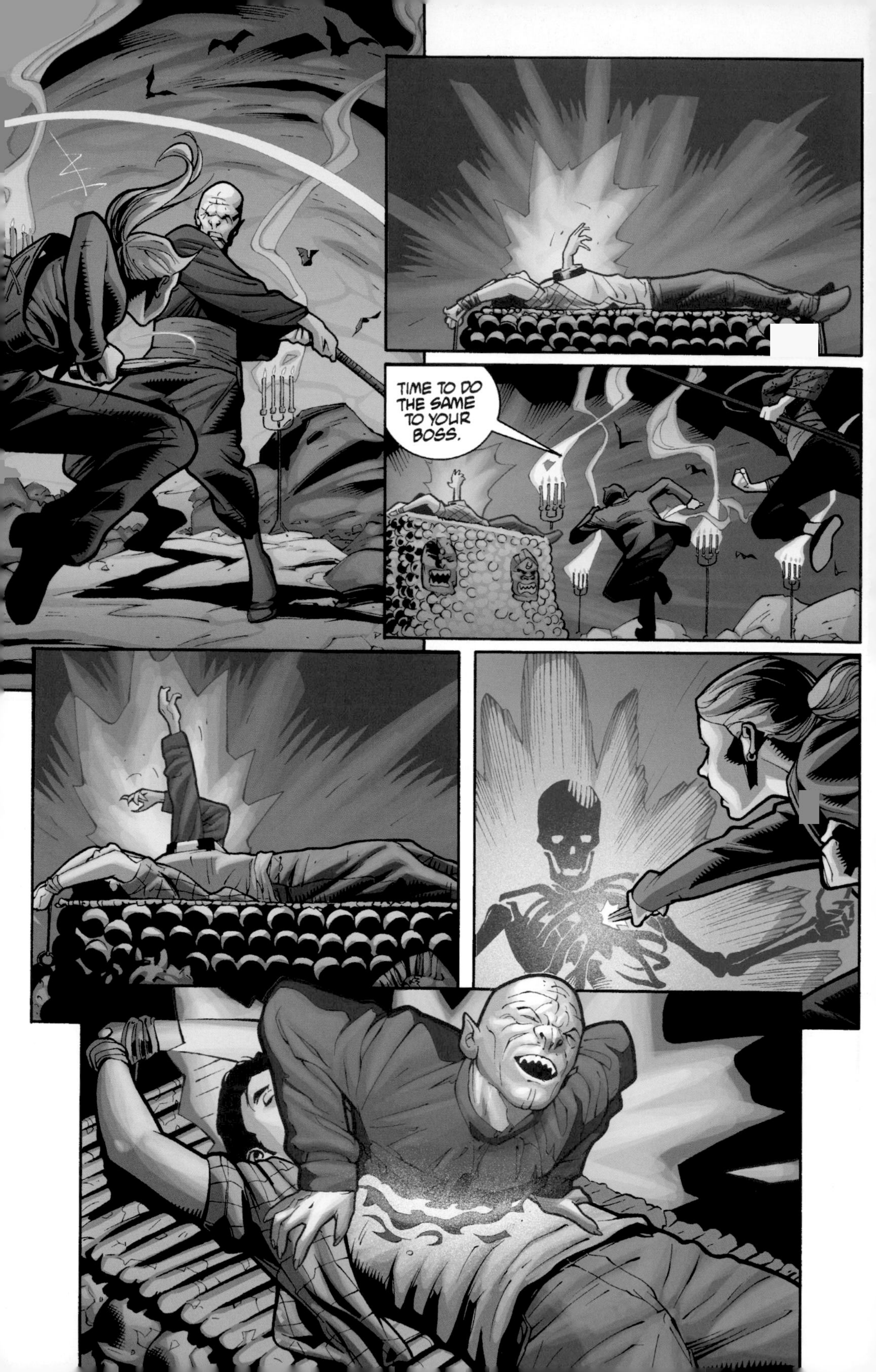
TIME TO DO THE SAME TO YOUR BOSS.

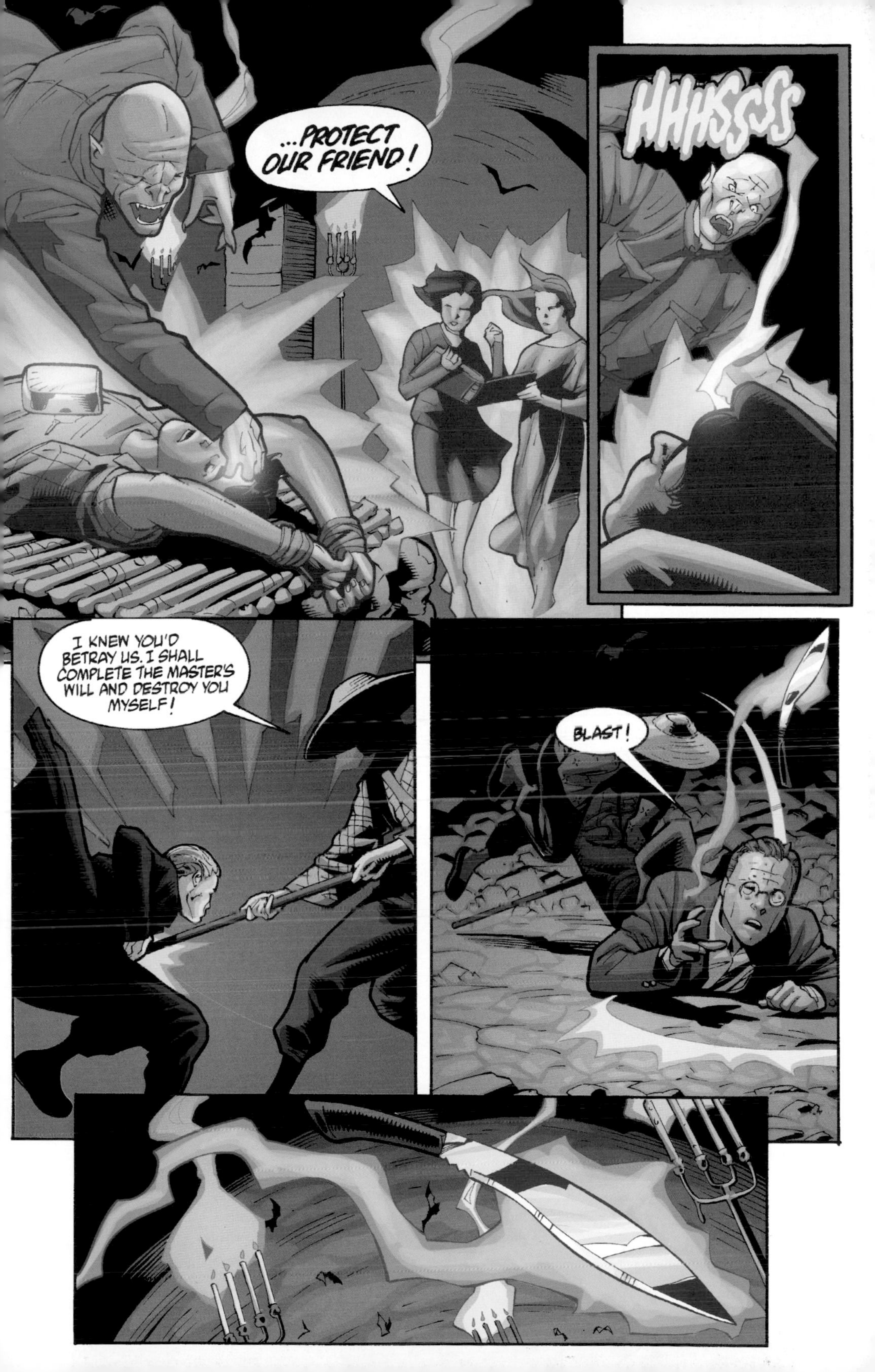
...PROTECT OUR FRIEND!
HHHSSSSS
I KNEW YOU'D BETRAY US. I SHALL COMPLETE THE MASTER'S WILL AND DESTROY YOU MYSELF!
BLAST!

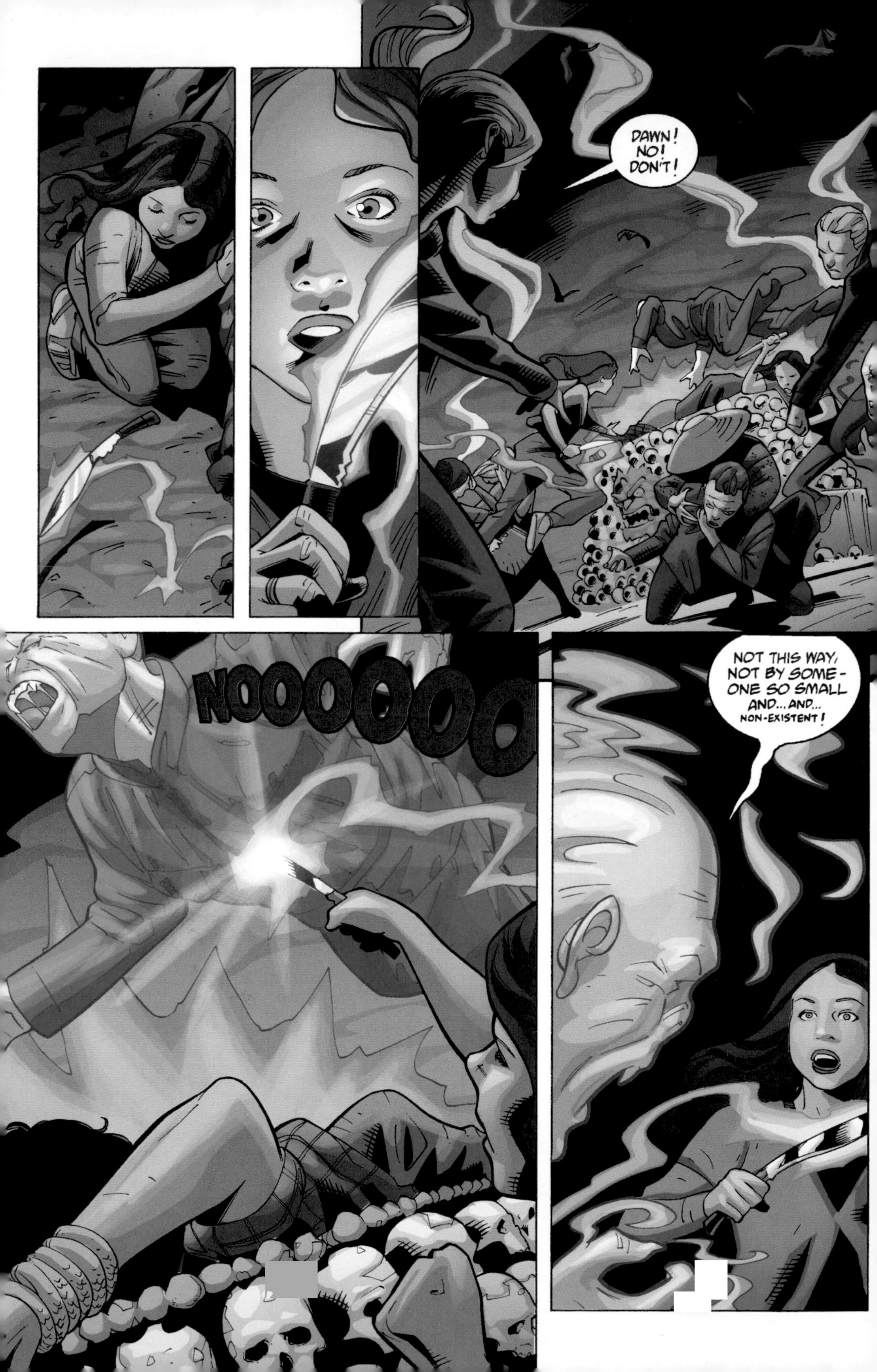
DAWN! NO! DON'T!
NOOOOOOO
NOT THIS WAY, NOT BY SOME-ONE SO SMALL AND...AND... NON-EXISTENT!

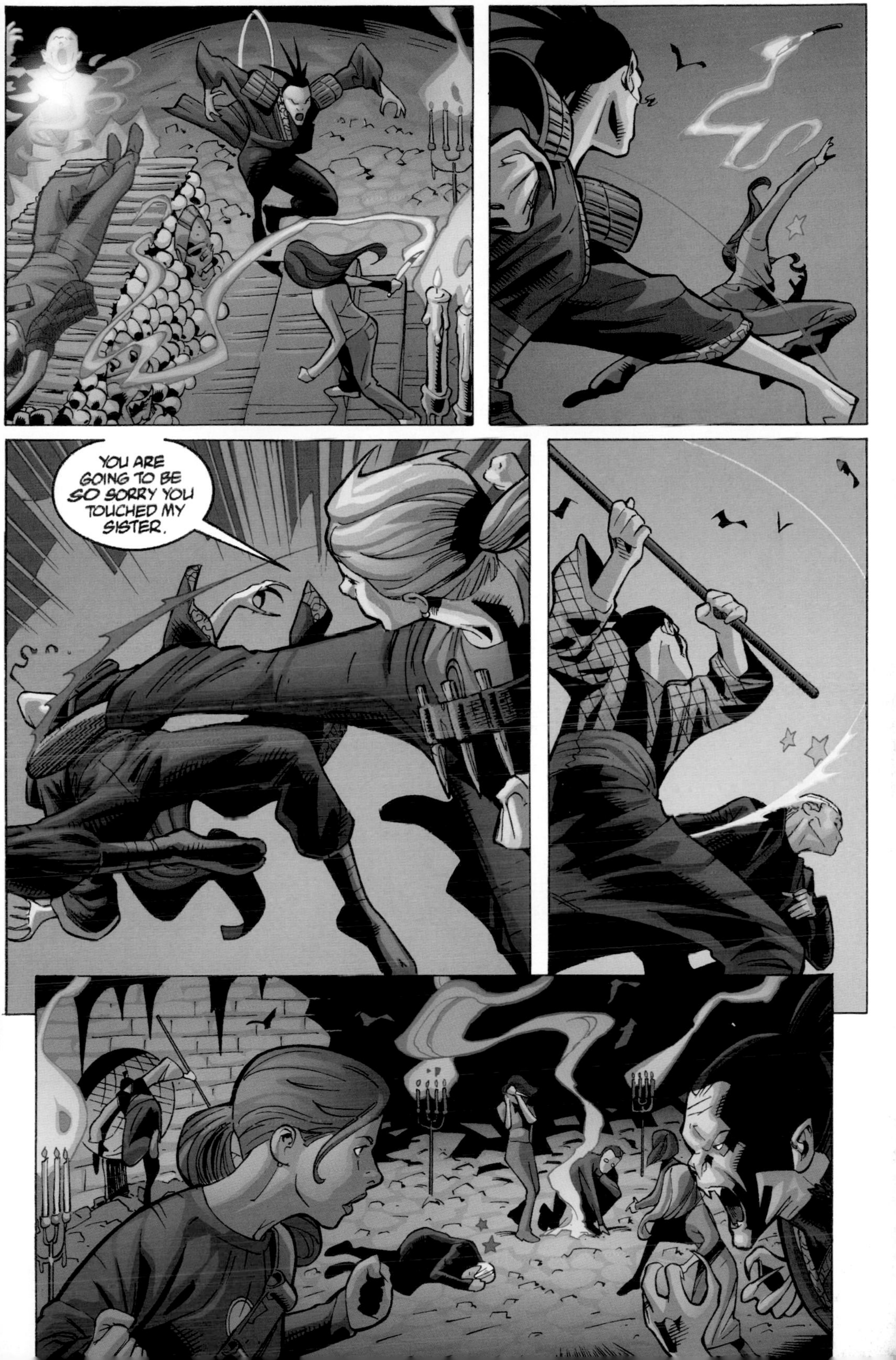
YOU ARE GOING TO BE SO SORRY YOU TOUCHED MY SISTER.

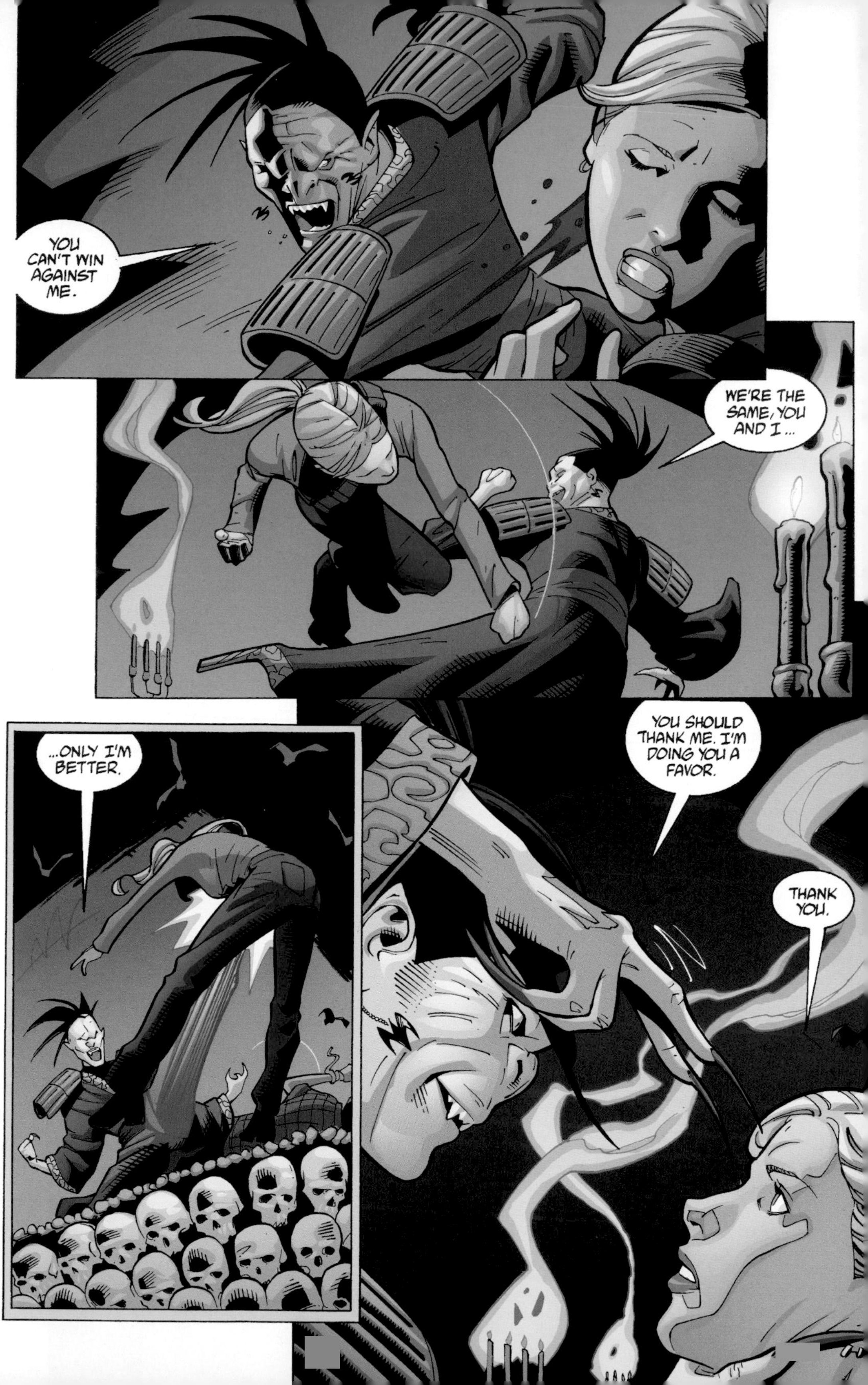
YOU CAN'T WIN AGAINST ME.
WE'RE THE SAME, YOU AND I...
...ONLY I'M BETTER.
YOU SHOULD THANK ME. I'M DOING YOU A FAVOR.
THANK YOU.

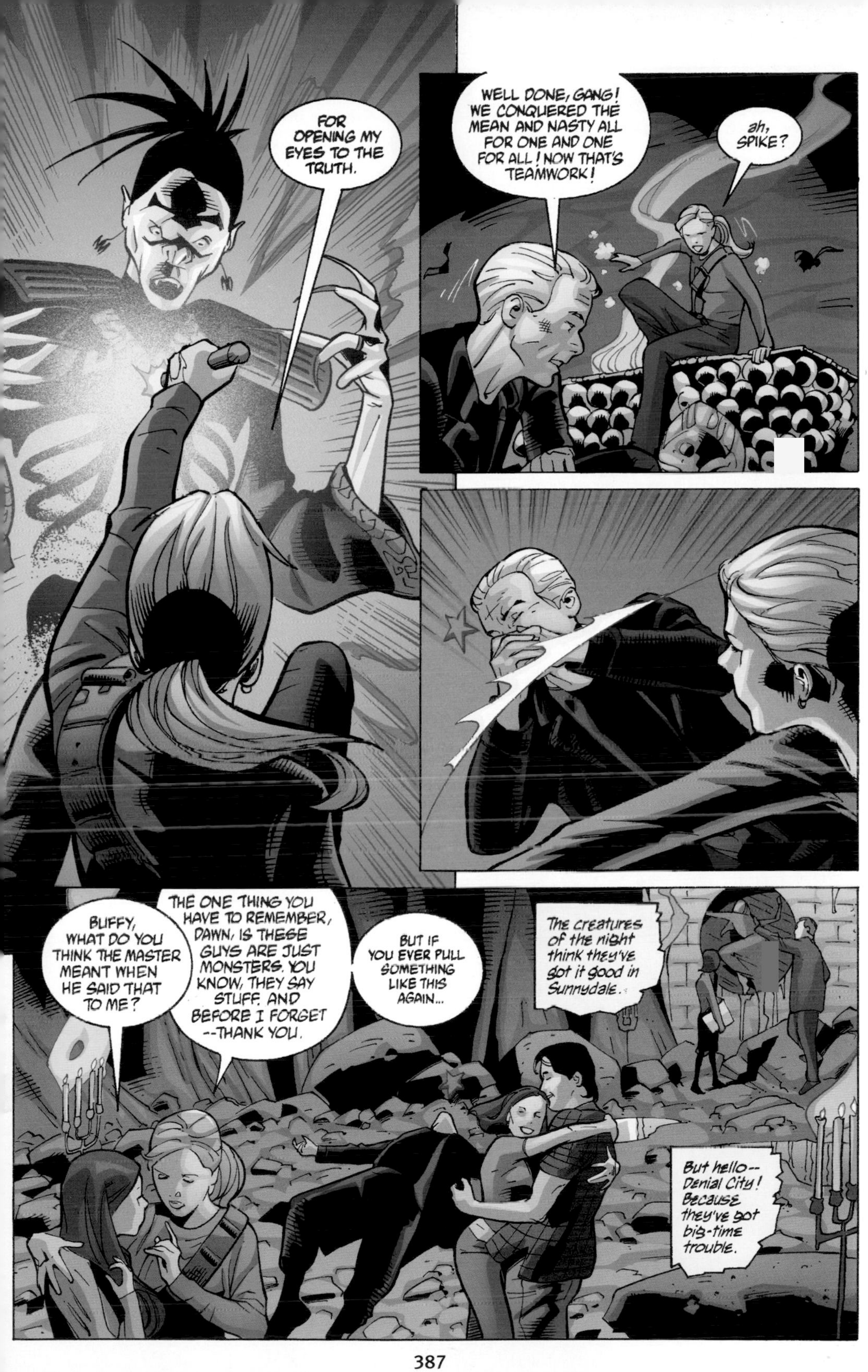
FOR OPENING MY EYES TO THE TRUTH.
WELL DONE, GANG! WE CONQUERED THE MEAN AND NASTY ALL FOR ONE AND ONE FOR ALL! NOW THAT'S TEAMWORK!
ah, SPIKE?
BUFFY, WHAT DO YOU THINK THE MASTER MEANT WHEN HE SAID THAT TO ME?
THE ONE THING YOU HAVE TO REMEMBER, DAWN, IS THESE GUYS ARE JUST MONSTERS. YOU KNOW, THEY SAY STUFF. AND BEFORE I FORGET --THANK YOU.
BUT IF YOU EVER PULL SOMETHING LIKE THIS AGAIN...
The creatures of the night think they've got it good in Sunnydale.
But hello-- Denial City! Because they've got big-time trouble.

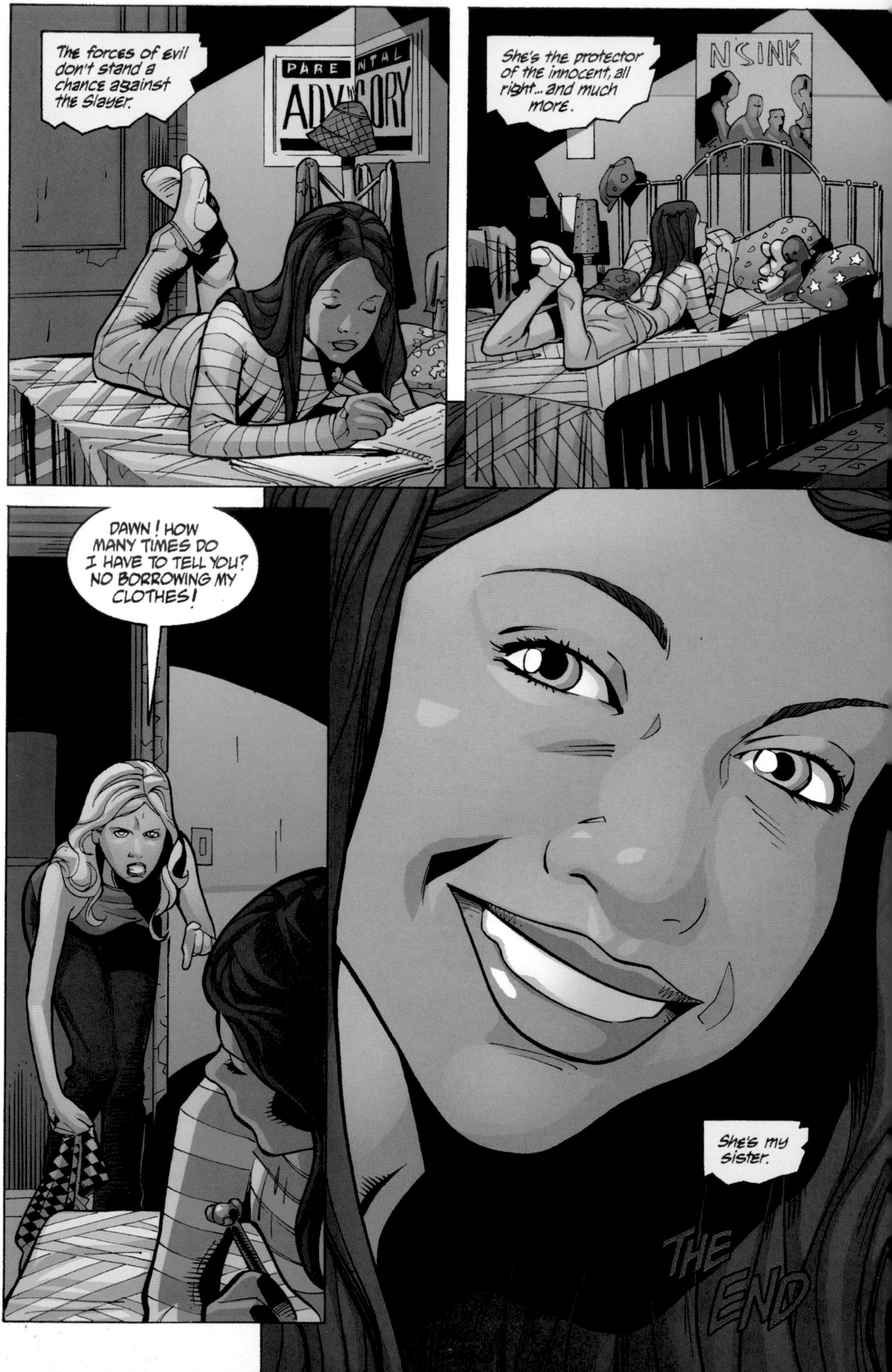

The forces of evil don't stand a chance against the Slayer.
PARENTAL ADVISORY
She's the protector of the innocent, all right... and much more.
NSINK
DAWN! HOW MANY TIMES DO I HAVE TO TELL YOU? NO BORROWING MY CLOTHES!
She's my sister.
THE END

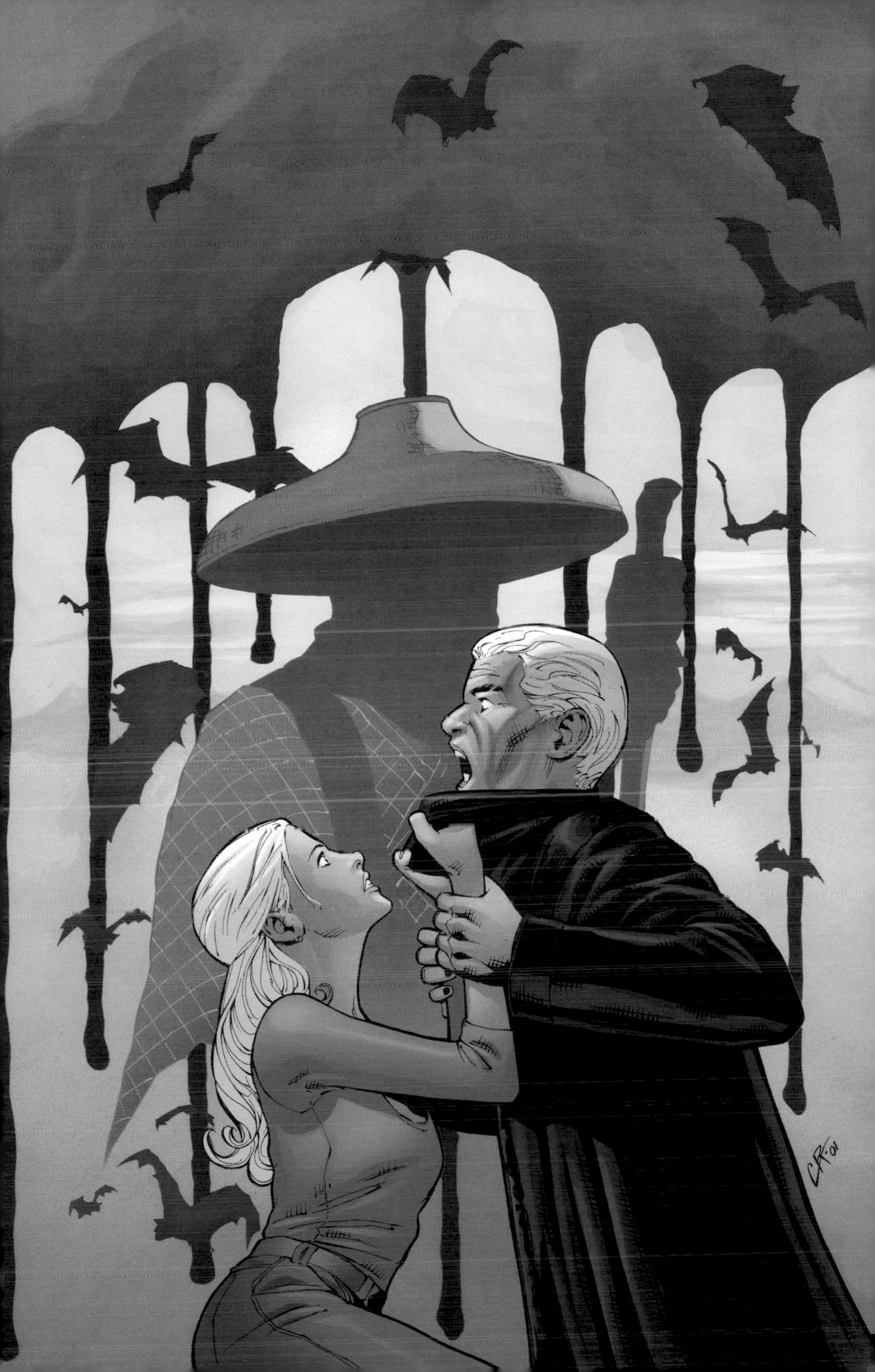

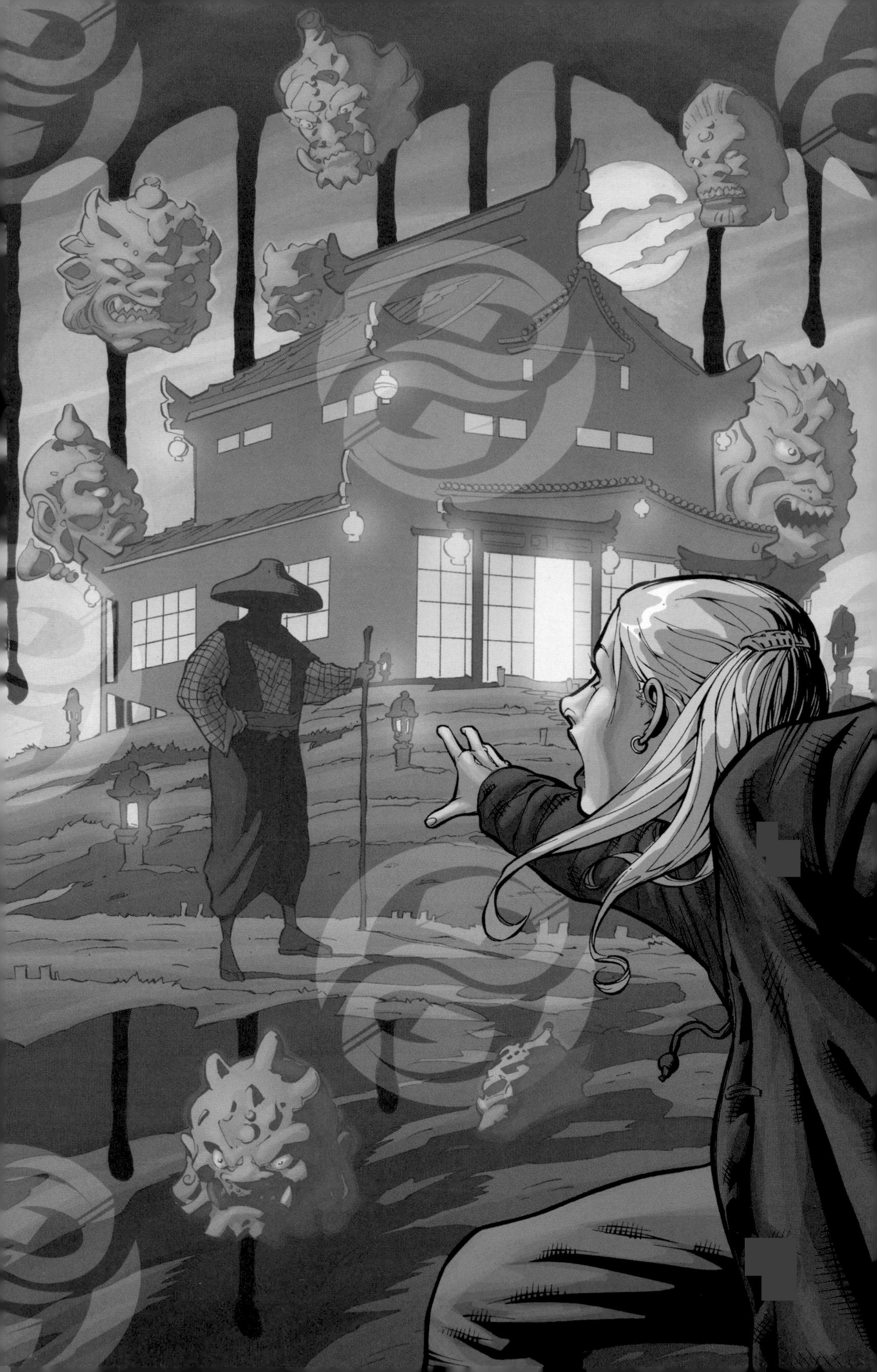

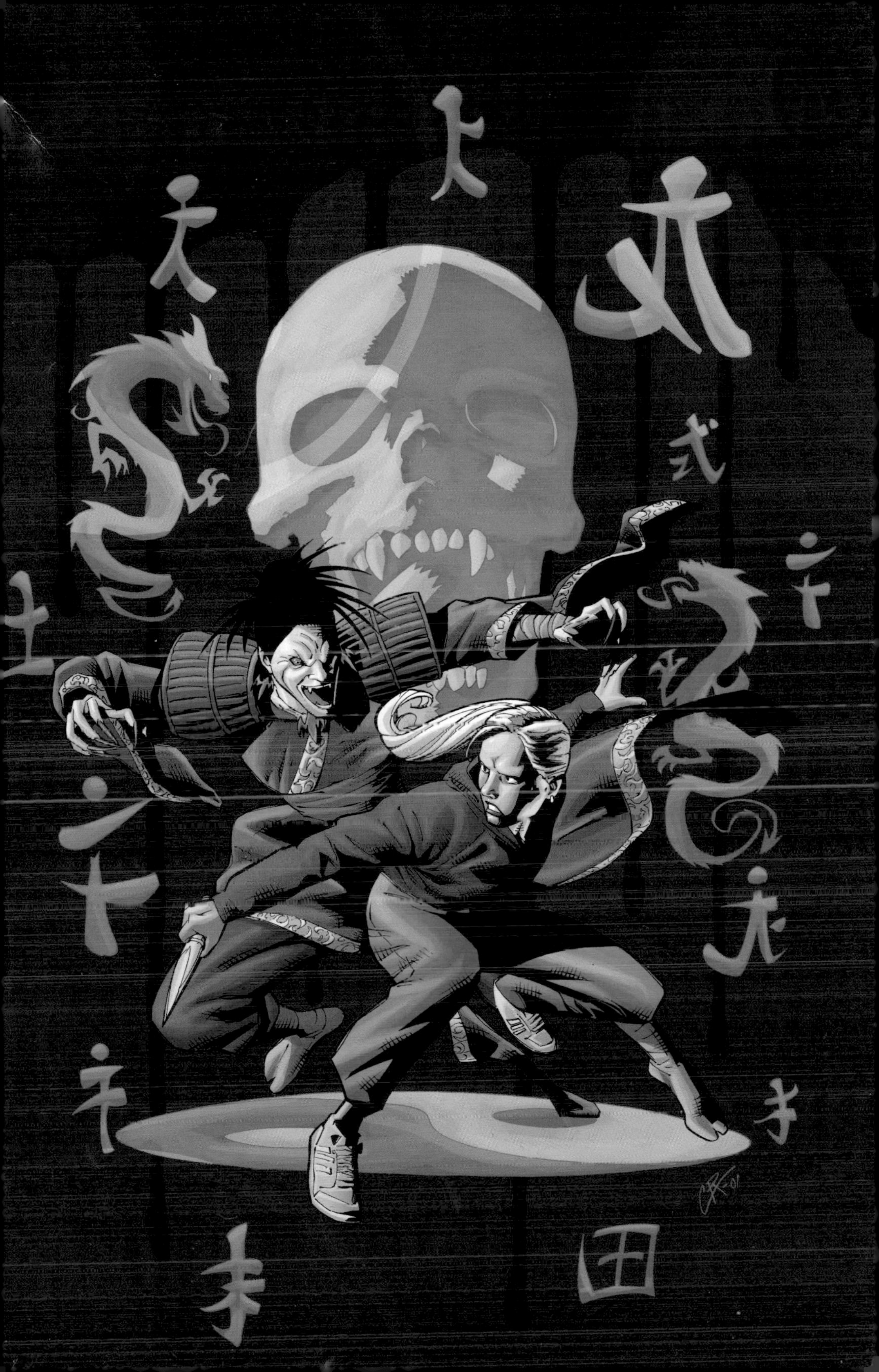

FROM JOSS WHEDON

BUFFY THE VAMPIRE SLAYER SEASON 8:

VOLUME 1: THE LONG WAY HOME
Joss Whedon and Georges Jeanty
ISBN 978-1-59307-822-5 | $15.95

VOLUME 2: NO FUTURE FOR YOU
Brian K. Vaughan, Georges Jeanty, and Joss Whedon
ISBN 978-1-59307-963-5 | $15.95

VOLUME 3: WOLVES AT THE GATE
Drew Goddard, Georges Jeanty, and Joss Whedon
ISBN 978-1-59582-165-2 | $15.95

TALES OF THE SLAYERS
*Joss Whedon, Amber Benson, Gene Colan, P. Craig Russell,
Tim Sale, and others*
ISBN 978-1-56971-605-2 | $14.95

TALES OF THE VAMPIRES
Joss Whedon, Brett Matthews, Cameron Stewart, and others
ISBN 978-1-56971-749-3 | $15.95

FRAY: FUTURE SLAYER
Joss Whedon and Karl Moline
ISBN 978-1-56971-751-6 | $19.95

SERENITY VOLUME 1: THOSE LEFT BEHIND
Joss Whedon, Brett Matthews, and Will Conrad
ISBN 978-1-59307-449-4 | $9.95

SERENITY VOLUME 2: BETTER DAYS
ISBN 978-1-59582-162-1 | $9.95

ALSO FROM DARK HORSE . . .
BUFFY THE VAMPIRE SLAYER OMNIBUS

VOLUME 1
ISBN 978-1-59307-784-6 | $24.95

VOLUME 2
ISBN 978-1-59307-826-3 | $24.95

VOLUME 3
ISBN 978-1-59307-885-0 | $24.95

VOLUME 4
ISBN 978-1-59307-968-0 | $24.95

VOLUME 5
ISBN 978-1-59582-225-3 | $24.95

BUFFY THE VAMPIRE SLAYER:
PANEL TO PANEL
ISBN 978-1-59307-836-2 | $19.95

BUFFY THE VAMPIRE SLAYER:
CREATURES OF HABIT
ISBN 978-1-56971-563-5 | $17.95

MYSPACE DARK HORSE PRESENTS, VOLUME 1
Featuring "Sugarshock" by Joss Whedon and Fábio Moon
ISBN 978-1-59307-998-7 | $17.95

DARK HORSE BOOKS®
darkhorse.com